TENNESSEE RECORDS

BIBLE RECORDS *and* MARRIAGE BONDS

COMPILED BY

JEANNETTE TILLOTSON ACKLEN
Vice President General, N. S. D. A. R.
President Nashville Chapter, Colonial Dames of America
National Vice Chairman, Historical Research

ASSISTED BY

ELIZABETH CARRIGER VAUGHT
Past State President, Daughters of 1812
Past Regent Julius Dugger Chapter, D. A. R.

MILDRED VAUGHN BOUTON
Lebanon

REBEKAH JETTON
Past Regent Capt. William Lytle Chapter, D. A. R.

LOUISE ALLEN OGDEN
Historian Cumberland Chapter, D. A. R.

CLEARFIE

Reprinted for
Clearfield Company, Inc. by
Genealogical Publishing Co., Inc.
Baltimore, Maryland
1992, 1994, 1995, 1997, 2000

Originally published: Nashville, Tennessee, 1933
Reprinted: Genealogical Publishing Co., Inc.
Baltimore, 1967, 1974, 1980
Library of Congress Catalogue Card Number 67-28618
International Standard Book Number 0-8063-0000-0
Made in the United States of America

BIBLE RECORDS

Marriages Solemnized by Robt. Boyte C. Howell
Norfolk, Virginia.

(Copied by Mrs. James B. Newman; Records loaned by Chancellor R. B. C. Howell, Nashville.)

1827

Mr. John Smith to Miss Mary Cook.
Mr. George Harvey to Miss Mary McHolland.
Mr. ——— Finn, to Miss Elizabeth Blount.
Mr. Edward Williams to Miss Jane Canby.
Mr. John Haywood to Miss Frances Angel.
Mr. Wm. D. Dunbar to Mrs. Jane Ross.
Mr. George Hammond to Miss Ellen Warren.
Mr. Nath'l. D. Wooten to Miss Ann Stewart.
Mr. Martin Meagher to Miss Susan Phillips.

(*In the Country*)

Sept. 27, Mr. George Wood to Miss Sarah Grant.

1828

Sept. 17, Mr. William Stopp to Miss Jane Granville.
Oct. 2, Mr. George W. Taylor to Miss Susan Green.
Oct. 21, Mr. Thomas Machen to Miss Elizabeth Grimes.
Oct. 23, Mr. Thomas Williams to Mrs. Ann Walker.
Nov. 1, Mr. William Hughes to Mrs. Hannah Burdick.
Dec. 18, Mr. James Chambers to Mrs. Eliza Smaw.

(*In the Country*)

April 28, Hugh H. Kelty to Miss Elizabeth A. L. Jordan.
Oct. 3, Charles Stevenson to Miss Sarah Forbes.

1829

March 25, John Robinson to Mrs. Elizabeth Morriss.
April 8, Wm. D. Seal to Miss Frances Gardner.
Aug. 26, Griffin Barnes to Eliza Jane Whiting.
Oct. 4, Wm. Thomas to Miss Frances Benthall.
Nov. 5, Joseph Walker to Miss Martha C. Mason.
Dec. 10, Isaac Clows to Mrs. Susan Parker (4 times a widow).
Dec. 15, Richard Stevens to Miss Louiza DeCovmis.

(*In the Country*)

June 3, James Halt to Miss Barbara Bolkin.
Dec. 15, John Davis to Miss Mary Ann Benthall.

1830

Feb. 13, Capt. Henry F. Harding to Miss Margaret Dixon.
March 23, John Goomly to Miss Hannah Mitchell.
April 13, Frederick Mayer to Miss Mary Ann Slack.
April 15, Ebenezer Parker to Miss Mary Ann Warren.
May 22, Wm. Albertson to Miss Bethia Crandal.
Aug. 26, David Williams to Miss Thirza Consolvo.
Sept. 1, Charles Ramsay to Miss Ellen Cunningham.
Sept. 16, Isaac Moore to Miss Ann Leslie.

(*In the Country*)

Feb. 9, Cornelius Hodges to Miss Ellen Hall.
Dec. 20, Major Wise to Miss Margaret A. W. Spires.

1831

Feb. 10, John Adams to Miss Emella Eemelina Filley.
Feb. 26, James E. Wickings to Miss Elizabeth White.
May 2, Amos Hillman to Miss Elizabeth Butt.
May 12, Col. John Harper to Miss Elizabeth Davis.
July 14, Thomas Davis to Mrs. Eliza Hill.
Aug. 19, Michael Keefe to Mrs. Mary Ann Gleason.

Oct. 5, Robert Gwine to Miss Mary Ann Baily.
Dec. 24, Edward Watson to Mrs. Elizabeth Stevenson.

(*In the Country*)

Dec. 23, Thomas Overman to Miss Jane Maxwell.

1832

Feb. 4, James Lloyd to Miss Ann Smoder.
Feb. 15, Davis Caddis to Miss Isabella Edwards.
Feb. 17, Wm. R. Boswick to Miss Susanna Sterrett.
March 3, Fitan Rudolph to Miss Dorothy Thrift.
May 1, Wm. B. Thomas to Miss Elizabeth G. Fanquier.
June 10, Seth March to Miss Virginia Jackson Gordon.
July 10, Marchant Woodard to Miss Rachel E. Baker.
Aug. 15, William Moore to Miss Margaret Benson.
Aug. 21, George W. Farrant to Miss Elizabeth H. Stevens.
Aug. 29, Thomas Dixon to Miss Ann Elizabeth L. Fatem.
Sept. 5, George Dosson to Miss Marion Wilson.
Sept. 20, Charles Tonkin to Miss Elizabeth L. Moore.
Sept. 21, John Collins to Mrs. Eliza Ann Colls.
Nov. 7, Wm. Harvey to Miss Emily Crouch.
Dec. 19, William Dey to Miss Margaret Waters.

(*In Country Places*)

Jan. 9, Francis Herbert to Miss Elizabeth Langly.
Nov. 1, John P. Howell to Miss Louiza La Perouse.
Nov. 19, Wm. Brown to Miss Ann Amelia Marks.

1833

Jan. 4, John Lumsden to Mrs. Elizabeth Finn.
Jan. 6, Edward James Davis to Miss Eliza A. Dryden.
Jan. 15, Wm. A. Brooks to Mrs. Mary Billifelt.
Feb. 9, Jacob R. Ashby to Miss Mary Ridley.
Feb. 12, Lewis Salisbury to Miss Mary Ann Awank.
Feb. 20, Samuel Parker to Miss Susan Belota.
Mar. 30, Henry McBride to Miss Eliza Jones.
Mar. 30, Shepherd Savage to Miss Sarah Belota.
Apr. 3, Washington Bowles to Miss Susan Manning.
Apr. 3, Thomas W. Roach to Miss Margaret A. Hodges.
Apr. 17, Joseph M. Bullock to Mrs. Mary A. Bullock.
June 13, Willard Smith to Miss Sarah Reeves.
July 6, Thomas A. Kirby to Miss Susan Davis.
July 7, Shelbone Mahone to Miss Mary Jordan.
Aug. 7, Wm. D. Dowley to Mrs. Martha Ann Black.
Oct. 2, James Drummond to Mrs. Helena Crossly.
Dec. 2, Wm. T. Anderson to Miss Catherine Jane Decker.
Dec. 10, Edward A. Barns to Miss Ann Forest.
Dec. 21, John Bonny to Miss Elizabeth T. White.

(*In the Country*)

Jan. 18, Thomas D. Deans to Miss Rebecca Ann Gray.
Jan. 21, John Herrington to Miss Mary Ann Baker.
July 27, Absolom Thrift to Miss Senea W. Wood.

1834

Jan. 30, Wm. Haywood to Miss Tabitha Grendall.
Feb. 7, William Taylor to Miss Frances Nimms.
Feb. 21, Hugh McCubbin to Mrs. Ann Munn.
Apr. 12, Louis E. Rogers to Miss Mary Seymore.
May 15, Wm. Haynes to Mrs. Margaret Brown.
July 1, Samuel Bryan to Mrs. Mary Ann Maddon.
Oct. 16, George W. Mitchell to Miss Jane Hill.
Nov. 6, Ransom Dibble to Miss Mary Ann Knight.

(*In the Country*)

Mar. 19, George Eshon to Miss Eliza Porritear.
Apr. 14, William Clark to Mrs. Ann T. Blow.

Marriages Solemnized by Robt. Boyte C. Howell From 1834 through December, 1849, in Nashville, Tennessee.

1834

—— Morgan to Miss —— Tindal.

1835

———— Parker to Miss Elizabeth Barry.
Philip L. Stump to Miss Susan B. Menefee.
Jonas H. Menefee to Miss Amelia E. Scales.

1836

Apr. 28, Amos Fox to Miss Sarah Jane Young.
Apr. 28, Joseph Sills to Miss Mary F. Young.
May 4, Theodore Tagundus to Miss Levinia Sanders.
May 5, Robert Stewart to Miss Sarah L. Clemens.
May 26, Rufus M. Morgan to Miss Jane L. Williams.
June 15, Orange Swann to Miss Sarah Jane McFarland.
July —, Simeon Leonard to Mrs. ——— ———.
Aug. 25, T. J. Cook to Miss Volantia Jane Caruthers.
Sept. 6, Bennett H. Beasly to Miss Susan Carper.
Dec. 13, Wm. W. Wallace to Miss Mary A. W. Barry.

1837

Mar. 8, Charles Arnold Fuller to Miss Susan Austin DeMoville.
May 11, Col. W. W. Woodfolk to Miss Ellen D. Horton.
May 24, John S. Fullmer to Miss Mary Ann Price.
June 7, Dr. John Brelsford to Miss Mary Ann Cook.
June 22, Wm. Higginbotham to Miss Amanda M. Sturdevant.
July 2, Andrew Morrison to Miss Sarah Lawrence.
Aug. 15, Alex H. Poston to Miss Adaline T. Bosley.
Aug. 17, Isaac Dreyfus to Mrs. Lecy Royster.
Aug. 26, Leroy G. Napier to Miss Fanny H. Robertson.
Sept. 28, Col. John A. Taliaferro to Miss Mary A. Taliaferro.
Nov. 23, Thomas L. Marshall to Miss Catharine Williams.

1838

Mar. 15, Gabriel Sanders to Miss Martha L. Reddick.
Mar. 18, Col. Hugh C. Armstrong to Mrs. Sarah Wilson.
July 1, Samuel Myers to Miss Julia Ann Cabler.
July 4, John W. Steel to Miss Mary J. Read.
Sept. 4, Robert J. Clow to Mrs. Evelina Ball.
Sept. 25, John J. Gowen to Miss Malvina Esta.
Oct. 21, Asa S. Dobbs to Miss Martha Smart.
Nov. 8, Elias Kirby to Miss Rachel Powell.
Dec. 16, David Moss to Miss Elizabeth Bartlett.
Dec. 27, Maini Ritter to Miss Emelie Atala Ravenal.

1839

Jan. 6, John W. Smith to Miss Emily J. Reed.
Apr. 11, Dempsey Weaver to Miss Mary D. Johnson.
May 16, Dr. James H. Bacon to Mrs. Sarah Luster.
June 5, Charles I. Love to Miss Julia E. L. Shrewsbury.
June 20, Joseph Brown to Miss Mary Staggs.
Aug. 22, Col. John W. Hewgley to Miss Jane C. Whitsitt.
Sept. 11, Andrew J. Hughs to Miss Elizabeth H. Ball.
Sept. 19, Col. Hame H. Ridley to Miss Amanda R. Joslin.
Oct. 11, Smith Criddle to Mrs. Belle Ann Bromaker.
Nov. 9, T. L. Budd to Miss Eliza Jane Maffit.
Nov. 12, Capt. W. Green Kerley (Texas Army), to Miss Susan L. Kay.
Nov. 19, George W. Williams to Miss Martha Ann Nava.

1840

Jan. 1, A. P. Cleaveland to Miss Lucinda Alderson.
May 21, James H. Hughes to Miss Amanda Hartley.
Oct. 5, Bennett A. Joice to Miss Sarah A. Buchanan.
Nov. 3, Rev. T. W. Haynes to Miss Jane T. A. Buchanan.
———, A. H. Hicks to Miss Mary W. DeMoville.

1841

Oct. 7, Prof. Cyrus Smith to Miss Dorinda Lamson.
Oct. 21, John W. Yandell to Miss Mildred Martin.
Oct. 26, Richard H. Barry to Miss Elizabeth J. Haynes.
Nov. 11, Dr. Thomas J. Finney to Miss Mary A. Slatter.
Dec. 22, Alpheus Lyon to Miss Carolina H. Topp.
Dec. 23, Hugh H. Bell to Miss Prudence L. Bradford.

1842

Jan. 8, Jarman M. Fletcher to Miss Mary Ann Hooper.
Feb. 1, Wm. E. Watkins, Jr., to Almira J. Cockrell.
Feb. 3, George B. Goodwin to Miss Martha A. Barnes.
Mar. 22, Robt. B. Porterfield to Miss Mary D. Figmes.
June 23, James H. Jones to Miss Tabitha Barnes.
July 20, A. M. Green to Miss Mary A. E. Buchanan.
Aug. 17, Jeremiah Scales to Miss Rachel G. Bosley.
Aug. 19, Zach Howell to Miss Lucy Mills (colored).
Sept. 8, Frances M. Mayson to Miss Anna W. Horton.
Oct. 2, Alexander Fall to Miss Elizabeth Horton.
Nov. 22, Col. Granville C. Torbit to Miss Louisa Barrow.

1843

Feb. 1, Charles W. Moore to Miss Julia Ann King.
Feb. 9, Alexander Ledbetter to Miss Elizabeth Stull.
Apr. 13, Wm. Langford to Miss Amanda A. Boon.
July 6, Lewis Y. Craig to Miss Mary E. Lowry.
July 11, John F. Thomas to Miss Sarah Elizabeth.
Nov. 22, W. S. Murfree to Miss Fanny Priscilla Dickinson.
Dec. 21, Smith Freeman to Miss Martha E. Butler.

1844

Jan. 1, Alfred H. Russell to Miss Elizabeth Baird.
Mar. 12, Harvey H. Holland to Miss Amanda M. H. Webb.
Apr. 2, Charles G. McLean to Miss Temple Joslin.
May 23, Wallace Smith to Miss Ann Eliza Cartwright.
June 27, Elijah T. Craig to Miss Sarah Dew.
Aug. 1, Robert Bradley, Jr., to Miss Margaret Perkins.
Aug. 6, J. N. Ward to Miss Ellen E. Norton.
Sept. 7, W. M. Brown to Miss Jane Morton.
Oct. 3, Irby Morgan to Miss Julia Ann DeMoville.
Oct. 15, James R. Mershon to Miss Susan M. Atwater.
Nov. 6, Thomas E. Stratton to Miss Sarah M. Morris.
Nov. 10, Summer R. Mason to Miss Mary J. Dibble.
Nov. 20, J. P. Coleman to Miss Emily H. Taylor.
Dec. 4, Edward Hall to Miss Mahala Craig.
Dec. 5, Jefferson R. Ritter to Miss Mary Conley.
Dec. 24, N. S. Anderson to Mrs. Nancy Hensley.
Dec. 29, Martin L. Shaub to Miss Catherine Caton.

1845

Jan. 30, James Reed to Miss Matilda Levi.
May 1, Wm. D. Cabler to Miss Louiza Harsh.
Sept. 11, George T. White to Miss Sarah Jane Stone.
Oct. 15, Dr. James M. Critz to Miss Ann Eliza Scales.
Oct. 21, Henry L. Schluder to Miss Elizabeth R. Pigg.
Nov. 4, Jacob O. Wright to Miss Elizabeth M. Staggs.
Nov. 4, James J. S. Billings to Lucinda America Nance.

Nov. 21, J. V. J. Goodwin to Miss Alsinea J. R. Gillman.

1846

Jan. 13, E. C. Mason to Miss Delilah A. Park.
Feb. 25, Samuel Brown to Miss Sarah E. Samuel.
Mar. 12, William S. Lord to Miss Ellen D. Smith.
Mar. 31, Thomas Compton to Mrs. Susan Murphey.
July 2, James F. Miller to Miss Sarah White (colored).
July 20, Thomas Chadwell to Miss Mary A. Childress.
Aug. 6, Charles B. Devinney to Miss Esther Rose.
Sept. 28, Everitt Owen to Miss Mary M. Cowen.
Oct. 8, Benj. A. Gailbreath to Miss Jane J. Gailbreath.
Nov. 4, Edward A. Mulford to Miss Catharine H. Scantland.
Nov. 26, Thomas G. Bourne to Miss Elizabeth J. Long.
Dec. 29, Luke C. Brennen to Miss Mary E. Young.

1847

Jan. 7, Henry C. Lockett to Miss Helen Ann Anthony.
Mar. 16, R. H. Bedford to Miss Lucinda Kesee.
Mar. 25, James A. Crutcher to Miss Pheribu C. McCullough.
Apr. 8, John Jordan, Sr., to Miss Mary E. G. Jeffreys.
June 2, John C. Darden to Miss Virginia DeMoville.
Aug. 12, Bushrod L. Doughty to Miss Martha Tindal.
Aug. 16, Wm. W. Ellis to Mrs. Susan Clarke.
Sept. 15, Lewis H. Booby to Miss Mary E. Horn.
Oct. 19, John H. Tandy to Miss Sarah H. Trice.
Oct. 28, Wm. McLaughlin to Miss Harriett Barry.
Nov. 26, James C. Champ to Miss Eliza Ann Alford.
Nov. 27, Bazil Rhodes to Miss Martha Dougherty.
Dec. 1, Dr. Levindas F. Gower to Miss Rebecca Webb.
Dec. 8, Josiah G. Brown to Miss Judith D. Stoott.
Dec. 12, Gen'l Ferrell H. Bratcher to Miss Ann Eliza Nugent.
Dec. 21, Edmund Turner to Miss Mary Moss.
Dec. 23, William H. Sturdevant to Miss Martha E. Bateman.

1848

Jan. 4, James L. Faulkner to Miss Margaret M. Howerton.
Feb. 8, William Harwood to Miss Mary E. Grizzard.
Mar. 18, Lemuel B. McConnico to Mrs. Priscilla R. Massey.
June 12, Thomas C. Webb to Miss Sophia P. Scovel.
July 5, Henderson Clinard to Miss Mary Jane Hoone.
Oct. 5, Henry H. Warder to Miss Elizabeth P. Singleton.
Oct. 22, James J. McDaniel to Miss Rowena C. Shivers.
Oct. 31, William C. McMurry to Miss Hannah E. Sloan.
Nov. 1, Alexander Bean to Miss Amanda S. Sloan.
Nov. 5, Silas N. Macey to Miss Caroline A. Grady.
Dec. 13, Littleberry W. Fussell to Miss Samuella R. Overton.

1849

Feb. 21, James L. Haynes to Miss Sarah G. Barry.
Apr. 18, John B. Cowley to Miss Nancy Kernel.
Apr. 21, James M. Hinton to Miss Olivia J. Andrews.
May 24, John J. Ham to Miss Mary Ann Louiza Haymore.
July 19, George W. Jarmon to Miss Isabella W. Fletcher, Murfreesboro.
Aug. 7, Rev. Wm. Shelton to Miss Virginia T. J. Campbell, Lebanon.
Aug. 23, L. W. Freeman to Mrs. Jane N. Hope.
Sept. 13, W. H. Blount to Miss R. H. Robertson.
Sept. 27, S. C. Godshall to Miss A. H. Webb.
Sept. 27, Chas. H. Blackman to Miss Sarah F. Gresham.
Oct. 23, Joseph P. Brown to Miss Jonah Whaley.
Nov. 16, William Wilson to Miss Sarah Johnson.
Dec. 16, George Kemper to Miss Mary Runnels.

1850

Jan. 16, R. S. Snell to Miss Letitia L. Lucas.

Jan. 16, John W. Woodson to Miss Mary C. Lucas.

Feb. 28, Wm. R. Cornelius to Miss Martha Dorris.

Mar. 21, John McIntyre to Miss Eliza Kinnear.

Apr. 4, Augustus C. Winn, M.D., to Miss Laura J. Rawooth.

MARRIAGES SOLEMNIZED BY ROBT. BOYTE C. HOWELL From May, 1850, through July, 1857, in Richmond, Virginia.

1850

May 9, John O. Taylor to Miss Tremanda T. Starke in Hanover County.

May 23, Marcellus T. Starke to Miss Harriet R. Savage in New Kent County.

Aug. 15, Francis Marshall to Miss Wilmoth Wilkinson.

Aug. 26, John Graeme, Jr., to Miss Virginia Booth.

Aug. 27, Charles Campbell to Miss Elizabeth Frances Ellyson.

Aug. 29, Francis N. Jones to Miss Henningham W. Goolsby.

Sept. 3, Benjamin G. Tapscott to Miss Charlotte W. Wallace.

Sept. 5, Rev. C. B. Jennett, Augusta, Ga., to Miss Mary Catharine Williams, Petersburg, Va., in Petersburg.

Oct. 8, Isaac J. Mercer to Miss Josephine Virginia Arsell.

Oct. 10, Charles W. Allen to Caturah J. Pardue.

Oct. 15, Samuel R. Booum to Miss Eliza T. Stevenson, in Norfolk.

Oct. 31, John J. Pendleton to Miss Mary Bath.

Nov. 21, Elisha H. Turpin to Miss Lucy Temple Redd.

Dec. 5, Robert B. Pettis to Miss Mary Jane Hankins.

1851

Mar. 4, Theophilus C. Bowers to Miss Sarah Ann Nuckols.

Apr. 20, Boswell B. Butts to Miss Pocahontas Stewart.

May 1, Christian Herring to Rebecca Poach, in Petersburg, Va.

June 5, Fountain B. Chappell to Miss Mary A. Goodman.

July 9, James E. Mayo to Miss Sarah M. Griffin.

Aug. 10, Silas Myatt to Miss Almeda R. Gwaltney.

Aug. 10, Wm. Washington Franklin to Miss Elizabeth Tyler.

Aug. 10, Henry Duke to Miss Sarah Jane Garrett.

Sept. 2, Henry Bull to Miss Mary W. Alvis.

Sept. 11, John W. Dennis to Miss Sarah Adaline Burnett.

Sept. 23, J. Lechler to Rosetta Williams.

Oct. 2, Thomas J. Beale to Miss Sophia B. Pemberton.

Oct. 22, George C. Bray to Miss Elizabeth B. Robinson.

Nov. 4, John B. Glazebrook to Miss Jane L. Green.

Nov. 4, Cornelius J. Eaton to Miss Eliza S. Manson.

Nov. 5, Joseph Boothe to Miss Lucy Ann Eppes.

Nov. 11, Daniel P. Mitchell to Miss Martha Ann Franklin.

Nov. 20, Ambrose F. Ransom to Miss Ellen Hall.

Dec. 2, John Frederick Brimmer to Miss Amelia Ford.

Dec. 24, Joseph A. Smith to Miss Virginia J. Phillips.

1852

Jan. 1, Joseph W. Traylor to Miss Sarah Jane Beims.

Jan. 21, Edward D. Keeling to Miss Ann Baker.

Jan. 28, Wm. L. Cowardin to Miss Camilla A. Gary.

Feb. 17, Flavins J. Lake to Miss Mary Elizabeth Grant.

Mar. 2, John Joy to Miss Ann Mitchell.

Mar. 6, George S. Lownes to Miss Catherine Williams.

Mar. 13, William Jenkins to Mrs. Matilda Lynn.

Mar. 27, Octavius Davies to Mrs. Elizabeth Jones.
May 22, Sylvanus Davis to Miss Mary Simon.
July 4, Jacob F. Breckenridge to Miss Sarah E. Mantlo (in Hanover County).
July 17, John G. Mosby, Jr., to Miss Frances Ellen Wade.
Aug. 2, William S. Crockett to Miss Desire E. Rankin.
Aug. 5, Junius B. Stark to Harriet Marcella B. Hutcheson.
Aug. 31, Wm. H. Mosby to Miss Matilda J. Henry.
Oct. 14, Thomas E. Talbot to Miss Mary A. R. Saunders.
Oct. 27, James W. Hamilton to Miss Sarah E. Boulware.
Oct. 28, James W. Shields to Miss Caroline E. Beck.
Nov. 3, Daniel L. Cabot to Miss Mary H. Wade.
Nov. 12, William Stanby to Miss Rosa Ann Simmons.
Dec. 11, Dr. A. C. W. Young to Miss Martha B. White.
Dec. 23, Austin Gibbons to Miss Mary Rees.
Dec. 26, Robert L. Page to Miss Paulina Elizabeth Blankenship.
Dec. 28, John Adolphus Houseman to Miss Eliza J. P. Lee.
Dec. 29, William F. Jenkins to Miss Frances M. Harris.
Dec. 30, Valentine Clutter to Miss Elvira Whitlock.

1853

Feb. 28, Robert Gordon to Miss Anna Jones.
Mar. 30, John H. Elmore to Miss Mary Jane Y. Johnson.
Apr. 21, John W. Moody to Miss Hanover Jones.
Apr. 21, John E. Baily to Miss Julia B. Powell .
May 11, Eugenius Garner to Miss Matilda A. Garrett.
June 13, Augustus Chapin to Miss Margaret H. Lea.
July 13, John Eubank to Miss Susan C. Belknap.
Aug. 2, Andrew J. Ford to Miss Mary Lucy Carter.
Sept. 12, Benjamin Henry Otto to Miss Rebecca Ann Cheatham.
Sept. 19, Jeremiah McCleary to Miss Sarah Garrison.
Sept. 21, Thomas Wells to Sally Ann Walton.
Oct. 6, John T. Flournoy to Miss Nora Perdue.
Oct. 6, Robert H. Vaden to Miss Elizabeth H. Faherty.
Oct. 11, William M. Burruss to Miss Mary A. Kelly.
Oct. 17, Jesse L. Johnson to Miss Margaret E. Atlee.
Oct. 17, John N. Jennings to Miss Sarah Ann Johnson.
Oct. 20, George H. C. Rowe to Miss Virginia G. Sledd.
Oct. 22, Wm. D. A. Cousins to Mrs. Ann Caswell.
Oct. 29, Southey L. Savage to Miss Susanna F. Gary.
Oct. 31, Carter Bethel to Miss Sarah Ann White.
Nov. 23, William T. Allen to Miss America M. Yarrington.
Nov. 23, Jefferson S. Robertson to Miss Caroline C. Yarrington.
Dec. 6, Oliver H. Hope to Miss Mary Pretty.
Dec. 14, Charles S. Pleasants to Miss Jacintha W. Totty.
Dec. 15, Samuel T. Allen to Miss Oteria Sullivan.
Dec. 15, John W. Bullington to Miss Henrietta R. Winston.
Dec. 20, Hites H. Bartoon to Miss Susan Garett.

1854

Jan. 4, James Richard Lee to Miss Mary Dickson.
Jan. 12, James J. Winston to Miss Mary F. Pemberton.
Jan. 26, John G. Hooker to Miss Sarah V. Beal.
Feb. 9, Andrew Jackson Hawkins to Miss Mary Jane Blankenship.
Mar. 4, Marcus M. Tankersley to Miss Elizabeth B. Vanfran.
Mar. 23, Wm. H. T. Stott to Mrs. Vianna Vial.
Apr. 8, James B. Winston to Miss Mary C. Pendleton.
June 14, George Strangham to Miss Sarah Holer.
July 13, John G. Howle to Miss Ann E. Jones.
Aug. 14, William S. Phillips to Miss Virginia Taylor.

Aug. 16, John T. Howell to Miss Margaret E. Morien.
Aug. 17, Frederick Swartz to Miss Sarah Martin.
Sept. 11, William B. Ratcliff to Miss Fanny J. Gregory (Chesterfield County).
Sept. 15, James Alfred Wallen to Miss Ann Eliza Perkinson.
Sept. 21, Marion Green to Miss Demaris H. Olphin.
Sept. 23, John Lester to Miss Barbara Dickinson.
Oct. 4, James H. Tanner to Miss Roseanna J. Salmon (Goochland County).
Oct. 12, John G. Wade to Harriet E. Grey.
Oct. 11, John F. Enroughty to Miss Sarah E. Roganns.
Oct. 18, William M. Kennedy to Mrs. Anne Rebecca Barfoot.
Oct. 21, James Kindlir to Miss Angelina Granger.
Nov. 4, Richard L. Nelson to Miss Elizabeth A. Sands.
Dec. 5, F. W. Doggett to Miss Mary S. Dabney.
Dec. 12, A. D. Quarles to Isaetta M. Quarles.
Dec. 19, Andrew F. Childress to Miss Mary E. Bowers.
Dec. 22, John Wesley Harding to Miss Ellowese Tinsley (Chesterfield County).
Dec. 28, Alpheus R. Timberlake to Miss Williametta A. Jones (Hanover County).

1855

Feb. 12, James G. Mason to Miss Ellen J. Timberlake.
Feb. 21, Dr. L. M. McLeskey to Miss Emily A. Lee.
Feb. 27, John Maroony to Mrs. Catharine J. Bowen.
Mar. 14, Alexander L. Landram to Miss Sarah C. Wingfield.
Apr. 3, Thomas Leighton to Miss Mary Ann Vest.
July 3, George T. Woodcock to Miss Emily E. Elvis.
July 31, Henry Lenchtenburg to Miss Mary Jane Miller.
Sept. 5, Thompson C. Martin to Miss Charlotte E. Anderson.
Sept. 8, Alexander Conner to Mrs. Arthenius Wilford.
Sept. 20, Dixon M. Daughton to Miss Margaret Eliza Tinsley.
Oct. 23, James Reilley to Miss Hannah Page.
Oct. 25, James J. Dorum to Miss Elizabeth J. Quarles.
Oct. 25, Wm. B. Illingsworth to Miss Lucinda E. Tinsley.
Nov. 22, Vernon J. W. Mountcastle to Miss Mary Ann Bradley.
Nov. 22, Ransom Dowden to Miss Mary E. Stiff.
Nov. 29, Joshua A. Walker to Miss Maria F. Bullington.
Dec. 3, J. H. Wight to Miss Agnis Adams.
Dec. 17, William J. Lydnor to Miss Mary C. Smith.
Dec. 19, John P. Harlow to Miss Lilly Ann Eddins.
Dec. 28, Samuel Stanly to Mrs. Susan Luke.

1856

Jan. 15, P. G. Coghlan to Miss Mary A. E. Nia.
Jan. 16, Alfred Mann to Miss Harriet A. Clay.
Jan. 21, Charles M. Smith to Miss Susan E. Tensoo.
Feb. 1, Henry Myers to Miss Mary A. Hudson.
Mar. 27, George Q. Eley to Miss Eliza E. Brooks.
Apr. 9, John Stewart to Miss Frances W. Johnson.
Apr. 24, Samuel McPherson to Mrs. Eleanor C. T. Hitchcock.
May 13, William Miller to Miss Betsey Ann Belknap.
May 14, R. E. Hughson to Miss Sally Ann Wright.
July 23, Joseph Stanley to Miss Margaret A. Morrison.
Sept. 8, James McDouall to Miss Mary Dowd.
Sept. 18, Patrick H. Woods to Miss Elizabeth Jones.
Oct. 11, Branch Elevsby to Miss Mary S. Walker (Chesterfield Co.)
Oct. 20, Andrew Miller to Miss Mary Susan Glenn.
Oct. 20, Joshua B. Walton to Miss Georgeanna Ivy.
Oct. 29, Benjamin Brooks to Miss Catharine Harper.
Oct. 29, Franklin Whiteford to Miss Rachel King.

Nov. 1, William Barnes to Miss Ann Martin.
Nov. 5, Amos E. Willis to Miss Nancy Wills.
Nov. 5, John H. McCarthy to Miss Lemira C. Barnes.
Nov. 14, D. L. Hall to Miss Elizabeth M. J. Butler.
Nov. 21, James G. Smith to Miss Mary F. Hudson.
Nov. 27, Robert T. Hackett to Miss Letty P. Hankins.
Dec. 11, Jeremiah D. Whitlock to Miss Octavia Thompson.
Dec. 20, L. A. Whiting to Miss Elizabeth M. Crump.
Dec. 23, Joseph Fuqua to Miss Maria G. Ellett.
Dec. 24, Warner B. Mahone to Mrs. Mary J. (Wilson) Mahone.
Dec. 25, Wm. J. Dabney to Miss Lavinia Saunders.

1857

Jan. 1, Robert Poat to Miss Mary Barker.
Jan. 1, John L. Bennett to Miss Elizabeth Reese.
Jan. 1, Thomas Hays to Miss Virginia E. Boulware.
Jan. 1, Edward Allen to Miss Frances Beazley.
Jan. 7, Wm. Edward Harrison to Miss Sallie Elizabeth Virginia Wicker.
Jan. 13, Lewis B. Thompson to Miss Sarah M. Moore.
Feb. 14, John L. Walker to Nannie H. Chiles (Chesterfield Co.).
Apr. 11, Hiram A. Davis to Miss Ellen Boulware.
Apr. 23, George B. Steel to Miss Mary A. Hartman.
Apr. 23, William M. Read to Miss Maria L. Langhorne.
June 25, Christopher Walker Saunders to Miss Julia Ellen Dabney.
July 7, Wm. F. Garrett to Miss C. T. Miller.

Marriages Solemnized by Robt. Boyte C. Howell From August, 1857, through January, 1868, in Nashville, Tennessee.

1857

Aug. 5, Harvey C. Watkins, M.D., to Miss Eliza D. Martin.
Aug. 11, Marquis D. Whitesides to Miss Ann Eliza Karr (Winson County).
Sept. 18, Raymond B. Sloan to Miss Mary C. Sloan (Cheatham County).
Oct. 12, William Brown, Jr., to Miss Marina Elam.
Nov. 6, Frederick J. Palmer to Miss Jane S. Pendleton.
Dec. 23, N. U. Smith, M.D., to Miss Sallie Ann Mullins.

1858

Jan. 20, Jesse Collins, Jr., to Miss Ann Eliza Burlington.
Jan. 25, John T. Pendleton to Miss Amelia Pinckney Webb.
Feb. 1, James A. Howard to Miss Lettie A. Everitt.
Mar. 18, Wm. G. Gilliam to Miss America J. Tarpley.
June 7, Leroy T. Cunningham to Miss Josephine H. Buie.
June 30, A. B. Cockrell to Miss Mary J. Brown.
Nov. 4, George W. Allen to Miss Susan E. Greenfield.
Dec. 15, Chas. T. Vanderford to Miss Florence Anderson.
Dec. 28, John H. Wells to Miss Mary E. Wade.

1859

May 30, Tillman A. Fox to Miss Mary E. Stewart.
June 14, H. C. Williams to Miss Martha Sutherlun.
Aug. 31, James S. Persley to Miss Ann W. Morgan.
Nov. 24, Edward Higgins to Miss Milley E. Crunk.
Oct. 28, David Rees to Miss Virginia A. Chilton.
Oct. 28, J. C. Head to Miss Ann Lowry.
Dec. 1, A. W. Overton to Miss Sallie Chambers (Sumner County).

Dec. 13, John Dupree to Miss Mary Poor (free colored).

1860

Feb. 22, Andrew J. Baker, M.D., to Miss Mary E. Torian.
Apr. 26, Robert Ruth to Miss Susan Dorris.
May 8, Frank A. Erwin to Miss Martha Strell.
May 24, Wm. T. Shull to Miss Clay Anna Moses.
May 24, John R. Robinson to Miss E. M. Scott.
Aug. 22, John David Crawford to Miss Catharine M. Crawford.
Sept. 4, James D. B. DeBow to Miss Martha E. Johns.
Oct. 31, Benjamin C. Young to Miss Elizabeth Blacklock.
Nov. 8, J. H. Bruce to Miss Mary E. Couch.
Nov. 13, P. Lindsley Nichol to Miss Sue M. Shaffer.
Nov. 15, John W. Hooberry to Miss Martha C. Stump.
Dec. 24, Charles D. Benson to Miss Elizabeth Pilcher.

1861

Mar. 21, T. J. Massey to Mrs. Mary J. Scales (Rutherford Co.).
Apr. 30, James W. Rutledge to Miss Sallie E. Belcher.
May 7, John H. Curry to Miss Mary T. Eastman.
Sept. 29, Wm. R. McFarland to Miss Josephine Collins.
Nov. 20, William R. Stewart to Miss Charlotte Garner.

1862

Feb. 20, Powhattan Bowling to Miss Gertrude Bosley.
Apr. 16, Peter Harris to Mrs. Ellen Truesdell.
Apr. 30, Jos. L. Weakly to Mrs. Mary L. Thomas.
May 23, Winfield D. Scott to Mrs. Maria Ibers.
May 28, Wellington B. Briggs to Miss J. Tennessee Shivers.
June 18, J. B. Holloway to Miss Laura Carter (U. S. A. Lieut.).
Sept. 24, Zechariah Howard to Miss Milly Johnson (colored people).

1863

Mar. 12, Hiram A. Stewart to Mrs. Margaret Miller.
May 13, Thomas W. Morton to Miss Addie Greenfield.
June 4, John B. Romans to Miss Mary Haley.
June 24, Joseph T. Cudworth, U. S. A., to Miss Fanny T. Davidson.
July 8, Frank M. McIntosh to Miss Ellen Maness.
July 8, Henry Hoover to Miss Mary Hyronemus.
July 21, George T. Weakley to Miss Emma Farmer.
Oct. 27, Joseph L. Stephens to Miss Medora Carter.
Nov. 25, Alfred A. Adams to Miss Maggie J. Gleaves.
Dec. 24, Wm. M. Duncan to Miss Carrie C. Eastman.

1864

Jan. 26, Henry D. McKinney to Miss Laura Erwin.
Feb. 25, George Latin (Sluthauer) to Miss Mary Johnson.
Feb. 29, Lieut. J. L. Roberts, U. S. A., to Miss Mollie Laflin.
Mar. 24, Lyson D. Harris to Miss Georgia E. Burton.
Apr. 16, Dr. Charles H. Mullen to Miss Mattie E. Bishop.
May 3, Ephraim Connelly to Miss Anna Cherry.
June 1, E. D. Stephenson (Rev.), to Mrs. M. J. Gowen.
July 2, Frank H. Riggs (Lieut. U. S. A.), to Miss Isabelle N. Dunham.
July 27, James W. Richardson (Lieut. U. S. A.), to Miss Belle Jones.
Aug. 9, B. F. Karsner to Mrs. Jennie E. Burgo.
Sept. 29, Edward DeLurue to Miss Martitia McCaleb.
Nov. 3, Wm. C. Weir to Miss Sarah E. Hill.
Dec. 13, Thos. Rice to Miss Mary Cox.
Dec. 22, Henry C. Jenkins to Miss Mary Florence Webb.
Dec. 28, Wm. G. Dashelle to Miss Georgiana Ingraham.

1865

Mar. 2, W. W. Craig to Miss Mary A. Baug.
Mar. 19, Jesse Tanksley to Miss Fanny E. Cockrum.
Apr. 11, Peter Forshaa to Miss Mary Jane Houseley.
Apr. 25, Joseph A. Kellogg to Miss Mary L. Overstreet.
Apr. 27, John H. Brown to Miss Hester L. Cooper.
May 5, Abraham Van Schoick to Miss Mary Jane Calkins.
June 5, Henry H. Goodwin to Miss Jane Wilson.
June 17, Charles Howard to Miss Julia E. Gibbs.
June 17, Louis Valentino to Miss Annie E. Samuel.
July 25, Orville Ewing, Jr., to Miss Irene Watkins.
July 30, S. V. Clevenger to Miss Mariana J. Knapp.
Aug. 1, A. Judson Graham to Miss Hannah H. Gay.
Oct. 10, George R. Calhoun to Miss Maria Roberts.
Oct. 13, Edwin McPhee to Miss Minerva Atkins.
Nov. 8, Albert G. Ewing to Miss Henrietta A. Cockrell.
Dec. 31, Henry Hall to Miss Maria Griffith.

1866

Feb. 26, Philip Roden to Miss Mary F. Berry.
Mar. 7, Albert Guyer to Miss Lucy P. Green.
Apr. 5, Aaron Jennings (col.), to Emiline Ward (col.).
Apr. 9, Simon Beck (col.) to Jane Newman (col.).
Apr. 15, Daniel North to Elizabeth Lester (colored).
Apr. 26, Oliver P. Fish to Miss Lucinda J. Barker.
June 6, James A. Jennings to Miss Olivia Currey.
June 6, James Skillman to Miss Sarah White.
Oct. 4, John W. Mathews to Miss Yeba M. Hewitt.
Oct. 11, George S. Vanvalkenburg to Miss Mary O. Peace.
Nov. 1, G. W. Whitesides to Miss S. Fannie Copeland.

1867

Jan. 20, W. S. G. Booth to Miss Mary Louisa Caldwell.
Jan. 24, James M. Eads to Miss Elizabeth A. Wilkerson.
June 13, Matt B. Pilcher to Miss Judith Winston.
July 1, Rev. W. H. Barksdale to Miss Lucy Donaho (Rutherford County).
Oct. 3, John McCafferty to Mrs. M. F. Puckett.
Dec. 19, Edward R. Campbell to Miss Mary Overton Winston.

1868

Jan. 12, W. W. Knox, Jr., to Miss Eliza J. Dunnavant (in the country).

Will of Aaron Parron

December 1st, 1818.

I, Aaron Parron of White County and State of Tennessee, though weak in body, yet in my perfect senses by the mercies of God, do make this my last will and testament. First, I ———— my soul to God who gave me. Next the payments of all my just debts, then as follows:

Elizabeth Parron, wife.
Edwin Breeding Parron, son.
Bate Parron, son.
John Parron, son.
Aaron Parron, son.
Samuel Parron, son.

Excerpts from the Will of Ann Quarles, October, 1829

I, Ann Quarles of Overton County and State of Tennessee, make this my last will and testament as follows, to wit:

William Hawes Quarles, son.
James Tomplins Quarles, son.

John Adams Quarles, son.
Catherine Baxter Quarles, daughter.
Frances Dorothy Little, daughter.
Letitia Ann (married Wm. Burton), daughter.
Sallie Wesley (married Adam Huntsman), daughter.
Stephen Decatur Burton, grandson.
Frances Ann Burton, granddaughter.
Daniel W. Hawes, grandson.
Lucinda F. Hawes, granddaughter.
George A. Hawes, grandson.
Mary Jane Hawes, granddaughter.
John Hawes, grandson.
James Oscar Hawes, grandson.
Ann Huntsman, granddaughter.

Children of William Quarles

Tabitha Tomplins, born 1784, married to Wm. Hawes.
Mary Goodloe, born 1786, married to Harrison Irby Hughes.
Nancy, born 1788, married to William Burton.
Elizabeth Jane, born 1790, married to Chas. Burton.
Wm. Hawes, born 1792, married to Ruth Hyden.
Frances Dorothy, born 1794, married to Thomas Little.
James Tompkins, born 1796, married to Mary Diana Simpson.
John Adams, born 1800, married to Sara Catherine Baxter.
Sallie Wesley, born 1798, married to Adam Huntsman.
Catherine Baxter, born 1802, married to Wm. Snodgrass.

Children of Thomas Barnes and Alice Bohannon Barnes
(1st Wife)
Mary (Polly Strain)
(2nd Wife)

The Bible from which this record was copied is in hands of Mrs. Robt. W. Lowe (Mary Alice Whitson), great-granddaughter of John Barnes.

Elizabeth Barnes was born July 8th, 1798.
Sarah Barnes was born May 5th, 1800.
John Barnes was born March 23, 1808.
Lewis Barnes was born Feb. 22nd, 1804.
Nancy Barnes was born Jan. 23rd, 1806.
William H. Barnes was born Dec. 7th, 1809.
Polly Barnes was born Feb. 26th, 1811.
Susanah Barnes was born Aug. 25th, 1814.
Rebeccha Rice Barnes was born Feb. 23rd, 1817.
Thomas Barnes was born Aug. 14th, 1819.
Riley Barnes was born Nov. 25th, 1822.
Lewisa Barnes was born May 30th, 1824.
Rhoda Barnes was born July 28th, 1825.
Jessie Barnes was born Nov. 30th, 1828.
James Marion Barnes was born March 24th, 1830.
Amanda Barnes was born March 2nd, 1832.
Lydia Barnes was born May 18th, 1834.

Earliest Records from Family Bible Owned by Miss Lillian Jetton and Miss Rebekah Jetton of Murfreesboro, Tenn.

Rebekah Thompson was born Jan. 27, 1752.
Lelia(?) Thompson was born Aug. 29, 1753.
Samuel Thompson was born June 18, 1755.
Robert Thompson was born March 15, 1757.
Thomas Thompson was born Oct. 2, 1759.
Ephriam Thompson was born June 23, 1761.
Levinah Thompson was born Jan. 28, 1763.
John Thompson was born Feb. 23, 1765.
Jason(?) Thompson was born May 27, 1767.

Records copied from two family Bibles published in London in the years 1696 and 1768 respectively, owned by Miss Lillian Jetton and Miss Rebekah Jetton, Murfreesboro, Tenn. Copied by Miss Rebekah Jetton, Murfreesboro, Tenn.

Lewis Jetton was born Jan. 24, 1749.
Priscilla Sharp, his wife, was born Sept. 1, 1750.
Elizabeth was born Feb. 17, 1773.
Jemima was born Jan. 3, 1775.
Mary was born Jan. 10, 1777.
John Lewis was born Dec. 16, 1778.
James Sharp was born June 18, 1782.
Alexander Brevard was born Nov. 25, 1783.
Asaph was born March 5, 1786.
Sally S. was born Jan. 16, 1788.
Isaac G. was born Mar. 25, 1791.
Rachel was born Oct. 3, 1793.
Ezekiel was born Sept. 25, 1795.
Priscilla was born July 6, 1798.

—

Lewis Jetton died Sept. 21, 1825.
Priscilla Sharp Jetton died May 13, 1838.
Rachel died Feb. 15, 1794.
Ezekiel died Oct. 13, 1820.
Sally S. died May, 1821.

—

Julia Thompson Goodloe, the daughter of Henry Goodloe and Rebecca, his wife, was born January 11, 1805.
Betsey Johnson Goodloe, the daughter of Henry Goodloe and Rebecca, his wife, was born June the 22 day, 1806.
Polly Goodloe, the daughter of Henry Goodloe and Rebecca, his wife, was born November the 13 day, 1807.
Rebecca Goodloe, the daughter of Henry Goodloe and Rebecca, his wife, was born September the 18th day, 1809.
Cynthia Goodloe, the daughter of Henry Goodloe and Rebecca, his wife, was born November the 16th dav, 1810.
Newton Cannon Goodloe, the son of Henry Goodloe and Rebecca, his wife, was born June the 22nd day, 1812.
Hannah Goodloe, the daughter of Henry Goodloe and Rebecca, his wife, was born July the 19th day, 1813.
Thompson Goodloe, the son of Henry Goodloe and Rebecca, his wife, was born December the 19th day, 1815.
Nancy Goodloe, the daughter of Henry Goodloe and Rebecca, his wife, was born October the 13th day, 1817.
Robert Henry Goodloe, the son of Henry Goodloe and Rebecca, his wife, was born November the 26th day, 1818.
Leodicea Goodloe, the daughter of Henry Goodloe and Rebecca, his wife, was born April the 10th day, 1820.
Alfred Miller Goodloe, the son of Henry Goodloe and Rebecca, his wife, was born the 27th day of March, 1822.

Samuel Jones Goodloe, the son of Henry Goodloe and Rebecca, his wife, was born the 5th day of March, 1824.

—

Henry Goodloe departed this life the 22nd day of July, 1846, aged 69 years, 5 months, 16 days.
Rebecca Goodloe, wife of Henry Goodloe, departed this life the 6th day of May, 1852, aged 68 years, 4 months, and 24 days.
Thompson Wright Goodloe departed this life the 21st day of August, 1847.

—

Lewis Jetton departed this life July 5, 1886.
Rebekah Goodloe Jetton, his wife, departed this life November 27, 1880.

—

Lewis Jetton, born May 26, 1807.
Rebekah Goodloe Jetton, his wife, was born Sept. 18, 1809.
Mary Elizabeth Jetton was born Dec. 17, 1829.
Granville Jetton was born Jan. 31, 1831.
Julia Amanda Jetton was born Feb. 11, 1832.
John Henry Jetton was born Oct. 16, 1833.
Lewis White Jetton was born Feb. 7, 1836.
Robert Newton Jetton was born March 20, 1838.
James Thompson Jetton was born Feb. 13, 1840.
William Marshal Jetton was born Sept. 8, 1842.
Charles Foster Jetton was born March 13, 1844.
Albert Jetton was born Nov. 3, 1845.
Sarah R. Jetton was born Sept. 25, 1848.

—

Julia Amanda Jetton died Aug. 5, 1833.
Mary E. Jetton McKnight departed this life Feb. 19, 1849.
Robert Newton Jetton died at Meridian, Miss. (in service in Confederate army), June, 1862.
Lewis White Jetton died at Tullahoma, Tenn., April 13, 1863 (in service in Confederate army).
Granville Jetton died May 18, 1868. (He had been a soldier in Confederate army).
William Marshal Jetton died Nov. 17, 1868 (from effects of wounds received while in service in Confederate army).
John Henry Jetton died —— —, 1872. (He had been a soldier in Confederate army).
James Thompson Jetton died —— ——. (He had been a soldier in Confederate army).
Albert Jetton died April 14, 1912.

—

Isaac Wright, Senior, departed this life 18th October, 1816.
Polly Dill, formerly Polly Wright, died the 7th June, 1818, aged 47. She was married 16th March, 1786, had 12 living children when she died; was a married wife 31 years.
Abraham Wright died in March, 1829, in the lower country on the Mississippi river.
Thompson Wright died the 9th June, 1834.
Hannah Statten died Nov., 1836.
Rebecca Wright departed this life 9th April, 1840.

—

Polly Wright was born the 17th day of November, in 1770.
Hannah Wright was born the 16th day of January, in 1772.
Abraham Wright was born October the 12th, in 1773.
Isaac Wright was born December the 23rd, in 1775.
Jacob Wright was born December the 25th, in 1777.
Thompson Wright was born December the 30th, in 1779.
Betsey Wright was born November the 2nd, in 1781.
Rebecca Wright was born December the 13th, in 1783.

—

Henry Goodloe, the son of George Goodloe and Priscilla Goodloe, his wife, was born January the 6th, 1777.
Rebecca Wright, the daughter of

Isaac Wright and Rebecca, his wife, was born December 12, 1783.

———

Lewis Jetton was born May 26, 1807.
Peggy Louisa was born ——, 1809.
Jacky S. was born Nov., 1810.
Polly was born Aug., 1812.
Jane was born April, 1816.
——— was born ———, 1817.
Sarah was born ———, 1819.
Nancy was born Aug. 19, 1821.
Alexander was born ———, 1824.
Robert White was born Sept. 14, 1826.
Elizabeth was born Mar. 2, 1829.

Bible records copied by Miss Essie Hancock for Miss Lillian Jetton.

William Palmer, born 1752; died 1824.
His wife, Caroline Dulaney, born 1757; died 1826; married 1773.

CHILDREN

Philip Palmer (died young).
William Palmer, born 1777; died 1857; married Susan Rankin.
Henry Dulaney Palmer, born 1781; died 1861; married Patsy Angel.
Susan Palmer (invalid).
Frances Rose Palmer, born 1789 (a noted Christian preacher).
Caroline Palmer (married Nelson).
Mary Palmer, born 1773; died 1848; married Charles Ready, 1807.

Copied from the family Bible of Mrs. E. W. Macon, Woodbury, Tenn., by Miss Eva Mai Atwood, of Murfreesboro, Tenn.

William Wharton was born February 14th, 1799, in Fauquier County, Virginia.
(and his wife)
Mariana Weedon was born March 8th, 1799, in Culpeper County, Virginia.

From tablet in First Presbyterian Church, Murfreesboro, Tenn. Copied by Annie E. Campbell, March 26, 1932.

IN MEMORIAM

Rev. Wm. Eagleton, D.D., born Blount County, Tenn., March 25, 1798; died at Murfreesboro, March 28, 1866. He came to us Dec., 1829, and for 37 years broke to us the bread of life. How good and true, how guileless and faithful, how sympathizing and affectionate this shepherd was, we, his flock only knew.

Record given by Miss Mary Robertson, Smyrna, Tenn.

Richard S. Keele was born in 1757, on the voyage from England to America. His father's name was Arthur Keele. Richard S. was for 7 (seven) years a soldier in the American Revolution.
From Pension Commissioner's Report, Washington, D. C., Survivor File No. 1979:
"It appears that Richard Keele enlisted in Henry County, Virginia, in the spring of 1776 in Capt. Jas. Lyons' and P. Harston's Company of Rangers. He served till July 19, 1777. After July, 1777, he married (Lydia Richmond) and removed to frontiers of North Carolina on Nolachucky River where he entered in Washington Co., a volunteer company under Samuel Williams which joined with Col. Sevier and was at the Battle of King's Mountain. He served here one month. He was

allowed pension on his application executed August 7, 1832, at which time he was seventy-four (74) years old and living in Rutherford County, Tennessee, with one of his sons."

Record copied from family Bible, found among old papers belonging to Mrs. Bettie Taylor Carlton, deceased, Rockvale, Tenn.

Sally S. Taylor was born January the 5th, 1807.
Benjamin B. Taylor was born December the 4th, 1808.
Martha Ann Taylor was born September the 13th, 1810.
Thomas Taylor was born Sept. the 6th, 1812.
Grizzy Taylor was born June the 6th, 1814.
Robert Taylor was born March 24, 1816.
Elizor Taylor was born November the 25th, 1817.
July Wilmoth Taylor was born February the 16th, 1820.
James Monrow Taylor was born January the 3rd, 1822.
Francis (Frances) Taylor was born November the 15th, 1823.
John Joseph Taylor was born August the 21st, 1826.
Maria Amandy Taylor was born February the 5th, 1828.
William Carol Taylor was born November the 6th, 1830.

Memoranda found among old papers belonging to Mrs. Bettie Carlton.

Edward Elam was born January the 20th, 1769; died Feb. 15th, 1830.
Jane Elam (wife of Edward) was born July the 29th, 1772; died March 7, 1846.
Daniel Elam was born March the 21st, 1809; died Dec. 22nd, 1829.

Copied from record in family Bible owned by Miss Annie E. Campbell, Murfreesboro, Tenn.

Samuel Campbell was born in Campbell County, Va., Jan. 15, 1769. He died in Rutherford Co., Tenn., Sept. 7, 1846. His wife was Nancy Mann of Georgia. The names of their children and birth dates follow:
Archibald Campbell was born Oct. 15. 1798.
Elizabeth M. Campbell was born July 5, 1800.
Mary M. Campbell was born Sept. 3, 1802.
Virginia B. Campbell was born Oct. 11, 1804.
Camilla T. Campbell was born Oct. 25, 1807.
Josiah Campbell was born Dec. 25, 1809.
Nancy Edmonson Campbell was born Feb. 15, 1812.
Samuel Campbell was born Jan. 9, 1816.
Martha Campbell was born July 15, 1818.

Obituary

This is taken from the Murfreesboro News, dated August 1, 1859.

Died at his residence in Rutherford County, 3rd Inst., Charles Ready, Sr. Esq. The deceased was born at Salsbury, in the State of Maryland, on the 1st of April, 1770, and was in the 90th year of his age, when he died. His father having died at the commencement

of the Revolutionary war, his widowed mother removed with him and an older brother to North Carolina where with limited means she raised her two sons to manhood. Shortly after the subject of this notice attained his majority, he married and settled in Edgefield District, S. C. From there he removed in 1797 to Sumner County, Tennessee, and in 1802 he removed to his late residence in Rutherford County. At the establishment of Rutherford County in 1803, he was appointed one of the Justices of the Peace, and presided at the first County Court held in Rutherford County. He was one of the Commissioners who located the town of Murfreesboro in 1812.
In his early life he became a member of the Presbyterian Church, and continued his membership till his death. For many years he acted as an elder in the Church and when death came he was "ready to be offered up."
He was energetic and industrious and even in his old age. He was kind to his family and neighbors. Frank in his associations with his fellows, prudent in the discharge of every obligation whatever, that rested upon him, and strictly honest with himself as well as with others. Proof of his punctuality and honesty is found in the fact no man ever brought a suit against him in any court whatever. His friends and acquaintances esteemed him highly in life. They will not forget him now that he is dead.
He leaves a numerous progeny who are scattered over the Southern and Western States. They will lament his departure but they will cherish his memory with pride and pleasure.

Marker inscription copied by Miss Katherine Haley, Murfreesboro, Tenn.

Road to Black Fox Camp Spring. Orr's Expedition, sent out by General Robertson, camped near this spring September 7, 1794. Erected by Captain William Lytle Chapter, National Society Daughters of the American Revolution. 1933.

From family Bible of John Haley, Sr. Sent by Miss Katherine Haley, Murfreesboro.

Jas. Garrett, born Feb. the 14th, 1781; died April the 7th, 1863.
Nancy Garrett, Jan. 17th, 1842.
Sallie S. Puckett, born Oct. 10, 1806.
(a) W. C. Powell, born April 21, 1830.
(b) Kate I. Powell, born Feb. 26, 1849.
(1) Emma G. Haley, born June 6, 1871.
(2) Eugene W. Haley, born Feb. 23, 1873.
Wilburn T. Haley, died Feb. 9, 1895.
Philip R. Haley, died Jan. 30th, 1862.
John Haley, died April the 2nd, 1851.
Mr. John C. Haley and wife, Talitha C. Garrett, were married June 6, 1833.
(a) Mr. W. A. McCord and wife, Sallie T. Haley, were married Dec. 16, 1875.
(b) J. M. Haley and Kate I. Powell were married Oct. 7, 1869.
(1) S. J. Hopkins and Emma G. Haley were married Feb. 20, 1895.
(2) E. W. Haley and Annie V. McCord were married Feb. 25, 1902.
(c) Mr. Philip B. Haley and wife, Sarah N. Carter, were married the 13th day of Dec., 1853.
(d) Mr. A. J. Wood and wife, Nancy C. Haley, were married Nov. the 28th, 1854.
(e) Mr. John C. Haley and wife, Mary B. Powell, were married Oct. 3, 1860.

Talitha Cumi Haley, born Dec. 5th, 1815; died May 16th, 1874.
John Haley, born Jan. 19th, 1806; died March 7, 1900.
(a) Philip Beasley Haley, born April 7th, 1834; died Aug. 13th, 1895.
(b) Nancy Elizabeth Haley, born Nov. 29, 1835; died Dec. 19, 1863.
(c) Sallie T. Haley, born Nov. 15, 1850; died June 2, 1878.
(d) William Carrol Haley, born Oct. 12, 1844; died 1930.
(e) Dorothy Caroline Haley, born April 7, 1841; died July 8, 1842.
(f) Jas. Garrett Haley, born April 12, 1837; died Oct. 9, 1838.
(g) John Carrington Haley, born July 14, 1838; died June 1, 1913.
(h) Joseph Madison Haley, born March 4, 1847; died June 19, 1913.

Records sent by Miss Anne Gray Sikes, Murfreesboro, Tenn. Family records out of old McCulloch Bible.

Births

Benjamin McCulloch, born April 16, 1789.
Sarah McCulloch, born June 27, 1790.
Adelaide McCulloch, born Dec. 30, 1812; daughter of Benjamin and Sarah McCulloch.
Henry McCulloch, born May 14, 1819.
Mary E. McCulloch, born Nov. 22, 1816.
Ann McCulloch, born Oct. 13, 1818.
Benjamin McCulloch, born Nov. 20, 1820.
Sarah McCulloch, born Oct. 25, 1822.
Phillip McCulloch, born Jan. 10, 1825.
Sarah McCulloch, born Oct. 1, 1827.
Ellen McCulloch, born Oct. 26, 1829.
John McCulloch, born Sept. 15, 1831.
Richard McCulloch, born May 13, 1839.
Thomas Eldridge Hord, born Sept. 16, 1846.
Ellen Lucretia Hord, born Jan. 24, 1849.
Mary Elizabeth Hord, born July 24, 1851.
Thomas Ewing, son of Josiah and Ada Ewing, born at Rose Hill on Sept. 2, 1856.
Thomas Hord Bibb, son of Sarah and Algernon Bibb, born at Rose Hill, April 4, 1858.
Amelia M. Lafon, born Jan. 29, 1820.
Tommie, daughter of Thomas and Amelia Hord, born May 30, 1861.
Thomas Epps Gibbons Hord, son of Thomas and Amelia Hord, born Feb. 27, 1863.
Ada Syd Bibb, born in Rutherford County, Tennessee, Nov. 25, 1861.

Deaths

Benjamin McCulloch, died Aug. 10, 1847, at McMinnville.
John McCulloch, died Sept. 16, 1847, at McMinnville.
Sarah McCulloch, wife of Benjamin McCulloch, died July 2, 1862.
Algernon S. Bibb, husband of Sarah A. Hord, died March 10, 1904, at the Confederate Home at Pewee Valley, Ky.
Sarah A. Hord Bibb, died March 13, 1923, in her 89th year.
Thomas Eldridge Hord, died Oct. 31, 1869, in Phillips County, Ark.
Ellen L. Hord Wendel, died April 11, 1877, at Murfreesboro.
Thomas Hord Bibb, died Jan. 12, 1882, at Helena, Ark.
Mildred Hord Washington, died May 9, 1912, at Nashville, Tenn. She was the daughter of Thomas and Amelia Hord and was born on May 30, 1861; married F. W. Washington, Dec. 1885.
Ada B. Hord Ewing, died April 16. 1920, at Bradentown, Florida, in her 85th year.
Sarah A. Hord, died Jan. 29, 1835. Oldest child of Thomas and Mary Hord. Algenon S. Bibb, husband of Sarah Hord, born June 4, 1827, in Morgan County, near Decatur, Ala.
Mary Adelaide Hord, died July 10, 1840, age 9 months and 11 days, at Knoxville, Tenn.

Mary Elizabeth Hord, died Sept. 16, 1851, in Rutherford County.
Jane Caswell Hord, died Oct. 31, 1852, at 15 years of age, in Nashville.
Mary Elizabeth Hord, Jr., died May 11, 1858, in Rutherford County.
Thomas Hord, died Sept. 15, 1865, in Rutherford County.
Amelia M. Hord, died July 15, 1892, in Rutherford County.

BIRTHS

Thomas Hord, born Aug. 31, 1802.
Mary Elizabeth McCulloch, born Nov. 22, 1816.
Sarah Ann Hord, daughter of Thomas and Mary Hord, born Jan. 29, 1835.
Ada Byron Hord, born Oct. 22, 1836.
Jane Caswell Hord, born Aug. 3, 1838.
Mary Adelaide Hord, born Sept. 28, 1839, at Spring Hill.
Benjamin McCulloch Hord, born March 20, 1842.
Alice Gray Hord, born Feb. 5, 1844.

MARRIAGES

Thomas Hord and Mary Elizabeth McCulloch, married by Rev. William Eagleton, April 3, 1834, at Spring Hill, Rutherford County, Tenn.
Thomas Hord and Amelia M. Lafon, married by Dr. Edgar in her Church in Nashville, Oct. 12, 1859.
Ellen L. Hord and William Wendel, married in Murfreesboro, Tenn., in the spring of 1874.
Sarah Ann Hord, oldest daughter of Mary and Thomas Hord, married to Algenon S. Bibb of Ala., by Rev. Dr. Edgar on Sept. 22, 1856, at Rose Hill, Rutherford County, Tenn.
Ada B. Hord and Josiah W. Ewing of Nashville, married by Rev. Dr. Edgar at Rose Hill, Nov. 21, 1855.
Benjamin McCulloch Hord and Annie Gray Warner, married by Rev. Dr. Tremble of Edgefield, Nov. 15, 1866.
Alice G. Hord and Joseph H. Warner, married by Rev. Jno. Grime, June 20, 1867, in the Christian Church at Murfreesboro, Tenn.
Ada Bibb and William E. Blackburn of Kentucky, married Oct. 25, 1881, by Rev. Dr. F. Patton, in the Presbyterian Church at Helena, Ark.

BAPTISMS

Sarah Ann Hord, Ada B. Hord, Jane C. Hord, Benjamin Hord, and Alice G. Hord were baptized in 1846 by the Rev. Dr. Edgar.
Eldridge Hord, Ellen Lucretia Hord, baptized in 1849, by Rev. Dr. Edgar.
Mary Elizabeth Hord, baptized 1858, by the Rev. Dr. Edgar.

Copied from family record taken by Mrs. Mary Hardeman from family Bible of her uncle, James Noailles Brickell, of North Carolina.

Matthias Brickell, my great-grandfather (of Mrs. Mary Hardeman), was born 23rd of March, 1725. Married to Rachiel Noailles Nov. 6, 1748; died 17th Oct. 1788.
Rachiel Noailles, his wife, was born 13th January, 1728; died 17th February, 1770.
Their children were as follows:
1. Marinia Brickell, born 6th Sept. 1749; died 8th Jan. 1762.
2. Lavenia Brickell, born 17th July 1750; died 1799.
3. William Brickell, born 30th March 1752; died 1810.
4. Martha Brickell, born 25th Sept. 1753; died 1809.
5. Bathsheba Brickell, born 28th Sept. 1755; died (drowned) 7th June 1782.
6. Sally Brickell (our grandmother), born 29th July 1757; died 19th March 1802.
7. Matthias Brickell, born 23rd Jan. 1759; died 3rd June 1797.
8. Thomas Noailles Brickell, born 11th March 1761; died Nov. 1810.
9. John Brickell, born 8th Sept. 1762; died 1798.
10. James Noailles Brickell, born

19th Jan. 1765; died 1841.
11. Jonathan Brickell, born 11th Feb. 1767; died Jan. 1807.
12. Joseph Brickell, born 23rd Dec. 1769; died 1802.
13. Ann Brickell.

Matthias Brickell's Second Marriage to Mrs. Jones

1. Benjamin Brickell, born 15th Dec. 1773; died 1812.
2. Marinia Brickell, born 28th May 1777.
3. Rebecca Brickell, born 14th June 1780.
4. Betsy Brickell, born 1st May 1783.
5. Nancy Brickell, born 17th Jan. 1786.

The children of my great-grandfather, Matthias Brickell, were married as follows:
1. Marinia.
2. Lavinia married Dickinson. Her children were Joe, Matt, and Rachiel. Joe married Peggy Gregory. Rachiel married Dr. Stimson, was afterward a widow and engaged to Kilby, but died and Kilby went deranged. Mrs. Lavenia Dickinson married the second time to Dr. Bembury. (Aunt Lavenia Burton was named for her).
3. William married Nancy Jones ("the blue hen"). They had no children.
4. Martha. Saved by her scissors chain fastening in the bridge.
5. Bathsheba was drowned by falling into the river. Her sister and herself were in a "double gig". The horse got frightened and backed off!
6. Sally (our grandmother) married Hardy Murfree 17th February, 1780.
7. Matthias.
8. Thomas married (————); their children were Rachiel, Betsy, Robert, Thomas, and Lavenia, who married Dr. Isaac Jones.
9. John.
10. James, married Betsy White of S. C. Their children were William and Henry. William married Miss Faust. Henry married Betsy Smith.
11. Jonathan married, had no children.
12. Joseph.
13. Ann married Dr. Hill of Franklin City, N. Carolina. Their children were Nancy, Lavenia and Natt. Nancy married Murfree Knight (a runaway match), was afterward divorced and married a second time to Mark Cook of Raleigh, N. C. Lavenia married Dr. Wheaton. Natt took arsenic through mistake and died!

Second Marriage to Nannie Jones

The children of my great-grandfather, Matthias Brickell, were married as follows:
1. Benjamin married Nancy Davis, had one child, "Benjamin Ann."
2. Marinia married 4 times; Rollins, Moore, Saxon, and Burns who was a Baptist preacher. Matilda Rollins, her daughter, married Moody.
3. Rebecca married Palmer. Matt, their son, was very talented. They had several children who lived in Winton, N. Carolina.
4. Betsy married Godwin. Ann and Eliza were their daughters.
5. Nancy married 7 (seven) times. Lemon, Dickinson, Dr. Clark, etc. She never had but one child and that was a daughter by the fifth marriage. She was so beautiful a rejected lover went deranged.

My great-grandfather, William Murfree, married Miss Mary Moore and had seven children, viz:
1. Hardy Murfree (our grandfather), born 5th June 1752; died 6th April 1809.
2. William Murfree.
3. James Murfree, married and left two daughters, Mary and Sarah.
4. Sarah Murfree, married Sam Cryer.
5. Patty Murfree, married Ben Banks.
6. Betty Murfree, married Richard Andrews.
7. Nancy Murfree, married Jonathan Roberts.

The children of my great-grandfather, William Murfree, were married as follows:

1. Hardy Murfree to Sally Brickell on Thursday, 17th Feb. 1780. Their children were:
William Hardy Murfree, born 2nd Oct. 1781; died ——.
Fanny Noailles Murfree, born 23rd Aug. 1783; died ——.
Mary Moore Murfree, born 9th March 1786; died 1st March 1848.
Matthias Brickell Murfree, born 26th July 1788; died ——.
Rachiel Dickinson Murfree, born 5th Oct. 1790; died 28th Aug. 1794.
Sally Hardy Murfree, born 12th Feb. 1793.
Lavenia Bembury Murfree, born 3rd April 1795.
A Girl, not named, born 27th May 1797; died same day.
A Girl, not named, born 17th June 1798; died June 19, 1798.
Martha Long Ann Croakley Murfree, born 22nd May 1801.

---

2. William Murfree.
3. James Murfree had two daughters. Mary married Thomas Finney, and Sarah married Henry Soresburg.
4. Sarah Murfree married Sam Cryer, had three sons and four daughters; James, George, and Johnny; Mrs. Parker, Mrs. Pipkin, Mrs. Saurie, and Mrs. Barrow were her daughters. James was the father of Hardy Cryer. John married his cousin, Polly Banks. George never married, but was blind half his life.
5. Patty Murfree married Ben Banks. Their children were Mrs. Boyers, of Gallatin, Tennessee. Polly, who married Cryer;. Sally, who married Britt. Mrs. F. E. Pitts was the daughter of Mrs. Britt. James and Hardy Banks married Harriet and Martha Sketchley. Alexander Banks.
6. Betty Murfree married Richard Andrews. They had three children, William, Sally and Patty. Sally married a sea captain called Dunstan—they had a son called William Hardy. The other two died of "black tongue" in 1812.
7. Nancy Murfree married Jonathan Roberts.

The children of Colonel Hardy Murfree and Sally Murfree married as follows:
1. William Hardy Murfree married Elizabeth Maney, 1808.
2. Fanny N. Murfree married David Dickinson, 22nd Aug. 1799.
3. Mary M. Murfree married Isaac Hilliard, 9th March 1803.
4. Matthias B. Murfree married Mary Roberts.
5. Sally H. Murfree married Dr. James Maney.
6. Lavenia B. Murfree married Colonel Frank Burton, Feb. 23, 1814.
7. Martha L. A. C. Murfree married William Maney, March 10, 1818.

Record from family Bible belonging to Miss Fanny Noailles Dickinson Murfree, Murfreesboro, Tenn.

William Hardy Murfree was born on Tuesday, 2nd October, 1781, at 11 o'clock p.m.; son of Hardy Murfree and Sally Murfree, his wife.
Elizabeth Mary Murfree, daughter of James Maney and Mary Maney, his wife, was born on the 28th October, A. D. 1787.
William Law Murfree, son of William H. and Elizabeth M. Murfree, was born on the 19th day of July, 1817.
Sally Brickell Murfree, daughter of William H. and Elizabeth M. Murfree, was born on the — day of September, A. D. 1821.
Elizabeth Maney Murfree, daughter of William H. and Elizabeth M. Murfree, was born on the 13th July 1826.
Married on the 22nd day of November, A. D. 1843, near Murfreesboro, Tenn., William Law Murfree, Esq., to Miss Fanny Priscilla Dickinson, daughter of David Dickinson, Esq., and Fanny N. Murfree Dickinson.
Fanny Murfree (Fanny Noailles Dickinson Murfree) daughter of

William L. and F. Priscilla Murfree, was born August the 2nd, A. D. 1846.
Mary Susan Murfree, daughter of William L. and F. Priscilla Murfree, was born January the 24th, A. D. 1850. This child's name by consent of both parents was changed to Mary Noailles Murfree.
William Law Murfree, Jr., son of William L. and Fanny Priscilla Murfree, was born on Sunday, March 26th, 1854.
Married on the 7th day of December, 1881, William Law Murfree, Jr., to Miss Louise, daughter of John Knostman, Esq.
William Law Murfree (III) and Louise Murfree, twin son and daughter of William L. Murfree, Jr., and Louise K. Murfree, were born at Woodlawn, near St. Louis, Mo., November 18th, 1882.
Dickinson Knostman Murfree, son of William L. Murfree, Jr., and Louise K. Murfree, was born at St. Paul, Minnesota, January 9, 1888.

DEATHS

Elizabeth Mary Murfree, consort of William H. Murfree, departed this life on the 13th day of July, A. D. 1826, in the 39th year of her age.
William H. Murfree departed this life on the 19th day of January, A. D. 1827, in the 41st year of his age.
Louise Murfree, daughter of William L. Murfree, Jr., and Louise K. Murfree, departed this life the 28th day of November, 1883, aged one year and ten days.
William Law Murfree, son of William Hardy Murfree and Elizabeth M. Murfree, departed this life August 23, 1892, at Murfreesboro.
William Law Murfree, Jr., son of William Law Murfree and Fanny Priscilla Dickinson Murfree, departed this life January 25, 1902, at Boulder, Colorado.
Fanny Priscilla Dickinson Murfree, daughter of David Dickinson (and Fanny Noailles Murfree Dickinson), and wife of William Law Murfree, departed this life, September 19th, 1902, at Murfreesboro, Tennessee, eighty-six years of age, having been born on the 24th of September, 1816.
Mary Noailles Murfree, daughter of William L. Murfree and Fanny Priscilla Dickinson Murfree, departed this life July 31, 1922, at Murfreesboro, Tenn.

From Family Record in Blank Book copied from record in the old Dickinson Bible. This paper is from the copy of the Blank Book record made by Miss Fanny Noailles Dickinson Murfree, of Murfreesboro, Tenn.

John Hare was born on the 24th day of March, 1720.
Priscilla Hare, wife of John Hare, was born the 14th day of December, 1723.
Priscilla Hare, wife of John Hare, departed this life 16th day of May, 1765.
Grace Hare, wife of John Hare, departed this life the 30th day of April, 1787.
The ages of John Hare and his wife, Priscilla, and their children:
Mary Hare was born in September, the 6th, 1742.
Luke Hare was born June, the 20th day, 1745.
Sarah Hare was born in December, the 14th, 1748.
Elizabeth Hare was born in October, the 24th day, 1750.
John Lawrence Hare was born in March, the 18th day, 1754.
Moses Hare was born in August, the 28th day, 1757.
Benjamin Hare was born in October, the 3rd day, 1760.
Penelope Hare was born in February, the 11th day, 1764.

The above list of the names and ages of the children of John Hare and his wife Priscilla Hare was

copied from an old blank book. The births of three other children are noted, probably by the second wife, Grace Hare (the date of whose death is given), as these dates are subsequent to the death of the first wife, Priscilla Hare, May 16, 1765.
These entries are as follows:
September 5th, 1766, Lucresey Hare was born.
Jesse Hare was born 14th day of May, 1769.
On another page is this entry:
Bryan Hare was born the 17th day of December, 1783.
On the intervening page occurs this entry:
Moore Steavenson and William Steavenson, sons of William Steavenson, were born the twelfth day of December, 1761.

In the same book occur these entries:
David Dickinson, son of David Dickinson, was born the 11th day of October, 1774.
David William Dickinson, son of David Dickinson, was born 10th day of June at 8 o'clock in the morning, Friday, 1808.

Old Memorandum Found Among Dickinson Papers

David Dickinson, son of John Dickinson and Rebeckah, his wife, was born June 2nd, 17—7 (third figure of date is obliterated by book-worm hole, but it may be presumed to be "3", making the date 1737, and his age at his marriage in 1764 twenty-seven).
Sarah Hare, daughter of John Hare and Priscilla, his wife, was born December the 14th, 1748.
David Dickinson and Sarah Hare were married Sept., 25th day, 1764.
Priscilla Dickinson, daughter of David Dickinson and Sarah, his wife, was born December 17, 1765.
Mary and Sarah Dickinson, daughters of David Dickinson and Sarah, his wife, were both born January 22nd day, 1770.
David Dickinson, son of David Dickinson and Sarah, his wife, was born November 13th day, 1774.
Luke Dickinson, son of David Dickinson and Sarah, his wife, was born December 10th day, 1776.
Sarah Dickinson departed this life February 27th, 1778.
David Dickinson departed this life the 25th of November, 1783.
John Hilliard is four years, four months and four days older than his wife.
(This is the last entry on the old memorandum.)

David Dickinson, son of David Dickinson and Sarah, his wife, was born November 13, 1774.
Fanny Noailles Murfree, daughter of Hardy Murfree and Sally Brickell Murfree, his wife, was born August 23, 1783.
David Dickinson and Fanny Noailles Murfree were married August 22, 1799.
Hardy Dickinson, son of David Dickinson and Fanny, his wife, was born in 1800; died in infancy.
Sarah Louisa Dickinson, daughter of David Dickinson and Fanny, his wife, was born in 1801, and died in 1832; married John Bell.
David William Dickinson, son of David Dickinson and Fanny, his wife, was born June 10, 1808; died 1845; married first Miss Eliza J. Grantland (died 1838), and second Miss Sallie Brickell Murfree, daughter William Hardy Murfree.
Lavinia Dickinson, daughter of David Dickinson and Fanny, his wife, was born next; died about thirteen or fourteen years of age.
Benjamin Dickinson, son of David Dickinson and Fanny, his wife, was born about 1814; died about 1824.
Fanny Priscilla Dickinson, daughter of David Dickinson and Fanny, his wife, was born Sept. 24, 1816; died 1902, Sept. 19; married Nov. 22, 1843, William Law Murfree.
William Dickinson, son of David Dickinson and his wife, Fanny, born ———, died about four years of age.
Martha Elizabeth Dickinson,

daughter of David Dickinson and Fanny, his wife, was born June 10, 1823, and died February 27, 1850; married Lewis G. Galloway Sept. 14, 1846.

James Dickinson, son of David Dickinson and Fanny, his wife, died in infancy.

Their last child was a daughter dying in infancy.

Copied by Rebekah Jetton from family Bible owned by Mrs. George Davis of Murfreesboro.

Dr. M. Hill and Mrs. Hardenia J. Read were married in 1849, in McMinnville, Tenn.

Laurenia Caroline Rankin and John Thomas Read were married Sept. 7, 1848.

Mary Hardenia Read and William Watson Frater were married Jan. 10, 1887.

Mary Watson Frater and George Davis were married Aug. 15, 1906.

Mary Hardenia Read was born April 17, 1854.

William Watson Frater was born July 31, 1855.

Mary Watson Frater was born Oct. 24, 1887.

Caroline Pickens Frater was born Sept. 15, 1889.

Hannah Sims Frater was born March 27, 1891.

Elizabeth Read Frater was born June 5, 1898.

Caroline Pickens Frater and Philip Sidney Beebe were married April 15, 1912.

Elizabeth Read Frater and Frederick U. Dickman were married Sept. 29, 1920.

Sion S. Read and Hardenia Jefferson Spencer (cousin of Thomas Jefferson) were married at Templeton, Rutherford County, Tenn.

Harrison Barksdale and Laura C. Read were married in 1837, in Rutherford County, Tenn.

Laura C. Read was born Oct. 14, 1820.

Lycurgus W. Read was born 1822.

John T. Read was born Dec. 2, 1825.

Harriet J. Read was born Sept. 11, 1828.

George G. Read was born 1831.

Edwin C. Read was born 1834.

Corin Read was born 1837.

Charles W. Read was born April 17, 1841.

(The family of S. S. Read and Hardenia J. Read).

Dr. M. Hill, died Aug. 3, 1860; buried in McMinnville, Tenn.

H. J. Hill, died Sept. 6, 1889; buried in McMinnville, Tenn.

Laura C. Barksdale died Jan. 9, 1886, in Mississippi.

Lycurgus W. Read, died Nov. 13, 1846, in Monterey, Mexico, and buried there.

George Granville Read, died 1833; 14 months old; buried in Rutherford County, Tenn.

Edwin C. Read, died in Kentucky from wounds received at the Battle of Perryville.

Sion S. Read, died Aug. 3, 1845, and was buried in McMinnville, Tenn.

John T. Read, died Jan. 12, 1900.

L. W. Read, died Jan. 3, 1903.

Wm. W. Frater, died June 30, 1901.

Hannah Sims Frater, died June 25, 1911.

Mary Read Frater, wife of Wm. Watson Frater, died Dec. 3, 1930.

Copied by Rebekah Jetton from family Bible owned by James Horton Davis, of Murfreesboro, Tenn.

Solomon and Rebecca Farmer were married July 2, 1829.

Solomon Farmer was born Jan. 5, 1807.

Rebecca Farmer was born Jan. 9, 1810.

Wm. Farmer was born Jan. 11, 1834.

Joseph Farmer was born Jan. 6, 1836.

Houston Farmer was born Sept. 25, 1837.

James Farmer was born Feb. 28, 1840.
Mary Farmer was born Jan. 10, 1842.
John Farmer was born Nov. 9, 1843.
Elizabeth Farmer was born June 28, 1846.
Houston Farmer deceased this life Aug. 29, 1856.
Rebecca Farmer deceased this life Oct. 14, 1881.
Solomon Farmer deceased this life Jan. 14, 1886.

Copied by Rebekah Jetton from Bible owned by Mrs. Oliver Mann, Sixth District, Rutherford County, July 26, 1933.

John Nash Reed and Polly Barksdale were united in marriage May 22, 1810.
Col. Clement Read, Jr., married Mary Nash Dec. 22, 1757.
William Allen, son of Robert Allen, was born in the Kingdom of Ireland, Feb. 2, 1711; married to Sarah Cox, his third wife, on Jan. 2, 1726; he died Jan. 9, 1800. Third wife died June 27, 1797.
James Allen, son of William Allen and Sarah, his wife, was born Oct. 15, 1769, and was married to Elizabeth Lee, daughter of David and Margaret Lee, Jan. 24, 1793. The said Elizabeth Lee was born April 22, 1775, and died March 1, 1820.
Names of children of James and Elizabeth Allen, his wife:
Margaret, their first-born, June 23, 1794.
Sarah, born July 2, 1796.
Mary, born March 6, 1798.
William, born Nov. 6, 1799.
Teresa, born Feb. 2, 1802.
Jane, born Jan. 2, 1804.
David Lee, born March 14, 1807.
Samuel, born Nov. 2, 1807.
James, born Dec. 17, 1808.
Samuel Cox, born Oct. 3, 1810.
Elizabeth, born Aug. 4, 1812.
Robert, born Sept. 7, 1814.
Lemuel, born March 23, 1818.

Mary, died 1811.
William died Sept. 22, 1842.
Jane died July 15, 1820.
Samuel died July 31, 1808.
James died Sept. 29, 1826.

William Allen, first son and fourth child of James Allen and Elizabeth, his wife, was born Nov. 6, 1799, and was married to Sarah W. G. Read, daughter of John Nash Read and Mary, his wife, April 22, 1828.
The said Sarah W. G. Read was born April 17, 1811.

John James, born July 31, 1829; died Tuesday, 12 o'clock, April 22, 1873.
Mary Elizabeth, born Feb. 4, 1837.
Susan Ann, born March 7, 1834; died July 28, 1835.
Juliet Teresa, born Sept. 26, 1836.
Wm. Harrison, born March 6, 1838; died Nov. 4, 1838.
Nathaniel Reed, born Feb. 3, 1840.
William, born July 2, 1842.

William Allen, son of James Allen and Elizabeth, his wife, and father of the above named children, departed this life on Thursday evening about 8 o'clock, Sept. 22, 1842. After an illness of a few days he was attacked on Friday preceding his death with a soreness in his breast, a chilliness and general debility. He expired under the influence of spasmodic action of the lungs and fell asleep in the arms of the Savior, in whom he had put his trust for more than twenty years.

W. A. Davis (Wilbert), son of J. W. and Ella Davis, born July 4, 1890, departed this life Feb. 7, 1920, at 7:05 a.m., after a short illness.
John B. Davis, son of Wm. K. Davis and Mary Elizabeth, his wife, fell asleep in Jesus Oct. 11, at 6 p.m., 1919. He is buried at Fresno, California.

Names of children of Wm. K. Davis and Mary Elizabeth Davis:

Sarah, born Jan. 29, 1855; died Oct. 8, 1862.
Travis, born Aug. 20, 1857; died Oct. 3, 1862.
Mary Davis, born Aug. 11, 1859; died Oct. 30, 1862.
Wm. Allen Davis, born Dec. 20, 1861; died 4:45 o'clock, Nov. 16, 1862.
Lucy Margaret, born April 15, 1871.

From family Bible owned by Mrs. T. E. Kerr, Fosterville, Rutherford County.

Philip J. Brown, born April 27, 1819.
Ann E. Brown, born Jan. 13, 1821.
John Thomas Brown, born Feb. 14, 1846; died Aug. 20, 1902.
Deborah Franklin Brown, born June 19, 1850; died March 1, 1927.

Bible records sent on July 28th to Rebekah Jetton by Mrs. Media Davis Sinnott, of Smyrna, Tenn.

Betsy Simmons, grandmother of Sam Davis, born March 6, 1806, Petersburg, Va.; died March 2, 1891, at Smyrna, Tenn.
Charles Louis Davis, father Sam Davis, born Petersburg, Va., 1800; died Oct. 19, 1873.
Jane Simmons, mother of Sam Davis, born in Petersburg, Va., 1823; died Jan. 23, 1874, Smyrna, Tenn.
Sam Davis, born Oct. 6, 1842; executed Nov. 23, 1863.
Maggie Davis, born Nov. 24, 1844; died Nov. 18, 1910.
Media Davis, born March 14, 1849; still living.
Elizabeth Davis, born Jan. 9, 1854; died June 22, 1889.
Fannie Davis, born 1856.
Everett Davis, born 1851; died 1853.
Charles Louis Davis, Jr., born June 19, 1859; died Sept. 19, 1929.
Hickman Davis, born Sept. 19, 1861; died June 1, 1927.

From family Bible of James G. Overall family. Sent by Miss Jetton.

Jas. G. Overall was married Oct. 26, 1837, to Rachel W. Davis of Daviess County, Ky.
Wm. Jefferson Overall was married Feb. 28, 1860, to Clementine Hutchinson.
Robt. Baxter Overall was married Oct. 18, 1870, to Euphronia Ramsey.
Asbury McKendree Overall was married May 8, 1878, to Hudie M. Lowe.
Luther Capers Overall was married Dec. 21, 1881, to Josephine Vaughan.
Nathaniel D. Overall was married Nov. 21, 1894, to Kate C. Moore.
A. M. Overall died Jan. 9, 1922, aged 77 years, 8 months, 19 days.
James G. Overall was born May 23, 1814.
Rachel W. Overall, his wife, was born July 13, 1819.
Birth of children:
Wm. Jefferson Overall was born Aug. 2, 1838.
Polly Ann Overall was born Oct. 2, 1839.
Robert Baxter Overall was born April 30, 1841.
Asbury McKendree Overall was born April 20, 1844.
James Abram Dow Overall was born Feb. 22, 1847.
Nace Preston Overall was born Oct. 6, 1848.
John Arthur Hopkins Overall was born Aug. 28, 1850.

Thos. Bascom Young Overall was born Sept. 23, 1853.
Landrum Luther Capers Overall was born May 23, 1857.
Nathaniel James Davis Overall was born Dec. 19, 1862.

Deaths

Polly Ann, died Jan. 28, 1842; aged 2 years, 3 months and 26 days.
James Abram Dow, died Nov. 1, 1859; aged 12 years, 8 months.
Euphronia Overall, wife of Robt. B., died Nov. 30, 1870.
Thos. Bascom Young, died Dec. 2, 1872; aged 19 years, 2 months.
James G. Overall, our father, died May 2, 1874; aged 59 years, 11 months.
Robt. B. Overall, died July 27, 1874; aged 33 years, 2 months and 27 days.
Rachel W. Overall, our mother, died Aug. 26, 1874; aged 55 years, 1 month and 13 days.
Nace Preston Overall, died April 1, 1894; aged 45 years, 5 months and 25 days.
Hudie M., wife of Asbury McK. Overall, died Feb. 22, 1903; aged 42 years.
John Hopkins Overall, died Jan. 29, 1905; aged 54 years, 5 months, 1 day.
William Jefferson Overall, died April 3, 1908; aged 69 years, 8 months, 1 day.

Genealogy

John Overall married Miss Christine Froman, in Frederick County, Va., about 1750.
Nathaniel Overall, son of above, married Miss Annie Thomas in Davidson County, Tenn., in 1783.
Robert Overall, 1785-1863, son of above, married Miss Mary Espey in Rutherford County, Tenn., Dec. 24, 1810.
Jas. Garnett Overall, 1814-1874, son of above, married Miss Rachel Webb Davis, in Daviess County, Ky., Oct. 26, 1837.
Asbury McKendree Overall, 1844-1922, son of above, married Hudie M. Lowe in Rutherford County, Tenn., May 8, 1878.

Sketch of Overall Family by A. M. Overall

John Overall was living in Shenandoah County, Va., in 1783, at time of first census. In 1753 he married Maria Christina Froman (born March 1, 1786, granddaughter of Hans Joist Hite and Anna Maria DuBois, of Strasburg, Germany). They settled on South River, Shenandoah Valley. Their children:
John, married Elizabeth Waters, 1773.
William, 1754-1793 (Capt. Wm.), went to Tennessee.
Nathaniel, went to Tennessee.
Nancy (Nancy married Abraham Bowman, Jr., according to one record), married Joshua Thomas.
Mary, married Mr. Espey.
Robert, went to Tennessee.
Christina.
Sons of John Overall and Elizabeth Waters were Abraham, Isaac and Jacob.
His second wife was Mrs. Mary Byrne, in 1785. Their children were: Elias, Elizabeth, Marion, John Froman and Christina W.
Abraham Overall married Hannah Leath in Virginia and came to Tenn in 1805. They had ten children: John W., Elizabeth, Eliza (married James Wood), Nancy, Harriet, Vadney, Louisa, Paralee (married Gen. Wm. B. Stokes), Malissa (married C. W. L. Hale), (Maj.) Horace A. (married Mary Caroline Owen.)
Nathaniel Overall, born ——, in Frederick County, Va., son of John and Maria Christina Overall; died in Rutherford County, Tenn., 1835. Married Anne Thomas, who died in 1844. Their second child was Robert Overall, who settled in Rutherford County about 1810, and who fought in the War of 1812.
Another child of theirs was Mary Overall, born 1783, died 1849, and married Wm. Ramsey, Jr., in 1803.

Their son, Nathaniel Jefferson Ramsey, 1809-1871, married, 1828, Frances Young Davis, born 1812, died 1862.

Overalls in America

The first settlement made by this family in America was in Stafford County, Va., about 1700. One member of this branch came to the Shenandoah Valley as soon as it was opened for settlement. This was John Overall, who married Maria Christina Froman, granddaughter of Joist Hite.

The Overalls are of Saxon origin and settled in Thuxsted, Essexshire, England, during the reign of Henry VIII.

George Overall died in 1561. He was the first of the name I have any knowledge of, and he left three sons, William, Nathaniel and John. The last named was said to have been the most learned man of his time in England.

The American Overalls are in direct descent from Bishop John Overall, who was author of the Convocation Book mentioned by Macaulay in his History of England.

(Sketch of Overall Family by Asbury M. Overall).

William Webb, 1745-1809, born Essex County, Va., died Granville County, N. C.; served as a private in Capt. John Ashley's Company, 3rd Virginia Regiment; married Frances Young, 1771.

Mary Webb, 1782-1833, married, 1801, Baxter Davis, 1773-1839.

Rachel Webb Davis, 1819-1874, married Oct. 26, 1887, Jas. Garnett Overall, 1814-1874.

L. C. Overall, married Dec. 21 1881, Josephine Price Vaughan.

Inscriptions on Markers at Readyville, Tenn., sent by Miss Jetton.

Charles Ready, Sr., born at Salisbury, Md., April 1, 1770. Lived from early childhood in North Carolina and emigrated in 1797 to Tennessee. Settled in what is now Readyville. Died Aug. 3, 1859.

Mary Ready, consort of Charles Ready, Sr., born in N. C., Sept. 4, 1773. Died Sept. 3, 1848.

Palmer-Ready Record

*Francis Palmer, born in King William County, Va. Lived in Fairfield District, South Carolina, later. Served in the Revolutionary War, some say under General Marion, others say under "Light Horse Harry" Lee. After war he emigrated with his family to Tennessee; settled on Duck River. His daughter, Mary Ready, and family settled near Murfreesboro, Tenn., at the same time.

*Francis Palmer married Caroline Dulaney (French descent). She was born on the east shore of Maryland. She had a sister who married Mr. Ready. Both sisters after they were widows lived with Charles and Mary Ready and are buried at Readyville, Tenn. (So says Mr. Van Armstrong. He may be mistaken).

Children of Francis Palmer and Caroline Dulaney

1. Phillip Palmer, died young.
2. William Palmer, born 1777, died

---

*This should be William Palmer, born 1752, died 1824, near Lebanon, Wilson County. Corporal in Capt. Wm. Johnston's and later Everard Meador's Company; Col. Daniel Morgan's Regiment, Virginia Troops, March 1, 1778. (From supplemental paper of Laura Lillian Jetton, 179060).

1857 in Lebanon, Tenn.; married Susan Rankin; 13 children as follows:

1. Nancy Palmer, married Joab Goodall; had 12 children; moved to Marion, Ill. (Mrs. Nannie Parks, Marion, Ill.).

2. John (Jack) Palmer, lived near Lebanon, Tenn.

3. William Palmer. (W. R. Chambers of Lebanon is a grandson of one of the Palmers; also Jonathan Palmer, a Congressman from North Carolina).

4. Frank Palmer, had no heirs.

5. Charles Palmer.

6. Victoria Palmer, married W. Phelps.

7. Elizabeth Palmer, married M. Phelps.

8. Mary Palmer, married James White.

9. Martha Palmer, married Cage Bennett.

10. Sarah Palmer, married Cicero Murphey. (Four Murphey brothers live near Lebanon).

11. Margaret Palmer, married Thomas Cox, Tennessee.

12. Susan Palmer, married Addison Reese; emigrated to Marion, Ill.).

13. Henry Palmer, died young.

---

3. Henry Dulaney Palmer, born Charleston, S. C., in 1781; died in Illinois in 1861; preacher; married Patsy Angel; had nine children.

4. Susan Palmer, who was an invalid.

5. Francis Rose Palmer, born in 1789; emigrated to Independence, Mo.; preacher; married; one child, Frances A. Palmer, who married Mr. Grant. Lee W. Grant of St. Louis, Mo., is a son.

6. Caroline Palmer, married Nelson. (Never have been able to get in touch with them).

7. Mary Palmer, born 1773; died 1848 at Readyville, Tenn.; married Charles Ready. They were first cousins, (so Mr. Van Armstrong says). They had ten children as follows:

1. Nancy Ready, married Haskell. William T. Haskell, the noted Tennessee orator, was their son. He is the author of the poem, "Ransomed".

2. Caroline Ready, born in Sumner County, Tenn., in 1800; married Dr. Benjamin Hancock in 1817; died in May, 1873. Was a widow 39 years; married Enoch Jones in 1861; had five children as follows:
Benjamin Hancock, died young.
Mary Hancock, married Mr. T. N. Wendel, of Mississippi. (David Longstreet of the Illinois Central is a grandson).
Harriet Hancock, married Mr. Stewart. Mrs. Mary Auguspath, of Little Rock, Ark., is a daughter.
Erasmus Darwin Hancock, born 1822; married Fannie Murfree in 1859; died 1891. (E. D. Hancock of Murfreesboro, Mrs. W. V. Whitson of McMinnville, Mrs. Fred Craig of Nashville, Tenn., Mrs. H. A. Cannon of Waycross, Ga., John Hancock, Murfreesboro, and Essie Hancock, of Murfreesboro, are the six living children).
John Hancock, died ——, no heirs.

3 and 4. Charles and Aaron Ready, twins. Aaron died; Charles married Martha Strong of Knoxville, Tenn. (Weavers, Cheathams, of Nashville; Martins of Lebanon).

5. Eliza Ready, married Lafayette Burrus. (G. W. Howse, Murfreesboro, Tenn.).

6. Mary Ready, married Mr. Holmes. (Mrs. Eugene Logan, daughter of Mrs. Mary Nichol, deceased, Murfreesboro, Tenn.; David Holmes, Readyville, Tenn.).

7. Lucinda Ready, died aged 19.

8. Jane Ready, married Dr. Donoho, afterwards Peter C. Talley. (Mrs. Emma Jetton, Murfreesboro; E. W. Talley, Lawrenceburg,

Tenn.; Haskell Talley, Murfreesboro, Tenn.; Dr. Matt Murfree, Murfreesboro, Tenn.; James Spence, Grenada, Miss.)

9. Maria Ready, married Dr. Armstrong. (Mr. Van Armstrong, of Peoria, Ill.).

10. William Ready, married ——. (Mrs. John Price, of Louisville, Ky.).

McGowan Records

Sent by Miss Jetton.

(Copy from the obituary of Eliza McGowan, of Charlottetown, England).

"Methinks I have as much of Heaven as I can hold." These were the last words of the Rev. John MacGowan, whose works including his "Shaver" and "Dialogue of Devils", have been published in two octavo volumes, and who died in London in the year 1780. . . John MacGowan was a native of Edinburg and had been intended for the Presbyterian ministry, but at the age of 19 he joined the rebel army of the Pretender; fought at Culloden, then retired to Durham, but afterwards settled at Stohton. He was converted to God by the agency of John Urtank, a zealous local preacher among the Methodists of that day, and for a time he stood for the truth as then preached by Wesley, but MacGowan was a Calvinist and became the minister of Devonshire Square Chapel, London.

Peter, the third son of Rev. John MacGowan, was a student of law in London and was admitted in Court of King's Bench in 1762. In early manhood he emigrated to New York, but was afterwards induced to move to Prince Edward Island. He arrived here in 1789, and in four years after that event he was made Attorney General of the Province by Gov. Fanning, which office he held up to the time of his death in 1810.

Rev. Ebenezer MacGowan was born in the city of London on the 17th day of February, 1767, and departed this life on the 30th day of April, 1850. He emigrated to the United States in his seventeenth year and settled in Dinwiddie County, Va., where he was married to Sally Stell in 1785, with whom he lived seven years, when she died leaving three children, viz: John, James and Elizabeth... After he lost his wife he lived a widower four years and married Frances Baugh, of Mechlenburg County, Va., in 1797. From Dinwiddie County he moved to Mechlenburg County, to St. Tamony. From St. Tamony in 1816 to Rutherford County, Tennessee.

(*Exact Copy of Original*)

Register of the Births, deaths, etc., of the family of John MacGowan, of London, correctly transcribed from the genuine Register accompanying this Bible, which being torn from its place occasioned this copy.—E. Macgowan.

John Macgowan, son of James Macgowan and Elizabeth, his wife, was born October 23, 1726, and married to Esther Rigby, daughter of James and Esther Rigby, of St. Helen's in Lancanshire, on August 18th, 1766, in the parish Church of Warrington.

They had issue:

James Macgowan, born July 18, 1756.

Elizabeth Macgowan, born March 25, 1758.

John Macgowan, born August 3, 1760.

Peter Macgowan, born March 21, 1762.

Esther, my wife, died March 30, 1762.

Married to Mary, the daughter of William and Mary Harper of Book-

ton, near Shiffnal in Shropshire, on May 15, 1766, in the Parish Church of Bridgenorth. Issue by this marriage:
Ebenezer Macgowan, born Feb. 17, 1767.
Nathaniel Macgowan, born May 27, 1768.
Joseph Macgowan, born —— 21, 1769.
Mary, my wife, died on March 6, 1779, of the Febricula.
Nathaniel died March 21, 1770, of a mortification in his forehead.
Joseph Macgowan died March 17, 1771, at Highgate.
Married to Mary Sherron, daughter of Simon and Mary Sherron of the Isle of Purbeck, in the County of Dorset, on Dec. 4, 1771, in the Parish Church of St. Leonard, Thoreditch, London.
Elizabeth Macgowan died Feb. 19, 1774, aged 16.
John Macgowan, Sr., departed this life the 25th day of November, 1780, leaving his wife and four children, James, John, Peter and Ebenezer surviving him.
James Macgowan died July 9, 1886, in London.
Mary, widow of John Macgowan, Sr., died Dec. 4, 1815, in the 90th year of her age.
(Thus far the transatlantic record).

John Macgowan, the son of John and Esther Macgowan, died April 14, 1816, at St. Bartholomew's.
Peter Macgowan, son of John and Esther Macgowan, died June 19, 1810, at Prince Edward's Island (formerly St. John's) Nova Scotia.

Record of the family of James Macgowan, son of Ebenezer and Sally Macgowan.
James Macgowan was born Nov. 10, 1790, and died Jan. 3, 1845.
He was married to Ann Bugg Lewis, born March 31, 1800.
Issue of this marriage:
Jane Lewis, born April 23, 1822, and died April 4, 1843.
John Stell, born Feb. 2, 1824.
James Ebenezer, born April 8, 1826.
Robert Lewis, born Nov. 26, 1828.
Ann Bugg, born Sept. 26, 1831; died Sept. 8, 1847.
Samuel Bugg, born May 11, 1834.
Henry Ballard, born Jan. 26, 1837.
Mary Elizabeth, born Jan. 15, 1840.

Record of the family of Peter Macgowan, son of Ebenezer Macgowan and Esther Macgowan, transcribed from one of his letters to E. Macgowan.
Peter Macgowan was married to Ann Stainforth in England, Nov. 23, 1788.
Issue from this marriage:
Elizabeth, born March 14, 1798.
A son, born May 18, 1799; died.
John, born July 30, 1800.
William Stainforth, born April 18, 1802; died June 24, 1802.
William Stainforth, born April 12, 1803.
Peter, born May 3, 1805.
Lydia Cambridge, born Nov. 27, 1809.
Mary, born June 30, 1807.
L. C. Macgowan was married Nov. 22, 1832, to Daniel Hodgson.

O March, most fatal of the twelve, my peace
By thee is robb'd, thy very name sounds harsh
Upon my throbbing heartstrings. Canst thou not walk
Thine annual round unaccompanied by death?
Dost thou delight in that grim meagre visage,
That still with thee he visits my poor Dwelling?
Steal from my little Cabinet the Gems
Of highest worth, well ev'n do thy worst,
——— too hast limits, beyond which one Torch
——— cans't not go. I know the worst of all
——— handy work, and dread thee not, fell Ruffian.

This Bible was the property of my father, the Rev. John Macgowan of London, and it was after his death retained by his Relict and by her bequeathed to me. It was accordingly forwarded by Mr. Luntly, her Executor, and came to hand Dec. 22, 1817, and is now the property of Ebenezer Macgowan.

(Records compiled by Mrs. Caswell M. Stockard of Rutherford County, Tennessee, a descendant of Ebenezer Macgowan.

Bible records of M. A. F. White's Bible, presented to her by her husband, R. H. White, 1854.

Copied by Mary Robertson, member of Capt. Wm. Lytle Chapter. Sent by Miss Jetton.

MARRIAGES

Richard H. White to M. A. F. Nelson, Oct. 23, 1834.
Daniel N. White to E. Satira Phillips, May 11, 1865.
Levi Black White to Fannie A. Sims, May 25, 1865.

BIRTHS

R. H. White, June 27, 1811.
M. A. F. Nelson, March 31, 1818.
Children of R. H. and M. A. F. White:
Mildred A. E. White, Monday, June 20, 1836.
Daniel M. White, Tuesday, Aug. 6, 1837.
Levi B. White, Saturday, Sept. 7, 1839.
Sallie O. White, Wednesday, July 23, 1842.
R. H. White, Friday, March 22, 1845.
Diodorus Circulus White, Wednesday, May 27, 1847.
Cleopatra White, Tuesday, May 30, 1848.
Dora Frances Ann White, Thursday, April 10, 1851.
Tludla White, Monday, July 4, 1853.
Wm. D. Nelson, Jr., July 5, 1839.

DEATHS

Mildred A. E. White, July 9, 1836.
Diodorus C. White, June 20, 1847.
Richard H. White, Sr., Sept. 21, 1854.
William D. Nelson, Aug. 15, 1861.
Daniel N. White, Aug. 28, 1868.
M. A. F. White, May 30, 1884.
Levi B. White, Jan., 1894.
Cleopatra White, Sept. 21, 1905.
H. D. Lowry, March 31, 1900.
Dora F. A. Lowry, Jan. 6, 1931.
Richard H. White, Dec. 25, 1911.
Sallie O. White, Nov. 13, 1932.

Bible of C. R. H. White, Jan. 17, 1871, Smyrna, Tenn.

BIRTHS

R. H. White, March 22, 1845, Saturday.
Nannie R. White, July 1, 1843, Saturday.
Minnie L. White, July 15, 1869, Thursday.
Wm. Henry Garrett White, Thursday, Aug. 8, 1867; son of R. H. and N. R. White.

DEATHS

G. T. James, Jan. 16, 1874, 28 years, 5 months, 9 days.
E. C. James, July 12, 1874, at 12:30 o'clock, aged 54 years, 9 months, 10 days.
Enie Rucker White, Willie's wife, June 20, 1895; buried in Mt. Olivet, near Nashville, Tenn., in 22nd year.
W. R. James, Oct. 19, 1897, at 8:50 o'clock, aged 89 years, 2 months, 4 days.
Annie Rudder White, March 25, 1903, at 11:10 p.m., aged 59 years, 8 months, 25 days. She was married 37 years, 7 months, 17 days, 3 hours.
R. H. White, Dec. 25, 1911, aged 66 years, 10 months, 3 days.

MARRIAGES

John and Hannah Ellison married Sept. 22, 1769.
Mary Ellison married June 25, 1772.
Adam Ellison married April 15, 1777.
Henry White and Hannah White married March 3, 1778.
Robert Marley White married April 14, 1805.
Levi White married Feb. 16, 1808.
Asa White married Oct. 3, 1811.
Henry White married Feb. 18, 1809, and again in 1817.
H. White married Mrs. Lucy Searcy Dec. 8, 1832.

BIRTHS

Henry White, Sr., July 1, 1755.
Children of John and Hannah Ellison:
Marey Ellison, born March 23, 1772.
Adam Ellison, born Aug. 20, 1775.
Children of Adam Marley, Sr., and Rosanna Marley, his wife:
Robert Marley, born Aug. 4, 1741.
Mary, born Sept. 17, 1743.
Catherine, born March 22, 1745.
Margaret, born Nov. 16, 1748.
Hannah, born March 25, 1754.
Adam, born Sept. 17, 1756.
Samuel, born Sept. 30, 1758.
Children of Henry and Hannah White:
Samuel White, born Jan. 20, 1779.
Robert Marley White, born Oct. 11, 1781.
Levi White, born Aug. 18, 1784.
Asa White, born May 2, 1787.
Henry White, born Feb. 6, 1790.
Children of Henry and Betsy White:
Martha, born Feb. —, 1809.
Richard, born June 27, 1811.
Levi B., born Feb. 18, 1813.
Betsy, born Nov. 15, 1814.
Robert M. White, born Oct. 14, 1818.

DEATHS

Samuel White, Aug. 20, 1801.
Betsy S. White, April 10, 1816.
Henry White, Sr., Oct. 6, 1830.
Nancy E. White, June 29, 1831.
Mildred Ann Elizabeth White, daughter of R. H. and M. A. F. White, July 9, 1836.
Hannah White, Nov. 19, 1840.
Robert M. White, Jr., Aug. 8, 1841.
Levi White, Sr., July 2, 1848.
Elyabeth White Searcy, March 23, 1891.
Catherine Marley, Dec. 8, 1747.
Margaret Marley, July 23, 1775.
Samuel Marley, Dec. 28, 1891.
Adam Marley, Aug. 27, 1813.

EPPS

Lafayette Epps and Rebecca Allen married Dec. 13, 1834.
Lafayette Epps born Nov. 15, 1815; died May 26, 1857.
Rebecca Epps, born Jan. 27, 1820.
John Richard Epps, son of Lafayette and Rebecca Epps, born Jan. 30, 1836; died March 21, 1858.
Eliza Matilda Epps, daughter of Lafayette and Rebecca Epps, born Nov. 2, 1841.
Rebecca Epps died Feb. 15, 1859.
Wm. Henry Epps, born March 10, 1844.
Elizabeth Frances Epps, born May 19, 1847.
Francis Bat Epps, born May 18, 1851.
James Alexander Epps, born Jan. 2, 1854.
Rebecca Jane Epps, born July 22, 1856.

MARRIAGES

W. B. Coleman and Dollie Barnes, Dec. 28, 1879.
Thos. Carter and Fannie Coleman, Feb. 11, 1874.
Tom Coleman and Jane Epps, Nov. 20, 1879.

BIRTHS

Wm. B. Epps, son of Bat and Madora Epps, Dec. 17, 1874.
Fannie Bell Pots, daughter of George and Della Pots, Dec. 18, 1874.
David and William Carter, the sons of Thos. and Fannie Carter, May 6, 1875.
Ada V. Epps, daughter of Bat and Madora Epps, Feb. 14, 1876.
Anora Eliza Jane Coleman, daughter of Wm. A. Coleman and Dolly

F. Coleman (his wife was Dolly Williams), born Nov. 17, 1818.
Rebecca H. Coleman, April 16, 1820.
Amandy Melvin Coleman, Dec. 30, 1823.

William Archer Coleman Bible, originally Lafayette Epps.

BIRTHS

Wm. Bellfield Coleman, June 5, 1829.
Leveny Frances Coleman, Aug. 12, 1833.
David Alexander Coleman, Jan. 23, 1837.
Dollie Coleman, Dec. 3, 1852.
Thos. et Coleman, son of W. B. and Dollie, June 15, 1881.
Caroline Coleman, Oct. 4, 1853.
Lula Rebecca Coleman, Oct. 31, 1880; died Nov. 19, 1880.
James Thomas Coleman, July 10, 1856.
Rebecker Jane Coleman, July 22, 1856.

DEATHS

Leveny Frances C., wife of Thomas Barnes, Sept. 12, 1854.
William A. Coleman, Oct. 12, 1869.
Rebecca Coleman, March 8, 1874.
William C. Coleman, Dec. 2, 1874.
Wm. B. Epps, Sept. 15, 1875.
Frances Coleman, born Jan. 22, 1802; died July 21, 1883.

FAMILY RECORDS

James I. Ward and Mary I. Leath, married June 18, 1850.

BIRTHS

Mary L. Leath, Dec. 20, 1824.
Louisa Ward, Sept. 25, 1819.
Mary E. Ward, Nov. 18, 1838.
Martha Ward, Sept. 5, 1840.
Isabeler Ward, Jan. 5, 1843.
Victora Ward, Jan. 4, 1845.
Josehene A. Ward, Oct. 18, 1846.
Andrew I. Ward, March 21, 1849.
William A. Ward, April 17, 1851.
Charles A. Ward, Jan. 15, 1852.
Frances C. Ward, Sept. 29, 1853.
Mifes Edwin Lewis, Nov. 10, 1870.
Mary I. Leath, Dec. 25, 1824.

WHITE FAMILY BIBLE RECORD

Family Bible records in the possession of H. J. Lowry, of Smyrna, Rutherford County, Tennessee., Capt. Wm. Lytle Chapter. Sent by Miss Jetton.

Henry White, Sr., Captain in Revolutionary War, born July 1, 1755; died Oct. 6, 1830; married March 3, 1778, to Hannah Marley (Mrs. Ellison), born March 25, 1754; died Nov. 19, 1840.
Children of Henry White and Hannah White:
Samuel White, born Jan. 20, 1779; died Aug. 20, 1801.
Robert Marley White, born Oct. 11, 1781; died ——; married (1) Elizabeth Banton, April 14, 1805; (2) Susan Isbell.
Levi White, born Aug. 18, 1784; died July 2, 1848; married Sarah O. Booth, Feb. 16, 1808.
Asa White, born May 2, 1787; married (not known), Oct. 3, 1811.
Henry White, Jr., born Feb. 6, 1790; died Oct., 1856; married Betsy S. Ward, Feb. 18, 1809.
Betsy S. Ward White, died April 10, 1811.
Henry White, Jr., married Nancy E. White, 1817.
Nancy E. White, died June 29, 1831.
Henry White, Jr., married Mrs. Lucy Searcy, Dec. 8, 1832.
Children of Levi White and Sarah O. (Booth) White:
Two died in childhood.
Children of Henry White, Jr., and Betsy S. (Ward) White:
Martha A. E. White, born Dec. 25, 1809; died in infancy.
Richard Henry White, born June 25, 1811; died Sept. 21, 1854; married M. A. Nelson, Oct. 23, 1834.
M. A. F. Nelson White, died May 30, 1884.
Levi B. White, born Feb. 14, 1813.
Betsy S. White, born Nov. 15,

1814; died 1891; married Anderson Searcy.
Children of Henry White, Jr., and Nancy E. White:
Robert M. White, born Oct. 14, 1818; died Aug. 8, 1841; married Ann Barksdale.
Children of Henry White, Jr., and Mrs. Lucy Searcy (none).
Children of Richard H. White and M. A. E. Nelson White:
M. A. E. White, born June 20, 1836; died July 9, 1836.
Daniel N. White, Lieutenant in Confederate Army, born Aug. 8, 1837; died Aug. 28, 1868; married E. Satira Phillips, May 11, 1865.
E. Satira Phillips White, died Nov., 1915.
Levi B. White, Captain in Confederate Army, born Sept. 7, 1839; died Jan. 15, 1894; married May 25, 1865, to Fannie Sims, born Feb. 26, 1843; died March 2, 1887.
Sarah O. White, born July 23, 1842.
Richard H. White, private in Confederate Army, born March 22, 1845; died Dec. 25, 1911; married (1) Aug. 8, 1865, to Nannie James; (2) April, 1905, to Minnie Sanders.
Diodorus C. White, born May 27, 1847; died June 20, 1847.
Cleopatra White, born May 30, 1848; died Sept. 21, 1900.
Dora F. A. White, born April 10, 1851; died Jan. 6, 1931; married July 2, 1871, to H. D. Lowry, born Dec., 1847; died March 31, 1900.
Ella White, born July 4, 1853; died Jan. 4, 1923; married June 6, 1872, to Garrett James.
Children of Daniel N. White and E. Satira (Phillips) White:
John H. White, born Sept. 2, 1866; died ——; married Jan. 17, 1892, to Loretta P. Hines.
Children of Levi B. White and Fanny Sims White:
Lula White, born April 17, 1866; married Oct. 6, 1898, to G. Lipscomb, born ——; died Feb. 20, 1910.
Viola White, born Feb. 13, 1868; married Nov. 26, 1896, to C. M. Gadsey.
Ella Beatrice White, born Nov. 8, 1869; married June 26, 1895, to A. J. Hamer.
L. Numa White, born Sept. 13, 1871; married March 11, 1896, to Christine Edmondson, born ——; died Feb. 2, 1913; married Feb., 1915, to Bessie Seward.
M. A. F. White, born Aug. 6, 1873; married Jan. 24, 1900, to S. Willard.
Lizzie White, born May 28, 1875; died Oct. 17, 1881.

Children of R. H. White and Nannie James White:
W. H. G. White, born Aug. 8, 1867; married Feb., 1893, to Evie Rucker.
Children of Dora F. A. White Lowry and H. D. Lowry:
Romars Lowry, born Sept. 9, 1872; died April 18, 1874.
David Lowry, born Oct. 17, 1874; died Dec. 19, 1874.
Wm. L. Lowry, born Jan. 7, 1876; married Dec. 22, 1904, to M. M. Kennedy.
M. A. F. Lowry, born Sept. 10, 1879; died Oct. 2, 1883.
Sallie H. Lowry, born Dec. 3, 1882; died Dec. 23, 1883.
Infant, born July 18, 1884; died July 30, 1884.
Henry Jackson Lowry, born Aug. 2, 1885; married Jan. 6, 1921, to L. M. Harris.

Children of Ella White James and Garrett James:
Lola Garrett James, born March 11, 1873; married June 22, 1892, to E. A. Hibbett.

Children of John H. White and Loretta P. Hines:
Mary Esther White, born Nov. 18, 1893.
John Daniel White, born Aug. 11, 1801.

Children of Ella Beatrice White Hamer and A. J. Hamer:
L. Buford Hamer, born Oct. 29, 1896.

L. Beatrice Hamer, born March 9, 1901.
J. G. Hamer, born May 2, 1905.

Children of L. N. White and Christine Edmondson White:
Tillis White, born Feb. 26, 1897.
Infant, born May, 1900; died May, 1900.
Laban E. White, born Dec. 23, 1902.

Children of L. N. White and Bessie Seward White:
Edwin Seward White, born Jan. 17, 1916.
Clide Sims White, born Aug., 1918.
Children of M. A. F. White Willard and S. Willard:
Viola Frances Willard.
S. J. Willard.

Children of Lola G. James Hibbett and E. A. Hibbett:
Garrett J. Hibbett, born July 22, 1893.
J. K. Hibbett, born Sept. 1, 1895.
E. A. Hibbett, Jr., born Sept. 16, 1897.
Horace I. Hibbett, born July 1, 1900.
Ella Mary Hibbett, born Dec. 1, 1902.
Hoffman Hibbett, born Jan. 4, 1909.
Lola D. Hibbett, born Jan. 8, 1913.

Children of Betsy S. White Searcy and Anderson Searcy:
Anderson Searcy, Colonel in Confederate Army, born 1832; died May 11, 1910; married April 25, 1855, to Amanda E. Batey.
Lucy Searcy, born March 26, 1836; died Dec., 1894; married June 2, 1856, to Steve M. Glenn.
Sallie E. Searcy, born Feb. 2, 1837; died Aug. 7, 1895; married April, 1856, to Wm. Davis.
Tabbie Searcy, born Feb. 17, 1838; died Aug. 1, 1910; married Nov. 28, 1859, to Wm. B. Batey.
Judy Searcy, born 1840; married (date unknown) to Mr. Dyer.

Children of Col. Anderson Searcy and Amanda E. Batey Searcy:
Lizzie L. Searcy, born April 15, 1856; married Nov. 13, 1878, to A. J. Matthews.
Evie A. Searcy, born May 15, 1858; married Nov., 1879, to J. B. Johns, Jr., and died July, 1883.
Benjamin B. Searcy, born Jan. 15, 1861; died March 18, 1930.
John H. Searcy, born Feb. 20, 1866; married Jennie Crutcher.
James B. Searcy, born Feb. 13, 1868.
Sallie D. Searcy, born Feb. 18, 1870; married Dec. 6, 1893, to A. G. Thompkins.
Kate B. Searcy, born March 5, 1871; married Oct. 22, 1913, to O. L. Wilkerson.
Newton Collier Searcy, born Nov. 29, 1873.
Anderson Searcy, Jr., born May 22, 1877; died Feb. 27, 1887.
Willie B. Searcy, born July 31, 1880; died May 22, 1881.

Children of Lizzie L. Searcy Matthews and A. J. Matthews:
Mary Eliza Matthews, born Oct. 7, 1879; died Sept. 5, 1880.
Batey Matthews, born July 11, 1881; died Aug. 13, 1910; married June 20, 1906, to Mary Banks.
Gladys Matthews, born July 31, 1883; died July 31, 1883.
Grover Cleveland Matthews, born Oct. 10, 1884.
Erline Matthews, born April 23, 1887; married June 3, 1909, to W. M. Erwin.
Epps Edwin Matthews, born Jan. 5, 1889.
May Matthews, born May 31, 1891; married Feb. 7, 1913, to W. W. Holloway.
Ben Searcy Matthews, born Dec. 13, 1896; died Sept. 4, 1897.

Children of Evie A. Searcy Johns and J. B. Johns, Jr.:
Will Anderson Johns, born Aug. 12, 1881; married Jennie Murray, June, 1908.
Albert Searcy Johns, born Dec., 1883.

Child of Erline Matthews Erwin and W. M. Erwin:
John Martin Erwin, born July 11, 1911.

Child of May Matthews Holloway and W. W. Holloway:
Lucy Elizabeth Holloway, born Oct. 23, 1913.

Child of Will Anderson Johns and Jennie Murray Johns:
John Palmer Johns, born March, 1909.
Children of Sallie E. Searcy Davis and Wm. Davis:
Robert O. Davis, born 1857; married Sept. 19, 1895, to Laura Johnson.
Mollie L. Davis, born April 9, 1859; married Nov. 27, 1883, to R. T. Bell.
Ella Davis, born 1861; married Joe Black.
John Davis, born 1863; married (1) Kim Morton; (2) Lizzie Elam.
Sam B. Davis, born Dec. 25, 1866; married 1898 to Florence Wells.

Children of Robt. O. Davis and Laura Johnson Davis:
Sarah C. Davis, born Jan. 27, 1897.
Robt. O. Davis, Jr., born April 30, 1903.

Children of Mollie L. Davis Bell and R. T. Bell:
R. T. Bell, Jr., born Nov. 17, 1884; married Kate Currin Rather, 1911.
Sadie E. Bell, born March 17, 1887; died Oct. 7, 1892.
Georgie Bell, born Sept. 17, 1889; married Oct., 1912, to Wm. F. Earthman.
Charlie E. Bell, born Dec. 17, 1891; died Oct., 1918.
Sam Davis Bell, born June 6, 1900.

Children of R. T. Bell, Jr., and Kate Currin Rather Bell (died 1922):
Kate Currin Bell, born Oct. 4, 1912.
Mary Catherine Bell, born 1922.

Child of John Davis and Kim Morton Davis:
Ella B. Davis, born 1900.

Children of Sam B. Davis and Florence Wells Davis:
Wm. L. Davis, died at age of 7 years.
Margarette Davis, born Sept., 1907.
Dorothy Wells Davis, born 1909.
Mary Louise Davis, born 1912.
Children of Tabbie Searcy Batey and Wm. B. Batey:
Eva A. Batey, born Sept. 23, 1860; died May 11, 1886.
Wm. B. Batey, Jr., born Feb. 26, 1862; died Jan. 30, 1901.
Bessie S. Batey, born Feb. 27, 1864; died Sept. 16, 1869.
Anderson S. Batey, born Aug. 24, 1866; married April 24, 1901, to Jennie Hooper.
Sallie L. Batey, born Jan 6, 1871; married Dec. 18, 1901, to W. N. Brown.
Mattie E. M. Batey, born July 23, 1873; married to I. R. Peebles April 12, 1899; died May 8, 1930.
Robert T. Batey, born June 30, 1876; married Marian Miller.
Jack G. Batey, born June 30, 1876; married Annie Watt Smith, Nov. 28, 1812.

Children of Sallie L. Batey Brown and W. N. Brown:
Jetton Jarratt Brown, born July 1, 1903.
Kathleen Searcy Brown, born Sept., 1904.
John Clark Brown.
Albert Johns Brown.

Children of Mattie E. M. Batey Peebles and I. R. Peebles:
Wm. B. Peebles, born Feb. 10, 1901.
Sarah A. Peebles, born Sept. 13, 1902; died Dec. 3, 1902.
Melvy Peebles, born Dec. 13, 1903.
Jennie M. Peebles, born Sept. 30, 1905.
Mollie W. Peebles, born Jan. 5, 1907.

Precious Tabbie Peebles, born Nov. 30, 1909.
Isham R. Peebles, born Nov. 25, 1911.
Leon P. Peebles, born Nov. 6, 1913.

—

Children of Robt. T. Batey and Marian Miller Batey:
Robert T. Batey, Jr., born April 24, 1905.
Wm. Newton Batey, born Oct. 29, 1913.
Child of Jack G. Batey and Annie Watt Smith Batey:
Martha Louise Batey, born April 10, 1915.

—

Children of Robt. M. White, Jr., and Ann Barksdale White:
Mary White, born 1840; married (1) Mr. Howse; married (2) Mr. Williamson.
Robt. M. White, born 1842; died 1863.

—

Child of Mary White Howse and Mr. Howse:
Arthur Howse, born 1860.

—

Children of Robt. Marley White, Sr., and Nancy Banton:
Judidah White, married (1) Mr. Fussell; (2) Mr. Lannom.
Aurelia White, married (1) ——; (2) Mr. Garrett.
Sarah White, married Wm. Fant.
Jackson B. White, married Ellen Cahal.
Louisa A. White, born Aug. 6, 1816; married Ellis Isbell; died 1905.
Henry White; died when grown.
Nancy White; married John Weaver.

—

Child of Judidah White Fussell and Mr. Fussell:
Wm. Fussell.

—

Child of Judidah White Fussell Lannom and Mr. Lannom:
Aurelia Lannom; died 1854.

—

Child of Aurelia (White) Furmault and Mr. Furmault:
Ann Furmault; married Jim Robins.

—

Children of Sarah White Fant and Wm. Fant, Sr.:
Wm. Fant, Jr.
Lou Fant.

—

Child of Jackson B. White and Ellen Cahal White:
Sarah A. White, died March 7, 1901.
Children of Louisa A. White Isbell and Ellis Isbell:
Robert Isbell.
George Louis Isbell.
Henry Isbell.
Ella Isbell, married Jim O'Riley.
Mollie Isbell.
Bettie Isbell.
John E. Isbell, born Nov. 27, 1852; married Oct. 29, 1873, to Anne S. Haris.
Lula Isbell.

—

Child of Ella Isbell O'Riley and Jim O'Riley:
Ellis O'Riley.

—

Children of Nancy White Weaver and John Weaver:
Fannie Weaver, married Mr. Roberts.
Robt. M. Weaver.
Sallie Lou Weaver.
James Weaver.
Kate Weaver.

—

Child of Will Fussell and Sallie Lou Fussell:
Kate Fussell.

—

Children of Ann Furmault Robin and Jim Robin:
Aurelia Robin.
Altie Robin.

—

Children of Aurelia Robin McGeehee and Mr. McGeehee (none recorded).

—

Children of Altie Robin Davis and Mr. Davis (none recorded).

Children of Robt. Fant and Mary Williams:
Lula Fant, married Holliday.
Nannie Faut, married Leatherwood.
Minnie Fant, married Hollinsworth.
Ellen Fant, married Gruner.
Fannie Fant.
Robert Fant.
Child of Lou Fant Roberson and Mr. Roberson:
Mollie Roberson; married Wm. Harris.

Children of J. E. Isbell and Anne S. Haris Isbell:
Wm. H. Isbell, born Nov. 3, 1874; married Horton Andrews, April 19, 1906.
Robert F. Isbell, born Jan. 1, 1876; married Ruby Neville, July 25, 1899.
Jack Gibson Isbell, born Aug. 9, 1879; married June, 1900, to Mary Sorbe.
Julia Katherine Isbell, born Nov. 30, 1882; married Sept. 14, 1904, to Victor Andrews.
Mary Ellis Isbell, born July 20, 1885; married June 29, 1904, to W. M. Watkins.
(?) Henry Wyatt Isbell, born Nov. 30, 1887; married ——.
Albert Edward Isbell, born March 11, 1889; married Jan., 1814, to Laura B. Meadows.
Anne Stratton Isbell, born Sept. 15, 1892; married June 26, 1911, to Edward W. Lee.
George Louis Isbell, born Aug. 12, 1894; married Grace Juanita Bond, Sept. 19, 1927.
Margaret Angela Isbell, born May 18, 1897; married Feb. 7, 1916, to J. G. Stephenson.

Children of Lucy White Searcy Glenn and S. M. Glenn:
John A. Glenn.
Willie H. Glenn.
Sallie L. Glenn, married Mr. Cobb.
Tabbie E. Glenn, married Mr. Barfield.
David M. Glenn.
Stephen M. Glenn.
Lula A. Glenn.
Minnie Glenn, married Mr. Foust.

Children of Willie H. Glenn and ——
Lloyd Glenn.
Tabbie Glenn.
Sadie Glenn.
Grover Glenn.
Ruth Glenn.
William Glenn.
James Glenn.
Virginia Glenn.

Children of Sallie L. Glenn Cobb and Mr. Cobb:
Lucy Cobb.
Kate Cobb.

Children of Tabbie E. Glenn Barfield and Mr. Barfield:
Harry Barfield.
Palmer Barfield.
Searcy Barfield.
Robert Barfield.
George Barfield.

Children of Stephen M. Glenn and ——:
Lucy Glenn, married Mr. Johnson.
Stephen Glenn, Jr.

Children of Minnie Glenn Foust and Mr. Foust:
Agnes Foust.
Catherine Foust.

Children of Lloyd Glenn and ——:
Ella Glenn.
Lloyd Glenn, Jr.
Joseph Glenn.

Child of Lucy Glenn Johnson and Mr. Johnson:
Frances Johnson.

Children of William H. Isbell and Horton Andrews Isbell:
William Isbell.
Laura Isbell.
Julia Isbell.

Child of Robert F. Isbell and Ruby Neville Isbell:

Children of Jack G. Isbell and Mary Sorbe Isbell:
Cheneza Isbell.
Willeaz Isbell.

Child of Julia Kathrine Isbell and Victor Andrews:
Victor B. Andrews.

Children of Mary Ellis Isbell Watkins and W. M. Watkins:
William M. Watkins.
Richard Wyatt Watkins.

Child of Albert Edward Isbell and Laura Bell Meadows Isbell:
John Ellis Isbell, born June 12, 1915.

Child of Ann Stratton Isbell Lee and Edward W. Lee:
Edward Lee.

Child of George L. Isbell and Grace J. Bond Isbell:
Patricia Catherine, born May 27, 1929.

W. E. Knox Bible Record

W. E. Knox Bible records copied by Rebekah Jetton.

Jane Knox, born June 11 (or 13), 1770; died May 25, 1842.
Samuel W. Knox, born Oct., 1814.
Eliza Knox, born Oct. 17, 1817; died Sept. 13, 1840.
Samuel W. Knox and Eliza Dill, married Feb. 22, 1838.
Samuel W. Knox and Mary A. Mabry, married Dec. 13, 1842.
Thomas Allison Knox, born April 14, 1722, and departed this life May 5, 1794.
Magdalene Allison, born Aug. 31, 1725, and departed this life May 17, 1794.
Theophilus Allison, born Feb. 1, 1740.
Alexander Allison, born Nov. 27, 1749, and departed this life May, 176—.
Magdalene Allison, born Dec. 20, 1751.
Theophilus Allison, born May 30, 1754.
Margaret Allison, born Aug. 29, 1756, and departed this life Sept. 24, 1779.
Thomas Allison, Jr., born Jan. 10, 1759.
Magdalene Knox, born Dec. 28, 1751, and departed this life Nov. 27, 1802.
Elizabeth Knox departed this life April 7, 1807.

Bible Records Copied by Mrs. W. P. Bouton, Lebanon, Tenn.

Bradshaw Bible, in possession of daughter, Kate Bradshaw-McFarland (Mrs. J. J. McFarland), Lebanon, R. F. D., Wilson County, Tenn.

Births

W. L. Bradshaw, born Feb. 18, 1825.
S. J. Bradshaw, born Jan. 27, 1832.
Mary E. Bradshaw, born Mar. 31, 1854.
Ida Bradshaw, born Sept. 19, 1858.
Frances G. Bradshaw, born Sept. 9, 1860.
Samuel S. Bradshaw, born May 5, 1863.
Jack Bradshaw, born Dec. 14, 1865.
Evaline Bradshaw, born Oct. 5, 1867.
Ben J. Bradshaw, born Aug. 17, 1870.
Kate Bradshaw, born Jan. 2, 1873.
Charlie Beverly Bradshaw, born Oct. 24, 1878.
Edgar Howard Oldham, born April 6, 1881.

Sadie May Oldham, born April 12, 1883.
Mary Oldham, born May 30, 1884.
Kate Oldham, born June 18, 1886.
Sallie Oldham, born Aug. 31, 1886.
Charlie Oldham, born April, 1889.

MARRIAGES

R. F. Woodroof and Mary E. Bradshaw, married Aug. 9, 1872.
W. H. Oldham and Ida Bradshaw, married Oct. 16, 1879.
Frank Bradshaw and James Oldham, married May 17, 1883.
S. S. Bradshaw and Susie Palmer, married Oct. 24, 1889.
J. H. Bradshaw and Marcie McClain, married Dec. 9, 1890.
B. J. Bradshaw and Kittie Goldston, married Nov. 25, 1891.

DEATHS

John Shepard, died June 2, 1836, aged 42 yrs., 3 mos., and 7 days.
Frances G. Shepard, died Oct. 4, 1860, aged 54 yrs., 10 mos., and 7 days.
Evie Bradshaw, died Nov. 29, 1886, aged 19 yrs., 1 mo., and 24 days.
Frank Oldham, died July 21, 1888, aged 27 yrs., 10 mos., and 12 days.

Young Bible, in possession of grandson, Orville Young, Mt. Juliet, R. F. D. No. 5, Wilson County, Tenn.

BIRTHS

William L. Young, born May 23, 1806.
Nancy Hewgley, born Nov. 15, 1808.
Tabitha Ann Young, born Nov. 1, 1830.
Charles W. L. G. G. B. Young, born Feb. 5, 1834.
Eliza Ann Young, born June 2, 1832.
Sarah H. Young, born Oct. 22, 1835.
Martha G. Young, born May 2, 1837.
James A. Young, born Dec. 7, 1838.
William H. H. Young, born Nov. 15, 1840.
Margaret E. Young, born Jan. 15, 1843.
Theodore F. H. Young, born Oct. 28, 1844.
John L. N. M. C. Young, born June 11, 1849.
Claud Viverett Young, born June 16, 1867.
Cora Young, born April 16, 1869.
Orvill Young, born May 8, 1870.
Ruth Young, born Jan. 25, 1872.
Ora Young, born Nov. 1, 1876.
Laurance W. Young, born July 30, 1880.
Floy B. Young, born April 15, 1876.
M. E. Young, born Aug. 3, 1876.
Ruby L. Young, born Jan. 2, 1872.
Bertha Clair Young, born Sunday morning, 6:30 a.m., Mar. 2, 1919, to Orvill and Bertha Young.
Vinsen Z. L. Harilson, born May 7, 1851.
Margaret A. Guill, born July 2, 1867.
Mattie Foust Guill, born Aug. 5, 1870.
Sarah B. Guill, born Feb. 16, 1871.
Ada W. Guill, born Mar. 2, 1874.
May S. Guill, born April 21, 1886.

MARRIAGES

William L. Young and Nancy Hewgley, married Jan. 14, 1830.
James L. Harilson and Eliza Ann Young, married Feb. 22, 1849.
E. M. Guill and Tabiyha Young, married Aug. 26, 1866.
N. C. Young and Viney Wallis, married Oct. 19, 1877.
Orvill Young and Bertha Clair Tipton, married April 2, 1914.

DEATHS

Margaret Elizabeth Young, died Aug. 1, 1844.
Cora Young, died Feb. 5, 1870.
Sarah H. Young, died Nov. 19, 1880.
Ora Young, died Nov. 25, 1880.
Tabitha Guill, died Jan. 7, 1882.
Nancy Young, died Feb. 21, 1883.
Novella Young, died Feb. 1, 1884.
W. L. Young, died Feb. 15, 1891.
E. M. Guill, died Feb. 2, 1896.
Eliza Ann Harilson, died Aug. 18, 1896.

Charles W. Young, died Oct. 26, 1905.
Martha G. Young, died Oct. 28, 1913, 7:30 a.m.
T. F. Young, died Dec. 7, 1913, at 1:30 p.m.
Infant son of Orvill and Bertha Young, born and died Feb. 10, 1917.
Bertha Clair Tipton Young, died Mar. 29, 1919, at 1:30 p.m.

Bible Records

(Copied by Mrs. W. P. Bouton, Lebanon, Wilson Co., Tenn.)

Records from William Montgomery Bell Bible in possession of granddaughter, Mrs. Robert Cox, Lebanon, Tenn.

Births

W. M. Bell, born Sept. 7, 1823.
Maredian M. E. McCullough, born June 29, 1829.
Pheriba Farnell Bell, born July 9, 1850.
Margarett M. Bell, born June 14, 1852.
Cate Henry Bell, born Dec. 17, 1854.
Maredian McCullough Bell, born March 27, 1859.
Willie M. Bell, born Jan. 3, 1862.
Hugh Barnet Hale, born Jan. 20, 1842.
J. Lizzie Catron, born Aug. 25, 1840.
Nathan C. Wilson, born Feb. 9, 1848.
William Hamilton Wilson, born April 25, 1878.
Meridian Elizabeth Wilson, born June 5th, 1880.
Mary Bell Wilson, daughter of J. M. and K. H. Wilson, born Sept. 7, 1881.
Bessie Franklin Wilson, born Dec. 11, 1884.
Ferrie Ola Wilson, born May 8th, 1883.
James McCollough, born Oct. 20, 1791.
Brancy Bender, born Jan. 18, 1799.
George Brite McCollough, born Dec. 21, 1824.
Ferriba Catherine McCollough, born March 21, 1827.
Maredian Mary Elizabeth McCollough, born June 29, 1829.
Brancy Bender McCollough, born Aug. 17, 1832.
James Bender McCollough, born Dec. 11, 1839.
Willie Hale, born Sept. 20, 1870.
Nannie Maredian Hale, born April 8, 1873.
Matthew Currie Wilson, born March 2, 1887.
Mary Alice Elliott, born May 17, 1883.
Lillie May Elliott, born Jan. 27, 1886.
Emma Bell Elliott, born Oct. 21, 1888.
Maryatt Rosni Elliott, born Jan. 13, 1891.
Samuel Elliott, son of W. F. and Willie Elliott, born Feb. 23, 1892.
Currie Teslie Elliott, born Sept. 25, 1898.
Thelma L. Elliott, born July 11, 1903.
Cate Henry Bell, born Dec. 17, 1854.
Margaret Frances Talley, born Sept. 26, 1906.
Wm. Marion Montgomery Bell Talley, born Aug. 2, 1908.
Margaret Elizabeth Wilson, born June 20, 1914.
James Curry Wilson, born Sept. 26, 1915.
Wm. Nathan Wilson, born Jan. 14, 1919.
Norris Cordell Wilson, born Feb. 8, 1923.
Baby girl of C. C. and Ferriola W. Talley, born and died Nov. 22, 1923.

Marriages

Wm. M. Bell and Maredian M. E. McCullough, married April 17, 1849.
Hugh B. Hale and Ferrie F. Bell, married June 3, 1869.
Nathan C. Wilson and Maggie Bell, married June 11, 1876.

I. G. Campbell and Katie Crutcher, married Dec. 27, 1877.
J. M. (Matthew) Wilson and Katie Bell, married Oct. 17, 1878.
W. F. Elliott and Willie Bell, married Sept. 6, 1881.
Carver Chalmers Talley and Ferrie Ola Wilson, married Dec. 20, 1905.
Robert Cox and Mary Bell Wilson, married Nov. 29, 1905.
Walter K. Purnell and Bessie Franklin Wilson, married Oct. 28, 1913.

DEATHS

Brancy Bender, died Aug. 26, 1854.
James McCollough, died April 25, 1870.
George Brite McCollough, died March 30, 1851.
Ferriba Catherine McCollough, died Jan. 30, 1888.
Brancy Bender McCollough, died Oct. 20, 1832.
Maredian McCollough Bell, died April 5, 1864.
Maredian McCollough Bell, died March 16, 1914.
W. M. Bell, died May 28, 1917.
Willie M. Bell, died July 27, 1911.
Readie Elizabeth Wilson, died Aug. 3rd, 1892.
J. Matthew Wilson, died June 2, 1924.
Kate Bell Wilson, died Feb. 13, 1931.
Mary Alice Elliott, died 1883.
Lillie May Elliott, died Sept. 9, 1886.
Willie Bell Elliott, died July 27, 1911.
Emma Bell Elliott, died July 25, 1905.
Currie Teslie Elliott, died Nov. 25, 1900.
W. F. Elliott, died Nov. 2, 1924.
Strube Ross Elliott, died Dec. 13, 1924.
I. G. Campbell, died Jan. 29, 1925.
John Wm. Hale, died Dec. 2, 1908.
H. B. Hale, died June 22, 1918.
Nannie Maredian Hale, died May 13, 1925.

Records Samuel Green Bible, possession great-granddaughter, Mrs. Charlie Hankins, Lebanon, Tenn.

BIRTHS

Samuel T. Green, born Oct. 13, 1830.
E. E. Shannon, born March 5, 1839.
Edger Green, born Feb. 13, 1870.
William H. Green, born March 12, 1871.
Asa E. Green, born April 11, 1873.
Josephine Green, born Aug. 21, 1868.
James H. Shannon, born Dec. 19, 1803.
T. J. Shannon, born Nov. 27, 1833.
N. C. Shannon, born Feb. 28, 1835.
C. F. Shannon, born June 14, 1837.
E. E. Shannon, born March 5, 1839.
E. K. Shannon, born March 22, 1841.
A. Shannon, born April 16, 1844.

MARRIAGE

Samuel T. Green and Ermanilda E. Shannon were married Sept. 13, 1866.

DEATHS

James H. Shannon departed this life June 16, 1870.
Issabeller Shannon departed this life April 19, 1876.

Records from James Young Bible in possession of Mr. Ben Young, Shop Springs, Wilson County, Tenn., a great-grandson.

BIRTHS

James Young, born Sept. 28, 1797.
Nancy Branch, born 8th March, 1800.
Benjamin Young, born 30th July, 1819.
Sarah Young, born Jan. 11, 1821.
Robert Young, born 7th May, 1822.

Frances Young, born 10th August, 1825.
David Young, born 25th July, 1827.
William Young, born 31st March, 1829.
Polly Young, born 16th Feb., 1831.
Martha Young, born 12th August, 1832.
Thomas Young, born 11th May, 1834.
John Young, born 6th Feb., 1836.
Bettie Young, born 12th Jan., 1839.
Nancy Young, born 25th Jan., 1843.

MARRIAGES

James Young and Nancy Branch, married Oct. 15, 1818.
Benjamin Young and Eliza Philips, married Jan. 30, 1839.
N. W. Philips and Sarah Young, married Feb. 10, 1839.
Robert Young and Nancy Neal, married Dec. 1, 1841.
W. M. Bryan and Frances Young, married Dec. 22, 1841.
David Young and N. C. Neal, married Nov. 21, 1848.
Pallis Neal and Polly Young, married Nov. 22, 1848.
William Young and Lucinda E. Cartwright, married August 11, 1852.
William Neal and Martha Young, married Dec. 9, 1855.
Thomas Young and Polly Neal, married Dec. 14, 1855.
John Young and Polly Ann Philips, married Feb. 22, 1857.
M. V. New and Bettie Young, married Jan. 29, 1868.
James Givans and Nancy Young, married Jan. 6, 1870.

Records from David Young, Sr., Bible in possession of great-grandson, Mr. Ben Young, Shop Springs, Wilson County, Tenn.

BIRTHS

David Young, Sr., born 6th day of 1774.
Sarah Young, Sr., born Sept. 9, 1776.
James Young, born Sept. 28, 1797.
Elizabeth Young, born March 22, 1799.
Delphy Young, born Dec. 19, 1800.
Joseph Young, born March 18, 1802.
Doke Young, born Jan. 12, 1804.
Carson Young, born Nov. (dim), 1806.
David Young, born July 17, 1808.
Sarah Young, born April 20, 1811.
Alexander A. Young, born Feb. 15, 1813.
Alpha Young, born July 4, 1814.
Nancy Young, born May 20, 1816.
Polly Young, born Aug. 12, 1818.
Louisiana Young, born April 11, 1820.
Fanny Young, born Feb. 7, 1822.

MARRIAGES

David Young and Sally Philips, married Dec. 9, 1796.
James Young and Nancy Branch, married Oct. 15, 1818.
Elizabeth Young and Edward B. Wheeler, married Oct. 24, 1818 (torn).
Doke Young and Sarah Reeder (Keeder)?, married May 12, 1825.
Mary Young and Beverly A. Cornwell, married Feb. 19, 1840.
Frances Young and Matthew Skeen, married Jan. 5, 1842.
(Several too dim to read).

DEATHS

David Young, Sr., died April 13, 1856, in 82nd year.
James Young, died June 7, 1881.
Nancy Young, died April 17, 1875.
Sarah Philips, daughter of James and Nancy Young, died Sept. 22, 1883.
Frances Branch, died April 13, 1868.

Gwynn records in possession of Mrs. Roy Crips, Lebanon, Tenn., granddaughter.

BIRTHS

Robert Gwynn, born Nov. 18, 1803.

Judith Perry Hilliard Wynn, born Feb. 3, 1813, in South Carolina.

Walter Davis Evertson, born April 5, 1819.

Ann Fatheree, born Aug. 30, 1831.

Joseph Granville Gwynn, son of Robert and Judith, born Dec. 22, 1831.

Hugh Thomas Gwynn, son of Robert and Judith, born June 21, 1837.

Wm. Dewitt Clinton Gwynn, son of Robert and Judith, born June 20, 1839.

Gideon Ransom Gwynn, son of Robert and Judith, born July 12, 1842.

Robert James Gwynn, son of Robert and Judith, born Sept. 22, 1848.

Alice Nicoll Evertson, born June 4, 1859, in Hinds Co., Mississippi.

MARRIAGES

Robert Gwynn and Judith Perry Hilliard Wynn, married Feb. 10, 1831.

Joseph Granville Gwynn and Virginia Ann Parham, married Oct. 22, 1856.

Hugh Thomas Gwynn and Martha Ann Sadler, married Sept. 8, 1859.

Wm. Dewitt Clinton Gwynn and Mary Blanche Hall, married Feb. 22, 1872.

Gideon Ransom Gwynn and Corrie Ann Peyton, married Oct. 28, 1869.

Robert James Gwynn and Alice Nicoll Evertson, married Dec., 1872.

DEATHS

Walter Davis Evertson, died Mar. 14, 1892.

Ann Fatheree, died Sept. 1, 1890.

Robert Gwynn, died May 29, 1888.

Judith P. H. W. Gwynn, died May 11, 1882.

Joseph Granville Gwynn, died April 26, 1883.

Hugh Thomas Gwynn, died May 26, 1912.

Martha Ann Sadler, wife Hugh T. Gwynn, died Dec. 26, 1904.

Wm. Dewitt Clinton Gwynn, died July 15, 1879.

Mary Blanche Hall, wife of W. D. C. Gwynn, died May 26, 1912.

Gideon Ransom Gwynn, died July 22, 1907.

Corrie Ann Peyton, wife of Gideon R. Gwynn, died Feb. 29, 1904.

Robert James Gwynn, died Jan. 14, 1908.

George Bloom Evertson, died Aug. 12, 1829, in Ithaca, N. Y.

Frances Mary Nicol, died March 24, 1861.

Jacob Rooters Evertson, died May 1, 1807, in Duchess Co., New York.

Margaret Bloom, wife of Jacob Evertson, died Nov. 18, 1807.

BIRTHS

George Bloom Evertson, father of Walter Davis Evertson, born Feb. 20, 1773, in Duchess Co., N. Y.

Frances Mary Nicoll, second wife of George Bloom Evertson, born Dec. 17, 1785.

Jacob Rooters Evertson, father of George Bloom Evertson, born Jan. 3, 1734, at South Amboy, New Jersey.

Margaret Bloom, wife of Jacob R. Evertson, born Aug. 29, 1744.

Virginia Ann Parham, wife of Joseph G. Gwynn, born Sept. 16, 1835.

Martha Ann Sadler, wife of Hugh T. Gwynn, born Nov. 6, 1841.

Mary Blanche Hall, wife of W. D. C. Gwynn, born Nov. 11, 1860, Harris Co., Texas.

Corrie Ann Peyton, wife of Gideon R. Gwynn, born March 7, 1848.

MARRIAGES

George Bloom Evertson and second wife, Frances Mary Nicoll, married April 13, 1809.

Jacob Rooters Evertson and Margaret Bloom, daughter of George Bloom, married Oct. 29, 1761.

Gilley Gromarrin Land Grant, 1687

Land Office, Richmond, Va.—Book 7, Page 562.

To all & whereas & now know ye that I Francis Lord Howard Govnr & hereby ye advise and Consent of ye Council of State accordingly give and Grant Gilly Gromeron a Tract of Land containing five hundred and thirty none acres lying and being in ye County of Henrico, and in ye parish of Varina, etc., on South Side of Chicahominy Swamp. Dist beginning at a corner of White Oak standing long Cattail branch being ye line of Mr. Henry Wyat, etc., running thence along his line East South East forty six poles to a Corner black oak, thence South South East thirty two poles to a corner Pockery, thence South South East forty four poles to a Corner black oak, thence East South one hundred four poles to a corner poplar, thence along Linoell Morris his line South South West sixty eight poles to a corner oak, thence South East ninety four poles to a corner Black Oak, thence leaving Morris his line and run South West by woods one hundred forty two poles to a corner black oak, thence West North West seventy-nine poles to a corner black oak, thence North North West twenty eight poles to a corner, thence West by North forty two poles to a corner, thence West North West one hundred sixty two poles to a corner black oak, thence North by West eighty eight poles to a corner black oak, thence North East and by North two hundred sixteen poles to a corner black oak, standing ten poles thence along his line South East South one hundred forty eight poles to place we began, including ye aforesaid five hundred thirty nine acres of land, for ye Transportation of eleven persons. To have and to hold and to be held, etc., yielding and paying, etc. Provided, etc., dated this twentieth day of April, Anno Domino, one thousand and six eighty seven.

	Edwd. Richards.
John Smith.	Tho. Cary.
Avis Colling.	Tho. Charles.
Hen Hicks.	Henry Brodsha.
Anne Colling.	Jno. Caddy.
Jno. Bestle.	Maria, a negro.
Margt. Swaine.	Xphor Pocking.
Rogor Morris.	

Great - great - great - great grandfather (maternal)—from copy.

Will of Gillee Gromarrin, from Richmond, Virginia, 1716.

I, Gillee Gromarrin of county and parish of Henrico, being perfect sense and memory, give soul to God in hope joyfull resurrection through Saviour Jesus Christ, body to be decently buried. (All lands entailed to others if no legal heirs of body).

Item: To son Franciss Gromarrin all divident land of mine whereon Warrum Esley now lives being 700 acres.

Item: To son Wiltsheir Gromarrin all land whereon I now live being about 580 acres.

Item: To son Gillee and daughter Arabella all tract or divident at Pickerocque being about 1490 acres.

Item: To daughter Anne all land or tract at poewhite being about 400 acres.

Item: To my two sons Francis and Wiltsheir all my tract of land on Tuckahoe being 500 acres more or less.

Item: To son Gillee and daughter Anne and all rest of my children full privilege of fishing place from the creeks mouth to all the privilege of landings, share and privilege alike.

It is my Will that all my children have two years schooling after my decease each of them alike.

My Will that Thomas Wood, Sr., shall continue to live and keep plantation whereon he now lives

during his own life and natural life of his wife Anne Wood, not be annulled, have plantation for use of his children two years after their decease to provide for themselves, paying the same rent.
All movable estate be equally divided between all my children.
Son-in-law, Luke Smith, Executor.
Signed: Gillee Gromarrin, 16th Oct., 1716. Witnesses: Richard Williams, Thomas T. W. Woods, Sr. (mark), James F. Frankling (mark), Peter P. Corbin (mark), proved at Court Henrico County, Nov. 5, 1716. Thos. Eldridge, Dep. Cl. Cur.
(This is abstract of Will of my great - great - great - great grandfather, Gillee Gromarrin (maternal), taken from photostat copy).

1747—Will of Gilley Marin, of Henrico County, Virginia, from Richmond.

I, Gilley Maren of Henrico, being in perfect sence, God be praised.
All children of wench Hannah, which I purchased of Thomas Cardwell, with Lucy, Jane & Ned, with all children they now have or may have, when my sons each come to age of 20 to have equal part of those negroes in quantity and quality, and daughters to receive equal part of negroes at age 17.
If unborn child is son to have equal part with Wiltshire. Wiltshire to have 100 pounds current money at age 20, horse and saddle worth ten pounds, five cows and calves. Unborn child if son to have same.
Loving wife during natural life six working negroes, viz: Jack, Robin, Bob, Temp & Bibb, Lucy.
I lend to Thomas Cardwell & wife Marthew one negro wench name Hannah during their natural lives, be returned to my wife Mary, at her death negroes and rest of estate be equally divided all my children.
Wife Mary appointed whole and sole executrix.
Signed, Gilley Marin. Janu. 28, 1746-7, in presence David Holt, John Holmes, Benjamin B. Bridgwater (his mark).
At Court for Henrico County first Monday in July, 1747, Will proved by John Holmes and Benjamin Bridgwater. Mary Marin, executrix. Bowler Cocke, junr., Dep. Ct. C.
(Abstract of Will of my great-great-great grandfather, Gilley Marin [Gromarrin] from photostat from Richmond Va. Maternal).

Family Records from Old Ledger of Wiltshire Gromarrin Pettipool.

Pines Ingram was born the 1st day of January.
Lucy Hamlette was born the 27th day of July.
Pines Ingram and Lucy Hamlette were married the 1st day of January, 1773.
Martha Ingram, daughter of Pines and Lucy, was born the 4th day of December, 1773.
Lucy Worsham Ingram, daughter of Pines and Lucy, his wife, was born the 6th day of May, 1775.
William Ingram, son of Pines and Lucy, his wife, was born the 5th day of April, 1778.
James Ingram, son of Pines and Lucy, his wife, was born the 7th day of October, 1781.
John Ingram, son of Pines and Lucy, his wife, was born the 10th day of October, 1783.
Samuel Ingram, son of Pines and Lucy, his wife, was born the 19th day of June, 1790.

Charles Cabaniss, Jr., was born December 22, 1773.

Lucy Worsham Ingram was born May 6, 1775.
Charles Cabaniss and Lucy W. Ingram were married Jan. 9, 1795.
Elizabeth Hamlette Cabaniss, daughter of Charles and Lucy, his wife, was born Dec. 14, 1795.
Patsey Worsham Cabaniss, daughter of Charles and Lucy, his wife, was born Dec. 11, 1797.
Caroline Clay Cabaniss, daughter of Charles and Lucy, his wife, was born June 8, 1800.
James Bryan Cabaniss, son of Charles and Lucy, his wife, was born April 4, 1802.
Caroline Clay Cabaniss was married to John A. Allen, April 4, 1819.
Patsey W. Cabaniss was married to Drury M. Allen, Jan. 28, 1818.
Caroline C. Allen departed this life August 7, 1821.
(Wiltshire G. Pettipool was my great grandfather [maternal] and I have copy from Ledger.)

W. G. Pettipool was born March 29, 1770 .
Martha Ingram was born December ye 4th, 1773.
Wiltshire Gromarrin Pettipool and Martha Ingram was married Dec. 22, 1792.
Son born Nov. 12, 1793, departed this life Nov. 23, 1793.
Mary Gromarrin Pettipool, daughter of Wiltshire and Martha, his wife, was born July 11, 1795.
Samuel Colwell Pettipool, son of Wiltshire and Martha, his wife, was born Dec. 30, 1798.
Nancy Pettipool, daughter of Wiltshire and Martha, his wife, was born Jan. 1, 1802.
Colwell Pettipool, son of Wiltshire and Martha, his wife, was born 8th of Sept., 1804.
John Pines Pettipool, son of Wiltshire and Martha, his wife, was born June 16, 1808.
Lucy Worsham Pettipool, daughter of Wiltshire and Martha, his wife, was born 4th March, 1814.

Mary G. P'Pool was married to Parham Booker, Jan. 28, 1819.
Colwell P'Pool and Elizabeth, his wife, were married Jan. 12, A. D. 1830.
Martha F. P'Pool, daughter of Colwell P. and Elizabeth, his wife, was born Nov. 23, 1830.
John H. Webster was born Dec. 17, 1801.
Nancy M. P'Pool was born 1802.
John H. Webster and Nancy M., his wife, married Nov. 28, 1822.
John Colwell Webster, son of John H. and Nancy M., his wife, was born April 24, 1824.
Sarah Elizabeth, daughter of John H. and Nancy M., his wife, was born Jan. 16, 1826, and departed this life Sept. 19, 1827.
John Colwell Webster departed this life June 14, 1831.
(I have copy from old ledger of my great grandfather, Wiltshire G. Pettipool.)

Abstract of Will, by Mrs. W. P. Bouton, Lebanon, Tenn.

Will of James Denny of Guilford County, North Carolina. Dated Dec. 10, 1790.
I, James Denny of county of Guilford, State of North Carolina, farmer, weak state as to bodily health.
1st, give unto each of my married children, viz: Mary Duck, Ann Bass, Maryanne Paisley, George Denny, Jane Hamilton, Agnes and Elizabeth Donnell and James Denny, one dollar each.
Give the loan of five pounds to son James for eight years without interest, at end term allow him pay said sum to grandson, James Denney, Georges Denny's son.
Give and bequeath to daughter Hannah her horse & saddle, 2 cows, 6 sheep, bed & its furniture, chest fifteen pounds pewter & iron pot. All that remains of my estate, I allow Agnes my wife and William my son to have equal during her natural life, at her death

her part to become his property, together with plantation on which I now live with appurtenances. If she choose rather to live with any of her children, allowed to have mare and saddle, bed and wheel and five pounds in money each year during life and any money remaining after his debts paid & can leave articles to whom she will.
Witnesses: John Rankin, Joseph McGaughy, Charles Wheeler.
Proved February Court, 1795, by Charles Wheeler.
Executors, William, my well beloved son, and John Donnell, my respected & trusty friend and son-in-law.
Guilford County, North Carolina, attested John Hamilton, C. C.

James Denny was great-great grandfather (maternal) of my husband, William Paisley Bouton (deceased), and I have copy.

Records, family Bible of Mr. and Mrs. George Washington Vaughan.

George Washington Vaughan, born Mechlenburg County, Va., Oct. 20, 1816.
Mary Marion Pettipool, born in Madison County, Ala., May 9, 1827.
Samuel Pool Vaughan, born Madison County, Ala., Oct. 14, 1847.
Bettie C. Vaughan, born Tippah County, Miss., Dec. 13, 1849.
William Lewis Vaughan, born Tippah County, Miss., July 10, 1851.
Laura Mildred Vaughan, born Tippah County, Miss., June 18, 1853.
Mary Marion Vaughan, born Tippah County, Miss., Dec. 8, 1855.
George Washington Vaughan, Jr., born Tippah County, Miss., April 1, 1857.
Virginia Vaughan, born Holly Springs, Miss., Nov. 18, 1859.
John Wiltshire Vaughan, born Holly Springs, Miss., Oct. 29, 1861.
Colwell Pines Vaughan, born Tippah County, Miss., Sept. 5, 1864.
Mildred Thomas Vaughan, born Tippah County, Miss., Nov. 1, 1867.
Lemuel Vaughan, born Tippah County, Miss., Oct. 7, 1869.
George Washington Vaughan and Mary Marion P'Pool were married in Madison County, Ala., Jan. 6, 1847.
Bettie C. Vaughan and Francis Marion Treadwell were married in Tippah County, Miss., Nov. 3, 1868.
Mary Marion Vaughan and Lucius Eugene Lipford were married in Benton County, Miss., Dec. 12, 1871.
Laura Vaughan and Bradley Thomas Kimbrough were married in Benton County, Miss., March 12, 1872.
Mildred Thomas Vaughan and William Paisley Bouton were married in Benton County, Miss., Dec. 18, 1884.
John Wiltshire Vaughan and Willa Aileen Ayres were married in Benton County, Miss., March 4, 1885.
Lemuel Vaughan and Clara Elinor Winborn were married in Benton County, Miss., May 12, 1889.
Caldwell Pines Vaughan and Leta Blanche Porterfield were married at Potts Camp, Marshall County, Miss., Dec. 18, 1895.
Samuel Pettipool Vaughan died Tippah County, Miss., Sept. 9, 1849.
William Lewis Vaughan, died Tippah County, Miss., Aug. 15, 1853.
Virginia Vaughan, died in Tippah County, Miss., Oct. 17, 1861.
George Washington Vaughan, Jr., died Tippah County, Miss., Nov. 23, 1862.
George Washington Vaughan, died in Benton County, Miss., June 21, 1871.
Laura Vaughan Kimbrough, died in Benton County, Miss., Aug. 21, 1874.
Elizabeth Morgan P'Pool, wife of

Samuel P'Pool, died in Benton County, Miss., Dec. 16, 1879.
Samuel P'Pool, died in Benton County, Miss., Feb. 9, 1880.
Mary Marion P'Pool Vaughan, died in Benton County, Miss., Aug. 25, 1890.

The Vaughan family Bible was the property of Lemuel Vaughan, youngest son. Mildred T. Vaughan Bouton, daughter, made copy from Bible, 1912, which is in her possession, Lebanon, Tenn., from which this is taken.

Isaac Taylor Family Bible.

Isaac Taylor was born 11th Dec., 1781.
Margaret Taylor was born 22nd May, 1792.
Louisa Jane Taylor, daughter of Isaac and Margaret Taylor, born 12th Oct., in year of our Lord, 1815.
Adrion G. Taylor, son of Isaac and Margaret Taylor, was born the 7th April, in the year of our Lord, 1817.
John Douglas Taylor, son of Isaac and Margaret Taylor, was born 3rd of February, in the year of our Lord, 1819.
Ann Eliza Taylor, daughter of Isaac and Margaret Taylor, was born 18th of July, in the year of our Lord, 1821.
Mary Rose Taylor, daughter of Isaac and Margaret Taylor, was born 10th of July, in the year of our Lord, 1823.
Altamira G. Taylor, daughter of Isaac and Margaret Taylor, was born 10th of Oct., in the year of our Lord, 1826.
Thomas Edward Taylor, son of Isaac and Margaret Taylor, was born 22nd of Sept., in the year of our Lord, 1829.
Isaac Taylor, son of Isaac and Margaret Taylor, was born 19th of Sept., in the year of our Lord, 1831.

John D. Taylor, son of John and Nancy Taylor, was born 15th Nov., 1836.
F. E. G. Taylor, daughter of John and ——— Price, was born 7th Feb., 1822.
Margaret J. Taylor, daughter of Lee T. and Sarah Blakemore, was born 27th June, in the year of our Lord, 1837.
Annie Cara Taylor, daughter of John D. and F. J. Taylor, was born June 14th, 1859.

Isaac Taylor married his wife, Margaret, the 19th of Dec., 1813.
Foster G. Finley married his wife, Altamira G. Taylor, daughter of Isaac and Margaret Taylor, 17th July, 1845.
Frederick O. Hunt married his wife, Mary A. Taylor, daughter of Isaac and Margaret Taylor, 23rd Feb. 1847.
John D. Taylor married his wife, Frances E. Jane Price, 15th July (dim) 1851.
Ammon L. Davis married his wife, a daughter of Isaac and Margaret Taylor, Louisa J. Taylor, on Tuesday, the 29th of May, 1838.
Bird S. Rhea married his wife, Anna E. Taylor, daughter of Isaac and Margaret Taylor, on Tuesday, the 14th day of January, 1845.
Isaac Taylor married his wife, Margaret Jane Blakemore, the 8th of July, 1856.

Furnished by great-great granddaughter, Mrs. George R. Bouton, from a copy in her possession.

Records from Robert Hewitt Family Bible.

Births

Robert Hewitt, born Nov. 23, 1755.
Anna Hewitt, wife of Robert Hewitt, born March 6, 1767.
Caleb Hewitt, born Oct. 5, 1788.
Elizabeth Hewitt, born Feb. 6, 1791.

Hazael Hewitt, born March 3, 1793.
Robert Hewitt, Jr., born March 26, 1796.
Matilda Hewitt, born Dec. 31, 1797.
Emella Hewitt, born Jan. 29, 1800.
Mary Hewitt, born Dec. 19, 1805.
Caroline Hewitt, born Sept. 6, 1809.

MARRIAGES

Robert Hewitt and Anna Shute, married Sept. 16, 1786.
Joseph P. Wharton, married to Caroline Hewitt by the Rev. William Hume on Sept. 21, 1830 A.D.

DEATHS

Elizabeth Hewitt departed this life May 12, 1794, was drowned in Phillip Shute spring; age 3 years 4 months.
Robert Hewitt, Jr., departed this life Sept. 22, 1803, was burned to death in a gin house, aged 7 years 4 months.
Caleb Hewitt departed this life on Sept. 9, 1816; age 27 years 11 months and 4 days; was murdered in Nashville.
Anna Hewitt, wife of R. Hewitt, departed this life Oct. 17, 1814; age 47 years 7 months and 10 days.
Mary Hewitt departed this life June 22, 1824; age 22 years 6 months and 3 days.
Robert Hewitt departed this life at the home of Joseph P. Wharton March 3, 1837.
(Made from a copy which is in possession of his great-great grand daughter, Mrs. George R. Bouton, nee Margaret Wharton Chambers, Lebanon, Tenn.)

Records from the James W. McCartney Bible, now in possession of Mrs. James W. McCartney, nee Emma Lignon, Lebanon, Tenn., R. F. D.

MARRIAGES

James W. McCartney married Petro Quincy Harrison Jan. 23, 1843.
Thweatt H. McCartney married Frances C. Ozment Aug. 17, 1866.
Silas J. Chapman married Mary F. McCartney Sept. 20, 1867.
Milliam T. Brinkley married Huldah Doak McCartney Sept. 20, 1876.
B. F. Holloway married Quincy Catherine McCartney Feb. 27, 1879.
John L. McCartney and Hattie Rogers were married Jan 20, 1881.
James W. McCartney, Jr., and Emma Ligon were married Jan. 20, 1881.
J. A. Brinkley and Bettie McCartney married Dec. 28, 1892.
C. L. McCartney married Corrie Crosson April 19, 1891.

BIRTHS

James W. McCartney, born July 29, 1821.
Petro Quincy McCartney, born Nov. 23, 1820.
Thweatt H. McCartney, son of above, born Nov. 1, 1843.
Mary Frances McCartney, born Aug. 14, 1846.
Nancy E. McCartney, born July 20, 1849.
John Lewis McCartney, born Feb. 11, 1852.
James W. McCartney, born April 8, 1855.
Quincy Catherine McCartney, born Sept. 26, 1857.
Frances Farmer, wife of T. Harrison and last wife of Charles Wade, born Dec. 11, 1792.
Kitty Harrison, born Aug. 6, 1817 Betsey Ann.
John Harrison, born June 24, 1819.
Huldah Doke McCartney, born Aug. 27, 1860.
Charles Lee McCartney, born Dec. 20, 1863.
John Peyton, son of J. W., Jr., and Emma McCartney, born June 13, 1882.
Andrew Wilson McCartney, born Oct. 13, 1883.
William Dudley McCartney, born June 7, 1885.

DEATHS

Thweatt Harrison, died ——— 7, 1823.
Betsy Ann John Harrison, died July 13, 1860.
Petro Quincy McCartney, died Aug. 15, 1869.
James W. McCartney, died March 2, 1901.
John Peyton McCartney, died Aug. 1, 1904.
J. L. McCartney, died April 28, 1930.

Records from William Bryan Bible, copied by Mrs. W. P. Bouton. Bible in possession of Robert Lee Bryan, a son, Wilson County, Tenn.

BIRTHS

William Bryan, son of Nelson and Mary, his wife, born Oct. 7, 1817 A.D.
Frances Young, daughter of James Young and Nancy, his wife, born Aug. 10, 1825 A.D.
Mary Elizabeth Bryan, daughter of Wm. and Frances Bryan, born Jan. 3, 1843 A.D.
James Nelson Bryan, son of Wm. and Frances Bryan, his wife, born Aug. 24, 1844.
Julia Bryan, daughter of Wm. Bryan and Frances, his wife, born Dec. 25, 1845.
Nancy Frances, daughter to Wm. and Frances Bryan, his wife, born Jan. 4, 1848.
Alva Curtis Bryan, son of Wm. Bryan and Frances, his wife, born Sept. 19, 1850.
Sarah Bryan, daughter to Wm. and Frances Bryan, his wife, born Oct. 5, 1851.
William Bryan, son of Wm. Bryan and Frances, his wife, born Oct. 10, 1853.
Robert Lee Bryan, son of Wm. and Frances Bryan, his wife, born July 2, 1866.
Ira Bryan, son of Wm. and Frances, his wife, born Feb. 2, 1868.

MARRIAGES

Wm. Bryan and Frances Young were married Dec. 22, 1841 A.D.
Julia Bryan and Jas. L. Hearn were married Oct. 16, 1866.
N. F. Bryan and Marcellus Turner were married Feb. 7, 1867.
Mary E. Bryan married to S. L. Turner Dec. 19, 1867.
J. N. Bryan married to Martha Morris July 29, 1869.
J. N. Bryan to E. R. Hearn in Oct., 1876.
A. C. Bryan to Cecelia Stewart June 22, 1875.
William Bryan to Amanda Borum Oct. 23, 1878.
Robert Lee Bryan married to Ida Simpson Oct. 19, 1890.

Records from Bible of Mrs. Isabella Neal Waters. Bible now in possession of Charles N. Waters' family, Wilson County, Tennessee.

BIRTHS

I. N. Waters, born Dec. 25, 1849.
Geo. W. Waters, born Feb. 14, 1830.
Mary P. Waters, born Oct. 14, 1832.
Walter Lee Waters, son of G. W. and Mary P. Waters, born Oct. 13, 1865.
Shelah Waters, born Dec. 27, 1867.
Sally Waters, born Sept 7, 1869.
George Waters, Jr., born Sept. 13, 1872.
Charlie Neal Waters, son of G. W. and I. N. Waters, born Oct. 25, 1878.
William Gregory Waters, born June 9, 1880.
Edgar Pallas Waters, born Sept. 2, 1882.

Mary Etta Waters, born April 19, 1885.
Robert Waters, born Feb. 9, 1890.

MARRIAGES

G. W. Waters and M. P. Waters were married Dec. 2, 1857 or ? 9.
G. W. Waters to Isabella Neal Jan. 7, 1875.
Geo. Waters, Jr., to Bettie Bass Nov. 30, 1899.
William G. Waters to Maude Grainger Nov. 27, 1902.
Charley N. Waters to Jennie Marler Oct. 26, 1906.
Mary E. Waters to William H. Bettes, Nov. 29, 1906.
Edgar P. Waters to Susie Johnson.
Robert Waters to Ariel E. Bryan Jan 16, 1916.
William G. Waters to Laura Sue Pitts Aug. 6, 1927.

DEATHS

Mary P. Waters, wife of G. W. Waters, died May 23, 1874.
Walter Lee Waters, died April 27, 1871.
George W. Waters, died Nov. 3, 1915.
Charlie Neal Waters, son of G. W. Waters and Isa Neal Waters, died July 30, 1918.
Mrs. Isa Neal Waters, died Sept. 7, 1928.

Records taken from the Rev. Samuel Donnell Bible, present owner, Horace E. Turner, Lebanon, Wilson County, Tenn.

BIRTHS

Samuel Donnell, born April 25, 1771.
Eliza Donnell (Carmichael), born 1780 A.D.
Jane Donnell Andrews, born March 15, 1786.
Eliza Carmichael Donnell, born Sept. 23, 10 o'clock at night, 1806.
Jane Clementine Donnell, born April 18, 1808, about sunset.
John Andrews Donnell, born Aug. 11, 1810, about 8 o'clock in morning.
Francina Louisa Donnell, born May 21, 1813, at 4 o'clock p.m.
Samuel Madison Donnell, born March 15, 1818, about 1 o'clock.
Jane Joanna, daughter of Edward McMillan and Eliza Seay, his wife, born Dec. 2, 1831.
Eliza Newel, daughter of Edward McMillan and Eliza Seay, his wife, born Dec. 2, 1831.
Martha Satoria, daughter of Edward McMillan and Eliza Seay, his wife, born Oct. 6, 1833.
John Donnell, son of Edward McMillan and Eliza Seay, his wife, born Sept. 22, 1835.

DEATHS

Eliza Donnell, daughter of the Rev. John Carmichael of Brandywine Hundred, Penn., departed this life Nov. 4, 1802 A.D.
Rev. Samuel Donnell departed this life Sept. 1, 1824.
John Andrew Donnell, died June 29, 1832, at 2 o'clock p.m.
Eliza Seay McMillan, died Sept. 26, 1835, at 40 minutes past 3 o'clock a.m.
Henry A. Major, died of conjested fever in the 28th year of his age, 1838, at a few minutes past 7 o'clock p.m.
John W. Wynne, died April 23, 1850, in the fourth year of his age.
John A. Major, died May 31, 1858, in the 53rd year of his age.
Jane Donnell, departed this life Oct. 29, 1861.
S. M. Donnell, died March 2, 1868.
John A. Owen, died March 6, 1885.

Bible Record from William D. Thompson Bible, now in possession of son, George P. Thompson, Leeville, Wilson County, Tenn.

BIRTHS

William D. Thompson, born Oct. 6, 1833.

Melvina Thompson, born Oct. 19, 1840.

Permelia Thompson, born March 30, 1841.

William Nathaniel Thompson, born Nov. 15, 1858.

George Pinkney Thompson, born Aug. 10, 1860.

James Wesley Thompson, born Nov. 14, 1864.

Mary Eveline Thompson, born March 7, 1870.

Selma J. Thompson, born Oct. 28, 1882.

Mamie Robert Thompson, born Jan. 18, 1892.

Joseph Wesley Thompson, born Feb. 24, 1894.

MARRIAGES

William D. Thompson and Melvina Wamack, married March 7, 1854.

William D. Thompson and Permelia Murrey, married Dec. 27, 1857.

George P. Thompson and Jennie Beard, married Nov. 28, 1881.

W. M. Thompson and Callie Ellis, married Jan. 16, 1890.

George P. Thompson and Jennie Marks, married Jan. 21, 1891.

DEATHS

Melvina Thompson, died Aug 24, 1857.

William D. Thompson, died Aug. 2, 1871.

Jennie Thompson, died Oct. 31, 1884.

Records from Charles Henry Oldham Bible, in possession of grandson, C. H. Oldham, near Laguardo, Wilson County, Tenn., copied by Mrs. W. P. Bouton, Lebanon, Tenn., 1933.

BIRTHS

Charles Henry Oldham, born Jan. 17, 1821.

Mary Baker Horn, born March 21, 1827.

Elizabeth Ann, daughter of C. H. and M. B. Oldham, born Feb. 3, 1852.

Laura Gee Oldham, born Aug. 17, 1853.

William Howard Oldham, born April 24, 1855.

James Horn Oldham, born May 17, 1857.

Mary Alice Oldham, born Nov. 11, 1858.

Sarah Tabitha Oldham, born Sept. 25, 1864.

MARRIAGE

Charles Henry Oldham and Mary Baker Horn, Sept. 10, 1850.

DEATHS

Mary B. Oldham, wife of C. H. Oldham, died July 7, 1872.

Elizabeth A., wife of R. A. Cartwright, died Feb. 2, 1874.

C. H. Oldham, died Oct. 9, 1891.

Mary Alice, wife of W. E. Smith, died Jan. 25, 1891.

Mary Poston, wife of C. H. Oldham, died Oct. 13, 1900.

William Howard Oldham, died March 7, 1912.

James Horn Oldham, died Nov. 4, 1932.

Records from William H. Oldham Bible in possession of a son, Charles H. Oldham, near Laguardo, Wilson County,

BIRTHS

William Howard Oldham, born April 24, 1855.

Ida Bradshaw Oldham, born Sept. 19, 1858.

Edgar Howard Oldham, born April 6, 1881.

Sadie May Oldham, born April 12, 1883.

Kate Oldham, born June 18, 1886.

Charles Henry Oldham, born April 22, 1889.
Alice Oldham, born Sept. 24, 1893.
Ida Elizabeth Oldham, born Nov. 8, 1896.

MARRIAGE

William H. Oldham, of Tennessee, and Ida Bradshaw, of Tennessee, Oct. 16, 1879, at Laguardo, by Early.

DEATHS

Sadie Mai Oldham, died Feb. 19, 1904.
Ida B. Oldham, died Oct. 29, 1909.
William Howard Oldham, died March 7, 1912.

Record from Levi Fisher Bible now owned by grandson, Talmage J. Fisher, Leeville, Wilson County, Tenn.

BIRTHS

Levi Fisher, born Dec. 22, 1803.
Martha E. S. Guthrie, born Oct. 20, 1816.
Richard W. B. Fisher, born April 15, 1837.
Chloe E. F. Fisher, born Nov. 11, 1842.
John W. F. Fisher, born Jan. 22, 1845.
Elizabeth Susan Fisher, born Sept. 1, 1866.
Richard Baird Fisher, born July 25, 1870.
Chloe Atkinson Fisher, born Oct. 30, 1873.
William Fletcher Fisher, born May 5, 1875.
Talmage Judson Fisher, born Aug. 23, 1885.
Clarissa Rosa Fisher, born Jan. 22, 1889.
Earl Lanburth Lanius, born May 16, 1896.
Paul Fisher Lanius, born Jan. 15, 1898.
William Lee Lanius, born July 2, 1904.
Lacy Mai Fisher, born Feb. 28, 1905.
Blanch Lynier Fisher, born July 14, 1911.
Cloe Clayton Fisher, born March 1, 1914.
Marion Fisher, born Oct. 24, 1902.
William Porter Fisher, born Feb., 1909.
John W. Fisher, born July 12, 1908.
Chloe Alice Fisher, May 13, 1910.
Talmage Ferrell Fisher, born July 1, 1921.
Lou Douglass Fisher, born July 22, 1922.
Mary Louise Hollingsworth, born Jan. 2, 1910.
Ruth Elizabeth Hollingsworth, born Sept. 2, 1912.
Martin Rayborn Hollingsworth, born Feb. 22, 1915.

MARRIAGES

Levi Fisher and Martha E. S. Guthrie, married May 5, 1835.
Chloe E. F. Fisher and William J. Atkinson, married Sept. 23, 1856.
Richard W. B. Fisher and Martha C. Robertson, married Aug. 23, 1857.
John W. F. Fisher and Louisa C. Baird, married Nov. 11, 1865.
Elizabeth S. Fisher and Robert W. Skeen, married Oct. 15, 1890.
Chloe A. Fisher and William L. Lanius, married Aug. 20, 1893.
Richard Baird Fisher and Cleo Russ, married Feb. 24, 1904.
Talmage J. Fisher and Nellie L. Ferrell, married Sept. 15, 1907.
Clarissa R. Fisher and G. G. Hollingsworth, married Feb. 18, 1909.
William F. Fisher and Lillie Lain, married May 5, 1898.

DEATHS

Rev. Levi Fisher, died Sept. 17, 1866.
Martha E. S. Fisher, wife of Levi Fisher, died July 21, 1898.
Richard W. B. Fisher, died Oct., 1870.
John W. Fisher, died Sept. 6, 1906.
Louisa C. Fisher, died June 1, 1911 (wife of John W. Fisher).
Chloe A. Lanius, died May 13, 1910.
Mary Louise Hollingsworth, died March, 1914.

Ruth Hollingsworth, died March, 1929.

Talmage Ferrell Fisher, died July 1, 1921.

McFarland Bible, in possession of daughter, Mrs. Richard Palmer, Lebanon, Wilson County, Tenn., R. F. D.

Births

James H. McFarland, born April 18, 1850.

Mattie C. McFarland, born Dec. 17, 1855.

Walter J. McFarland, son of J. H. and Mattie C. McFarland, born Oct. 17, 1877.

Jack Chambers McFarland, born May 4, 1879.

Edna Walker McFarland, born Mar. 1, 1882.

Bertha McFarland, born Aug. 23, 1885.

Sallie Leila McFarland, born Aug. 14, 1888.

Edna Chambers, born Aug. 30, 1812.

Marriages

James H. McFarland and Mattie H. Chambers, married Sept. 21, 1876.

Edna McFarland and J. H. Hobson, married Feb. 24, 1904.

Bertha L. McFarland and Richard H. Palmer, married Nov. 7, 1906.

Sallie L. McFarland and Richard H. Adams, married Aug. 21, 1909.

Deaths

John Chambers, died April, 1865.

Edna Chambers, died Sept. 20, 1878.

Walter J. McFarland, died Aug. 26, 1896.

James H. McFarland, died Sept. 22, 1901.

Mattie C. McFarland, died July 29, 1911.

Will

Copied by Mrs. W. P. Bouton, Lebanon, Tenn.

Will of John Crawford, from copy in possession of Dr. T. E. Halbert, Lebanon, Tenn., R.F.D. 2, a great-grandson.

I, John Crawford, of County of Lincoln, State of Tennessee. His farm and all that pertains to it, my dwelling and in general all my property to wife, Elizabeth, during her natural life. At death of wife, Elizabeth, sons, John and Ezekiel, to have three hundred and two acres land on north side of farm and one hundred and forty acres woodland north side of hilly tract purchased of McConnell Estate. Remaining lands, negroes and other property to be divided, sold, as to make each equal share after accounting for advancements. John and Ezekiel, after having each one-third of landed property, to have no more.

Some of older children in Arkansas and some in Tennessee have had sums as follows: Hay (or his heirs), $809; Wm. D., $927; James, $434.75; Naomi, $367; Eleanor, $403; Rachel, $228; Nancy, $228; Andrew A., $317.50; Mary, $270; Margaret, $162; Elizabeth, $192; which amounts are charged to them on my book of accounts.

If any older children found to have received more than an equitable share shall not be required to refund, John and Ezekiel, after death of wife, two-thirds of the lands only.

Proceeds of estate after death of wife equally divided among my following named children: Hay's heirs, William D., James, Naomi, Eleanor, Nancy, Andrew A., Mary and Margaret, Elizabeth, Emily and Martha Lucinda and Rachel.

Executors: Alexander McDonald of Fayetteville, William F. Kerchenal, Esq., of Fayetteville, and my son, John Crowford.

Dated Jan. 10, 1846.

Witnesses: H. C. Marcell, A. S. Boone.

Copy test: H. Kelso, Clerk.

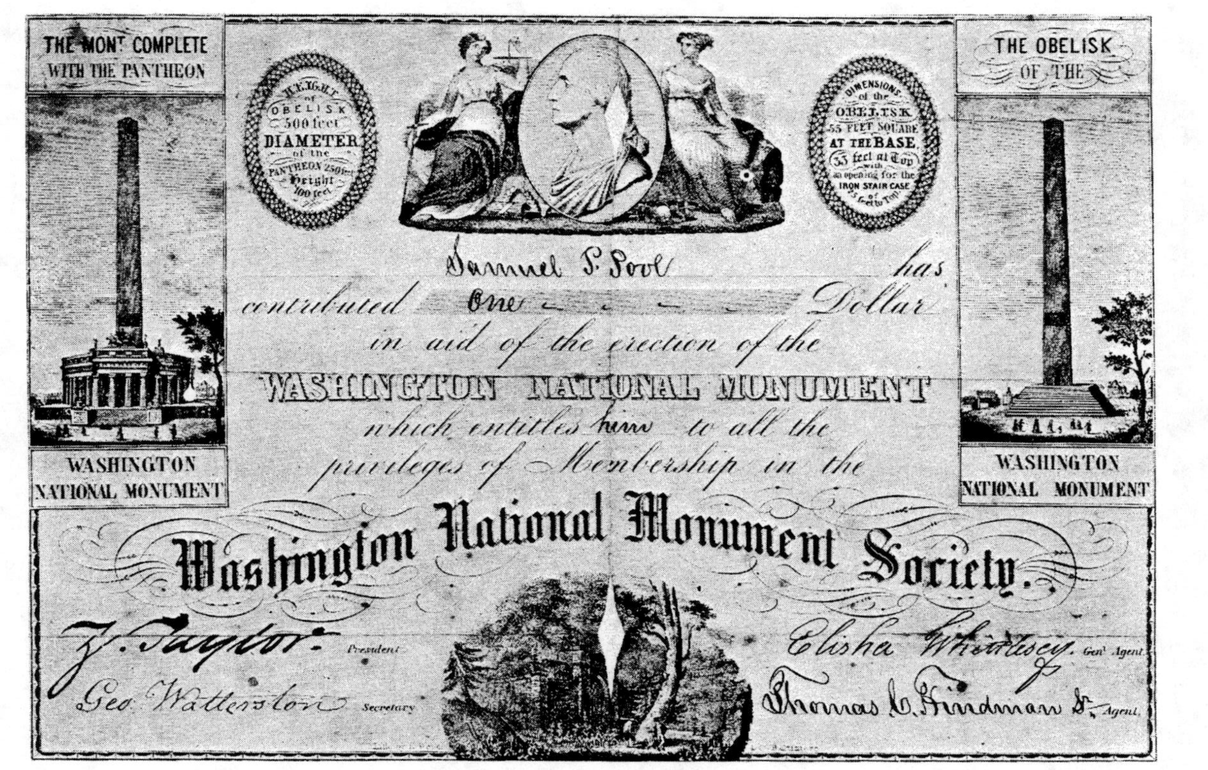
THE MONT. COMPLETE WITH THE PANTHEON

HEIGHT of OBELISK 500 feet DIAMETER of the PANTHEON 250 feet Height 100 feet

Samuel P. Pool has contributed One Dollar in aid of the erection of the

WASHINGTON NATIONAL MONUMENT

which entitles him to all the privileges of Membership in the

Washington National Monument Society.

DIMENSIONS of the OBELISK 55 FEET SQUARE AT THE BASE. 35 feet at Top with an opening for the IRON STAIR CASE

THE OBELISK OF THE WASHINGTON NATIONAL MONUMENT

WASHINGTON NATIONAL MONUMENT

Z. Taylor President

Geo. Watterston Secretary

Elisha Whittlesey Genl. Agent

Thomas C. Hindman Sr. Agent

Membership Certificate in the Washington Monument Association, issued to Samuel P'Pool, ancestor of Mrs. Mildred Vaughan Bouton

Bible Records

Copied by Mrs. W. P. Bouton, Lebanon, Tenn.

Thomas Turner Bible, in possession of Horace E. Turner, Lebanon, Tenn., a grandson.

Births

Thomas Turner, July 15, 1809.
Penelope L. Turner, wife of Thos. Turner, Sept. 30, 1813.
Mathew J. Turner, April 20, 1832.
William S. Turner, Oct. 14, 1833.
John Wesley Turner, Dec. 28, 1834.
Amanda J. Turner, Sept. 28, 1836.
Edward Asbury Turner, Aug. 8, 1838.
Stephen Leonidas Turner, June 17, 1840.
Penelope Josephine Turner, Jan. 26, 1842.
Thomas Marcellus Turner, Jan. 23, 1844.
Frances Elizabeth Turner, Feb. 10, 1846.
Marion H. N. Turner, Dec. 24, 1847.
Almira Lucinda Turner, Dec. 12, 1849.
Adeline Olivia Turner, May 25, 1852.
Rufus Wilson Turner, Oct. 5, 1853.
Peter Cartwright Turner, April 25, 1856.

Marriage

Thomas Turner and Penelope S. Cartwright, married April 28, 1831.

Deaths

Thomas Turner, Oct. 14, 1871.
Penelope S. Turner, wife of Thomas Turner, Aug. 9, 1888.
Mathew J. Turner, Jan. 29, 1913.
William S. Turner, Oct. 28, 1834.
Amanda Jane Turner, Aug. 29, 1857.
Edward A. Turner, June 21, 1871.
Frances Elizabeth Turner, Dec. 4, 1850.
Almira L. Turner, Dec. 20, 1850.
Adaline Olivia Turner, July 6, 1852.
Rufus Wilson Turner, June 18, 1877.
Peter C. Turner, May 1, 1856.

Major Bible record, in possession of Horace E. Turner, Lebanon, Tenn.

Births

Jane C. Major, April 18, 1806.
Martha Eliza Major, Aug. 7, 1837.
Lemuel Henry Major, March 23, 1839.
Nancy E. Eugene Major, Nov. 28, 1849.
Francine Louisa Donnell, May 21, 1813.
John W. Wynn, June 6, 1810.
William Madison Wynn, April 27, 1854.

Marriages

Henry A. Major and Francine L. Donnell, married Sept. 29, 1836.
John Wynn and Francine L. Major, married Jan. 27, 1852.
Benjamine Phillips and Francine L. Wynne, married Dec. 18, 1861.

Deaths

Lemuel Henry Major, March 7, 1849.
William Madison Wynne, April 5, 1860.
Benjamine Phillips, March 26, 1879.
Jane Donnell, Oct. 29, 1861.
Lemuel L. Phillips, Jan. 16, 1897.
Nancy E. Eugene Owen, April 11, 1885.

Nathaniel Murray Bible, in possession of Mrs. R. T. Reeves, Lebanon, Tenn., R. F. D. No. 5, a descendant.

Births

Nathaniel Murray, Oct. 8, 1809, in Halifax County, Va.
Jane Hearn, May 6, 1814, in Wilson County, Tenn.
George W. Murray, July 1, 1822.

Joseph Pitts Murray, Aug. 25, 1826.
Permelia Murray, March 30, 1821.
Mary Mallissa Murray, Sept. 20, 1838, in Wilson County, Tenn.
Tobitha Jane Murray, Dec. 29, 1839.
Mathew Nathaniel Murray, Feb. 9, 1845.
Sarah Murray, Dec. 18, 1849.
John Burr Murray, Jan. 26, 1852.

MARRIAGE

Nathaniel Murray and Jane Hearn, married Dec. 26, 1837.

DEATH

Nathaniel Murray, Feb. 14, 1886.

William C. Guthrie Bible, in possession of Walter Smithwick, a descendant, Lebanon, Tenn.

BIRTHS

Henry Guthrie, Jan. 23, 1785.
John Guthrie, Nov. 4, 1786.
Rebecca Guthrie, Dec. 16, 1788.
Sallie C. Guthrie, Jan. 11, 1790.
Abigial S. Guthrie, Jan. 25, 1792.
Thomas Guthrie, Dec. 16, 1794.
James B. Guthrie, Dec. 14, 1796.
Susana L. Guthrie, Dec. 28, 1798.
William M. Guthrie, Dec. 26, 1800.
Daniel J. Guthrie, April 20, 1803.
Mary G. Guthrie, Jan. 4, 1806.
Susanna L. Guthrie, March 7, 1821.
Wm. C. Guthrie, June 26, 1823.
Thomas H. Guthrie, Nov. 14, 1825.
Samuel J. Guthrie, Dec. 22, 1827.
Martha A. Harlan, June 22, 1832.
Mattie J. Shanks, April 14, 1850.
J. J. Hartsfield, March 3, 1826.

MARRIAGES

Wm. C. Guthrie and his wife, Obedience (Mucklerey), married March 17, 1784.
James B. Guthrie, married Teresa McLerey, Oct. 27, 1819.
John J. Hartsfield, married Martha A. Harlan, Dec. 19, 1847.
J. J. Hartsfield, married Martha J. Shanks, June 29, 1870.

DEATHS

William C. Guthrie, Nov. 14, 1823.
Henry Guthrie, Oct. 24, 1808.
Sallie C. Guthrie, Nov. 29, 1839.
Susanna L. Guthrie, Sept. 19, 1816.
William M. Guthrie, Jan. 14, 1822.

William B. Guthrie Bible, in possession of daughter, Lizzie Guthrie Wynne (Mrs. M. C. Wynne), Lebanon, Tenn.

BIRTHS

William B. Guthrie, Nov. 20, 1818.
Mary Elizabeth Jackson, wife of William B. Guthrie, Dec. 18, 1819.
Asa Jackson, Sr., Feb. 14, 1792.
Nancy Jackson, wife of Asa Jackson, Sr., July 18, 1800.
John Guthrie, Nov. 4, 1786.
John A. Guthrie, Dec. 20, 1844.
William H. Guthrie, May 13, 1846.
Nancy C. Guthrie, Sept. 2, 1847.
Abram B. Guthrie, Dec. 23, 1848.
Mary J. Guthrie, Oct. 3, 1850.
Sim J. Guthrie, Aug. 4, 1855.
Thomas E. Guthrie, Nov. 30, 1857.
Lizzie E. Guthrie, May 9, 1861.
M. C. Wynne, 1860.
Eva M. Wynne, Jan. 4, 1886.
Mary Pauline Wynne, June 11, 1888.
J. A. Gordan Wynne, March 18, 1894.
Graften Guthrie Wynne, Dec. 13, 1897.
Haidee Earl Wynne, May 10, 1901.

MARRIAGES

William C. Guthrie and Obedience Mucklerey, married March 17, 1784.
John Guthrie and Chele Babb, married Jan. 17, 1816.
William B. Guthrie and Mary E. Jackson, married Nov. 16, 1843.

DEATHS

William C. Guthrie, Nov. 14, 1823.
John Guthrie, son of William C. Guthrie, March 12, 1858; buried in Babb Graveyard, west of Lebanon, Tenn.

Asa Jackson, Sr., Aug. 30, 1870.
Nancy Jackson, wife of Asa Jackson, Sr., Feb. 20, 1833.
William B. Guthrie, June 25, 1909.
Mary Elizabeth Jackson, wife of William B. Guthrie, May 23, 1881.
William H. Guthrie, July 5, 1909.
John Asa Guthrie, 1929.
Sim Jackson Guthrie, 1923.
Nannie C. Guthrie, wife of J. S. Sullivan, July 11, 1921.
J. A. Sullivan, July 11, 1924.
Thomas E. Guthrie, March 22, 1932.

Nathaniel Cartmell Bible, in possession of Mrs. W. H. Bettis, Lebanon, Tenn., whose husband (deceased) was a great-grandson.

BIRTHS

Rachel E. Cartmell, Jan. 15, 1819.
James S. Cartmell, Oct. 27, 1820.
William M. Cartmell, June 15, 1822.
Mary P. Cartmell, Aug. 30, 1824.
Martha Ann Missouri Cartmell, Aug. 12, 1826.
Henry P. Cartmell, March 1, 1829.
Eliza Jane Cartmell, Feb. 26, 1831.
Sophia I. Cartmell, Feb. 10, 1833.
Mary E. Cartmell, Nov. 17, 1854.
John M. Powell, Feb. 28, 1841.
James H. M. Powell, Oct. 5, 1843.
Martha E. Powell, July 15, 1845.
William H. Cartmell, Sept. 14, 1846.
Sophia J. Cook, May 1, 1849.
Ann E. D. Cook, July 1, 1851.
Nathaliel G. Cook, July 11, 1854.
Maryella Cartmell, Nov. 17 (18), 1854 (?).
Henry T. Cartmell, Oct. 29, 1851.
Sophia S. Cartmell, April 29, 1855.
Chole I. Cartmell, March 20, 1861.
John Nathaniel Cartmell, Nov. 26, 1865.
Sofa S. Cartmell, April 29, 1855.

MARRIAGES

Nathaniel Cartmell, married Isabela Gleaves, Sept. 18, 1817.
Rachel E. Cartmell, married William T. Powell, March 23, 1837.
James S. Cartmell, married Mary E. S. Guthrie, April 26, 1843.
W. H. Cartmell, married Nannie Eatherly, Nov. 17, 1870.
John W. Bettis, married Sue Cartmell, Sept. 25, 1879.
James M. Eatherly, married Belle Cartmell, Sept. 8, 1881.

DEATHS

Rachel Gleaves, Sr., Sept. 7, 1735.
Rachel E. Powell, daughter of Nathaniel and Issabella Cartmell, July 21, 1846; age 27 years 6 months 6 days.
Mary P., daughter of Nathaniel and Issabella Cartmell, Dec. 13, 1846; age 22 years 5 months 13 days.
Martha A. M., daughter of Nathaniel and Issabella Cartmell, March 18, 1848; age 22 years 5 months 16 days.
Sophia I., daughter of Nathaniel and Issabella Cartmell, Aug. 21, 1849; age 16 years 6 months 11 days.
Eliza I. Cook, daughter of Nathaniel and Issabella Cartmell, March 18, 1854; age 23 years 20 days.
Henry T. Cartmell, Aug. 10, 1855.
Issabella Cartmell, wife of Nathaniel, June 24, 1857.
Nathaniel Cartmell, Nov. 11, 1863.
William M. Cartmell, June 19, 1876.
James S. Cartmell, April 3, 1893.
Mary E. S. Guthrie, wife of James S. Cartmell, July 1, 1887.
James M. Eatherly, Feb. 4, 1906.
Belle Cartmell, wife of James M. Eatherly, Jan. 4, 1919.
John W. Bettis, Feb. 12, 1926.
Sue Cartmell, wife of John W. Bettis, Sept. 8, 1823.

Foster Bible (John Donnell Foster), in possession of grandson's widow, Jennie Charlton Foster (Mrs. John Stephen Foster), Lebanon, Tenn.

BIRTHS

John D. Foster, Dec. 11, 1784, in North Carolina.
Elizabeth H. Foster, Dec. 25, 1795, in North Carolina.
Rufus H. Foster, Oct. 4, 1814, in Tennessee.
Wm. M. Foster, March 1, 1817, in Tennessee.
Nancy S. Foster, Aug. 5, 1819, in Tennessee.
Benjamin T. Foster, Dec. 3, 1821, in Tennessee.
John D. Foster, Aug. 5, 1824, in Tennessee.
Marthy R. Foster, Dec. 5, 1826, in Tennessee.
James A. Foster, Feb. 25, 1828, in Tennessee.
Elizabeth T. Foster, July 29, 1832, in Tennessee.
Erastus A. Foster, May 29, 1834, in Tennessee.
Mary E. Foster, March 14, 1837, in Tennessee.
These ten are the children of John D. Foster and Elizabeth H., his wife.

DEATHS

John D. Foster, Sr., Feb. 28, 1838.
Wm. M. Foster, March 13, 1838.
James A. Foster, Oct. 3, 1832.
Benjamin T. Foster, Sept. 25, 1847.
Erastus A. Foster, Oct. 31, 1861.
John D. Foster, June 29, 1863, in White County, Tenn.
Elizabeth H. Foster, Dec. 11, 1873.
(John Donnell Foster married Elizabeth "Betsey" Rogers, daughter of Solomon Rogers and Rebecca Smith.)

BIRTHS

Rufus H. Foster, Oct. 4, 1814.
Sarah Ann (Spain) Foster, July 5, 1817.
Frances Hardenia Foster, Sept. 27, 1842.
William Alexander Foster, Dec. 25, 1843.
Robert Verell Foster, Aug. 12, 1845.
John Stephen Foster, March 9, 1847.
Mary Adalaide Foster, Dec. 24, 1848.
Charlotte Elizabeth Foster, Jan. 16, 1851.
Son of Rufus and Sarah Foster, born and died June 23, 1853.
Benjamin Smith Foster, Feb. 1, 1855.

MARRIAGES

Rufus H. Foster and Sarah Ann, his wife, were married Nov. 18, 1841.

DEATHS

Frances Hardenia Foster, Jan. 21, 1843.
William A. Foster, Nov. 3, 1862.

Sherrill Bible records, in possession of Mr. William Sherrill, Lebanon, Tenn., R. F. D.

BIRTHS

Samuel Wilson Sherrill, March 21, 1758.
Elizabeth Sherrill, his wife, July 29, 1764.
Hugh Sherrill, Dec. 26, 1782.
Peggy Sherrill, Sept. 14, 1784.
Archibald Sherrill, May 26, 1786.
Samuel Wilson Sherrill, July 26, 1788.
Hulda Sherrill, Feb. 27, 1791.
Anne Sherrill, Feb. 14, 1793.
Betsey Thomas Sherrill, Sept. 14, 1796.
Rebeckah Sherrill, June 6. 1800.
Rouanna Sherrill, Aug. 7, 1802.
Hughe Sherrill, May 5, 1806.
Alanson Newnan Sherrill, Sept. 9, 1805.
Newton Sherrill, Oct. 30, 1824.
R. H. Sherrill, July 21, 1847.
W. A. Sherrill, Dec. 17, 1849.
Pleasant Annie Sherrill, April 16, 1852.
Edith Agnes Sherrill, Dec. 19, 1855.
R. H. Mason, Dec. 23, 1797.
Elizabeth Moss, May 20, 1806.
Parthenea Mason, April 23, 1824.

MARRIAGES

Samuel Wilson Sherrill and Elizabeth, his wife, married Jan. 17, 1782.
R. H. Mason and Elizabeth Moss,

married Jan. 12, 1826.

Newton Sherrill and Parthenea H. Mason, married Jan. 13, 1846.

DEATHS

Samuel Wilson Sherrill, Oct. 12, 1823, about 25 minutes after 3 o'clock in the evening, in the 66th year of his age.

Elizabeth Sherrill, June 30, 1851; age 86 years 11 months 1 day.

Alanson Newnan Sherrill, March 1, 1832, in the 24th year of his age.

Ricanna Peirkins, May 20, 1846; age 43 years 4 months.

Hugh Sherrill, July 28, 1836; age 30 years 2 months 23 days.

Samuel Hannah Bible record, in possession of great-granddaughter, Jennie Charlton Foster (Mrs. John Stephen Foster), Lebanon, Tenn.

BIRTHS

Samuel Hannah, July 2, 1767.

Mary Hannah, Dec. 8, 1768.

Melinda Hannah, Dec. 4, 1791.

Milecinda S. Hannah, March 24, 1794.

William Davison Hannah, Friday, Oct. 25, 1799.

John M. Hannah, Saturday, Jan. 25, 1802.

Jeany Hannah, Monday, Nov. 28, 1796.

Betsey Matilda Hannah, Monday, March 23, 1805.

Samuel Wilson Hannah, Tuesday, Nov. 29, 1807.

Joseph Harvey Hannah, Friday, April 13, 1810.

Elizabeth Hannah, second consort of Samuel Hannah, Oct. 7, 1792.

Mary Agnes Hannah, daughter of Sam. W. and Juliet Hannah, Oct. 29, 1831.

Virginia Tennessee Hannah, Thursday, Oct. 10, 1833.

Caroline Melinda Hannah, Saturday, Oct. 31, 1835.

Hardenia Trigg Hannah, Friday, Aug. 31, 1838.

Frances Elizabeth Hannah, Thursday, Nov. 19, 1840.

Sarah K. Hannah, Oct. 16, 1844.

MARRIAGES

Samuel Hannah and Mary McMillen, married Sept. 15, 1790.

Samuel Hannah and his wife, Elizabeth, married Jan. 24, 1833.

John M. and Amelia Hannah, married Jan. 8, 1828.

Samuel W. and Julyet Hannah, married Dec. 9, 1830.

Elizabeth Metilda Hannah and Logan McCarver, married Nov. 13, 1832.

Meceenda S. Hannah and Larken Sweazea, married Aug. 3, 1837.

DEATHS

William Davison Hannah, Nov. 6, 1803; age 4 years 12 days.

Jeany Hannah, Sept. 27, 1816; age 19 years 10 months 1 day.

Mary Hannah, consort of Samuel Hannah, Sabbath morning, about 9 o'clock, Jan. 16, 1825; age 56 years 1 month 8 days.

Joseph Harvey Hannah, Monday, Aug. 13, 1827; age 17 years 4 months.

John M. Hannah, Monday night, 11 o'clock, March 28, 1831; age 29 years 2 months 5 days.

Elizabeth Hannah, consort of Samuel Hannah, Thursday morning, 3 o'clock, Aug. 22, 1839; age 46 years 10 months 15 days.

Samuel Hannah, Monday, about 12 o'clock midnight, Aug. 24, 1840; age 73 years 1 months 22 days.

Caroline Melinda Hannah, third daughter of Sam W. and Juliet, Friday night, Dec. 1, 1837.

Hardenia Trigg Hannah, Thursday evening, Nov. 25, 1841.

Sarah K. Hannah, Oct. 19, 1845.

S. W. Hannah, Nov. 2, 1845.

Juliet Hannah, June 21, 1880.

John Skeen Bible, in possession of Mrs. D. M. Lane, a granddaughter of John Skeen (nee Ruthie Skeen), Lebanon, Wilson County, Tenn.

BIRTHS

John Skean, Aug. 1783.
Edith Skean, June 16, 1789.
Hannah Skean, Sept. 6, 1809.
Martin Skean, June 5, 1813.
Mathew Skean, June 10, 1815.
Elizabeth Skean, Nov. 30, 1817.
Hope H. Skean, Jan. 20, 1820.
William S. Skean, Jan. 5, 1824 (?).
David Lain, March 16, 1844.
Crist Lain, Feb. 25, 1850.
America J., daughter of D. M. and R. H. Lain, June 18, 1867.
William J. Lain, Jan. 24, 1869.
Mary J. Lain, May 1, 1872.
W. D. Hawkins, March 27, 1890.

MARRIAGES

Levin Clifton and Hannah Skean, married Nov. 8, 1826.

Hope H. Skean and Winnie J. Vanhook, married Nov. 23, 1842.

William S. Skean and Martha H. New, married Sept. 7, 1860.

David M. Lain and Ruthie H. Skean, married Feb., 1865.

DEATHS

John Skean, May 11, 1850.

Edith Skean, March 5, 1873.

Winnie J. Skean, July 7, 1896.

Mary J. Covington, March 15, 1900.

America J. Fields, March 7, 1891.

David Hankins, Aug. 18, 1893.

Charlie Lain, April 5, 1895.

Hope H. Skean, Oct. 19, 1856.

Eli Reed Bible, in possession of G. H. Reed, a son, Lebanon, Tenn., Wilson County.

BIRTHS

Margret Reed, July 24, 1771.
Eli Reed, Nov. 24, 1813.
Elizabeth Jane Reed, Sept. 6, 1834.
Cathrine Reed, May 12, 1836.
Mary Frances Reed, April 24, 1839.
Sophs H. Reed, March 13, 1841.
James D. Reed, July 19, 1843.
Joseph S. Reed, Jan. 18, 1848.
G. H. Reed, Aug. 12, 1850.

MARRIAGE

Elizabeth Jane Reed and A. B. Comer, married Nov. 29, 1857.

DEATHS

Margret Reed, March 28, 1875.
Saley Reed, Sept. 21, 1881.

Jacob Castleman Bible, in possession of Val Castleman, a great-grandson, Wilson County, Tennessee.

BIRTHS

Jacob Castleman, Oct. 6, 1788.
Anna Cassilman, wife of the above, Feb. 11, 1795.
Elizabeth Cassilman, daughter of the above, May 14, 1812.
Robert B. Cassilman, March 12, 1814.
John L. Cassilman, April 29, 1816.
Nancy R. Cassilman, March 22, 1818.
Polly Ann Cassilman, Feb. 7, 1820.
Jacob M. Cassilman, Sept. 24, 1821.
Thomas K. Cassilman, June 28, 1823.
Joseph W. Cassilman, April 18, 1825.
Rachel Amandy Cassilman, May 23, 1827.
Martha Hariett Cassilman, daughter of the above, Nov. 15, 1828.
Lazarus G. Cassilman, July 16, 1830.
Willis Durrum Cassilman, March 16, 1833.
Margret Reed Cassilman, March 8, 1836.

Easther Jane Cassilman, Aug. 5, 1840.
James Cassilman Reed, Nov. 20, 1832.
Anne Cisco Reed, Nov. 19, 1834.
Son born, Robert and Araminty Cassilman, Dec. 31, 1835.
Hariet M. Reed, Jan. 31, 1837.
Margret W. Reed, Feb. 15, 1839.
Rachel A. Reed, Aug. 7, 1841.
Jacob H. Reed, Dec. 13, 1844.
Sarah J. Reed, Jan. 14, 1848.

DEATHS

Jacob Castleman, July 10, 1847; age 58 years 9 months 4 days.
Anna Castleman, wife of the above, Sept. 24, 1844; age 51 years 6 months 13 days.
Easther Jane Castleman, daughter of the above, Sept. 26, 1847; age 6 years 1 months 20 days.
Elizabeth Reed, April 13, 1848, and Sarah Jane, April 14.
Rachel Amanda Hudson, April 6, 1848; age 20 years 10 months 14 days.
Nancy R. Clemmons, April 4, 1850; age 31 years 9 months 14 days.
Araminta Castleman, Sept. 12, 1885.
Joseph W. Castleman, son of Jacob and Ann, his wife, July 15, 1825.
Polly Ann Cassilman, Jan. 20, 1827.
Martha Hariet Cassilman, daughter of the above, June 15, 1829.
Esther Ricketts, July 10, 1828.
Eve Turmham, Oct. 27, 1831.
Willes Durham Cassilman, May 29, 1833.
John Listen Cassilman, Aug. 9, 1836.

MARRIAGES

Jacob Cassilman, married Anna Ricketts, his wife, Aug. 29, 1811.
Robert Reed, married Elizabeth, his wife, Jan. 5, 1832.
J. M. Cassilman, married Marthie Hancock, his wife, Nov. 16, 1848.

John Liston Castleman Bible, in possession of Jeff Castleman, a son, Lebanon, Tenn.

BIRTHS

Jacob Cassilman, Oct. 6, 1788.
Anna Ricketts, wife of Jacob Cassilman, Feb. 11, 1795.
Robert B. Castleman, son of Jacob and Anna Castleman, March 12, 1814.
Araminta Reed, wife of Robert B. Castleman, March 9, 1812.
John Liston Castleman, son of Robert B. and Araminta Castleman, Jan. 15, 1838.
Sarah Josephine Holloway, wife of John Liston Castleman, March 15, 1837.
Jefferson Liston Castleman, son of John Liston and Sarah Josephine Castleman, April 22, 1861.
Lula Harris, wife of Jefferson Liston Castleman, May 22, 1867.
Edward Castleman, son of John Liston and Sarah Josephine Castleman, Oct. 12, 1866.
Elizabeth Octavia Shelton, wife of Edward Castleman, Oct. 6, 1870.
Andrew Liston, son of Edward and Elizabeth Octavia Castleman, May 18, 1903.
Andrew Castleman, son of John Liston and Sarah Josephine Castleman, Sept. 4, 1868.
Val Castleman, son of John Liston and Sarah Josephine Castleman, Sept. 2, 1872.

MARRIAGES

Jacob Cassilman and Anna Ricketts, married Aug. 29, 1911.
Robert B. Castleman and Araminta Reed, married Nov. 22, 1834.
John Liston Castleman and Sarah Josephine Holloway, married Sept. 28, 1859.
Jefferson Liston Castleman and Lula Harris, married Jan. 20, 1892.
Val Castleman and Effie Baird, married May 17, 1896.
Edward Castleman and Elizabeth Octavia Shelton, married Dec. 29, 1901.

DEATHS

Jacob Cassilman, July 10, 1847.

Anna Ricketts, wife of Jacob Cassilman, Sept. 24, 1844.
Robert B. Castleman, April 29, 1896.
Araminta Reed Castleman, wife of Robert B. Castleman, Sept. 2, 1885.
John Liston Castleman, Dec. 11, 1915.

Sarah Josephine Holoway Castleman, July 22, 1905.

Andrew Castleman, son of John Liston Castleman, June 14, 1869.

Elizabeth Octavia Shelton Castleman, wife of Edward Castleman, Nov. 25, 1928.

Joseph Franklin Harris Bible, in possession of daughter, Lula Harris Castleman (Mrs. Jeff L. Castleman), Lebanon, Tenn.

BIRTHS

Alfred H. Harris, Dec. 23, 1790.

Elizabeth Woodrum, wife of Alfred H. Harris, Nov. 7, 1800.

Elihugh Caraway, Feb. 4, 1813.

Mary (Polly) Donaldson Richmond, wife of Elihugh Caraway, July 20, 1819.

Joseph Franklin Harris, April 20, 1836.

Louisa Frances Caraway, wife of Joseph Franklin Harris, Aug. 7, 1839.

CHILDREN

Alfred Rufus Harris, July 13, 1860.

Mary Susannah Harris, May 14, 1862.

Joseph Alexander Harris, Nov. 15, 1864.

Lula P. Harris, May 22, 1867.

Cromwell Kidder Harris, Oct. 5, 1869.

Sarah Elizabeth Harris, June 6, 1872.

Richmond Woodrum Harris, July 19, 1876.

Walter Caraway Harris, July 7, 1879.

Carrie Lena Harris, Nov. 30, 1882.

MARRIAGES

Joseph Franklin Harris and Louisa Frances Caraway, married Jan. 13, 1858, by Rev. D. B. Moore.

Joseph A. Harris and Cora A. Bell, married Dec. 30, 1889.

Mary Sue Harris and M. K. Hollister, married Aug. 6, 1891.

Lula P. Harris and Jeff L. Castleman, married Jan. 20, 1892.

Richmond W. Harris and Nellie B. Campbell, married Dec. 23, 1896.

A. Rufus Harris, married, first, Mertie Rogers, Aug. 31, 1898.

A. Rufus Harris, married, second, Hattie Donnell, Nov. 30, 1905.

Sarah Elizabeth Harris and Oscar Everett Gardner, married June 22, 1904.

Carrie Lena Harris and Andrew Oscar Eskew, married June 30, 1904.

Walter Caraway Harris and Mary Wilson, married March 2, 1906.

DEATHS

Alfred H. Harris, March 22, 1876.

Elizabeth Woodrum Harris, Aug., 1889.

Elihugh Caraway, Nov. 18, 1892.

Mary Donaldson "Polly" Richmond Caraway, June 23, 1894.

Cromwell Kidder Harris, Aug. 12, 1883, Gladeville, Tenn.

Edward Lee Harris, May 14, 1894, Weatherford, Texas.

O. E. Gardner, Jr., March 4, 1906, Greenfield, Tenn.

Carrie Lena Harris Eskew, Dec. 4, 1908, Lebanon, Tenn.

Frank C. Gardner, Jan. 8, 1911, Greenfield, Tenn.

Joseph Franklin Harris, Nov. 24, 1920, Gladeville, Tenn.

Louisa Frances Harris, March 25, 1927, Gladeville, Tenn.

A. Rufus Harris, May 21, 1929, Berlin, Okla.

James Shannon Record, in possession of great-grandson, Walter Jackson Baird, Lebanon, Tenn.

Henry Shannon, born Jan. 10, 1766, in Virginia; died Sept. 25, 1844, in Wilson County, Tenn.; married Jane Hayes, born March 22, 1772, in Virginia; died Dec. 10, 1832, in Wilson County, Tenn.; settled on Bartons Creek, Wilson County, and buried in Reland Graveyard on Wool Factory Road.

Robert "Robin" Shannon, born in Virginia, 1768; married April 11, 1790, in Sumner County, Rebeccah Buchanan, daughter of Archibald Buchanan; settled in Wilson County, Tenn., on Pond Lick Creek, near Gladeville. Henry Shannon and Robin Shannon were brothers.

James Shannon, son of Robin Shannon and Rebeccah Buchanan, born Dec. 10, 1795; died Aug. 7, 1867; married Dec. 31, 1816 (cousin), Mary Hayes Shannon, daughter of Henry Shannon and wife, Jane Hayes, born Nov. 20, 1794; died Aug. 12, 1865; settled 8 miles southwest of Lebanon, northeast of Central Pike in Wilson County, Tenn., where nine children were born:

Lucinda Hayes Shannon, born Aug. 13, 1817; died June 25, 1864; married as second wife of Byrd Moore.

Sarah Emily Shannon, born Dec. 6, 1819; died Sept. 25, 1887; married 1835 or 1836, James Madison Swain, born June 6, 1812; died Sept. 24, 1865; issue, three sons, five daughters.

William Washington Shannon, born Sept. 26, 1822; died Dec. 1, 1822.

Ethelbert J. Shannon, born June 1, 1824; died Aug. 11, 1900; married, first Sarah E. Mosely, died 1855; three children; married, second, Nancy Justice; married, third, Mary Justice, born 1830; died 1890.

James Buchanan Shannon, born Oct. 11, 1826; died April 23, 1828.

George Washington Buchanan Shannon, born Jan. 22, 1829; died Sept. 22, 1863; married 1847, Mary Caroline Baird, born Jan. 28, 1832; died Oct. 22, 1908; issue, four children.

Henry Jefferson Shannon, born Jan. 18, 1832; died July 31, 1890; married, first, Miss Mosely; married, second, Anna Tansil.

Mary Jane Shannon, born April 3, 1835; died May, 1894; married Willis D. Martin, died Dec. 10, 1892; issue, two children, son and daughter.

Rebecca Bowen Shannon, born May 27, 1838; died Dec. 9, 1914; married Oct. 24, 1861, John Summerfield Brown, born in Warren County, Tenn.; issue, 4 children.

James Madison Swain Record, in possession of grandson, Walter Jackson Baird, Lebanon, Tenn.

James Madison Swain, son of William Swain, born Jan. 6, 1812; died Sept. 24, 1865; married, 1835-6, to Sarah Emily Shannon, daughter of James Shannon and wife, Mary Hayes Shannon, born Dec. 6, 1819; died Sept. 25, 1887; settled on Stewart Ferry Road, east of Gladeville, Wilson County, Tenn., where both are buried in unmarked graves; issue, 8 children:

America Emeline Swain, born Oct. 22, 1837; died Feb. 23, 1919; married Sept. 22, 1855, James Franklin Baird, born Feb. 10, 1836; died Jan. 2, 1910; issue, 7 sons and 2 daughters.

Mary Angeline Swain, born Oct. 13, 1839; died Jan. 2, 1877; married, first, wife of John Randolph Lain; married 1866; issue, 2 children.

Lucinda Jane Swain, born Dec. 13, 1841; died ——; married Robert Baxter Cotton; issue, 5 children.

James Bowen Swain, born March 22, 1844; died Aug. 26, 1863, in Civil War; unmarried.

Frances Jackson Swain, born Oct. 9, 1846; died March 28, 1931; married Nov. 1, 1870, George Washington Vannatte, born Nov. 1, 1846; issue, 5 children.

William Washington Swain, born Jan. 19, 1850; died Nov. 6, 1929; married Oct. 13, 1870, Mattie C. Claxton; issue, 8 children.

Josephine Jefferson Swain, born June 9, 1852; died July 4, 1926; married Dr. William Thompson Ragsdale, born March 20, 1851; died April 24, 1903; issue, — children.

Henry Edgar Swain, born Sept. 25, 1856; living Sept., 1933, on the old home place of his father in Wilson County, Tenn.; married Jan. 8, 1890, Ella Frances Estes (living); issue, 7 children.

Clinton Baird Record, in possession of grandson, Walter Jackson Baird, Lebanon, Tenn.

Clinton Baird, son of John Baird and first wife, name not known, was born April 28, 1800-1; married in Wilson County, Tenn., Aug. 7, 1822, Patsey (Martha) Harris, born 1798; settled 7 miles southwest of Lebanon, Tenn., north of Central Pike, where their ten children were born. He married, second, Nancy Thompson Sullivan; no children. Clinton Baird, died Dec. 28, 1878. Patsey Harris Baird, his first wife, died March 21, 1861; both buried on home place in private graveyard.

CHILDREN

Henry Alexander Baird, born June 9, 1823; died Feb. 2, 1913; married Aug. 9, 1846, Almada H. Lane, born April 22, 1827; died March 11, 1899; issue, 5 children.

Eliza Ann Baird, born July 20, 1825; died July 12, 1907; married William James Rogers, born April 2, 1819; died July 10, 1871; issue, 9 children.

Houston Baird, born April 16, 1827; died Sept. 2, 1896; married April 9, 1852, Elizabeth Cassandra Donnell, born Sept. 25, 1831; died Oct. 31, 1923; issue, 5 children, 1 son, 4 daughters.

Wilburn Christopher Baird, born Oct. 28, 1829; died Aug. 2, 1875; married Martha Donnell, born July 22, 1833; died April 26, 1906; issue, 6 children.

Mary Caroline Baird, born Jan. 28, 1832; died Oct. 22, 1908; married, 1847, George Washington Buchanan Shannon, born Jan. 22, 1829; died Sept. 22, 1863; issue, 3 sons, 1 daughter.

John Baird, born 1834; killed in saw mill when quite young.

James Franklin Baird, born Feb. 10, 1836; died Jan. 2, 1920; married Sept. 22, 1855, America Emeline Swain, born Oct. 22, 1837; died Feb. 23, 1919; issue, 9 children, 7 sons, 2 daughters.

Clementine Baird, born June 1, 1838; died Oct. 20, 1917; married March 19, 1874, second wife of Richard Edward Willis Wray, born Oct. 25, 1826; died April 11, 1909; issue, 1 daughter.

Newton Harris Baird, born Aug. 7, 1840; died Nov. 24, 1912; married Jan. 16, 1868, Margaret "Maggie" Bishop; issue, 1 son.

Clinton Baird, Jr., born June 25, 1843; died 1862, in war, C. S. A.; unmarried.

Ezekial Holoway, grandfather of Jefferson Liston Castleman, Lebanon, Tenn.

Ezekial Holoway, born Feb. 10, 1803; died Aug. 5, 1864; married March 24, 1825, Jane Shannon, daughter of Henry Shannon and wife, Jane Hayes, born April 15, 1802; died July 23, 1851.

CHILDREN

Jasper A. Holoway, born Dec. 20, 1825; died Sept. 4, 1826.

Minerva J. Holoway, born Sept. 12, 1827; died April 8, 1851; married Jan. 8, 1850, Martin Steed.

Levi Durham Holoway, born Nov. 16, 1829; died Oct. 24, 1868; married Oct. 18, 1866, Louisa Viverett.
Judith A. F. Holoway, born June 17, 1832; died March 5, 1875; marmarried 1867, William Hancock.
Eunice Emelina Holoway, born July 21, 1834; died 1865; married Aug. 22, 1850, William A. Jones.
Sarah Josephine Holoway, born March 15, 1837; died July 22, 1903; married Sept. 28, 1859, John Liston Castleman.
Thomas Jefferson Holoway, born June 18, 1839; died July 3, 1863, in Battle at Gettysburg, Pa.
Harriet Almedia Holoway, born Nov. 14, 1842; living 1933; married Oct. 5, 1865, James Houston Hancock, born July 19, 1832; died ——.
Andrew Jackson Holoway, born Jan. 14, 1846.

John Morgan, great-grandfather of Mildred T. Vaughan Bouton (Mrs. William Paisley Bouton), Lebanon, Wilson County, Tennessee.

John Morgan and Sarah Neblett (Niblett), married in Lunenburgh County, Va., by the Rev. John Neblett, M. E. minister, Dec. 21, 1797; lived in Lunenburgh County, Va., where their children were born; later lived in Madison County, Ala.; were with their son, Dr. William Neblett Morgan, at Germantown, Tenn., when Sarah Neblett Morgan died, Feb. 16, 1849, and buried there in private graveyard of her son in unmarked grave.

John Morgan, her husband, was living at that time but was feeble.

I have not the exact date of his death. Tradition is that Sarah Neblett Morgan was a cousin of the mother of William Henry Harrison, ninth President of the United States.

Children

Edward R. Morgan (house carpenter), married in Lunenburgh County, Va., Nov. 25, 1822, Elizabeth "Betsey" Goodwin; issue, 3 children—John, Andrew and Sarah.

Francis N. Morgan (M.D.), died a young man.

Elizabeth "Betsey" Morgan, born in Lunenburgh County, Va., Jan. 14, 1804; died in Benton County, Miss., Dec. 16, 1879; married in Madison County, Ala., April 10, 1824, Samuel Pettypool (P'Pool), born in Davidson County, Tenn., Dec. 30, 1798; died in Benton County, Miss., Feb. 9, 1880; issue, 1 child—Mary Marion; married George Washington Vaughan.

John Harrison Morgan, born 1805; died 1841; buried at Uniontown, Pa., where he served as pastor, being a Cumberland Presbyterian minister; married Margaret Craft; issue, 4 children—Frances, married Baird; Sarah Virginia, married Dr. J. R. Brown, minister; William and John.

Thomas Morgan, married Eliza Mason; 1 child—daughter, Frances.

Mary Morgan, married John Irby (lived in Alabama); issue, 11 children—McCana, Sarah, John, Marsellus, Ellen, Rebeccah, Virginia, John, Josephine, Richard, Bettie.

William Neblett Morgan, M.D., lived at Germantown, Tenn.; married Mary Welburn (Wilburn); issue, 8 children—Cassie, William, Mary Neblett, married Robert McDonald; John Harrison, married Mary Rogers; Frances Grisselda, married Joseph Robinson; Chrosia; Frank, married Addie Leake. William Neblett Morgan, M.D., died and buried at Germantown, Tenn.; his widow, Mary Wilburn Morgan, after his death lived with her family at Ashland, Benton County, Miss, and is buried in the Vaughan Graveyard in an unmarked grave.

Sarah Morgan, died at 12 years of age.

John Paisley Family Record, in possession of great-great-granddaughter, Ethel Bouton Baird (Mrs. W. J.), Lebanon, Tenn.

John Paisley, son of the emigrants, William Paisley and his first wife, Eleanor McLean, was born in Pennsylvania in 1745; moved to North Carolina with his father in 1765; married, 1769, Maryanna Denny, born 1750, daughter of James Denny, 1715-1795, and wife, Agnes ———. John Paisley was early identified with the military forces of North Carolina. He was appointed by the Council as Major of 1st Battalion, Minute Men of Salisbury District, 1775. He was a field officer for Guilford County, being Lieutenant Colonel of Guilford Regiment. In 1776 he joined General Rutherford to subdue the "Over-hill" Cherokee Indians. He was appointed to pay for salt taken from Revolution.

John Paisley, 1745-1811, and wife, Maryanna Denny, 1750-1833.

CHILDREN

William Denny Paisley, 1770-1857; married, 1798, Frances Mebane; issue, 8 daughters. He was a Presbyterian minister.

James Paisley, 1772-1849; married, 1795, Hannah Denny (cousin); moved to Giles County, Tenn.; had large family.

Nancy Paisley, 1774-1852; married, 1794, Robert Hanner(h); issue, 5 girls, 3 boys. He left to go West prospecting and never heard from by his family; supposed murdered.

John Paisley, Jr., 1776-1845; married, 1799, Hannah Donnell; 5 girls and 3 boys.

Nellie (Eleanor) Paisley, 1780-1856; married Rev. Samuel Paisley (cousin).

George Paisley, 1782-1830; married Betsey Freeland; 2 girls, 2 boys.

Elizabeth Paisley, 1785-1846; married, 1810, Moses Gibson, 1783-1857.

Maryanna Paisley, 1787-1857; married, 1812, Joseph Gibson; no children.

Jean Paisley, 1790-1797.

Anna Paisley, 1793-1796.

Lieut. Col. John Paisley lived on his farm on Birch Creek, a small tributary of Little Alamance Creek, in Guilford County, N. C.

William Paisley Family Record, in possession of great-great-granddaughter, Ethel Bouton Baird (Mrs. W. J.), Lebanon, Tenn.

After the Earls of Tyrone, Ireland, had fled, leaving their vast estates of land to the mercy of the King of England, these lands were given to peoples of other countries who would pledge allegiance to the King. At that time the Paisleys of Western part of Scotland were suffering persecution with other Protestants, as they were Presbyterians. In 1637 they took refuge in Tyrone, Province of Ulster, Ireland. It was from these ancestors our emigrant, William Paisley, descended. Of a large family, he and his brother, John, were only ones to come to America. John Paisley went into Delaware, and we know nothing of him. William Paisley was born about 1700-1708 in Tyrone, Ulster, Ireland, and came to America in 1736-37. Landing at Philadelphia, he settled about 20 miles above Philadelphia on the Schuylkill River on rented land, where by industry and management he reared his six children and saved enough to buy them homes or land in North Carolina, when they moved there about 1765. He was married three times; first, to Eleanor McLean in Ireland, just before coming to America, 1736-7. She was mother of his six children and died in Pennsylvania; married, second, to Catherine Hamilton in Pennsylvania, who died soon after they moved to North Carolina. He married, third, in North Carolina to Elizabeth Denny. William Paisley settled in bounds of Alamance Presbyterian Church and was among the first elders of that church, and many of his family were members of that church and buried in its churchyard. He is said to have been low of stature, heavy build, and stood very erect. He died in North Carolina in 1777; buried at Alamance Presbyterian Church.

William Paisley's first wife, Eleanor McLean, had two brothers and three sisters to come to Pennsylvania from Ireland and settle there.

William Paisley and his first wife, Eleanor McLean, emigrants from Tyrone, Ulster, Ireland, to Pennsylvania, 1736-7.

CHILDREN

Jane Paisley, born in Pennsylvania, 1737; married, first, in Pennsylvania, John White; died in North Carolina; married, second, in North Carolina, William Cowdy, died in North Carolina. She moved to Kentucky with daughter, Martha, wife of Joseph McDowell, where she died in 1804.

Robert Paisley, born in Pennsylvania, 1739; married in Pennsylvania, Margaret Majors (cousin); moved from North Carolina to Kentucky in 1797; issue, 5 sons, 4 daughters.

William Paisley, Jr., born Dec. 23, 1741, in Pennsylvania; married in Pennsylvania, 1763, to Deliverance Paine; issue, 6 sons, 1 daughter.

John Paisley, born in Pennsylvania in 1745; married in North Carolina, 1769, Maryanna Denny; issue, 4 sons, 6 daughters.

Margaret Paisley, born 1747, in Pennsylvania; married in North Carolina, William Denny; issue, 10 children.

Mary Paisley, born 1750, in Pennsylvania; married in North Carolina, James Doak; issue, 4 sons, 4 daughters.

William Paisley, the emigrant, born in Ireland, 1700-1708; died in North Carolina, Guilford County, 1777; married three times; married, first, in Ireland, Eleanor McLean, 1736-7; married, second, in Pennsylvania, Catherine Hamilton, before 1765; married, third, in North Carolina, Elizabeth Denny.

Eleanor McLean had two brothers and three sisters to come from Ireland and settle in Pennsylvania.

John McLean, married Jane Marshall; their children: Joseph, John, Thomas, Robert, Marshall, Nelly, Jane, Margaret, Polly, Nancy and Betsey.

Joseph McLean, married Nancy Marshall, sister of John's wife; children: Catherine, Martha, John, Joseph, William, Thomas.

Her sister, Martha McLean, married Mr. Adams.

Her sister, Margaret McLean, married Thomas Majors.

Her sister, Isabell McLean, married Mr. Sterling.

Moses Gibson Records, in possession of his great-granddaughter, Ethel Bouton Baird (Mrs. W. J.), Lebanon, Tenn.

Moses Gibson, son of the emigrant, Andrew Gibson and wife, Jane Freeland, was born in Guilford County, N. C. He was a farmer, and an elder in the Bethel Presbyterian Church for twenty-five years. In 1841, with his family, he moved to Jackson County, Ark., arriving at Dunbar farm on Black River Dec. 24. In the spring of 1842 he moved to Litchfield, the old county seat, and rented the entire farm, including the old court house, and put in a ten-horse crop of corn. In Dec., 1842, he moved down the river about 30 miles to a point called Taylor's Bay, where he remained until the fall of 1844, when he moved back by wagons, bringing family, negroes and household goods, crossed the Mississippi River at Memphis and on through Holly Springs into Tippah County, Miss. He bought 160 acres of land, being the northeast quarter of Section 5, Township 2, Range 2, east, about four miles south of the Tennessee line, in what was then Tippah County, Miss., after 1870, Benton County, Miss. There he built his home and lived until death, being buried only a few hundred yards southwest of his home in his family plot, by the side of his wife.

BIRTHS

Moses Gibson, born Feb. 9, 1783, in Guilford County, N. C.
Elizabeth Paisley, born June 25, 1785, in Guilford County, N. C.

CHILDREN

Eliza Ann Gibson, born April 17, 1811, in Guilford County, N. C.
John Paisley Gibson, born Aug. 10, 1813, in Guilford County, N. C.
Andrew Fin Gibson, born July 1, 1815, in Guilford County, N. C.
Joseph Washington Gibson, born Dec. 22, 1817, in Guilford County, N.C.
Lemuel Newton Gibson, born Sept. 29, 1819, in Guilford County, N. C.
Anna Jane Gibson, born July 2, 1821, in Guilford County, N. C.
William Paisley Gibson, born Dec. 17, 1825, in Guilford County, N. C.
Two boys, died in infancy.

MARRIAGES

Moses Gibson and Elizabeth Paisley, daughter of Lieut. Col. John Paisley and wife, Maryanna Denny, married Feb. 15, 1810, in Guilford County, N. C.
John Paisley Gibson, married, first, May 14, 1838, Demaris Porter, Rockingham County, N. C.; married, second, Jan. 28, 1847, Susan Gatlin, Tippah County, Miss.; married, third, Oct. 23, 1864, Sallie Gatlin, Tippah County, Miss.
Andrew Fin Gibson, married Dec. 19, 1837, Agnes Ann Porter, Guilford County, N. C.
Joseph Washington Gibson, married Nov. 16, 1843, Elizabeth Childress, in Jackson County, Ark.
Lemuel Newton Gibson, married Oct. 1, 1846, Ann H. Pegram, Tippah County, Miss.
Anna Jane Gibson, married Feb. 9, 1843, Dr. Ralph Leonard Bouton, in Jackson County, Ark.
William Paisley Gibson, married Dec. 16, 1852, first Araminta R. Belote; married second, Feb. 16, 1863, America A. Conway.

DEATHS

Eliza Ann Gibson, died Aug. 13, 1830, in Guilford County, N. C.
Moses Gibson, died Dec. 8, 1857, in Tippah County, Miss.
Elizabeth Paisley Gibson, died July 23, 1846, in Tippah County, Miss.
John Paisley Gibson, died Sept. 18, 1883, in Benton County, Miss.
Andrew Fin Gibson, died 1885, age 70 years.
Joseph Washington Gibson, died Nov. 6, 1848, Tippah County, Miss.
Lemuel Newton Gibson, died June 25, 1853, Tippah County, Miss.
Anna Jane Gibson Bouton, died Oct. 24, 1901, buried in Ashland Cemetery, Ashland, Benton County, Miss.
Dr. Ralph Leonard Bouton, died Dec. 15, 1900; buried in Ashland Cemetery.
William Paisley Gibson, died June 11, 1881, in Tate County, Miss.
Araminta R. Belote Gibson, died Oct. 17, 1860.

Andrew Gibson Records, in possession of great-great-granddaughter, Ethel Bouton Baird (Mrs. W. J.), Lebanon, Tenn.

Andrew Gibson, son of James Gibson and wife, Jane Fin, was born in Edinborough, Scotland, 1750. When a boy, early in his teens, he was apprenticed to a silversmith of that city. The silversmith emigrated to America, landing in Charleston, S. C. Against the wishes of his parents, Andrew came with him, then at the age of about 15. After Andrew Gibson became of age he moved to Cheraw, S. C., and opened a store of his own. About 1775 he moved to Guilford County, N. C., and operated a general store. He sued a man for debt before Esquire Freeland of Orange County; while at the Esquire's home he met his daughter, Jane Freeland, and fell in love with her, and they were married the latter part of 1776. Andrew Gibson, emigrant, died 1823, and buried at Gibsonville, N. C., place named for his family, and the town has bought land adjoining his burying ground for the town cemetery.

Andrew Gibson, born 1750; died 1823; married 1776, Jane Freeland, born 1757; died 1827.

THEIR CHILDREN

James Gibson (M.D.), 1777-1843; married Sarah Nicks, daughter of George Nicks (Nix).

John Freeland Gibson, 1780-1823; unmarried.

Moses Gibson, 1783-1857; married Feb. 15, 1810, Elizabeth Paisley, 1785-1846.

Joseph Gibson, 1785-1857; married, 1812, Marianna Paisley, 1787-1857.

Robert Gibson, 1787-1798; died young.

Elizabeth (Betsey) Gibson, married, 1812, William A. Causey, 1790-1842.

Jane (Jennie) Gibson, 1792-1873; married Jesse Thompson, 1800-1857.

Nancy Unity Gibson, 1805-1857; married George B. Clapp, 1809-1866.

John Wharton, great-great-great-grandfather of Margaret Chambers-Bouton (Mrs. George Ralph Bouton), Lebanon, Wilson County, Tenn.

REPORT FROM WAR DEPARTMENT,
WASHINGTON, D. C.

"The records of this office show that one John Wharton, Jr., served in the Revolutionary War as a private in Capt. Gustavus B. Wallace's Company, Third Virginia Regiment, commanded by Col. George Weeden. The date of enlistment is not shown. His name first appears on the company pay roll covering this period from Oct. 8 to Dec. 7, 1776, and is last borne on the company pay roll covering the period from Jan. 1 to March 1, 1777.

"The records also show that one John Wharton, Sr., served in that war in the same company and regiment. The date of enlistment is not shown. His name first appears on the company pay roll covering the period from Oct. 8 to Dec. 7, 1776, and last on pay roll from Jan. 1 to March 1, 1777. The records further show that one John Wharton served in said war as a soldier of Virginia Infantry, organization not further indicated. His name appears on a record under the following heading: 'A list of Virginia soldiers of the Virginia Line on Continental Establishment who have received certificates for the balance of their full pay agreeable to an Act of Assembly passed Nov. Session, 1781, which shows that on April 21, 1785, the sum of S. 13-D4 was received by one William Arnold.'"

John Wharton, born about 1746, married Rhoda Morris of Hanover County, Va.; settled in Albemarle County, near North Garden, Va., and reared his family of seven sons. Late in life he and his wife lived with his son, Jesse Wharton, at Nashville, Tenn., where he died March 3, 1816, of influenza. His wife died in 1827. They are both buried in Mt. Olivet Cemetery, Section 3, Lot 86.

CHILDREN

George Wharton, born 1765, in Virginia; died Aug. 21, 1824, in Davidson County, Tenn.; married, first, Elizabeth Farrar; married,

second, Elizabeth Harris.
William H. Wharton, born in Virginia; died in Nashville Feb. 3, 1816; married Judith Harris, who died five days after her husband.
John Wharton, Jr., born in Virginia; died Feb. 7, 1845, in Bedford County, Va.; married Sally Lilbourn Logwood, daughter of Thomas Logwood.
Austin Wharton, M.D., born in Virginia; resided at Cartersville, Va., later Goochland County, Va.; died in Mississippi, 1835; married, first, Jane Logwood, of Powatan County, Va.; married, second, Lucy Goode; married, third, Mrs. Spears, nee Bates.
Jesse Wharton, born in Albemarle County, Va.; died in Nashville, Tenn., July 22, 1833; married, first, April 29, 1804, Mary "Polly" Philips, daughter of Joseph Philips and wife, Milbrey Horn, born in Edgecomb County, N. C., Sept. 6, 1786; died in Davidson County, Tenn., April 11, 1813; children: John Overton, Joseph Philips, Rhoda Ann, Sarah Angelina, Mary Philips. Married, second, Elizabeth Auston Rice, of Virginia, cousin; children of second marriage: Thomas Jefferson, Jane, Ramsey, Fedelia and two others.
Samuel Leake Wharton, born in Virginia; died in Davidson County, Tenn.; married Lucinda Farrar.
Dabney Wharton, married Anna T. Swan.

Joseph Philips Wharton, great-grandfather of Margaret Chambers-Bouton (Mrs. George Ralph Bouton), Lebanon, Tenn.

Joseph Philips Wharton, son of Jesse Wharton and his first wife, Polly Philips, born in Davidson County, Tenn., Oct. 10, 1806; died in Wilson County, Tenn., Sept. 26, 1866; married Sept. 21, 1830, in Nashville, Tenn., by Rev. William Hume, to Caroline C. Hewitt, daughter of Robert Hewitt and Anna Shute, born Sept. 6, 1809; died Jan. 20, 1881.

CHILDREN

Mary Ann Elizabeth Wharton, born Oct. 1, 1831; died 1924; married Frank Buchanan.
Robert Hewitt Wharton, born April 1, 1885; died Oct. 29, 1917; married Feb. 16, 1864, Margaret Taylor Davis; born Nov. 29, 1843; died Feb. 16, 1916.
Joseph Philips Wharton, Jr., born Aug. 23, 1837; died May 9, 1865; C. S. A. at Rock Island.
Jesse Wharton, born Aug. 19, 1839; killed in Battle of Murfreesboro, Tenn.

Sarah Caroline Wharton, born Jan. 9, 1841; died Oct. 18, 1843.

Matilda Emma Wharton, born Feb. 22, 1833; married, first William W. Price; married, second, Ellis Harper.

Margaret Isabella Wharton, born Aug. 7, 1845; died March 24, 1901.
Mary Caroline Wharton, born Feb. 17, 1848; died Jan. 20, 1900; married Jan. 20, 1870, Joseph Balie Peyton.

Joseph Philips Wharton lived on his farm, three miles east of Lebanon, Tenn., where he built a water mill on Spring Creek. He and his wife are buried in private graveyard on the place, which is now owned by his descendants.

Joseph Philips, great-great-great-grandfather of Margaret Chambers-Bouton (Mrs. George Ralph Bouton), Lebanon, Tenn.

Joseph Philips was an early settler, emigrated in 1891 with his wife, Milbrey Horn, from Edgecomb County, N. C., to Davidson County, and settled six miles north of Nashville. His ancestry for several generations, both paternal and maternal, were natives of Edgecomb Province under the Colonial Government.

"Joseph Philips served as guide for the Continental forces and participated in the Battle of Kings Mountain. Mathew Philips, brother of Joseph Philips, commanded a regiment of troops and died preceeding the Battle of Kings Mountain, from an overdraught of water."

Joseph Philips served as Justice for Davidson County in 1796.

Joseph Philips was born in Edgecomb County, N. C., Oct. 31, 1763; died in Davidson County, Tenn., May 22, 1832; married, 1785, Milbrey Horn, born in Edgecomb County, N. C., Dec. 4, 1764, daughof Henry Horn, Jr., second husband of Sarah Battle, Hiliard, widow, died in Davidson County, Tenn., Dec. 19, 1851.

CHILDREN

Mary "Polly" Philips, born Sept. 6, 1788, in North Carolina; died in Davidson County, Tenn., April 11, 1813; married April 29, 1804, as first wife of Jesse Wharton.

Sarah "Sallie" Philips, born in North Carolina Aug. 1, 1788; died in Davidson County, Tenn., Jan. 19, 1859; married Feb. 11, 1807, William Williams, born April 15, 1776; died March 6, 1862.

Rebecca Philips, born in North Carolina April 16, 1790; died in infancy.

Martha Philips, born in Davidson County Dec. 11, 1792; married Thomas Martin.

Charlotte Philips, born Nov. 25, 1795; drowned in Cumberland River July 23, 1811.

Henry Horn Philips, born Sept. 5, 1797; died Oct. 4, 1816; unmarried.

Margaret "Peggy" Thomas Philips, born Sept. 20, 1799; died ——, 1844; married, 1815, Josiah Fredrick Williams.

Joseph Hooper Philips, born Jan. 2, 1803; died in infancy.

William Duncan Philips, born June 10, 1804; died June 5, 1879; married, first, 1825, Susan B. Clark; died without issue; married second, 1828, Eliza Dwyer, born Aug. 3, 1801, in Ireland; died Nov. 10, 1871.

The homestead of Joseph Philips, six miles north of Nashville, Tenn., was known as "Sugar Tree Grove." He and his family are buried in private burial ground on his home place.

John Seay, great-great-great-grandfather of Margaret Chambers-Bouton (Mrs. George Ralph Bouton), Lebanon, Tenn.

John Seay and wife came from Virginia about 1805, settled on the Troudale Ferry Pike, in the edge of Smith County, about 8 miles east of Lebanon, Wilson County, Tenn. The farm is now owned by Dan Seay, a descendant. John Seay and wife, Sarah McCarty, are buried in private graveyard in rocked up box tomb, no inscription.

"Tradition is that John Seay went to Revolutionary War at the age of 16 years. He was so interested in seeing what was going on when Cornwallis surrendered, he stepped forward out of line and was reprimanded by an officer."

John Seay was born in Virginia April 29, 1764; died in Tennessee Sept. 13, 1830; married in Virginia, Sarah McCarty, who died Thursday morning, Oct. 6, 1831.

CHILDREN

Polly Seay, born Nov. 27, 1789, in Virginia; died July 17, 1835, in Tennessee; married William Spears.

Sally Seay, born Jan. 7, 1791, in Virginia; died in Tennessee; married about 1811, James Johnson.

Jacob Seay, born Sept. 21, 1792, in Virginia (must have died young).

John Seay, Jr., born Oct. 9, 1794;

died Feb. 19, 1885; unmarried; minister in M. E. Church.
Elizabeth Seay, born Feb. 27, 1797, in Virginia; married Hearn.
Charles H. Seay, born May 30, 1799, in Virginia; married Miss Beard.
William Washington Seay, born April 2, 1801, in Virginia; died March 24, 1874; married July 13, 1825, Ann W. Stanfield, born Jan. 8, 1805; died Sept. 21, 1872.
Daniel Seay, born Jan. 23, 1805; died July 13, 1875; married Sept. 5, 1832, Elizabeth Ledbetter, born Sept. 17, 1811; died May 9, 1880.

John Chambers, great-grandfather of Mrs. Margaret Chambers-Bouton, Lebanon, Wilson County, Tenn.

John Chambers, born in Wilson County, Tenn.; settled on Spring Creek, about five miles north of Lebanon; born 1806; died April, 1865; son of Lewis Chambers and first wife, Annie Hunter; married about 1830-31.
Edna Johnson, daughter of James Johnson and wife, Sarah Seay, wife of John Chambers; born Aug. 30, 1812; died Sept. 20, 1878.

Children

James Lewis Chambers, born March 12, 1832; died June, 1863; married March, 1854.
Louisa Palmer, daughter of John Palmer and wife, Margaret Reese, born Dec. 7, 1833; died June 20, 1900.
Elizabeth Chambers, born March 5, 1834; died ——; married ——.
William Chambers, born Nov. 21, 1836; died ——; married ——.
Sarah "Sallie" Chambers, born March 29, 1839; died ——; married ——.
Hugh Alexander "Bob" Chambers, born Dec. 23, 1841; died ——; married, 1866, Marcia Holman, born Aug. 20, 1844, daughter of William S. and Sophia A. Holman; issue, 8 children—Lelia, Eugene, Pearl, Hortense, Daisy, Sophia, Pauline and Bessie.
John Dana "Jack" Chambers, born Sept. 17, 1844; married, 1874, Woody Miller, born Dec. 19, 1840, daughter of John and Mary Miller.
Sooky Chambers, born March, 1846.

Thomas Meacham Chambers, born March 7, 1849 (living 1933 in Wilson County); married Martha McFarland, daughter of Dr. James Harvey McFarland and wife, Charlotte Walker (Mrs. Chambers, living 1933 in Wilson County).

David Chambers, born Sept. 20, 1852.

Martha "Mat" Chambers, born Dec. 17, 1855; married James McFarland.

Lewis Chambers, great-great-grandfather of Margaret Chambers-Bouton (Mrs. George Ralph Bouton), Lebanon, Wilson County, Tenn.

Lewis Chambers was an early settler on Cedar Creek, about nine miles north of Lebanon, Wilson County, Tenn. He died during the Civil War, and is buried in an unmarked grave on his home place.

Lewis Chambers was twice married; first to Annie Hunter, who was the mother of his ten children; married, second, late in life to Mrs. Jane Reasonover Durham, a widow.

Children

Children of Lewis Chambers and his first wife, Annie Hunter:
John Chambers, born in Wilson County, Tenn., 1806; died 1865; married about 1830-31, Edna Johnson, daughter of James and Sarah Seay, born Aug. 30, 1812; died Sept. 20, 1878.
Edward "Ned" Chambers, married, first, Hunter; married, second, Elizabeth Debow.

Nicholas "Nick" Chambers, married Betsey Norris.
Alexander "Alex" Chambers, married Jan. 25, 1838, Jane Hunter.
James Chambers, married Susannah Chandler.
Lewis Chambers, died young .
Elizabeth Chambers, married Wright Hunter.
Eliza Chambers, married Spencer Duncan.
Jane Chambers, married Randall McDonald.
Mary Chambers, died unmarried.

Francis Palmer, great-great-great-grandfather of Margaret Chambers-Bouton (Mrs. George Ralph Bouton), Lebanon, Wilson County, Tenn.

Francis Palmer (or William Francis Palmer), was born in King William County, Va., about 1752. It is said he served in the Revolutionary War under Gen. Francis Marion, some say under Light Horse Harry Lee. He lived after marriage in North Carolina and South Carolina.

Francis Palmer, married Caroline Dulaney of the eastern shore of Maryland or Virginia. Caroline Dulaney, had a sister who married Charles Ready, whose son, Col. Charles Ready, married her daughter, Mary Palmer.

Children

Children of Francis Palmer and wife, Caroline Dulaney:

Mary Palmer, born in North Carolina Sept. 4, 1773; died Sept. 30, 1848; married, 1797, her first cousin, Charles Ready, born April 1, 1770; died Aug. 3, 1859.

William Palmer, born in North Carolina in 1777; died March 12, 1857; married, 1803, to Sarah Rankin, born 1781; died Nov. 4, 1859.

Henry Dulaney Palmer, born in Charleston, S. C. in 1781; died in 1861; married Patsey Angel. He was a minister and moved to Illinois; issue, 9 children.

Caroline Palmer, married Nelson.

Francis Rose Palmer, born 1789; married unknown. He was a minister and moved to Independence, Mo. He had one child, a daughter, Frances A. Palmer, who married a Mr. Grant of St. Louis.

Phillip Palmer, died young.

Susan Palmer, was an invalid.

Family Records

Copied by Mrs. W. P. Bouton, Wilson County, Lebanon, Tenn.

John Palmer, great-grandfather of Margaret Chambers Bouton (Mrs. George Ralph Bouten), Lebanon, Tenn.

John Palmer, son of William Palmer and wife, Sarah Rankin, settled five miles north of Lebanon, Wilson County, Tenn., on Spring Creek.

John Palmer, born in Wilson County, Tenn., April 13, 1804; died Feb. 23, 1892; married Aug. 25, 1825, to Margaret "Peggy" Reese, daughter of Thomas B. Reese, and wife, Peggy Thompson, born Jan. 11, 1803; died Jan. 5, 1874. He and his wife are both buried on his home place, now owned by his grandson, James Lewis Chambers.

Children

James R. Palmer, born July 6, 1826; died April 28, 1833.

Margaret Ann Palmer, born Oct. 20, 1828; died Jan. 5, 1874; married Jan., 1850, H. W. Robb.

Sarah Palmer, born March 16, 1831; died Sept. 14, 1865; married Jan., 1849, A. B. Douglas.

Louisa Palmer, born Dec. 7, 1833; died June, 1900; married March, 1854, James Lewis Chambers, born March 12, 1853; died June, 1865.

Richard H. Palmer, born Jan. 3, 1835; died ———; married Nov., 1868, Nancy Jane Miller.

Ellan Palmer, born July 30, 1841; died Nov. 17, 1895; unmarried.

Henry Clay Palmer, born June 17,

1844; died ———; married, 1883, Bettie Blair Ross (widow).

———

William Palmer, great-great-grandfather of Margaret Chambers Bouton (Mrs. George Ralph Bouton), Lebanon, Tenn.

The records of this office show that William Palmer served in the War of 1812 as a private in Capt. James A. Black's Company of Infantry, Third (Roulston's) Regiment, West Tennessee Militia from ——— 13, 1814 to May 13, 1815. The records indicate that this Regiment was in expedition to New Orleans, the transportation paid on the baggage of William Palmer from Wharton, La., to Tennessee. Nothing further relative to this man has been found. Adjutant Gen. H. T. McCain.

William Palmer, son of Francis Palmer and wife, Caroline Dulaney, born in North Carolina, 1777; died in Tennessee March 12, 1851; married in 1803.

Sarah Rankin, daughter of James Rankin and wife, Hannah, born 1781; died Nov. 4, 1859.

CHILDREN

John Palmer, born April 13, 1804; died Feb. 23, 1892; married Aug. 25, 1825.

Margaret "Peggy" Reese, born Jan. 11, 1803; died Jan. 5, 1874.

Nancy Palmer, married Joab Goodall, moved to Marion, Ill.; issue, 12 children.

William Palmer, married Louisa Green.

Francis Palmer, married Sept. 3, 1838, Polly Bumpass.

Victoria Palmer, born Sept. 10, 1807; died Nov. 2, 1871; married Robert Phelps.

Charles Palmer, married Elizabeth "Betsy" Talley.

Henry Palmer, born Dec. 24, 1818; died Oct. 16, 1844 (probably a bachelor).

Elizabeth Palmer, married George Washington Phelps.

Martha Palmer, born Dec. 24, 1822; died Oct. 28, 1848; married M. T. "Cage" Bennett.

Mary Palmer, married James W. White.

Susan Palmer, married Addison Reese.

Sarah Palmer, married Cicero L. Murphey, born Nov. 8, 1822; died Dec. 17, 1892.

Margaret Palmer, married Thomas Cox.

William Palmer lived and died on his farm, near Linwood, Wilson County, Tenn., east of Lebanon.

Hardin Phillips Record, in possession of Mrs. E. S. Bowers, Lebanon, Tenn.

BIRTHS

Hardin Phillips, May 11, 1848.
Lizzie Phillips, April 22, 1851.
Josiah Phillips, Nov. 4, 1869.
Hattie Phillips, June 28, 1873.
Rossey M. Phillips, Sept. 18, 1878.
Davie Phillips, April 26, 1850.
Bennie Phillips, April 24, 1852.
Wilson Phillips, Jan. 1, 1854.
Zemana Roberts, May 5, 1890.
Gussie Roberts, Sept. 16, 1896.
Roger Dale, Aug. 26, 1904.
Fred Cleveland Barbour, Sept. 24, 1915.
Mary Zemma Barbour, May 22, 1919.
Ann Augusta Barbour, Nov. 12, 1922.

MARRIAGES

Hardin Phillips and Lizzie Pendleton, married Oct. 15, 1868.

J. W. Phillips and Susia Kidwell, married Dec. 1, 1885.

H. C. Roberts and Hattie Phillips, married June 9, 1889.

Fred Cleveland Barbour and Willie Augusta Roberts, married Sept. 19, 1914, at Lebanon, Tenn.

DEATHS

Josiah Phillips, 1868.
Rossey M. Phillips, Oct. 12, 1879.
Malinda Phillips, Dec. 23, 1882.
Hattie Phillips, Feb. 14, 1912.
Hardin Phillips, March 23, 1912.
David Phillips, March 10, 1912.
J. W. Phillips, Feb. 11, 1931.

Bell Bible, in possession of Judge E. G. Walker, Lebanon, Tenn.

BIRTHS

John S. Bell, Aug. 9, 1825.
Mary J. Bell, Jan. 24, 1826.
Mary L. Bell, May 1, 1846.
Almira A. Bell, Oct. 17, 1847.
Isabella W. Bell, May 26, 1853.
Emma T. Bell, July 31, 1861.
J. C. Weir, June 24, 1799.
Mary B. Weir, Jan. 20, 1801.
Nancy I. Weir, April 5, 1828.
W. T. Weir, April 5, 1835.
Ozella Foster, Jan. 28, 1871.
Johnnie Dell Foster, Jan. 8, 1874.

MARRIAGES

John S. Bell, married Mary J. Weir, Feb. 28, 1844.
J. S. Bell, married Maggie M. Collinsworth, May 4, 1865.
John S. Bell, married Mollie E. Collinsworth, Feb. 5, 1866.
A. E. Foster, married Mary L. Bell, Jan. 8, 1868.
H. F. Shutt, married A. A. Bell, Feb. 23, 1875.

DEATHS

Nancy I. Weir, Sept. 8, 1853.
William T. Weir, May 1, 1859.
Mary J. Bell, Dec. 7, 1859.
Maggie M. Bell, Aug. 12, 1865.
Susannah T. Bell, June 8, 1863.
Jefferson Bell, Nov. 9, 1839.
Mollie E. Bell, July 5, 1869.
Ozella Foster, Oct. 1, 1871.
John S. Bell, May 12, 1872.
Emma T. Bell, Aug. 7, 1874.
Johnnie Bell Foster, Nov. 28, 1874.
Mary L. Foster, July 12, 1876.
James C. Weir, Dec. 21, 1879.

Shutt Bible, in possession of Judge E. G. Walker, Lebanon, Tenn.

BIRTHS

Ruth D. Carless, Dec. 30, 1824.
Mary F. Carless, Dec. 17, 1826.
Robert W. Carless, April 9, 1828.
George H. Shutt, Feb. 1, 1808.
Clement W. Shutt, July 30, 1831.
Elizabeth A. S. Shutt, March 31, 1833.
Margaret H. Shutt, Nov. 2, 1835.
George M. Shutt, March 22, 1838.
William J. S. Shutt, Feb. 19, 1841.
Henry F. Shutt, Jan. 18, 1843.
Martha Hanah Shutt, Dec. 27, 1845.
Virginia Miller Shutt, March 31, 1848.
Thomas Owen Shutt, Oct. 25, 1850.
Emma Taylor Shutt, Jan. 16, 1853.
Hannah C. Stokes, March 13, 1809.
Lizzie Alice Kimbro, Nov. 3, 1851.
Willie Ann Kimbro, May. 25, 1853.
Robert Albert Franklin, Oct. 15, 1860.
Mary Jessie Franklin, Feb. 8, 1863.
George Henry Smith, Wednesday, Dec. 2, 1868.
Walter Hill Smith, Tuesday, Nov. 15, 1870.
Stokes Shutt Smith, Wednesday, Oct. 4, 1876.
Owen Smith, Monday, July 29, 1878.
Mary Hill Shutt, Sunday, Feb. 20, 1881.
Hays H. Shutt, Nov. 29, 1883.

MARRIAGES

George H. Shutt and Hannah H. Carless, married Oct. 22, 1830.
D. S. Dew and Ruth D. Carless, married Oct. 28, 1841.
William M. Kimbro and Mary A. Carless, married Nov. 26, 1850.
Thomas Miller and Elizabeth H. Shutt, married Jan. 18, 1855.
J. S. Franklin and Mary A. Kimbro, married Sept. 1, 1859.
George M. Shutt and Josephine E. Fransieli, married Jan. 25, 1866.
Martha H. Shutt and Henry C. Smith, married Oct. 29, 1867.
James A. Leiper and Alice Kimbro, married March 13, 1869.
E. P. Duvall and Virginia M. Shutt, married June 18, 1874.
Henry F. Shutt and Mira A. Bell, married Feb. 23, 1875.
Emma T. Shutt and Henry C. Smith, married Sept. 27, 1875.

DEATHS

Robert W. Carless, Jan. 18, 1851.

William W. Kimbro, July 4, 1853.
George H. Shutt, Oct. 9, 1853.
Clement W. Shutt, Dec. 20, 1853.
Willie A. Kimbro, Nov. 24, 1853.
Ida Miller, Dec. 16, 1861.
Jordan W. Shutt, March 6, 1865.
Jesse Slade Franklin, March 20, 1866; age 43.
Robert Albert Franklin, April 20, 1870; age 9 years.
George Henry Smith, Monday, Oct. 17, 1870; age 22 months.
Walter Hill Smith, Jan. 30, 1872; aged 14 months.
Martha H. Smith, Dec. 3, 1873.
Lizzie H. Miller, Feb. 12, 1873.
H. H. Shutt, Nov. 2, 1873.
Jennie S. Duvall, May 4, 1875.
Thomas O Shutt, June 22, 1876.
Emma Shutt Smith, June 25, 1882.
Margaret H. Shutt, June 18, 1885.
Mary Hill Shutt, Feb. 20, 1882.
George M. Shutt, March 24, 1890.
Mary Ann Francis Franklin, Nov. 12, 1904.

Bible of Lazenby family in shop of C. L. Hooberry. Copied by Mrs. Acklen.

MARRIAGE

Sidney Lawrence Lazenby and Eudora Alice Smith were married Oct. 27, 1897.

BIRTHS

Sidney Lazenby, born Sept. 8, 1871.
Eudora Alice Lazenby, born Nov. 6, 1877.
Mildred Lazenby, born July 17, 1915.
John Harvy Lazenby, date torn off.
Eli Smith, born Jan 28, 1835.
Mary E. Smith, born May 22, 1839.
Nannie Smith, born June 15, 1868.
James A. Smith, born April 1, 1870.
Belle Smith, born May 12, 1874.
Dora Smith, born Nov. 6, 1877.

MARRIAGES

Nannie was married Dec. 25, 1892.
Belle was married Dec. 25, 1894.
Dora was married Oct. 27, 1897.
Papa and Mama married Feb. 13, 1867.
Jimmie was married Jan. 7, 1913.

DEATHS

Nannie Nomia Lazenby, died July 29, 1903.
Mary E. Smith, died May 13, 1916.
Mary E. Lazenby, died Sept. 19, 1918.
Eli Smith, died Feb. 10, 1922.

Bible found in book shop on Church Street, Nashville. Copied by Mrs. Oscar F. Noel.

This certifies that Samuel B. Fry of Carroll County, Tennessee, and Marium Humphrey of Carroll County, Tennessee, were joined by me in the bonds of Holy Matrimony at residence of Bride on the 20th day of September, in the year of our Lord 1857.
Signed, John Neely, M. G.
In the presence of family and friends. Robert Bledsoe and W. K. Davis.

BIRTHS

Samuel Benton Fry, born March 11, 1832.
Marium Fry, born April 18, 1833.
Millard Fillmore Fry, born Dec. 1, 1858.
Virginia Bell Fry, born Nov. 6, 1860.
W. G. Brownlow Fry, born Sept. 29, 1862.
W. T. Sherman Fry, born Aug. 13, 1865.

DEATHS

Samuel B. Fry, died April 16, 1914.
Mrs. Marium Fry, died July 21, 1918.
Virginia Bell Fry, died Aug., 1862.
W. G. Brownlow Fry, died May 21, 1914.
Sherman Fry, died May 28, 1922.

Bible of J. J. H. Burgess. Bought in June, 1853. Found in the shop of C. L. Hooberry and copied by Mrs. Joseph H. Acklen.

MARRIAGE

J. J. H. Burgess and E. R. Chambliss were married December 17, 1846.

BIRTHS

Henrie Anna Burgess, born Nov. 5, 1847.

Mary Elizabeth E. Burgess, daughter of J. J. H. and E. R. B., born April 26, 1849.

Lorrimer Stith D. and Laura J. D., twin daughter and son of J. J. B. and E. R. Burgess, born April 8, 1851.

Grace Lillian, daughter of J. H. and E. R. Burgess, born July 22, 1854.

DEATHS

Henrie Anna Burgess, daughter of J. and E. B., died Sept. 21, 1849.

Laura Jane D., daughter of J. J. and E. R. Burgess, died Oct. 13, 1853.

Lorrimer Stith D., son of J. J. H. and E. R. B., died June 11, 1856.

Henry Chambliss, son of Nathaniel Chambliss of Sussex County, Virginia, died Jan. 26, 1848.

Bible found in the shop of C. L. Hooberry, Nashville, Tennessee. Copied by Mrs. Joseph H. Acklen.

M. R. H. Dale's Book, given to him by his Father and Mother. God give him grace to study it and profit by it to the good of his deare sole.

MARRIAGES

John E. Dale and Ann, his wife, were married Oct. 20, 1808 A.D.

Austin Frirks and Mary E. F. P. Frirks, his wife, were married July 4, 1833.

Thos. J. G. Dale and Elizabeth Moor, his wife, were married July 18, 1836.

John G. W. Dale and Jane F. Pruett, his wife, were married Dec. 29, 1836.

Mr. Isaac A. Dale was married to Miss Nancy Dale Oct. 8, 1840.

Mr. George Brittle was married to Miss Melissa A. Dale Aug. 28, 1867.

Mr. J. G. W. Dale and Mrs. Virginia Turner were married Nov. 29, 1849.

N———— (illegible), date is Feb. 4, 1852 or '33.

James M. Dale and Emma M. Penkins were married Sept. 4, 1886.

BIRTHS

John E. Dale, born May 12, 1785. Y 55, M 4, D 11.

Ann F. Dale, wife of John E. Dale, born April 16, 1794 A.D.

Mary E. F. P. Dale, daughter of John E. Dale and Ann, his wife, born Nov. 17, 1809.

Thomas Joseph Green Dale, born March 7, 1812.

John George Washington Dale, born March 28, 1814.

Melissa Ann Dale, born July 11, 1816.

Flavius Josephus Williamson Dale, born May 15, 1820.

Isaac Alexander Dale, born Jan. 1, 1823.

Ursula Jane Anderson Dale, born April 8, 1825.

Narsissa Elizabeth Dale, born Nov. 23, 1827.

Matthias Robert Handy Dale, born ——— 22, 1830.

Mary R. Green, daughter of Joseph Green and Mary, his wife, born June 21, 1798.

Matthias R. H. Dale, born Nov. 22, 1830. (Printed)

James Monroe Dale, born Oct. 5, 1833.

Elizabeth Dale, wife of Thos. J. G. Dale, born March 9, 1813.

First written Rufus William, changed to William Rufus Dale, born Aug. 7, 1837.

Drusilla R. J. Dale, born June 15, 1832.

DEATHS

Ursula Jane Dale, daughter of John E. Dale and Ann, his wife, died April 14, 1833, age 8 years and six days.

William Rufus departed this life Aug. 10, 1838.

Drusilla R. J. Dale, died Sept. 26, 1840.

John E. Dale departed this life Oct. 23, 1840, in the 55th year of his life. He died as he had lived, a disciple of the Lord. Blessed.

M. R. H. Dale, killed at the Battle of Sharpsburg, Md., Sept. 17, 1863.

Ann F. Dale, died Nov. 18, 1869.

John E. Dale, 1822.

W. Dale was born May 15, 1820, and am now 20 years and 3 months old.

My father is gone and left me to mourn. He lived a Christian and died as he lived. He departed this life the 23rd of October, 1840. If Matty never comes to get this Book I want James M. Dale to have it. (Signed) Ann F. Dale.

BIRTHS

John G. W. Dale, born March 28, 1819.

Jane F. Dale, his wife, born Dec. 21, 1819.

John R. H. Dale, born July 3, 1838.

William R. H. Dale, born Sept. 25. 1840.

Bible of Mrs. C. B. Tucker, found in the shop of C. L. Hooberry. Copied by Mrs. Joseph H. Acklen.

MARRIAGES

Isaac Benton Kinkead and Hannah A. Thornburg were married Jan. 20, 1856.

William Wallace Kinkead and Lizzie H. Mason were married Dec. 2, 1882.

Edgar B. Kinkead and Nellie M. Snyder were married Jan. 20, 1883.

R. Grant Kinkead and Anna Marshall were married March 6, 1884.

Clinton B. Tucker and Helen A. Kinkead were married Nov. 14, 1889.

William Wallace Kinkead and Emma Warner were married Nov. 14, 1894.

William Wallace Kinkead and Ella Cook.

BIRTHS

Mabel Kinkead, born Oct. 16, 1884.

Helen Mar Kinkead, born Dec. 5, 1885.

Robert Benton Kinkead, born Feb. 23, 1888.

Clara Elizabeth Tucker, born Feb. 23, 1891.

Willie Adelia Tucker, born May 11, 1892.

Majorie Marshall Kinkead, born Jan. 21, 1895.

Robert Thornburg Tucker, born Oct. 12, 1899.

DEATHS

Lizzie Mason Kinkead, wife of W. W. Kinkead, died May 27, 1887.

Clara Elizabeth, daughter of C. B. and H. A. Tucker, died March 9, 1891.

Isaac Benton Kinkead, died Oct. 12, 1894, in Nashville, Tenn.

Emma W. Kinkead, died July 17, 1895.

Helen Adelia Tucker died Jan. 15, 1912-13.

BIBLE FOUND IN SHOP OF C. L. HOOBERRY, NASHVILLE, TENN. In the front is "Hill's Book". Copied by Mrs. Joseph H. Acklen.

MARRIAGES

Hezekiah Hill and Ann D. Humphries were married June 28, 1821.

Jeremiah Hill and Margret Isora Marshall were married Dec. 4, 1845.

Sarah C. Hill and Madison Monroe Henry were married Feb. 23, 1854.

Francis M. Hill and Mary A. E. Davis were married Jan. 11, 1855.

BIRTHS

Hezekiah Hill, born Nov. 29, 1800.

Ann D. Hill, born July 13, 1805.

Spencer Hill, born Sept. 22, 1822.
Jeremiah Hill, born Nov. 6, 1823.
Benjamin Humphreys Hill, born Jan. 15, 1825.
Sarah Catherine Hill, born April 13, 1826.
Penelope Jane Hill, born Dec. 7, 1827.
William Washington Hill, born April 16, 1829.
Daniel Jones Hill, born July 2, 1830.
Peter Eaton Hill, born April 22, 1832.
Francis Marion Hill, born Dec. 21, 1833.
Aljournal Jackson Hill, born Oct. 31, 1835.
John Atkinson Hill, born Nov. 6, 1836.
Henry Clay Harrison Hill, born April 15, 1840.

DEATHS

Daniel J. Hill departed this life Dec. 11, 1832.
Peter E. Hill departed this life March 20, 1833.
Aljournal J. Hill departed this life Oct. 31, 1935.
Penelope J. Hill departed this life June 21, 1851.
Benjamin H. Hill departed this life Dec. 18, 1853.
Ann D. Hill departed this life Oct. 15, 1858.
H. C. H. Hill departed this life April 12, 1864.

The foregoing are true copies of entries in old, badly worn Bible, with the paper yellowed with age, of Alfred J. Lester. The writing is all apparently very old.

There was also in the Bible an old sheet of paper with the following writing thereon:

JUNE, 1853

5th June, Robert M. Lester, died 15 minutes after 11 a.m.
5th June, Wm. A. Lester, died 15 minutes before 12 a.m.
6th June, James N. Lester, died 15 minutes before 10 a.m., June 6, 1853.
7th June, Emma E. Lester, died at 9 p.m.
11th June, Christopher C. Lester, died 11 a.m.

The fly leaf of the Holy Bible contains the following:

PHILADELPHIA:
Printed and Published by M. Carey
No. 121 Chesnut Street
1816

The fly leaf of the Concordance to the Bible bears the following:

PHILADELPHIA:
Printed and Published by
Mathew Carey
No. 121 Chesnut Street
1815

Copied from Family Bible of Charles Binns Jones, great-grandfather of Henry Harrison Eager, present owner of the Bible. Bible printed by Collins Co., New York, 1813. No other dates. Sent by Mrs. Clarence Jones, Chattanooga.

BIRTHS

Charles Binns Jones, born July 5, 1798, Virginia.
Caroline M. Dubrutz, born Aug. 2, 1799, North Carolina; married Dec. 10, 1818.
Deborah Ann Jones, born Jan. 29, 1820, North Carolina.
Elizabeth Hamilton Jones, born Dec. 2, 1821, North Carolina.
Sarah P. Jones, born Feb. 28, 1824, North Carolina.
Caroline Dubrutz Jones, born Dec. 31, 1827, North Carolina.
Marian Carusoe Jones, born May 29, 1830, North Carolina.
Elizabeth Hamilton Jones, born Aug. 15, 1833, North Carolina.
Louise Josephine Jones, born Dec. 7, 1835, North Carolina.
Charles Binns Jones, born Sept. 5, 1839, Alabama.
Georgiana Jones, born April 15, 1841, Maring County, Alabama.
George Hamilton Jones, born Jan. 20, 1844, Maring County, Alabama.

Copy from Bible of Thomas Smith Jewell and his wife, Amanda Lawrence Jewell. Sent by Mrs. Clarence Jones.

BIRTHS

Thomas Smith Jewell, born May 24, 1819.
Amanda Lawrence Jewell, born Feb. 13, 1823.
William Jewell, born 1846.
Benn Jewell, born 1849.
Bell Jewell, born 1852.
Newton Jewell, born Aug, 12, 1855.
Mattie Jewell, born 1860.

MARRIAGES

Thomas Smith Jewell, married Amanda Lawrence Sept. 25, 1844.
Bell Jewell, married James Doelsins, 1872.
Newton Reily Jewell, married Sallie Sams, Dec. 4, 1878.

DEATHS

Thomas Smith Jewell, died Dec. 28, 1866.
Amanda Jewell, died June 20, 1907.
William Jewell, died 1849.
Benn Jewell, died 1852.
Bell Jewell, died March, 1893.
Newton Riley Jewell, died Dec. 30, 1910.
Mattie Jewell, died June, 1879.

Copy from Bible of Newton Rilly Jewell and his wife, Sallie Dupuy Sams Jewell.

BIRTHS

Newton Riley Jewell, born Aug. 12, 1855.
Sallie D. Sams Jewell, born July 16, 1861.
Ethel Thomasson Jewell, born Nov. 17, 1879.
Stella Dupuy Jewell, born March 30, 1881.
Rosco Newton Jewell, born Jan 26, 1883.
Urmey Griffin Jewell, born Oct. 14, 1884.
Minnie Jewell, born July 20, 1889.
Sallie Bessie Jewell, born June 13, 1891.
William Aurther Jewell, born April 6, 1893.
Helen Josephine Jewell, born March 26, 1895.
Ray Norris Jewell, born Nov. 13, 1897.
Jesse Lawless Jewell, born Aug. 3, 1900.
Mary Dupuy Lawless, born Aug. 3, 1899.
Sarah Manie Lawless, born April 15, 1901.

Cathryn Jewell Lawless, born July 11, 1906.

MARRIAGES

Newton Riley Jewell, married Sallie D. Sams, Dec. 4, 1878.
Stella Dupuy Jewell, married John W. Lawless, June 3, 1898.
Sallie Bessie Jewell, married Geo. Samuel McCarty, Aug. 4, 1908.
William Aurther Jewell, married Hattie Fay Harris, Aug. 4, 1916.
Helen Josephine Jewell, married Thomas Fletcher Sims, March 11, 1924.
Ray Norris Jewell, married Sarah Leach, Sept. 14, 1929.
Sarah Marie Lawless, married Joseph N. Jones, March 24, 1920.

BIRTHS

Geo. Samuel McCarty, Jr., born Feb. 15, 1910.
Stella Joyce McCarty, born March 4, 1914.
Dorris Jewell, born April 2, 1918.
Margueart Jewell, born Sept. 9, 1919.
Sara Cathryn Jones, born Oct. 24, 1921.

DEATHS

Newton Riley Jewell, died Dec. 30, 1910.
Ethel Thomasson Jewell, died March 17, 1891.
Rosco Newton Jewell, died March 12, 1891.
Urmey Griffin Jewell, died March 9, 1891.
Ellen Thomas Jewell, died Feb. 25, 1891.
Minnie Jewell, died March 6, 1891.
Mary Dupuy Lawless, died Aug. 3, 1899.

Inscriptions on Broyles Monument in little old cemetery called Mt. Cumberland, near Dalton, Georgia.

Mother.
Lucinda Nash Broyles, widow of Major Cain Broyles, deceased.
Born Aug. 10, 1790.
Died Oct. 9, 1868.
Son.
Walter L. Broyles.
Born July 25, 1832.
Died a Confederate soldier at Lynchburg, Va., Nov. 13, 1862.
Son.
Marcellus F. Broyles, a Confederate soldier.
Born July 16, 1837.
Fell at Battle of the Wilderness May 6, 1864.

Inscription on tomb of Major Cain Broyles in Shady Grove Churchyard, Calhoun, South Carolina.

Erected by his children to the memory of Major Cain Broyles.
Born Jan. 12, 1788.
Died April 20, 1864.
(Maj. Cain Broyles was my great-great-grandfather, Lucinda Nash Broyles was his wife. Mrs. John G. Burton sends this. Chattanooga.)

Copied from the Bible of Major William Kelly and his wife, Redsy Smith.

BIRTHS

Major William Kelly, born in Ireland, 1735.
Redsy Smith, born 1737.

MARRIAGE

Major William Kelly married Redsy Smith, 1755.

BIRTHS

Samuel, 1756.
Permelia, 1758.
James, 1759.
Elizabeth, 1761.
William, 1763.
Jane, 1766.

Joseph, Jan. 29, 1767.
Mary, 1769.
Griffin, 1770.
Nancy, 1773.
Washington, 1777.

MARRIAGES

William Kelly married Nancy Cave.
Jane Kelly married Thomas Sims, 1781.
Joseph Kelly married Elizabeth Mallory, 1787.
Griffin Kelly married Sarah Sutton, Dec. 26, 1793.
Nancy Kelly married Jessie Bowlin.

DEATHS

Major William Kelly, died 1783.
Joseph Kelly, died Oct. 16, 1853.
Griffin Kelly, died March 17, 1855.
Sarah Kelly, died Feb. 4, 1859.
Elizabeth Kelly, died March 30, 1830.

Copy from the Bible of Capt. Joseph Kelly and wife, Elizabeth Mallory.

MARRIAGES

Joseph Kelly married Elizabeth Mallory, 1787.
Samuel Kelly married (Sarah) Patsy Sutton.
Permelia Kelly married James Sams, Dec. 24, 1806.
James Sams married Eliza Duvall.
Elizabeth Kelly married, first, Fielding Lacklin; second, Thomas Showmaker.
William Kelly married Susan Hayden.
Jane Kelly married, first, William Kelly; second, Dr. Whitehead.
Joseph Kelly married, first, Nancy Smith; second, Harriet Jones.
Mary Kelly married Joel P. Thomasson, 1821.
Griffin married Rebecca Jane Smith.

BIRTHS

Joseph Kelly, born Jan. 29, 1767.
Elizabeth Mallory, born March 24, 1771.
Samuel, born Sept. 22, 1788.
Permelia, born June 18, 1791.
James, born July 1, 1793.
Elizabeth, born Oct. 10, 1795.
Sarah, born Jan. 29, 1798.
William, born April 12, 1800.
Jane, born May 30, 1802.
Joseph, born June 13, 1804.
Ariel, born June 20, 1806.
Polly (Mary), born Sept. 18, 1807.
Griffin, born Jan. 25, 1810.
Nancy, born April 28, 1812.

MARRIAGE

Nancy Kelly married Burgess Acton.

DEATHS

Joseph Kelly, died Oct. 16, 1853.
Elizabeth, the wife of Joseph Kelly, died March 30, 1830.
Samuel Kelly, died Feb. 26, 1871.
Patsy, wife of Samuel, died May 4, 1857.
Permelia Sams, died July 26, 1855.
Uriel Kelly, died 1807.
Mary Kelly Thomasson, died April, 1879.

Copy from the Bible of James Sams.

BIRTHS

James Sams, born 1785.
Permelia Kelly, born 1791.

MARRIAGE

James Sams married Permelia Kelly, Dec. 24, 1806.

CHILDREN OF JAMES SAMS

Joseph, born Nov. 8, 1808.
Elizabeth, born May 24, 1810.
William G., born Jan. 18, 1812.
Polly D. (Mary), born Nov. 6, 1813.
F. W., born May 20, 1815.
Sallie A., born Jan. 18, 1817.
Eliza D., born Sept. 6, 1818.
James, born June 6, 1819.
Ariel Mallory, born April 18, 1823.
John, born April 9, 1825.
Nancy, born July 18, 1827.
Jane Kelly, born April 4, 1829.

Griffin, born May 2, 1831.
Permelia, born June 8, 1833.

MARRIAGES

Joseph Sams married Delia White, 1828.
William Sams married Lucinda Kelly, April 7, 1833.
Polly D. (Mary) Sams married James Kelly, April 4, 1839.
Sallie A. Sams married Dennice Van Anyce, Jan. 1, 1832.
Eliza D. Sams married Anston Duncan, Jan. 26, 1837.
James Sams married, first Casanda Cox, Feb. 11, 1841; second, Darah Wills, Feb. 22, 1855; third, Angine Lale.
Ariel Mallory Sams married Sarah Dupuy Thomasson, Feb. 28, 1845.
John Sams married Margueart Jackson, April 18, 1841.

BIRTHS

George Washington Sams, son of John Sams, born Oct., 1843.
Belle Morse, daughter of G. W. and Permelia Morse, born about Oct. 5, 1851.

MARRIAGES

Nancy Sams married John Forbis, Oct. 31, 1845.
Jane Kelly Sams married William Lucas, Sept. 1, 1846.
Griffin Sams married Elizabeth Neal, April 13, 1852.
Permelia Sams married Geo. Morse, Jan., 1850.

OTHER BIRTHS IN THIS OLD BIBLE

Lenora Sams, daughter of Griffin Sams and Elizabeth, his wife, born Feb. 9, 1859.
George Cox, born July 16, 1868.
Nanie Cox, born Dec. 13, 1869.
Emma Cox, born April 24, 1871.
Liza Cox, born May 11, 1873.

DEATHS

Elizabeth Sams, died 1811.
William Sams, died June 15, 1900.
Polly D., died May 12, 1896.
F. W. Sams, died 1817.
Lucinda Sams, died April 25, 1877.
Uriel Mallory Sams, died April 8, 1863.
Jane K. Lucas, died Dec., 1898.
Griffin Sams, died May 2, 1917.
James Sams, died Feb. 26, 1849.
Permelia, his wife, died July 26, 1855.

Copy from Bible of Uriel Mallory Sams.

MARRIAGES

Uriel Mallory Sams married Sarah Dupuy Thomasson Feb. 28, 1845.
Griffin J. Sams married Katherine Bryant Feb. 25, 1877.
Joanna Sams married Feb. 4, 1869.
Martha Frances Sams married Amos D. Houston May 23, 1872.
Sallie Dupuy Sams married Newton Riley Jewell Dec. 4, 1878.

BIRTHS

William, born Aug. 29, 1846.
Joel Poindexter, born Feb. 8, 1849.
Griffin J., born Aug. 17, 1851.
Jonna, born Oct. 15, 1853.
Martha Frances, born Nov. 8, 1856.
Sallie Dupuy, born July 16, 1861.

DEATHS

William Sams, died July 13, 1847.
Joel P. Sams, died 1886.
Griffin J., died Feb. 6, 1931.
Uriel Mallory Sams, died April 8, 1863.
Sarah Dupuy Sams, died Nov. 10, 1910.

BIRTHS

John Thompson, born Jan. 5, 1794., son of P. Thomasson.
Joseph M. Thompson, son of P. and Sallie Thompson, born Feb. 17, 1796.
William Thompson, son of P. and Sarah Thompson, born Oct. 8, 1798.
Joel Dupuy Thompson, born July 10, 1799, son of P. and S.
Nelson Thompson, son of P. and S., born Jan. 17, 1806.
Elias Thompson, son of P. and S., born Jan 22, 1810.
Uriel M. Sams, born April 18, 1823.
Sarah D. Sams was the wife of Uriel Sams, born May 5, 1828.

Births

William R. Sams, the son of Uriel Sams, born Aug. 29, 1846.
Joel P. Sams, born Feb. 6, 1849.
Griffin J. Sams, born Aug. 17, 1851.
Joanna Sams, born Oct. 15, 1853.
George Chilton, born Dec. 13, 1848.
Married Joanna Sams Feb. 4, 1869.
Edgar Chilton, born Aug. 28, 1870.
Amos D. Humston, born ——— 6, 1850, married Martha F. Sams May 23, 1872.

Deaths

Poindexter Thompson, departed this life Friday, Sept. 1, 1833.
Sarah Dupuy Thomasson, departed this life May 23, 1851.
Joel D. Thomasson, the son of Poindexter and Sarah Dupuy Thomasson, departed this life July 4, 1862.
William P. Thomasson, the son of Joel D. Thomasson and Polly D. Thomasson, died Sept., 1868, at the age of 41 years.
Harriet A. McKee departed this life Feb. 25, 1867, age 41.
Joel D. Sams, died March 2, 1867, age 18 years.
Cramus, son of Elisa, died May 14.

Births

Martha F. Sams, the daughter of Uriel M. and Sarah D., born Nov. 8, 1856.
Sallie Dupuy Sams, the daughter of Uriel M. and Sarah Dupuy Sams, born July 16, 1861.

Marriages

Griffian J. Sams was married to Kate Bryant Feb. 25, 1877.
Sallie Dupuy Sams married Newton R. Jewell Dec. 4, 1878.
Newton, born Aug. 12, 1855.
Poindexter Thompson and Sarah Dupuy were married March 21, 1793.
John Thomasson married, first, Sarah Coleman; second, Elizabeth MacIntosh.
Joseph Thomasson married Martha Bartlett.
William married Charlett Levard.
Joel D. Thomasson married Mary Kelly, 1821.
Nelson never married.
Elias Thomasson married Miss Snead.
Poindexter Thompson and Sarah Dupuy married March 21, 1793.
Joseph H. Thompson married Dec. 6, 1821.
William P. Thompson and Charlott Lenard were married March 28, 1828.

PARENTS RECORDS

Father

Uriel Mallory Sams, born in the year 1823, married to Sarah D. Thomasson in the year of 1845, Feb. 25. Elder R. Ricketts officiated, a Predestinated Baptist.

Mother

Sarah D. Thompson was born in the year 1828, May 5. Was married to Uriel M. Sams in the year 1845, Feb. 25.

Negro Births

Mary's children's ages:
Kitty, born Oct., 1810.
Ferdinand, born Sept., 1814.
Nancy's children's ages:
Belford, born 1813.
Mathley, born 1816.
Elisa's children's ages:
Mary Jane, born Oct. 30, 1824.
Herrit, born July 25, 1826.
Georganna, born Sept. 30, 1828.
Betty, born Nov. 15, 1830.
Annia, born March 1, 1833.

Negroes' Ages

James, born Nov. 31, 1835.
Catherine, born Aug. 13, 1837.
Harriet Ann, born Oct. 16, 1839.
Lucy Jane, born Sept. 9, 1841.

Deaths

Joseph Dupuy, died on Thursday, June 22, 1815.
John Dupuy, aged 57 years, died on Friday, Jan. 28, 1820.
William R. Sams, the son of Uriel Sams, died July 13, 1848.
Agnes Maccon, the wife of James Maccon, died Nov. 16, 1850.
George Sams, the son of John Sams, born Oct., 1843, died Feb. 3, 1878.

I have personally examined and carefully studied the records contained in the Bible owned by Mrs. Joannia Chilton, the one mentioned in these records as Joannia Sams, daughter of Uriel Mallory Sams and his wife, Sarah Dupuy Thomasson Sams.

These records plainly show the name of Thompson and Thomasson are one and the same—for instance note Poindexter Thompson has his wife as Sarah Thomasson and the birth of their children spelled Thompson, and their marriages spelled Thomasson.

This Bible was owned by Poindexter Thompson first, then by his son, Joel Dupuy Thomasson second, then by his daughter, Sarah Dupuy Thomasson Sams, third, then by her daughter Joanna Sams Chilton, the present owner. The records are in good condition.

Bible Records copied from fly leaf of Bible of James Harris. Sent by Blanche Pickle and Mrs. Leo Schwartz.

BIRTHS

Ann Thomson, born Oct. 29, 1780.
James Harris, born Feb. 10, 1777.
James Stapleton Harris, born Feb. 23, A.D. 1799, and died Aug. 7, 1800.
Ann Wallis Harris, born Feb. 8, A.D. 1801.
John Thompson Harris, born July 6, A.D. 1804.
Hiram Harris, born Oct. 20, 1806.
Betsy Harris, born June 5, 1809.
Elvira Harris, born Sept. 23, 1813.
Cely Ann Freeman, daughter of Nancy (Ann Wallis), born Feb. 27, A.D. 1824.

Copied from a later Bible of James Harris.

James Harris, born Feb. 10, 1777.
Ann Harris, born Oct. 28, 1780, in Charleston, S. C.
James Stapleton Harris, born Feb. 28, 1799.
Ann Wallace Harris, born Feb. 8, 1801.
John Thompson Harris, born July 6, 1804.
Hiram Harris, born Oct. 20, 1806.
Elizabeth Harris, born Sept. 28, 1813.
Sarah Turrentine Harris, born Dec. 1, 1816.
Almeida J. Harris, born June 10, 1818.
James Harris and Nancy Thompson were married June 28, 1797, in Union City, S. C.
Joseph Williams, born in Orange County, North Carolina, Oct. 10, A.D. 1782.
Charity Turrentine, born in Orange County, North Carolina, Oct. 6, 1796.
Joseph Williams and Charity Turrentine were married January 21, 1813, by John Thompson, Esq., Bedford County, Tennessee.
Joseph Williams, died May 12, 1876.
Charity Williams, died Nov. 1, 1878.

David Williams, born 1815, died Sept., 1887.
Sarah Turrentine Williams, died Oct. 4, 1910.
Almeida J. Collins, born Oct. 6, 1837, died May 28, 1888.

Mary Jenkins, born Aug. 2, 1859, died July 14, 1889.

Louvenia, born Sept. 6, 1839, died February 25, 1900.

Ann Green, born July 7, 1841.

James Green, born July, 1843.

TOMBSTONE RECORD

James Harris, born 1777, died 1863.

Nancy Thompson Harris, wife of James Harris, born 1781, died 1870.

Records from the family Bible of Miss Augusta Lincoln Brown, Greeneville, Tennessee.

BIRTHS

Alexander Brown, Sr., born Jan. 1, 1737.

Elizabeth Brown Alexander, born in the fall of 1780 (Pa.).

Joseph Brown, born Sunday, Aug. 9, 1767.

Peggy Rutherford Brown, born Monday, May 18, 1802.

John Alexander Brown, born Friday, Aug. 10, 1804.

James Brown, born Saturday, March 28, 1807.

Polly Grace Brown, born Sunday, Aug. 6, 1810 (or 12).

Joseph Brown, Jr., born Sunday, May 5, 1814.

William Brown, born Monday, Feb. 17, 1819.

Alfred Brown, born Friday, April 23, 1825.

David Alexander, born Nov. 26, 1801.

Mary Eliza Alexander, born Thursday, Sept. 21, 1826.

Anna Amelia Alexander, born Thursday, Nov. 13, 1828.

Malinda Jain Alexander, born Nov. 26, 1830.

MARRIAGES

Joseph Brown and Elizabeth Brown Alexander, married Sept 10, 1801.

Peggy R. Brown was married to David Alexander Tuesday, Nov. 8, 1825.

Mary C. Brown was married to G. M. Spencer Tuesday, Feb. 1, 1842.

Joseph R. Brown was married to Frances Josephine Broyles Sept 12, 1843.

William R. Brown was married to Mary Lincoln Feb. 14, 1852.

John A. Brown was married to Mrs. R. L. Rabe Jan. 3, 1861.

DEATHS

Alexander Brown, Sr., died Dec. 2, 1820.

James Brown, died Sept. 27, 1808.

Anna Amelia Alexander, died Feb. 4, 1830.

Peggy R. Alexander, died May 13, 1833.

Joseph Brown, Sr., died Nov. 2, 1854, born in Dublin.

Elizabeth Alexander Brown, died Nov. 18, 1865, Saturday.

John Alexander Brown, died Dec. 2, 1880.

From Bible in possession of John M. Scott, Washington College, Tenn. Sent by Mrs. W. P. Diehl and Mrs. J. M. Scott.

Samuel Scott, born Feb. 16, 1790.

Sussannah Alison, born May 8, 1792.

Samuel Scott and Susannah Alison were married Nov. 6, 1811.

THEIR CHILDREN

John Marshall Scott, born Aug, 1818.

Mary Jane Scott, born Nov. 9, 1819.

Elizabeth Amanda Scott, born Aug. 19, 1821.

Robert Franklin Scott, born Feb. 28, 1824.

Samuel Warren Scott and Susannah Evaline Scott, born Jan. 4, 1830.

Elizabeth Alison Scott, born Oct. 24, 1825.

Seeton-Craig (Knoxville and Knox Co.) family Bible, in possession of Mrs. W. S. Hickey, Jonesboro, Tennessee.

BIRTHS

James Seeton, Sr., born Feb. 27, 1788.
Elizabeth Love, born Sept. 25, 1792.
Margaret R. Seeton, born Sept. 25, 1812.
James N. Seeton, born April 3, 1815.
Ann Amelia Gilkerson Seeton, born May 25, 1817.
John Love Seeton, born Dec. 17, 1819.
Mary Ann Elizabeth Seeton, born Dec. 11, 1823.
Martha Jane Seeton, born May 11, 1825.
William Martin Fleming Seeton, born June 16, 1828.
George Thomas Love Seeton, born Dec. 8, 1830.
Lovey Sarah Ann Seeton, born June 4, 1833.

MARRIAGES

James Seeton, Sr., was married to Elizabeth Love by the Rev. Samuel G. Ramsey, Sept. 5, 1811.
William Walker was married to Margaret R. Seeton by the Rev. William A. McCampbell, Feb. 18, 1830.
James N. Seeton, Jr., was married to Rachel Craig by the Rev. Dr. Samuel Doak, Nov. 26, 1834.
William Craig was married to Ann Amelia Gilkerson Seeton by the Rev. William A. McCampbell, Nov. 26, 1835.
William H. Swan was married to Mary Ann Elizabeth Seeton by the Rev. A. A. Mathes, Nov. 30, 1841.

JAMES IRELAND TIPTON BIBLE RECORD
(John Sevier Chapter, D. A. R.)

Copied March 8, 1932, from the Bible of James I. Tipton, by Mary Hardin McCown, Johnson City, Tenn. Bible dated 1828. Published in New York by Daniel D. Smith, 120 Greenwich St.

MARRIAGES

James I. Tipton, married to his first wife, Nancy Patterson, June 21, 1812.
James I. Tipton, married to his second wife, Joanna Gourley, Oct. 14, 1824.
N. A. C. Tipton was married Oct. 3, 1848, to P. D. Tilson.
Mary E. A. Tipton was married Feb. 6, 1855, to James M. Cameron.

BIRTHS

Births of James I. Tipton's children by his first wife:
Eliza Tipton, born Feb., 1814.
Samuel P. Tipton, born July 22, 1816.
Martha Jane Tipton, born Jan. 2, 1819.
Albert Jackson Tipton, born Dec. 26, 1820.
Susanna Tipton, born July 2, 1822.
Births of James I. Tipton's children by his second wife:
Edmund W. Tipton, born Jan 12, 1826.
A nameless son born Jan. 24, 1828.
Nancy Ann C. Tipton, born Feb. 27, 1829.
Alfred Taylor Tipton, born Jan. 18, 1831.
Mary Eliza Adeline N. Tipton, born Jan. 23, 1833.
Harriet Jane N. Tipton, born Feb. 18, 1835.
James I. Tipton, born Oct. 14, 1792.
Joanna Tipton, his second wife, born Jan. 16, 1805.

DEATHS

Nancy Tipton, first wife of James I. Tipton, died July 14, 1823.
Eliza Tipton, died Dec., 1814.

Alfred Taylor Tipton, died Aug. 9, 1832.

(End of Record.)

NOTES BY MARY HARDIN MCCOWN, JOHNSON CITY, TENN.

The Bible of James I. Tipton is in possession of a great-granddaughter, Mary Hardin McCown, Johnson City, Tenn. James I. Tipton died Jan. 20, 1861, and is buried in Green Hill Cemetery below Elizabethton, Tenn. He was born near where Elizabethton, Tenn., now stands, and was the son of Samuel Tipton (born June 7, 1752, died July 21, 1833, buried in Green Hill Cemetery) and second wife, Susanna Reneau (born ——, died Feb. 10, 1853, age 85 years 3 months 26 days, buried in Green Hill).

Samuel Tipton was the oldest son of Col. John Tipton (born 1732 in Maryland, died 1815, and buried at home on Sinking Creek, Washington County, Tenn.) and his first wife, Mary Butler (born ———, died June 8, 1776, in Virginia).

Col. John Tipton was in the Revolutionary War from Shenandoah County, Va., coming to Tennessee with his family and second wife, Martha Denton Moore, a widow (married July 22, 1777, in Shenandoah County, Va., to John Tipton). He was very prominent in the life of the Watauga Settlement. He is particularly remembered for his loyalty to North Carolina during the short existence of the state of Franklin. His home is standing today just south of Johnson City. Samuel Tipton was also a Revolutionary soldier of Virginia. He came probably with his father, Col. John Tipton, in 1783 to Watauga County, and Samuel Tipton owned large lands in Carter County. He owned the land where Elizabethton now stands. The first court held in Carter County was in his house. He was a member of the Shenandoah Baptist Church, Shenandoah County, Va., and brought his letter from that church, dated Sept. 6, 1783 or 85, and presented it to the Sinking Creek Baptist Church on his arrival in Watauga County. This letter was signed by James Ireland, moderator. So that is where James Ireland Tipton may have got his name. Samuel was very active in the Baptist Church in East Tennessee.

James Ireland Tipton was a preacher in the Christian Church. This church gathered most of its members in East Tennessee from the Buffalo Ridge and Sinking Creek and Cherokee Creek Baptist Churches. James I. Tipton was one of the earliest preachers in the Christian Church in Tennessee.

Joanna Gourley Tipton, second wife of James I. Tipton, was born Jan. 16, 1805, and died in Springfield, Ill., May, 1867. She was a daughter of James Gourley (born Feb. 10, 1782, died Aug. 21, 1848) and wife, Mary Patton (born 1787, died 1861).

James Gourley was a son of Capt. Thomas Gourley, a Revolutionary soldier in Pennsylvania, who was discharged at Yorktown in 1781, and his wife, Martha McNeely.

James I. Tipton's daughter, Mary Eliza Adeline N. Tipton, married Dr. James M. Cameron, Elizabethton, Tenn. They were the parents of Nola F. Cameron who married George Williams Hardin Feb. 2, 1888, and were the parents of Mary Hardin McCown, the writer of above.

Peter Miller Bible Record
(John Sevier Chapter, D. A. R.)

Bible printed in New York by the American Bible Society, 1844. Copied March 8, 1932, by Mary Hardin McCown, Johnson City, Tenn.

The Record:

Marriages

Peter Miller, born June 22, 1792.
Mary Hunt, born Oct. 10, 1798.
Peter Miller and Mary Hunt were married Aug. 27, 1817.
William R. Miller and Nanie Perry were married Jan 18, 1865.

Births

Samuel H. Miller, born July 18, 1818.
Elbert S. Miller, born April 11, 1820.
Elizabeth Miller, born April 3, 1822.
Sarah C. Miller, born April 10, 1825.
James S. Miller, born Oct. 21, 1827.
Nancy C. Miller, born Jan. 9, 1830.
Mary F. Miller, born Sept. 14, 1832.
Margaret J. Miller, born Nov. 16, 1834.
William R. Miller, born May 19, 1837.
Emily S. Miller, born Oct. 21, 1839.

Marriage

Alexander McNeil and Elizabeth Miller were married Oct. 6, 1853.

Births

James P. McNeil, born Oct. 8, 1855.
William McNeil, born May 29, 1858.
Charlie McNeil, born Feb. 1, 1860.
Mary McNeil, born June 7, 1862.

Deaths

Mary Miller, consort of Peter Miller, departed this life May 19, 1852, age 53 years 7 months 9 days.
Peter Miller, died April 27, 1863, aged 70 years 10 months and 25 days.
Elizabeth McNeil, died Dec. 21, 1873.
Emma S. Rodes, died March 24, 1880.
Mary Thompson, died Nov. 7, 1874.
Sarah Pouder, died April, 1875.
Margaret J. Miller, departed this life Jan. 22, 1836, aged 1 year 2 months and 6 days.
Alexander McNeil, born Aug. 20, 1824, departed this life Aug. 16, 1870.
Willie McNeil, died Nov. 7, 1877.

(End of Record.)

Notes by Mary Hardin McCown

The above Bible is in possession of Mrs. Mary McNeil Hunt (S. H.), Johnson City, Tenn.

Peter Miller was the son of Peter Miller and Elizabeth Boone, who came to Tennessee from near Woodstock, Va. Peter Miller I. was a Revolutionary soldier. Peter Miller II. was in the War of 1812.

"Peter Miller served in the War of 1812 as a first lieutenant in Capt. Andrew Lawson's Company, Third Regiment (Johnson's) East Tennessee Militia, from Sept. 20, 1814, to May 3, 1815. Place of residence was given as Washington county, Tennessee."

The following data will supplement the Bible data:

Samuel Hunt Miller married Eliza Range and had children. Julia married J. M. Carr; Elberts married Addie Miller; William P. married Sue (died March 8, 1832, at Johnson City, Tenn.); Susan M. married Henry Carr; Alice never married; Peter Q. married Sallie Miller; Jacob R. married Addie Miller.

Elbert Sevier Miller married first, Maria James and had children; Addie married Dr. E. S. Miller, Jr.; Mary married Thomas Elam; Dr. Walter J. married, first,

Sarah Haynes; second, Sanna Taylor.

Elbert Sevier Miller married second, Betty Evans of Blountville, Tenn.

Elbert Sevier Miller married third, Queen Patterson and had children. Dr. Samuel Rush Miller of Knoxville, Tenn.

Sarah Caroline Miller married Leonard Andrew Pouder and had children. Francinia Jane never married; Samuel Hunt married Mary Emma Swingle; Wm. James died young; Elbert Alex died young; Chas. M. died young; twins, Peter H. and Mary Elizabeth, died young; Sallie Maria.

James S. Miller married Mary Evans and had children. Evans Miller of Atlanta, Ga.; Margaret married Harry W. Lyle; James, Joe and Lou died.

Nancy C. Miller married Vincent Easley and had children, Peter, Eldridge and Vincent Easley.

Mary F. Miller married Joel Thompson, no children.

Wm. R. Miller married Nanie Perry and had children. Charlie, Perry, Lee (daughter) and Emma married, first Bailey; second, Campbell.

Emily S. Miller married Iverson K. Rhodes and had children. Thomas; James E.; Arthur; William; Henry; Twyman; and Mary married George Good.

Peter Miller is buried in the Hunt Mamily Cemetery, south of Johnson City, Tenn. The following inscriptions are copied from tombs in that cemetery by Mary Hardin McCown; 1928.

Peter Miller, died April 27, 1863, aged 70 years 10 months and 5 days.

Mary, consort of Peter Miller, who departed this life May 19, 1852, aged 53 years 7 months and 9 days.

Samuel H. Miller, born July 18, 1818, married 1840 to Eliza A. Range, daughter of Jacob and Susan Range, died June 17, 1894.

Mary F. Miller, wife of J. C. Thompson, born Sept. 14, 1832, died Nov. 7, 1874. She gave me her hand in youth, and also at death. Naught but death could separate us.

Thomas Vincent, born Feb. 20, 1790, died Jan. 20, 1864. A model husband and father, a soldier of the War of 1812.

Sarah C., wife of Leonard A. Pouder, born April 10, 1825, died April 6, 1876, aged 50 years 11 months 26 days.

Elizabeth McNeil, consort of Alexander McNeil and daughter of Peter Miller, born April 3, 1822, died Dec. 23, 1873.

Alexander McNeil, born in Scotland Aug. 20, 1824, died Aug. 16, 1870.

Samuel Hunt, died July 21, 1852, age 79 years 9 months and 24 days.

Sarah, consort of Samuel Hunt, died Aug. 29, 1852, age 73 years 9 months 13 days.

Joseph Hunt, born Dec. 2, 1806, died March 15, 1848.

Lorina T. Hunt, born Aug. 11, 1828, died Oct. 20, 1905, wife of Franklin Hunt, born March 19, 1818, died Dec. 27, 1900.

James S. Hunt, born Dec. 24, 1820, died June 5, 1905.

Mary F. Easley, first wife of Jas. S. Hunt, born Jan. 15, 1821, died Dec. 18, 1855.

Peter Miller's will is on file in Washington County, Jonesboro, Tenn.

JACOB MILLER BIBLE RECORD
(John Sevier Chapter, D. A. R.)

Copied Feb. 23, 1932, by Mary Hardin McCown, Johnson City, Tenn. Bible printed 1816. Brattleborough, Vermont. Printed by John Holbrook. The record:

Jacob Miller and his wife, Elizabeth, were married July 31, 1798.
Jacob Miller and Hannah Broiles were married June 29, 1845.

BIRTHS

Jacob Miller, born June 30, 1779.
Elizabeth Miller, his wife, born Jan. 21, 1777.
Mary Miller, their daughter, born June 16, 1799.
Peter Range Miller, their son, born Nov. 13, 1800.
Abraham Elias Miller, their son, born Oct. 19, 1802.
Katherine Miller, their daughter, born Dec. 25, 1804.
Jacob Miller, their son, born Jan. 12, 1807.
Elizabeth Miller, their daughter, born May 30, 1809.
Eliza Miller, their daughter, born March 6, 1811.
Matilda Miller, their daughter, born Feb. 18, 1813.
John Miller, their son, born March 15, 1815.
Chelnisse, their daughter, born April 5, 1817.
Abraham T. Broyls, born Nov. 1, 1839.
Samuel N. Broyls, born July 22, 1841.

DEATHS

Elizabeth Miller, wife of Jacob Miller, Sr., departed this life Aug. 25, 1843, aged 66 years 7 months 4 days.
Jacob Miller, departed this life Nov. 18, 1858, aged 78 years 4 months 18 days.
Elizabeth Bowman, departed this life July 21, 1876, aged 67 years — months 21 days.
Daniel Bowman, departed this life April 27, 1879.

(End of Record.)

(The above Bible is in possession of Ralph Ingersoll Barkley, 706 West Pine Street, Johnson City, Tenn.)

NOTES

The Jacob Miller above was the son of Peter and Elizabeth Boone Miller who were early settlers in East Tennessee. His wife, Elizabeth Range, was a daughter of Peter and Susan Range, also early settlers in Washington County. Peter Miller, Sr., and Elizabeth Boone Miller had Jacob Miller, born 1779; James Miller; Peter Miller, born 1792, and in War of 1812; and Mary Miller, married a Reeves.
Peter Miller, Sr., was born in Germany, and after coming to Tennessee he was an elder in the Old Hebron German Baptist Church on Knob Creek, Washington County, Tennessee. The Miller (Mueller) family migrated from Pennsylvania down through Virginia into North Carolina (later Tennessee). Peter Miller, Sr., is buried at his old home between Johnson City and Jonesboro, close by where now runs the Southern Railway (a flag stop called Miller's Switch). Peter Miller, Sr., served in the Revolution in Pennsylvania.

MICHAEL MASENGILLE BIBLE RECORD
(John Sevier Chapter, D. A. R.)

Copied March 1, 1932, by Mary Hardin McCown, Johnson City, Tenn. Bible printed by McCarthy & Davis, No. 171 Market St., Philadelphia, Pa., 1834.

The Record:

Michael Masengille and L. B. Cobb, married Jan 9, 1817.
Wm. R. Tipton and B. F. Masengille, married April 12, 1828.
Leander M. King and Penelope L. Masengille, married Nov. 3, 1839.
B. L. Dulaney and R. C. Masengille, married Sept. 17, 1846.

R. H. Masengille and Harriet Stuffle, married Oct. 1, 1850.
Henry Hyder and Sally Masengille, married May 25, 1852.
Mich'l Masengille and Hannah Torbett, married March 20, 1834.
T. H. B. Wolf and Lucretia S. Masengille, married Sept. 19, 1860.
W. A. Masengille and D. L. Masengille, married Feb. 11, 1872.

BIRTHS

Michael Masengille, born Oct. 10, 1792.
L. B. Cobb, born Feb. 26, 1801.
Penelope Masengille, daughter of Michael and L. B. Masengille, born Feb. 14, 1818.
Barshaba S. Masengille, daughter of Michael and L. B. Masengille, born Dec. 25, 1821.
Rebecca C. Masengille, daughter of Michael and L. B. Masengille, born Jan. 17, 1825.
Richard H. Masengille, son of Michael and L. B. Masengille, born March 10, 1828.
Infant daughter, born 1820.

DEATHS

Infant daughter of Michael and L. B. Masengille, died 1830.
L. B. Masengille, departed this life Jan. 10, 1930.
Rebecca Cobb Masengille, departed this life Feb. 7, 1842.
Michael Masengille, departed this life Sept. 3, 1856.
Hannah Masengille, departed this life May 17, 1887.

BIRTHS

Hannah Torbett, born Aug. 29, 1807.
Sallie Masengille, daughter of Michael and Hannah Masengille, born —— 15, 1835.
Jos—— Masengille, —— of M—— and H——, born —— 10, 1837.
Lucretia E. Masengille, daughter ————, born March 22, 1839.
Lucinda Masengille, daughter of ———, born —— 22, 1842.
Susan Masengille, daughter of ———, born —— 16, 1844.
Infant son of M. and H. Masengille, born Feb. 11, 184—.
William Allen Masengille, son of M. and Hannah Masengille, born June 18, 1849.
Joe M. Wolf, born July 11, 1861.
Thomas C. Wolf, born March 30, 1865.

DEATHS

Infant son of M. and H. Masengille, departed this life Feb. 20, 1848.
I. T. Masengille, departed this life March 10, 1865.
T. H. B. Wolfe, ——— this life —— 22, 1865. --

BIRTHS

Hannah J. Masengille, daughter of Wm. A. and D. L. Masengille, born Jan. 7, 1873, died March 7, 1901.
Mary Lucretia Masengille, daughter of Wm. A. and D. L. Masengille, born Aug. 1, 1875.
Sallie Blanche, daughter of Wm. A. and D. L. Masengille, born Jan. 17, 1878.
Maggie Alice Masengille, daughter of Wm. A. and D. L. Masengille, born Dec. 22, 1880.
John Michael Masengille, son of Wm. A. and D. L. Masengille, born Dec. 17, 1882.
George Alex Masengille, son of W. A. Masengille, born Nov. 24, 1888.

DEATHS

Fannie C. Masengille, daughter, born Nov. 7, 1884, died Aug. 23, 1891.
Wm. A. Masengille, died July 20, 1896.
Eva Masengille, died April 24, 1902.

MARRIAGES

C. H. McFall and Jennie Masengille, married July 29, 1900.
Jennie McFall, died March 7, 1901.
B. B. Wolf and Maggie Masengille, married Sept. 15, 1901.
E. E. Robertson and Lula Masengille, married Aug. 28, 1902.
(End of Record.)

NOTES BY MARY HARDIN MCCOWN

This Bible is in possession of Mrs. D. L. Bayless, 209 W. Holston Ave., Johnson City, Tenn. She was the wife of Wm. A. Masengille, then married Bayless.

Michael Masengille is called Michael II., named for an uncle, brother of his father, Henry Masengille, Jr. (called Hal). Henry Masengille, Jr., was born in Southhampton County, Virginia, Oct. 1, 1758, the son of Henry Masengille and Mary Cobb (a sister of Wm. Cobb). Henry Masengille, Jr. (Hal), was enlisted at the age of 18 in the Revolutionary War and served two years and three months on frontier and in North Carolina. He married his cousin, Penelope Cobb, daughter of William and Mary Cobb. They were married in Womack"s Fort on the Holston River during an Indian invasion while the fort was surrounded by Indians.

Michael Masengille, born Oct. 10, 1792, died Sept. 3, 1856, married Louisa Buckingham Cobb (daughter of Richard Caswell Cobb and Rebecca Buckingham). Michael Masengille lived in the old Cobb house which was used as the first Capitol of the Territory Southwest of the River Ohio by Gov. Wm. Blount in 1790.

William Cobb, Sr., and Henry Masengille, Sr., left East Tennessee early. William Cobb, Sr., was living in Grainger County, Tennessee, on March 8, 1799, and died between Sept., 1802, and Sept., 1803.

Henry Masengille, Sr., left Washington County after 1798 and died at the home of his daughter, Mary, who married Wm. Atkinson, and lived in Grainger County, Tennessee.

The Masengille Cemetery on the Hal Masengille homestead in Sullivan County, Tennessee, has the following:

Michael Masengille, born Oct. 10, ——, died Sept. 3, 1856.

Henry Masengille, who was a Revolutionary soldier, born A.D. 1760 (should be 1758, S. E. Masengille), died Sept. 25, 1837, age 77 years. "Honor the brave; rest, soldier, thy warfare over."

Sacred to the memory of Louisa B., consort of Michael Masengille, died Jan. 10, 1930, age 28 years 11 months and 16 days.

Sacred to the memory of David Stuart, died April 12, 1827, age 32. David Stuart, died Aug. 3, 1830.

Penelope, consort of Henry Masengille, Jr., died Sept. 1, 1810, age 49 years ——.

Sacred to the memory of Alcey Masengille, died Aug. 14, 1809, age 11 months.

J. Masengille, died Aug. 6, ——, age 15 years 7 months 1 day.

Elizabeth, wife of Henry Masengille, died Sept. 28, 1875, age 85 years 1 month 4 days.

——— Masengille, died Aug 9, ——, age 9 years 7 months 26 days.

Sacred to the memory of Deborah Masengille, consort of Wm. Masengille, died Sept. 7, 1833, aged 46 years 11 months.

Hannah, wife of Michael Masengille, born Aug. 29, 1807, died May 17, 1887.

Deborah, wife of F. D. Masengille, died March 28, 1874, age 63 years 9 days.

Martha Masengille, wife of F. D. Masengille, born May 1, 1844, died July 3, 1890.

Felty Devault Masengille, born April 30, 1815, died March 30, 1894.

John Masengille, born 1816, died Feb. 28, 1895, age 78 years 5 months.

Mary J., wife of John Masengille, died June 20, 1909.

(The above cemetery record, as well as the Masengille records, outside of the Michael Masengille Bible, are taken from the Masengille, Masengiles and Variants, 1472-1931, by S. E. Massengill, 1931. The other notes are my own.—M. H. McC.)

Michael Masengille lived in Sullivan County, Tenn.

Michael Hyder, Jr., Bible Record
(John Sevier Chapter, D. A. R.)

Copied May 27, 1929, by Mary Hardin McCown, Johnson City, Tenn. Bible was printed 1816 at Brattleborough, Vt.

The Record:

Marriages

Michael Hyder, Jr., married, first, Martha Locherd, March 9, 1797.
Michael Hyder, Jr., married, second, Sarah Simmerman (widow), Nov. 18, 1813.
Eleanor Hyder, married Dec. 28, 1817.
Benj. Hyder, married Feb. 14, 1822.
John Hampton Hyder, married Oct. 23, 1823.
Eliz. Hyder, married Dec. 15, 1825, in Roane County.
Jacob Hyder, married Sept. 29, 1836.
Martha Ann, married Jan. 25, 1849.
Catherine, married Nov. 23, 1824.

Births

Michael Hyder, Jr., born Oct. 24, 1767, died Oct. 6, 1861.*
Martha L. Hyder, born Aug. 1, 1775, died Aug. 8, 1812.*
Benj. Hyder, son to Michael Hyder, born Dec. 31, 1797.
Ellenor Hyder, born May 31, 1799.
Johnathan Hampton Hyder, born Jan. 15, 1801.
Michael Hyder, III., born April 26, 1803.*
Eliz. Hyder, born Jan. 4, 1807.
John W. Hyder, born Feb. 23, 1809.*
Jacob Hyder, born Oct. 21, 1814.
Adam Hyder, born Feb. 21, 1816.*
Samuel Williams Hyder, born Aug. 21, 1817.*
Joseph Hyder, born Jan. 20, 1820.*
Eliza Haynes, born June 15, 1819.
Michael Hyder Haynes, born July 25, 1821.
Elizabeth Haynes, born Aug., 1823.

Deaths

Martha Hyder, died Aug. 8, 1812.
Michael, son of Michael, died Sept. 6, 1805.*
Adam, died May 13, 1816.*
Adam, died May 13, 1816.
Benj., died Aug. 19, 1831.
Eliz., died Jan. 7, 1834.
John Haynes, died Aug. —, ——.
Elizabeth Hyder, died Jan. 3, 1841, aged, as we suppose, 96.*
Michael Hyder, Sr., died Oct. 6, 1861.*
John Hyder, died Oct. 20, 1870.*
Lavinia E. Fair, died Sept. 15, 1874.*
Michael E. Hyder, died March 19, 1885.*
Samuel C. Hyder, died Sept. 6, 1886.*
Samuel W. Hyder, died Sept. 25, 1897.*
Julia C. Fair, died Jan. 14, 1899.

David R. Hyder and Julia A. Persinger were married Jan. 5, 1893.

Children

Dora Maud Hyder, born Dec. 5, 1897.
Julia A. Hyder, born Feb. 4, 1913.
Sarah Jane Hyder, born Nov. 17, 1823.
Wm. F. M. Hyder, born Jan. 20, 1824.
Catherine Hyder, born Nov. 23, 1824.
Henry Hampton Hyder, born Jan. 9, 1825.
John Hyder, born Feb. 3, 1841.
Sary Hyder, born May 19, 1842.
Michael Hyder, born Oct. 26, 1844.
Nath. H. Hyder, born Feb. 15, 1847.
Luvenia J. Hyder, born April 20, 1849.*
Margaret Ann Hyder, born Oct. 26, 1852.
Joseph Hyder, born May 7, 1856.
David Hyder, born Dec. 16, 1861.
Sam'l Hyder, born Dec. 24, 1863.

Sarah Hyder, died May 6, 1865.*

Julia C. Hyder, born May 31, 1865.
Chester B. Hyder, born Dec. 6, 1868.

Luvisa E. Hyder, died April 5, 1870.*

Samuel W. Hyder, married, second, Sallie E. Fair July 2, 1872, by Nathaniel Hyder.

(End of Record.)

NOTES BY MARY HARDIN McCOWN

The above Bible is in possession of Mrs. Pearl Hyder Treadway, Oak Grove, on Powder Branch, Carter County, Tennessee. She lives in the old Michael Hyder, Jr., homestead. Close by is the old Hyder Cemetery where the Michael Hyder I., and also Michael II. are buried.

Michael Hyder I. came from Hampshire County, Virginia, to the Watauga Settlement about 1766 or 68. He was one of the earliest settlers on the Watauga. He served in the Revolutionary War and was at the Battle of King's Mountain Oct. 8, 1780. His tombstone inscription reads:

"Erected by His Descendants
to
MICHAEL HYDER, SR.
Died June 25, 1790.

Member of Watauga Association. In Watauga Fort June 21, 1776. Took part in all the early Indian wars in Tennessee under Shelby, Sevier and Christian. Was in the following battles of Revolution: Thickety Fort, Cedar Springs, and Musgroves Mills in South Carolina. Was detailed from King's Mountain Expedition to defend Watauga Settlement from Indian invasion."

The will of Michael Hyder,, Sr. dated May 20, 1790, is in Jonesboro, Washington County, Tennessee. Will No. 1, p. 21, names wife, Elizabeth; sons, John, Jonathan, Michael, Adam, Jacob and Joseph; there were several daughters not named in will. They were Polly, Nancy, Katy and Martha Hyder.

All names in Bible record marked * are buried in the Hyder Cemetery on Powder Branch, Carter County, Tennessee.

Martha Locherd is spelled Lockhart in Carter County marriage bond.

Sarah Simmerman, second wife of Michael, Jr., was an Isenberg. Her old Bible in German is in possession of Sam J. Hyder, Milligan College, Tenn. The inscription inside is "Sarah Isenberg, Nov. 14, 1812, for 6 shillings."

The marriages of the children of Michael Hyder, Jr., were as follows:

Eleanor Hyder, married James Haynes.

Benj. Hyder, married Elizabeth Taylor, daughter of Isaac Taylor.

John H. Hyder, married, first, Mary Williams (born May 25, 1805, died Nov. 23, 1832); second, Aug. 25, 1833, to Martha King (Washington County).

Elizabeth Hyder, married John Haynes in Roane County, Tenn.

Jacob Hyder, married Elizabeth Bean in Washington County, by Jacob Hartsell.

Catherine Hyder, married Hampton H. Edens.

John H. Hyder (born Jan. 14, 1801, died Aug. 7, 1865) and wife, Mary Williams, are buried in Andrew Taylor Cemetery on left side of Powder Branch, Carter County, Tenn.

Benj. Hyder (died Aug. 19, 1831, in Illinois). His wife, Elizabeth Taylor, died in Illinois and John Hyder went after their three children, Henry Hampton Hyder (born Jan. 9, 1825, see Bible record); Martha, married ——— King, and Jane married ——— Stonicipher.

Sam. W. Hyder, married, first Lavicia Eliz. Edens, daughter of James Edens, Jr.

Sam. W. Hyder, married, second, Sarah E. Fair (see Bible record). Children of John H. Hyder and

Mary Williams as given in Bible record are: Sarah Jane Hyder, Wm. F. M. Hyder.
Children of S. W. Hyder and L. E. Edens are: John, born 1841; Sary, born 1842; Michael, born 1844; Nath. Henry, born 1847 (living today at Milligan College); Luvenia J.; Martha Ann; Joseph, born 1856; David, born 1861; Samuel, born 1863; Julia C., born 1865; Chester B.
Elizabeth Hyder, died Jan. 3, 1841, aged, as we suppose, 96, was the Elizabeth Wood(s), wife of Michael Hyder, Sr., who were married in 1764.

Jacob Hartsell Family Data
(John Sevier Chapter, D. A. R.)

Copied March 8, 1932, by Mary Hardin McCown (Mrs. L. W.), Johnson City, Tenn., from a "Diary of Capt. Jacob Hartsell, a Soldier in War of 1812." The Diary was kept from Oct. 12, 1813, through January 27, 1814.

The Record:

This is a memorandum of Jacob Hartsell and his wife, Nancy Hartsell. They were married October 3 the day, 1805.
This is the following record of the names of their offsprings.
In the year of our Lord 1807, May 26th day, between 10 and 11 o'clock, was born Mary Hartsell, daughter of Jacob and Nancy Hartsell.
January 11th day, in year of our Lord 1809, was Anthony Hartsell born, between 11 and 12 o'clock, son of Jacob and Nancy Hartsell.
In the year of our Lord 1811, February 23 day, about 4 o'clock in the afternoon, was Delilah Hartsell born, daughter of Jacob and Nancy Hartsell.
March 17th day, 1813, about 1 o'clock in the morning, was Russell Bean Hartsell born, son of Jacob and Nancy Hartsell.
May 29th day, 1815, was Hannah Hartsell born, between 4 and 5 o'clock in the afternoon, daughter of Jacob and Nancy Hartsell.
July 25th day, 1817, was Marton Luther Hartsell born, about 4 o'clock in the afternoon, son of Jacob and Nancy Hartsell.
June 24th day, 1819, about 6 o'clock in the morning, was Emeline Hartsell born, daughter of Jacob and Nancy Hartsell.
July 4th day, 1821, about 4 o'clock in the morning, was Isaac Washington Hartsell born, son of Jacob and Nancy Hartsell.
July 11th day, in the year of our Lord 1823, was Nancy Hartsell born, about 9 o'clock in the morning, daughter of Jacob and Nancy Hartsell.

This is a memorandum of the property that I, Jacob Hartsell, gave to my daughter Mary when she was married to Joney Lilbourn and her age so that all of my children may know how things will stand at my departure of this life. Mary was aged 17 years and 7 months when she was married.
First to one side saddle and plated bridle, cost $30.00.
To one cow and calf at $15.00.
To one bureau and table at $30.00.
To one sorrel horse at $100.00.
To one bedstead and furniture at $30.00.
To household furniture at $20.00.
To one cupboard at $20.00.

My daughter Delilah was aged when she was married about 17 years and 5 months to Thomas E. Jackson.
First to one side saddle and plaited bridle, $30.00.
Second, to one cow, $12.00.
Third, to one bureau and table, $30.00.

Fourth, to one bedstead and furniture, $30.00.
Fifth, to household furniture, $20.00.
Sixth, to one sorrel horse, $90.00.
Which is equal to the time she did not stay with as long as Polly, therefore I think they are nearly even as to their property so far.

My son Anthony was aged 21 years and 6 months when he left me and I gave him in boot of horses ten dollars in money and one patent plough, single trees and two pairs of gears for two horses and clevises and the cupboard that was at the Harrison house and table and one set of split-bottom chairs worth three dollars and fifty cents. This was in boot of horses, then I agreed to give him the rent of the Harrison place (part of) five years at fifty dollars a year to make him even with the two girls as I believe is fair for his services in that he stayed longer than the girls.
To say one horse and the boot, worth $100.00.
To one rifle gun, $25.00.
To one cow, $10.00.
To one saddle at $25.00.
To one bed and furniture at $20.00.
Then the rent of the place after paying me $50.00 a year is worth something like $20.00 a year—$100.00.
And that will be what thing is right and even.

January 9th day, 1834, my daughter Hannah Hartsell married Norvill P. Nelson and left me at the age of 18 years and 7 months, which was longer than either of the other daughters stayed.
1 article—one saddle and plated bridle, $30.00.
2—to one cow, worth $12.00.
3—to one bureau and dressing table, $30.00.
4—to one bedstead, worth $35.00.
5—to household furniture, $30.00.
6—to one sorrel filly, worth $80.00.
7—to one set of split-bottom chairs, $3.50.
Which will make ten dollars and fifty cents more than Delilah got for her time of staying so much longer, which will make all of them even as yet.

November 15th day, 1836, my daughter Emeline Hartsell married James Carr and left me at the age of 17 years and 5 months.
1 article—one saddle and plated bridle, $27.50.
2—to one cow and heifer, worth $13.00.
3—to one bureau and dressing table, worth $33.00.
4—to one bedstead, worth $35.00.
5—to household furniture, worth $25.00.
6—to one sorrel mare by name of Fenox, $85.00.
Which will make her, by not staying so long as Hannah, nine or ten dollars more than she ought.

January, 1842, 17th day, my daughter, Nancy Hartsell, married Wm. Love and left me at the age of 18 years and 6 months.
1 article—one side saddle and plated bridle at $30.00.
2—to one bureau at $20.00.
3—one cow, $12.00.
4—to one bedstead at $35.00.
5—to household furniture worth $25.00.
6—to one sorrel mare worth $75.00.

May, 1838, Martin Hartsell, my son, was married in May and left in July and he was not of age by something like two months.
1 article—one rifle gun worth $25.00.
2 article—one bay mare and sorrel filly, worth $100.00.
3 article—one common bed, worth $20.00.
4 article—one saddle and bridle, worth $25.00.
5 article—to one suckling colt, worth $20.00.
6 article—to one plow, 2 pair gears, worth $15.00.

Isaac W. Hartsell left me and married in the month of Sept, 1842, at the age of 21 years 3 months. He married Mrs. Rebecky Brown.
1 article—one bay horse, Prince, worth $80.00.
2 article—one rifle gun, worth $25.00.
3 article—one cow, called the Garland cow, $13.00.
4—one bedstead and table, worth $30.00.
5 article—one saddle and bridle, $30.00.
6—one plow and 2 pair of gears, worth $18.00.

(End of the Record.)

NOTES BY MARY HARDIN McCOWN

Jacob Hartsell was a resident of Washington County, Tenn. His home was in the Cherokee Creek district of said county. It is not known who his wife Nancy was before her marriage, but the Washington County 1850 census gives living at her home:

Nancy A. Hartsell, aged 62, born in Tennessee.
Rosamond Bean, aged 75, born in North Carolina.
N. M. Harry, aged 22, born in North Carolina.
Bird B. Brown, laborer, born in Tennessee.
Eleanor Luttrell, born in Virginia.

Could Nancy have been a Bean or a Luttrell? It is not known just when she died.

Jacob Hartsell is buried in the Cherokee Creek Baptist Church yard, Washington County, Tenn. Following inscription: "In memory of Col. Jacob Hartsell, died May 2, 1843, aged 57 years."

Jacob Hartsell served in the War of 1812 as captain of a company of East Tennessee Volunteers in the Second (Col. Lillard's) Regiment. Service from Oct. 12, 1813, to Feb. 8, 1814.

The diary above referred to is in possession of a great-great-granddaughter, Mrs. Minnie Jones Cargille, Garbers, Tenn.

JOHN HARDIN BIBLE RECORDS
(John Sevier Chapter, D. A. R.)

Copied 1928 by Mrs. Nannie K. Hardin from the Bible in Salem, Ore. Copied March 8, 1932, from her copy by Mary Hardin McCown, Johnson City, Tenn.

The Record:

BIRTHS

John Hardin, born May 29, 1795.
Charlotte Hardin, born April 16, 1795.
John H. Snider, son of George and S. S. Snider, born June 15, 1857.
George Henry Snider, son of John and Martha E. Snider, born Sept. 24, 1870.
Jordan C. Snider, son of George W. Snider and Sarah S. Snider, born May 17, 1863.
Martha Alice Snider, daughter of George W. and Sarah S. Snider, born Jan. 22, 1867.
John C. Snider, born Aug. 25, 1839.
Henry Hardin, son of John and ——— Hardin, born Sept. 29, 1821.
Sarah S. Hardin, born Jan. 1, 1826.
Elizabeth A. Hardin, born Sept. 29, 1828.
Jordan C. Hardin, born Aug. 3, 1830.
Martha E. Hardin, born Feb. 11, 1834.
John G. Powell, born Aug. 14, 1828.
James H. Hardin, son of Henry and Lucinda Hardin, born Oct. 19, 1847.
Joseph D. Powell, son of John G. and Elizabeth Adeline Powell, born March 25, 1848.
John Hardin, son of Henry and Lucinda Hardin, born Feb. —, 1850.
William Hamilton Hardin, son of

H. W. and Lucinda Hardin, born Feb. 13, 1852.
Martha E. Powell, daughter of John G. and Elizabeth A. Powell, born March 8, 1850.

MARRIAGES

John Hardin and Charlotte Councill, his wife, married Aug. 15, 1820.
Henry Hardin, son of John and Charlotte Hardin, and Lucinda Horton, married Sept. 3, 1846.
John G. Powell and Elizabeth Adeline Hardin, married May 9, 1847.
George W. Snider and Sarah Salina Hardin, married Dec. 25, 1856.
Jordan C. Hardin and Julia C. Williams, married Dec. 4, 1861.
John Snider and Martha E. Hardin, married Oct. 20, 1867.
George H. Snider, son of John and Martha Snider, was married to Arvilla M. Dawson, Nov. 24, 1897.

DEATHS

Fannie Snider, wife of Mikel Snider, departed this life Oct. 24, 1867.
Mikel Snider, departed this life June 19, 1887.
John C. Snider, departed this life Dec. 15, 1902.
Martha E. Powell, daughter of John D. and Elizabeth Powell, departed this life Oct. 7, 1850.
Charlotte Hardin, departed this life Nov. 1, 1843.
John Hardin, departed this life Sept. 16, 1869.
Sarah S. H. Snider, departed this life Oct. 10, 1883.
Julia C. Hardin, departed this life May 28, 1886.
Jordan C. Hardin, departed this life June 27, 1898.
Mary E. Epps, daughter of J. C. and Julia Hardin, departed this life Dec. 17, 1899.
Catherine Hardin, wife of Henry Hardin, departed this life Feb. 3, 1847.
Henry Hardin, husband of Catherine Hardin, departed this life Oct. 23, 1856.
Elizabeth A. Powell, departed this life June 13, 1860.

(End of Bible Record.)

NOTES BY MARY HARDIN MCCOWN

John Hardin, born May 29, 1795, lived in Ashe County, N. C. He died Sept. 16, 1869, and is buried at Elk Park, N. C. He represented Ashe County, N. C., in Legislature in 1820 (see Wheeler's N. C.). Senator from Ashe, 1818.
Charlotte Hardin, wife of John Hardin, was a daughter of Jordan Council (born 1769, died Dec. 10, 1839) and wife, Sarah Howard (born Oct. 21, 1771, died ——) who lived at Boone, N. C. Charlotte Hardin is buried at Boone, N. C.
John Hardin was a son of Henry Hardin (born Sept. 18, 1765, died Oct. 23, 1856, aged 91 years 1 month, 5 days, buried on Beaver Creek, Ashe County, N. C.) and his wife, Catherine Cox (died Feb. 3, 1847, aged 74 years 4 months 15 days). Catherine Cox was a daughter of Capt. John Cox, a Revolutionary soldier of Virginia, and wife, Margaret Davis. John Cox moved from Virginia into Wilkes County (now Ashe), N. C.
Henry Hardin, father of John, was a Revolutionary soldier from North Carolina. He was a son of William and Sallie Hardin. William Hardin was in the Revolutionary War.
The writer has not the data at hand, but she knows that the Hardins were French Hugenots, as several cousins have joined that society on Hardin ancestry.
(The above is my own line.)
The Bible of John Hardin is in possession of a grandson, Geo. H. Snider, in Salem, Ore.

JAMES EDENS RECORD
(John Sevier Chapter, D. A. R.)

This record is written on a hand made scroll, with a bird

drawn in red ink, the writing being in blue ink. It was the work of an itinerant Scotchman named McDougal.

The Record:

James Edens was born Oct. 7, 1774.

Eve Shultz, now Eve Edens, wife of James Edens, was born Feb. 17, 1773.

Alexander Edens, their first child and son, was born in the year 1797, June 11, and died, aged ——.

Elizabeth Edens, their first daughter, was born April 11, 1798, and died Aug. 17.

Nathaniel T. Edens, their second son, born April 4, 1801; died, 1824.

Washington Edens, their third son, born Feb. 26, 1805, died March 20, 1805.

"In infancy his spirit flew away,
And soared to regions of celestial day,
Where now he dwells in happiness above—
And tastes the sweets of a Redeemer's love."

———

A record of the births and deaths of the family of the Rev. James Edens and Eve Edens, his wife; as also of the births and deaths in the family of Nathaniel Edens, his son, and Levinah Edens, his wife: May peace, friendship, harmony and love attend them here and celestial joys be their ultimate inheritance.—I. S. G.

———

Nathaniel Edens, son of James Edens, was married to Levinah Hyder Nov. 29, 1820.

Levinah Hyder, now Levinah Edens, wife of Nathaniel Edens, born Nov. 18, 1802.

Hampton H. Edens, first child and son of Nathaniel Edens and Levinah, his wife, born March 29, 1822.

Lavicia Elizabeth Edens, first daughter of Nathaniel T. Edens and Levinah, his wife, born Feb. 6, 1824.

Rosanna Edens, their second daughter, born June 28, 1826, died Jan. 5, 1828.

"On angel's wings her infant soul did fly,
And found a rest, in realms beyond the sky.
Ye earthly parents, who are left behind,
Let thoughts of death be ever in our mind,
And by a life of purity prepare
To soar to Heaven and meet Rosanna there."

———

A daughter, born without perceptible life Aug. 6, 1828.

Margaret Edens, their third daughter, born July 6, 1829.

John J. Edens, their second son, born Aug. 21, 1831.

Lucinda Jane Edens, born May 23, 1826.

Julian Edens, born Nov. 11, 1837.

William G. B. Edens, born Feb. 5, 1840.

Nancy Ann Edens, born May 15, 1842.

Joseph P. Edens, born March 18, 1844.

MEMENTO MORI.

A record of the names, ages of William and Nancy and Andrew Jackson, lawful heirs of Sarah and James Jackson, former inhabitants of the state of North Carolina (county unknown), likewise temporary residents of Wythe County, Va., and bound by the court of Carter County, Tenn., the sons, Wm. and Andrew, to the Rev. James Edens, the daughter, Nancy, bound as aforsesaid to Nathaniel Edens, son of aforesaid James Edens.

William Jackson, born May —, —.

Nancy Jackson, born Aug. 9, 1819.

Andrew Jackson, born Aug. 9, 1821.

———

"May Andrew rise to eminence and fame—
And cast a luster on Old Hickory's name.

Be great in goodness, rise to high renown,
On acts of —— cast the contemptuous frown.
May he the weapons of destruction wield,
Fight the Old Hickory, drive his foes away,
Nor suffer them within his clime to stay."
(End of Record.)

NOTES BY MARY HARDIN MCCOWN

This was copied Feb. 14, 1932, by M. H. McCown from original owned by Mrs. John Birchfield, Milligan College, Tenn.

James Edens was a resident of Carter County, Tenn. Was son of James Edens, Sr., one of the early settlers on the Watauga region.

James Edens, Sr., settled on Gap Creek above the Big Spring. He married in Rockingham County, Va., in 1768 to Martha Sassine, a French girl. They came to North Carolina (now Tennessee) about 1770. James Edens was at the Battle of King's Mountain (tradition has it that he was one of those detailed to protect the Watauga women and children against the Indians while the others went to the battle). He was a pioneer Baptist preacher and was a member of the Sinking Creek Baptist Church. The following is list of children of James Edens, Sr., and Martha Sassine:

James Edens, Jr., born Oct. 9, 1774, died 1855.

Austin Edens, born 1791. Went to Mississippi.

Isaac Edens.

Washington Edens, died young.

Jean (Jane) Edens, married Jonathan Hyder Feb. 13, 1821.

Martha Edens, married Dr. Moore.

Rhoda Edens, married Joseph Hyder.

James Edens, Sr., died ———, and is buried in an unmarked grave in the Edens Cemetery on his home place above the Big Spring, Carter County.

James Edens, Jr., was likewise a Baptist preacher and member of Sinking Creek Church. He married, first, Evanna Shultz (born Feb. 17, 1773, died 1847) in Oct., 1796. Evanna was daughter of George Shultz, a Revolutionary soldier of Pennsylvania.

James Edens, Jr., married, second, Feb. 11 or 12, 1850, to Elizabeth Berry of Carter County, Tenn.

DRAPER RECORDS
(John Sevier Chapter, D. A. R.)

Copied 19— by Mrs. J. A. Drake, of Cookeville, Tenn., from the old Draper Bible in the possession of Mrs. Geneva Draper Anderson, Gallatin, Tenn. Copied March 16, 1932, from Mrs. Drake's copy by Mrs. Lula Holladay, Cookeville, Tenn.

The Record:

Thomas Draper, Sr., born Sept. 15, 1768, died Aug. 20, 1840.

Sally Draper, born Oct. 17, 1766, died Sept. 22, 1844.

Thomas and Sally Draper, married Aug. 9, 1787, on Salt Lick.

A RECORD OF AGES OF CHILDREN OF THOMAS AND SALLY DRAPER

Elizabeth Draper (alias Young), born July 27, 1788.

James Draper, born May 8, 1790.

Sally Draper (alias Evans), born Jan. 4, 1792.

Thomas Draper, born May 4, 1793.

Henrietta Draper (alias Holladay), born Feb. 28, 1795.

Anne Draper (alias Rogers), born Sept. 8, 1796.

Lucy Draper (alias Pate), born May 8, 1799.

Lawson and Luranna Draper, born Dec. 4, 1801.
Edward B. Draper, born March 18, 1804.
Brice Mathis Draper, born March 16, 1806.
Milton Draper, born July 1, 1808.

DEATHS

Henrietta D. Holladay, died April 10, 1851.
Anne D. Rogers, died Oct. 20, 1849.
James Draper, died Feb. 1, 1873.
Edward Draper, died March 2, 1888.
Brice M. Draper, died Sept. 16, 1845.

MARRIAGES

Elizabeth Draper to James Young, Nov. 27, 1806.
James Draper to Jane Moore Fitzgerald, Feb. 20, 1819.
Sally Draper to Obadiah Evans, Nov. 4, 1820.
Henrietta Draper to Stephen Holladay, Jan. 20, 1820.
Anne Draper to John Rogers, Nov., 1821.
Lawson Draper to Eleanor Jones, Nov. 30, 1828.
Luranna Draper to Thomas Huddleston, March 25, 1827.
Lucy Draper to Edward Pate, Nov. 12, 1829.
Thomas L. Draper to Elizabeth Huddleston, Nov. 4.
Edward Draper to Emily W. Goodbar, June 2, 1850.

Thos. Draper, Sr., born Sept. 15, 1768, died Aug. 20, 1840.
Sally Draper, born Oct. 17, 1766, died Sept. 22, 1844.
Elizabeth Draper Young, died Nov. 24, 1871.
Milton Draper, died July 22, 1871.
Thos. and Sally Draper were married Aug. 9, 1787.
Edward G. Draper, born Aug. 14, 1851.
Nancy G. Draper, born Jan. 9, 1854.
Thos. P. Draper, born April 9, 1855, died Oct. 28, 1856.
Sallie Draper, born June 25, 1864.
Jas. Hillery Draper, born Dec. 27, 1866.

(End of the Record.)

Notes on the Draper Records by Clara C. Coile, Johnson City, Tenn.:

Thomas Draper (called Thomas Draper, Sr., in the above record) was born in Berkeley County, S. C., the fifth child of Thomas (died 1795, buried in Monk's Corner, S. C.) and his wife Lucy Coleman (buried in Monk's Corner, S. C.) Draper (see page 219, "Drapers in America," by Thomas Waln-Morgan Draper). Thomas, the son, married, in 1787, Salley Lyle in South Carolina, county not known. (The above Bible record is in error in stating that Thomas and Salley Draper were married on Salt Lick [Tennessee].) In 1797 Thomas Draper came to Tennessee and bought land in Sumner County (see Sumner County Deeds, Book 2, page 243). He returned to South Carolina and in 1800 brought his wife and seven small children to Tennessee. They settled near Bagdad, Jackson (then Smith) County, where their five other children were born and where Thomas and Salley died and are buried.

JOSEPH CROUCH BIBLE RECORD
(John Sevier Chapter, D. A. R.)

Copied March 1, 1932, by Mary Hardin McCown, Johnson City, Tenn. Bible printed Oct. 27, 1802, in Philadelphia, for Matthew Carey, No. 118 Market St.

The Record:

Joseph Crouch and Pegge, his wife, were married Feb. 21, 1778.
John Crouch, the son of Joseph and Pegge, his wife, was married Dec. 13, 1805.
George Crouch, the son of Joseph

Crouch and Pegge, his wife, was married April 19, 1807.
Joseph Crouch, son of Joseph and Pegge, his wife, was married Feb. 10, 1814.
William Crouch, the son of Joseph and Pegge, his wife, was married May 26, 1815.
Sary Crouch, the daughter of Joseph Crouch and Pegge, his wife, was married Dec. 26, 1797.
Elizabeth Crouch, the daughter of Joseph Crouch and Pegge, his wife, was married Oct. 17, 1805.
Patty Crouch, the daughter of Joseph Crouch and Pegge, his wife, was married January 7, 1819.
Sanford Crouch was married Sept. 12, 1822 (the son of Joseph Crouch and Pegge, his wife).

BIRTHS

Sary Crouch, the daughter of Joseph Crouch and Pegge, his wife, born Nov. 16, 1778.
John Crouch, the son of Joseph Crouch and Pegge, his wife, born June 22, 1781.
George Crouch, the son of Joseph Crouch and Pegge, his wife, born June 14, 1784.
Elizabeth Crouch, the daughter of Joseph Crouch and Pegge, his wife, born April 17, 1787.
Joseph Crouch, the son of Joseph Crouch and Pegge, his wife, born Dec. 30, 1791.
William Crouch, the son of Joseph and Pegge, his wife, born July 2, 1793.
Patty Crouch, the daughter of Joseph Crouch and Peggy, his wife, born Feb. 14, 1796.
Sanford Crouch, the son of Joseph Crouch and Pegge, his wife, born Dec. 1, 180—.

BIRTHS

Colored children of Stephen and Grace that are to be free at the age of 31, according to the will of Joseph Crouch, deceased.
Lydia, born Feb. 22, 1815.
Matildy, born Jan. 22, 1817.
Mark, born June 15, 1818.
Solomon, born March 4, 1821.
Samuel, born Oct. 4, 1824.
Henderson, born Sept. 4, 1827.

DEATHS

John Crouch, the son of Joseph Crouch, died Jan 26, 1813, in the 33rd year of his age.
Sanford Crouch, the son of Joseph Crouch, died Nov. 5, 1856 (or 36), age 35 years 11 months.
George M. Crouch, born ——.
Ceny Crouch, the wife of William, departed this life June 4, 1843.
Joseph Crouch, died Sept. 8, 1830, age 81 years.
Margaret Crouch, the wife of Joseph Crouch, deceased, departed this life April 13, 1844, age 82 years within five days.
Sarah Hunt, the daughter of Joseph Crouch and Margaret, his wife, died Aug. 29, 1852, aged 73 years 9 months 10 days.
Samuel Hunt, Sr., departed this life July 21, 1852, aged 79 years 9 months and 24 days.
Joseph Hunt, the son of Samuel Hunt and Sarah, his wife, died March 15, 1840, aged 36 years.
(End of Record.)

NOTES BY MARY HARDIN McCOWN

Sanford Crouch, married Elizabeth Bean Sept. 12, 1822 (Washington County).
Sarah Crouch, married Samuel Hunt, Sr., Dec. 26, 1797.
George Crouch, married Susan Gresham April 19, 1807.
In Hodges Cemetery on Boone's Creek, Washington County, Tenn., is following grave stone: "George Crouch, born June 14, 1784, died June 6, 1866."
Mary Hunt, daughter of Sarah Crouch and Samuel Hunt, was the wife of Peter Miller, Jr., a soldier in the War of 1812 (see Peter Miller Bible record, also compiled by Mary Hardin McCown).
There are many Crouch descendants in Washington County, Tenn. The Crouchs were members of Old Buffalo Ridge Baptist Church. Again we find them as charter members of the oldest Christian Church in Tennessee—the Boone's Creek Christian Church, organized about 1828 or 30. (Records are in existence from 1834.)

CHARLES BURTON BIBLE RECORD
(John Sevier Chapter, D. A. R.)

Copied March 18, 1932, from the original by Clara C. Coile, Johnson City, Tenn.

The Record:

BIRTHS

Charles Burton, son of William and Frances Burton, born Nov. 4, 1782.
Elizabeth Jane Quarles, daughter of Wm. and Ann Quarles, born March 27, 1790.
Frances Ann Louesia Penn Burton, daughter of Charles and Jane, born May 13, 1811.
Stephen Decatur Burton, son of Charles and Jane, born Friday, Oct. 8, 1813.

MARRIAGES

Charles Burton and Eliza Jane Quarles, married Dec. 14, 1808.
Stephen D. Burton and Polly Goodbar, married July 19, 1835.

DEATHS

William Burton, Sr., father of Charles Burton, died Jan. 7, 1811.
William Quarles, father of Eliza Jane Quarles, murdered on the road near White Plains April 2, 1814.
Departed this life Oct. 21, 1814, Eliza Jane Burton, after a severe illness of seventeen days.
Departed this life March 30, 1831, Frances Ann Louisa Penn Burton, after a severe illness of seventeen days, in the 20th year of her age.
Frances Burton, mother of Charles Burton, died Oct. 8, 1835.
Departed this life Aug. 17, A.D. 1842, Charles Burton, father of Stephen D. Burton, after a severe illness of fifteen days.

(End of the Record.)

(This record is copied from the family Bible record of my great-great-grandfather, Charles Burton, of White Plains, Putnam County, Tenn. The Bible, now in my possession, was printed and published in 1813 by M. Carey, No. 121 Chesnut St., Philadelphia.)

NOTES BY CLARA C. COILE

Wm. (Wm. P.) Quarles, born about 1752 in Caroline County, Va., one of the ten children of Roger (born 1720, died 1790) and Mary Goodloe (born about 1731) Quarles. He served as Ensign and Lieutenant in the First Virginia Regiment during the Revolutionary War (see Heitman's Historical Register of Officers of the Continental Army), and was a member of the Society of the Cincinnati in Virginia. In 1783 he married Ann Hawes (died 1844, Putnam County, Tenn.), daughter of William and Tabitha Tompkins Hawes, and to them were born ten children, seven girls and three boys. Sometime around 1800 William moved his family to Bedford County, Va., and thence in 1809 to White Plains, Putnam (then White) County, Tenn., where he was murdered in 1814, according to the above Bible record. His will is recorded in the Clerk's office (pages 22 and 23 in the Will and Inventory Book) of White County, Tenn. In 1931 a government marker was placed at the grave of Wm. Quarles in the family cemetery just off the old Walton Road, three miles east of Cookeville, Tenn.

BIBLE RECORDS
(Old Glory Chapter, Franklin.)

Bible of Joseph L. Parkes, late of Franklin, Tennessee, now owned by his daughter, Mrs. R. H. Crockett, of Franklin, Tennessee.

Holy Bible, published by Jasper Harding, Philadelphia, 1856.

FAMILY RECORD

Joseph Parkes, son of William and Elizabeth Parkes, born May 1, 1806, at Upton Forge, in County of Sallop, England.

Mary Ann Leonard, daughter of Samuel and Betsy Leonard, born May 2, 1812, at the Level, Parish of Kingswinford County, Stafford, England. We were married at Kingswinford Church Feb. 1, 1829.

Betsy Parkes, their daughter, born Feb. 1, 1830, died Feb. 20, 1830.

William Parkes, their son, born Jan. 30, 1831.

Thomas Parkes, their son, born Dec. 21, 1832, died Feb. 21, 1834.

Joseph Parkes, their son, born Feb. 11, 1835.

Henry Parkes, their son, born March 26, 1837, died April 7, 1839.

Martha Parkes, their daughter, born April 6, 1839.

Leonora Parkes, their daughter, born May 29, 1841.

Leonard Parkes, their son, born Jan. 9, 1844.

Mary Ann Parkes, their daughter, born March 13, 1846, died Feb. 17, 1849.

Elizabeth G. Parkes, their daughter, born June 24, 1848, died 1899.

Lydia Alice Parkes, their daughter, born May 14, 1851, died March 8, 1854.

Mary Lucena Parkes, their daughter, born Oct. 24, 1853.

They emigrated from Cradley Forge to Lawrenceburg, Tenn., and arrived Oct. 12, 1855, with their then living children, William and Joseph being already there.

William Parkes, son of Elizabeth and Wm. Parkes, born Dec. 5, 1786, at Knockin, in the County of Sallop, England.

Thomas Parkes, born Nov. 25, 1794.

John Parkes, born April 19, 1801.

Joseph Parkes, born May 1, 1806, at Upton Magna, in County Sallop, England.

Eliza Parkes, born at Upton Magna, Aug. 2, 1808.

Martha Parkes, born at Upton Magna, Mar. 18, 1814.

Bible of Mrs. Judith A. Walker, late of Franklin, Tennessee, now owned by her granddaughter, Mrs. R. H. Crockett, of Franklin, Tennessee.

Holy Bible, containing, etc., published by R. White & Hutchison & Dwier, Hartford, 1835.

FAMILY RECORD

MARRIAGES

Silas C. Walker and Judith A. Word were married at Brandon, Rankin County, Miss., May 27, 1834.

Joel C. Stevens and America Call Walker were married at Franklin, Tenn., by Prof. J. M. Sharpe, May 31, 1857.

Joseph L. Parkes and Louisa E. Walker were married at Franklin, Tenn., by Rev. Ira Marey, Friday, June 11, 1858.

Dr. James P. Hanner and Mary L. Walker were married at Franklin, Tenn., by Rev. A. N. Cunningham, Thursday, Nov. 30, 1865.

BIRTHS

Louisa Everly Walker, the first child of Silas Call Walker and Judith A. Walker, born April 7, 1836.

America Call Walker, the second child of Silas C. Walker and Judith A. Walker, born Sept. 6, 1838.

Mary Ann Walker, the third child of Silas C. Walker and Judith A. Walker, born Nov. 30, 1841.

DEATHS

America J. Walker, our dear mother, departed this life June 15, 1858. She breathed her last on Tuesday evening at 15 minutes past 7 o'clock and was borne to the Methodist Church on Wednes-

day evening at 4 o'clock, where her funeral was preached from the 23rd Psalm by Rev. W. D. T. Sawrie.
America Call Stevens, second daughter of Silas C. and America J. Walker, died at 5:30 p.m., Nov. 11, 1905.
Louisa Everly Walker Parkes, the first child of Silas C. and America J. Walker, and the wife of Joseph L. Parkes, departed this life at 6:30 p.m., April 7, 1908, aged 72 years.
Mary L. Walker Hanner, third child of S. C. and J. A. Walker, died Jan 1, 1914, aged 73 years.
John Word Parkes, second child of J. L. and L. E. Parkes, departed this life on Sunday, Feb. 16, 1862, at 4:45 p.m.
J. L. Parkes, departed this life May 22, 1911, at 12:15 a.m., aged 76 years.
William Walker Parkes, first child of J. L. and Louisa W. Parkes, departed this life at 6:20 p.m., Sept. 24, 1924.

Bible of Hugh Brown, contributed by Mrs. Eliza Brown Wallace, Old Glory Chapter, Franklin, Tennessee, No. 37,491, great-great-granddaughter of Hugh Brown.

This Bible was printed in London, England, in 1784, by Charles and Mark Kerr, *His Majesty's Printers.* Volume now in possession of Frederick Heiskell McCampbell, of Straw Plains, East Tennessee, great-great-grandson of Hugh Brown.

Record as follows:

Hugh Brown, born in Ireland Nov. 14, 1728, died 1792. He married Jane Kyle Sept. 17, 1755.
Joseph Brown, born in Ireland June 19, 1759, died Monday morning, 8 o'clock, May 15, 1843.
Hugh Brown (son of Joseph), born Sept. 4, 1791.
Mary Ann Susan Rice, born April 26, 1814, died about 2 o'clock on Friday morning, June 28, 1838, aged 24 years 2 months and 2 days.
Hugh Brown (son of Joseph), was married to Mary Ann Susan Rice at Rogersville on Thursday, April 5, 1832.
Eliza Brown (daughter of Joseph), born in Jonesboro, Tenn., Oct. 24, 1797. (Married F. S. Heiskell, 1816.)
Nancy Brown, born Dec. 15, 1802.
Eliza Brown Heiskell had the following children:
Margaret Brown Heiskell, born Feb. 11, Friday, 10 o'clock in the morning, 1820, died on Monday evening, Aug. 10, 1827.
Joseph Brown Heiskell, born on Wednesday at 2 p.m., 1823, Nov. 5.
Hugh Brown Heiskell, born on Monday, at 6 o'clock in the morning, Feb. 13, 1826.
Ann Eliza Peay Heiskell, born Jan. 27, 1829.
Margaret Alexander White Heiskell, born on Sunday, June 12, 1831 (married Jesse G. Wallace, 1851).
Susan Jacobs Heiskell, born March 28, 1834.
Carrick White Heiskell, born July 25, 1836.

Records from the family Bible of Mrs. Mary Roberts Truett, Franklin, Tennessee, published by Joseph Harding and Sons, Philadelphia, 1857.

BIRTHS

R. R. Roberts, born Oct. 16, 1828, Madison County, Ala.
Roshe Hamilton Robinson, his wife, born July 22, 1834, in Madison County, Miss.
Augustus Walton Robinson, born in State of Georgia Dec. 24, 1799.

Judith Amanda Truly, wife of Augustus, born April 28, 1801, Adams County, Miss.

CHILDREN OF AUGUSTUS AND JUDITH ROBINSON

John McCaleb Robinson, born Sept. 28, 1823.
George Milton Robinson, born Aug. 21, 1825.
Mary Caroline Robinson, born Dec. 9, 1826.
Derrick January Robinson, born Oct. 28, 1829.
Cordelia Ann Robinson, born June 10, 1832.
James Benjamin Robinson, born March 5, 1837.

CHILDREN OF ROSCHE HAMILTON ROBINSON AND R. R. ROBERTS

William Clifton Roberts, born Oct. 9, 1858, Chick County, Ark.
Richard Augustus Roberts, born March 12, 1861, Helena, Ark.
John Robinson Roberts, born May 10, 1865, Limestone County, Ala.
Mary Medora Roberts, born June 4, 1869, Pulaski, Tenn.

Records from family Bible of Col. John McGavock, late of Franklin, Tennessee, now in possession of his daughter, Mrs. Hattie McGavock Cowan, of Franklin, Tennessee, published by American Bible Society, 1846.

Col. John McGavock, born April 2, 1815, died June 7, 1893.
Caroline E. Winder, wife of Col. McGavock, born Sept., 1829, died Feb. 22, 1905, married Dec. 5, 1848.
George Limerick Cowan, born in Derry County, Ireland, Oct. 15, 1842, died Sept. 18, 1919.
Harriett Young McGavock, wife of George L. Cowan, born July 2, 1855, married January 3, 1844 (still living).
Winder McGavock, son of Col. John McGavock, born July 13, 1857, died June 3, 1907.
Susie Lee Ewen, wife of Winder McGavock, born April 4, 1863, died Oct. 25, 1931, married Feb. 5, 1883.

Records from the family Bible of Mr. and Mrs. James Newton Prather, Harrodsburg, Kentucky, published by J. B. Lippincott and Company, Philadelphia, 1859, now in possession of their daughter, Mrs. Freeman J. Hyde, Franklin, Tennessee.

George Robertson, LL.D., was born in Mercer County, Ky., Nov. 18, 1790, died May 16, 1874.
Eleanor Bainbridge Robertson, wife of George Robertson, born April 17, 1794, died Jan. 13, 1865, married Nov. 28, 1809.
Dr. David Bell, born July 9, 1810, died March 4, 1888, married Charlotte Corday Robertson, daughter of George Robertson, June 5, 1834.
Charlotte Corday Robertson Bell, born June 14, 1837, died March 11, 1894.
Alexander McIntosh, born 1705, died Nov. 18, 1780.
Eleanor James, wife of Alexander McIntosh, born Dec. 8, 1721, married May 3, 1737.
Dr. Peter Bainbridge, cousin of Commodore Bainbridge, born Oct. 8, 1739, died 1802.
Eleanor James McIntosh, wife of Dr. Peter Bainbridge, born Nov. 2, 1743, died 1793, married Jan., 1760.
Henry Prather, born Nov. 16, 1759, died Nov. 23, 1830.
Elizabeth G. Prather, wife of Henry Prather, born Dec. 3, 1765.
Joseph Glass Prather, son of Henry Prather, born July 5, 1806, died May 29, 1849.
Elizabeth L. Prather, wife of Joseph G. Prather, born Jan. 12, 1811, died April 18, 1888.
James Newton Prather, son of Joseph G. Prather, born Nov. 13,

1838, in Mercer County, Ky., died July 17, 1912; married March 17, 1859.

Nannie Holmes Bell, wife of James N. Prather, born Feb. 13, 1841, died Feb. 25, 1912.

Records from the family Bible of Samuel Crockett, of Augusta County, Virginia, later of Williamson County, Tennessee, now in the possession of his great-grandson, Dorsey T. Crockett, of Franklin, Tennessee, published and sold by Collins and Company, New York, 1814.

The family record is as follows:

BIRTHS

Samuel Crockett, born Feb. 1, 1772.
Joannah Sayers, born Nov. 20, 1772, married 1792.
Andrew Crockett, born Nov. 13, 1793.
David Crockett, born 1795.
Louisa Crockett, born Oct. 27, 1797, married Jan., 1821.
Mary Sayers Crockett, born Aug. 20, 1799, married McNeil.
Sally Elliott Crockett, born Sept. 20, 1801.
John Sayers Crockett, born May 30, 1803.
Samuel Crockett, born Feb. 13, 1805, married Margaret Lindsley.
Nancy Hamilton Crockett, born Nov. 27, 1806, married Ed Upshaw.
Robert B. Crockett, born May 27, 1808, married an Indian.
Esther Thompson Crockett, born Jan. 21, 1810, married E. Chapman.
Lucinda Joannah Crockett, born Feb. 1, 1812.

DEATHS

Samuel Crockett, died Jan. 30, 1827.
Joannah Sayers Crockett, died Sept. 17, 1812.
Andrew Crockett, died Sept. 12, 1852.
David Crockett, died 1799.
Louisa Crockett Johnson, died Aug. 1, 1833.
Mary Sayers Crockett McNeil, died June, 1838.
Sally E. Crockett Bain, died Jan. 27, 1878.
John Sayers Crockett, died Oct. 2, 1861.

Records from the Bible of Mrs. Catherine Walker Bell Crockett, wife of Andrew Crockett, the younger, presented to her upon her marriage April 4, 1818, by her father, Samuel Bell, of Davidson County, Tennessee.

In addition to the family record, this Bible has the following entry made in the handwriting of Mrs. Crockett:

"This is the property of Catherine Crockett, 12th of September, 1819."

This volume printed by and for William W. Woodward, No. 52 Second Corner of Chestnut Street, Philadelphia, 1813. The title page of the New Testament, included in the volume, bears the imprint:

"Philadlphia, printed by W. W. Woodward, No. 52 Corner of Second and Chestnut Streets, 1811."

Entries in handwriting of Mrs. Crockett as follows:

Andrew Crockett, born Nov. 13, 1793.
Katherine Bell, born Feb. 21, 1798.
Joanna Margaret Crockett, born March 4, 1819.
Samuel Crockett, born Nov. 17, 1820.
John Bell Crockett, born Nov. 11, 1822.
Andrew James Crockett, born Feb. 17, 1825.
Robert Thomas Crockett, born June 28, 1827.
Catherine Ann Eliza Crockett, born Nov. 29, 1829.
George Washington Bell Crockett, born July 13, 1832.
Ferdinand Crockett, born Dec. 9, 1834.
Rufus Alphonso Crockett, born June 18, 1837.
William Alonzo Crockett, born March 24, 1841.
Henry Theodore Crockett, born Feb. 1, 1845.
Andrew Crockett, married Katherine Bell April 8, 1818.
Andrew Crockett, died Sept. 12, 1852.
Samuel Crockett, son of A. and K. Crockett, died Feb. 9, 1822.
Robert Thomas Crockett, died Aug. 11, 1830.
Ferdinand Crockett, died May 24, 1836.

Records from the Bible of James J. Sayers, late of Williamson County, Tennessee. Publishers and date of publication of this Bible not known, title page having been mutilated and other parts of the Bible destroyed. But the pages having the family record have been preserved, in the handwriting of Mrs. Ann M. Sayers, the wife of James J. Sayers, who survived him for many years, and who died April 8, 1886.

The entries made by Ann M. Sayers, in the order as made, read as follows:

DEATHS

Robert Sayers, departed this life March 10, 1847.
James J. Sayers, departed this life April 6, 1863, at 8 o'clock a.m.
Robert B. Sayers, born Dec. 24, 1836.
Mary E. Sayers, born Oct. 18, 1839.
Ann J. Sayers, born April 8, 1844.
Sarah Josephine Sayers, born Nov. 19, 1846.
James J. Sayers, born March 14, 1801.
Ann M. Sayers, born March 16, 1806.
James J. Sayers and Ann M. Sayers, married Jan. 29, 1835.

MURPHEY BIBLE RECORD

Sent by Mrs. Eugene McDade, Mountain City.

Abraham Murphey, father of Sterling, Keren, Hawkins P., John, Kemp and Elbert, born May 18, 1796, and died Feb. 6, 1882.
Mary Murphey, mother of John, Kemp and Elbert, died Oct. 14, 1856.
Catherine Murphey, wife of Abraham Murphey, born March 9, 1812, died Thanksgiving Day, Nov. 22, 1904; married Sept. 13, 1857, by A. J. Brooks, minister.
Kemp Murphey and Susan C. Wills, married Nov. 11, A.D. 1869, by Abraham Murphey.

DEATHS

Susan C. Murphey, died Feb. 23, 1902.
Judge Sherman Murphey, died Oct. 21, 1893.
John G. Murphey, died Feb. 26, 1899.

Births

Hawkins P. Murphey, born June 1, 1816.
Kemp Murphey, born July 20, 1841.
Susan C. Murphey, born April 16, 1853.
James Hawkins Murphey, born Nov. 5, 1870.
John Grant Murphey, born July 21, 1872.
Ollie May Murphey, born March 17, 1874.
Hugh Elbert Murphey, born May 30, 1876.
Hattie Belle Murphey, born March 9, 1880.
Annie Eliza Murphey, born June 25, 1882.
Jessie Murphey, born Oct. 3, 1884.
Kate Murphey, born July 21, 1888.
Judge Sherman Murphey, born June 22, 1891.
Ruth Rebekah Murphey, born Sept. 11, 1895.

———

(The Berry, Donnelly, Keys, Murphey, Morrison and Walker records are copied from family Bibles.)

Walker Bible Record

George Walker, departed this life July 16, 1833, and William, our son, departed this life July 27, 1833.
George Walker was 35 years and 2 days old when he departed this life.
George Walker and Mary, his wife, were married on Dec. 19, 1822.
William Walker, their son, born Friday, April 10, 1824.
Mitchell Walker, born Thursday, Oct. 6, 1825.
Cornelia Ann Walker, born Jan. 6, 1828.
G. E. Walker, born Thursday, March 11, 1830.
Abner Walker, born Thursday, Jan. 11, 1833.
John Murphey, born Saturday, Nov. 23, 1839.
Kemp Murphey, born Tuesday, July 20, 1841.
Elbert Murphey, born Saturday, Aug. 2, 1846.

Morrison Bible

Sarah West, born April 22, 1818.
James Morrison, born Nov. 25, 1817.
James Morrison and Sarah West were married Nov. 14, 1834.
Sarah Jane Morrison, born Aug. 6, 1853.
Margaret Isabell Morrison, born April 17, 1856.
Margaret Isabell Morrison, departed from life March 2, 1860.
Martha Morrison, wife of James Floyd Morrison, died May 2, 1873.
Anna Embrosia Thompson, born Feb. 26, 1868.
William Oliver Morrison, born Aug. 17, 1872.
J. T. Beaty, born Sept. 21, 1827.
Nathaniel Morrison, born Dec. 28, 1836.
Hetha C. Morrison, born Nov. 8, 1838.
David Morrison, born March 14, 1840.
Benjamin H. Morrison, born Jan. 8, 1842.
Nancy A. E. Morrison, born March 8, 1844.
William T. Morrison, born May 4, 1846.
John R. Morrison, born March 2, 1848.
James T. Morrison, born Aug. 3, 1850.

Record from the Old Donnelly Bible

Births

Catherine Brown, born Feb. 29, 1772.
Henery Brown, born May 20, 1775.
Mary Morley, born Aug. 4, 1776.
Elizabeth Shaver, born March 31, 1778.
Wm. Brown, born Dec. 26, 1780.

Presented to Continental Hall Library by Mrs. Eugene McDade in honor of the State Regent, Mrs. Joseph Hayes Acklen

Peter Brown, born Dec. 31, 1782.
George Brown, born April 12, 1784.
Joseph Brown, born Feb. 6, 1786.
Richard Donnelly, born Aug. 17, 1790.
William Donnelly, born Feb. 15, 1792.
Lucy Donnelly, born Dec. 20, 1794.
Catherine Donnelly, born July 9, 1798.
Mary Donnelly, born Aug. 13, 1808.
Robert Donnelly, born in Ireland, April 27, 1760.
Sarah McQueen Donnelly, born June 4, 1801.
Rebecca Gwyn McQueen, born Nov. 13, 1773.
Richard Alex. Donnelly, born Nov. 5, 1824.
William Kendrick Donnelly, born Jan. 14, 1827.
Rebecca Jane Donnelly, born Oct. 2, 1829.
Nancy Ann Elizabeth Donnelly, born May 7, 1832.
Robert Henry McMullin Donnelly, born Jan. 2, 1835.
John McKillup Donnelly, born Feb. 25, 1837.
James Carter Donnelly, born Oct. 20, 1839.

Deaths

William Donnelly, departed this life Feb. 16, 1842, in his 51st year.
Sarah Donnelly, departed this life Dec. 24, 1876, in her 75th year.
William McQueen, departed this life May 16, 1860, in his 88th year.
Eve Donnelly, departed this life Dec. 19, 1806.
Franky Donnelly, departed this life Jan 29, 1827.
Robert Donnelly, departed this life Aug., 1832, in his 73rd year.

Marriages

Robert Donnelly, married to Eve Donnelly (Sevely Brown) Aug. 29, 1789.
Robert Donnelly, married Franky Donnelly (Jennings) Aug. 20, 1807.
William Donnelly, married Sarah (McQueen) Donnelly Feb. 26, 1824.
Richard A. Donnelly, married Matilda (Sullivan) Donnelly, Jan. 30, 1850.
Thomas J. Crosswhite, married Rebecca Donnelly Oct. 29, 1851.
Benjamin W. Jenkins, married Nancy A. E. Donnelly Jan. 16, 1853.
Robert H. Donnelly, married Eloza Jane Allen April 15, 1860.
James C. Donnelly, married Careloin Elizabeth Rominger April 7, 1861.
William Kendrick Donnelly, married Rachel Alice (Moore) Kiser Aug. 31, 1865.

Berry Bible Record

Marriages

James W. McQuowen was married to Rachel Ann Wills June 7, 1841.
Robert E. Berry was married to Rachel A. McQuowen, Sept. 27, 1857.
William E. Scott was married to Margaret R. McQuown, June 18, 1866.
A. T. Berry and Rhoda L. Crockett were married Aug. 7, 1883.

Births

James W. McQuown, born April 14, 1819.
Rachel Ann McQuown, born July 18, 1825.
John Russel McQuown, born March 29, 1847.
Margaret Rebecca McQuown, born Jan. 25, 1849.
Laura Jane McQuown, born June 2, 1851.
James L. W. McQuown, born June 12, 1853.
Lucinda Wills, born Oct. 31, 1813.
Peter D. Wills, born Jan. 16, 1816.
Susannah Wills, born Feb. 21, 1818.
R. B. Wills, born July 7, 1820.
Rebecca Wills, born Jan. 15, 1823.
R. L. Crockett, born March 12, 1863.
Robert E. Berry, born Feb. 1, 1831.

Rachel A. Berry, born July 18, 1825.
Alexander Thomas Berry, born Oct. 21, 1858.
Will E. Scott, born Sept. 27, 1842.
Maggie McQuown, born Jan. 25, 1849.
Charles R. Scott, born May 2, 1867.
John Walter Scott, born Jan 2, 1869.
Moses Berry, born April 16, 1803.
Dorcos L. Berry, born Aug. 28, 1802.
Lewis Wills, born April 1, 1784.
Catherine Wills, born Aug. 24, 1783.
James Berry, born May 20, 1833.
Thomas T. Berry, born Feb. 12, 1835.
James W. Scott, born July, 1870.
Bertie F. Scott, born Feb. 29, 1872.
Elizabeth Wills, born Dec. 9, 1865.
Mary Wills, born Jan. 30, 1808.
James Wills, born Nov. 21, 1809.
Nancy S. Wills, born Nov. 21, 1811.

Deaths

James W. McQuown, died July 26, 1853.
Lewis Wills, died July 29, 1855.
Catherine Wills, died Nov. 15, 1874.
R. B. Wills, died Jan. 21, 1876.
R. D. Wills, died July 14, 1878.
Margaret R. Scott, died Jan. 13, 1873.
William E. Scott, died March 22, 1875.

Keys Bible

Births

Robert W. Keys, born Jan. 9, 1814.
Susan Wills Keys, born Feb. 27, 1818.
Marcus A. Keys, born Oct. 1, 1841.
Caina Hesteline Keys, born April 4, 1843.
Emma Louise Keys, born Nov. 2, 1844.
Zachary Taylor Keys, born Sept. 18, 1846.
Veteria Ann Keys, born Nov. 10, 1848.
James Donnelly Keys, born Oct. 1, 1850.
Margaret Catherine Keys, born Sept. 2, 1852.
Mary Adaline Keys, born Nov. 6, 1854.
Robert Russell Keys, born May 3, 1857.
Susan Rebecca Keys, born Nov. 12, 1863.

Marriages

Robert W. Keys and Susan Wills, Dec. 3, 1840.
Marcus A. Keys and Mary E. Smith, March, 1861.
Emma P. Keys and Landon H. Hawkins, Dec. 5, 1867.
Veteria Ann Keys and Jacob Cornett, Oct. 25, 1866.
Margaret C. Keys and Liley Thomas, April 29, 1875.
Mary A. Keys and Richard D. Hawkins, Jan. 25, 1877.
David D. Keys and Martha Ellen Ramsey, Jan. 28, 1877.

Bible Record

William H. Nave, born 1843; died 1924.
Wife, Mary E. Dugger Nave, born 1841; died 1920.
David Henry Nave, born 1866.
Wife, Amelia Moore Nave, born 1874.
Joel Eastridge, born 1837; died 1927.
Wife, Sarah Rominger Eastridge, born 1838; died 1902.

Wagner

Daniel Wagner, born 1746; died 1827; buried in the grave yard of the Bethany Reformed Church in Davidson County, North Carolina. Matthias Wagner, born 1765; died 1835; buried in the Wagner grave yard, 4 miles south of Mountain City, Tenn. He had four sons, Joseph, Matthias, Jacob and Fredrick.

From Joseph Wagner's family Bible:

Joseph Wagner, born Dec. 5, 1799; died Dec. 5, 1899; married Nancy Wagner, born 1810; died 1887. They had 13 children:
Andrew C., born 1828; married Hiley Baker.
Alexander B., born 1831; married Nancy Catherine Baker.
Margaret A., born 1832; never married.
Susanah, born 1834; married Andrew Smith.
Matthias W., born 1836; married Sarah Howard.
Sarafine C., born 1838; married Andrew Shoun.
David, born Dec. 20, 1839; married Nancy Dugger.
Rachel, born 1841; married John B. Vaught.
Mary Ann, born 1843; married Dugger Pierce.
Joseph, born 1845; married Louise Smith.
Jacob, born 1847; married Mary Reece.
Nancy Catherine, born 1850; never married.
Daniel, born 1852; married Alice Smith.

From Alexander B. Wagner's Family Bible. Sent by Mrs. James Wagner, Mountain City.

Alexander B. Wagner, born 1831; married Nancy Catherine Baker. They had five children:
Andrew J., born 1851; married Sarah Jane Whitehead.
Amanda Elizabeth, born 1853; married John M. Donnelly.
James P., born 1855; married Titia Voncannon.
David W., born 1858; married Susan Maples.
Nancy Naomi, born 1860; married Lafayette Wagner.

From John M. Donnelly's family Bible:

Amanda Elizabeth Wagner married John M. Donnelly in 1878. They had five children:
Alexander C., born July 4, 1880.
Kendrick S., born 1882.
Parlee, born 1884.
James O., born 1886.
Robert W., born 1888.

From the family Bible of Matthias Miller Wagner:

Matthias Miller Wagner, born June 30, 1801, died Feb. 15, 1887; married to Mary Fyffe in 1829. They had 11 children:
Isaac R., born 1830; never married.
Caroline E., born 1832; married Thomas J. Faw.
Alzenia P., born 1833; married Samuel D. Jackson.
Matthias F., born 1834; married Titia Worth.
Daniel W., born 1835; never married.
James F., born 1837; never married.
Mary M., born 1838; died in infancy.
Luke Lee, born 1839; died in infancy.
Joseph H., born 1841; married Sallie White.
Noah J., born 1844; married Nellie King.
Wiena Safronia, born 1846; never married.

From the family Bible of Noah J. Wagner:

Noah J. Wagner, born April 16, 1844; died Feb. 26, 1931; married to Nellie King Sept. 14, 1869. They had seven children.
Charles M., born 1870; married May Murphey.
Joseph Hugh, born 1872; never married.

Julia Mary, born 1875; married W. White Newberry.
Carrie, born 1878; married Richard E. Donnelly.
James I., born 1880; married Mae Hill.
Addie Boyd, born 1883; married Robert P. London.
Noah King, born 1886; married Martha Sorrell.

From the family Bible of James I. Wagner:

James I. Wagner, born March 8, 1880; married to Mae Hill Sept. 12, 1906. They have one child, Louise Linville Wagner, born Sept. 18, 1909.

From the family Bible of Joseph H. Wagner:

Joseph H. Wagner, born Jan. 14, 1841; died June 16, 1910; married to Sallie K. White June 18, 1874. They had eight children:
Mary, born 1875; married J. B. Johnson.
Matthias M., born 1878; married Belle Milburn.
Noah J., born 1880; died in infancy.
Fletcher, born 1882; died in infancy.
Joe White and George White, twins, born 1884. Joe married Winfred Church; George married Sandol Chapman.
Martha Faw, born 1887; married Archie Leslie.
Nell, born 1890; married Dudley C. Wiley.
Sarah, born 1893; married Walter Robinson.

From the family Bible of I. W. Nave:

Parlee Donnelly, born June 8, 1884; married to I. W. Nave, 1907. They have four children:
Marilyn, born 1908; married Wallace B. Carden.
Catherine; born 1910; married Chas. Evert Kepley.
Dick, born 1912.
Hal, born 1918.

From family Bible of Wallace B. Carden:

Marilyn Nave, born April 20, 1908; married Walace B. Carden Nov. 3, 1930. They have one child: Walace B. Carden, Jr., born July 9, 1932.

Bible Records

(Spencer Clack Chapter, Sevierville, Mrs. Stanley McMahan, Regent.)

Births

Wellington McMahan, the son of James McMahan and Rachel McMahan, born Sept. 16, 1817.
Catherine Hammer, the daughter of Jonathan and Sarah Hammer, born May 3, 1818.
Julia Ann McMahan, the daughter of Wellington and Catherine McMahan, born July 5 1844.
Sarah McMahan, the daughter of Wellington and Catherine McMahan, born Jan. 28, 1847.
Isaac Calvert McMahan, the son of Wellington and Catherine McMahan, born April 28, 1849.
Rachel Emy McMahan, daughter of Wellington and Catherine McMahan, born March 14, 1852.
Robert Bruce McMahan, the son of Wellington and Catherine McMahan, born May 28, 1855.

Boulder of white quartz brought from the Great Smoky Mountains, dedicated in honor of Spencer Clack during the regency of Mrs. Stanley MacMahon, by the Spencer Clack Chapter, D. A. R.

Paul Wellington McMahan, the son of Wellington and Catherine McMahan, born May 24, 1858.
(The record above was formerly owned by Katherine Hammer McMahan and is now the property of Mr. Bruce McMahan, Sevierville, Tenn.)

Bible Records

Births

Richard West Crowson, born July 8, 1810.
Nancy Allen Crowson, born March 26, 1818.
Mary C. Crowson, born Nov. 27, 1838.
Martha Jane Crowson, born Jan. 10, 1841.
William Crowson, born Sept. 26, 1843.
Aaron Crowson, born Jan. 9, 1846.
James Wells Crowson, born Oct. 6, 1848.
Joseph Crowson, born March 21, 1851.
Richard West Crowson, born Jan. 24, 1854.
Sarah Elizabeth Crowson, born Dec. 31, 1857.
Nancy Caroline Crowson, born Jan. 8, 1860.
(This record is the property of Mr. Robert Bruce McMahan, who now resides in Sevierville, Tenn., and was the property of Katherine Hammer McMahan, the mother of Mr. Bruce McMahan.)

Bible Records

The oldest Bible record I have been able to find is the property of Mrs. Sallie Mullendore Massey, who now resides in Sevierville, Tennessee, who is also the oldest living descendant of the Spencer Clack for whom our chapter was named, and following is some of this record:

Births

Jno. Mullendore, Oct., 1800.
Dialtha P. Mullendore, Feb. 11, 1810.
Abraham Lafoyett Mullendore, June 11, 1830.
Mary Amanda Mullendore, April 26, 1832.
William Wallace Mullendore, Feb. 21, 1834.
Elijah Leonadas Mullendore, Dec. 15, 1835.
Robert Bruce Mullendore, Jan. 26, 1842.
Jno. Newton Mullendore, Feb. 6, 1840.
Susanne Katherine Mullendore, Feb. 25, 1842.
Nancy Matilda Mullendore, April 17, 1844.
Jane Elizabeth Mullendore, April 16, 1846.
Malvina Caroline Mullendore, Jan. 29, 18—.
David R. Mullendore, March 8, 1851.
Dialtha N. Mullendore, May 31, 1854.
Sally Josephine Mullendore, June 24, 1855.

Bible Records

Births

Geo. McCown, born July 5, 1790.
Polly Porter, born Dec. 11, 1795.

Their Children

Penelope C. McCown, born June 13, 1813.
John P. McCown, born Aug. 19, 1815.
Mitchell W. McCown, born Oct. 21, 1817.
Eliza C. McCown, born April 22, 1820.
Matilda E. McCown, born June 3, 1822.

George W. McCown, born Oct. 29, 1828.
Melville McCown, born July 16, 1837.

Sarah M. Runyan, born Dec. 28, 1823 (second wife of George McCown).

THEIR CHILDREN

Aaron Marcus McCown, born June 23, 1840.
Arthur McCown, born Jan. 26, 1859.

MARRIAGES

George McCown and Polly Porter were married July 24, 1812.
Benjamin C. Mathis and Penelope C. Mathes were married Sept. 11, 1834.
Joshua Nichol and Eliza C. McCown were married Dec. 2, 1842.
Flail Nichol and Matilda E. McCown were married Feb. 11, 1844.
George McCown and Sarah M. Runyan were married Sept. 4, 1845.

DEATHS

Polly McCown, wife of Geo. McCown, died Sept. 28, 1837, aged 41 years 9 months and 17 days.
Melville McCown, died Sept. 30, 1837, aged 2 months 14 days.
Sarah McCown, wife of Geo. McCown, died March 23, 1865, aged 41 years 4 months and 23 days.
George McCown, died July 28, 1871, aged 81 years and 23 days.
(The above record was the property of Sarah Runyan McCown and is now the property of Mrs. Sallie Houk, Sevierville, Tenn.).

JAMES WHITE BIBLE

Sent by Miss Kate White, Honorary State Historian.

James White, founder and owner of Knoxville. Bible now in the Cal McClung collection in the Lawson McGhee Public Library, the gift to the library by William W. French, a direct descendant of James White.

MARRIAGES

James White and Mary Lawson were married April 14, 1770.
Cynthia Berry White was married to Thomas A. Smith Sept. 17, 1807.

BIRTHS

Margaret White, born April 8, 1771.
Hugh Lawson White, born Oct. 30, 1773.
Moses White, born April 22, 1775.
Andrew White, born May 9, 1779.
Mary McConnell White, born Nov. 11, 1782.
Cynthia Berry White, born April 7, 1786.
Millenda White, born Feb. 15, 1789.
Lucie Ann Smith, born Nov. 11, 1812.
James White Smith, born Sept 5, 1851.

DEATHS

Hugh Lawson White, departed this life April 10, 1840, in his 67th year.
Elizabeth Carrick White, his wife, departed this life March 25, 1831.
My granddaughter, Isabella White, departed this life Nov. 30, 1805.
Samuel I. Carrick, departed this life July 8, 1814, aged 35 years.
The Rev. Samuel G. Ramsay, departed this life July 5, 1817.
Mary Lawson White, departed this life March 10, 1819, 3:30 in the morning, age 77 years.
Gen. James White, departed this life Aug. 14, 1831.
Andrew White, died Oct. 6, 1806.
Rev. Samuel Carrick, departed this Aug. 18, 1809.
Rebecca L. Williams, our granddaughter, departed this life July 22, 1810, aged 10 months.
James White Williams, departed this life April 30, 1817, age 10 months.
Dr. F. T. May, departed this life Nov. 26, 1817, age 40 years.

The Hugh Lawson White Bible was a gift to the library by Miss Mary Alcesta Legerwood of Knoxville, a granddaughter of the late John H. Crozier.

HUGH LAWSON WHITE BIBLE RECORDS

Hugh Lawson White and Elizabeth Carrick were married by the Rev. Samuel G. Ramsay, Dec. 14, 1789. She died March 25, 1831, leaving a son.

Charles Andrew Carrick White, their son, born Dec. 22, 1797; died Jan. 18, 1826, leaving a wife and three children; buried in Knoxville.

James Moon May White, their second son, born Oct. 23, 1801; died Nov. 16, 1828, at Tuscaloosa, Ala., where he was buried, leaving a wife and son and daughter, Polly Lawson White.

Betsy Moon White, their oldest daughter, born Aug. 23, 1803; married John Newton Scott in 1818, who died 1819. She died Nov. 12, 1828, leaving one daughter, Nancy Scott.

Polly Lawson White, their second daughter, born Oct. 16, 1805; married William Swan in 1827, and died May 13, 1828, leaving no children, and was buried in Knoxville.

Lucinda Blount White, their third daughter, born Sept. 19, 1807; died March 20, 1827; never married; buried in Knoxville.

Peggy Ann White, their fourth daughter, born Nov. 17, 1809; married Ebenezer Alexander. Their oldest child, Elizabeth, died June 1, 1831, and was buried at Judge Overton's place near Nashville, Tenn.

Peggy Ann, died at her father's home in Knoxville, Aug. 25, 1831, and buried in Knoxville.

Cynthia Williams White, their fifth daughter, born July 29, 1812; died Jan. 3, 1829; unmarried; buried in Knoxville.

Malinda McDowell White, their sixth daughter, born May 21, 1815; died April 3, 1830.

Hugh Lawson White, their third son, born Aug. 16, 1818; died Jan. 20, 1819.

Isabella Harvey White, eighth daughter, born May 19, 1820.

Samuel Davis Carrick White, their fourth son, born May 26, 1825.

GRANDCHILDREN

Nancy N. Scott, daughter of Betsy Moon White, born 1819.

Sophia Elizabeth, Hugh Lawson and James Park, children of Charles A. C. White, James White, died 1827; buried in Knoxville.

James, John and Elizabeth, children of James Moon May White.

Elizabeth Alexander, daughter of Peggy Ann White, born 1830; died June, 1831.

JAMES PARK BIBLE RECORDS

BIRTHS

James Park, born in County Donegal, Ireland, April 14, 1770.

Sophia Moody Park, born in Wilmington, Del., April 2, 1770.

Park, Nancy Aiken, born Dec. 7, 1804.

Nancy Aiken Park, born Dec. 7, 1804.

Andrew Park, born March 2, 1806.

William P. Park, born Dec. 10, 1807.

Sophia Park, born Nov. 7, 1809.

Eliza Park, born Sept. 6, 1811.

Mary Park, born Aug. 25, 1813.

Harriet Park, born Aug. 25, 1813.

Hugh Park, born Jan. 15, 1816.

Margaret Park, born Oct. 10, 1817.

Jean Park, born Sept. 18, 1819.

James Park, born Sept. 18, 1822.

Carrick White Park, born Oct. 2, 1826.

Sophia Eliza Park, born March 27, 1822.

Hugh Lawson White Park, born March 7, 1824.

James White Park, born Dec. 24, 1825.

Georgean Washington English, born Oct. 13, 1834.

Marriages

James Park and Sophia Moody, married Feb. 23, 1804.
Nancy Aiken Park, married Charles A. C. White, Oct. 25, 1821.
Sophia Park, married George Moon White, March 9, 1827.
Andrew Park, married Ananda M. Morgan, April 22, 1830.
William Park, married Sarah Jane Crockett, April 28, 1836.
Eliza Park, married Charles H. Coffin, Jan. 4, 1837.
Mary Park, married George W. English, Oct. 13, 1833.
Margaret Park, married James M. Welcker, Dec. 11, 1860.
Jean Park, married Langdon Bowie, Sept. 28, 1841.
Sophia Eliza Park, married Robert Craighead, Sept. 28, 1841.
Mary England Park, married William S. Kennedy, Jan 1, 1843.
James Park, married Phebia C. Alexander, May 27, 1847.
Carrick White Park, married Jane Deadrick, Dec. 8, 1859.

Deaths

Sophia Park, died Oct. 14, 1816.
Charles A. C. White, died Jan. 18, 1826.
Nancy Aiken White, died Jan. 3, 1827.
James White Park, died Jan 27, 1826.
Hugh Lawson Park, died May 12, 1843, in his father's home.
Sophia Elizabeth Park Craighead, died Jan. 19, 1850.
James Park, Sr., died Sept. 19, 1853.
James M. Welcker, died April, 1858.
Margaret Welcker, died March 10, 1892.
Andrew Park, died in St. Louis, Mo., Feb. 21, 1892.
Carrick White Park, died Sept. 18, 1890.
Sophia Moon Park White, died April 30, 1894.
George Moon White, died Dec. 18, 1889.
William Park, died Nov. 24, 1895.
Sophia Park Brooks, died April 28, 1886.
James Park Craighead, died at the home of Rev. James Park.
Robert Craighead, died in Nashville Oct. 1, 1829.
Carrick White Park, died Sept. 28, 1890.
Sophia Moody Park, died Jan. 16, 1812.
John Craighead, died April 14, 1853.

Charles McClung Bible Records

Mr. Charles McClung came to the territory south of the Ohio before it was a territory. He was the first land surveyor in Knox County. Charles McClung married Margaret White, daughter of James White, the founder and owner of Knoxville, Oct. 20, 1790.

Births

Polly Lawson McClung, born May 28, 1792.
Hugh M. McClung, born May 22, 1794.
Matthew McClung, born Oct. 10, 1795.
James White McClung, born June 6, 1798.
Charles McClung, born July 28, 1800.
Betsy Jones McClung, born May 6, 1803.
Martha McClung, born June 18, 1805.
Hugh Lawson McClung, born May 26, 1811.
Ann Malinda McClung, born Oct. 26, 1812.

Marriages

Polly Lawson McClung, married to Thomas S. Williams, Aug. 5, 1811.
Matthew McClung, married to Cynthia Morgan, Jan. 9, 1818.
Betsy Jones McClung, married to John McGhee, Sept. 5, 1820.

Charles McClung, married to Malivna Louise Miller, July 3, 1824.
James White McClung, married to Sarah Elizabeth Mitchell, April 29, 1823.
Hugh Lawson McClung, married to Rachel Kibby Trig Morgan, Nov. 5, 1829.
Margaret M. McClung, married to Ebenezer Alexander, Jan. 31, 1833.
James White McClung, married Elizabeth Spottswood, his second wife, March 1, 18—.
Hugh Lawson McClung, married to Ann Gillespie, his second wife, daughter of George Gillespie and his wife, Elizabeth Carter, daughter of Landon Carter and his wife, Elizabeth McLinn, who lived in Carter County, Tenn., were married at Clover Field, the family residence, July 31, 1845.
Blanch McClung, their daughter, born in Knoxville April 10, 1846.
Iredell Lawson McClung, their son, born at Clover Field June 2, 1855.

BIRTHS

Charles McClung, son of Matthew McClung of Lecock Township, Lancaster County, Penn., and his wife, Margaret Cunningham, who was a sister of James McCampbell, who owned Campbell County, Va., May 13, 1761.
Margaret White, born in Iredell County, N. C., April 8, 1771.

CHILDREN

Children of Polly L. McClung and Thomas Williams:
Rebecca Williams, born Oct. 21, 1812.
Charles Williams, born Nov. 20, 1815.
Margaret Williams, born Oct. 7, 1817.
Malinda Williams, born Feb. 9 1820.
Betsy Williams, born June 4, 1823.
Morgan Williams, born ———.

———

Children of Betsy J. McClung and John McGhee:
Margaret McGhee, born July 2, 1821.
Barckly McGhee, born Sept. 2, 1823.
Charles McClung McGhee, born Jan. 23, 1828.

———

Children of James and Sarah E. Mitchell McClung:
Charles William McClung, born March 13, 1824.
Mary Ann McClung, born Dec. 6, 1825.
David Bridie Mitchell McClung, born April 2, 1827.
Hugh Lawson White McClung, born May 11, 1829.

———

Children of Matthew McClung and Elizabeth Morgan McClung:
Calvin Morgan McClung, born May 14, 1823.
Margaret McClung, born May 15, 1822.
Sarah Ann McClung, born July 5, 1824.
Charles James McClung, born Aug. 26, 1826.
Franklin H. McClung, born Nov. 25 1828.
Lawson Smith McClung, born ——.
Matthew McClung, born ——.
Amanda McClung, born ——.

———

Children of Charles and Mary L. Miller McClung:
Charles McClung, born Sept. 17, 1822.
Pleasant Miller McClung, born Aug. 19, 1824.
Albert Stewart McClung, born ——.

———

Children of H. L. and R. K. T. Morgan McClung:
Margaret McClung, born Dec. 8, 1830.
Rufus Morgan McClung, born May 20, 1830.
James White McClung born April, 1834; died June 31, 1834.
Lizzie Trigg McClung, born April 20, 1836.
Mary Frances McClung, born Jan. 16, 1838.
Rachel Filmore McClung, born Sept. 9, 1840.
Charles Oliver McClung, born Oct. 24, 1842.

Deaths

Margaret M. McClung, died Aug. 27, 1827.
Charles McClung, died Dec. 25, 1827.
Robert L. Williams died June 16, 1828.
Betsy Jones Miller, died April 8, 1829.
Matthew McClung, died Oct. 5, 1844.
James White McClung, died May 21, 1848.
Margaret McClung Alexander, died July 27, 1864.

Births

Children of Margaret McClung and Ebenezer Alexander:
Margaret McClung Alexander, born Oct. 31, 1833.
Charles McClung Alexander, born Jan. 5, 1835.
Eliza Janes Alexander, born Oct. 11, 1829.
Mary Hill Alexander, born Nov. 22, 1842.

J. M. Murphy Family Bible

Marriages

Malachi Murphy, born Feb. 19, 1765.
Dorcas Murphy, born May 29, 1780.
Malachi Murphy and Dorcas Dobbins, married Sept. 6, 1796.
Hugh Murphy, son of Malachi, married Rebecca Barnett, March 8, 1822.
Joel Gossett, married Margaret Murphy, Feb. 21, 1828.
Wiley Murphy, married Mary Robinson, Sept. 14, 1836.
Dennis Murphy, married Margaret Hill, July 27, 1826.
James K. D. Murphy, married Rebecca Fad, Jan. 2, 1859.
Ruth Spark Murphy, married John Smith, June 21, 1836.
Daniel Franklin Murphy, married Martha Fad, Jan. 15, 1859.
Almira Chapman Murphy, married William Robinson, Jan. 16, 1842.
Nancy Bell Murphy, married —— Airheart, Nov. 18, 1824.

Births

Hugh Murphy, born Oct. 6, 1787.
Margaret Johnson Murphy, born June 30, 1789.
Dennis Claiborn Murphy, born May 7, 1801.
Mary Bird Murphy, born March, 1803.
Mary Ann Jackson Murphy, born Jan. 11, 1805.
Willie Blount Murphy, born June 10, 1807.
Richard Sevier Murphy, born May 12, 1810.
Jackson Dobbins Murphy, born Nov., 1811.
Ruth Sparks Murphy, born May 21, 1813.
Daniel Franklin Murphy, born Nov. 26, 1814.
Mary Booth Murphy, born Sept. 29, 1816.
Rebecca Jane Murphy, born Oct. 25, 1820.
Almira Chapman Murphy, born Feb. 15, 1826.
Keeble Manley, born July 3, 1807; died Jan. 1, 1882.
James Kennedy Mickels, born Nov. 5, 1852.
Elizabeth Jane Mickels, born Jan. 25, 1854.
Dorcas Emily Mickels, born July 24, 1856.

Deaths

Willey B. Murphy, died July 3, 1842, age 32 years.
Alice B. Murphy, died March 14, 1850.
Ruth S. Murphy, died June 15, 1819.
Jane M. Murphy, died May, 1854, age 35 years.
Dennis C. Murphy, died May 18, 1834.
Dennis Murphy, died Nov. 21, 1837.
Jacob Mickles, died Sept. 14, 1828.
Mary Jackson Mickles, died Sept. 11, 1838.
Hugh Murphy, died Sept. 30, 1833.
Malachi Murphy, died Feb. 12, 1841, age 75 years.

KENNER FAMILY BIBLE

BIRTHS

Marther Kenner, born Dec. 8, 1828.
Mary Kenner, born Oct. 29, 1830.
Jane Kenner, born Oct. 16, 1830.
Maurina Kenner, born Oct. 6, 1824.
John M. Kenner, born Aug. 8, 1834.
Licinda Kenner, born March 25, 1839.
Franklin Kenner, born ——— 12, 1841.
Christopher Kenner, born Oct. 1, 1843.
Nancy Kenner, born Sept. 27, 1845.
Virginia Kenner, born Jan. 19, 1850.

MARRIAGES

James Kenner, married Susan Mitchell, Jan. 19, 1828.
John Davis, married Martha Kenner, March 3, 1841.
George F. Ferguson, married Vane Kenner, March 31, 1850.
Mary Kenner, married N. P. Baldwin, March 14, 1852.
Maurina Kenner, married William Tayers, April 20, 1853.

DEATHS

Susan Kenner, died Jan. 6, 1881.
James Kenner, died July 21, 1870.
C. E. Kenner, died Dec. 21, 1870.
John M. Kenner, died June 28, 1875.
Lucinda K. Water, died Feb. 16, 1924.
Sue Water, died Jan. 10, 1924.
Margaret Water, wife of James, died Dec. 4, 1925.
Virginia K. Sneed, died Jan. 30, 1870.

BIRTHS

James Kenner, born May 14, 1803.
Susan Kenner, born Jan. 28, 1810.
John Waters was a soldier in the Confederate Army.

SHEDDAN BIBLE RECORDS

MARRIAGES

Charles Kelso Sheddan and Ann McClain Wilson, married Feb. 17, 1822.
Thomas Sheddan and Jane McClung, married March 28, 1851.
Robert C. Sheddan and Nancy Duncan, married Aug. 8, 1850.
James A. Sheddan and Mary B. Rankin, married March 19, 1851.
James McClung and Martha Sheddan, married Nov. 1, 1855.
Joseph C. Sheddan and Margaret Malcome, married Oct. 21, 1855.
William E. Sheddan and R. E. Blackwell, married Nov. 22, 1857.
William D. West and Nancy C. Sheddan, married Jan. 14, 1867.
John E. Sheddan and Belle Davis, married Sept. 21, 1869.
William Stuart and Talutha Sheddan, married Sept. 27, 1870.

BIRTHS

Charles E. Sheddan, born Feb. 5, 1799.
Ann McClain Sheddan, born June 3, 1815.
James A. Sheddan, born Feb. 21, 1824.
Thomas W. Sheddan, born Oct. 4, 1825.
Robert C. Sheddan, born Dec. 5, 1827.
William E. Sheddan, born Nov. 18, 1829.
John E. Sheddan, born March 9, 1832.
Joseph Sheddan, born May 24, 1834.
Martha J. Sheddan, born May 27, 1800.
Talitha Sheddan, born June 16, 1827.
Charles C. Sheddan, born Aug. 19, 1839.
Newton H. Sheddan, born Feb. 17, 1842.
Nancy C. Sheddan, born Dec. 16, 1845.
Andrew Sheddan, born Feb. 23, 1847.
Jane Eakin, born Sept. 29, 1784.
John Eakin, born Nov. 19, 1788.
Jane Sheddan, born Jan., 1797.

Charles Kelso Sheddan, born Feb. 5, 1799.

DEATHS

Margaret J., wife of Thomas Sheddan, died Feb. 28, 1842, age 82 years.

Thomas Sheddan, died Aug. 6, 1845; born 1765.

Charles C. Sheddan, died Sept, 1757, at Big Springs, Blount County.

Martha J. McClung, died Sept. 24, 1857.

Martha H. Sheddan, died Sept. 24, 1857.

Joseph C. Sheddan, died Oct. 25, 1859.

James A. Sheddan, died Oct. 25, 1857.

Andrew S. Sheddan, died Oct. 24, 1879.

Charles Kelso Sheddan, died March 2, 1879, age 70 years.

Ann McClain Sheddan, died Nov. 5, 1882, age 79 years.

William E. Sheddan, died Aug. 30, 1887.

T. W. Sheddan, died Feb. —, 1902.

J. E. Sheddan, died Sept. 26, 1908.

Robert Cooper, died Aug. 7, 1922.

Tame Pamplan, died July 16, 1825, age 86 years.

Mrs. Nancy Caroline West, died June 19, 1825.

Records from a Bryan family Bible owned by Joe Bryan, Coffee County. Sent by Mrs. James Elkins, McMinnville.

John Bryan, born March 7, 1780; married Sarah Bucy May, 1803, North Carolina.

Abner Bryan, born Jan. 17, 1804; married Abnedo Roberts.

Matthew Bryan, born Oct. 23, 1805; married Fanny Stroud.

David Barton Bryan, born Aug. 4, 1807; married Nancy M. Powell.

Enoch Bryan, born March 22, 1810.

John Alexander Bryan, born March 2, 1812.

Joseph Bryan, born March 4, 1814.

William H. Bryan, born March 13, 1816.

Sarah Elizabeth Bryan, born Sept. 28, 1930; married Cyrus Browne.

James Issac Bryan, born March 8, 1821.

Isham Bryan, born March 18, 1823.

Marquis LaFayette Bryan, born Dec. 31, 1824; married Selma Catherine Wagner; died Jan. 1, 1865.

Sarah E. Bryan, died Dec. 1, 1849.

John Bryan, died Oct. 28, 1854.

Family Bible of Frank Smartt and Wife, Margaret Davidson Smartt, Warren County. Sent by Mrs. Elkins.

MARRIAGES

Frank Smartt, son of Wm. Cheek Smartt and Margaret Davidson, daughter of John Davidson, married Sept. 1, 1825.

David Vance McLean and Margaret M. Smartt, widow of Frank, married April 4, 1844.

Geo. N. Whitson and Caroline Smartt, married April 29, 1845.

Robt. B. McLean and Martha Smartt, married June 20, 1848.

BIRTHS

Martha C. Smartt, born Jan. 28, 1831.

Caroline Smartt, born Sept. 19, 1826.

Margaret Smartt, born Dec. 29, 1828.

Wm. D. Smartt, born Sept. 23, 1832.

Bettie A. Jones, born April 25., 1850.

DEATHS

Frank Smartt, died March 17, 1843, age 38 years.

Martha L. McLean, died Dec. 19, 1849.

Caroline Whitson, died Feb. 24, 1864.

David Vance McLean, died April 29, 1871, age 69 years.

Margaret (Davidson, Smartt, McLean) Gwyn, died May 14, 1881, age 73 years.

Bible of Joseph Colville. Sent by Mrs. Elkins.

Joseph Colville, born June 18, 1764.
Sarah Lusk, his wife, born June 15, 1765.
Peggy (Margaret) Colville, born March 25, 1787.
Samuel Colville, born March 9, 1789.
Lusk Colville, born May 27, 1791.
Elizabeth Colville, born April —, 1793.
Joseph and Sallie Colville, born June 15, 1797.
Davidson Colville, born June 27, 1795.
Catherine Colville, born Nov. 10, 1799.
Sallie Cheek Colville, born Jan. 10, 1804.
Jane (Lowery) Colville, born March 7, 1809.
Joseph Colville, died Jan. 1, 1834.
Martha Colville, died Jan. 25, 1837.
Joseph Colville, married Martha Cheek Smartt, mother of Wm. Cheek Smartt, Dec. 25, 1801.
Joseph Colville, married Sarah Lusk.

Bible of John Davidson, Bedford County, Tenn.:

Hugh Davidson, born Jan. 29, 1795.
James Davidson, born Sept. 12, 1796.
William Davidson, born July 8, 1798; died Nov. 3, 1816.
George Davidson, born March 10, 1800.
Lorenzo D. Davidson, born June 29, 1804.
Margaret Davidson, born Dec. 26, 1807.
Andrew M. Davidson, born Oct. 22, 1811.
Mary Davidson, born Oct. 4, ——.

CHILDREN OF MAJ. WM. DAVIDSON OF NORTH CAROLINA

John Davidson, born Oct. 4, 1764.
George Davidson, born Jan. 5, 1768.
Jane Davidson, born June 1, 1772.
Sarah Davidson, born July 29, 1774.
Ruth Davidson, born Nov. 2, 1777.
William M. Davidson, born June 2, 1780.
Samuel W. Davidson, born April 2, 1782.
Elizabeth Vance Davidson, born July 1, 1775.

Copied from Rodham Kenner's family Bible, Rodgersville, Tennessee. Sent by Mrs. Elkins.

Francis Kenner and wife, married ——.
Rodham Kenner, born ——.
Malinda Paine.
Howser Kenner, son, born Feb. 4, 1787.
Rutha Kenner, born April 15, 1789.
Bettie Kenner, born May 25, 1791.
Sallie Kenner, born Oct. 7, 1793.
James Kenner, born March 7, 1796.
Matilda Kenner, born April 15, 1798.
Polly Kenner, born Aug. 12, 1800.
Francis Kenner, born Nov. 12, 1802.
Eliza Kenner, born Jan. 30, 1805.
Rodham Kenner, born March 15, 1807.
Cummings McCoy, born Oct. 10, 1800.
Francis Kenner McCoy, born Dec. 17, 1825.
Bettie Kenner, died Feb. 4, 1810.
Rodham Kenner, died July 18, 1812.
Sallie Kenner, died Sept. 23, 1814.

FAMILY NAMES

Cyrus D. F. Browne, born Aug. 14, 1871, S. C.; died Feb. 2, 1859, Coffee County.
Sarah Elizabeth Browne, born April 28, 1820, Coffee County, Tenn.; died Oct. 29, 1858.

Gidean Rufus Browne, born Oct. 16, 1843, Coffee County; died Dec. 20, 1861, Nashville, Tenn.

London Bucy Browne, born Oct. 4, 1844, Coffee County, Tenn.; died Sept. 28, 1899, Warren County.

Nancy Caroline Browne, born March 6, 1846, Coffee County, Tenn.; died Aug. 24, 1860, Warren County, Tenn.

John Driies Browne, born Sept. 9, 1847, Coffee County, Tenn.; died Nov. 27, 1869, Warren County.

Sarah Eliazbeth Browne, born April 9, 1849, Coffee County, Tenn.; died Jan. 20, 1916, Warren County.

Abner Moore Browne, born Aug. 13, 1850, Coffee County, Tenn.; died March 10, 1866, Coffee County, Tenn.

Catherien Adella Browne, born Aug. 16, 1852, Coffee County, Tenn.

Eliza Ferrwice Brown, born in Coffee County, Tenn.; died March 29, 1893, Franklin County, Tenn.

Cyrus Adeon Browne, born Feb. 6, 1856, Coffee County, Tenn.; died Oct., 1888, Viola, Tenn.

Leyrenssee Frances Browne, born Sept., 1858, Coffee County, Tenn.

PARKER—CRYER—KING—MANNING—BROWN

Bertie County—Wills and Marriages, North Carolina Register, Vol. 2, page 65. Sent by Ethel Ward Patton, Nashville.

On Oct. 7, 1780, Richard Parker married Elizabeth King.

Also is found the will of Richard Parker mentioning son, King Parker. The following information as told to Kenneth Paine Brown by his great-aunt, Tennessee (Tennie) Brown Matthews, age 82, who was a granddaughter of King Parker. She says she often played in the old white satin-lined carriage which brought King Parker's family from North Carolina.

King Parker married (in N. C.) Elizabeth Cryer, and brought their children to Tennessee, settling in Sumner County near Gallatin. They also brought slaves and furniture, building a log cabin later, burning their own brick and erecting a lovely brick home, which still belongs to his descendants, "the Browns."

The writer, Ethel Ward Patton, mother of Kenneth Paine Brown, great-great-grandson of King Parker and Elizabeth Cryer Parker, often talked to Mrs. Annie Brown, wife of Thos. H. Brown (grandson of King Parker), who for many years lived in the old home. She said sometime in the improving of this house a part was walled in, which held an old trunk and other things which may be of great value and interest to the descendants today.

She also had some beautiful old furniture, a sugar chest, a clock, a rope-spool bed and other antiques from this home.

(Kenneth Brown is very interested in his family and feels that there is much material that can be compiled through the combined efforts of descendants of the Parker-Cryer-King and Brown and Manning families.)

CHILDREN OF KING PARKER AND ELIZABETH CRYER

Elizabeth married Barton B. Brown, who was reared in Georgia by his grandparents.

Cherry married an Ellis.

Mary married a Perry.

Hardy, Samuel, John, Tom, and George.

CHILDREN OF BARTON B. BROWN AND ELIZABETH CRYER PARKER

1. Robert King, Methodist minister, whose children were Jimmie Franklin, no children; Sophia Manning, seven children; Madeline Moore, no children.

CHILDREN OF ROBERT KING BROWN AND SOPHIA MANNING

(a) Manning, married Elizabeth Long of Hopkinsville, Ky, whose children were: (1) Manning, Jr., married, 1 child, a doctor in Mayo's Clinic, Honolulu; (2) Robert King, married, one child, a chemist in China; (3) Madeline, married McFarland Wood, U. S. Army, one child.
(b) Erle, married, one adopted child, lives in California.
(c) Robert, died while student at Vanderbilt University, age about 25.
(d) Julian, unmarried.
(e) Kenneth Paine, married Ethel Dake Ward Nov. 1, 1908; one son, Kenneth Paine, Jr., born Dec. 28, 1909.
(f) Virginia, died young, about 8.
(g) Mary, died in infancy.
2. Martha, married Charles Clarke, whose children were: (1) Fulton, married, lives in Birmingham; (2) Jimmie; (3) David; (4) Brown; (5) Emma, known as Bird.
3. Alfred Douglas, fought all through the Civil War in Virginia; married Ellen Clarke, sister of Chas. Clarke.
4. Thomas H., married Annie Hunt, whose children were: (1) Alfred, married, two children; (2) Barton B., married Harriet Mills, one daughter, Betty; (3) Charles, married; (4) Thomas, married Catherine Acklen, four children: Catherine, Thomas, Janet, and Ann Hunt.
5. Virginia (called Jennie), married Chas. Adams, one son, died young.
6. Tennessee (called Tennie), married John W. Matthews, no children.
7. Wesley.
8. Hardy, was chaplain in Braggs Army, married Louise McGhee, four children: (1) Robert; (2) Lula, married E. K. Campbell, whose daughter, Mary, married Lewis Underwood, son of Oscar Underwood; (3) Floy Bell, now Mrs. Ohme; (4) Ed.

JOHN HAYS BIBLE

Facts obtained from the family Bible of John Hays. Bible now in possession of Mrs. Frieda Hays Pate, who lives at 1043 W. Greenwood Ave., Nashville, Tenn. Sent by Anne Carver Graves, Nashville.

Robert Hays, father of John Hays, born Nov. 11, 1800, died July 26, 1870; married Methursy Wilson, Dec. 27, 1827, by William Saunders.
Methursy Wilson, born May 5, 1805, died June 6, 1872.
Henry Hays, father of Robert Hays, who died in 1812; married Nancy Tate in Virginia.
William Wilson, father of Mathursy Wilson, married Elizabeth Craven, Aug. 17, 1803.
The children of Robert and Mathursy Hays were:
Anderson Hays, born Dec. 20, 1841.
Mary Jane Hays, born Nov. 16, 1837.
Martha Hays, born 1843.
John Hays, born Feb. 17, 1845, died May 27, 1920.
George Melvin, father of Mahala Melvin, born Oct. 1, 1828, died April 11, 1863; married Hess Obryant, Feb. 5, 1846.
Hess Obryant, born Oct. 3, 1831, died about 1910.
Edward Melvin, father of George Melvin, married Mrs. Nancy Cowgill, Dec. 22, 1825, by Absolum Gleaves.
John (Jack) Obryant, father of Hess Obryant, married Mahala Wilson, Dec. 21, 1826, by Absolum Gleaves.
John Hays married Mahala Wilson in 1868.
The children of George and Hess Melvin were:
Mahala Melvin, born Sept. 9, 1848; died April 13, 1921.
John Melvin, born 1850.

Mollie Melvin, born 1852; died about 1913.
The children of John and Mahala Hays were:
George Robert Hays, born Nov. 9, 1870, died Aug. 13, 1917.
Junius Hays, born 1872, died March, 1904.
Dr. John Hays, born March 7, 1876.
Ada Beatrice Hays, born 1780, died Oct., 1904; married John Pomeroy in 1903; one infant child, who died Oct., 1904.
George Robert Hays, son of John and Mahala Hays, of Davidson County, Tenn., born Nov. 9, 1870, died Aug. 13, 1917; married Flora Adeline Carver, Dec. 20, 1890.
Flora Adeline Carver, daughter of Alexander J. and Almeda Adeline Carver, born Feb. 20, 1873, died March 24, 1920.
The children of Geo. Robert and Flora C. Hays are:
John Oakley Hays, born Dec. 15, 1891.
Freida Bethman Hays, born March 4, 1896.
Adeline Beatrice Hays, born Oct. 12, 1902.
Mahala Hays, born Aug. 14, 1906.
Flora Edith Hays, born Aug. 7, 1910.
John Oakley Hays, married Leona Cunningham, Oct. 15, 1914.
The children of John Oakley and Leona C. Hays are:
J. O., Jr., born April 6, 1922.
Dorothy Leona Hays, born June 4, 1923.
Frieda B. Hays, married Earl Graves Pate, Jan. 6, 1919.
The children of Frieda Hays and Earl Graves Pate are:
Miriam Louelle Pate, born Oct. 12, 1919.
Earl Graves Pate, born June 4, 1923.
Frieda Jean Pate, born Nov. 25, 1924.
Lloyd Whitefield Pate, born July 26, 1926.
Adeline B. Hays married John Henry Pate, May 14, 1925.
The children of Adeline Hays and John Henry Pate are:
Joe Henry Pate, born March 28, 1926.
Virginia Adeline Pate, born May 31, 1928.
Robert Hays Pate, born Oct. 12, 1929.

JOSEPH SHACKLEFORD BINKLEY BIBLE

Facts obtained from the family Bible of Joseph Shackleford Binkley, born in Davidson County, Tenn. Bible now in possession of his son, Henry Clay Binkley, 902 Chicamauga Ave., Nashville, Tenn.

Frederick Binkley, father of Joseph S. Binkley, born Feb. 15, 1774, died Sept. 18, 1857; married Adeline Shackleford, daughter of Roger Shakleford and Nancy Carter, born in Virginia May 17, 1789, died Sept. 15, 1868; Fredrick and Adeline Shackleford were married Dec. 24, 1804.
Joseph Shackleford Binkley, born Nov. 19, 1810, died Aug. 21, 1887; married Martha Buchanan Steele, July 18, 1833.
Martha Buchanan Steele, daughter of Samuel Steele and Patience Shane, born Dec. 9, 1811, died July 28, 1859.
Samuel Steele, son of Andrew Steele and Martha Buchanan, born May 13, 1782, died March 7, 1864; married Patience Shane, June 19, 1805.
Patience Shane, daughter of Morris Shane and Phoebe Castleman, born Sept. 2, 1787, died June 4, 1852.
The children of Joseph S. and Martha Steele Binkley were:
Mary, born Oct. 13, 1834, died Aug. 8, 1884.
Fredrick Summerfield, born June 22, 1836, died June 23, 1836.
Benjamin Franklin, born May 3, 1837, died Dec. 17, 1903.

Malvina, born May 1, 1839, died June 12, 1852.
Amanda Rebecca, born Oct. 21, 1841.
Almeda Adeline, born Nov. 18, 1843, died April 14, 1887.
Ann Leady, born Nov. 11, 1845.
Henry Clay, born Nov. 25, 1847.
Martha Elizabeth, born Dec. 24, 1849, died June 18, 1852.
Samuel Steele, born Oct. 2, 1851, died March 7, 1883.
Joseph Pitts, born May 14, 1854, died April 8, 1921.
David C. Kelley, born June 30, 1857; died Aug. 14, 1928.
Joseph S. Binkley's second wife was Elizabeth Ivey Holland, daughter of Jaret and Elizabeth Ivey, died July 15, 1879.
Their daughter was Elizabeth Clark, born May 5, 1862, died Dec. 6, 1879.
Joseph S. Binkley's third wife was Mrs. Hettie Ellis Young, married Oct. 31, 1885.

Marriages

Frederick Binkley, son of John and Johanna Leedy Binkley, born in North Carolina, Feb. 15, 1774, died Sept. 18, 1857, married Dec. 24, 1804, to Adeline Shackleford, daughter of Roger and Nancy Carter Shackleford, born in Virginia May 17, 1789, died Sept. 15, 1868.
Samuel Steele, son of Andrew and Martha Buchanan Steele, born in Virginia May 13, 1782, died March 7, 1864; married, June 19, 1805, to Patience Shane, daughter of Morris and Pheobe Castleman Shane, born in Tennessee, Sept. 2, 1787, died June 4, 1852.
Joseph Binkley and Martha Buchanan Steele, married July 18, 1833.
Their children were:
Mary Binkley and Samuel Steele, married Jan. 12, 1851.
Amanda Rebecca Binkley and Frederick Marshall Binkley, married Jan. 7, 1862.
Almeda Adeline Binkley and Alexander Jefferson Carver, married Feb. 18, 1866.
Benjamin Franklin Binkley and Matilda Markham, married March 25, 1866.
Ann Leedy Binkley and Joshua Beadle, married April 8, 1868.
Henry Clay Binkley and Ree J. McGee, married April 16, 1874.
Joseph Pitts Binkley and Alice Moss, married April 30, 1876.
David Campbell Kelley Binkley and Florence Dickson, married May 13, 1883.

Historical Facts of the Binkley Family

Peter and John Binkley came to Pennsylvania in or about 1717 from Herrnhut, Saxony. At least one other brother came with them and he remained in Pennsylvania while Peter and John came to North Carolina.
They were in North Carolina in 1727 and were present when a committee met on March 24, 1727, to establish the line between Virginia and North Carolina. Peter Binkley's home had been recommended as a place for the surveyors to stay while at work in that section. The state line ran by John Binkley's property.
Peter Binkley later went to Monakasy, Md., near Frederickstown, and was connected with the Moravians there. In 1770 he came to Wachovia, N. C., as a Communicant Brother and bought 300 acres of land. In 1771 he bought 309 acres more.
He was born in 1704. He spent much of his time preaching and visiting in the homes. He had his Memoir written by Sr. Cramer July 12, 1782. He died in 1793.
Seven sons survived—John, Adam, Joseph, Jacob, Peter, Jr., Frederick and Christian.
Adam and Jacob came to Tennessee about 1782. John Binkley's fourth child, Frederick, came to Tennessee with his uncles. Adam Binkley settled with his family on Sycamore Creek in Cheatham Co., and Jacob Binkley went to Robert-

son County, near Springfield. Frederick Binkley bought and built on Stones River, twelve miles from Nashville, Tenn. His old home is now owned and occupied by a Gleaves family.

John Binkley and two other sons and their families came to Tennessee in 1779.

There were several different ways in which the name Binkley was spelled when they first came to America. Among them were: Pinkley, Pinkly, Prinkley, Binkel, Brinkley and later Binkley, since 1780.

John Binkley married Johanna Leedy in Pennsylvania and they came to Stokes County, N. C., in 1772. Their children were:

Peter.

Elizabeth, who married a Mr. Childress.

John, who married Elizabeth Wright.

Frederick, born in 1774, and married Adeline Shackelford in 1804.

Jacob, who married Miss Frey.

Joseph never came to Tennessee.

Henry, who married in Missouri.

Abraham, who married in Missouri.

Daniel, who married Catherine Moser.

George, who married Isaac Earthman's daughter.

Katherin, who married Henry Frey.

Sarah, the youngest child, married Peter Frey.

Steele Family History

Samuel Steele, father of Andrew Steele, born 1709, died 1790, in Virginia.

Andrew Steele, born about 1755. He married Martha Buchanan in 1780. Martha Buchanan was the daughter of Archibald and Agnes Bowen McFerrin Buchanan, born 1762. Andrew Steele came to Tennessee from Montgomery County, Va., and bought land on Caney Fork in 1793.

The children of Andrew and Martha Buchanan Steele were:

Archibald Steele, who married and left a family near Natchez, Miss.

John and James Steele, who were twins. John married a Miss Compton. James married on Caney Fork.

Andrew Steele, who married on Caney Fork.

Mary Steele, who married Perry Magnes.

Nancy Steele, who married Charles Hall.

Samuel Steele, born 1782, and married Patience Shane 1805.

The children of Samuel and Patience Shane Steele were:

Rebecca, who married Thomas Wood.

James Steele, who married Judith Wood.

Polly Steele, who married William Harper Wright.

Martha Buchanan Steele, born in 1811, and married Joseph Shackleford Binkley in 1833.

Shane Family History

Morris Shane (McShane) ran away from his home in Ireland when very young. He came to Tennessee in the early part of 1780. He entered 640 acres near Goodlettsville in 1785.

He married Phoebe Castleman about 1785. They were present at the Buchanan Fort the night of the Indian attack Sept. 30, 1792. Morris Shane was on guard in the block house nearest the creek and was the first to discover and fire on the Indians who were congregating at the fort gate. Mrs. Buchanan and Mrs. Shane sprang from their beds without taking time to dress and started molding bullets and passing them to the men, along with brandy and words of cheer.

Phoebe Castleman Shane was the daughter of Jacob and Rhoda Robertson Castleman, the sister of John, Jacob, Andrew, Benjamin and Joseph (?).

The children of Morris and Phoebe Castleman Shane were:

John Shane, who married Nancy Drennon.

Jacob Shane, who married a Miss Bowles.

Andrew Shane, who married Martha Green.

James B. Shane, who married Asenath Guthrie.

Cornelius, who never married.

Nellie and Nancy were twins. Nellie never married. Nancy married William Melvin, Aug. 12, 1812.

Sarah Shane, who married Jeff Stephens.

Rebecca, who never married.

Rhoda Shane, who married Thomas Strong.

Margaret Shane, who married William Baldwin.

Patience Shane, born Sept. 2, 1787; married Samuel Steele, June 19, 1805.

The children of Roger and Nancy Carter Shackleford, all born in Virginia, were:

Elizabeth, who married a Mr. Busby.

Nancy Anne, born Oct. 8, 1779, died April 26, 1870; married Henry Guthrie, Nov. 24, 1796.

Adeline, born May 17, 1789, died Sept. 15, 1868; married Frederick Binkley, Dec. 24, 1804.

John.

The children of Frederick and Adeline Shackleford Binkley were:

Henry John, who married a Miss Gleaves.

John Henry, who married Mary Walker.

William Blackman, who married Emiline Wilson.

Joseph S., born Nov. 19, 1810, died Aug. 21, 1887; married Martha Buchanan Steele, July 18, 1833.

Franklin, who married Indiana ———.

Frederick, who married Catherine Crockett.

James Guthrie, who married a Miss Daniel.

Jasper Newton, who married Amanda Yorbrough.

Nancy, who married John Dickson.

Almedia, who married Jacob Kirk.

Robert Foster, who married Isabella Steele.

Martin David, who married Emma Caskey.

Sallie, who married Alfred Bass.

Andrew.

Carver Family Bible

Facts obtained from the family Bible of the Carver families. The older Carver Bibles were destroyed by fire. The following information obtained from the family Bible now in possession of Mrs. Anne Carver Graves, Belle Meade Drive, Nashville, Tenn. Many facts obtained from Mrs. Graves' father, A. J. Carver, who spent the most of remaining years with her. He died March 23, 1930, aged 88 years.

Thomas and Clara Carver of North Carolina came to Tennessee about 1800. Some of their children were:

William Carver, died 1856.

Thomas Carver.

Benjamine Carver.

Isaac Carver, born Oct. 19, 1791, died July 16, 1858; married Mary Hummer Hughly, Oct. 12, 1817.

The children of Isaac and Mary Carver were:

Isaac Newton Carver.

William H. Carver.

George Washington Carver.

Henry Carver, born Jan. 20, 1820, died Aug. 18, 1868; married Elizabeth Annis Hamblen, Dec. 24, 1840.
Frances Carver, married Mr. Clements.
Mary Carver, married Levi W. Wright.
Rachel Carver, married Charlie Cook.

The children of Henry and Elizabeth Carver were:
Alexander Jefferson Carver, born March 5, 1842, died March 23, 1930; married Almeda Adeline Binkley, Feb. 18, 1866.
Joseph Madison Carver, born 1844, died in 1863, while in Confederate service.
Pleasant S. Carver, born Nov. 24, 1846, died April, 1902.
Patrick Carver, born 1853, died 1916; married Mattie Wright.
James H. Carver, born April 5, 1855, died May 21, 1911; married Fannie Hamilton.
Henry Isaac Carver, born Nov. 27, 1852, died June 12, 1927; married Araminta A. Carver; second wife, Elizabeth Steele.
Martha Jane Carver, born July 13, 1848, died March 16, 1870.
Sarah Ellen and Mary Emily Carver, born Oct., 1850. Sarah married Albert Hardy Ellis, Nov. 6, 1870, and died Aug. 20, 1892; Mary married James E. Bridges, Dec. 19, 1867, and died Nov. 1, 1880.
Annis Tryphena, born March 20, 1860, died Jan. 15, 1913; married Bell Smart.
Nicie Carver, born 1858, died 1900; married James Cook about 1875.

The children of Alexander J. and Almeda Adeline B. Carver are:
Martha Elizabeth Carver, born Feb. 11, 1867, died Sept. 21, 1883.
William Owen Carver, born April 10, 1868; married Alice Hughes Sheppard, Dec. 29, 1897.
Joseph Binkley Carver, born Jan. 14, 1870; married Mary Maude Mann, Feb. 13, 1892.
Henry Barnett Carver, born Aug. 21, 1871; married Alma Wright, March 13, 1895.
Flora Adeline Carver, born Feb. 20, 1873, died March 24, 1920; married Geo. R. Hays, Dec. 20, 1890.
Allie Cawthorn Carver, born June 16, 1874, died April 19, 1889.
Alexander Jefferson, Jr., born March 4, 1876, died Nov. 7, 1896.
Anne Tryphena Carver, born Feb. 23, 1878; married Geo. B. Graves, Nov. 25, 1901.
Benjamine Joshua Carver, born June 24, 1880; married Sada Palmer, Aug. 18, 1905.
David June Carver, born Aug. 12, 1882; married Hally Council, 1907.
Granville Williams Carver, born June 14, 1885; married Lillie Hughley, 1906.

The children of William Owen and Alice S. Carver are:
William Owen Carver, Jr., born April 21, 1900; married Peggy Clemmons.
James Edward Carver, born April 30, 1902.
George Alexander Carver, born 1904; married Saxon Rowe, 1929.
Ruth Carver, born Sept. 26, 1898; married Norfleet Gardner, 1921.
Dorothy Sheppard Carver, born Oct. 10, 1909.
Alice Hughes Carver, born Feb. 26, 1912.

The children of Joseph B. and Maude Carver are:
Christine Carver, born Aug. 11, 1893, died June 2, 1930; married Bruce Lunsford, 1913.

The children of Flora C. and Geo. R. Hays are:
(See Hays family records.)

The children of Anne C. and Geo. R. Graves are:
(See Graves family records.)

The children of Ben. J. and Sada P. Carver are:
Palmer Carver, born March 6, 1906; married Orville Lena Eskew, Nov. 25, 1931.
Anne Graves Carver, born May 23, 1908, died March 16, 1910.

Ben. J., Jr., born July 14, 1910, died Sept. 1, 1914.

The children of David J. and Hally C. Carver are:
Margaret Binkley Carver, born Nov. 1, 1910.
David June, Jr., born 1915.
Anne Council Carver, born May 11, 1918.

The children of Granville W. and Lillie H. Carver are:
Douglas Preston Carver, born April 6, 1908.
Granville Ervin Carver, born July 29, 1909.
Duncan Alexander Carver, born Feb. 12, 1911.
Joseph Binkley Carver, born May 13, 1912.

The children of Alexander J. and Lucy Dement (second wife) Carver are:
Ollie Delle Carver, born Oct. 23, 1888; married Boone W. Taylor, Dec. 17, 1920.
Nannie Belle Carver, born July 20, 1890; married William Carlos Raines, Oct. 8, 1913.
Grace Carver, born July 4, 1893; married Roy C. Goodall, Nov. 25, 1914.
Byron Graves Carver, born Oct. 27, 1891, died July 15, 1916.
Gertrude Carver, born Jan. 26, 1895.
Lona Carver, born Jan. 3, 1897; married Robt. S. Busby, May 25, 1915.
Zena Mae Carver, born Sept. 4, 1899; married Roland G. Bloomfield, April 29, 1823.
Fields Bernard Carver, born Aug. 2, 1902.
Iona Carver, born Feb. 16, 1905, died March 5, 1905.

The children of Nannie Belle C. and Carlos Raines are:
Charles Carver Raines, born Aug. 13, 1914.
Alexena Raines, born Dec. 29, 1916.

The children of Grace C. and Roy C. Goodall are:
Roy Carver Goodall, born April 24, 1917.
Lucy Ellen Goodall, born July 9, 1919.
David Truett Goodall, born July 14, 1921.

The child of Lona C. and Robt S. Busby is:
Erlene Rose Busby, born March 25, 1916.

The children of Ruth C. and Norfleet Gardner are:
Lelia Gardner, born Oct. 9, 1923.
Alice Ruth Gardner, born May 10, 1923.

The child of Christine C. and Bruce Lunsford is:
Bruce Lunsford, born May 29, 1920.

The child of Geo. and Saxon R. Carver is:
George Alexander Carver, Jr., born Jan. 14, 1930.

The child of James E. and Isabelle Carver is:
James Edward Carver, Jr., born Aug. 26, 1930.

The children of J. O. Hays and Leona Cunningham are:
(See Hays family records.)

The children of Freida H. and Earl Graves Pate are:
(See Hays family records.)

The children of Adeline H. and J. Henry Pate are:
(See Hays family records.)

Wade Hampton Graves Bible

Facts obtained from the family Bible of Wade Hampton Graves, born on Salt Lick, Jackson County, Tenn. Bible now in possession of his son, Geo. B. Graves, Belle Meade Drive, Nashville, Tenn.

Beamon Graves, father of Wade Hampton Graves, born Jan. 13, 1788, died July 12, 1865.
Susannah Pate Graves, wife of Beamon Graves, born 1793, died Sept. 26, 1892.
Wade Hampton Graves, born Nov. 10, 1932, died Aug. 28, 1901; married Elvira Elizabeth Teel, Jan. 1, 1857.
Elvira E. Teel Graves, born July 29, 1840, died Jan. 22, 1912.

The children of Wade Hampton and Elvira T. Graves were:
Bernetta Susan, born April 7, 1860.
Josephine, born April 27, 1862, died July 9, 1862.
Cartez Henry, born March 21, 1864, died Jan. 5, 1874.
George Beamon, born Jan. 14, 1868.
Verlena Edna, born Aug. 17, 1875.
Lee Hatton, born March 3, 1872, died Feb. 28, 1875.
Infant daughter, born 1858, died 1858.

Bernetta Graves and James Radford Draper were married Dec. 7, 1879. They had one child, a son, who lived only a few days.

Lena Graves and Joseph J. Pate were married July 25, 1895. Their children were:
Earl Graves, born June 14, 1896.
Willie George, born Oct. 5, 1897, died July 28, 1902.
John Henry, born June 29, 1899.
Alberta Teele, born June 25, 1812.

George Beamon and Anne Carver Graves were married Nov. 26, 1901. Their children were:
Martha Marna, born Aug. 10, 1906.
Anne Elizabeth, born Aug. 24, 1912.

Mrs. Nettie Graves Draper married J. W. Draper, Jan. 18, 1891.
She married J. A. Montgomery, Nov. 1, 1916.
She married J. R. Richmond, Nov. 28, 1920.
She was faithful to each husband unto death.

Earl Graves Pate and Frieda B. Hays were married Jan. 6, 1919. Their children were:
Miriam Louell, born Oct. 12, 1919.
Earl Graves, Jr., born June 4, 1923.
Frieda Jean, born Nov. 25, 1924.
Lloyd Whitefield, born July 26, 1926.

John Henry Pate and Adeline B. Hays were married May 14, 1925. Their children were:
Joe Henry, born March 28, 1926.
Virginia Adeline, born May 31, 1928.
Robert Hays, born Oct. 12, 1929.

Beamon Graves and Susannah Pate were married about 1810.
Sally Graves, married Phillip Ray.
Susannah (Puss) Graves, married Jim Ray.
Armannilla Graves, died about the age of 15.
Jerry Graves, who moved to St. Joseph, Mo., and there left a large family.
John Gassaway Graves, died while a young man.
Octavos (Tobe) Graves, married Elvira Thaxton.
Wade Hampton, married Elvira Elizabeth Teele.
Henry Mickelberry Graves, married Jennie Pate, died during the Civil War and was buried in Richmond, Va.
Beamon Graves was the son of Easom Graves and Judith Parrott of Halifax County, Va., who were married Jan. 11, 1787. They came to Tennessee in 1805.
Easom Graves was the son of John Graves of Spotsylvania County, Va.
Some of John Graves children were:
Reuben Graves, born 1760; married

Elizabeth Yarbrough, Nov. 28, 1786. He fought in the Revolutionary War.
Polly Graves, married Akin Roberts, 1794.
Frances Graves, married John Shepard.
William Graves, married Rebecca East.
Winfield Graves.

Susannah Pate Graves was the daughter of Stephen and Polly Pate.
Stephen Pate, born 1768, died 1846.
Anthony Pate, son of Edward and Martha Pate, and father of Stephen Pate, fought in the Revolutionary War.
Thomas and Leroy were also the sons of Anthony and Sarah Pate.
Edward and Martha Pate's children were: Matthew, Anthony, Jeremiah, Thomas and Judith.

PATE BIBLE RECORDS

Facts obtained from Stephen H. Pate family Bible.

Stephen H. Pate, son of Jubal E. and Martha Holiday Pate, born Feb. 3, 1834, died Feb. 2, 1928; married Lucy Emiline Whitefield, Dec. 26, 1865.
Lucy Emiline Whitefield, daughter of Josiah and Dicey Perkins Whitefield, born June 2, 1842, died March 29, 1921.
Jubal E. Pate, son of Stephen and Polly Pate, born 1805, died 1895; married Martha Holiday, 1827.
Stephen Pate, son of Anthony and Sarah Pate, born 1768, died 1846.
Anthony Pate, son of Edward and Martha Pate; fought in the Revolutionary War, and died after 1795.
Edward Pate, died 1764.
Jubal Josiah Pate, son of Stephen and Lucy W. Pate, born Aug. 29, 1870; married Lena Graves, July 25, 1895.
Willie Belle Pate, daughter of Stephen and Lucy W. Pate, born March 30, 1867; married Dr. Howard K. Edgerton.

The children of Stephen and Polly Pate were:
Sallie Pate, married a Mr. Bentley.
Elizabeth Pate, married Phillip Draper.
Agnes Pate, married Johnnie Bluford.
Susannah Pate, married Beamon Graves.
Peggy Pate, married James King.
Harriet Pate, married Leroy Carter.
Payton Pate.
Calib Pate.
Hampton Pate, never married.
Booker Pate.
Jubil Pate, married Martha Holiday.
(For further Pate information, see Graves family records.)

JOHNSTON BIBLE

Copied from my mother's Bible, Jan. 13, 1917, Edna Holliday, given by Mrs. W. A. Ogden, Cumberland Chapter.

BIRTHS

L. B. Johnston, born Oct., 1792.
Mary Johnston (Polly Cochran), born Jan. 6, 1787.
A. M. Johnston, born Nov. 3, 1817 (grandmother).
Oscar L. Jones, born Oct. 21, 1819.
O. L. B. Johnston, born April 22, 1825.
O. H. T. Johnston, born Sept. 27, 1827.
David Cochran, born Nov. 2, 1824.
Polly Cochran, born 1787.

MARRIAGES

H. K. Chism and A. M. Johnston, married Oct. 7, 1834.
O. D. Johnston and L. M. Peyton, married Jan. 15, 1845.
O. L. Johnston and M. Granberry, married Oct. 6, 1848.
O. H. Johnston and M. J. Peyton, married Dec. 25, 1847.

E. A. Peyton and A. M. Chism, married Jan. 2, 1848.
S. O. Herring and C. L. Chism, married Sept. 6, 1855.
T. M. Little and S. M. Chism, married Feb. 18, 1864.
Mathew Walker Allen and Demaris Porter Chism, married May 23, 1872.
J. P. Herring and M. R. Chism, married June 22, 1876.
G. H. Clint and J. C. Payton, married, ———.

BIRTHS

Clifford J. Chism, born July 12, 1835.
Damaris Chism, born Sept. 23, 1838.
Adelbert D. Chism, born Jan. 8, 1841.
Senhora Chism, born Aug. 30, 1843.
Mary R. Chism, born Sept. 8, 1846.
Mat. W. Allen, Jr., born in Nashville, Tenn., Feb. 28, 1875.
Hiram Chism Allen, born in Nashville, Tenn., Aug. 2, 1876.
Louise Clifford Allen, born in Nashville, Tenn., Nov. 5, 1880.

DEATHS

Leonard B. Johnston, died Aug. 28, 1845.
Mary Johnston, died Sept. 11, 1846.
Hiram K. Chism, died Oct. 26, 1846.
Oscar B. Johnston, departed this life Feb. 5, 1847.
A. D. Chism, died Jan. 27, 1862; killed in Battle of Richmond.

JAMES BARLOW BIBLE

Entries in old Bible of James Barlow, great-grandfather of Mrs. Ewin L. Davis. Said Bible owned by her.

Sent by Hilda Thoma, Tullahoma.

MARRIAGES

James Barlow, born Feb. 18, 1791.
Amelia Barlow and A. J. Lester, married June 26, 1834.

William Barlow and Amanda Allen, married June 27, 1837.

Louisa Barlow and Arthur Wellesley Preston, married May 13, 1840.

John H. Barlow and Louisiana Daves, married Dec. 22, 1841.

Wade J. Barlow and Jane H. Brown, married Tuesday, June 1, 1847.

Susan Barlow and Joseph Summers, married Thursday, July 23, 1847.

James Barlow, married, Dec. 19, 1810, to Rebecca Harvin.

James Barlow, married the second time, May 13, 1832, to Winnifred J. Caldwell.

Samuel David Caldwell,, son of Spencer R. and Catherine Caldwell was born Oct. 1, 1828.

S. D. Caldwell, born Oct. 1, 1829.
Mary Rebecca Summers, daughter of Joseph and Susan Summers, born Friday, Sept. 1, 1848.

BIRTHS

William W. Barlow, son of James and Rebecca Barlow, born Sept. 24, 1811.

Amelia Barlow, daughter of James and Rebecca Barlow, born Sept. 24, 1813.

John Harvin Barlow, son of James and Rebecca Barlow, born Feb. 9, 1816.

James Madderson Barlow, son of James and Rebecca Barlow, born April 3, 1818.

Wade Barlow, son of James and Rebecca Barlow, born Jan. 20, 1820.

Louisa M. Barlow, daughter of James and Rebecca Barlow, born Aug. 13, 1823.

Susannah Barlow, daughter of James and Rebecca Barlow, born Feb. 26, 1826.

James Jodgson Barlow, son of James and Rebecca Barlow, born Dec. 12, 1830.

James M. Barlow, son of James and Winnifred J. Barlow, born Feb. 16, 1833.

Mary Jane Barlow, daughter of

James and Winnifred J. Barlow, born Sunday, May 18, 1834.
Jane Green, daughter of Thos. and Catharin Green, born Oct. 8, 1821.
Oliver E. Green, son of Thos. and Catharin Green, born March 2, 1823.
Christopher C. Barlow, son of James and Winnifred J. Barlow, born Friday, Jan. 15, 1836.
Sarah Winnifred Barlow, born May 4, 1838.
Ann Eliza Victoria Barlow, daughter of James and Winnifred Barlow, born Jan. 22, 1840.

DEATHS

James M. Barlow, son of James an Rebecca Barlow, died Saturday, Oct. 20, 1821, age 3 years 6 months 17 days.
Rebecca Barlow, wife of James Barlow, died Sunday night, Dec. 19, 1830, age about 36 years, consort of James Barlow 20 years to a day.
Samuel Mansfield Barlow, son of James and Winnifred J. Barlow, died Tuesday morning, March 11, 1834, at 2 o'clock, age 12 months 26 days.
Christopher Caldwell Barlow, son of James and Winnifred J. Barlow, died Friday, June 23, 1837, age 1 years 4 months 28 days.

Ann Eliza Victoria Barlow, died Saturday, Feb. 17, 1844, age 4 years 24 days.

Susan Summers, wife of Joseph Summers, daughter of James and Rebecca Barlow, died July 3, 1851, age 24 years 8 months 5 days.

Winnifred J. Barlow, wife of James Barlow, died Aug. 2, 1852, age 50 years 5 months 16 days, consort of James Barlow 20 years 2 months 20 days.

James Judson Barlow, son of James and Rebecca Barlow, died in Americus, Ga., June 19, 1855; joined the Baptist Church at Rocky Creek and baptized July 9, 1848.

John and Jane Barlow, the wife of John Barlow, both died Oct. 4, 1827.

James Barlow, died Sept. 19, 1855, age 64 years 7 months 1 day.

Mary Jane Hill, died July 18, 1860, age 26 years 2 months.

The foregoing are true copies of entries in old, badly worn Bible, with the paper yellowed with age, and with the words, "James Barlow's Book", inscribed on the book. The writing is all apparently very old. The Bible has the Apocrypha in it. The book was "Printed and Published by M. Cary & Son, No. 126 Chestnut Street, Philadelphia," and bears the printed date of 1818.

ALFRED J. LESTER BIBLE

Entries in old Bible of Alfred J. Lester, now owned by Mrs. Ewin T. Davis.

FAMILY RECORD

MARRIAGES

A. J. Lester and Amelia Barlow, married June 26, 1834.

John T. Windsor and Emily A. Lester, married April 24, 1870.

William H. McAlister and Hattie Amelia Windsor, married Feb. 17, 1897.

Ewin Lamar Davis and Callie Windsor, married Dec. 28, 1898.

BIRTHS

Lester Windsor, born Oct. 29, 1871.

Hattie Amelia Windsor, born Dec. 25, 1873.

Callie Windsor, born July 21, 1876.

James J. Lester, son of Nixon Lester, born Nov. 16, 1801.

Silas M. Lester, born Oct. 8, 1803.

Nathan N. Lester, born May 23, 1806.

Alfred J. Lester, born Feb. 23, 1808.
Thomas J. Livingston, son of P. Livingston, born Nov. 25, 1805.
Louisa Livingston.
Caroline Livingston.
Emily Jane Livingston, born Jan. 23, 1817.
Frances Amanda Livingston, born Aug. 14, 1819.
Sarah E. Livingston, born May 26, 1821.
Amelia B. Barlow, daughter of James Barlow, born Sept. 24, 1813.
James Nixon Lester, son of A. J. and Amelia B. Lester, born Sept. 20, 1835.
William Alexander Lester, born Sept. 3, 1838.
John Westley Lester, born Feb. 27, 1841.
Sarah Rebecca Lester, born Jan. 7, 1845.
Robert Milton Lester, born Nov. 3, 1846.
Christopher Columbus Lester, born Nov. 24, 1848.
Emmah Eugenia Lester, born Dec. 22, 1851.
Emily Amelia Lester, born Feb. 5, 1855.

DEATHS

James Nixon Lester, son of A. J. and Amelia B. Lester, died June 6, 1853, age 17 years 8 months 17 days.
William Alexander Lester, died June 5, 1853, age 14 years 9 months 2 days.
Robert Milton Lester, died June 5, 1853, age 6 years 7 months 2 days.
Christopher Columbus Lester, died June 11, 1853, age 4 years 6 months 18 days.
Emmah Eugenia Lester, died June 7, 1853, age 1 years 5 months 16 days.
John W. Lester, died March 26, 1863, age 22 years 1 month, died at Richmond, Va., in the defense of his country.
Frances Amanda Livingston, died Sept. 22, 1822, age 3 years 1 month 6 days.
Peter L. Livingston, died Nov. 23. 1832.
Sarah Livingston, wife of Peter L. Livingston, died Nov. 27, 1832.
Silas M. Lester, died Jan. 17, 1835.
Nathan N. Lester, died Feb. 22, 1841.
Sarah Rebecca Lester, daughter of A. J. and Amelia B. Lester, died June 29, 1849, age 4 years 5 months 22 days.
James J. Lester, son of Nixon Lester, died Sept. 23, 1869.
A. J. Lester, son of Nixon Lester, died Feb. 4, 1874, age 66 years.
Amelia Barlow Lester, died June 4, 1898, age 84 years 6 months.

DEATHS OF NEGROES

Jerry, died April 25, 1825.

The foregoing are true copies of entries in old, badly worn Bible, with the paper yellowed with age, of Alfred J. Lester. The writing is all apparently very old.

There was also in the Bible an old sheet of paper with the following writing thereon:

JUNE, 1853

5th June, Robert M. Lester, died 15 minutes after 11 a.m.

5th June, William A. Lester, died 15 minutes before 12 p.m.

6th June, James N. Lester, died 15 minutes before 10 a.m., June 6, 1853.

7th June, Emma E. Lester, died at 9 p.m.

11th June, Christopher C. Lester, 11 a.m.

The fly leaf of the Holy Bible contains the following:

PHILADELPHIA
Printed and Published by M. Carey
No. 121 Chesnut Street
1816

The fly leaf of the Concordance to the Bible bears the following:

PHILADELPHIA
Printed and Published by
Matthew Carey
No. 121 Chesnut Street
1815

Emerson Bible

Entries in old Bible of Hiram S. and Mary H. Emerson. Said Bible now in the possession of their granddaughter, Miss Hilda Thoma, Tullahoma, Tennessee.

Hiram Sharon Emerson, born (in Kentucky) July 11, 1799.
Mary Hipkins (Child) Emerson, born (in Fairfax County, Va.) Dec. 22, 1805.
Hiram Sharon Emerson and Mary Hipkins Child, married Sept. 15, 1825 (Burksville, Ky.).

Births

Elizabeth Sharon Emerson, oldest daughter of H. S. and Mary H. Emerson, born July 24, 1826 (Kentucky).
Catherine Johnson Emerson, second daughter of Hiram S. and Mary H. Emerson, born Oct. 21, 1827 (Kentucky).
John Francis Emerson, first son of Hiram S. and Mary H. Emerson, born May 25, 1829.
Gabriel Demilion Emerson, second son of Hiram S. and Mary H. Emerson, born Dec. 5, 1830.
Sarah Susannah Emerson, third daughter of Hiram S. and Mary H. Emerson, born July 23, 1833.
Thomas Mansfield Emerson, third son of H. S. and M. H. Emerson, born July 25, 1835.
Burr Hamilton Emerson, fourth son of H. S. and M. H. Emerson, born May 14, 1837.
Mary Ann Emerson, fourth daughter of H. S. and M. H. Emerson, born Oct. 26, 1838 (one of twins, the other one born dead).
Nancy Gillenwater Emerson, fifth daughter of H. S. and M. H. Emerson, born May 2, 1841 (seven months old when the family moved to Manchester, Tenn.).
Unice Francesco Emerson, seventh daughter of H. S. and M. H. Emerson, born May 5, 1846.
Virginia Acanthus Emerson, eighth daughter of H. S. and M. H. Emerson, born July 20, 1851 (Manchester, Tenn.).

Marriages

Pleasant H. McBride and Elizabeth S. Emerson, married Aug. 17, 1848 (at Manchester, Tenn.).
Gabriel D. Emerson and Louise Jane Young, married Dec. 15, 1845, at Clinton, Hickman County, Ky.
Francis W. Emerson and Sarah Susannah Emerson (cousins), married Nov. 1, 1859.
Thomas M. Emerson and Sarah Amanda Koger, married Sept. 25, 1861.
Burr H. Emerson and Hattie Rosetta Buss, married Sept. 3, 1862.
Nancy G. Emerson and James Thom, married April 4, 1872, at Manchester, Tenn.
Jonathan W. Brixey and Helon M. Emerson, married Dec. 11, 1866.
William A. Thoma and Virginia A. Emerson, married May 25, 1870.

Deaths

Elizabeth S. McBride, died at Manchester, Tenn.
Catherine J. Emerson, died ——.
John Francis Emerson, died July 17, 1830 .
Sarah Susannah Emerson, died of pneumonia Jan. 12, 1892, at her residence in Manchester, Tenn.
Thomas M. Emerson, died of heart failure at Manchester, Tenn., Dec. 27, 1906.
Burr H. Emerson, died of white-swelling (caused from a jump when a boy) at Manchester, Tenn.
Mary Ann Emerson, died of pleurisy at the home of her sister, Mrs. Virginia Thoma, in Tullahoma, Tenn.
Nancy G. Thom, died at Manchester, Tenn., Dec. 6, 1886.
Unice Francisco Emerson, died Oct. 17, 1849.
Virginia T. Thoma, died of acute bronchitis Oct. 27, 1924, in Tullahoma, Tenn.
Mary Hipkins Child Emerson, died of pneumonia Dec. 9, 1876, at Manchester, Tenn.
Hiram S. Emerson, drowned in Whiteman Pond on main branch of Duck River, March 39, 1878.

HAMMOND FAMILY REGISTER

Family register of Job Hammond, father of Nancy Duncan, mother of George Duncan.

This is copy of records taken from the Bible of Geo. W. Duncan now in possession of Margaret Brevard Haynes.

Job Hammond, born May 4, 1754.
Nancy Stone, his wife, born Oct. 6, 1760.

THEIR CHILDREN

William Hammond.
James Hammond.
Mildred Hammond.
Rebecca Hammond, born Feb., 1784.
Nancy Hammond, born July 11, 1786.
Sarah Hammond.
Elizabeth Hammond.
Gervis Hammond.
Mary Hammond.
Eli Hammond.
Davis Hammond.

Family register of Colman Duncan, father of Sandford Duncan, father of George Duncan.

Colman Duncan, born Feb. 21, 1742.
Mary Lynn, his wife, born March 7, 1749.

THEIR CHILDREN

Thomas, born Dec. 16, 1769.
Henry, born Aug. 12, 1772.
Charles, born June 21, 1774.
James, born Sept. 16, 1779.
Rebecca, born March 21, 1782.
George, born Aug. 25, 1784.
Sandford, born Oct. 25, 1786.
Mary, born Oct. 18, 1789.
Fanny, born March 24, 1792.

George W. Duncan, born Jan. 12, 1826, son of Sanford Duncan and Nancy Hammond Duncan, and Dorinda Ann Puryear, born Jan. 30, 1837, were married Sept. 4, 1866, by the Rev. Henry Hail in Smith County, Tenn.

THEIR CHILDREN

Willie P. Duncan, born Aug. 22, 1861, died Aug. 3, 1864.
Thos. J. Duncan, born July 4, 1863, died Oct. 4, 1864.
Mary Sanford, born Aug. 2, 1865, died Sept. 26, 1916.
Charles A. Duncan, born Feb. 5, 1868.
Nannie Rebecca, born Aug. 12, 1870, died July 24, 1871.
George Henry, born Aug. 25, 1872.
William Adolph, born March 31, 1877.

BREVARD BIBLE RECORDS

Records found in the Bible of Zebulon Brevard, Sr.
Copy certified to by Margaret Brevard.

Zebulon Brevard, Sr., born March 29, 1724.
Ann Templeton, his wife, born Nov., 1733.

Records found in the Bible of Thomas Brevard.

Zebulon Brevard and Ann Templeton, married March 7, 1754.

THEIR CHILDREN

Mary Brevard, born Aug. 5, 1755; married Benjamin Wallace, 1773.
David Brevard, born March 18, 1755.
Elizabeth Brevard, born Dec. 30, 1758; married William Beard, 1783.

Jane Brevard, born May 29, 1760; married William Givans.
Sarah Brevard, born June 5, 1762; married William Wilson.
Ann Brevard, born Jan. 6, 1766; married David Edmiston.
Zebulon Brevard, born Feb., 1769; married, first, Izabelle Edmiston; second, Widow Burton.
James Brevard, born March 3, 1771.
Rhoda Brevard, born July 21, 1773; married William McFee, 1813.
Thomas Brevard, born Sept. 25, 1775; married, first, Sarah S. Jetton, March 1, 1808; second, Elizabeth Troutte, May 9, 1822.
Sarah Sharpe Jetton, born June 16, 1788, died May 7, 1821.
Elizabeth Troutte, born Oct. 3, 1798.
Thomas Brevard, died Oct. 16, 1846.
(The Zebulon Brevard, Sr., mentioned above, was the son of Jean Brevard, the French Hugenot, who is mentioned in Wheeler's History of North Carolina.)

Records found in the private papers of Zebulon Brevard, son of Thomas Brevard.

CHILDREN OF THOMAS BREVARD

James Hall Templeton Brevard, born Dec. 24, 1808, died Sept. 24, 1829.
Nancy E. Brevard, born Feb. 17, 1811; married Daniel Vance, Jan. 3, 1833, died Sept. 26, 1867.
Zebulon L. Brevard, born Sept. 5, 1813; married Margaret Ferrell, Aug. 24, 1853; died Nov. 10, 1900.
Thomas B. Brevard, born April 13, 1816; married Jane W. Fugitt, Nov. 2, 1847.
Mary Caroline Brevard, born April 13, 1819; married Edward R. Vance, Feb. 21, 1839; died May 4, 1853.
John J. Brevard, born Sept. 17, 1826.

Record of Daniel Vance, who married Nancy E. Brevard:
Daniel Vance, born Feb., 1811, died Jan. 27, 1845. His children are:
Thomas Jefferson Vance, born April 23, 1835.
Sarah Sharp Vance, born Feb. 25; ——; married Isaac Turner.
Hall Vance, born ——, killed in battle at Murfreesboro, Tenn.
Daniel Vance, married Elizabeth Brewer.

CHILDREN

Record of Edward R. Vance, who married Carolian Brevard. Their children are:
Eliza Ann Vance, born Nov. 11, 1840.
Mary Ellen Vance, born Jan 31, 1846, died Feb. 5, 1847.
Joseph Thomas Vance, born May 6, 1848.
Zebulon Brevard Vance, born Dec. 31, 1850.
Sarah Caroline Vance, born Dec. 20, 1852.
James Hall Vance, born May 28, 1843, died May 16, 1862.

Copied from the family Bible of Jacob Augustus Cox and wife, Elizabeth Turner Cox. Sent by Nettie B. Stoops Brown, Chattanooga.

MARRIAGES

Jacob Augustus Cox, son of Jacob and Lydia Stephens Cox, born Dec. 5, 1815; at 23 years of age was married to Elizabeth Turner, April 24, 1838.
Elizabeth Turner, his wife, born Feb. 22, 1815.
Nancy Ann Cox, daughter of Jacob Augustus and Elizabeth Cox, born May 31, 1839; at 22 years of age married to Andrew Jackson Stoops, Jan. 16, 1862, at Cincinnati, Ohio, First M. P. Church, by Joseph G. White, pastor.
William Filmore Cox, son of Ja-

cob Augustus and Elizabeth Cox, born June 28, 1855; at 20 years of age married to Mary Jane Hudson, Aug. 26, 1875, at New Trenton, Ind.

BIRTHS

Nancy Ann Cox, daughter, born May 31, 1839.
Lydia Ann, born Jan. 21, 1842.
Hannah Minerva, daughter, born June 16, 1851.
William Filmore, son, born June 28, 1855.

DEATHS

Lydia Ann, daughter, died April 20, 1849, age 7 years 2 months 29 days, at Logan, Ind.; buried in Braysville Cemetery, New Trenton, Ind.
Elizabeth Cox, mother, died July 11, 1891, age 76 years 4 months 19 days, at Logan, Ind.; buried in Braysville Cemetery, New Trenton, Ind.
Jacob Augustus Cox, father, died Jan. 2, 1894, age 78 years 1 month, at Logan, Ind.; buried in Braysville Cemetery, new Trenton, Ind.
Andrew Jackson Stoops, husband of Nancy Ann Cox, died March 20, 1910, age 72 years 4 months 6 days, at Chattanooga, Tenn.; buried in National Cemetery, Chattanooga, Tenn.
Nancy Ann Cox, daughter, died June 25, 1922, age 83 years 25 days, at Lookout Mountain, Tenn.; buried in Forest Hill Cemetery, Chattanooga.
Hannah Minerva Cox, daughter, died Oct. 30, 1922, age 71 years 4 months 14 days, Lookout Mountain, Tenn.; buried in Forest Hill Cemetery, Chattanooga, Tenn.
Mary Jane Hudson Cox, wife of William Filmore Cox, died April 7, 1925, age 70 years 8 months 23 days; buried in Edgewood Cemetery, Clarence, Mo.

Copied from the family Bible of Andrew Jackson Stoops and wife, Nancy Ann Cox Stoops.

This certifies that the rite of Holy Matrimony was celebrated between Andrew Jackson Stoops of Cincinnati, Ohio, and Nancy Ann Cox of Dearborn County, Ind., on Jan. 16, 1862, at Cincinnati, Ohio, by Rev. Joseph White, pastor Sixth Street M. P. Church. Witness: J. B. Frisbee and Mary E. Burt.

MARRIAGES

Harry Eugene Stoops and Mary Josephene Wood, at Nashville, Tenn., May 29, 1889, by father.
Nettie Bell Stoops and Joseph Nelson Brown, at Chattanooga, Tenn., June 11, 1885, by Rev. L. Warner.
Edith Nancy Brown, daughter of Nettie S. and Joseph N. Brown, and William Franklin Stone, at Lookout Mountain, Tenn., by Rev. Barney Thompson, Sept. 25, 1912.
Irene Eugenia Stoops, daughter of Harry E. and Mary Wood, and Walter W. Terry, July 25, 1912, at Chattanooga, Tenn.; (2) E. Bell Garrison, at Toledo, Ohio, Nov. 26, 1827.
Elizabeth Jeanet Stoops, daughter of Harry E. and Mary J. Wood, and Arthur Pleasant Sibold, at Chattanooga, Tenn., Aug. 24, 1919.

BIRTHS

Andrew Jackson Stoops, Bridgewater, Beaver County, Pa., Nov. 14, 1837.

Nancy Ann Cox, Logan, Dearborn County, Ind., May 31, 1838.

Harry Eugene Stoops, Cincinnati, Hamilton County, Ohio, Aug. 30, 1963.

Nettie Bell Stoops, Covington, Kenton County, Ky., Oct. 11, 1865.

Frank Filmore Stoops, Covington, Kenton County, Ky., Jan. 3, 1871.

Charles Andrew Stoops, Chattanooga, Hamilton County, Tenn., Feb. 5, 1876.

DEATHS

Andrew Jackson Stoops, Chattanooga, Tenn., March 20, 1910; buried in National Cemetery, Chattanooga, Tenn.

Charles Andrew Stoops, Lookout Mountain, Tenn., Feb. 25, 1916; buried in Forest Hills Cemetery, Chattanooga, Tenn.
Nancy Ann Cox Stoops, Lookout Mountain, Tenn., June 25, 1922; buried in Forest Hills Cemetery, Chattanooga, Tenn.
Harry Eugene Stoops, Chattanooga, Tenn., July 14, 1922; buried in Forest Hills Cemetery, Chattanooga, Tenn.

From old family Bible belonging to Syley S. Embry, Winchester, Tennessee.

Jesse Embry—Children:
Willis, Merril, Orvin, Joel Henrietta, Sally, Polly, Tampa, Julia, Muvy.
Willis Embry—Children:
Willis, Mary Anne, Wiley S. Embry I., Merril D., born 1868, married Charaty Evaline Simmons, daughter of Reuben Simmons; Parker; Eliza, married Willie Ragnor; Elizabeth, married B. F. Russey.
Merril D. Embry, married Charaty Evalin Simmons—Children:
Eliza, Charaty Evalin, Jesse, John Wesley, Willis, Alexander, Wiley S. Embry II. (1830-1910), married Nannie or Anne, daughter of Elisha Meridith; Hannah Stevens, born 1837, married 1857; Mary Elizabeth, Merril III., Wilburn B., Julia Anne.
Wiley S. Embrey II. (1830-1900), married Anne Meridith, A.B. degree, Mary Sharp College—Children:
Julia (1858-1884), Hugh H. (1860-1925), married Cecelia C., daughter of W. B. Tyler and Eliza Nichilas Hawes; Sally (1862-1863); Wiley S. III. (1864-1864); Elizabeth Merril, born 1863), married W. H. Carmack; Wiley S. Embrey IV., married Jimmie Lindsay; Avalina Alliene, born 1873, married John Edgar Carmack; Meridith Porter (1875-1912); Edward A. Embrey, born 1878.
Hugh H. Embrey and Cecelia C. Tyler—Children:
Julia Howard, born 1884, married J. Read Moore, in Hong Kong, China;; Hartley C., born 1886, married Dr. P. L. Sherman; Hugh H., born 1889, died 1911; Cecelia Tyler, born 1890, married L. S. Daniels; Edwin Tyler, born 1894.
Julia Howard and Read Moore—Children:
Julia E. (1911-1923), Jane Darnaby, Cecilia Tyler.
Hartley C. and Dr. P. L. Sherman—Children:
Hugh S., Edwin E.

MARRIAGES

Samuel Dixon Robertson and Sallie Dudley Garrett, married March 6, 1862.

BIRTHS

Samuel Dixon Robertson, born in Fairfield District, S. C., Oct. 24, 1837.
Sallie Dudley Garrett, born in Hinds County, Miss., Feb. 5, 1843.

DEATHS

Samuel Dixon Robertson, died Sept. 22, 1911, at Anding, Miss.
Sallie Dudley Robertson, wife of Samuel D. Robertson, died at Cameron, Milam County, Texas, the morning of May 28, 1877.

BIRTHS

Annie Garrett Robertson, daughter of Samuel Dixon and Wallie Dudley Robertson, born in Tuscaloosa County, Ala., Aug. 24, 1865.
Amelia Mattie Robertson, daughter of Samuel Dixon and Sallie Dudley Robertson, born in Yazoo County, Miss., Feb. 27, 1869.
Samuel Garrett Robertson, born Sept. 13, 1872, in Yazoo County, Miss.

DEATHS

Annie Garrett Robertson Kelly, died Jan. 5, 1890.
Amelia Mattie Robertson, died Aug. 20, 1870.

BIRTHS

Mable Clare Robertson, daughter of Samuel Dixon and Sallie Dudley Robertson, born in Yazoo County, Miss., Dec. 4, 1870.

Garrett Robertson, son of Samuel Dixon and Sallie Dudley Robertson, born in Hinds County, Miss., March 26, 1874.

DEATHS

Samuel Garrett Robertson, died Feb. 23, 1873.
Garrett Robertson, died at Cameron, Texas, Feb. 13, 1876.

McMINN FAMILY

From the Bible of Joseph McMinn, who was governor of the state of Tennessee from 1815 to 1821, and at whose grave in the cemetery at Calhoun, Tenn., the state of Tennessee has erected a marble shaft; we have copied the following records:
Joseph McMinn, son of Robert and Sarah McMinn, born June 22, 1758, near West Chester, Pa., and married to his wife, Hannah Cooper, May 9, 1785, she being the daughter of James and Rosanna Cooper, and was born June 20, 1760, Chester County, Pa., near Piquea Church.
Second Marriage—Joseph McMinn was married to his wife, Rebecca Kincaid Jan 5, 1812. She was born in Carter's Valley, Hawkins County, and state of Tennessee, Oct. 7, 1793, and was the daughter of David and Mary Kincaid.
Third Marriage—Joseph McMinn was married to his wife, Nancy Williams, at South West Point, Roane County, and state of Tennessee, on Aug. 4, 1816, she being the daughter of James and Phenobie Glasgow, and was born in Greene County, state of North Carolina, April 22, 1770.
Hetty McMinn, daughter of John and Mary McMinn, married to Robert Morrison, both of Hawkins County, Tenn., on May 11, 1823.
Jane McMinn, daughter of Joseph and Hannah McMinn, born Aug 27, 1787, at 1 o'clock, a.m., in Hawkins County, now state of Tennessee.
The aforesaid Jane was married to Hugh Campbell, Esq., merchant, Rogersville, on May 9, 1804, in Hawkins aforesaid, who died Sept. 27, 1804, in Rogersville, aforesaid, of a cholera-morbus, and something like yellow fever.
Jane Campbell, relict of Hugh, aforesaid, was married to Major James Gaines, Nov. 20, 1808, in neither of those marriages had she any issue.
Hetty McMinn, daughter of John and Mary McMinn, born May 13, 1801, in Hawkins County, and on the death of her mother , was adopted into my family, and was in all respects attended to as one of its members.
Robert Morrison, son of Thomas and Jane Morrison, born Jan 7, 1796.
Mary J. Morrison, daughter of Robert and Hetty Morrison, born Sept. 25, 1829.
Joseph L. Morrison, son of Robt. and Hetty Morrison, born Jan 2, 1824.
George W. Morrison, son of Robt. and Hetty Morrison, born Jan. 4, 1826.
William H. Morrison, son of Robert and Hetty Morrison, born Sept. 29, 1827.
Eldridge H. Morrison, son of Robert and Hetty Morrison, born Sept. 25, 1831.
Sarah Ann Morrison, daughter of Robert and Hetty Morrison, born Nov. 17, 1833.
Marthy Ann Morrison, daughter of Robert and Hetty Morrison, born Aug. 31, 1843.
Hannah McMinn, wife of said Joseph McMinn, died Feb. 27, 1811, of an inward inflamation, which terminated her life in five days' illness, age 49 years 8 months 7 days, and departed at her own dwelling in Hawkins County, Tenn.
Rebecca McMinn, wife of Joseph McMinn, died Jan. 11, 1815, of a nervous fever of 29 days' continuation, age 21 years 9 months.
Jane Gaines, wife of James T. Gaines and daughter of Joseph

and Hannah McMinn, died Jan 27, 1815, of what was called the cold plague or epidemic, in an illness of something less than three days from a perfect state of good health, age 27 years 9 months.

Joseph McMinn, died Oct. 17, 1824. Sarah Ann Morrison, daughter of Robert and Hetty Morrison, died Nov. 3, 1836, with the measles and whooping cough, age 2 years 10 months.

George Morrison, son of Robert and Hetty Morrison, died Feb. 2, 1842, about 4 o'clock in the p.m., age 16 years 28 days.

Robert Morrison, husband of Hetty Morrison, died April 19, 1854, of flux, age 59 years 4 months.

On the fly leaf of the Bible we find, "Joseph McMinn Bible; bought of David Wendlo, Jan., 1819; price, $16.00."

After the governor's death, through a flaw in the wording of his will, by which he intended to leave his property to his adopted daughter, Hetty, she was cut off and the property was all put up and sold at public auction and the proceeds turned over to the state of Tennessee. This old Bible was bought by Hetty McMinn Morrison and passed from her to her daughter, Martha Ann Morrison Knox, and thus to its present owner, Mary Knox Harle (Mrs. Frank J. Harle of Cleveland).

The records of Joseph McMinn's marriages, his wives' deaths and the records concerning his daughter, Jane, and his adopted daughter, Hetty, are all in the same handwriting, evidently that of Mr. McMinn himself. The records concerning the births and death of the children of Hetty McMinn Morrison are all written by another person, while the deaths of Joseph McMinn and Robert Morrison are recorded in two entirely different scripts. Mrs. Harle identifies the writing in which Gov. McMinn's death is recorded as that of her father, Thos. J. Knox.

Mrs. Harle has another very interesting old family Bible. This one is the "First American Edition of Henry's Exposition of the Old and New Testaments," and is in six volumes. These books were the property of David Lucky Knox, the father of Thos. J. Knox, who married Martha Ann Morrison, daughter of Hetty McMinn.

In the front of the first volume we find the following family records:

David Lucky Knox, married to Elizabeth Montgomery, March 9, 1820.

Cintha Ann Knox, married to James Parkes, July 13, 1841.

Samuel Knox, married to Mary Elizabeth Griles, Jan. 15, 1846.

James M. Knox, married to Nancy Ann Camp, Feb. 10, 1848.

Christopher Columbus Knox, married to Malida Jane Weir, Feb. 21, 1850.

Juliet Eliza Knox, married to Williard H. McKamy, Nov. 2, 1854.

Margaret Knox, married to Henry Rice, Jan. 8, 1857.

Mary J. Knox, married to E. A. Freeman, Jan. 13, 1858.

William Knox, married to Tennessee Smith, March 14, 1861.

Caroline Elizabeth Knox, married to Alex' C. Robison, Nov. 10, 1859.

Joseph S. Knox, married to Miss M. E. Carlock, Oct. 9, 1860.

Thos. J. Knox, married to Miss Martha Morrison, Aug. 29, 1859.

David L. Knox, born March 25, 1801.

Elizabeth Montgomery, born April 20, 1800.

Cynthea Ann Knox, born April 11, 1821.

James Montgomery Knox, born July 11, 1822.

Hugh Crawford Knox, born Aug. 23, 1823.

Samuel Knox, born Oct. 17, 1824.

Mary Jane Knox, born Jan. 13, 1826.

Christopher Columbus Knox, born Feb. 21, 1827.

William Knox, born Sept. 10, 1828.

Joseph Scot, born Nov. 10, 1829.

Margaret Knox, born April 15, 1831.

Thomas Jefferson Knox, born Jan. 10, 1833.

Juliett Elizar Knox, born May 28, 1834.
Nancy Agnes Knox, born, Oct. 17, 1836.
Carolie Elizabeth Knox, born Dec. 28, 1838.
Henry Harrison Knox, born July 16, 1840.
Harriet Elizabeth Knox, born Feb. 11, 1847, a daughter of Samuel Knox.
James Knox, born June 5, 1775, the father of David.
Ann Cowen, born Oct. 1, 1777, mother of David L. Knox.
David L. Knox, died at his residence in Bradley County, Tenn., May 2, 1854, at 4:15 o'clock p.m.
Cynthia A. Parks, died March 4, 1858.
Ann Cowan, mother of David L. Knox, died Aug. 8, 1858.
Elizabeth Knox, died Feb. 7, 1859.
Nancy Agnes Knox, died July 30, 1891.
William Knox, died July 1, ——.
James Montgomery Knox, died Jan. 2, 1894.
Hugh Montgomery, father of Elizabeth Knox, died Jan. 22, 1852.
Margaret Montgomery, mother of Elizabeth Knox, died July 28, 1848.
Mary Jane Freeman, died April 27, 1894.

Abstracts of the Will of Major Peter Helphenstine. Probated Court House, Frederick County, Va., May 4, 1779. Sent by Mrs. J. M. Ferguson, Erwin.

I, Major Peter Helphenstine, of the town of Winchester, County of Frederick, and Colony of Virginia, make this my last will and testament.

I will the third part of my estate to my dear wife, Catherine Helphenstine, with all wearing apparel, plate and the two-thirds to be equally divided between my sons, Phillip, Peter, William and Henry, and my daughters, Catherine, Rosanna, Charlotta and Elizabeth, sons to be paid at age of 21, daughters paid at age of 18 or days of marriage.

I witness hereunto, I set my hand and seal, this 24th day of March, 1776.

Abstracts of the will of James Black of the Township of Martic, County of Lancaster, State of Pennsylvania.

I bequeath to my dearly and well beloved wife, Jane, her bed and furniture, all pewter and two pots, one cow and four sheep of her own choosing. I also allow her one-third of my real estate during her life in the manner the law directs.

To my dutiful and beloved daughter, Mary, I bequeath 20 pounds, in which is to be included, her saddle and bridle, bed and bed clothes. To my beloved son, Thomas, I give 2 pounds, 10 shillings. To my beloved son, James, I give 5 pounds.

My beloved children, David, Margaret and John, are yet in their minority and will require more education.

It is my will that David receives schooling to the value of 5 pounds, Margaret to the value of 5 pounds and John to the value of ten pounds. I also bequeath Margaret 20 pounds.

It is my will that David and John go to a trade as they arrive at the age of 16.

It is my will my books be divided between my wife and children, my wife to choose her own.

The residue of my estate after everything else is paid, to be divided among my sons, Hugh, David and John.

It is my desire that Mary and Margaret receive each an additional 10 pounds. My sons, Thomas, Black and James Black are appointed executors of this my last will and testament.

I have set my hand and seal this 23rd day of August, in the year of our Lord 1805.

(Probated Feb. 7, 1806, Lancaster County, Pa., Martic Township.)

Abstracts of the will of Thomas Harry of the Township of Pennsbury, County of Chester, State of Pennsylvania.

I give and devise unto my two sons, Amos Harry and Isaac Harry, all the plantation of land I live on in the Township of Pennsbury, they to pay the following legacies.

To my sons, Evan Harry and Jacob Harry, and daughters, Mary Hollingsworth, Hannah Walter, Betsey Harlen and Sarah Vernon, the sum of one hundred dollars each. My daughter, Lidia Walker, the sum of five dollars; Grandson, Samuel Harry, son of my daughter, Lidia Walker, the sum of ninety-five dollars. I give and bequeath unto my son, Amos Harry, the sum of four hundred dollars to be paid from my personal estate. To my daughter, Rachel, one hundred dollars worth of my household and kitchen furniture of her own choice. To my two sons, Amos and Isaac, all the residue of my estate to be equally divided between them. My two sons, Amos and Isaac to be executors of this my last will and testament.

I hereunto set my hand and seal the 12th day of 8th month in the year of our Lord 1824.

(Wills in possession of Julia Elizabeth Sprint Ferguson, descendant.)

CARRIE HARPER CHEEK DATA

Carrie Harper Cheek (Mrs. H. E.), descent of John Harper, Sr., who was born 1740, died Sept., 1812, in Sumner County, Tenn. The daughter of James George Harper and Emma Hunt Harper. George, the son of Thomas, who was the son of John Harper, Jr., who married Martha Snead Oldham, daughter of Major George Oldham, who was born Feb. 25, 1779, died April 25, 1845. John Harper, Jr., the son of John Harper, Sr., and Margaret Morrow, born 1750, died Dec. 6, 1835, married 1772. He was of English descent. Margaret Morrow's parents came from Ireland.

Children of John Harper, Sr., and Margaret Morrow:

Rebecca Harper, born May 16, 1773.
William Harper, born Jan. 1, 1775.
Hugh Harper, born Sept. 22, 1776.
John Harper, Jr., born Feb. 25, 1779.
Anna Harper, born Sept. 8, 1781.
Andrew Harper, born Oct. 3, 1784.
James Harper, born June 6, 1786.
Elizabeth Harper, born March 25, 1788.
Asa Harper, born Aug. —, 1790.
Enos Harper, born July 2, 1793.
Jesse Harper, born Dec. 1, 1795.
Margaret Harper, born Nov. 29, 1799.

John Harper, Jr., owned a large tract of land in Anderson County. He was for many years a Justice of the Peace. An old account book, a hundred years old, contains an account of these transactions, in possession of his grandson, James George Harper, Seneca, S. C. He and his wife are buried at Big Creek Cemetery.

John Harper, Jr.'s will is on record at Anderson Court House. A letter written by Wm. L. Harper from Tennessee to South Carolina relatives in 1851, July 17, says he is the son of Jesse Harper, who is the son of John Harper, married Sarah Gregory in 1826. Six children were born to them—Wm. Lafayette, Leander Franklin, Mary Ann Elizabeth, Eliza Caroline, Sarah Louise and Margaret Catherine Harper. This letter is in possession of Carrie Harper Cheek, was mailed at Gallatin, Tenn., July 17, 1851, to John Harper or family, Anderson, S. C.

This sketch was contributed by Mrs. R. W. Brown, Chairman of Historic Spots, D. A. R. Sent by Mrs. J. M. Ferguson, Erwin. First child born in Erwin, Tenn., after the County of Unicoi was formed.

In the month of June, 1876, near the bank of the beautiful Nolachucky in the county of Unicoi on Nolachucky Avenue in the town of Erwin a baby girl was born. Her parents named her "Nolachucky," and not only being the first child born in Erwin after the formation of the county, but she was the first child of George H. Scott and his wife, Eleanor V. O'Brien Scott. This site was marked by the Unaka Chapter, Daughters of the American Revolution, in the year 1925, and was the first historic spot marked by the Chapter. This marker in marble is in the corner of the building owned by Brown and Burleson on Nolachucky Avenue, the site where Nolachucky was born, and was unveiled by her granddaughter, Mary Jane Allen, who at the time of placing the memorial was 15 months of age.

The Unaka Chapter was happy to place this memorial to the memory of this baby. She has grown to womanhood and is one of our fine Christian characters. She is a charter member of the Unaka Chapter. Nola, as she is called by her friends, descends from a long line of men and women who served America from the Revolution to this day. Her father, George H. Scott, was a teacher in the public schools when Nola was born, training children to be good citizens. Her mother, Eleanor V. O'Brien Scott, did her part in training her children, a family of seven. George H. Scott is the son of James Scott and Christiana Moltern. James Scott was a minister of the gospel; he assisted in establishing the First Christian Church in Johnson City, Tenn., at that time called Johnson's Junction. Christiana Moltern was the daughter of John Moltern and his wife, Sally Hart. Sally Hart was the daughter of Leonard Hart and his first wife, Sally Goodman. Leonard Hart was a Revolutionary soldier; he was with the King's Mountain patriots. He was a surveyor and was appointed to survey a great road from Shoels to the Holston River. Nolachucky Scott attended school at Columbus Powell and Science Hill, Johnson City, and Milligan College, Milligan, Tenn. She married Jake Waltenbeiger. They lived in Johnson City, Greeneville, Rockwood, Tenn. Mr. Waltenbeiger died in Rockwood, leaving his wife with two small daughters, Clara and Grace. In 1907 Nola married B. M. Allud, coming back to live at Erwin, the place of her birth. Since the death of Mr. Allud Nola has spent most of her time in New York with her daughter, Grace, Mrs. Gentry, returning every summer to visit her daughter, Clara, Mrs. Will Allen, and sister, Mrs. W. C. Toney, and relatives and friends. Nolachucky Scott's (Mrs. B. M. Allud's) work in Nolachucky Chapter has gone down in history. Erwin and Unicoi County will ever be proud of her first baby born in Erwin after the county was formed in 1876.

Florence G. Booth, born Nov. 21, 1874, died Jan. 8, 1885, age 11 years 1 month 12 days; buried on family plot on Erwin Old Road.

Jobe Cemetery

Saba Nelson, wife of Wm. White, born Oct., 1887, died Aug. 4, 1911.
Mary, wife of Landon Anderson, born Oct. 16, 1876, died July 9, 1911.

Wm. S. Baker, born April 24, 1892, died Jan. 28, 1916.

Ina May Worthen, wife of Chas. F. Duncan, born 1886, died 1922.

John Wiley Campbell, born April 3, 1878, died Dec. 21, 1927.

Carl F. Dryman, born 1894, died 1928.

S. C. Morgan, born April 22, 1851, died Sept. 20, 1923.

John S. Broyles, born 1845, died 1916.

Margaret ,wife of John S., born 1854, died 1920.

Rhoda E. Toney, born May 4, 1838, died Feb. 23, 1893.

Rachel S., wife of J. J. Toney, born Jan. 14, 1840, died Dec. 19, 1910.

Will H. Hunt, born Dec. 27, 1868, died Oct. 6, 1890.

John R. Elliott, born April 12, 1870, died Nov. 19, 1907.

Margaret Don Turnbull, wife of S. K. Cloyd, born March 5, 1855, died July 27, 1927.

Mollie L. T. McNabb, wife of W. B. McNabb, born Jan. 27, 1853, died June 19, 1887.

G. W. Harrison, born July 19, 1860, died Nov. 28, 1913.

Isac G. Burlison, born Aug. 7, 1856, died July 25, 1914.

Peter Wills, Son of Lewis Wills

Peter Wills, married to Susan Weitzel. To them were born the following children (Bible records, Mrs. B. G. Wills, Mountain City, Tenn.):

Mary, born Jan. 6, 1807; married Adam Shoun; died June 22, 1885.

John, born Dec. 16, 1808; married Polly Neal of Virginia; died Nov. 27, 1886.

Lewis, born Sept. 6, 1810; married Sara Crabtree of Virginia.

Catherine, born March 9, 1812; married Rev. A. Murphey; died Nov. 24, 1904.

Caleb, born Nov. 6, 1813, died March 3, 1903.

William, born Oct. 3, 1815, died Aug. 15, 1886.

David, born Sept. 5, 1817, died young.

Margaret, born Feb. 24, 1820, died at age of 16.

Adam, born April 12, 1822; married Amanda Orr of Virginia; died Dec. 17, 1898.

James, born Aug. 22, 1824; married Eliza Orr, sister to Amanda and Sara Orr; died Feb. 16, 1908.

Peter, born Aug. 26, 1827; married Sara Orr. sister to Amanda and Eliza Orr; died Feb. 6, 1863.

Susanna, born Aug. 3, 1829; married Clifford Donnelly; died July 3, 1903.

Wills Family, Johnson County, Tenn.

Sent by Mrs. W. L. Cook.

Lewis Wills landed at Philadelphia in 1748 at the age of 4 years. His father died at sea during the voyage to America from Germany.He had a step-mother who took little interest in him. He was adopted by a family in Lancaster, Pa. He remained there until he was married at the age of 21, to Catherine Dick. Seven children were born to them (Bible record):

John, born 1772; married Miss Snodgrass, 1794.

Peter, born Dec. 23, 1776; married Susan Weitzel, 1806.

Elizabeth, born 1778; married Alfred Smith, 1808.

Mary, born 1779; married Henry Smith, 1800.

Barbary, born 1782; married Thomas McQueen, 1802.

Lewis, born April 1, 1784; married Catherine Wetzel, 1804.

Sara, born 1786.

Lewis, Sr., lost his wife and married Ellen Martha King at New River, Ash County, N. C., in 1808. To them five children were born: Jacob, born 1809.

Robert, born 1811.
Sophia, born 1813.
Ellen, born 1815.
Martha, born 1817, died 1904.

From papers in Revolutionary War pension claims w-1018, it appears Lewis Wills enlisted in Virginia May 1, 1781, served eighteen months in Capt. Lammes' Company and Col. Gaskin's Virginia Regiment and was at the Battle of Jamestown and the capture of the army at Cornwallis. He was allowed a pension on his application.

Lotspeich-Browder Bible Record

(Bible in possession of C. D. Browder, near Sweetwater, Tenn.) Sent by Mrs. C. L. Clark.

Marriages

John J. Browder and Elizabeth J. Lotspeich, married Dec. 12, 1844.
Charles David Browder and Nettie Adkins, married Nov. 7, 1888.
Mildred Browder and Fred Reeves, married Oct. 14, 1919.
Eli Jefferson Browder and Helen Warren, married Dec. 26, 1930.
Ernest T. Browder and Helen Andrews, married Aug. 16, 1926.

Births

John J. Browder, born Nov. 9, 1818.
Elizabeth Lotspeich, born March 7, 1875.
Elizabeth A. Browder, born Oct. 10, 1845.
Mary F. Browder, born Aug. 24, 1847.
Amanda J. Browder, born April 12, 1849.
William L. Browder, born Nov. 29, 1850.
Sarah A. Browder, born Aug. 13, 1852.
John W. Browder, born April 1, 1854.
Charles D. Browder, born Jan. 27, 1856.
Nancy E. Browder, born Feb. 19, 1858.
Julia E. Browder, born Feb. 16, 1862.
Alice G. Browder, born March 11, 1866.
Samuel L. Browder, born Sept. 10, 1868.
Mildred E. Browder, born Aug. 14, 1889.
Ernest T. Browder, born Dec. 9, 1890.
Eli Jefferson Browder, born May 27, 1894.
Margaret Louise Browder, born Oct. 29, 1897.

Deaths

Sarah A. Browder, died Sept. 4, 1867.
Julia E. Browder, died Sept. 25, 1873.
William L. Browder, died July 1, 1878.
Nannie E. Browder, died March 26, 1882.
John W. Browder, died April 18, 1890.
John Jefferson Browder, died July 14, 1903.
Alice Browder Hardin, died Oct. 9, 1919.
Elizabeth Lotspeich Browder, died Jan. 12, 1921.
Bettie A. Browder, died Sept. 16, 1921.
Mary F. Cleveland, died Dec. 25, 1921.
Samuel L. Browder, died Dec. 30, 1927.
Amanda Browder Dickey, died Dec. 24, 1929.
Mildred Browder Reeves, died Oct. 18, 1921.

Bible Record

The records copied below are taken from an old Bible given to Mrs. James A. Reagan, Sweetwater, Tenn., several

years ago by a great-aunt who was born and lived most of her life in New England. In the possession of Elizabeth Hammond Reagan.

MARRIAGES

Grandparents of Mrs. Lettes Hammond: Amasa Fuller to Chloe.
Lucy Fuller, daughter of Chloe and Amasa Fuller, to Joshua Fosket.
Margaret, daughter of J. and L. Fosket, to Lettes Hammond, June 12, 1800.

Children of M. and L. Hammond:
Jeduthan Hammond to Sophira Bicknell, Oct. 29, 1827.
Margaret Hammond to Aaron F. Wells, Sept. 23, 1829.
Joshua F. Hammond to Eliza Ann Leake, April 1, 1832.
Elizabeth H. Hammond to Ephraim E. Wiley, Feb. 18, 1833.
Samuel Hammond to Margaret M. ———, Feb. 16, 1848.

Children of Jeduthan and Mary Hammond:
Jane Hammond to Ephraim Landress.
Paul Hammond to Sarah Edson.
Elizabeth Hammond to Asa Hacket.
Jeduthan Hammond to Hannah Haman.
Jedediah Hammond to Nancy Brooks.
Mary Hammond to Elisha Gaswell.
Lidia Hammond to Bishop Ashley.
Hepsibah Hammond to ——— Hedley (?).
Lettes Hammond to Margaret Fosket.

BIRTHS

Mary Jenny Hammond, mother of Lettes Hammond, born May 18, 1743, in Dartmouth or New Bedford, Mass.
Jeduthan Hammond, father of L. Hammond, born April 14, 1740, in Rochester, Mass.
Lettes Hammond, March 28, 1778.
Margaret Fosket, his wife, Dec., 1784.
Lucy Fosket, mother of Margaret Fosket, born Aug. 27, 1764 (?).
Paul Hammond, son, born in Rochester, Mass., May 20, 1772, died May 5, 1795.
Paul Hammond, Jr., born in Rochester, Mass., May 13, 1795.

Children of Lettes and Margaret Hammond:

BIRTHS

Jeduthan, March 15, 1802.
Joshua, July 27, 1805.
Margaret, March 10, 1807.
———, Jan. 2, 1809.
Joshua Fosket, April 14, 1810.
Elizabeth Harket, Sept. 12, 1813.
Penelope Keys, July 14, 1820.
Samuel, Feb. 3, 1823.

Children of Samuel Hammond and wife:

BIRTHS

Adeline L., Feb. 15, 1849.
Emma B. (?), Sept. 6, 1851.

Penelope K. Hammond joined the South Congregational Church July 7, 1839, at Middletown, Conn.

Children of Jeduthan Hammond and Sophira, his wife:

BIRTHS

Caroline H., July 25, 1823.
Mary E., June 20, 1831.
Ellen A., Aug. 8, 1841.
Samuel Edson, May, 1843.

Children of Margaret Hammond and Aaron Wells, her husband:
Edward, died at 3 months.
Edward Hubbard II., Ephraim Wiley, Samuel Osgood, George Eugene, Francis Henry.

Children of Joshua Hammond and wife:
Edward Niles, William Emmerson, Charles, Penelope Maria, Cornelia, Joshua, Ann Eliza, Henry Wayne, Julia, Frank.

Children of Elizabeth Hammond and husband, Ephraim:
Emerson Wiley, Margaret Ann, Frances Elizabeth, William Har-

low, a son not living, Virginia Watson, Olin Fiske, George Ephraim, Charles Sherwood.

DEATHS

Lettes Hammond, died Sept. 2, 1852, age 74 years 5 months.
Aaron F. Wells, son-in-law of Lettes Hammond, died Dec. 28, 1855, age 49 years 11 months.
Samuel Hammond, died April 3, 1856, age 33 years 2 months.
Margaret F. Hammond, wife of Lettes Hammond, died April 22, 1861, age 76 years 4 months.
Sophira Bicknel, daughter-in-law, died July 4, 1861, age 53 years.
Joshua, son of L. and M. Hammond, died Sept. 20, 1805, age 1 year 2 months.
A son, age 2 days, died Jan. 4, 1803.
A son, died Sept. 12, 1812.
A daughter, died April 17, 1816.
Joshua F. Hammond, died April 27, 1874, age 64 years 13 days.
Jeduthan Hammond, died May 10, 1876, age 74 years.
Margaret Hammond Wells, died May 20, 1888, age 81 years, 2 months.

Elizabeth Hammond Buchanan, wife of James A. Reagan, daughter of Frances Elizabeth Wiley (Buchanan), daughter of Elizabeth Harket Hammond (Wiley), daughter of Lettes Hammond, son of Jeduthan Hammond.

YOAKUMS BIBLE RECORD

The Yoakums emigrated to America with the first Dutch settlers on the Island of Manhattan, the present site of New York City.

They were of Welsh extraction. In the Welsh language the original name was so uncouth and knotty that our fathers of three or four hundred years ago agreed to have it changed into "Iugum," or "Jagum," which is the latin term for "Yoke." A short time under the influence of their English neighbors, it was again changed into "Yocum" and finally "Yoakum."

The given names of the Yoakums in the City of New York are not known, but Valentine, a son of one of them, moved to South Potomac on Potomac on Peach Creek. After he married, Valentine Yoakum (1721), youngest of seven sons, moved to Muddy Creek, Greenbrier County, Va., and settled Yoakum's Station (1771). He was there tomahawked by a Shawnee Indian. With him were his wife and children—all killed but young George, who was swift of foot and of great strength, killing three Indians with a frying pan handle, which he jerked from one as he passed through. He was afterwards in Battle of Point Pleasant. At 25 years of age he married the daughter of Isaac Van Bibber, who fell in that battle. George Yoakum I. continued to live at Muddy Creek, Va., until he became father of three sons, the youngest of whom was George II., when they moved to Powell's Valley.
This was written by Franklin Yoakum (born 1819), son of George Yoakum and Mary Ann Maddy, and given to him by his father, George Yoakum I.—now the property of Chas. H. Yoakum, of Los Angeles, Calif.

HENDERSON YOAKUM'S BIBLE

Sent by Mrs. C. L. Clark.

George Yoakum II., born July 30, 1783, in County of Greenbrier, Va., died March 31, 1841, at Madisonville, Tenn.,; married Mary Ann Maddy, May 27, 1809, at Yoakum's Station, Claiborne County, Tenn.; she was born Nov. 25, 1792, died April 27, 1848. My grandfather, George Yoakum I., with the Van Bibbers, his brother-in-law, established that station about 1790. George Yoakum I. was killed in a bear hunt in the Cumberland Mountains. He was buried near the station.

My father and mother (George Yoakum II. and Mary Ann Maddy) are both buried in Madisonville, Tenn., Monroe County, in church yard of Methodist Church.

Martha Aurelia Yoakum, born Oct. 9, 1827, in Madisonville, Tenn.; married James Askew Wright, May 25, 1848. Martha died Aug. 19, 1852, in Sweetwater, Tenn., and is buried beside her parents, George II. and Mary Ann Yoakum.

George Yoakum of Yoakum's Station in Powells Valley, Tenn., built a fort fourteen miles of Cumberland Gap and named it Yoakum's Fort. He married Margaret Van Bibber and had seven children.

BIRTHS

Isaac Yoakum; married —— Davis, of Powells Valley.

Peter Yoakum; married Sally Stinit, of Powells Valley.

Feltz Yoakum; married Sally Reynolds, of West Illinois.

Robert Yoakum; married —— Berry, of Tennessee.

Margaret Yoakum (called Peggy); married —— Condra, of Powells Valley.

Nancy Yoakum; married ——

George II., born July 30, 1783; married Mary Ann Maddy in 1807.

Children of George and Mary Ann Yoakum:

Henderson, born Sept. 6, 1810, died Nov. 31, 1856.

Marie Louise, born Aug. 2, 1812, died Sept 7, 1854, of cholera.

Washington, born Oct. 6, 1814, died July 20, 1869.

Emily, born Dec. 12, 1816, died Aug. 24, 1854, of cholera.

Franklin, born Nov. 14, 1819, died 1891.

Madison, born March 12, 1822, died 1885.

Celia Ann, born Nov. 19, 1824, died Aug. 24, 1854, of cholera.

Martha Aurelia, born Oct. 9, 1827, died Aug. 19, 1852.

Mary Ann, born Jan. 28, 1830, died Aug. 2, 1857.

Lavinia W., born Sept. 17, 1832, died Sept. 23, 1833.

Adaline, born Aug. 30, 1835, died Dec. 29, 1858.

MARRIAGES

Henderson Yoakum and Eveline Cannon.

Louise Yoakum and Dr. Ben Bayless.

Washington Yoakum and Mary Elizabeth Tunstill.

Emily A. Yoakum and Wertz Stephens.

Franklin Yoakum and Fannie Holt.

Madison Yoakum and Mrs. Elkins (nee Dillard).

Celia Ann Yoakum and George Montgomery Cuson.

Martha Aurelia Yoakum and James A. Wright.

(Three others never married.)

---

1. Henderson Yoakum and Eveline Cannon — Texas Historian — the daughter of Robert Cannon and Ann Galbraith. Children:

Eliza, married D. G. Campbell.

Martha, unmarried.

Mary, married W. T. Robinson.

Annie, unmarried.

Emily, died at age of 3 years.

Houston, married Fannie Dailey.

Robert, unmarried.

George, died in hospital, Richmond, Va.; member of Company 4, 5th Texas Regiment.

Henderson, died at age of 10 years.

---

2. Louise Yoakum (first wife) and Dr. Ben Bayless had no children. Harriet Humphrey (second wife) had one child, Letitia Bayless.

---

3. Washington C. Yoakum, married Mary E. Tunstill—children born in Leavenworth, Kan.:

William, born July 28, 1840; married Caroline McBride.

Mary E., born Oct. 17, 1841; married —— Singer .

Wyndan, born April 8, 1843.

Iodine, born March 28, 1845.

Franklin A.

Lavenia A.

Steven T.
George W.
Hedger.
David M.

---

4. Emily A. Yoakum, married Wertz Stephens—children:
B. T. Stephens.
George W. Stephens, lives at Gyp, Okla.

---

5. Franklin L. Yoakum, married Fannie Holt—children:
William H., married Miss Bass, Waco, Texas.
Charles H., married Ollie ——, member of Congress.
By second wife, Narcissa C. Teague—children:
Dr. Finis, married Mollie Hood, Los Angeles, Calif.
Caledonia B., married J. L. Modrall, Los Angeles, Calif.
Robert D., unmarried.
B. F. Yoakum, married Bettie Porter.
Lillian May, died at age of 16.

Madison S. Yoakum, married Mrs. Elkins; one child:
Matt, Dallas, Texas.

---

7. Celia Ann Yoakum, married George M. Cuson—children:
Ada Aurelia, married Jos. H. Cozart, Philadelphia.
George Oliver, never married, East Tennessee.
John Franklin, married Eliza Poesy.

8. Aurelia Martha Yoakum (first wife), married James A. Wright—one child:
Mary E., married George H. Holliday, Atlanta, Ga.—children:
Mabel, married John T. Moody.
Ethel, married Joseph C. Crankshaw.
George H. Jr., married Leola G. Houser.

---

9. Mary Ann Yoakum, married ——— Lemons, Texas.

---

10. Lavenia A. Yoakum, died at age of 1 year.

---

11. Adaline A. Yoakum, unmarried.

Children of Aurelia Cuson and Joe H. Cozart, who married in Philadelphia, Tenn., and moved to Waukomis, Okla., after children were born—children:
Olive, born Dec. 16, 1872; married John McQuigg in Oklahoma.
Julia, born March 10, 1874; married Earl Douglas, Colorado.
Ethel, born Feb. 29, 1876; married J. M. Childress, Texas.
Ada, born Nov. 20, 1877; died May 11, 1878.
Hattie Glenn, born Nov. 10, 1880; married Will Gregg.
Hugh H., born Jan. 14, 1883; married Verna Burford.
George Henry, born June 4, 1885; married Bessie McFarland.

Reagan-Love Bible Record

Bible in possession of Mira Love Lowry (Mrs. J. W.), Sweetwater, Tenn. Sent by Mrs. C. L. Clark.

Marriages

James H. Reagan and Mira A. Lenoir, married Sept. 3, 1835.
James R. Love of Jackson County, N. C., and Julia Reagan of McMinn County, Tenn., married Nov. 18, 1868.

Births

William Ballard Lenoir Reagan, born May 31, 1838.
Julia Reagan, born Sept. 4, 1843.
James Avery Reagan, born Jan. 7, 1846.
John Martin Reagan, born Feb. 20, 1848.
Franklin Reagan, born July 14, 1851.
Infant son, born Feb. 19, 1854.
James Robert Love, son of John B. and Margaret E. Love, born Aug. 19, 1832.
Infant son of Julia R. and James

R. Love, born Jan. 12, 1871, at Reagan Station, E. T., Va. and Ga. R. R.
Mira Lenoir Love, daughter of Julia R. and James R. Love, born at 12:30 o'clock p.m., June 19, 1872, at Reagan Station, McMinn County, Tenn.
Margaret Bell Love, daughter of Julia Reagan and James R. Love, born at Webster, Jackson County, N. C., Aug. 4, 1874.
Julia Love, daughter of Julia Reagan Love and James R. Love, born at Webster, Jackson County, N. C., March 30, 1876.
James Reagan Love, second son of Julia Reagan Love and James R. Love, born near Sweetwater, Tenn., Dec. 24, 1877.
Elizabeth Avery Love, fourth daughter of Julia and J. R. Love, born Sept. 3, 1879.
Robert John Love, third son of Julia and J. R. Love, born Sept. 19, 1881, named for his great-grandfather, Robert, and grandfather, John B. Love .
Hattie Franklin Love, fifth daughter of Julia R. and J. R. Love, born Feb. 6, 1884.

DEATHS

Infant son, died Feb. 19, 1854.
Franklin Reagan, died Nov. 30, 1862.
John Martin Reagan, died July 17, 1870.
Infant son of Julia R. and James R. Love, died Jan. 12, 1871.
James H. Reagan, died Oct. 15, 1864.
Mira A. Reagan, died March 9, 1879.
Maggie Bell Love, died Jan. 7, 1885.
Col. Jas. R. Love, entered into rest Nov. 10, 1885, at his home near Sweetwater, Tenn. A member of the House of Representatives at the time of his death from his adopted County, Monroe, Tenn. He was an honored son of his State, North Carolina, having served in both branches of the Legislature. A Colonel in the Confederate States Army, he won distinction in arms, etc. His brother, D. L. Love.

DICKEY-BROWDER BIBLE RECORD

(Bible in possession of C. O. Browder, near Sweetwater, Tenn. Presented by D. H. Dickey, as a token of affection, to his daughter and son-in-law, Mr. and Mrs. David A. Browder, March, 1860.)

Sent by Mrs. C. L. Clark.

MARRIAGES

David Asbury Browder and Rachael Letitia Dickey, married Oct. 14, 1858.
William D. Browder and Adalou Peak, married Oct. 5, 1887.
Charles O. Browder and Georgia Elizabeth Duncan, married June 5, 1906.
Hattie Mae Browder and Jacob Elijah Ewing, married Feb. 9, 1923.
Hubert Wesley Browder and Katherine Bonner, married April 14, 1827.
Betty Letitia Browder and Dr. Joseph A. Hardin, married Dec. 27, 1921.

BIRTHS

David Asbury Browder, born March 2, 1835.
Rachael Letitia Browder, born April 27, 1837.
William Dickey Browder, born July 9, 1859.
Bettie Letitia Browder, born Aug. 5, 1861.
David Houston Browder, born Sept. 29, 1863.
Franklin Edward Browder, born May 21, 1867.
Charles Oscar Browder, born Dec. 9, 1870.
Infant son, born Jan. 17, 1872.
Hubert Wesley Browder, born Oct. 24, 1878.

Hattie Mae Browder, born April 6, 1895.
Infant son of W. D. and Adalou Browder, born and departed this life June, 1888.
David Duncan Browder, born May 29, 1907.
Charles O. Browder, Jr., born Sept. 23, 1909.
Mary Elizabeth Browder, born Dec. 5, 1914.
William Robert Ewing, born July 3, 1926.
Ada Lou Ewing, born Aug. 8, 1928.

DEATHS

David Asbury Browder, died April 6, 1883.

Infant son of David and R. L. Browder, died Jan. 19, 1872.

Rachael Letitia Browder, died Jan. 21, 1912.

William Dickey Browder, died July 26, 1929.

LACKEY-BROWDER BIBLE RECORD

(Bible in possession of C. O. Browder, near Sweetwater, Tenn.)

MARRIAGES

William Browder and Elizabeth Lackey, married March 30, 1815.
Maryline Browder and James Stone, married Feb. 9, 1833.
William D. Browder and Sarah A. Deatheridge, married Oct. 24, 1844.
John J. Browder and Elizabeth J. Lotspeich, married Dec. 12, 1844.

BIRTHS

William Browder, born Feb. 10, 1792.
Elizabeth Browder, born Aug. 28, 1793.
Maryline Browder, born Dec. 25, 1815.
John Jefferson Browder, born Nov. 9, 1818.
William Dixon Browder, born Jan. 25, 1823.
James Madison Browder, born Oct. 16, 1824.
Nancy Jane Browder, born May 17, 1827.
Polly Ann Browder, born Oct. 30, 1829.
Darius Powel Browder, born June 2, 1832.
David Asbury Browder, born March 2, 1835.

DEATHS

Polly Ann Browder, died Aug. 30, 1830.
Maryline Browder Stone, died Aug. 7, 1839.
Mother Lackey, died Sept. 5, 1848.
Father Lackey, died Sept. 1, 1837.
Mother Browder, died Nov. 9, 1851.
Sary Campbell, died Sept. 15, 1851.

BIBLE RECORD OF REV. CHARLES TALIAFERRO

(Bible in possession of C. P. Taliaferro, Loudon, Tenn.)
Sent by Elizabeth Taliaferro.

BIRTHS

Charles Taliaferro, born March 5, 1799.
Elizabeth A. Eldredge, born ——.
John Whitlock Taliaferro, born Feb. 25, 1823.
Mark Harden Taliaferro, born Dec. 9, 1824.
Sally Catherine Taliaferro, born April 15, 1827.
Charles P. Taliaferro, born March 12, 1829.
Bethilda Anne Taliaferro, born Oct. 29, 1831.
Richard Dickerson Taliaferro, born May 28, 1841.
William Judson Taliaferro, born Aug. 6, 1843.
Samuel Love Taliaferro, born April 6, 1845.

MARRIAGE

Charles Taliaferro and Elizabeth A. Eldridge, married Oct. 22, 1839 (second wife).

DEATHS

Rev. Charles Taliaferro, died May 23, 1856, at 3 o'clock in the evening.

Jane Eldredge, died ——.

Sarah Jennie Eldridge, died June 29, 1860, at 2 o'clock.

Isabella Jane Eldridge, died Sept. 7, 1854; age 21 months 7 days.

BIBLE RECORD OF DAVID LOW

(Bible in possession of Mrs. Margaret Low Burke, R.F.D., Sweetwater, Tenn.)

Sent by Elizabeth J. Taliaferro.

David Low, born Oct. 1, 1802.

Margaret Currier, born Dec. 25, 1810.

CHILDREN

William E. Low, born —— 11, 1830.

Martha E. Low, born March 12, 1832.

James D. Low, born —— 2, 1834.

John L. Low, born, Dec. 12, 1837.

Margaret E. Low, born Aug. 2, 1844.

Samantha Low, ——.

BIBLE RECORD OF WILLIAM HARRISON

(Bible in possession of Mrs. Jennie Mae Harrison Yearwood, Loudon, Tenn.)

William Harrison, born June 7, 1821.

Martha E. Harrison, born March 6, 1832.

Marshall Leander Harrison, born Jan. 30, 1852.

Mary E. Harrison, born Nov. 30, 1854.

William L. Harrison, born Dec. 6, 1863.

Margaret J. Harrison, born Dec. 6, 1863.

Charles Author Harrison, born July 29, 1869.

Samuel Estel Harrison, born Nov. 21, 1894.

William Benjamin Harrison, born Nov. 7, 1900.

Callie Harrison, born April 25, 1864.

MARRIAGES

William Harrison and Martha E. Lowe, married Feb. 11, 1851.

William L. Harrison and Callie Thomas, married Nov. 26, 1893.

Charlie A. Harrison and Hattie M. Willson, married June 12, 1894.

DEATHS

Marshall L. Harrison, died Sept. 20, 1862.

William Harrison, died Sept. 26, 1891.

Martha E. Harrison, died March 11, 1915.

Thos. L. Upton, died March 23, 1877 .

Maggie's baby, died June 10, 1889.

Mollie Pennington's funeral was preached from Hosea 13: 14, Sunday, May 20, 1883, by Mr. Ingram.

BIBLE RECORDS

(From C. M. Hotchkiss family Bible, now in possession of his daughter, Mrs. Sarah Hotchkiss, Lenoir City. Tenn.)

DEATHS

Sallie Hotchkiss, died Aug. 4, 1889.

Claiborne H. Hotchkiss, died Jan. 26, 1893.

Jackson S. Johnston, died Oct. 17, 1925.

MARRIAGES

Sarah Wyly, married C. M. Hotchkiss, Nov. 20, 1840.

Louisa Hotchkiss and John Lauderdale, married Jan. 12, 1887.

BIRTHS

Betsy Ann Hotchkiss, born Nov. 6, 1841.

Artymeas Hotchkiss, born in Roane County, Tenn., Aug. 12, 1843.

Louisa Hotchkiss, born in Roane County, Tenn., Nov. 23, 1845.

Martha Isabellah Hotchkiss, born in Roane County, Tenn., April 16, 1848.

Claibourne Meigs Hotchkiss, Jr., born in Roane County, Tenn., Tuesday, —— 12, 1851.

C. M. Hotchkiss, born in Roane County, Tenn., Sept. 22, 1802.

Sarah Wyly, his wife, born in Madison City, Ala., Sept. 14, 1811.

GEORGE N. WELCH BIBLE RECORD

Putnam County, Tenn.

Sent by Mrs. Arthur Harrison.

George Nathaniel Welch, born Jan. 28, 1879, and Effie Florence Walker, born Sept. 25, 1880, were married, Nov. 25, 1900.

CHILDREN

Mildred, born Sept. 19, 1901.
Ruth, born Oct. 22, 1903.
George N., Jr., born Aug. 26, 1906.
Robert Lee, born Dec. 31, 1912.
Effie Florence, born April 13, 1915.
Luray, born Jan. 11, 1821.
Mary Walker, born March 16, 1925.

MARRIAGES

Mildred to Arthur Porter Harrison, June 20, 1923.
Ruth to Andrew F. Mason, June 29, 1929.

GRANDCHILDREN

Samuel Arthur Harrison, born Feb. 23, 1925.
Ruth Boyd Harrison, born Sept. 29, 1927.
Betty Ruth Mason, born April 29, 1930.

FAMILY RECORD OF GEORGE WASHINGTON LEE

Monroe County, Tenn.

BIRTHS

George Washington Lee, born Oct. 17, 1813, son of William Carroll Lee.
Mary Blackston Lee, born Jan. 14, 1814.
Thursa Lee, daughter, born Nov., 1837.
William M. Lee, son.
John Blackston Lee, son.
James Argil Lee, son.
Isaac Carroll Lee, son, born April 4, 1846.

MARRIAGES

George Washington Lee to Mary Blackston, Dec. 25, 1836.
Thursa Lee to Berry Slaton, 1857.
William M. Lee to Athalona Reagan, Jan., 1868.
John Blackston Lee to Martha Carden.
James Argil Lee to Bettie Snider, Sept., 1895.
Isaac Carroll to Laura Reagan, July 3, 1870.

DEATHS

George Washington Lee, died Feb. 3, 1889.
Mary Blackston Lee, died Dec. 2, 1894.
Thursa Lee Slaton, died, 1924.
William M. Lee, died Sept., 1900.
John Blackston Lee, died, 1910.
James Argil Lee, died, 1902.
Isaac Carroll Lee, died Nov. 12, 1919.

Family Record of Erasmus Reagan

Sweetwater, Tenn.

Births

Erasmus, son of Jeremiah and Rachael Reagan, born Jan. 15, 1818, in Brickingham County, Va.; married Nancy Amner Mize of Alabama and moved to Monroe County, Tenn.; served in the Confederate Army, 1862 to 1863.
Athalonia Reagan, Feb. 11, 1849.
Laura Amner Reagan, Dec. 8, 1851.
LaUna Reagan, Jan. 4, 1854.
Pan Dora Reagan, March 7, 1857.
Dixie Reagan, Aug. 10, 1860.
John Fletcher, April 6, 1864 (John Fletcher Reagan).
Mary Lee Reagan, June 6, 1868.
Landon Carter, Aug. 14, 1871.

Marriages

Athalonia Reagan, to William Lee, Jan., 1868.
Laura Amner Reagan, to Isaac Carroll Lee, July 3, 1870.
LaUna Reagan, to Robert Thompson, Feb., 1893.
Pan Dora, to Andy K. Harper (Pan Dora Reagan).
Dixie Reagan, to Samuel L. Crandal.
John Fletcher Reagan, to Mallie Cobb.
Mary Lee Reagan, to R. A. Autry.

Deaths

Erasmus Reagan, March 8, 1899.
Nancy Mize Reagan, Dec. 3, 1886.
Athalonia Reagan Lee, June 30, 1919.
LaUna Reagan Thompson, April, 1926.
Dixie Reagan Crandal, April 24, 1931.
Landen Carter Reagan, Jan. 21, 1884.

Family Record of Isaac Carroll Lee

Monroe County, Tenn.

Births

Isaac Carroll Lee, born April 4, 1846; married to Laura Reagan July 3, 1870.

Erasmus Reagan Lee, son, born Aug. 2, 1871.

Washington Lee, son, Aug. 5, 1873.

Mary Lillian Lee, daughter, Oct. 5, 1875.

Dixie Rosaline Lee, daughter, April 17, 1878.

James Franklin Lee, son, Feb. 12, 1880.

Robert Taylor Lee, son, Feb. 17, 1884.

Arnold Reece Lee, son, Jan. 14, 1887.

Ivanho Rex Lee, son, Jan. 28, 1889.

Nancy Lou Lee, daughter, June 22, 1893.

Marriages

Erasmus Reagan Lee, to Mary McCollum, Sept., 1894.
Mary Lillian Lee, to John Leonard Mize, July, 1899.
Dixie Rosaline Lee, to Calloway Sloan.
James Franklin Lee, to Beatrice Patterson.
Robert Taylor Lee, to Prudie Blankenship.
Arnold Reece Lee, to Racheal Stephens, Dec., 1909.
Arnold Reece Lee, to Minnie Tallent, Dec., 1914.
Ivanho Rex Lee, to Eva Crandal.
Nancy Lou Lee, to John Taylor, Sept. 9, 1916.

Deaths

Isaac Carroll Lee, Nov. 12, 1919.
Washington Lee, June 12, 1874.
Rachael Stephens Lee, 1914.

FAMILY RECORD IN JOHN MIZE BIBLE
Loudon, Tenn.

John Shepard Mize, father, born June 24, 1827.
Jane Keeling Mize, mother, born Aug. 23, 1832.
Mary Jane Mize, sister, born Oct. 10, 1854.
Julia Carrie Mize, sister, born Oct. 21, 1855.
Sarah Frances Mize, sister, born Sept. 9, 1857.
Nannie Rolina Mize, sister, born Oct. 2, 1859.
James Keeling Mize, brother, born June 24, 1862.
Elizabeth Annie Mize, sister, born Aug. 21, 1866.
Lena May Mize, sister, born May 19, 1871.
John Leonard Mize, born May 18, 1874.
Carrie Lou Mize, daughter, born May 2, 1900.
Ethel Lee Mize, daughter, born March 15, 1902.
Mary Katherine Mize, daughter, born April 20, 1911.

MARRIAGES

*John Leonard Mize, to Mary Lillian Lee, July 18, 1899, Madisonville, Tenn.
Ethel Lee Mize, to Max Parker, Dec. 30, 1927, Loudon, Tenn.

DEATHS

Sarah Frances Mize, June 5, 1857.
James Keeling Mize, Jan. 11, 1868.
Elizabeth Annie Mize, June 2, 1870.
Lena May Mize, May 19, 1871.
Nannie Rolina Mize, Aug. 29, 1876.
Jane Keeling Mize, Dec. 29, 1899.
John Shepard Mize, Aug. 7, 1906.
Julia Carrie Mize Johnston, June 2, 1918.

JOHN H. RAY BIBLE RECORD
Overton County

*John H. Ray, born Aug. 17, 1837 (Ray).
Sarah Ann Officer, born April 10, 1841; married April 18, 1859.

CHILDREN

*Lou Cynthia, born Nov. 8, 1861.
W. B., born Feb. 29, 1860.
Robert Lee, born Jan. 1, 1865.

MARRIAGE

*Lou Cynthia, to James C. Walker, Dec. 18, 1879.
James C. Walker, born Aug. 11, 1853.

CHILDREN

*Effie Florence, born Sept. 25, 1880 (Walker).
Robert Elmo, born Sept. 25, 1882.
Sarah Bell, born Aug. 31, 1884.
Willie, born Nov. 23, 1886.
Joseph Hubert, born March 17, 1890.
James Edward, born Aug. 31, 1903.
Father and mother of James C. Walker:
Andrew Jackson Walker, born June 12, 1829.
Clementine Verble, born Sept., 1831; married Jan. 23, 1851.
(Father of A. J. was Benjamin, who married the Widow Sehon, who owned the Standing Stone Inn on the old Walton Road. *Tradition.*)

---

*Indicates line. See George N. Welch Bible record for continuance.

JOSEPH LEE BIBLE RECORD
Overton County

John W. Lee, first son of Augustine and Rachel (Nichols) Lee of White County, born Feb. 8, 1823, near Muddy Creek in Roane County.
*Martha Lee, daughter of Augustin and Rachel Lee, born 1837.
(Record of Zach, Jackson, Rachel,

---

*See John Welch Bible record.

Ruth, Kathrine, George W., and Polk, other children of Augustin, unrecorded here. See will of Augustin in White County.)

LEONARD RAY BIBLE RECORD

Overton County

*Leonard Ray (here spelled Rea) was born Oct. 23, 1780; married "Rebecca," Jan. 7, 1803.

CHILDREN

John C., born Sept. 1, 1804.
*Benjamin B., born Sept. 8, 1806.
Biddy, born Feb. 25, 1809.
Nancy Lee, born Feb. 23, 1811.
George A., born June 22, 1814.
Theney, born Sept. 28, 1824.
Washington, born April 29, 1828.
*Benjamin B., married Catherine Sehon (date missing).

CHILDREN

*John H. Ray, born Aug. 17, 1837.
Martha Jane, daughter of John C., born April 19, 1836.
James K. Polk Ray, born Aug. 15, 1844.

DEATHS

Sister Nancy Cox, died May 29, 1814. (Signed) Leonard Rea.

Leonard Ray, died Sept. 10, 1853.

Letter inclosed dated Jan. 19, 1860, addressed to Rebecca, whose death is unrecorded.

*B. B. Ray, died Nov. 8, 1852.

His wife, Catherine Sehon Ray, died Sept. 19, 1886.

---

*Indicates line of descent. See John H. Ray Bible record.

WILLIAM ALEXANDER OFFICER BIBLE RECORD

Overton County

William Alexander Officer, born Feb. 22, 1812.
Cynthia Holford, born Jan. 1, 1819; married Feb. 11, 1836.

CHILDREN

Alexander Officer, born Feb. 1, 1837.
Henrietta Officer, born Aug. 11, 1838.
*Sarah Anne Officer, born April 10, 1841.
Margaret Officer, born May 7, 1843.
John Holford Officer, born July 7, 1845.
Frances Marchbanks Officer, born March 29, 1847.
James Lancaster Officer, born May 24, 1853.
Leanne Officer, born March 6, 1857.

MARRIAGES

*Sarah Anne, to John H. Ray, April 18, 1859.
John Holford Officer, to Ida Chowning, May 5, 1870.
Henrietta, to A. F. Capps, March 18, 1856.

DEATHS

Lieut. Alexander Officer, died May 20, 1862, at Columbus, Miss. His tombstone was marked with the first letters of his name.
Cynthia, wife of Alexander, Sr., died Sept. 22, 1877. (Wounded severely by Union soldiers during the War Between the States, as she tried to defend six wounded Southerners harbored in her house. The six were, nevertheless, tied to the gate post and shot. The post still stands with some of the bullets lodged in it, on the William Alexander Officer homestead in Overton County, later known as Gib Boswell Farm.)
William Alexander Officer, died Sept. 8, 1886.
John Holford, died March 10, 1912.

MARRIAGES

Frances, to J. Johnson, Aug. 30, 1867.
James L., to P. Emma Hampton, Nov. 28, 1878.

---

*See John H. Ray Bible record for descendants of Sarah Anne.

JOHN W. WELCH BIBLE RECORD

Putnam County

*John Wesley Welch, born Feb. 21, 1859.
Julia Ann Ford, born March 26, 1857; married Aug. 19, 1877.

GRANDPARENTS

*Nathaniel Welch, born April 11, 1833;died Feb. 14, 1905.
Martha Lee, born 1837.
(Marriage unrecorded. See D. Catherine Welch Bilbrey Bible record below for birth date of first child.)

Abraham Ford, born Jan. 3, 1821; died Dec. 12, 1890.
Nancy Womack, born Dec. 26, 1819.

CHILDREN

Children of John W. and Julia: Martha.
*George Nathaniel, born Jan. 26, 1879.
Abraham P., born May 28, 1881.
Charles, born Sept. 11, 1883.
Nancy Ethel, born Aug. 16, 1890.
Ova Ellen, born Feb. 10, 1894.

From Catherine Welch Bilbrey Bible:

Catherine Welch, daughter of Nathaniel and Martha, born Jan. 1, 1858.

---

*See Geo. N. Welch Bible record for continuance.

TOMBSTONE RECORDS

Nathaniel Welch, born April 11, 1833; died Feb. 14, 1905.

Martha (Lee) Welch, born 1837; died July 8, 1899.

A REAL DAUGHTER

Sent by Mrs. Oscar Knox, Ocoee Chapter, Cleveland, Tennessee.

This paper was written by Emma L. Hampton, a granddaughter of Benjamin Isbell, eldest son of Thomas Isbell.

Marks only grave of a "Real Daughter" in this immediate section of the State.

Thinking of a "Real Daughter," the mind intuitively wanders back to her ancestor who was willing to sacrifice all, even life, if necessary, for his country.

Such a one we find in Thomas Isbell, who when a brave, gallant youth of 18 years, enlisted in the Army of the Revolution, continuing in active service five years.

At King's Mountain Thomas Isbell and four brothers were in the regiment of Colonel Benjamin Cleveland, their father's neighbor and friend, which regiment was the first to reach the summit, and fought gallantly throughout the Battle of King's Mountain (Oct. 7, 1780, which continued only an hour; short but decisive).

I might say, in passing, that while visiting the haunts of my ancestors in Western North Carolina I had the pleasure of seeing the home of Benjamin Cleveland, parts of which are more than a hundred years old; and near by stands an old mill (still in use) in which corn was ground for Cleveland's regiment.

It is also interesting to note that our town, Cleveland, Tenn., was named for this hero of King's Mountain fame.

It was while returning home after the Battle of King's Mountain that as Thomas Isbell stopped to rest in the home of Benjamin Howard he first met the daughter of the house, Discretion Howard, who afterward became his wife.

In their home on the Yadkin River

they reared a large family, five generations of which have occupied the same home.

The youngest daughter, Mary Isbell, so beautiful that she was called "Pretty Polly," was so attractive that she was soon won by young Joseph Tucker, son of a prominent neighbor, and they "emigrated" to Tennessee, established a home about a mile southwest of Cleveland, where she retained throughout a long life her attractive manner which drew to her a host of friends to whom she dispensed lavish hospitality.

Her children never tired of her thrilling accounts of the hardships and privations of that period, suffering by her soldier father. She said he had ridden through deep snow with hungry wolves camping at the stirrups of his saddle. She also said that he bore the title "Captain of the Light Horse," though no official proof of that statement has ever been found. She told further that at the sight of a "Red Coat" (British) the horses would rear and plunge to make a charge. We prize these reminiscences of a "Real Daughter."

His eldest son, Benjamin, said that he was slightly wounded in one battle and that his health was impaired by exposure during the war.

It was with pride that Ocoee Chapter, after having borne on her roll twelve descendants of this Revolutionary soldier, should assume the marking of the grave of his most distinguished daughter; so, on December 21, 1924, anniversary of her birth, a large number of descendants and friends wended their way to her grave in Fort Hill Cemetery; and while the Regent, Mrs. John Milne, presided, they listened eagerly to a tender, most touching tribute by the late Dr. Harry B. Duncan; and as all were stirred by strains of soft music, the veil concealing the beautiful bronze marker was withdrawn by Mary Stamper, Anne Stamper, Joe Corn and Charlie Hardwick, great-great-grandchildren of that revered daughter of Isbell family.

This paper could have no more fitting climax than the addition of this incident:

On January 21, 1927, in the beautiful Yadkin River Valley of Western North Carolina, encompassed by the everlasting hills and sponsored by Colonel Ninian Bell Chapter, D. A. R., of Lenoir, N. C., Ocoee Chapter had the pleasure and the honor of marking the graves of two Revolutionary heroes, Thomas Isbell and Benjamin Howard, father and grandfather of our "Pretty Polly," our only Real Daughter of the American Revolution.

Stott, Holden, Cashmere, Noble, of England and American West Bromwich, Staffordshire, England.

John Cashmere, an officer (medical) in the English Army, died in India.

Daughters:

Anna Maria Smythe Weld Fitzherbert (wife of George IV.).

Elizabeth Cashmere, married John Holden.

Nancy Holden, married Jeremiah Stott.

Jane Stott, married James Noble.

Nancy Holden Stott, neice of Mme. Fitzherbert, born Sept. 14, 1801; died April 5, 1881.

CHILDREN

Sarah Stott (Woo), born Sept. 18, 1820; died Sept. 28, 1904.

Charlotte Stott, born Oct. 20, 1821; died in early childhood.

Elizabeth Stott, born Oct. 25, 1823; died in early childhood.

Harriet Stott (Jones), born Nov. 22, 1824; died Aug., 1898.

Jeremiah Stott, born Aug. 23, 1826; died Aug. —.

Isaac Stott, born July 8, 1828.

Jane Stott (Noble), born Dec. 29, 1829; died Nov. 14, 1906.

Isiah Stott, born March 25, 1831; died Sept. 18, 1890.

Ann Stott (Bricker), born Jan. 8, 1834; died Aug. 16, 1901.

Rachel Stott, born July 3, 1834; died Aug. 16, 1901.

Rachel Stott, born July 3, 1835; died Aug. 16, 1901.
John Stott, born Jan. 26, 1838.
James Holden Stott, born Dec. 4, 1840; died July 2, 1911.
Benjamin Stott, born Nov. 10, 1842; died Jan., 1897.
Martha Stott.
Matilda Stott.
Elijah Stott.
Jane Stott, married James Noble, Aug. 4, 1849.

Mary Attaway Noble, daughter of James and Jane Noble, born Jan. 29, 1865; married William Francis Teate, Dec. 13, 1822.

Mary Sherley Teate, daughter of William and Mary Noble Teate, born Sept. 25, 1893; married Donald Bain Todd, Jan. 27, 1913.

Mme. Anna Maria Fitzherbert, great-great-aunt of Mrs. Donald Bain Todd, married George IV. (then Prince of Wales) in 1736; Mme. Fitzherbert was of the Roman Catholic faith, and was the object of the King's most lasting attachment.

In the year 1786-1787 the Queen received the wife of the Prince, Mrs. Fitzherbert, in the most courteous manner in public. London, Nov. 11, 1907, by permission of King Edward, the Daily Chronicle asserts a package of papers consigned to the care of Coutts Bank, by Mrs. Fitzherbert (Maria Anne Smythe Weld), under the understanding that it was not to be opened for a long time, has now, after seventy years, been opened, and proved that to be the marriage certificate and other indisputable proofs that George IV. was actually married to Mrs. Fitzherbert.

Mrs. Fitzherbert was the daughter of Dr. John Cashmere. Her mother died while she was an infant, her father being in the Army, she was reared by her uncle, Mr. Walter Smythe, a country squire in Hampshire, and took the name of Smythe.

At 28 years of age Mrs. Fitzherbert married in 1775 Mr. Edward Weld, uncle of the Cardinal of that name, a family held in high esteem by the King, who paid many visits to his castle at Lulwarth.

Mr. Weld died in the first year of their marriage, and she espoused later Mr. Fitzherbert of Swimmerton in Staffordshire, who died in May, 1781, leaving her a most attractive person, with a fortune of two thousand pounds a year. Looking at her portrait by Conway, and by Romney, we can see of what kind were the blooming charms that so fascinated "an august person," the exquisitely cut lips, the round features, the store of refined good humor. On her death, in 1837, she enjoyed an annuity of 6,000 pounds, procured for her from the Prince, through the late Queen, and the Duke of York, strange to say, both her best friends. She was buried at Brighton, living to be nearly 40 years of age.

References

Papers in Coutt's Bank, sealed, and opened by Edward, King of England.
Mortgage on Palace at Brighton.
Certificate of Marriage, Dec. 21, 1785.
Letters from the late King, relating to the marriage, signed, George IV.
Will written by the late King (George IV.).
Memorandum by Mrs. Fitzherbert, attached to letters written by the clergyman who performed the ceremony.

Copied from the family Bible of Jeremiah Stott and wife, Nancy Nan Cashmere Holden Stott, now in the possession of Jerry Stott, son of Jeremiah and Nancy Stott, and cousin to Mrs. D. B. Todd, Etowah, Tenn.

SHERLEY, BROWN, BROOKS AND TEAT RECORDS

From the Bible of Richard Charles Sherley, now owned by Mrs. D. B. Todd (Mary Sherley Teat), of Etowah, Tenn.

Great-great-grandfather of Richard Charles Sherley. On the front leaf of said Bible appears the following: "Richard Charles Sherley, 1817, Jones County, Ga."

Edmund, John, Richard, James and William Sherley, brothers, were born in Scotland and came to Virginia in the early part of 1700. They settled in Augusta County, Va., became satisfied, separated, one going into Kentucky, another into South Carolina. Later James, John, Edmund and William settled in Georgia, in the year 1775. He had then a wife and five children, and was granted 250 acres of land at the Ford of McBeans Swamp and 150 acres at Chicasaw Old Path, 200 acres each in the Parishes of St. Paul and St. George.

William Stubly Sherley, Jr., son of the William Sherley mentioned, was born Aug. 31, 1757, in Washington County, Ga.; died May or June 3, 1799, in Jones County, Ga., while on a visit to his Richard Charles.

William Stubly Sherley and Elizabeth Maxwell were married Jan. 27, 1780, in Washington County, Ga.

Elizabeth M. Sherley, born Feb. 7, 1762, in Washington County, Ga.; died May 9, 1807.

Richard Charles Sherley, son of William S. and Elizabeth Sherley, born Sept. 25, 1781, in Jones County, Ga.; died Oct. 10, 1833.

Richard C. Sherley, màrried Sarah Brooks, daughter of John Hanna Brooks, Jones County, Ga., Aug. 5, 1804.

Sarah Brooks Sherley, died Dec. 2, 1824; born Dec. 5, 1787.

Elizabeth Sherley, daughter of Richard and Sarah Sherley, born April 25, 1897; died March 23, 1866; buried in Tallapoosa County, Ala.

Elizabeth Sherley married John Gaillard Brown, Jones County, Ga., May 19, 1825.

John Gaillard Brown, born Dec. 1, 1801, Jones County, Ga.; died in Tallapoosa County, Ala., Jan. 7, 1889.

Sarah Jane Brown, daughter of John Gaillard Brown and Elizabeth Sherley Brown, born in Jones County, Ga., Feb. 11, 1831.

Sarah Jane Brown died in Tallapoosa County, Ala., March 13, 1890.; married William Francis Teat, son of John Marshall and Martha Ball Scott Teat, Dec. 24, 1846, Jones County, Ga.

William Francis Teat, born July 25, 1857, in Tuskgee, Ala.; married Mary Attaway Noble, Dec. 13, 1882, in Jenifer, Ala.

Mary Sherley Teat, born Sept. 25, 1895, in Anniston, Ala.; married Donald Bain Todd, Jan. 27, 1913, at Etawah, Tenn.

Children of William Stubly Sherley and wife, Elizabeth: Edward Sherley, Mahaley Parker, Mary Sherley, Richard Charles (Nathaniel, James Nathen, Samuel, which were triplets), Elizabeth and William, Jr., twins, born 1790.

Children of Richard and Elizabeth Sherley:

Elizabeth, married John Gaillard Brown.

Phoebia, married Uriah Porter.

Kisire (called Kissie), married George King.

Thomas, Nathaniel, Edward, and Aaron.

Children of John Gaillard Brown and wife, Elizabeth Sherley Brown:

William Richard, born March 20, 1836; died Oct. 8, 1856.

Benjamin Thomas, born Jan. 25, 1829; died Oct. 8, 1856.

Charnick Tharp, born May 4, 1833; died June 8, 1862.

Jeremiah, born Sept. 6, 1835; died May 3, 1863.

NOBLE

The name of Noble was first taken up in England a little before the Norman conquest under King Edward the Confessor in 1060, but

was never fully established until after the time of Edward II. in 1307, except for that branch of William de Grenoble, who came from Normandy with William the Conquerer.
The said William de Grenoble went to Kent, where he died, but his descendants went to Lincolnshire, Devonshire, Barning and then to Cornwall. Barning is the county adjoining Cornwall. Their Coat of Arms were granted to the descendants of William de Grenoble for his bravery at the Battle of Hastings, there being on Arms until 1189, when Richard I. introduced their use. Sir John Noble was on March, 1426, a priest of Salisbury; in 1486, William, son of Sir John Noble, married Matilda, daughter of John Blone. William, son of William, was Manucaptor to Thomas le Taggler Burgess return from Farham. In 1566 or 68, Stephen Nichils, son of William, was instituted, on Sept. 13, as "Rector of All Saints" and made trustee of the "Poor Fund." In 1600, James, son of Stephen. In 1640, William, son of James, was heir to the estate of his uncle, George Noble of "Kippernnock." In 1669, John, son of William, wife ——— (record too dim). In 1699, John David Noble, married Susannah (faded), had a son, George, born May 13, 1671; baptized June 13, 1671. George married in 1724 (wife's name faded in records); their son, Samuel, born 1726; married Caroline; their son, Samuel, married Sarah, in 1746. Their son married Susannah Tucker in 1891 (family Bible says 1802). Their son, James, born April 17, 1805; baptized May 5, Cornwall, England; married Jenifer Ward, Dec. 24, 1826.
The above was signed and sealed as a true copy of the Parish Record, Cornwall, England, Certified Copy of Parish Recorder. Signed by R. de Ceyat, Crowan Parish, Cornwall, England, Vic.
James Noble and Susannah Tucker Noble had eight children, viz.: James, John, William, Eliza (died age 19 months), Elizabeth, married Lanyon of France; Mary, married John Vivia; Sarah, married Rhoda; Susan, married Trevenion.
James Noble, son of James and Jenifer Ward Noble, born in Cornwall, England, July 28, 1832; died in Anniston, Ala., Feb. 10, 1908; married Jane, daughter of Jeremiah and Nancy Holden Stott, Aug. 4, 1849.
Jane Stott, wife of James, born Dec. 29, 1829, in West Bromwich, Straffordshire, England; died Nov. 14, 1906, Anniston, Ala. Their children were:
James Ward Dizon, born March 15, 1851; died Jan. 16, 1916.
Charlotte Elizabeth, born July 2, 1852; died Aug. 18, 1853.
Charles Milton, born June 7, 1854.
Jane Stott (Jennie), born Oct. 28, 1855; died Feb. 15, 1908.
Annie Holden, born Feb. 26, 1856.
George Henry, born Feb. 2, 1860.
Mary Attaway, born Jan. 29, 1862.
Harriet Mabry, born July 27, 1864; died Aug. 18, 1865.
Walter Edwin, born Jan. 28, 1866; died Oct. 23, 1866.
Mary Attaway Noble, daughter of the above James and Jane Noble, married William Francis Teate, Dec. 18, 1882.
Mary Shirley Teat, daughter of Mary Noble and William Francis Teat, born Sept. 25, 1895; married Donald Bain Todd, Jan. 27, 1913.

Exact Copies of Bible Records of the Following Families
Sent by Mrs. E. E. Pearson, Nashville

Edwards family, Sumner County, Tenn.
James Douglass, Cage's Bend, Sumner County.
Mark Rickman, Sumner County, Tenn.
Stark family, Sumner County, Tenn.
Primm family, Stafford County, Va., and St. Clair County, Ill.
Jacob Cartwright, Davidson County, Tenn.

Enoch Cunningham, Davidson County, Tenn.

Mrs. Henry Hart, Davidson County, Tenn.

Charles Leslie Pearson, London, England, and Perry County, Tenn.

Henry Hart, Jr., Robertson and Davidson Counties, Tenn.

Robert Cartwright, Princess Ann County, Va., and Davidson County, Tenn.

Capt. John English, King George County, Va., and Sumner County, Tenn.

Alexander Cotton Cartwright, Davidson County, Tenn.

Henry Hyde, Davidson County, Tenn.

Edwin and Willie Drake Hyde, Davidson County, Tenn.

Edwards family, near Gallatin, Tenn., in possession of Judge B. D. Bell, Nashville, Tenn.

William Edwards, born July 31, 1752; died Jan. 14, 1828.
Sally Edwards, born March 31, 1752; died Jan. 21, 1826.
Elizabeth Edwards, born June 25, 1774; died Feb. 9, 1838.
Tabitha Edwards, born Oct. 2, 1776.
Nancy Edwards, born Dec. 17, 1778.
Peggy Edwards, born Dec. 30, 1779.
Lovey (?) Edwards, born March 8, 1782.
Richard Edwards, born Jan. 27, 1784; died Oct. 7, 1823.
William Edwards, born May 10, 1786.
Sally Edwards, born Nov. 4, 1788.
Cullen Edwards, born Aug. 20, 1796; died Oct. 6, 1823.

Rueben Douglass, born April 6, 1763; died Aug. 25, 1832.
Betsy Douglass (Elizabeth Edwards), his wife, born June 25, 1774.

Willie J. Douglass, born Sept. 21, 1792; died March 18, 1866.
Sophia Douglass, born July 28, 1794; died Jan. 25, 1872.
Peggy Douglass, born Dec. 25, 1796; died Saturday, Aug. 30, 1828.
Evelina Aurville Douglass, born Jan. 23, 1799; died April 4, 1855.
Sally Douglass, born Nov. 18, 1800.
Malissa Douglass, born Nov. 21, 1801; died June 22, 1833.
Bennett E. Douglass, born April 27, 1804; died Jan. 7, 1868.
Patsey Alexander Douglass, born March 18, 1806; died June 24, 1883.
William R. Douglass, born June 24, 1808; died April 5, 1829.
Emma Douglass, born Aug. 21, 1810; died Dec. 10, 1881.
Betsy Douglass, born Aug. 29, 1812; died March 28, 1884.

Lewis and Peggy Green, married Dec. 3, 1815, and first child, William Lauderdale Green, born Feb. 12, 1817; died June 20, 1850.
Reuben Douglass Green, born Dec. 1, 1818.
Sarah Green, born April 20, 1820.
Betsy Green, born July 29, 1821.
Sophia Green, born Oct. 13, 1823.
Edward Livingston Green, born March 16, 1825.
Peggy Green, born Oct. 27, 1826.

Willie and Eliza Douglass, married June 15, 1820.
Lewis and Peggy Green, married Dec. 3, 1815.
William and Evelina Franklin, married Oct. 7, 1821.
William S. and Emma Clark, married March 22, 1831.

Exact copy of family Bible record of James Douglass, Cages Bend, Sumner County, Tennessee, in possession of Judge B. D. Bell, Nashville, Tenn.

MARRIAGES

James Douglass, married Maria A. Hunt, his wife, Sept. 1, 1807.
Merry C. Abston, married Mary Ann Douglass, April 5, 1832.
Robert B. Douglass and Delia Ann Mitchell, married Dec. 15, 1835.
Albert G. Douglass and D. A. Turner, married Aug. 11, 1840.
Chas. E. Boddie and Evaline A. Douglass, married Jan. 24, 1839.
DeWitt C. Douglass and Martha A. Maney, married Jan. 2, 1850.

BIRTHS

James Douglass, Aug. 14, 1783.
Marina A. Douglass, Nov. 5, 1785.
Patsy Douglass, June 6, 1808.
Mary A. Douglass, June 30, 1810.
Robert Douglass, April 3, 1812.
Wm. J. Douglass, April 25, 1819.
Albert Douglass, Feb. 22, 1817.
Harry H. Douglass, June 13, 1819.
Evalina Douglass, Nov. 21, 1821.
Sally Douglass, April 14, 1824.
DeWitt Clinton Douglass, May 20, 1829.

DEATHS

Wm. J. Douglass, Oct. 2, 1817.
Harry H. Douglass, Sept. 23, 1821.
Sarah T. Douglass, Aug. 14, 1845.
Evalina A. Boddie, Nov. 10, 1855.
James Douglass, July 13, 1857.
Albert G. Douglass, May 7, 1863.
Martha H. Douglass, May 10, 1868.
Marina Douglass, Oct. 24, 1869.
Robert B. Douglass, May 11, 1895.
Mary Ann Abston, May 10, 1899.
DeWitt Clinton Douglass, Aug. 11, 1910.

Rickman family, Sumner County, in possession of Mrs. W. C. Minns, Nashville, Tenn.

Mark Rickman, married Mary Harper, Feb., 1786, in Halifax County, N. C. Their children were:
William Rickman, born April 9, 1787.
Sallie Rickman, born Feb. 12, 1789.
Elizabeth Rickman, born Nov. 28, 1791.
Robert Rickman, born June 7, 1794.
Nancy Rickman, born May 2, 1797.
Frances Rickman, born Nov. 8, 1799.
Rebecca Rickman, born Dec. 10, 1803.
Samuel H. Rickman, born Jan. 29, 1805.
Mark Rickman was the son of Robert Rickman and Boyce Tatum, his wife, and was born in Halifax County, N. C., in 1762.
Mary Harper Rickman, wife of Mark Rickman, was born ——, 1763.
Mark Rickman, died in Sumner County, Tenn., Aug. 14, 1805. He was a Revolutionary soldier.
Wm. Rickman, died unmarried.
Sallie Rickman, married John Owen.
Elizabeth Rickman, married William Stovall.
Robert Rickman, married Kathren Read.
Nancy Rickman, married William Carter.
Frances Rickman, married James Martin.
Rebecca Rickman, married Joel Stovall.
Samuel H. Rickman, married Frances E. Henry.
Samuel H. Rickman, born Jan. 29, 1805.
Frances E. Henry Rickman, his wife, born July 13, 1829.
Samuel and Frances Rickman, married Nov. 5, 1846, in Sumner County, Tenn. Their children were:
Louisa M. Rickman, born Aug. 24, 1847.
Marcus D. Rickman, born Aug. 18, 1849.
John H. Rickman, born Feb. 14, 1852.
Sallie Rickman, born June 1, 1854.
Bobbie Rickman, born Nov. 15, 1856.
Nancy Emma Rickman, born Feb. 22, 1859.
Mary Bettie Rickman, born Feb. 15, 1861.

Carney H. Rickman, born April 6, 1864.
William S. Rickman, born Sept. 26, 1866.
Louisa M. Rickman, married John W. Ray.
Marcus D. Rickman, married Ella Mills.
John H. Rickman, married Mattie D. Key.
Sallie Rickman, unmarried.
Bobbie Rickman, unmarried.
Nancy Emma Rickman, married M. M. Cocreham (?).
Mary Betty Rickman, married Wilson C. Nimmo, Feb. 6, 1885.
Carney H. Rickman, married Cora Pearson.
William S. Rickman, married Lucie F. Wood.

Wilson Carey Nimmo and Mary Bettie Nimmo, his wife, are parents of the following children:
Samuel Rickman Nimmo, born June 26, 1888.
Mabel Ray Nimmo, born Feb. 3, 1891.
Wilson Carey Nimmo, Jr., born March 11, 1901.
Samuel Rickman Nimmo and Charlotte Lucile Pearson, his wife, were married ——; issue, Betty Ann Nimmo, born Nov. 15, 1918.
Mable Ray Nimmo, married Kenneth Cayce. Their children:
Kenneth Cayce, Jr.
Samuel Nimmo Cayce.

Wilson Carey Nimmo, Jr., married Nancy Bicknell.

Stark family, of Sumner County, Tennessee, in possession of Mrs. J. W. Roscoe, Goodlettsville, Tenn.

Jeremiah, son of James Stark, who came to Virginia from Scotland, was born and reared in Stafford County, Va.
John, son of Jeremiah Stark, born in Stafford County, Va., Nov. 22, 1748; died in Sumner County, Tenn., May 16, 1814.
His wife, Sarah English, was born in King George County, Va., July 4, 1749; died in Sumner County, Tenn., Sept. 28, 1820. They were married in King George County, Va., Jan. 4, 1769, by the Rev. Brook at 10 o'clock in the morning.
John Stark, born May 8, 1788.
Margaret Primm, born Oct. 1, 1787.
John Stark and Margaret Primm were married by Rev. Mr. Arnet on Sunday evening, Sept. 6, 1812.
Their children:
James Stark, born Jan. 30, 1814; died in infancy.
Elizabeth Stark, born Jan. 30, 1815; died Oct. 10, 1846.
Lydia Stark, born April 16, 1816.
Joseph Carter Stark, born Dec. 30, 1817.
Louisa Stark, born May 30, 1819.
Sarah Anne Stark, born Sept. 4, 1820.
Mary Magdalene Stark, born Dec. 25, 1821.
Evalina Stark, born April 8, 1823.
John Primm Stark, born Aug. 29, 1824.
Margaret Malvina Stark, born April 19, 1826.
Catherine Hansbrough Stark, born Jan. 13, 1828.

Deaths

James Stark, Dec. 5, 1814.
Lydia Stark Judd, July 28, 1848.
Evalina Stark, Feb. 23, 1843.
Elizabeth Stark, Oct. 10, 1846.
Louisa Stark Patton, Aug. 12, 1852.
Margaret Malvina Stark, July 28, 1853.
Catherine Stark, July 18, 1821.
Joseph C. Stark, Nov. 6, 1890.
John Primm Stark, April 1, 1891.
Mary Stark Cartwright, Aug. 19, 1891.
Sarah Anne Stark Cunningham, Dec. 4, 1908.
John Stark, died May 28, 1862.
Margaret Primm Stark, consort of the above John Stark, died Dec. 10, 1872.
John W. Judd, Sr., born Feb. 8, 1812, died Feb. 20, 1861.
Thomas Carter Judd, born April 4, 1837.
John Walters Judd, son of same parents, was born Sept. 6, 1839.

Jeremiah Stark was a Lieutenant in King George's War.
John Stark, son of Jeremiah, was a Captain in the Revolutionary Army and saw four years of service.

Primm family record, in possession of Mrs. J. W. Roscoe, Goodlettsville, Tenn.

John Primm, born May 17, 1750.
Elizabeth Hansborough, wife of John Primm, born Jan. 5, 1761.
John Primm and Elizabeth Hansborough, married in 1777.
William Primm, born Sept. 1, 1778.
John Primm, born July 25, 1780.
Thomas Primm, born May 11, 1782.
James Primm, born Sept. 10, 1783.
Peter Primm, born June 25, 1785.
Daniel Primm, born June 23, 1786.
Margaret Primm, born Oct. 1, 1787.
Enoch Primm, born Dec. 15, 1788.
Elijah Primm, born March 8, 1790.
Silar Primm, born Jan. 6, 1792.
Betsy Primm, born May 26, 1793.
Parmenas Primm, born Oct. 26, 1794.
Joseph Primm, born Sept. 8, 1795.
Levi Primm, born June 11, 1797.
Aram Primm, born July 28, 1799.
Lydia Primm, born Jan. 31, 1801.
Mary Primm, born July 31, 1804.
John Primm and his wife were natives of Stafford County, Va., and emigrated to St. Clair, County, Ill., with their family, except the oldest son, Wm. John Primm, who was a Captain at Yorktown and served seven years in the Revolutionary Army.

Jacob Cartwright Bible record, Davidson County, Tennessee, in possession of Charles Smiley, Goodlettsville, Tenn.

Jacob Cartwright, born Feb. 22, 1767; died Oct. 12, 1828.
Patience Cartwright, his wife, born Nov. 3, 1785; died July 25, 1837; married Nov. 23, 1803. Their children:
Lorzettie Cartwright, born Aug. 20, 1804.
Harriett Cartwright, born Dec. 15, 1807; died Nov. 7, 1874.
Tabitha Cartwright, born April 5, 1809.
John H. Cartwright, born Jan. 1, 1812.
Johnson Cartwright, born July 21, 1816.
Robert Hobdy Cartwright, born July 21, 1816.
Alexander Cotton Cartwright, born July 16, 1823.
Marcus Lafayette Cartwright, born July 31, 1825.
Allen Mathes, born Oct. 19, 1779; died Mar. 29, 1848, aged 70 years.
Allen Mathes and Harriett Cartwright were joined in holy matrimony May 1, 1825.
Allen P. Mathes, born Feb. 27, 1826.
Narcissa A. Mathes, born Oct. 30, 1827.
Eliza H. Mathes, born Nov. 2, 1830.
Allen P. Mathes married Bettie Perry, Jan. 13, 1859.
William Connel and Narcissa Mathes, married Feb. 22, 1843.
R. D. Goodlett and Eliza Jane H. Mathes, married Sept. 14, 1847.
Andrew Milam and Talitha Cartwright were joined in holy matrimony June 24, 1830.
James Milam, born April 2, 1831.
William Wallis Milam, born Feb. 21, 1832.
Allen E. Goodlett, born July 15, 1845.
Adam Rush Goodlett, born Oct. 19, 1850.
Anna Elizabeth Goodlett, born Oct. 24, 1853.
Allen Physic Connell, born Feb. 29, 1844.
Harriett A. Connell, born Mar. 7, 1851.
Enoch Walton Connell, born ——.

Cunningham record, Davidson County, Tennessee, in possession of Mrs. J. W. Roscoe, Goodlettsville, Tenn.

Enoch Cunningham, Sr., was reared in Lanquier Co., Va., near Alexandria (the county seat); married Lucy BaShaw, 1778, of Virginia. He bought the Robt. Cartwright homestead and other lands from the Robt. Cartwright estate and moved to the old Robt. Cartwright home in the year 1810. Enoch Cunningham, Jr., was born in Virginia, Sept. 29, 1809, and was married to Sarah Anne Stark, his third wife, May 1, 1854.
Joseph Alexander Cunningham, born Feb. 1, 1855.
Malvina Louisa Cunningham, born Mar. 27, 1856.
Mary Catherine Cunningham, born Mar. 20, 1859.
Oliver Cromwell Cunningham, born Nov. 21, 1857.
Anne Margaret Cunningham, born April 9, 1862.

Copied from Bible record of Mrs. Henry Hart, Davidson County, Tennessee, in possession of Mrs. E. E. Pearson, Nashville, Tenn.

Our grandfather, Leonard Keeling, died Nov. 5, 1832.
Our grandmother, Martha Sugg Keeling, aged 84, died 1860.
My mother, Mary Ann K. Hooper, born Sept. 24, 1805; died Mar. 28, 1840.
Dr. Geo. Keeling, born Sept. 8, 1807; died May 28, 1841.
Sally K. Moorman, born Aug. 13, 1809; died 1842.
Elizabeth K. Lowe, born Aug. 29, 1811; died 1861.
Nancy K. Moore, born Feb. 17, 1814; died May 4, 1843.
Andrew J. Keeling, born Dec. 16, 1817; died Nov. 30, 1837.
Henry Hart, born Nov. 21, 1822; died Oct. 25, 1896.
Huldah Hooper Hart, born Jan. 21, 1832; died Dec. 19, 1915.
Edwin H. Hart, born Nov. 3, 1850; died Sept. 27, 1863.
Leonard H. Hart, born Feb. 2, 1853; died Feb. 14, 1908.
Mary Henry Hart Cartwright, born Nov. 18, 1854; died Nov. 29, 1918.
Thomas M. Hart, born Aug. 3, 1859; died Jan. 22, 1914.
Samuel B. Hart, born Sept. 20, 1864; died Aug. 21, 1914.
Claiborne Young Hooper, born April 21, 1797; died June 27, 1848.
Mary Ann K. Hooper, born Sept. 24, 1805; died Mar. 28, 1840.
Martha H. Hooper, born Dec. 24, 1826; died Nov. 5, 1831.
Leonard K. Hooper, born June 6, 1828; died May 31, 1877.
Sallie Hooper Phillips, born Nov. 22, 1829; died April 3, 1888.
Huldah Hooper Hart, born Jan. 21, 1832; died Dec. 19, 1915.
Elizabeth Hooper Meness, born May 27, 1834; died April 24, 1861.
Andrew J. Hooper, born Dec. 28, 1835; died Mar. 6, 1895.
Georgianna Hooper Mizell, born Dec. 8, 1828; died Jan. 12, 1903.
May we all meet in heaven.

Bible record of Charles Leslie Pearson of Linden, Perry County, Tennessee, formerly of London, England, in possession of E. E. Pearson, Nashville, Tenn.

Father:
Henry Robert Pearson, born in London, England, Aug. 24, 1790.
Ann Harris, born in London, England, May 7, 1797.
Charlotte Cousens, born Mar. 20, 1810.
Charles Leslie Pearson, sixth son of Henry Robert and Ann Pearson, born in London, England, Nov. 20, 1831.

Mother:

George Anson Brooks, born in Philadelphia, U. S. A., Feb. 2, 1819.

Sarah Ann Elizabeth Burgess, born in Virginia, July 12, 1822.

George Anna Priscilla Brooks, born in Williamson Co., Tenn., July 29, 1846.

Births

George Wilberforce Pearson, born in Perry Co., Tenn., Oct. 28, 1866.

Robert Brooks Pearson, born in Linden, Perry Co., Tenn., Oct. 11, 1868.

Lucy Eleanor Pearson, born in Linden, Perry Co., Tenn., June 5, 1870.

Chas. Leslie Pearson (6), born in Linden, Perry Co., Tenn., July 22, 1871.

Arabella Thornton Pearson, born in Linden, Perry Co., Tenn., May 20, 1873.

Henry Alfred Pearson, born in Linden, Perry Co., Tenn., Dec. 9, 1874 .

Wilfrid Norman Pearson, born in Linden, Perry Co., Tenn., April 6, 1876.

Percival Edwin Pearson, born in Linden, Perry Co., Tenn., Sept. 24, 1878.

Mary Ella Pearson, born in Linden, Perry Co., Tenn., Feb. 18, 1880, and baptized Aug. 8, 1880, by Rev. D. H. Merryman, P. C.

Elbert Edward Pearson, born in Linden, Perry Co., Tenn., Mar. 25, 1882.

This certifies that Elbert Edward Pearson was baptized by me at Linden, July 22, 1882—(Signed) J. B. McFerrin, M.G.D.D.

Henry Cousens Pearson, born in Linden, Perry Co., Tenn., Aug. 9, 1883.

This certifies that Henry Cousens Pearson was baptized by me at Linden, Tenn., Sept. 23, 1883—G. W. McBride.

Archibald F. Pearson, born in Linden, Perry Co., Tenn., Sept. 11, 1884.

This certifies that Archibald Francis Pearson was baptized by me at Linden, April 5, 1885—G. W. McBride.

Nora Charlotte Lucile Pearson, born in Linden, Dec. 10, 1888, and was baptized by me Mar. 29, 1889 —S. L. Fain, P.E.

This certifies that George Wilberforce, Chas. Leslie, and Arabella Thomtom Pearson were baptized by me at Linden, Aug. 10, 1873— A. G. Dinwiddie, P.E.

This certifies that Henry Alfred Pearson was baptized by me at Linden, May 30, 1875—J. G. Bolton, P.E.

Wilfrid Normal Pearson, born in Linden, April 6, 1876.

This certifies that Wilfrid Normal Pearson was baptized by me at Linden, May 21, 1876—J. G. Bolton, P.E.

This certifies that Percival Edwin Pearson was baptized by me at Linden, Dec. 8, 1878—John W. Rookey, P.C.

Marriages

Henry Robt. Pearson and Ann Harris, married Aug. 24, 1819.

Henry Robt. Pearson and Charlotte Cousens, married Jan. 23, 1838.

Chas. Leslie Pearson and Anna P. Brooks, married Mar. 8, 1865.

George Anson Brooks and Sarah A. E. Burgess, married Aug. 16, 1843.

Deaths

Ann Pearson, departed this life April 9, 1833, London, England.

Lucy Eleanor Pearson, departed this life Sept. 2, 1870.

Robt. Brooks Pearson, died Oct. 4, 1870.

Henry Alfred Pearson, died July 21, 1875.

Arabella Thornton Pearson, died Sept. 1, 1877.

Wilfrid Norman Pearson, died Oct. 15, 1877.

Henry Cousens Pearson, died Nov. 16, 1883.

Geo. A. Brooks, died Feb. 22, 1849.

Henry Robt. Pearson, died Nov. 16, 1870, London, England.

Charlotte Pearson, died April 5, 1892, London, England.

Chas. Leslie Pearson, Sr., died Mar. 11, 1906.
George Anna P. Pearson, departed this life Jan. 20, 1913.

MEMORIAL CARD

In loving memory of Julius Alexander Pearson, Doctor of Civil and Canon Law, F. S. A., etc. Fifth surviving son of the late Henry Robert Pearson, of 46 Hyde Park Square, London, Esq., born December 4, 1838, and entered into rest April 29, 1871.

Record copied from Bible of Henry Hart, Jr., Robertson and Davidson Counties, Tennessee, in possession of Mrs. E. E. Pearson, Nashville, Tenn.

MARRIAGES

Henry Hart, Jr., and Huldah Hooper, married in Davidson Co., by Rev. J. B. McFerrin, Oct. 30, 1849.
Henry Hart, Sr., and Judith Taylor Pickering, married Sept. 22, 1813.
Joseph Hart and Nancy Sugg, married in Davidson Co., Tenn., Aug. 21, 1791.
Mary Ann Hart, married to D. G. Baird, April 18, 1833.
John Spencer Hart, married to Martha Mumford (Miller), July 27, 1843.
Amanda M. Hart, married G. F. Neill.
Judith Taylor Caroline Hart, married G. F. Neill.
Williams W. Hart, married Laura Peebles.
Edwin T. Hart, married to Mattie Brown, Dec. 29, 1853.
Emily A. Hart, married J. R. Finch, Nov. 1, 1855, by Rev. A. R. Erwin, in Robertson.
Eneas Hooper and Anne Young, married in Davidson Co., Tenn., Mar. 10, 1796.
Daniel Young and Anne Greyson, married in Jonesboro, Tenn.
Anne Greyson was daughter of William Greyson.

BIRTHS

Henry Hart, Jr., born in Robertson Co., Nov. 21, 1822.
Huldah Hooper, born in Davidson Co., Tenn., Jan. 21, 1832.
Edwin Hooper Hart, born in Davidson Co., Tenn., Nov. 3, 1850.
Leonard Keeling Hart, born in Davidson Co., Feb. 2, 1853.
Mary Henrie Hart, born in Davidson Co., Nov. 18, 1854.
Thomas Menees Hart, born Aug. 3, 1859, in Robertson County.
Samuel Brown Hart, born in Robertson Co., Sept. 20, 1864.
Henry Hart, born June 22, 1792, in Davidson Co., Tenn.
Judith Taylor Pickering, born Aug. 17, 1793, in N. C.
Joseph Hart, born June 14, 1814, in Robertson Co.
Mary Ann Hart, born July 27, 1816.
John Spencer Hart, born July 25, 1818.
Amanda Malvina Hart, born May 4, 1820.
Henry Hart, Jr., born Nov. 21, 1822.
Nancy Hart, born Aug. 21, 1823.
Judity Hart, born May 2, 1826.
Wm. Wesley Hart, born April 26, 1828.
Edwin T. Hart, born Aug. 8, 1830.
Emily Augusta Hart, born Jan. 25, 1834.

DEATHS

Leonard Keeling, died Nov. 5, 1832.
Martha Sugg Keeling, died 1861.
Edwin Hooper Hart, died in Robertson Co., Sept. 27, 1863.
Henry Hart, Jr., died Oct. 25, 1896, near Nashville, Tenn.
Leonard Keeling Hart, died Feb. 14, 1908, near Nashville, Tenn.
Thomas Menees Hart, died at Duncan Hotel, Nashville, Tenn., Jan. 22, 6 p.m., 1914.
Samuel Brown Hart, died at 4 p.m., Friday, Aug. 21, 1914, at his home, Russellville, Ky.
Huldah Hooper, died at her home, Dec. 19, 1915, Sunday, 7:20 a.m.
Mary Hart Cartwright, died Nov. 29, 1918, at the home of her daughter, near The Hermitage, Tenn.

Joseph Hart, died in Dandridge, Tenn., 1793.
Nancy Sugg Hart Robertson, died Feb., 1845, Adairville, Ky.
Henry Hart, Sr., died Dec. 24, 1856, Robertson Co., Tenn.
Judith Taylor Pickering Hart, died June 3, 1865, Robertson Co.
Joseph Hart, died Nov. 4, 1818, in Robertson Co., Tenn.
Nancy Hart, died Sept. 23, 1832, in Robertson Co., Tenn.
Amanda M. Neill, died Sept. 28, 1841, Carrollton, Miss.
Caroline Hart Neill, died Aug. 10, 1859, Carrollton, Miss.
Williams W. Hart, died May 27, 1884, Lodi, Miss.
Edwin T. Hart, died Nov., 1888, Dresden, Tenn.

MARRIAGES

Len K. Hart and Lucy Carr Eastman, married Oct. 2, 1877.
Jacob Andrew Cartwright and Mary Henry Hart, married Nov. 10, 1881.
Thomas Menees Hart, married ———, 1884.
Samuel Brown Hart and Susan Moss Ewing, married ———.
Mathew Archie Henderson and Laniza Cartwright, married at West End Methodist Church, Nashville, Tenn., 6:30 a.m., July 10, 1907.
Elbert E. Pearson and Mary Edwin Cartwright, married Monday, July 5, 1909, at 1506 Sigler St., Nashville, by Bishop O. P. Fitzgerald of the M. E. Church.
Ewing Ambrose Grizzard and Helene Cartwright, married Dec. 28, 1909, at 1506 Sigler St., Nashville, Tenn.
Henry Hart Cartwright and America Forster Rees, married Dec. 8, 1915, 8 p.m., in Presbyterian Church, Winchester, Ky., by Rev. Cummins, pastor of the church.

———

Emily Augusta Hart Finch, died in Nashville, Jan. 9, 1875.
Mary Ann Hart Baird, died in Robertson Co., Tenn., Sept. 16, 1878.
John Spencer Hart, died Mar. 4, 1890, Nashville, Tenn.

BIRTHS

Mathew Archie Henderson, born at 1506 Sigler St., Nashville, Tenn., Sept. 24, 1908.
Andrew Cartwright Henderson, born May 30, 1911, in Wilson Co., Tenn.
Geo. Andrew Henderson, born at 1313 Colvin Ave., Nashville, Tenn., May 16, 1914.
Margaret Cartwright Henderson, born Mar. 5, 1921.
Anne Harris Pearson, born Nov. 17, 1910, at 1506 Sigler St., and was baptized April (Easter) at McKendree M. E. Church, Dr. French, Pastor, officiating, Nashville.
Mary Hart Pearson, born June 12, 1917.
Lanniza Cartwright Pearson, born Nov. 20, 1918.
Helen Cartwright Grizzard, born May 5, 1911.
Ewing Ambrose Grizzard, Jr., born Oct. 29, 1915.
Charles Rees Cartwright, born Feb. 6, 1918, in Winchester, Ky.
Mathew A. Henderson, Jr., was baptized by Bishop O. P. Fitzgerald of the M. E. Church, South, July 5, 1909, and died Sept. 4, 1927.

Record in Robert Cartwright Bible, in possession of John Beasley, Goodlettsville, Tenn.

Robt. Cartwright and Anne, his wife, married Aug. 15, 1745.
Wm. Cartwright, son of Robert Cartwright and Anne, his wife, born July 4, 1746.
Robert Cartwright and Anne, his wife, daughter of Robert Hugins and Mary, his wife, married Aug. 15, 1745; as it was God's pleasure to take this loving ——— (marked out) ——— March 17, Anne Cartwright died March 17, 1747.
Robert Cartwright and Mary, married April 20, 1749.

Martha Cartwright, daughter of Robert and Mary, born May 14, 1750.
Mary Cartwright, daughter of Robert and Mary, born Aug. 11, 1753.
Anne Cartwright, daughter of Robert and Mary, his wife, was born June 2, 1755.
Susannah, daughter of Robert Cartwright and Mary, his wife, born Sept. 4, 1757.
Robert Cartwright, son of Robert and Mary Cartwright, born Dec. 17, 1759; died March 23, 1776.
Aug. 11, 1760, found a pin betwixt the skin and his ribs, which remained to Oct. 20, and then was cut out by Doctor Wright, out of my son, Robert Cartwright's, side. Written by, father of the child.
John Hunter Cartwright, son of Robert and Mary Cartwright, born Feb. 26, 1762.
Mary Cartwright, wife of Robert Cartwright and daughter of Mr. John Hunter and Jacamine, his wife, died Jan. 22, 1764.
Thomas Cartwright, son of Robert and Pemmy Cartwright, born Nov. 20, 1763 or 68 (?).
Pemmy Cartwright, daughter of Robert and Pemmy, his wife, born Feb. 28, 1765.
Jacob Cartwright, son of Robert and Pemmy, his wife, born Feb. 21, 1767.
James Cartwright, son of Robert and Pemmy, his wife, born Feb. 14, 1770.
William Hunter Cartwright, son of Robert and Pemmy, born Oct. 4, 1772.
Elizabeth Cartwright, daughter of Robert and Pemmy, born Sept. 2, 1776.
(Here the record ends, although there were three other children in this family, viz:
David, born 1782.
Robert, born 178—.
Jesse Hunter, born 1778.

Record from Bible of Capt. John English of King George County, Virginia, in possession of Mrs. E. E. Pearson, Nashville, Tenn.

Sara English, daughter of John English, born July 23, 1749.

Lettice English, daughter of ——.

John English, in the year of our . . . and Saviour Christ, Feb. 23, 1751.

John English, son of John English, born June 31, ——.

Margaret English, daughter of John English, born Oct. 4, ——.
Robert English, son of John English, born July 25, 1756.
William English, son of John English, born ——. (This record is badly worn and there may have been other children whose record has been torn off.)
Sarah English (Stark), died in Sumner County, Sept. 28, 1720.

Record of Alexander Cotton Cartwright, Davidson County, Tennessee, in possession of Mrs. E. E. Pearson, Nashville, Tenn.

A. C. Cartwright and Mary M. Stark, married Jan. 7, 1844.
A. C. Cartwright, born July 16, 1823.
Mary M. Stark, born Dec. 25, 1821.
Jacob Cartwright, born Feb. 22, 1767; died Oct. 12, 1828.
Patience Hobdy Cartwright, born Nov. 3, 1785; died July 25, 1837.
John Stark, born May 3, 1788.
Margaret Primm, born Oct. 1, 1787.
John and Margaret Stark, married Sept. 6, 1812.
John Stark and Sarah English, married in Virginia, Jan. 4, 1769.
Jacob Andrew Cartwright, born Nov. 27, 1844.
Talitha Cotton and Robt. Hobdy, married near Halifax, N. C.; came to Sumner County, Tenn., in 1791, in wagons. Robt. Hobdy, died about 1800, and Talitha Hobdy married Dempsey Powell.

Mary Hart Cartwright, born Nov. 18, 1854.
Jacob A. Cartwright and Mary Hart, married Nov. 10, 1881, in Davidson County, Tenn.
Louis Henry Lanier and Lamiza Ann Cartwright, married July 13, 1869.
Mathew Archie Henderson and Lamiza Ann Cartwright, daughter of Jacob A. Cartwright, married July 10, 1907.
Elbert Edward Pearson and Mary Edwin Cartwright, married July 5, 1909.
Ewing Ambrose Grizzard and Helen Hooper Cartwright, married Dec. 29, 1909.
Talitha P. Cartwright, died Nov. 16, 1846; age 5 months 7 days.
Alexander Cartwright, died Oct. 6, 1861; age 3 weeks 5 days.
Mary M. Cartwright, died Aug. 19, 1891.
A. C. Cartwright, died Feb. 18, 1899.
Jacob Andrew Cartwright, died June 20, 1909.
Mary Hart Cartwright, died Nov. 29, 1918.
Mathew Archie Henderson, died Sept. 4, 1927.
The children of Louis Henry Lanier and Lamiza Cartwrigt Lanier are:
Thomas Lanier, born 1870; died Nov. 15, 1882.
Mary Jean Lanier, born 1872.
Louis Henry Lanier, Jr., born 1874.
Lamiza Lanier, born 1876.
Alexander Lanier, born 1878.
Jacob Andrew Lanier, born 1881; died 6 weeks later.
Martha Lanier, born 1889; died April 4, 1931.
Talitha Patience Cartwright, born June 9, 1846.
Lamiza Ann Cartwright, born Nov. 15, 1847.
Alexander Cartwright, born Sept. 10, 1861.

———

The children of Jacob Andrew Cartwright and Mary Hart Cartwright:
Mary Edwin Cartwright, born July 25, 1882.
Lamiza Ann Cartwright, born Oct. 19, 1883.
Helen Cartwright, born June 13, 1886.
Henry Hart Cartwright, born Jan. 14, 1888.
Margaret Cartwright, born March 26, 1890.
Jacob Andrew Cartwright, Jr., born April 30, 1892.

Henry Hyde family record, Davidson County, Tennessee, in possession of Drake Hyde, Nashville, Tenn.

Said in history to have been the richest settler on the Cumberland. Hyde's Ferry Pike ran through his property.

MARRIAGES

Jonathan and Eliza Drake, married Dec. 24, 1808.
Jordan Hyde and Susan S. Drake, married March 3, 1825.
Taxwell Hyde and Ann E. Drake, married Aug. 14, 1828.
Daniel Young and Ellen Hyde, married May 1, 1848.
Napoleon B. Hyde and Mollie A. Rayan, married Oct. 6, 1857.
Tazwell Hyde and Sallie Young, married Sept. 20, 1858.
Tazwell Hyde and Susan Drake, married Nov. 30, 1815.
Robt. W. Barnes and Martha Hyde, married Feb. 17, 1853.
——— Davice and Louisa Hyde, married Sept. 27, 1858.

BIRTHS

Felix R. Hyde, Feb. 6, 1817.
Edmund J. Hyde, Oct. 12, 1819.
Lucinda L. Hyde, May 24, 1829.
Eli Hyde, May 14, 1831.
Henry Hyde, Saturday, March 16, 1833.
Napoleon B. Hyde, Sunday, March 29, 1835.
Maria Louiza Hyde, Nov. 30, 1837.

———

Tazwell Hyde, died May 3, 1838 (son of Tazwell and Susan).
Ann Eliza Drake, born Sept. 22, 1810.
Mary Jane Drake, born Jan. 30, 1813.
Alfred A. Drake, born Dec. 2, 1815.
Susannah C. Drake, born Sept. 6, 1817.

Jonathan Drake, born March 6, 1819.
William McNary Drake, born Jan. 17, 1823; died Oct. 31, 1824.
Jonathan Drake, died Nov. 30, 1842.
Tazwell H. Young, born April 11, 1849.
Daniel Young, Jr., born Dec. 6, 1850.
Cara Ida Young, born May 10, 1852.
Lenard H. Young, born April 20, 1854.
Ann Barnes Young, born March 15, 1856.
Mattie Lou Young, born May 3, 1857.
Napoleon B. Hyde, killed in Battle of Shiloh, Miss., Sunday morning, 11 o'clock, April 6, 1862; Confederate Army.

DEATHS

Jordan Hyde, died Dec. 10, 1827.
Henry Hyde, father of John Henry, Rebecca, Richard, Benjamin, Edmund, Jordan and Tazwell, died March 12, 1812.
Rebecca Hyde, wife of Henry Hyde, died Aug. 31, 1829.
Tazwell Hyde, died May 3, 1838.
Susan S. Hyde, wife of Jordan, died Dec. 24, 1825.
Susan Hyde, wife of Tazwell, died June 16, 1820.
Felix Hyde, son of Tazwell and Susan Hyde, died Jan. 14, 1832; age 14 years.
A. E. Barnes, died April 19, 1836, at 9:30.
Rev. Jno. P. Hyde, president of the Leonah Female College, Martinsburg, Va., is one of the heirs to the immense Hyde estate in England. Mr. Hyde has the documents to prove his ancestry back to 1760. (Newspaper clipping pasted in old Hyde Bible.)
On the fly leaf of this old Bible is the following:
"Presented to my son, Napoleon B. Hyde. Read this book and follow its writings. Affectionately, your father, Felix R. Hyde, 1823."

Edwin Hyde's descendants and kindred families. In possession of Mrs. Sam M. Fite, Nashville, Tenn.

MARRIAGES

W. H. Hyde, to P. A. Morilove, April 18, 1850.
W. F. Williams, to Lula M. Hyde, June 24, 1869.
E. H. Hyde, to Willie P. Drake, Dec. 20, 1877.
Clarence Drake Hyde, to Grace Darling Smith, Dec. 6, 1905.
Samuel McClary Fite, to Laura Lucille Hyde, Dec. 1, 1909.

BIRTHS

Christiana H. Hyde, born Feb. 14, 1808.
Wellington H. Hyde, born April 8, 1830.
Susan D. A. Hyde, born July 28, 1832.
Mary Lula Hyde, born June 11, 1851.
Laura C. Hyde, born Oct. 15, 1853.
Edwin H. M. Hyde, born Feb. 26, 1855.
Richard R. Hyde, born Aug. 22, 1835.
Jerome B. Hyde, born March 16, 1837.
Samuel McClary Fite, born March 1, 1878.
Susie May Williams, born Wednesday, May 25, 1870.
Ida M. Young, born May 10, 1852.
Clarence D. Hyde, born Sept. 17, 1878.
Laura Lucille Hyde, born July 19, 1883.
Mildred Lucille Fite, born July 16, 1912.
Edwin Drake Fite, born May 28, 1915.
Elizabeth Richardson Hyde, born July 4, 1914.

DEATHS

Christians H. Hyde, died Aug. 24, 1854.
J. B. Hyde, died July 2, 1864.
R. R. Hyde, died Aug. 11, 1864.
Edmond Hyde, Sr., died March 15, 1849.
Edmund W. Hyde, Jr., died Oct. 14, 1865.
Edwin H. Hyde, died Dec. 16, 1890.
Willie Patience Drake Hyde, died Jan. 11, 1925; age 73 years 6 months 24 days; born June 18, 1851.

Ida M. Young, died Dec. 8, 1874.

Laura C. Hyde, died Feb. 11, 1854; age 4 months.

Edwin H. Hyde, died Dec. 16, 1890; age 36.

Susie M. Williams, died Sept. 10, 1893; age 23.

William F. Williams, died Jan. 16, 1894.

Mary Lula Williams, died Oct. 11, 1898; age 47.

Susan P. M. Hyde, born July 28, 1832; died Dec. 30, 1908.

Wellington H. Hyde, born April 8, 1830; died June 5, 1911.

From the family Bible of John Rolfe Hudson, in the possession of his granddaughter, Mrs. John H. DeWitt, Nashville, Tenn. Sent by Mrs. DeWitt.

FAMILY REGISTER

Births

John Wills Napier, son of Richard Claiborne Napier and Mary Wills, born near Augusta, Ga., April 1, 1785.

Cassandra Williams, daughter of Daniel Williams and Sally Nixon, born near Wilmington, N. C., May 18, 1799.

John Rolfe Hudson, son of Charles Hudson and Anna Goode, born in Mecklenburg County, Va., Dec. 13, 1802.

Araminta Claiborne Napier, daughter of John Wills Napier and Cassandra Williams, born in Dickson County, Tenn., Feb. 20, 1817.

Amanda Eliza Hudson, born in Dickson Co., Tenn., Feb. 10, 1838.

Susan Florence Hudson, born in Dickson County, Tenn., Aug. 20, 1840.

Lucy Hudson, born in Dickson County, Tenn., Oct. 3, 1844.

Mary Cassandra Hudson, born in Dickson County, Tenn., Nov. 7, 1847.

Florence Isabel Hudson, born in Nashville, Tenn., Nov. 12, 1850.

Minnie Claiborne Hudson, born in Nashville, Tenn., May 28, 1853.

John Wills Hudson, born in Nashville, Tenn., July 8, 1857.

Jennie Hill Brown, daughter of Robert Weakley Brown and Florence Isabel Hudson, born Aug. 26, 1870, in Nashville, Tenn.

Florence Isabel Brown, daughter of Robert Weakley Brown and Florence Isabel Hudson, born July 8, 1872, in Nashville, Tenn.

Marriages

John Wills Napier, married Cassandra Williams, Dec. 23, 1815.

John Rolfe Hudson, married Araminta Claiborne Napier, Dec. 7, 1834.

William Eldred Ward, married Amanda Eliza Hudson, Feb. 24, 1859.

Robert Weakley Brown, married Florence Isabel Hudson, July 13, 1869.

Benjamin Christopher Robertson, married Mary Cassandra Hudson, Nov. 3, 1870.

Robert L. Morris, married Lucy Hudson, June 20, 1872.

Minnie C. Hudson of Nashville, Tenn., and Preston H. Miller of Savannah, Ga., married at home in Nashville, Oct. 4, 1877, by Dr. Wm. E. Ward.

Deaths

John Wills Napier, died in Nashville, Tenn., Aug. 31, 1864.

Cassandra Napier, died in Dickson County, Tenn., Nov. 9, 1836.

Susan Florence Hudson, died in Dickson County, Tenn., Jan. 18, 1846.

Florence Isabel Hudson, died in Nashville, Tenn., Sept. 25, 1872, wife of R. W. Brown; age 21.

Benjamin Christopher Robertson, died in Tallahassee, Fla., Feb. 7, 1872.

Jennie Hill Brown, died in Nashville, Tenn., Nov. 8, 1876.

Florence Isabel Brown, infant, died in Nashville, Tenn., Oct. 8, 1872.

NOTE

Daniel Williams, born Jan. 5, 1751; died July 16, 1831.
Sarah Nixon, born Feb. 11, 1757; died Sept. 14, 1828.
Daniel Williams and Sarah Nixon, married March 3, 1782.
(From the Williams family Bible, at the Daniel Williams home, Dickson County, Tenn.

Records in M. B. DeWitt family Bible.

BIRTHS

M. B. DeWitt, born March 8, 1835.
M. E. DeWitt, born Dec. 28, 1839.
Marcilee, daughter of M. B. and M. E. DeWitt, born Nov. 27, 1868.
John Hibbett, son of M. B. and M. E. DeWitt, born Sept. 21, 1872.
Daisy Searcy, daughter of M. B. and M. E. DeWitt, born Jan. 27, 1875.
Paul, son of M. B. and M. E. DeWitt, born March 24, 1878.
Mary Marshall, daughter of B. M. and Marcilee Settle, born April 6, 1898.
Simon DeWitt, son of B. M. and Marcilee Settle, born Sept. 18, 1899.
Ward, son of John and Rebekah DeWitt, born Aug. 20, 1900.
Mary Elizabeth, daughter of W. A. and Daisy DeWitt Skelton, born Feb. 15, 1905, at 711 Woodland St.
John Hibbett, son of John Hibbett and Rebekah, born Feb. 20, 1906.
William Abner, son of William Abner and Daisy DeWitt Skelton, born March 24, 1913, Nashville, Tenn., Inglewood.

MARRIAGES

Marcus B. DeWitt and Mary E. Hibbett, married Feb. 13, 1860.
Marcilee DeWitt and Benjamin Marshall Settle, married Dec. 26, 1895.
Daisy DeWitt and William Abner Skelton, married Nov. 18, 1897.
John Hibbett DeWitt and Rebekah Williams Ward, married Nov. 14, 1899.
Paul DeWitt, M.D., and Jennie Harrison Peebles, married Nov. 18, 1909.

DEATHS

Marcus Bearden DeWitt, died Feb. 25, 1901; age 65 years 11 months 17 days.
Mary Elizabeth Hibbett DeWitt, died Oct. 16, 1912; age 72 years 9 months 18 days.
Mrs. Nancy Caroline Hibbett, died April 7, 1886; age 78 years 7 months 8 days.
Mrs. Mary Eliza DeWitt, died May 7, 1889; age 86 years 3 months 10 days.
John J. Hibbett, died Dec. 16, 1893; age 87 years 6 months 15 days.

From the M. B. DeWitt family Bible, in possession of John H. DeWitt.

BIRTHS

Washington John DeWitt, M.D., born Sept. 23, 1799, in Darlington District, S. C.
Mary Eliza (Bearden) DeWitt, born Jan. 26, 1803, at Knoxville, Tenn.
Richard Bearden, born in Granville County, N. C., Sept. 23, 1770.
Nancy Ann (Bennett) Bearden, born Oct. 17, 1774.
Elizabeth (Pomfret) Bennett, born Jan. 15, 1753, in King William County, Va.
Peter Bennett, born in Virginia, about 1750.
John Pomfret, father of Elizabeth Bennett, born in 1718.
John Johnston Hibbett, born May 30, 1806, in Smith County, Tenn.
Nancy Caroline (Parker) Hibbett, born Aug. 30, 1807, in Sumner County, Tenn.
Her father, Thomas Parker, and her mother, Susan (Rogers) Parker, were born in Virginia. His father, Nathaniel Parker, was born in Virginia in 1724.

Thomas Parker, born Feb. 29, 1768.
Susan Parker, born April 11, 1773.
David Crawford, born in Ireland in 1740.
Mary (Young) Crawford, born in 1745, probably in Lancaster County, Pa.

MARRIAGES

James Hibbett and Nancy Crawford, daughter of David and Mary Crawford, were married Dec. 28, 1792, in Mecklenburg County, N. C.
John Johnston Hibbett and Nancy Caroline Parker, married in 1829.
John Pomfret, married Anne Hunt.
Elizabeth Pomfret, married Peter Bennett in 1773.
Nancy Ann Bennett, married Richard Bearden, June 23, 1793.
Mary Eliza Bearden, married Washington John DeWitt in 1819.
Harris DeWitt, married Elizabeth Brockington, a daughter of Richard Brockington, of South Carolina.

DEATHS

Harris DeWitt (a soldier of the Revolution, 2nd South Carolina Regiment), died in Cocke County, Tenn., Dec. 6, 1829.
His son, Washington John DeWitt, M.D., died in Little Rock, Ark., in 1852.
Richard Bearden, died June 16, 1845, in Knox County, Tenn.
Nancy Ann (Bennett) Bearden, died June 24, 1855, in Knox County, Tenn. Her father, Major Peter Bennett, was born about 1750; died in 1822 in Knox County, Tenn. His wife, Elizabeth (Pomfret) Bennett, died July 7, 1845, in Knox County, Tenn.
Thomas Parker, died Aug. 8, 1846.
Susan Parker, died Oct. 25, 1838.
David Crawford, died Aug. 6, 1820.
Mary (Young) Crawford, died May 15, 1820.
James Hibbett, died in 1821.
Nancy (Crawford) Hibbett, died in 1856.
Nathaniel Parker, died in 1811, in Sumner County, Tenn.

FAMILY RECORD

Sent by Miss Mary Webb, Nashville.

This book was purchased Anno Domini 1805, by James Carlen.

William Carling, son of James and Pattasy Carling, born Oct. 16, 1795.
Their daughter, Sarah, born April 29, 1797.
Their second son, Hugh Webb, born Jan. 28, 1799.
Their second daughter, Hannah, born April 29, 1801.
Their third son, Daniel, born May 6, 1803.
Their third daughter, Elizabeth, born May 14, 1804.
Their son, James Carling, born Oct. 4, 1806, 1813.
(On another page.)
Their fourth son, James Carlen, born Oct. 11, 1806.
Their fifth son, Isham, born Jan. 17, 1809.
Their sixth son, Spencer, born Jan. 17, 1811.

MARRIAGE

Hugh, son of Patsy Carlen, married May 13, 1819.

William Carlen, born May 7, 1824.

(On another page.)

Their third son, Daniel, died June 26, 1803.

Their third son, born the 17th day of the month.

Their fifth son, Isum, born Jan. 17, 1808.

Sally Carlin Jun (?), born April 30, 1814.

(On another page.)

Their third son, James, born April 5, 1803.

Their sixth son, Isum Carlin, born Jan. 17, 1811.

Their son, Spencer, born Jan. 17, 1811.
Francis Rogan, born Sept. 14, 1778 (?) or 98.

DEATHS

James Carlin, died Sept. 23, 1813.
Their third son, Daniel, died June 26, 1803.
James Carlen, died Aug. 15, 1826.
Hannah Carlen, died Oct. 22, 1827.
(On another page.)
James Carlen, Jr., died Aug. 15, 1826.
Ann Webb, died Dec. 29, 1827.
Patsy Carlen Seignor, died May 3 (?), 1848.
(On back of cover.)
State of Tennessee, Wilson County.
William Carlen, Sunday, June 18, 1826, at Mother's.
James Carlen, 1826.
William Carlen.

Lewis Williams, born in Brunswick County, Va., Jan. 21, 1755; died Jan. 26, 1836, in Mecklenburg County, Va.; married Feb. 6, 1777.
Sarah Oslin, born Oct. 25, 1761; died June 27, 1828.
Children of Lewis and Sarah Williams:
Nancey Williams, born June 22, 1778; married Mr. Bennett.
Isaac Williams, born July 6, 1780.
Patsy Williams, born May 26, 1782.
Sally O. Williams, born March 20, 1784.
John Williams, born Feb. 28, 1786; married Mary Pettus, Dec. 2, 1813.
Elizabeth Williams, born Dec. 3, 1787.
Lucy Williams, born Oct. 25, 1789; married Mr. Rainey.
Winney Williams, born Sept. 29, 1791.
Lewis Williams, born April 2, 1796.
Mary J. Williams, born May 26, 1798; married Thomas Williams.
Matthew Williams, born June 7, 1800; married, first, Nancy J. Blanch, Nov. 14, 1821; second, Elizabeth Myrick, Dec. 30, 1826; third, Rebecca M. Daves, Dec. 22, 1841.
George Williams, born May 30, 1803.

The above record was given me by Mr. George W. Williams, son of Matthew Williams and his wife, Rebecca M. Daves. He secured it from his father, Matthew Williams' Bible. Mr. George W. Williams was living in Savedge, Virginia, at the time.

Records sent by Matie Fletcher.

Jesse Oslin, born in Kent County, Va., March 31, 1729; died in Mecklenburg County, Va., July, 1813; married Winney ——, born ——; died 1822.
Children of Jesse Oslin and Winney, his wife:
Samuel Oslin.
Isaac Oslin.
William Spencer Oslin.
Sarah Oslin, born Oct. 25, 1761; married Lewis Williams, Feb. 6, 1777.
Polly Oslin.
Rebecca Oslin.

In the will of Jesse Oslin (Osling) probated Jan. 17, 1814, at court held in Mecklenburg County, Virginia, Jesse Oslin mentions the six children listed above; also sons-in-law Thomas Binford and Meredith Moss, and grandson, Osling Binford.

The above mentioned will is on file in Will Book 8, page 30, Mecklenburg County, and a copy is in my possession.

Record of Pettus Family

I. Ashmead & Co., Printers, 1833.

Sent by Miss Mary Webb, Nashville.

This is a correct copy of record of Pettus family, contained in Bible given my mother, Mrs. Sophia Adaline Jordan, who was Sophia Adaline Pettus, by her brother, Musgrove Lamb Pettus, and I presume was his father's, Samuel Pettus.

This Bible was translated out of the original tongues, and with the former translations diligently compared and revised by the special command of His Majesty, "King James I of England."

Thomas Pettus, son of John Pettus and Anne, his wife, was married to Amey Walker, daughter of David Walker and Mary, his wife, Nov. 10, 1735.

Births of Their Children

John Pettus, born Sept. 24, 1736.
Overton Pettus, born Oct. 13, 1739.
Thomas Pettus, born March 10, 1741.
Mary Pettus, born Nov. 6, 1746.
Ann Pettus, born Jan. 31, 1749.
Samuel Overton Pettus, born March 1, 1751.
William Pettus, born April 30, 1753.
David Walker Pettus, born July 3, 1755.
Rebecah Pettus, born June 21, 1759.

Thomas Whitworth and Elizabeth Southerlan were married.

Births of Their Children

Samuel Whitworth, born Dec. 14, 1745.
Ann Whitworth, born Oct. 30, 1750.
Thomas Whitworth, born June 29, 1748.
Elizabeth Whitworth, born Oct. 29, 1752.
Mary Whitworth, born July 30, 1755.
Fendal Whitworth, born Oct. 17, 1757.
John Whitworth, born Oct. 17, 1759.
Loviney Whitworth, born March 9, 1762.
William Whitworth, born May 8, 1764,
Sarah Whitworth, born Sept. 1, 1766.
Southerland Whitworth, born Dec. 24, 1769.
Rebecah Whitworth, born Jan. 17, 1774.

David Walker Pettus, son of Thomas Pettus and Amy, his wife, married to Ann Whitworth, daughter of Thos. and Elizabeth Whitworth, Nov. 28, 1776.

Births of Their Children

Elizabeth Pettus, born Sept. 24, 1777.
Thomas Pettus, born Feb. 27, 1779.
David Pettus, born Dec. 20, 1780.
Samuel Pettus, born Aug. 22, 1784.

Births

A daughter, born Aug. 13, 1782; died Aug. 14.
A son, born July 6, 1783; died July 6.
A daughter, born April 19, 1786; died April 19.
John Pettus, born March 29, 1787; died Aug. 19, 1790.
A son, born Jan. 1, 1789; died same day.
Mary Pettus, born March 15, 1790; died July 12, 1790.
A son, born June 10, 1792; died June 10, ——.
A son, born May 31, 1793; died same day.
Nancy Pettus, born April 21, 1795; died in Nov., 1805.
Thomas Pettus, son of John Pettus and Anne, his wife, born Dec. 25, 1712.
Amey Walker, daughter of David

and Mary Walker, his wife, born Feb. 25, 1717.
David W. Pettus, son of Thos. and Mary Pettus, born July 3, 1755.
Anne Pettus, daughter of Thos. and Elizabeth Whitworth, born Oct. 30, 1750.
Thos. Whitworth, born June 26, 1726.
Elizabeth Whitworth, wife of Thos. Whitworth, formerly Southerland, born Feb. 2, 1726.
Thomas Pettus, died March 18, 1780.
Amy Pettus, died Oct. 22, 1778.
David Pettus, died Nov. 8, 1805.
Ann Pettus, died March 13, 1802.
Thomas Whitworth, died July 4, 1802.
Elizabeth Whitworth lived to the age of 93 or 94 years.
Samuel Pettus, son of David W. Pettus and Ann, his wife, was married to Sophia Musgrove.
Lamb, born Sept. 20, 1784, daughter of Richard and Clarissa Lamb, died May 29, 1806.

BIRTHS OF THEIR CHILDREN

Clarissa Ann Pettus, born July 23, 1807.
Musgrove Lamb Pettus, born Oct. 11, 1808.
Elizabeth Harriott Pettus, born Nov. 20, 1811.
John Richard Pettus, born Sept. 12, 1818.
Sophia Adaline Pettus, born April 17, 1820.

Samuel Pettus, died Sept. 10, 1857.
Sophia M. Pettus, died March 19, 1861.
Clarissa Anne Stone, died Dec. 23, 1878.
John Richard Pettus, died Sept. 26, 1870.
Musgrove Lamb Pettus, died Sept. 3, 1881, in his 73rd year.
Sophia Adaline Jordan, died 1898.

FAMILY RECORD

MARRIAGES

John Williams, born Feb. 28, 1786.
Mary, his wife, born Jan. 6, 1792.
John Williams and Mary, his wife, married Dec. 2, 1813.
John Williams and Mary L. Humphrey, married Dec. 2, 1858.
Mary L. Williams, born May 18, 1812.

FAMILY RECORD

BIRTHS

David P. Williams, born Sept. 12, 1814.
Lewis Williams, born April 15, 1816.
Samuel Williams, born Oct. 13, 1817.
John F. Williams, born June 10, 1819.
Elizabeth J. Williams, born April 10, 1821.
Mary L. Williams, born March 5, 1823.
Salley A. Williams, born May 20, 1826.
Charles Williams, born Oct. 2, 1828.
Susan Y. Williams, born July 8, 1829.
Richard H. Williams, born Dec. 23, 1830.
James O. Williams, born March 24, 1832.
Martha H. Williams, born Dec. 3, 1833.

FAMILY RECORD

DEATHS

Samuel Williams, died Jan. 2, 1817.
Elizabeth J. Williams, died Jan. 7, 1825.
Charles Williams, died March 4, 1831.
Richard H. Williams, died Sept. 7, 1844.
James O. Williams, died Nov. 3, 1852.
Mary Williams, mother of the above, died Jan. 4, 1856.

John Williams, father of the above, died Oct. 20, 1870.

From family records, we know the initials to stand for the following middle names: (all children of John Williams and Mary Pettus): David Pettus, Lewis, Samuel, John Fletcher, Elizabeth Jane, Mary Lucas, Sally Ann, Charles, Susan Young, Richard Henry, James Oslin, Martha Hannah.

Mary Pettus was the daughter of Samuel Overton Pettus of Mecklenburg County, Va., who was a Lieutenant in the Virginia Regiment of Guards, Revolutionary War. She was a granddaughter of Thomas Pettus of Lunenberg County, Va., and Cumberland Parish, who was a member of the Virginia House of Burgesses and signer of the protest against the importation or purchase of British manufacturers. The name of Thomas Pettus appears on the monument erected in Williamsburg, Va., in 1904.

Will of Thomas Pettus, probated April 14, 1780, Lunenberg County, dated Jan. 14, 1779.

Will of Samuel Overton Pettus, probated March 15, 1819, Mecklenburg County, dated Jan. 8, 1819. Will Book 9, page 9.

John Williams was the son of Lewis Williams, a Revolutionary patriot.

Will of Lewis Williams, probated Feb. 15, 1836, at Boydton, Mecklenburg County, Va. Will Book 14, page 41.

Lewis Williams and his wife, Sarah Oslin, were buried in the garden on the old plantation near La-Cross, Va.

A Register of the marriage of John C. and Sarah Ann Gaut and their sons and daughters.

John C. Gaut and Sarah Ann McReynolds, married Sept. 26, 1839, at the home of Isaac Lane.

We then went to Cleveland, Tenn., to live, where the said John C. Gaut had lived from Feb. 19, 1839. We lived in Cleveland from the date of our marriage until April 20, 1865, when we left Cleveland, moving to Nashville, Tenn., arriving in the latter place on the morning of the 22nd of April, 1865.

John C. Gaut of Nashville and Mrs. Sallie A. Carter of Franklin, Tenn., married Feb. 16, 1875, by the Rev. F. A. Thompson.

John M. Gaut and Miss Michal M. Harris and Miss Ann E. Gaut and Patrick H. Manlove were married May 5, 1870, at 8:30 o'clock p.m., at the First Cumberland Presbyterian Church in Nashville, Tenn., by Dr. A. J. Baird, pastor of the said church, in the presence of a large assemblage of friends and invited guests.

John M. Gaut and Miss Sallie Crutchfield were married Oct. 25, 1876, at the bride's father's residence, near Chattanooga, Tenn., by Dr. A. J. Baird.

John C. Gaut, born Feb. 27, 1813.

Sarah Ann Gaut, born June 22, 1817, in Cahaba, Dalas County, Ala.

Mrs. Sallie A. Carter, born July 12, 1826.

CHILDREN

Mary Lucinda Gaut, born July 11, 1840.

John McReynolds Gaut, born Oct. 1, 1841.

Ann Elizabeth Gaut, born Oct. 15, 1843.

Hugh Lawson Gaut, born Nov. 22, 1845.

Albert Colman Gaut, born Aug. 23, 1851.

An infant daughter of John C. and Sarah Ann Gaut, born dead on the morning of Sept. 26, 1855.

Horace Conaway Gaut, born Dec. 19, 1856, at 4 o'clock in the morning.

John Gaut Manlove, son of Patrick H. and Ann E. Manlove and grandson of John C. and Sarah Ann Gaut, born Nov. 22, 1871 at 5 o'clock a.m.

Joseph Edward Manlove, son of P. H. and Ann E. Manlove, born Sept. 12, 1874, at 1 o'clock p.m.
Horace Henry Manlove, son of P. H. and Ann E. Manlove, born Aug. 5, 1877, at 4 o'clock p.m.
Thomas Crutchfield Gaut, son of John M. and Sallie Gaut, born Aug. 21, 1877, at 4 o'clock a.m.
Sallie McReynolds Gaut, daughter of John and Sallie Gaut, born June 17, 1879, at 4 o'clock a.m.
Amanda King Gaut, daughter of John M. and Sallie Gaut, born July 19, 1881.
Mary Ann Gaut, daughter of John M. and Sallie Gaut, born Nov. 10, 1883.

Deaths of the children of John C. and Sarah Ann Gaut:
Albert Colman Gaut, son of John C. and Sarah Ann Gaut, died May 24, 1854, with scarlet fever, and perhaps worms, which precipitated his death.
Hugh Lawson Gaut, son of John C. and Sarah Ann Gaut, died about 10 o'clock at night May 28, 1854, with scarlet fever.
An infant daughter of John C. and Sarah Ann, born dead on the morning of Sept. 26, 1855.
Horace Conaway Gaut, son of John C. and Sarah Ann Gaut, died at 15 minutes before 8 o'clock in the morning of July 17, 1863, with scarlet fever, the same disease with which his brothers, Hugh L. and Albert C. Gaut, died. Horace C. Gaut was 6 years old when he died.
Miss Mary Lucendia Gaut, died in the City of Nashville on May 12, 1865, at 2 o'clock and 15 minutes p.m.; age 24 years 11 months and 1 day. Her disease was inflamation of the stomach and bowels. She died from internal hemorrhage of the bowels. She was perfectly in her right state of mind, and met death with a resignation and composure not excelled by any one. She believed that she would go to heaven and eternal happiness and exhorted us all to so live and prepare to meet her in heaven.
Mrs. Sarah Ann Gaut, wife of John C. Gaut, died of cholera in Nashville, Tenn., on the morning of June 9, 1873, at a quarter to 10 o'clock. She and her husband had been married, at the time of her death, 33 years 8 months and 14 days.
John Gaut Manlove, son of P. H. and Ann E. Manlove, died of diphtheria Dec. 12, 1879, at 6 o'clock and 25 minutes p.m.
John M. Gaut, son of John C., died Dec. 19, 1918.
Sallie C. Gaut, wife of John M., died April 19, 1930.
Thomas Crutchfield Gaut, son of John and Sallie Gaut, died of diphtheria July 24, 1885, at 4 o'clock a.m.; age 7 years 11 months 3 weeks.
Horace Henry Manlove, son of P. H. and Ann E. Manlove, died of diphtheria March 30, 1886, at 7 o'clock p.m.; age 8 years 7 months 5 days.
John Gaut, grandfather of John C. Gaut, born in Ireland, 1760; died March 5, 1833; 73 years old.
Lutitia McAll, his wife, born Sept. 25, 1768; died Oct. 25, 1849.

THEIR CHILDREN

James Gaut, father of John C. Gaut, born Sept. 19, 1786; died Feb. 13, 1875; married Feb. 18, 1812.
Mathew, born July 17, 1788; died 1878; married Feb. 26, 1812.
Benjamin, born Feb. 8, 1790; married March 3, 1829.
Polly, born Sept. 28, 1791; died Sept. 20, 1867; age 76 years.
John, born Dec. 28, 1793; died Nov. 4, 1886; age 86 years; married Dec. 27, 1821.
William, born Aug. 19, 1797; married Feb. 24, 1820.
Samuel, born Aug. 19, 1797; died Sept. 6, 1814; age 33 years.
Joseph, born July 16, 1798; died March, 1885; age 89 years; married Sept. 2, 1830.
Robert, born Aug. 6, 1800; died Feb., 1865; age 64 years; married May 9, 1822.
Nancy, born Nov. 26, 1802; died May 16, 1888; age 85 years.
Betsy (real name Elizabeth), born Nov. 10, 1804; died May 18, 1868; age 63 years; never married.

Patsey (real name Martha S.), born Oct. 12, 1806; died Jan. 28, 1878; age 71 years; never married.

George W., born Feb. 13, 1809; died May 7, 1903.

James Gaut's Family

Rozamond Irving, his wife, born Aug. 25, 1792; died July 12, 1869; age 76 years.

John C., born Feb. 27, 1813; died July 4, 1895.

Mahala S., born Oct. 31, 1814; died Nov. 4, 1857.

George W., born Dec. 9, 1816; died July 14, 1874.

Nancy, born Oct. 21, 1817; died March 9, 1866.

Mary E., born Feb. 15, 1821; died Jan. 9, 1846.

Jessie H., born Nov. 25, 1824.

Minerva, born Feb. 21, 1827; died Sept. 28, 1852.

James C., born Aug. 9, 1828; died June 28, 1837.

Robert D., born May 19, 1831; died June 2, 1837.

Mahala S., married John Dorsey.

George W., married Adeline Dorsey, 1841.

Nancy; never married.

Mary E., never married.

Jessie H., married, first Sarah E. Isbel, Dec. 8, 1849; second, Ella A. Luckey.

Minerva, married A. Taft.

Gaut Family

They were known as "Scotch-Irish," a term which is almost synonomous with brain and brawn. The family Bible of Jessie H. Gaut, Cleveland, Tenn., says that "John Gaut, from whom we are descended, was born in Ireland in 1760, and died at his home place on the French Broad river near Dandridge, Tenn., March 5, 1833, leaving a wife and thirteen children."

Tirrill Bible

From the family Bible of Henry and Louisa Tirrill. Now belongs to their son, Willard Oakes Tirrill, 3609 Richland Avenue, Nashville, Tenn. Sent by Mrs. W. O. Tirrill, Nashville.

Jecariah Snell, born 1705; died May, 1767.

Issachar Snell, his son, born 1732; died June 30, 1829.

Mehitable Snell, born 1771.

Abigail Snell, born 1772; died 1798.

Issachar Snell, born 1778; died Oct. 27, 1861.

Mehitable Tirrill, born June 13, 1806; died March, 1832.

Charlotte Tirrill, born April 12, 1808; died July 2, 1874.

Eliza Ann Tirrill, born Nov. 15, 1809; died Dec. 21, 1895.

Jacob Porter Tirrill, born Oct. 19, 1811; died June, 1874.

Hannah Snell Tirrill, born Aug. 3, 1815.

Willard Tirrill, born June 9, 1817; died July 5, 1856.

Oakes Tirrill, Jr., born May 31, 1820; died Nov., 1862.

Henry Tirrill, born July 2, 1823; died April 13, 1877.

Hannah Snell, married Oakes Tirrill, 1805.

Francis Cooke line, from family Bible of Henry and Louisa Tirrill, now owned by their son, Willard Tirrill.

Francis Cooke came over in the Mayflower, 1620, leaving his wife, Esther, maiden name unknown, and her three children, Jacob, Jane and Esther, who followed later in the ship "Ann" in 1628. He was born in 1600 and died in 1689.

Jane, their daughter, married Experience Mitchell, who came over in the "Ann" in 1628.

Hannah Mitchell, their daughter, married Deacon Joseph Haywood of Bridgewater, about 1683 or 1684.

Abigail Haywood, their daughter, born Aug. 30, 1702, married Zachariah Snell, 1731; died about 1800.

Issacher Snell, their son, born at Bridgewater, 1732; married Sarah, daughter of Benjamin Haywood, 1769, and died June 30, 1829.

Hannah Snell, their daughter, born at Bridgewater; married Oakes Tirrill, 1805.

Henry Tirrill, their son, born at Abbington, Mass., July 2, 1823; married Louisa Klinefelter, Aug. 6, 1857.

Willard Oakes Tirrill, their son, born Aug. 16, 1874; married Aphra Ann Eve, April 25, 1900.

Willard Oakes Tirrill, Jr., born May 29, 1906; married Bessie Thompson Brown, Aug. 24, 1929.

TWIGGS

From the family Bible of Aphra and Willard Tirrill, Nashville, Tenn.

Thomas Twiggs, or Triggs, died in Virginia, 1614. From mention of his name in private papers, he came, in 1608, from Devonshire, England. His son, Thomas, died near James City, Va., 1622-23. His son, Thomas, came in "The Hopewell," Feb., 1634; married Mary Southwood, or Southard; had several children. George, born 1640-41, married Mary; had Thomas, who married Eunice Ball, June 1, 1670; had George, born 1702, married Ann Williams; had George, born 1728, who first married Dorothy Carr, who lived three months; second, in 1749, married, Dec. 25, to Elizabeth Bryan; had John, born Dec. 12, 1750. John married Ruth Emanuel; had five sons and one daughter—George, David, Levi, Abraham, Acy and Sarah.

This is from the family Bible of John and Anna Ball of Virginia.

John and Anna Ball had four children—three daughters and one son. Ann, married Job Williams, Jan. 28, 1668; daughter, born May 12, 1672; baptized June 25, 1672, "Ann." Eunice married Thomas Twiggs, June 1, 1670; son, born April 2, 1672; baptized April 2, 1672, "George." Eunice Twiggs died at early candle light, April 2, 1672; buried April 4. On March 9, 1728, George Twiggs married Ann Williams. Eunice's boy, Ann's daughter. The other children of John and Ann Ball were John III., Dorothy IV.

The above records were furnished by Eugenia Williams, who got it from a descendant of Dorothy.

George L. Twiggs, the son of John Twiggs and Ruth Emanuel, married Sarah Low. Will of George L. Twiggs is in Augusta, Ga.

George L. Twiggs' daughter, Sarah Louisa Twiggs, born May 12, 1815; died April 10, 1851; married Paul Fitzsimons Eve, Dec. 20, 1832.

Paul F. Eve, born June 27, 1806; died Nov. 3, 1877.

Their first child was George Twiggs Eve, born April 3, 1835; died Feb. 6, 1897; married Jennie Sutherland, May 6, 1869.

Jennie Sutherland, born March 2, 1844; died May 16, 1924.

Their daughter, Aphra Ann Eve, married Willard Oakes Tirrill, April 25, 1900.

John Alden line, from the family Bible of Henry Tirrill and Louisa Klinefelter, now owned by their son, Willard Oakes Tirrill, 3609 Richland Avenue, Nashville, Tennessee.

John Alden, the Pilgrim, came to Plymouth on the "Mayflower" in 1620; married Priscilla Mullin, or Molines, of the "Mayflower," in 1621 or 1622. Priscilla died between 1680-87, before her husband.

Zachariah Alden, their son, born before 1650; died after 1699; married Mary (maiden name unknown).

Anna Alden, their daughter, married Josiah Snell of Bridgewater, Dec. 21, 1699; died 1705. The said Josiah lived till 1753.

Zachariah Snell, their son, born March 17, 1704; married Abigail Haywood, March, 1731. Abigail was born Aug. 30, 1702.

Issachar Snell, their son, born 1732; married Sarah Haywood in 1769. He died June 30, 1829. She died Nov., 1824.

Hannah Snell, born Jan. 1, 1781; their daughter married Oakes Tirrill, 1805.

Henry Tirrill, their son, born July 2, 1823; married Louisa Klinefelter, Aug. 6, 1857. Louisa Klinefelter was born May 7, 1839.

Willard Oakes Tirrill, their son, born Aug. 16, 1874; married Aphra Ann Eve, April 25, 1900. Aphra Ann Eve, born Jan. 26, 1878.

PRITCHARD

Paul Pritchard, an emigrant from Scotland, was a ship builder in Charleston, S. C. He was handsome and so wild that his friends put him on board a vessel. Sick with fever, he was left on the coast of Africa. When he regained consciousness he found himself being nursed by an old Negro man, in the wilds of Africa.

Years afterwards he was buying two young slaves in Charleston for his plantation, when he was touched by an old man, in whom he recognized the one who had saved his life, so he bought him and cared for him till his death.

In his will he left all his great possessions to his children—William, Paul, Aphra Ann and Catherine.

Catherine, married Christopher Fitzsimmons, and had issue.

Owen Pritchard.

Anna, married Wade Hampton.

Catherine, married James Hammond.

Aphra Ann, married Oswell Eve, June 29, 1783.

John Carmichael, married Rachel Davis, May 3, 1874. She was one of twins; of the other nothing is known.

Rachel D. Carmichael, died Dec. 26, 1805, and was buried at Kiokee, formerly Davis' Mills, in Columbia County. Kiokee is a large brick Baptist Church.

Sarah Davis, daughter of John and Rachel Carmichael, was born Feb. 19, 1805; married John P. Eve, Jan. 16, 1823; died Nov. 4, 1851. She was buried at the Eve Graveyard in Floyd County, Ga.

EVE

Oswell Eve, Sr., was a sea captain, owning and commanding the British brig "Roebuck," and some other twenty-five vessels. He filled many positions of trust in Philadelphia where he owned much property, and lived in a handsome stone house, where he raised a large family. He was of Quaker descent.

He and Ann Moore were married at Christ Church, June 2, 1744. When the war broke out he went to Nassau, where he died in his son Joseph's house.

Oswell Eve's walking stick was a

bamboo cane cut out on the Ganges more than one hundred and fifty years ago. "Eve" is cut in the ivory head. It has been used also by Oswell Eve, Jr., by John P. Eve, and by John C. Eve, and now belongs to Oswell Battey Eve, his great-great-grandson.

Oswell Eve married Ann Moore, and left five children:

1. John, married Jane Campbell.
2. Oswell, married Aphra Ann Pritchard.
3. William, married Mary Clarke.
4. Joseph, married Hannah Singleterry.
5. Sarah, died two weeks before she was to marry Dr. Rush.

Oswell Eve, married Aphra Ann Pritchard, June 29, 1783, and had issue:

1. Ann Pritchard, married Charles Cunningham.
2. Sarah, married John Strong Adams.
3. Catherine, married Andrew Watkins, Robert Campbell.
4. Mary Eliza, married John Carmichael.
5. Martha Henrietta, married Gilbert Longstreet.
6. Maria Fitzsimmons, married John Bones.
7. Emmeline, married William Smith.
8. John P., married Sarah Davis Carmichael.
9. Joseph William, married Filo Casey.
10. Paul Fitzsimmons, married (1) Louisa Twiggs, (2) Sarah Ann Duncan.

---

3. William, married Mary Clarke of Charleston and had issue: Joseph C. and William.

Joseph, married Jane Ringland and had issue: Joseph, John C., Emma, Mary, and Louisa.

Mary Isabel Eve, married John S. Wright.

May Wright, married E. C. Sofgee, had issue: Carrie, Hattie, Katie, Thodore and John.

Carrie, married Marshal Horsey, and had issue: Marshal, Charlie, and Daisy.

Katie, married Bignon.

Theodore, married Maude Roberson.

---

4. Joseph, married Hannah Singleterry, and had issue:

(1) Mary Roma, married James C. Campbell, had issue: Henry and Robert C.

Henry F., married Sarah Sibley.

Robert C., married Sibley.

Left issue: James, Robert, Josie, Mary R., Sallie and Nina.

(2) Joseph Adams Eve, married Sarah Garland Combs, and had issue:

Mildred, married Walton Timberlake.

Lizzie, married J. V. H. Allen.

Robert, married Willie Harmon.

Left issue: Osell R., Harold, Robert C., Joe, and Harmon..

John and Reginald.

Sterling, married Laura Baker, and left issue: Archie, Hinton, Sarah G., Josie and Katie.

Sarah, married Campbell.

Celeste, married Baker.

Joe.

William F., married Ida Evans, had issue: Allie, Sarah, Fred and Ida.

Allie Married Cabiness.

Fred, married Grace Boykin.

(3) Edward A. Eve, married Sarah Jane Raiford, had issue: Henrietta, Maria Lou, May.

William, married Betty Hammond, had issue: Catherine, Janie, Annie, Blue Eyes, and Edward.

Phil, married, had issue: Clara, Will.

(4) Frances, unmarried.

John P. Eve, son of Oswell and Ann Pritchard, married Sarah Davis Carmichael and Mary M. Olive; had issue by Sarah:

Rachel Davis, married Joshua Scott Key.

2. John Carmichael, married Mary L. Miller.
3. Mary Hill, married J. Newton Russell; had issue: Susie, Newton, and Charlton.

Susie, married Curtis.

4. Anna P., married R. Chancey Robbins.

5. Oswell Bones, married Ann Helen Hall; had issue, Ben Hall, John P., Robert C., and Oswell.

---

1. Ben Eve, married Addie Trowbridge; had issue: Marie, Annie, Addie, Allene, Edgworth, Robert, and Willie.
Marie, married W. W. Hume; had issue: Witzel, and Mary Adriene.
Annie, married Wm. Ward; had issue: William and ———.
2. Robert C., married Martha Parkman.
3. John P., married Mattie Lovelace; had issue: Lovelace, Embry, and Mattie.
6. Sarah Adams Eve, died July 26, 1886.
John C. Eve, married Mary E. Miller, and had issue: Oliver, Davis, Willie Miller, Oswell Battey, Mary Magruder, and Sarah Anna.
Oswell B. Eve, married Edith Davis.
Oswell and Ann P. Eve, married June 29, 1783.
Ann Pritchard, born June 28, 1784.
Sarah, born Oct. 27, 1785.
Catherine, born March 12, 1787.
Mary Eliza, born Nov. 22, 1788.
Elizabeth, born May 13, 1790.
Martha Henrietta, born Jan. 22, 1792.
Oswell, born Nov. 16, 1793; died Dec. 2, 1793.
Oswell, born Jan. 16, 1795; died in Liverpool, July 12, 1812.
Maria Fitzsimmons, born April 22, 1797.
Emmiline, born Nov. 16, 1798.
John Pritchard, born June 24, 1800.
Augusta Belinda, born Oct. 24, 1802; died July 24, 1803.
Joseph William, born Dec. 17, 1804.
Paul Fitzsimmons, born June 27, 1806.
Aphra Watkins, born June 4, 1808; died Sept. 16, 1808.

Oswell and Ann Eve, married June 29, 1783.
Ann Pritchard Eve, their daughter, born June 28, 1784.
Sarah Eve, their daughter, born Oct. 27, 1785.
Catherine Eve, their daughter, born March 12, 1787.
Mary Eliza Eve, their daughter, born Nov. 23, 1788.
Elizabeth Eve, their daughter, born May 13, 1790.
Martha Henrietta, their daughter, born Jan. 22, 1792.
Oswell Eve, their son, born Nov. 16, 1793; died Dec. 2, 1793.
Oswell, their son, born Jan. 16, 1795.
Maria Fitzsimmons, their daughter, born April 22, 1797.
Emmeline, their daughter, born Nov. 16, 1798.
John Pritchard, their son, born June 24, 1800.
Augusta Belinda, their daughter, born Oct. 24, 1802; died July 24, 1803.
Joseph William, their son, born Dec. 17, 1804.
Paul F., their son, born June 27, 1806.
Aphra Watkins, their daughter, born June 4, 1808; died Sept. 16, 1808.
Oswell, their son, died in Liverpool, July 12, 1812.
Ann Pritchard Eve, married to Charles Cunningham.
Sarah Eve, married John Strong Adam, March ——.
Catherine Eve, married Anderson Watkins, Jan. 26, ——.
Mary E. Eve, married John Carmichael, Dec. 3, ——.
Martha Henrietta Eve. married Gilbert Longstreet, March 6, ——.
Maria F. Eve, married John Bones.

FAMILY BIBLE, PROPERTY OF CHRISTOPHER NOEL, 1789

Copied and diligently compared from old Bible by Mrs. Wm. H. Lambeth.

Bible bought by C. L. Hooberry, dealer in rare books and curios.

BIRTHS

Christopher Noel, born July 10, 1789.
Catharine Noel, daughter of Christopher and Esther Noel, born Jan. 12, 1814.
Eliza Anne Noel, daughter of Christopher and Esther Noel, born Oct. 12, 1815.
William Noel, son of Christopher and Esther Noel, born Nov. 21, 1817.
Mary Noel, daughter of Christopher and Esther Noel, born Aug. 26, 1819.
Thomas M'Fall, born June 21, 1824.
Abraham Hertzler, born July 3, 1781.

DEATHS

Christopher Noel, died Oct. 31, 1819; age 30 years 3 months 21 days.
Abraham Hertzler, died Jan. 10, 1846; age 65 years 5 months 13 days.

FAMILY BIBLE, PROPERTY OF JOHN KEEL, 1806

Copied and diligently compared from old Bible by Mary Weeks Lambeth (Mrs. W. H. Lambeth), Nashville, Tenn., Bible bought by Mr. C. L. Hooberry, dealer in antiques.

John and Katherine Keel were married Aug. 3, 1806.
John and Ann Keel, married Oct. 8, 1812.
Charles Keel, son of John and Ann Keel, died Aug. 2, 1816.

BIRTHS

Peter Lane Keel, son of John and Catherine Keel, born March 8, 1807.
George Monnater (?) Keel, born Feb. 22, 1809, the son of John and Catherine Keel.
William Keel, son of John and Catherine Keel, born July 17, 1811.

DEATHS

William Keel, son of John and Catherine Keel, died July 29, 1811.
Catherine Keel, died Aug. 12, 1811; age 24 years 3 months 18 days.
Eliza Keel, daughter of John and Ann Keel, died Jan. 16, 1814.
Margaretta Keel, daughter of John and Ann Keel, died Sept. 22, 1816; age 19 months.
George and Hannah Keel, married March 5, 1834.
Peter L. and Mary Keel, married May 23, 1839.
George N. Keel, son of John and Catherine Keel, born Feb. 22, 1809.
William Keel, son of John and Catherine Keel, born July 17, 1811.
Eliza Keel, daughter of John and Ann Keel, born Sept. 26, 1813.
Margarett Keel, daughter of John Keel, born Feb. 28, 1815.
Frances A. Keel and William Stevenson, married Oct. 22, 1844.
Charles Keel, son of John and Ann Keel, born Aug. 1, 1816.
Frances Ann, daughter of John and Ann Keel, born Oct. 22, 1817.
Sarah Samson Keel, daughter of John and Ann Keel, born Aug. 20, 1819.
Elizabeth Smith Keel, daughter of John and Ann Keel, born Aug. 2, 1821.
Anna Maria Keel, daughter of John and Ann Keel, born March 30, 1824.

DEATHS

William Keel, son of John and Catherine Keel, July 29, 1811.
Catherine Keel, wife of John Keel, Aug. 12, 1811.
Eliza Keel, daughter of John and Ann Keel, Jan. 16, 1814.
Charles Keel, son of John and Ann Keel, Aug. 2, 1816.
Margarett Keel, daughter of John and Ann Keel, Sept. 22, 1816.
Ann, wife of John Keel, Jan. 11, 1847.
John Keel, Nov. 23, 1858, in the 76th year of his age.
Peter L. Keel, Jr., son of George N. and Hannah Keel, born June 5, 1834.

Bible of F. F. V. Schmittou, born in Prussia, served under Andrew Jackson at New Orleans. In the possession of a descendant, S. R. Potts, Cumberland Furnace, Tenn. German Bible dates 1803. Copied by Mrs. Acklen.

Some distance from Mr. Potts' house is the graveyard where Dr. Schmittou and many others are buried. Mr. Potts showed us the grave of the Doctor, which had been by a very large cedar tree, the stump of which is now by the rough field headstone. The graves are marked with field stones, but no names or dates are on them. The burying ground is on what was the farm of the Schmittou family.

In the front is "Abeyette Schmittou, her "Book and a present to G. D. Schmittou. Registered in the Register office Cortton."

F. F. V. Schmittou's Book—Was born in Prussia, Jan. 6, 1772; landed in America Nov. 22, 1806, at New Orleans, La.

Francois F. Schmittou was born in Prussia Jan. 6, 1772; landed in America in 1806; was married July 20 to Ally Reynolds.

BIRTHS OF CHILDREN

Obriant Livingston, born May 29, 1812.

Obigalla Schmittou, born Oct. 23, 1813.

Robert Livingston, born Feb. 1, 1816.

Antinette Omally Terasia, born Feb. 12, 1818.

Francois Ferdinand, born April 12, 1820.

Francois Frank, born March 9, 1822.

Sterling Brewer, born Feb. 10, 1824.

Mary Elizabeth, born Aug. 15, 1826.

Octavus Adolphus, born Dec. 11, 1828.

Charlotte Livingston, born April 18, 1831.

George Diederich, born July 21, 1833, the last child of Ally Schmittou, wife of F. F. Schmittou.

GAMBLE FAMILY BIBLE RECORD

Sent by Mrs. Charlton Rogers.

MARRIAGES

William Gamble and Jane McFarlan, in *Philadelphia*, Pa., April 25, 1805.

Eliza Gamble, to A. S. Burnett, in New Albany, Ind., April 19, 1829.

James F. Gamble and Sarah Jane Logan, in Shelbyville, Ky., June 25, 1840.

BIRTHS

William Gamble, son of John Gamble, of Ghouston, Ireland, March 15, 1774.

Jane McFarlan (alias), Jane Gamble, daughter of Walter McFarlan of the town of Newtonstewart, Ireland, May 11, 1773.

Eliza Gamble, daughter of Wm. and Jane Gamble, in Louisville, Ky., April 25, 1807.

William, son of Wm. and Jane Gamble, in Shippingsport, Ky., March, 1809.

Jas. McFarlan, son of Wm. and Jane Gamble, in Bardstown, Ky., Jan. 7, 1811.

John Alexander, son of Wm. and Jane Gamble, in Bardstown, Ky., April 25, 1812.

John Wellington, son of Wm. and Jane Gamble, in Louisville, Ky., Nov. 24, 1815.

George Wm. G. Burnett, son of Alex S. and Eliza Burnett, in New Albany, Feb. 25, 1830.

CHILDREN

Children of Walter and Eliza McFarlan in Ireland:

Jas. McFarlan, born May 3, 1771.

Jane McFarlan, born May 11, 1773.

Patrick McFarlan, born Aug. 31, 1775.

Mary McFarlan, born Dec. 3, 1779.
Walter McFarlan, son of Patrick, which was the son of Andrew McFarlan, who was in the land service of his country under the reign of William II. of England and lost his life in the Bay of Biscay in going to Flanders.

DEATHS

William Gamble, Jan. 17, 1824, in Louisville, Ky.
John Alex, son of above, in Bardstown, Ky., Dec. 23, 1812.
Eliza Burnett, in New Albany, Ind., Dec. 6, 1830.
Anna Anderson, daughter of J. F. Gamble, April 1, 1843.
Mrs. Jane Gamble, mother of Eliza, William, James McFarlan, John Alexander, and John W. Gamble, Aug. 28, 1847.
Edmonia Barbour, daughter of James F. Gamble, Dec. 26, 1847.
Annie Gamble, daughter of James F. Gamble, Nov. 30, 1851.

LATER BIRTHS

Jane McFarlan, daughter of Jas. F. Gamble, March 21, 1841, in Louisville.
Anna Anderson, daughter of J. F. G., March 15, 1845, in Jefferson County.
Catherine Mary, daughter of J. F. and Sarah Jane Gamble, June 2, 1844, in Jefferson County, Ky.
Edmonia Barbour, daughter of Jas. F. and Sarah Jane Gamble, April 15, 1846, in Jefferson County, Ky.
Sarah Elizabeth, daughter of Jas. F. and Sarah Jane Gamble, Jan 15, 1848, in Jefferson County, Ky.
Annie Gamble, daughter of Jas. F. and Sarah Jane Gamble, Nov. 19, 1849, in Louisville, Ky.
Logan Gamble, son of Jas. F. and Sarah Jane Gamble, Oct. 28, 1851, in Louisville, Ky.
Laura Gamble, daughter of Jas. F. and Sarah Jane Gamble, Oct. 6, 1853.

RECORDS FROM THE ROGERS FAMILY BIBLE

BIRTHS

Bernard F. Rogers, son of Joseph and Susan Rogers.

Charlton B. Rogers, son of Bernard F. Rogers and Mary A. Rogers, born June 30, 1842.

Mary E. Coons, daughter of Martin Coons and Mary White Coons.

Jane M. Gamble, daughter of James F. Gamble and Sarah Logan Gamble, born March 26, 1841.

Joseph M. Rogers, Charlton B. Rogers, and Susan C. Rogers, children of B. F. Rogers.

Charlton B. Rogers' and Jane M. Rogers' children:

Sarah Logan Rogers, born at Bryan Station, Jan. 22, 1868.

Mary Rogers, born at Bryan Station, April 9, 1870.

Margaret Fleming Rogers, born at Bryan Station, May 21, 1873.

Charlton Bernard Rogers, born at Bryan Station, Oct. 4, 1876.

Joseph McFarlan Rogers, born at Engleside, Bullitt County, Ky., Oct. 16, 1879.

MARRIAGES

Charlton Bernard Rogers and Jane McFarlan Gamble, married in Louisville, Ky., Dec. 5, 1867.

Joseph M. Rogers, married Kate Gamble.

Susan C. Rogers, married William Herod.

Charlton Bernard Rogers, Jr., married Linell Chenault, Nov. 8, 1905.

Records sent by Mrs. Edgar Foster, Gallatin Road, Nashville, Tenn.

Gen. Wm. Trousdale, born in Surrey County, N. C., in 1790.
Chas. W. Trousdale, born in Gallatin in 1738, son of Gov. Wm. Trousdale, born 1790.
J. N. Turner, born in 1839, son of Nelson B. Turner, born in Virginia in 1797.
T. S. Vaughn, M.D., born in Wilson County, 1820, son of Rev. M.

S. Vaughn, born in Georgia in 1797.
Josiah Walton, born in Sumner County in 1829, son of Josiah Walton, Sr., born in 1788; was private secretary of Andrew Jackson in 1818.
Elihu N. Mitchner, born in Sumner County in 1829, son of Wm. B. Mitchner, born in North Carolina in 1775.
Maj. W. S. Munday, born in Virginia in 1827, son of Walker Munday, born in 1807.
Jonas Nickelson, born in Gallatin in 1821, son of John Nickelson, born in New England in 1782.
A. Parham, born in North Carolina in 1825, son of Geo. Parham, born in 1785.
Chas. B. Rogan, born in Sumner County in 1839, son of Frank Rogan, born in 1798.
J. M. Shute, born in Sumner County in 1832, son of Lee Shute, born in 1797.
Daniel and William Calgy, born in 1830 and 1840, respectively, sons of Hugh Calgy, born in 1788.
James Campbell, born in Sumner County in 1816. His father was Colin Campbell and was born in Virginia in 1792.
James Darnell, born in Sumner County in 1827, son of John S. Darnell, born in Maryland in 1784.
A. B. C. Dickinson, born in Virginia in 1817. His father was born in Virginia in 1774.
J. B. Donelson, born in Hendersonville in 1850, son of Gen. D. S. Donelson, born in 1801.
Cullen E. Douglass, born in 1825. His father was Wm. Howard, born in 1782.
Capt. C. S. Douglass, born in Sumner Co., in 1839, son of Col. Young N. Douglass, born in N. C. in 1762.
Reuben Douglass, born in Sumner Co. in 1831. His father, Wiley J. Douglass, born in 1792.
J. Edwards, born in Virginia in 1815. His father, Thos. Edwards, born in 1765.
Dr. John W. Franklin, born in Sumner Co., 1819, son of John Franklin, born 1776.
R. G. Gillespie, born Sumner Co. in 1826, son of Jacob Gillespie, born N. C., 1779.
Geo. Gillespie, born Gallatin 1828, son of Jacob Gillespie, born N. C. in 1773.
Isaac Guthrie, born in Kentucky in 1810, son of James Guthrie, born Virginia, 1779.
M. J. Hassell, born in Sumner Co., 1827, son of Jennett Hassell, born in N. C., 1787.
Dr. James M. Head, born Sumner Co., 1818, son of Henry Head, born 1770.
James House, born in Sumner Co., 1832, son of James House, born in N. C., 1795.
James Alexander, born in Sumner Co., Sept. 27, 1813. His father was David Alexander, born in 1790 in Mecklenburg Co., N. C.
Hon. B. F. Allen (attorney), born in Sumner Co., in 1826. His father was John Allen, born in 1776 in Pennsylvania.
J. R. Barry, born in Gallatin in 1836, son of Thos. Barry, born 1806.
Dr. Humphrey H. Bate, born in 1844. His father was born in N. C., in 1779.
James W. Bullock, born in Kentucky, 1817. His father was James P., born in Virginia, 1789.
Thos. F. Witherspoon, born in 1825 in Kentucky, son of John R. Witherspoon, born 1774, in S. C.
Dr. Thos. N. Woodson, born in 1830, Sumner Co., son of Rev. Lewis M. Woodson, born Montgomery Co., Tenn., in 1806.
Col. A. R. Waynne, born in Sumner Co., in 1800, son of Robt. Waynne, born in N. C.

Records taken from Bible purchased by John Williamson July 22, 1803. Sent by Mrs. Edgar Foster.

John Williamson, born Dec. 16, 1764.
Margaret, his wife, born Jan. 24, 1766.

CHILDREN

Sallie Williamson, born April 4, 1782.
Margaret, born Jan. 29, 1784.
John, born April 14, 1786.
Rebecca, born Nov. 22, 1788.
George, born Oct. 10, 1795.
Betsy, born March 8, 1790.
Rachel, born Oct. 12, 1800.
James, born Jan. 18, 1798.
Ann, born Jan. 1, 1804.
William, born Sept. 14, 1806.
Thos. H., born July 2, 1809.

Henry A. Burge, son of Epaphroditus and Mary Burge, of the state of Virginia, born March 15, 1800.
Eliza Channing, daughter of Ann P. and Thomas Channing, born June 5, 1804.
Henry A. Burge and Eliza Channing, married Nov. 30, 1820.
Thomas C. Burge, son of Henry and Eliza, born Nov. 9, 1821.
Austin Gresham and Eliza Burge, married July 17, 1829.
Sarah F., daughter of Eliza and Austin, born Aug. 30, 1830.
William, son of Eliza and Austin Gresham, born July 12, 1833.

DEATHS

Henry A. Burge, died Aug. 30, 1826.
Eliza C. Burge Gresham, died June 17, 1834.
Austin Gresham, died Sept. 7, 1836.
William, son of Eliza and Austin Gresham, died Aug. 21, 1834.
Thomas C. Burge, died Dec. 22, 1860.
Sarah F. Blackman, died Aug. 25, 1863.
Julia F. Blackman, died Oct. 7, 1889.
Julia F. Burge, consort of Thomas C. Burge, departed this life Aug. 10, 1851.
Charles M. Blackman and Sarah F. Gresham, married Sept. 27, 1849, by the Rev. Dr. R. B. C. Howell, D.D.
W. A. Blackman, married to Ann Williams, Aug. 11, 1878.
Julia T. Blackman, died Oct. 7, 1889.
Robert Chadwell, born Sept. 24, 1820.
Mary Ann Burge, born March 7, 1824.
Robert Chadwell and Mary Ann Burge, married Jan. 23, 1845.
Irene, daughter of Robert and Mary Chadwell, born July 22, 1847; died Sept. 12, 1847.
Wm. Thomas, son of Robert and Mary Chadwell, born Feb. 27, 1849; died Oct., 1907.
John Thompson, son of Robert and Mary, born Oct. 17, 1851.
Roberta Love, daughter of Robert and Mary, born May 17, 1857.
Henry Burge, son of Robert and Mary, born Dec. 15, 1859.
Mary Ann Burge Chadwell passed into life eternal, Feb. 22, 1896.
Robert Chadwell passed into life eternal, May, 1900.
John T. Chadwell, married to Sue Litton, May 15, 1879.
Roberta Love Chadwell, united in marriage to Robert Exum Love, Feb. 1, 1883.
Henry Burge Chadwell, married to Beulah Vaughn, Feb. 21, 1889.
Duke William Sumner, born April 27, 1778; died May 15, 1844.
Mary Sumner, his wife, born Nov. 27, 1779; died June 22, 1832.
Edmund Burke Sumner, born Mar. 26, 1817.
Amanda Caroline Sumner, born Oct. 31, 1851.
Edmund Burke Sumner, married to George Ann Emett, Aug. 29, 1848.
Edmund Burke Sumner, born Sept. 1, 1849.

Bible of James McCasland, in the possession of Mrs. James Napier. Sent by Mrs. J. D. Howley.

James J. Wyly, born Dec. 23, 1824.
Eliza Jane, his wife, born April 30, 1824.
Thomas K. Wyly, born Saturday, September 30, 1848.
Margaret H. Wyly, born Monday, March 11, 1850.

Artemis Wyly, born Nov. 17, 1852.
Hester Wyly, born Monday, Jan. 5, 1857.
James J. Wyly, born Friday, July 23, 1858.
William M. Wyly, born Sunday, Feb. 10, 1861.
C. K. Wyly, born Friday, Aug. 7, 1863.
Wyly Wyly, born Monday, April 10, 1866.
George Humble, born June 15, 1773, Humphreys County.
Sarah Humble, born Oct. 16, 1770.
Margaret Humble, born Oct. 8, 1796.
Jacob Humble, born July 30, 1798.
John Humble, born March 6, 1800.
Mary Humble, born Dec. 17, 1801.
Elizabeth Humble, born Aug. 30, 1804.
Martha Humble, born July 29, 1807
David Humble, born Oct. 6, 1809.
Sarah Jane Humble, born Oct. 10, 1811.
George Humble and Sarah Humble, married July 31, 1795.
Eilliam McCasland and Margaret Humble, married July 31, 1823.
William McCasland, born July 20, 1788.
Margaret McCasland, born Oct. 8, 1796.
Eliza Jane McCasland, born April 30, 1824.
James J. Wyly, born Dec. 23, 1824.
James J. Wyly and Eliza Jane McCasland, married Oct. 12, 1847.
Thomas K. Wyly, born Saturday, Sept. 30, 1848.
Margaret H. Wyly, born Monday, March 11, 1850.
James Wyly Napier, born May 20, 1878.
William McCasland, departed this life Aug. 21, 1844.
Margaret McCasland, departed this life April 6, 1860.
Wyly Wyly, died Jan 24, 1873, aged 6 years and 9 months.
Sarah Humble, died 1852.
John H. Wyly, departed this life Feb. 23, 1855.
Hester Wyly, departed this life Sunday, June 21, 1857.
Wyly Wyly departed this life Jan. 24, 1873.
Willie M. Wyly, third son of J. J. Wyly and Eliza Jane Wyly, died at Waverly, Tenn., at 6 p.m., July 21, 1884.

Williams' Ancestors

Copied from data gathered by George T. Williams, uncle of John T. E. Williams. Record now owned by John T. E. Williams.

Sent by Mrs. Jos. Prichett, Nashville.

Begins with:
Edman Williams, from Wales. His wife was Lucretia Adams, of the noted Adams family. (Uncle George said a brother-in-law of John Adams).

Children

George Williams, married Rebecca Taylor.
Archibald Williams, married Rhoda Taylor.
(Rebecca and Rhoda Taylor were sisters).
John L. Williams, married Elizabeth Price.
Samuel H. Williams.
Joshua Williams.
Trophenia Williams, married Jonathan Smalling.
Sarah Williams, married John Hoss.
Lucretia Williams, married Johnathan Tipton.

George Williams, wife Rebecca Taylor, daughter of old Andrew Taylor.

Children

Labon Williams, married.
Vina Williams, married Boyd.
George C. Williams, accidentally killed on Gap Creek.
Levi Williams, single.
Elcana Williams, first wife, Edmonson; second wife, Lock.
(Dr. E. D. Williams, son of Elcana Williams, of Chinano, Texas).
Wilson Williams, single.

Archibald Williams, without heirs.
Trophosa Williams, married John K. Ensor.
Elizabeth Williams.
Pleasant Williams, wife, Sarah Smith Peters.
Trophenia Williams, wife of John Longmires.
Rhoda Williams, wife of Bartlett Boren.
Montgomery Williams, married Margaret Payne.
Albert Galiton Williams, never married.
Matthew Williams, without heirs.
Sam J. Williams, married Theodora Taylor.
Lucretia Williams, married Ware (had two children, both died).

Archibald Williams' wife was Rhoda Taylor.
This couple were John T. E. Williams' great-grandparents.

CHILDREN

Samuel Wilson Williams, bachelor.
Edman Williams, married Anna Ellis.
George D. Williams, married Lucinda Haun.
Joshua Williams (grandfather), married Elizabeth Lane.
Nathaniel S. Williams, bachelor.
Anna Williams, first husband, Drake; second, Callison.
Lucretia Williams, married Joseph Young.
Serphina Williams, married Dr. Joseph Rhea, son of Sam Rhea and Nancy Breden.
Children: Nannie, Archie W., Rhoda J., Sam W. (1850).

John L. Williams, wife, Elizabeth Price.

CHILDREN

Pinkney P. Williams, married Rosanna Haun.
Edman Williams, married Sarah Cox, of N. C.
Joshua Williams, bachelor.
Phineas Williams, bachelor.
Samuel Williams, married Racheal Pugh.
Lucretia Williams, married Jessy Dickson.
Ruhama C. Williams, married James A. Ruble (Preacher M. E.).
Names of Ruhama Ruble's children were: Rachel Ruble, Hanna Ann Ruble, Elizabeth Ruble, Nancy T. Ruble, Mary A. Ruble, Sarah A. Ruble, Hamett A. Ruble, Altha A. Ruble.
Nancy Williams, married Solomon Pugh.
Their children were: David Pugh, Elizabeth Pugh, Rachel Pugh, Solomon, called Solly.

Samuel H. Williams.
Joshua Williams.
Trophenia Williams, married Johnathan Smalling.
Sarah Williams, married John Hoss.

CHILDREN

Landon Hoss, Elcana Hoss, Math Hoss.

Samuel Wilson Williams, never married; died June, 1877, in his 82nd year.
Edman Williams' wife was Anna Ellis.

CHILDREN

Rhoda Williams, married Jas. I. R. Boyd.
George D. Williams, married Jane Hampton.
John E. Williams, married Pett Luckey.
Julia Williams, married Wm. Range.

George D. Williams, wife, Lucinda Haun.

CHILDREN

Anna Eliza Williams, married, first, Marion Willims; second, William Carroll.
Jane E. Williams (died Sept., 1906), married Tip Anderson, of Georgia (died May 12, 1910).
Mary E. Williams, married John W. Cameron.
S. W. H. Williams (died 1886), married Edna Miller.
Julia C. Williams, married Jordan C. Hardin.
Margaret Williams, married C. P. Toncray.
Louvena Williams, married James Anderson, of Georgia.
Frances T. Williams, married C. C. Taylor, died June, 1922.

Joshua Williams, died Oct. 17, 1895, in his 88th year; wife was Elizabeth Lane, died Oct. 18, 1885, in her 76th year.

CHILDREN

Rhoda Ann Williams, married P. A. J. Crockett.
Archibald Williams, married Sarah E. Hyder.
Nathaniel L. Williams, married Martha Daniels.
Robert Been Williams, married Martha McCorkle.
Samuel J. Williams, married Angeline Birchfield.
George T. Williams (died Aug. 4, 1922), married Nannie S. Barker.

Archibald Williams, who is John T. E. Williams' father, married Sarah Elizabeth Hyder.

CHILDREN

Maggie Williams, married James Love.
Nat R. Williams, married Ella Taylor.
Anna R. Williams, married John W. Williams.
Two children died young.
John T. E. Williams, married Cainie Carson.
Joseph Williams, married Dessie Range.

John T. E. Williams, wife, Cainie Carson.

CHILDREN

Velma Carson Williams, married Joseph W. Pritchett.
John Arch Williams, married Eleanor Lynn Baxter.
Ervin Maurice Williams, married Bertha B. Bradshaw.
A daughter died at 8 days old.
George Alex Williams.
Cainie Sue Williams.

Here are some more names Uncle George had and the way he had them written:
Andrew Taylor, wife, Anna Taylor (nee Wilson).

CHILDREN

Nathaniel Taylor, married Mary Patton. (He is the father of James P. Taylor and is the father of N. G. Taylor).
Isaac Taylor, married Jane Cunningham.
Andrew Taylor, Jr., married Sarah Rochhold.
Matthew Taylor, married Rachel Peoples.
Rebecca Taylor, married George Williams.
Rhoda Taylor, married Archibald Williams.
Elizabeth Taylor, married David McNabb.
(Written after this in pencil, said "Carter blood").
By itself was written on the last page the following:

ANDREW TAYLOR

His son, Gen. Nat Taylor; wife, Mary Carter, daughter of Col. John and sister of Landon.
His son, Jas. P. Taylor; wife, Mary Carter, daughter of Landon.
His son, Hon. N. G. Taylor.
His sons: Bob (R. L.); Alf (A. A.); J. P. (James P.).

John Adams was Edman Williams' brother-in-law.
This is taken from the Britannica Encyclopedia:
John Adams, second president of the U. S., was born on 30th of October, 1735, in that part of Braintree, that is now Quincy, Massachusetts; died on the 4th of July, 1826. In 1764 Adams married Miss Abigail Smith. She was born 1744; died 1818. Her grandfather was John Quincy, who was born 1689 and died 1767. He was for many years a prominent member of the Massachusetts legislature. Mrs. Adams was a woman of much ability, and her letters, written in an excellent English style, are of great value to students of the period in which she lived.
President John Quincy Adams was their eldest son.
Braintree, a township of Norfolk County, Mass., on the Monatiquot river, about 10 miles south of Boston.

Biography of the Williams Family

By N. E. Hyder

Edman Williams, a native of Wales, emigrated to America, settling in Massachusetts, and married Lucretia Adams, sister of John Adams, second president of the U. S.; born Oct. 19, 1735; died July 4, 1826.

Between the years 1775 and 1779 Edman Williams moved to the "Great West," making his home on Buffalo Creek (now Carter County, Tenn), Washington County, N. C. He was a man of splendid education, as most all the wills, and deeds of his neighbors are in his handwriting, which is good and legal expressions and forms closely observed. He was in the battle of Kings Mountain, and he was one of the first magistrates in Washington County, N. C., and was, it is thought, Chairman of the County Court, as he was addressed as Judge Williams. He disposed of 1,918 acres of the best farming land on Buffalo Creek, and elsewhere, also nine negroes in his will, which bears date Sept. 16, 1795, and was probated Nov. 1795. He was buried at the old homestead, about one mile above Milligan. The following were the children of Edman and Lucretia Adams Williams:

George D., married Rebecca Taylor.

Archibald, born 1777, married 1797, Rhoda Taylor, born 1773, sister of General Nathaniel Taylor.

Samuel H., married Ruth Davidson, of Buncom Co., N. C.

Joshua, married Sara Davidson, sister of Ruth, and daughter of William Davidson.

John Lindsey, married Elizabeth Price.

Triphenia, married Jesse Whitson first, and then Jonathan Smalling.

Sara Adams, married John Hoss.

Lavinia, married Jonathan Tipton, Jr.

Archibald, second son of Edman and Lucretia Adams Williams, married Rhoda Taylor, to whom the following children were born:

Samuel (single), member of the Legislature several times; died 1877.

Edman, married Anna Ellis. A Justice of the Peace and many years Chairman of the County Court.

George Duffield, married Lucinda Haun.

Joshua, married Elizabeth Lane.

Nathaniel T. (single), a private in the Mexican war.

Ann, first married a Drake, and second a Callison.

Lucretia, married Joseph Young.

Sarafina, married Joseph Rhea.

Pinkney P., married Rosana Haun, was a son of John Lindsey, who married Elizabeth Price.

The Williams family has been aggressive in politics. George D. was County Court Clerk from 1796 to 1806. George T., the same office from 1878 to 1886. George C., Circuit Court Clerk from 1836 to 1840. Archibald, Sr., was sheriff from 1805 to 1813. Thomas Joshua, trustee 4 years, died September, 1910.

John Adams, second president of the U. S., born in Braintree, Mass., Oct. 19, 1735, a great-grandson of Henry Adams, who, emigrating from Great Britain in 1640, founded in America a family made famous by many illustrious names. The father of John Adams was a Puritan deacon. So we are back to the Mayflower.

A copy of the "Lineage Form" used by Velma Carson Williams, when joining the National Society of the Daughters of the American Revolution, Washington, D. C.

Descendant of Andrew Taylor

Lineage

I, Velma Carson Williams, being of the age of eighteen years, and upwards, hereby apply for membership in the following line from Andrew Taylor, who was born in Augusta Co., Va. (on the —— day of ——) before 1735, and died in Washington Co., N. C., in 1782.

I was born in Telford, Washington Co., Tenn.

I am the daughter of John T. E. Williams, born April 18, 1873, died ———, and his wife, Cainie Carson Williams, born June 2, 1872, died ———; married Dec. 25, 1894.

2. The said John T. E. Williams was the son of Archibald Williams, born Nov. 24, 1834, died Jan. 24, 1895, and his wife, Sarah Hyder, born May 19, 1842, died Mar. 9, 1920; married August 19, 1858.

3. The said Archibald Williams was the son of Joshua Williams, born 1808, died Oct., 1895, and his wife, Elizabeth Bean Lane, born Jan. 26, 1810, died Oct., 1885; married 1830.

4. The said Joshua Williams was the son of Archibald Williams, born 1777, died ———, and his wife, Rhoda Taylor, born 1773, died ———; married 1797.

5. The said Rhoda Taylor was the daughter of Andrew Taylor, born before 1735, died 1782, and his wife, Anna Wilson, born ———, died ———; married ——.

And he, the said Andrew Taylor, is the ancestor who assisted in establishing American Independence, while acting in the capacity of Patriot.

(See National number 183392).

Give below reference, by volume and page, to the documentary or other authorities upon which you found your record. (180740).

Family Record copied from old Bible belonging to Rev. Green Hill. Sent by Mrs. Waters and Mrs. Woodcock.

This Bible was published in London, England, in 1756.

Green Hill, Sr., born Nov. 20, 1714.
Grace Bennett, born April 26, 1721.
They were married in March, 1739.
Children born to them:
Henry, born Feb. 12, 1740.
Green, born Nov. 14, 1741.
Hannah, born Aug. 24, 1745.
Bennett, born Dec. 1, 1747.
William, born Feb. 20, 1750.
Mary, born May 11, 1754.
Sarah, born April 27, 1756.
Temperence, born Feb. 10, 1761.
Elizabeth, born July 25, 1763.

Green Hill, born Nov. 14, 1741.
Nancy Thomas, born July 26, 1745.
They were married Oct. 13, 1763.
Children born to them:
Jordan, born Oct. 17, 1765.
Hannah, married Thomas Stokes, of North Carolina; born May 28, 1766; died July 13, 1800; left large family.
Nancy, married Thomas Knibb Wynn, of North Carolina; born Jan. 25, 1768; died 1791; left children.
Martha, married Jeremiah Brown, of North Carolina, Jan. 22, 1790; born Oct. 2, 1769. Removed to Wilson County, Tenn. She departed this life Jan., 1863, at a ripe old age, leaving a long line of descendants.
Richard, born Sept. 14, 1771; died Jan. 26, 1772.
Nancy Thomas Hill, wife of Rev. Green Hill, died Thursday, Jan. 16, 1772.

Rev. Green Hill, married June 3, 1773, to Mary Seawell, daughter of Benjamin Seawell, born Aug. 5, 1751.
Their children:
Green Hill III, born May 5, 1774; married Mary Long; moved to Alabama; died at advanced age, leaving large family.
Lucy, born July 20, 1776; married Joshua Cannon, Williamson County, Tenn.

John, born Nov. 23, 1778.
Thomas, born Sept. 15, 1781; left children.
Sally Hicks, born Nov. 16, 1783; died July 27, 1810; never married.
Mary Seawell, born Oct. 1, 1786; died Sept. 29, 1859; married Abrum Maury de Graffenried.
William, born Jan. 24, 1792; married Nancy Peebles.
Their son, Richard Hill, Methodist Preacher, Memphis Conference.
Joshua Cannon Hill, born Aug. 10, 1795; died 1827; married Lamiza Lanier.
Their son, Col. William Hill, Williamson County, gave this old Bible to Vanderbilt University, but it was afterward given to Mrs. Ferguson, his niece, and is now in possession of Mr. Hill Ferguson of Birmingham.

Bible Records of the Dodson, Wren, Brown, Chappell and Davidson Connections, With Other Intermarriages With These Families

Copied by Ralph H. Dodson, Trevecca College, Nashville, Tennessee.

Martha Chappell, born April 30, 1793, married James Brown of Obion County, Tennessee. This is taken from the book by Philip E. Chappell, "Genealogies, Chappell, Dickie, and Kindred Families," Revised Edition 1900, on page 262. This book will take the line back to about 1635 in America. The DeGraffenreids mentioned in this book can be traced back to 1191 A. D., and the records are published in the "Book of the DeGraffenreids" and a copy is in the State Library in Nashville, Tennessee.

The above is given in order that a connection can be made by anyone wishing to trace these records farther back than this copy.

The records that I give first are taken from an old Bible, now in my possession, and was bought by James Brown (above) from S. R. Roberts on the 25th day of August, 1818. The records are as follows:

James S. Brown was married the 23rd day of August, 1810, to his wife, Martha, the daughter of John Chappell, Senator of Virginia, Halifax County, Virginia.
To this union were born the following children:
Nancy D. Brown, born Sept. 11, 1811.
William A. Brown, born Jan. 8, 1813.
James C. Brown, born Aug. 25, 1815.
Mary B. Brown, born Oct. 24, 1817.
George Washington Brown, born May 27, 1820.
John Richard Brown, born Dec. 21, 1821.
Thomas Jackson Brown, born April 18, 1824.
Napoleon Bonepart Brown, born July 13, 1831.
Martha Ann Brown, born July 29, 1833.
Isoriah Brown (record defaced and faded).

Marriages

Nancy D. Brown, married Thedia Staley, Sept. 11, 1828.
Mary B. Brown, married —— Head, June 24, 1834.
James C. Brown, married Ruth Parnelipar Davidson, Aug. 15, 1843.
William A. Brown, married —— ——, first, Sept. 15, 1835; second, Aug. 9, 1845.

G. W. Brown, married ———, May 23, 1843.
Martha Ann Brown, married ——, Aug. 16, 1849.
Isoriah Brown, married M. V. Harris (no date given).
Thomas J. Brown, married Senora Reeves, Sept. 30, 1852.

DEATHS

Nancy D. Staley, died Mar. 5, 1848.
William A. Brown, died Jan. 8, 1849.
Mary B. Head, died Dec. 10, 1850.
Martha Chappell Brown, died July 26, 1851.
John R. Brown, died ——— ——, 1856 (faded).
Isoriah Harris, died April 12, 1861.
James S. Brown, died Oct. 15, 1863.
James C. Brown, died Jan. —, 1870.

James C. Brown and Ruth Parnelipar Davidson, who married August 15th, 1843, kept a record of their family, but the Bible was not preserved after their deaths, but the records were not thrown away as was the remainder of the Bible. However, they were badly handled and I came into possession of them just in time to prevent their complete destruction. The records that I shall give now are copied from those records, some of which were too badly defaced to be certain about some of the dates; but with the help of my cousin, Mrs. Ruth Haislip Collins, who now lives at 932 Woodland Street, Nashville, Tennessee, I was able to figure out the most of them, I think fairly accurate.

BIRTHS

Catherine F. Brown, born Sept. 24, 1844.
James A. Brown, born April 1, 1846.
Martha Elizabeth Ann Brown, born Sept. 11, 1848.
Nancy L. Brown, born Aug. —, 1850.
William Caldwell Brown, born Oct. —, 1852.
Rebeccah Housten Brown and Abner B. Brown, born Sept. 21, 1854.
George B. Brown, born June 5, 1857.
Sarah Jane (Jennie) Brown, born Feb. 21, 1860.

MARRIAGES

Catherine F. Brown, married Leroy Key, Oct. 5, 1865.
Martha E. A. Brown, married M. V. Harris, March 1, 1870.
(His first wife was her aunt, Isoriah Brown).
Rebeccah Housten Brown, married Labon Haislip, about 1850 (record too faded).
Sarah Jane (Jennie) Brown, married Wren Dodson, Dec. 24, 1879.
Abner B. Brown, married Mattie Dabney, about 1883(?).
James A. Brown, married Ella Wade, March 31, 1886.
William C. Brown, (1) married Annie Colbert; (2) married Lillian Willson.

Another old record that I found on a loose page from an old Bible, and very badly defaced, gives another line of this same family, all of whom I am sure, from what I can find out, died in Obion County, Tennessee. The following is the copy of this old record.

Andrew White and Nathan P. Davidson were born March 24, ——.
A. W. Davidson, born April 3, 1795.
Catherine R. Caldwell, born June 26, 179—.
Edmond W. Caldwell, born June 25, 1825.
Nancy W. Caldwell, born July 27, 1828.
William White Caldwell, son of E. W. and Nancy White Caldwell, was born Dec. 18, 1845.
Martha Maria Caldwell, daughter of E. W. and Nancy W. Caldwell, was born July 4, 1848.
James P. Davidson, died Aug. 22, 1824.
Rebeccah Elizabeth Davidson, died March 19, 1833.
Abner B. Davidson, died Aug. 16, 1833.
Andrew White Davidson, died June 30, 1834.
Sarah Jane Davidson, died Aug. 28, 1834.
Catherine Caldwell, born June 15, 1850.
Ruth Dinnie Caldwell, born Sept. —, 1853.
Catherine R. Caldwell, died Dec. 3, 1866.

The above record is copied as it was written in the original. There are more names on another part of the page, but I could not read them because of the faded condition.

I have all the original records in my possession at my home on Trevecca College Campus, Nashville, Tennessee, where I am teaching.

The following is copied from an old Bible, kept by my father's family in Maury County, Tennessee, and is now in the possession of my brother, Percie Brown Dodson, at Barlow, Kentucky.

Edmond Lacy Dodson, born April 20, 1810.

Nancy (Wren) Dodson, born April 20, 1815.

Selina Dodson, born Feb. 23, 1836.

Martha A. Dodson, born Oct. 8, 1839.

Sarah A. Dodson, born Oct. 9, 1841.

Joseph A. Dodson, born Sept. 25, 1845.

Elizabeth C. Dodson, born June 14, 1848.

Wren Alexander Dodson, born May 13, 1851.

(Note: These are all dead now).

Joseph A. Dodson, died Nov. 14, 1864.

Nancy (Wren) Dodson, died Aug. 13, 1877.

Edmond L. Dodson, died April 12, 1886.

Wren Alexander Dodson, died Nov. 3, 1925.

Copied from the family Bible of Mrs. E. W. Macon, Woodbury, Tenn.

William Wharton, born Feb. 14, 1799, in Fauguier County, Va.

Mariana Weedon, born March 8, 1799, in Culpeper County, Va.

From Batey Family Bible

Copied by Miss Minnie Batey, Murfreesboro, Captain Wm. Lytle Chapter.

Elizabeth Puckett, died June 11, 1859.

Mrs. Elizabeth Batey, died Aug. 14, 1862, wife of William P. Batey, who died July, 1883.

Charles L. Batey, died June 6, 1864.

Copied by Miss Minnie Batey, Murfreesboro

Capt. William Batey, born May 1, 1760.

Christopher Batey, born Sept. 9, 1792.

Mahala Batey, born Dec. 30, 1804.

Maryann E. Batey, born Nov. 14, 1822.

William P. Batey, born Dec. 8, 1824.

Martha Charlott Batey, born Nov. 22, 1828.

David C. Batey, born Dec. 22, 1832.

Martha Jane Weatherly, born Feb. 19, 1839.

Charles Lewallen Batey, born 1840.

Henry Jackson Batey, born Jan. 7, 1842.

Christopher T. Batey and Mahala C. Puckett, married Jan. 17, 1822.

James M. Weatherly and Maryann Elisabeth Batey, married Aug. 3, 1837.

John S. Wright and Martha C. Batey, married Jan. 17, 1844.

H. R. Kirby and M. P. York, married July, 1866.

W. P. Batey and Elizabeth A. Hoskins, married.

David C. Batey and Sallie W. Hunt, married Dec. 26, 1861.

Henry J. Batey and F. A. Huddleston, married June 14, 1865.

Clarence M. Batey and Myrtle Yeargan, married Sept. 30, 1892.

Charles C. Batey and Flora B. Jackson, married Jan. 22, 1896.

Wm. P. Ferguson and Belle Bowman Batey, married Feb. 26, 1896.

William Batey, Jan. 11, 1835.

Christopher T. Batey, died April 22, 1849.

Mrs. Martha Ann Puckett, consort of B. F. Puckett, born Nov. 23, 1824, married Nov. 30, 1843; died Nov. 7, 1853.

King Family Bible Record

Bible now in the possession of Mrs. Bryant Reeves, Edmonson Pike, Nashville, Tenn.

Copied by Mrs. Acklen.

Miles King, born Oct. 8, 1729, and married his wife, Elizabeth, Jan. 5, 1752, and died Feb. 25, 1799.

Elizabeth King, born April 8, 1835.

Children of Miles and Elizabeth King:

Ann King, born Jan. 12, 1753; died Sept, 1765.

Juliet King, born Nov. 1, 1754; died same month.

William King, born March 13, 1756; died Aug. 14, 1814.

Miles King, born Oct. 25, 1758.

George King, born Jan. 26, 1760.

Edward King, born May 3, 1763.

David King, born Aug. 18, 1770.

John King, born May 2, 1702; died March 1, 1758.

Anne King, born Dec. 28, 1705; died March 2, 1750.

Children of John and Anne King:

John King, born Nov. 3, 1726.

Mary King, born Oct. 9, 1728; died Oct. 20, 1728.

M—— King, born Oct. 7, 1729; died April 17, 1772.

Anne King, born April 4, 1730; died Dec. 5, 1771.

Susanna King, born May 5, 173—; died Jan. 3, 1745.

Michael King, born Nov. 26, 1738.

David King, born Feb. 20, 1740.

Charles King, born July 31, 1744.

George and Susann King, married Dec. 31, 1780.

Elizabeth King, our daughter, born Oct. 23, 1782.

Thomas L. King, our son, born July 11, 1784.
Catharine King, born July 8, 1799.
Alpheus King, son of Thomas and Catharine, born Aug. 24, 1822.
Elizabeth A. King, born Aug. 10, 1824.
Geo. King, born June 25, 1826.
Joel King, born March 31, 1828.
Pansey King, born Nov. 1, 1838.
Mecleius Franklin King, born April 7, 1841.
Sam C. DeWitt King, born Feb. 7, 1843.
Alphius King, son of Thos. and Catharine King, died Oct. 20, 1854.
Martha K. King, daughter of Thos. and Catherine King, died Oct. 3, 1854.
Pansey King, died Jan. 3, 1855.
Mearry, her maid, died Jan. 8, 1855.
Thomas L. King, son of George King and Susan King, died Feb. 13, 1862; lived to be 77 years of age; born July 11, 1754.
DeWitt King, the youngest child of Thomas and Catharine King, died March 27, 1864. He was 21 years old the 7th of Feb.

———

Thomas L. King, born July 11, 1784.
Katharine King, wife of Thos. L. King, born July 8, 1800.
Children of Thomas L. King:
Alphius King, born Aug. 24, 1822; died Oct. 20, 1854.
Betsey Ann King, born Aug. 10, 1824.
George King, born June 5, 1826.
Joel P. King, born March 31, 1828.
Martha K. King, born March 10, 1830; died Oct. 3, 1854.
Thomas L. King, Jr., born Feb. 20, 1832.
Harry O. King, born Dec. 22, 1833; died Oct. 23, 1854.
Philo King, born Aug. 9, 1836; died March 28, 1855.
Penny King, born Nov. 1, 1838; died Jan. 3, 1855.
Medicus F. King, born April 7, 1841.
DeWitt King, born Feb. 7, 1843.

Mrs. Albert Ewing III Records

Ward Bible Records

Information from the Ward Bible in the possession of William Eldred Ward, Jr., Harding Road, Nashville, Tenn. The Bible was presented to Rev. William Eldred Ward, founder of Ward's Seminary, by the first graduating class of the school.

Births

John Rolfe Hudson, born Dec. 13, 1800.

Ariminta Claiborne Hudson, born Feb. 20, 1817.

William Eldred Ward, born Dec. 21, 1829.

Eliza Hudson Ward, born Feb. 10, 1838.

Sallie Clark Ward Conley, born Dec. 21, 1859.

Minnie Claiborne Ward, born Dec. 21, 1859.

Mary Florence Ward, born Aug. 25, 1861.

Eunice Robertson Ward, born April 28, 1864.

Mary Robertson Ward, born April 28, 1864.

Willie Ward (girl), born April 28, 1864.

Elise Ward, born Nov. 30, 1869.

William Eldred Ward, Jr., born Nov. 4, 1873.

Rebecca Williams Ward, born Nov. 4, 1873.

Sara Ward Conley, born July 28, 1883.

Elise Ward Chaffe, born Nov. 24, 1881.

John Robert Chaffe, born Aug. 25, 1883.
William Walter Holt, born Oct. 28, 1891.
William Eldred Ward III, born Sept. 4, 1900.
Ward DeWitt, born Aug. 20, 1900.
Ward Napier Holt, born ———.
Ward Chaffe, born Dec. 20, ——.
John Hibbett DeWitt, Jr., born Feb. 20, 1906.
James Eatherly Ward, born April 30, 1906.
Ward DeWitt, Jr., born Oct. 15, 1925.
William Eldred Ward IV, born April 6, 1928.
Jean Lynn Ward, born June 13, 1929.

MARRIAGES

William Eldred Ward to Eliza A. Hudson, Feb. 24, 1859.
Mary Florence Ward to Robert Hodges Chaffe, Nov. 30, 1880.
Sally Clark Ward to John Withrin Conley, April 27, 1882.
Eunice Robertson Ward to William Day Holt.
William Eldred Ward, Jr., to Anne Martin Burney, Nov. 14, 1899.
Rebecca Williams Ward to John Hibbett DeWitt, Nov. 14, 1899.
John Robert Chaffe to Helen Miller Kirksey, May, 1925.
William Walter Holt to Minnie Tight Holt.
Ward DeWitt to Elizabeth Graves Smith, Oct. 15, 1924.
William Eldred Ward III to Rosa Lee Lynn, April 2, 1925.
John Hibbett DeWitt, Jr., to Elise Martin, April 29, 1929.

DEATHS

Minnie Claiborne Ward, died Aug. 10, 1860.
Mary Robertson Ward, died Jan. 4, 1865.
Willie Ward, died June 10, 1865.
Elise Ward, died Jan. 16, 1865.
John W. Conley, died May 18, 1883.
Sara Ward Conley, Jr., died Jan., 1886.
William Eldred Ward, Sr., died July 20, 1887.
John Rolfe Hudson, died Dec. 26, 1887.
Florence Ward Chaffe, died Sept. 8, 1892.
Mary Craig Holt, infant, died March 16, 1897.
Eunice Ward Holt, died March 17, 1897.
Ward Napier Holt, died April, 1899.
Eliza H. Ward, died March 22, 1900.
Elise Ward Chaffe, died June 30, 1900.
Ariminta C. Hudson, died March 5, 1904.

WAR OF 1812-1815.

J. W. Napier, Quartermaster, enlisted Jan. 28, 1814, under Col. R. C. Napier, 1st Regiment, West Tennessee Infantry.
Richard Napier, Lieut.-Col., enlisted May 13, 1813, 6th Brigade, Infantry.
R. C. Napier, Colonel, enlisted Jan. 28, 1814, 1st Regiment, West Tennessee Infantry.
E. W. Napier, Surgeon, enlisted Jan. 28, 1814, under Col. R. C. Napier, 1st Regiment, West Tennessee Infantry.

STUBBLEFIELD BIBLE RECORDS

Information from Stubblefield Bible, published in Philadelphia, 1803. It is now in the possession of Mrs. Duncan Eve, Jr., 3823 Whitland Ave., Nashville, Tenn.

Robert L. Stubblefield and Sarah Easley, married together on Thursday, July 15, 1772.
Thomas Stubblefield and Patsey Bond, married June 12, 1806.
Geo. Stubblefield and Mary Jeffries, married Jan. 16, 1799.

William Stubblefield and Willmuth Bond, married March 5, 1800.

H. B. Stubblefield and Mary S. Cain, married June 22, 1843.

G. J. Stubblefield and M. A. Rankin, married Nov. 15, 1849.

Births

Robert Loxley Stubblefield, born June 8, 1751.
Sarah, his wife, born Dec. 1, 1752.
The ages of Robert L. Stubblefield and Sarah Stubblefield's children:
William, their son, born June 4, 1773.
Nancy, their daughter, born May 27, 1775.
Thomas, their son, born Dec. 18, 1776.
Mary, their daughter, born June 29, 1778.
George, their son, born July 6, 1780.
Keziah, their son, born July 30, 1782.
Anna, their daughter, born Jan. 7, 1785.
Sarah, their daughter, born Dec. 18, 1787.
Stephen, their son, born Jan. 6, 1789.
Susannah, their daughter, born Jan. 25, 1792.
Betsey, their daughter, born June 28, 1793.
Winney, their daughter, born Nov. 11, 1797.
Patsey Stubblefield, wife of Thomas Stubblefield, born Feb. 13, 1791.
Nathaniel Carrol, son of John and Betsey Carrol, born Jan. 1, 1812.
Robert, their son, born Sept. 30, 1814.
Nancy Stubblefield, daughter of Thomas Stubblefield and Patsey, his wife, born Jan. 27, 1808.
Polly, their second daughter, born April 20, 1810.
Sally, their third daughter, born Jan. 4, 1812.
Willy, their fourth daughter, born May 29, 1814.
Marian Jasper Stubblefield, born Aug. 28, 1826.
William Lafayette Stubblefield, born Feb. 27, 1832.
John Bruce Stubblefield, born Dec. 22, 1834.
Josephine Jeffries Stubblefield, born Feb. 27, 1832.
George Stubblefield, born July 6, 1780.
Mary, his wife, born Jan. 17, 1783.

Their Children

Robert Loxley Stubblefield, son of George Stubblefield and Mary, his wife, born May 19, 1801.
Thomas Stubblefield, born April 5, 1803.
William Stubblefield, born April 10, 1805.
Martha Stubblefield, born April 27, 1808.
Sarah Stubblefield, born July 28, 1810.
John Stubblefield, born April 21, 1812.
Hiram Stubblefield, born Sept. 25, 1814.
George Jeffries Stubblefield, born Dec. 3, 1817.
James C. Stubblefield, born Feb. 10, 1819.

Deaths

James C. Stubblefield, son of George and Mary Stubblefield, died April 8, 1847, in Alabama.
Mary, wife of George Stubblefield, died April 18, 1857, in Tennessee; 74 years old.
R. L. Stubblefield, son of George and Mary Stubblefield, died Feb. 3, 1858, in Texas.
H. B. Stubblefield, son of George and Mary Stubblefield, died Jan. 17, 1861, in Tennessee; 47 years old.
George Stubblefield, died Oct. 15, 1866, in Tennessee; 86 years old.

Bell Bible Records

Information in the Bell family Bible in the possession of Mrs. W. H. Knox, Jr., Iroquois Ave., Nashville, Tenn.
Sent by Mrs. Ewing.

Samuel Bell, married Margaret Edmiston, June 16, 1791.
Samuel Bell, born Feb. 11, 1766.
Margaret Bell, wife of Samuel Bell, born Jan. 23, 1773; died July 6, 1830.

Sarah, daughter, born July 3, 1792.
Robert, son, born April 11, 1794.
John, son, born Feb. 18, 1796.
Catherine, daughter, born Feb. 21, 1798.
Thomas, son, born Sept. 26, 1802.
Martha E. Bell, daughter, born Jan. 15, 1805.
Sarah A. Crockett, born Sept. 2, 1825.
Margaret Jane Crockett, born Oct. 17, 1829.
Martha Washington Crockett, born March 19, 1833.
Charles Crockett, born March 12, 1835.
James B. Crockett, born March 29, 1838.
Charley Crockett, died Aug. 19, 1858.
Mary E. Crockett, born June 26, 1849.
Martha W. Crockett and James P. Moore, married Oct. 23, 1860, by Rev. Dr. Langdon.
Willie A. Moore, oldest son of Jas. P. Moore and Mattie Moore, born June 1, 1862.
Augusta Bell Crockett, born Dec. 24, 1872, daughter of J. B. Crockett and Pauline Cocke.
Margaret Bell, died July 6, 1830.
Margaret Jane Crockett, born Oct. 17, 1828; died Dec. 8, 1847, about 1 o'clock.

Autobiographical Sketch of John Cockrill

The following is copied from John Cockrill's Bible, being in his own handwriting.

Sent by Mrs. Ewing.

Nashville, Tenn., July 27, 1833.—This is a sketch of part of my life from my 17th year, 1774, the day after a tremendously big frost, about the 3rd or 4th of May. As my father and step-father were both dead and left a very poor family, so of course there was nothing left for me, so my mother bound me to a blacksmith and I stayed with him well on five years, and learned that trade, and also to make buns, but I was drafted in the time, I believe twice. I went one time to Watauga as the Indians had attacked their fort. I helped to carry in one of the wounded on Holsten as we went along on the way to Wautauga. Then I went on another trip. I think they said we were to join Gen. McIntosh's army against the Indians. We traveled in snow knee deep and were out a good part of the winter and had run out of provisions. There were six days I had not as much nourishment as would make one good meal, and three days without one mouthful. The news came from the General, "Discharge the ——, and don't give them a mouthful to eat," but the officers said take as much flour as will do you. We did so but the weather was so bad we could not get along fast, but I got home and served out my time, and one other year, and got fixed, and in the fall of 1779 I came to this country from Virginia, where I learned the trade. The first winter we had peace, but at corn-planting time the Indians began. They were bad, and every two or three weeks they would be doing some mischief, either killing or wounding or stealing horses. Then in the spring of '81 there came 333 against us. There were only 40 men in the fort at that time; 6 or 7 had gone to hunt their town to get some horses, for they had got most of ours. These 40 were all that lived on this side of the Cumberland. Of this 40, 20 of us went out to meet them, not knowing their number. They were lying behind the bank of the branch just from the stone bridge up to where it turns toward the tan-yard, then in a circle so as to surround, and did come very near it. They came in about three or four steps of me. I dodged to the river bank. Three pursued me and I had gained two or three steps and turned around where there was three in a row. I fired and killed the foremost one, if no more, and they were shooting and knocking about among our men and killed six before they went off. There was one of our men in their nation. He gave us the account. Then there were some contrary folks who would not join to make corn, and we were in a bad way, for we got out of bread again. At first it was nine or ten months we had none, and in the fall of '81 was hard times, for the Indians were still very bad and our bread ran out. There was for a time they were so bad we could scarcely go out but what they would shoot at us. As it happened that I married a woman in the year 1780, that had three children. It had been about three days that we had very little to eat. I had gathered up my tools and I went in from my shop, such as it was. The children were following their mother about the cabin and saying, "Mammy, I'm hungry." I said, "I can't stand that; I must have meat or die," so I took my gun and started. My wife and several others said, "You had better come back; you will never see the fort again." I said, "The children are starving; I must go. I can see as good as the Indians, and I will not follow any path, so they cannot waylay me." So I went on and got something like three or four miles, shot one bear down, but it got up and got away, so I could not find it. Then I was hunting along and came across another and killed that and cut off his skin with most of the meat to it, wrapped it up in the skin and took it on my back and carried it home and cut it from the skin and weighed it. I had brought in one hundred pounds on my back, and they came around us as my wife was helping to cut it. They said, "Do give me a little." Some would say, "I have had nothing for three or four days." Others would say, "My children are starving." My wife said, "What shall we do?" I said, "Divide it out; only save us some for tomorrow. I think the Indians are gone, for I saw no sign of them and I will go again tomorrow." So we went for a while and got provisions again. I have had several ups and downs with the Indians. They shot at me five different times. One time up the river on Goose creek there were seven of them and seven of us. None got hurt, only I fell down and sprained my ankle chasing them. We killed three of them and took twenty horses from them they had got from three companies of our hunters that they had defeated. The night and morning that we met them in the defeats they killed and wounded two or three of our men. Another time here at Nashville, where I think there were forty or fifty guns fired at me and never so much as touched my clothes, as I know of. Another time was here by the penitentiary they shot my mare through the neck. Then another time I was out in the day on a scout and some of our men stopped out to try to waylay the Indians as we had found signs of them, and they sent me home to let the folks know that they were trying to waylay them. But the Indians had got by the place and as I went home in the night four or five shot at me not ten or twelve steps. Never struck me nor my horse. Another time two men and I went out to see if we could see any sign of them, as they had been very much about for several weeks, and out by that lick where Chas. Bosley lives, about ten or twelve shot at me. As I was about seventy or eighty yards nearer to them than the other men, they shot me through the arm and side, but touched no bones, shot my mare through the brains as she was wheeling and threw her on my leg and held me till they got in about six steps of me. I got loose and rose up with my gun and killed the nearest one to me, and that surprised the others so I got off and got home, etc.

This manuscript is not signed, but is in John Cockrill's handwriting.

On the back of the paper is this: "Received nine dollars of Alex Bausley for a pided cow, Oct. 4, 1833. John Cockrill."

John Cockrill evidently meant to add more to the above manuscript.

The sketch of John Cockrill's interesting life in the early days of Fort Nashborough was copied and sent, with the explanatory note, to relatives in Tennessee, by the owner of the manuscript, Mr. Mark Cockrill, of Great Falls, Montana.

Cockrill Bible Records

The following information came from Mr. Mark Cockrill, of Great Falls, Montana, who owns the Cockrill Bible at the present time.

John Cockrell, born Dec. 19, 1757.
Ann Cockrell, born Feb. 10, 1757.
John Cockrell, Jr., born July 8, 1781.
Nancy Cockrill, born Feb. 1, 1783, Pulliam.
Sterling R. Cockrill, born March 7, 1785.
James Cockrill, born Jan. 28, 1787.
Mark R. Cockrill, born Dec. 2, 1788.
Susannah Cockrill, born Sept. 2, 1790, Bunting.
Sarah Cockrill, born May 15, 1794, Beasley.
Patsey Cockrill, born Nov. 5, 1800; married three times.
Ann Cockrill, died Oct. 13, 1821.
John Cockrill, died April 11, 1837; recorded by Mark R. C.
Susan C. Cockrill, died Aug. 3, 1871; recorded by Mark S.

Mark R. Cockrill, died June 26, 1872; recorded by Mark S.

This is an old, much worn, leatherback Bible, about 10x10x3 inches. The fly leaves are gone and there is nothing to show when it was printed. There is a little slip pasted inside of the cover which reads, "H. Elliot, bookbinder, Nashville, Tenn.," so I suppose that H. Elliot either re-bound it or sold it to John Cockrill. It contains no provision for recording births, deaths and marriages. This list that I am sending is written on the back of a picture or woodcut of which it contains several.

Ewing Bible Records

The Bible containing the following records is in the possession of Miss Mary Ewing, Gillespie Ave., Nashville, Tenn.

Register of Births

Albert Gallatin Ewing, born Oct. 30, 1836.
Henrietta Cockrill Ewing, born Dec. 9, 1840.
Rowena Thompson Ewing, born Nov. 11, 1866.
Albert G. Ewing, Jr., born Jan. 27, 1868.
Susan Milbrey Ewing, born May 31, 1869.
Mark Cockrill Ewing, born Dec. 29, 1870.
Orville Ewing, Jr., born May 5, 1872.
Mary Ewing, born Sept. 15, 1874.
Edgar Ewing, born March 7, 1875.
Milbrey Williams Ewing, born July 6, 1876.
Henrietta Cockrill Ewing, born March 16, 1878.
Robertson Collingsworth Ewing, born April 1, 1880.
Margaret Julia Ewing, born Aug. 28, 1884.

Register of Marriages

A. G. Ewing, to Henrietta Cockrill, Nov. 8, 1865, by R. B. C. Howell.
Risley P. Lawrence, to Rowena Thompson Ewing, Oct. 7, 1884.

Albert Gallatin Ewing, Jr., to Leila Berry, Oct. 27, 1897.
Mark C. Ewing, to Mabel Roberts, Nov. 9, 1898.
Orville Ewing, to Mary Berry, Dec. 14, 1898.
Milbrey Williams Ewing, to James H. Gordon, Sept. 30, 1902.
Henrietta Cockrill Ewing, to Alex. C. Harsh, Oct. 11, 1905.
Margaret Julia Ewing, to W. Dayton Phillips, Aug. 23, 1905.

REGISTER OF DEATHS

Susan Milbrey Ewing, March 13, 1870.
Edgar Ewing, Aug. 24, 1875.
Robertson Collingsworth Ewing, April 13, 1880.
Mrs. Henrietta Cockrill Ewing, Aug. 31, 1910.
Mr. Albert Gallatin Ewing, May 21, 1924.
James H. Gordon, March 9, 1931.

BERRY BIBLE RECORDS

Information copied from the Berry family Bible and sent to me (Mrs. Albert Ewing III), by Mrs. Varina Berry Pruden, of Rome, Ga., daughter of John Marshall Berry and Mary Margaret Rawlins.

BIRTHS

James Enfield Berry, April 5, 1790, in Washington County, Va.
Sarah C. McChesney Berry, July 31, 1819.
Thomas Berry III., Sept. 21, 1820.
Margaret McChesney Berry, Aug. 12, 1824.
James Enfield Berry, Dec. 9, 1826 (see records, his Bible).
Elizabeth Hamilton Berry, Aug. 13.
William Hamilton Berry, March 7, 1832.
John Marshall Berry, Aug. 27, 1835 or 37 (?).
Joseph Walker Berry, Oct. 17, 1844.
Augustus Berry, Aug. 4, 1846.

MARRIAGES

James Enfield Berry, Sr., to Rebecca Crawford McChesney, Aug. 13, 1818.
Sarah C. McChesney Berry, to William Clark, Feb. 27, 1840.
James Enfield Berry, Sr., to Araminta McLester, Nov. 2, 1843.
James Enfield Berry, Jr., to Mary Jane Evans, Sept. 23, 1863.
Elizabeth Hamilton Berry, to Thomas Anderson.
William Hamilton Berry, to Josephine Daniel.
John Marshall Berry, to Tennessee Russell.
John Marshall Berry, to Mary Margaret Rawlins, April 5, 1866.

DEATHS

Margaret McChesney Berry, 1826.
Rebecca Crawford McChesney Berry, Aug. 24, 1841.
Augustus Berry, Sept., 1846.
Elizabeth Hamilton Berry Anderson, Nov. 22, 1852.
James Enfield Berry, 1857, in Jacksonville, Fla.
Joseph Walker Berry, June 8, 1866.
James Enfield Berry II., Oct. 2, 1879.
Mary Jane Evans Berry, Nov. 28, 1880.

Information from the Bible of James Enfield Berry I, in the possession of Mr. Charles E. Berry, Rome, Georgia, who furnished the information.

James Enfield Berry I., born Dec. 9, 1826.
Mary Jane Evans, born Dec. 23, 1844.
They were married Sept. 23, 1863.
Their children were:
Emma Rebecca Berry, born Aug. 1, 1864.

James Enfield Berry II., born Nov. 1, 1866.
Charles Evans Berry, born May 17, 1869.
Sarah Leila Berry, born Oct. 11, 1871.
Mary Elizabeth Berry, born Aug. 23, 1874.
Charles Evans Berry and Mary Ellena Abernathy (born Jan. 10, 1871), married at the Church of the Good Shepherd in Cave Spring, Ga., Oct. 22, 1891. Their children were:
James Enfield Berry III., born June 22, 1892.
Robert Evans Berry, born Aug. 19, 1895.
Amelia Caroline Berry, born June 7, 1898.
James Enfield Berry III., married Margaret Smith in Rome, Ga., on June 3, 1928.
A son, James Enfield Berry IV., born June 23, 1930.
Robert Evans Berry, married Dorothy Todd in Gary, Ind., Aug. 12, 1930.
Amelia Caroline Berry, married Albert R. Rush, M.D., Feb. 20, 1929; lives at Hawkinsville, Ga.

DEATHS

James Enfield Berry II., July 28, 1879.
James Enfield Berry I., Oct. 2, 1879.
Mary Jane Evans Berry, Nov. 28, 1880.
Emma Rebecca Berry, Dec. 7, 1880.

HILL BIBLE RECORDS

Family record copied from an old Bible belonging to Rev. Green Hill. This Bible was published in London, England, 1756. Information from Mrs. George Waters, 2613 Belmont Blvd., Nashville, Tenn. Sent by Mrs. Ewing.

Green Hill, born Nov. 20, 1714.
Grace Bennett, born April 26, 1721.
They were married in March, 1739.
Children born to them:
Henry, born Feb. 12, 1740.
Green Hill, Jr., born Nov. 14, 1741.
Hannah Hill, born Aug. 24, 1745.
Bennett Hill, born Dec. 1, 1747.
William Hill, born Feb. 20, 1750.
Mary Hill, born May 11, 1754.
Sarah Hill, born April 27, 1756.
Temperance Hill, born Feb. 10, 1761.
Elizabeth Hill, born July 25, 1763.
Green Hill, Jr., married Nancy Thomas (born July 26, 1745), Oct 13, 1763. Their children:
Jordan Hill, born Oct. 17, 1765.
Hannah Hill, born May 28, 1766; married Thomas Stokes; died July 13, 1800; left large family.
Martha Hill, married Jerre Brown; moved from North Carolina to Lebanon, Wilson County, Tenn.
Green Hill, Sr., lived in Brunswick County, Va. His will proved in Northampton County, N. C. (Added as note in Bible.)

The following information was taken from the Hill Bible, in the possession of Mr. Claude Ernest Hill, 1904 Pearl St., Austin, Texas. Mr. Hill is a great-great-grandson of the Revolutionary soldier, Daniel Hill, who originally owned the Bible.

Dan Hill, born Oct., 1756; married 1779; died May 28, 1826.
Martha Hickman, born Oct. 16, 1758; died April 20, 1845.
Children of the above:
Sarah Hill, born July 28, 1780; married Nathan Ewing.
Mary Hill, born Sept. 4, 1782; married Henry Bateman.

Nancy Hill, born April 7, 1785; married John Creecy; died Jan. 27, 1829.

Wm. Hickman Hill, born May 1,

1788; married Sally Brown, Sept. 20, 1810; died Aug. 12, 1867.
Green Hill, born Oct. 15, 1790; unmarried; died Feb. 7, 1825.
Mildred Hill, born July 8, 1793; married Burrus.
Elizabeth Hill, married March 14, 1796; married Henry Clayton Ewin; died March, 1855.
Lucinda Hill, born March 14, 1796; married Wm. Garner; died Feb. 4, 1885.
Susanna Smithers Hill, born Aug. 20, 1800; died Dec. 12, 1807.

Barnhill Bible Records

The following records have been copied at various times by members of the family, prior to the destruction by fire, of the original Barnhill family Bible, and have been placed in more recent Bibles where they may be found at the present time. Mrs. Rainey I. Hall, of Corinth, Miss., possesses one of these Bibles.

Register of Births

William Barnhill, Sr., 1735.
Isabella Barr, 1759.

Children

William Barnhill, Jr., born 1774.
Robert Barnhill.
Samuel Barnhill.
John Barnhill.
Hannah Barnhill.
Mary Barnhill.
Isabella Barnhill.
Children of William Barnhill, Jr.:
Daniel Barnhill.
William Hodge Barnhill.
John Newton Barnhill, born Oct. 21, 1811.
Pleasant A. Barnhill, born 1816.
Ann Barnhill.
Cynthia Barnhill.
Emily Barnhill.
Elizabeth Barnhill.
Isabella Barnhill.
Children of John Newton Barnhill:
Nancy Barnhill, born March 5, 1831.
Thomas LeRoy Barnhill, born Sept. 25, 1834.
Virgil DeKalb Barnhill, born Aug. 7, 1837.
William Newton Barnhill, born May 13, 1840.
Elizabeth Barnhill, born May 5, 1846.
John Taylor Barnhill, born Nov. 8, 1848.
Robert Pleasant Barnhill, Oct. 8, 1851.
Children of Thomas LeRoy Barnhill:
Rebecca Jane Barnhill, born Aug. 2, 1862.
Mary Elizabeth Barnhill, born March 22, 1864.
Dr. Robert Young Barnhill, born July 14, 1866.
Children of Mary Elizabeth Barnhill Waits:
Mary Ernestine Waits, born Jan. 29, 1899.
Katherine Waits, born Feb. 2, 1902.

Register of Marriages

William Barnhill, Sr., to Isabella Barr, 1773.
William Barnhill, Jr., to Cynthia Hodge, 1796.
Hannah Barnhill, to James Glass.
Mary Barnhill, to John McGinnis.
John Newton Barnhill, to Elizabeth Chambers, Jan. 25, 1830.
Nancy Barnhill, to J. N. W. Derryberry.
Thomas LeRoy Barnhill, to Mary Katherine Young, Feb. 27, 1861.
Elizabeth Barnhill, to Col. Giles Springer.
John Taylor Barnhill, to Theodocia Rosson, Feb. 22, 1880.
Rebecca Jane Barnhill, to Rainey I. Hall, Nov. 11, 1886.
Mary Elizabeth Barnhill, to Ernest F. Waits, Oct. 1, 1891.
Dr. Robert Young Barnhill, to Effie Small, Oct. 1, 1891.

REGISTER OF DEATHS

William Barnhill, Sr., May 4, 1810.
Isabella Barr Barnhill, Aug. 7, 1826.
Isabella Barnhill, Feb. 13, 1826.
William Barnhill, Jr., 1838.
Cynthia Barnhill, 1848.
Virgil DeKalb Barnhill, Oct. 8, 1862 (killed in the Battle of Perryville, Ky., in the Civil War).
John Newton Barnhill, Aug. 14, 1881.
Elizabeth Chambers Barnhill, April 22, 1893.
Dr. Robert Young Barnhill, May 31, 1899.
Mary Katherine Young Barnhill, April 13, 1900.
John Taylor Barnhill, Jan. 3, 1909.
Mary Ernestine Waits, Dec. 4, 1914.
Thomas LeRoy Barnhill, Sept. 29, 1918.
Robert Pleasant Barnhill, Feb. 7, 1919.
Rainey I. Hall, Jan., 1926.
Nancy Barnhill Derryberry, June, 1927.

MACKEY BIBLE RECORDS

Records copied on March 6, 1911, from a Mackey Bible, by Mr. A. B. Mackey of West End Drug Co., Birmingham, Ala., a son of John W. Mackey named in the Bible.

Information copied from a Mackey Bible in the possession of Hannah Mackey Yeater. The Bible was burned some years ago, but the authenticity of the copied notes was sworn to by Mrs. Lillie Mackey Camp, great-niece of Hannah Yeater, on her D. A. R. application papers. Her national number is 246322. She lives at 48 S. Twelfth Ave., Mount Vernon, N. Y.

John Mackey, born Nov. 21, 1782; died May 24, 1855.
Mary Mackey, born Jan. 3, 1787; died Nov. 20, 1850.
Alexander J. Mackey, born Dec. 31, 1806.
George H. Mackey, born Aug. 10, 1809.
Henry H. Mackey, born Jan. 21, 1813.
Margaret S. Mackey, born Jan. 11, 1815.
John W. Mackey, born Sept. 21, 1816, in Pickins District, S. C.
Nancy Mackey, born July 27, 1818.
Mary A. Mackey, born Oct. 18, 1820.
Galesberry Mackey, born June 12, 1822.
Hulda H. Mackey, born June 6, 1826.

John Mackey I. was born in Ireland, where he married Ann Alexander in 1751 and came directly to America, accompanied by his brothers, William and Thomas. They landed in North Carolina, where John and his wife remained. William went to Pennsylvania. It is not known what became of Thomas. He probably died in North Carolina.

John and Ann Mackey were the parents of ten children—Mary, James, Elizabeth, Nancy, Anne, Jane, William, Alexander, Thomas, John II.

The Husband and father died in North Carolina, after which the mother and children moved to Tennessee.

YOUNG BIBLE RECORDS

The following records in Bible owned by the Rev. Robert Young, whose daughter, Mary Katherine, was my grandmother. The Bible is now in my possession.—Mrs. Ewing.

Nathan Young, born in 1712; married Nancy Hogan (no date; died May 22, 1818, in Scott County, Ky.
Nathaniel Young, son of Nathan, born in 1765; married Nancy Paxton, daughter of Samuel and Margaret Paxton, in 1810; died in 1830. His children were:
Robert Young.
Nathaniel Young II.
Felix Young.
Nancy Young, married John Hill.
Polly Young, married A. G. Tooms.
Margaret Young, married Robert Hudspeth.
Rev. Robert Young, son of Nathaniel, born Jan. 5, 1816; married, first, Mary Jane Wray, daughter of Rev. John Wray of Giles County, Tenn. She was born June 20, 1823, in Ireland. They were married Nov. 25, 1838, in Giles County. Their children were:
Martha Louise Young, born Dec. 30, 1839.
Mary Katherine Young, born Sept. 20, 1842.
Nancy M. Young, born Oct. 16, 1844.
Margaret Ann Young, born Dec. 24, 1846; died June 7, 1868.
John Wray Young, born Nov. 1, 1848; died July 8, 1861.
Margery G. Young, born Oct. 17, 1850; died Oct. 13, 1851.
Robert Felix Young, born Aug. 6, 1852.
Juline L. Young, born March 15, 1854.
Mary Jane Wray Young, died July 3, 1855.
Rev. Robert Young, married, second, Jemima Jane (Merrill) Burrows, May 18, 1856. Their children were:
Frances Elizabeth Young, born March 18, 1857.
Laura L. Young, born April 8, 1859.
Edmona Young, born July 2, 1860.
Jemima Jane Young, died May 17, 1894.
Rev. Robert Young, died June 14, 1894.

Sharp Bible Records

Records copied in 1931 from the Sharp Bible by Mary Pearl Sharp, Mrs. James Anthony McAmis, of Corinth, Miss., daughter of Tom Jeff Sharp, and Julia Ann Latta.

Sent by Mrs. Ewing.

Births

Henry Raiford Sharp, Oct. 21, 1809.
Mary Chambers, 1820.

Children

Sam Sharp, born Feb. 20, 1838.
John William Sharp.
Nannie Sharp.
Tom Jeff Sharp, born Aug. 5, 1845.
Mary Winfred Sharp, born Dec. 10, 1850.
Sarah E. Sharp, born Nov. 25, 1853.
Dave H. Sharp, born May 25, 1856.
Mary Pearl Sharp, daughter of Tom Jeff Sharp, born Jan. 25, 1878.

Marriages

Henry Raiford Sharp, to Mary Chambers (born 1820), 1837.
Sam Sharp, to Idstha Fulghum (born May 26, 1841), June 19, 1866.
Tom Jeff Sharp, to Julia Ann Latta (born March 23, 1844, in South Carolina), Dec. 17, 1867.
Mary Winfred Sharp, to Thomas Jordan Hurley (born Feb. 19, 1848), May 19, 1868.
Sarah E. Sharp, to E. H. Prince (born March 14, 1858), March 14, 1878.
Dave H. Sharp, to Zilpha Meeks (born Nov. 20, 1868), Feb. 3, 1886.

Deaths

Henry Raiford Sharp, April 25, 1875.
E. H. Prince, Jan. 17, 1888.
Major Sam Sharp, Dec. 15, 1906.
Mary Chambers Sharp, 1907.
Dave H. Sharp, May 13, 1812.

Mary Winfred Sharp Hurley, July 7, 1915.

Idstha Fulghum Sharp, July 15, 1921.

Tom Jeff Sharp, April 3, 1923.

Sarah E. Sharp Prince, Sept. 13, 1823.

Thomas Jordan Hurley, Sept. 27, 1923.

Julia Ann Latta Sharp, March 22, 1924.

Foster Bible Records

The pages of the Bible containing the births and marriages were destroyed by Federal soldiers during the Civil War, according to Mrs. Edward W. Foster, owner of the Bible, 2108 West End Ave., Nashville, Tenn. The following record copied by Mrs. Albert Ewing III.

Ephraim McNairy Foster, died at White's Creek Spring Aug. 10, 1827; age 3 years 4 months 18 days.

Jane M. Foster, consort of E. H. Foster, died at Mansfield, near Nashville, Tenn., Nov. 12, 1847; age 55 years 1 month 18 days.

Julia A. Hood, consort of P. M. Hood and daughter of E. H. and J. M. Foster, died at Florence, Ala., Oct. 13, 1848; age 18 years 8 months 27 days.

Jane E. Cheatham, consort of E. G. Cheatham and daughter of E. H. and J. M. Foster, died at Nashville, Tenn., June 20, 1851; age 29 years 7 months.

Ephraim H. Foster, died near Nashville Sept. 6, 1854; age 59 years 11 months 20 days.

John D. Foster, died at New Orleans, La., Nov., 1867; age 41 years 8 months.

Robert C. Foster III., died at Nashville, Tenn., Dec. 28, 1871; age 53 years 3 months 15 days.

John Dickinson, died at Nashville July 7, 1815, son of Elihu and Belinda Dickinson.

Belinda E. Dickinson, died Aug. 23, 1816, at Franklin, Tenn.

Henry Dickinson, died near Nashville Sept. 14, 1845, at 6:15 o'clock a.m.

Jane Mebane Foster, consort of Eph. H. Foster, died at Mansfield, near Nashville, Nov. 12, 1847, at 3 o'clock p.m.

Funeral Announcement Pasted in Bible—"The friends and acquaintances of E. H. Foster are invited to attend the funeral of his son, Ephraim, on tomorrow morning, 9 o'clock, Saturday, Aug. 11, 1827."

Thompson Bible

Sent by Mrs. Samuel Orr, Nashville.

Family Record—Maxwell Bible

Ann Elizabeth Thompson, born Sept. 12, 1834, daughter of John and Martha Thompson.

Robert Henry Rollings, born April 7, 1829, son of Henry Rollings.

John Thompson, Jr., born Aug. 14, 1852, son of John and Mary Thompson.

Joseph Hamilton Thompson, born Jan. 14, 1854, son of Mary and John Thompson.

Emma Thompson, daughter of Joseph H. and Ella Thompson, born Oct. 25, 1875.

Mary Thompson, born April 30, 1879, daughter of John and Mary McConnell Thompson.

Harriet Thompson, born Feb. 20, 1881, daughter of John and Mary McC. Thompson.

Con. Overton Thompson, daughter of John and Mary McC. Thompson, born Jan. 21, 1883.

John Thompson, Jr., born April 2,

NASHVILLE INN

Courtesy Tennessee State Library

Scene of many historic events. On June 6, 1819, James Monroe, President of the United States, was the honor guest of a dinner given at four o'clock at the Inn. He was the first President to visit Nashville.

1885, son of John and Mary McC. Thompson.
Overton Thompson, born Feb. 23, 1888, son of John and Mary McC. Thompson.
Ida H. Thompson, daughter of Jos. H. and Ella Vaughn Thompson, born June 24, 1884.
Jos. H. Thompson, son of John and Mary McC. Thompson, born April 3, 1890.
Joseph H. Thompson, Jr., son of Jos. H. and Ella Vaughn Thompson, born Sept. 25, 1890.
Elizabeth Thompson, daughter of John and Mary McC. Thompson, born June 16, 1892.
Jos. H. Thompson, Jr., son of Jos. H. and Willie DeMoville Thompson, born Oct. 29, 1900.
John Orr, son of Samuel H. and Mary Thompson Orr, born Oct. 28, 1903.
Gordon P. Paine, Jr., son of Gordon and Emma Thompson Paine, born March 4, 1903, in Baltimore.
Joseph H. Thompson Paine, son of Gordon and Emma Thompson Paine, born March 4, 1903, in Baltimore.
Joseph H. Thompson Paine, son of Gordon and Emma Thompson Paine, born April, 1906, in Baltimore.
Mary McConnell Overton Thompson, daughter of Margarette and John Thompson, Jr., born Nov. 6, 1907, at Glen Leven.
Henry Dickinson, Jr., son of Ida Thompson and Henry Dickinson, born in Seattle, Wash., Aug. 9, 1908.
Conn Overton Harris, daughter of Conn Thompson and Albert W. Harris, born Feb. 26, 1909.
John Thompson III., son of John Thompson, Jr., and Margarette Wade Thompson, born at Glen Leven, Sunday, July 18, 1909.
Mary Hamilton Thompson Orr, daughter of Samuel H. and Mary Thompson Orr, born on Saturday, Dec. 18, 1909.
John Overton Dickinson, son of Henry and Ida Thompson Dickinson, born in Seattle, Wash., Dec. 9, 1910.
Joseph Hamilton Thompson Dickinson, son of Henry and Ida Dickinson, born in Seattle, Wash., Oct. 1, 1913.
Anne McGavock Dickinson, daughter of Henry and Ida Dickinson, born in Seattle, Wash., Nov. 19, 1914.
Margaret Allison Thompson, daughter of Overton and Margaret Lipscomb Thompson, born in New Orleans, La., March 15, 1913.
Jacob McGavock Dickinson, son of Henry and Ida T. Dickinson, born Oct. 17, 1820, at Brightwood, Nashville, Tenn.
Overton Thompson, Jr., son of Overton and Margaret Lipscomb Thompson, born June 25, 1915, at Glen Leven.
William Gilliam Kennon, Jr., son of Elizabeth Thompson Kennon and William Gilliam Kennon, born Sunday, Aug. 6, 1916, Nashville, Tenn.
Joseph Hamilton Thompson, Jr., son of Joseph Hamilton Thompson and Florence Fonde Thompson, born June 8, 1919.
Harriet Maxwell Orr, daughter of Mary Thompson Orr and Sam. H. Orr, born Nov. 1, 1920.
Alice Broun Thompson, daughter of Florence Fonde Thompson and Joseph H. Thompson, born at Glen Leven, Jan. 21, 1922.

DEATHS

Mary E. Thompson, died April 24, 1826, daughter of Thomas Washington, deceased, and wife of John Thompson.
Elizabeth N. Thompson, died Sept. 12, 1831, daughter of Thomas Turly, deceased, and wife of John Thompson.
Nancy Thompson, wife of Thomas Thompson, died Aug. 23, 1828; age 59 years 10 months 8 days.
Robert Thompson, died Sept. 26, 1820, son of Thomas and Nancy Thompson.
Thomas Thompson, died March 24, 1837; age 77 years 5 months.
John Thompson, Jr., died Feb. 18, 1832, son of John and Elizabeth N. Thompson.
Margaret Adelaid Thompson, died April 23, 1841, daughter of John and Mary E. Thompson.

Mary E. W. Thompson, died Feb. 8, 1844, daughter of John and Mary E. Thompson.
Martha Thompson, died Oct. 6, daughter of Michael C. Dunn and wife of John Thompson.
Sarah Bronaugh Buchanan, wife of Thomas Plater and daughter of Robert and Elizabeth Buchanan, died March 18, 1867, at the Nashville Female Academy.
John Thompson, son of Thomas and Nancy Thompson, died April 18, 1876; age 82 years 10 months 18 days.
Harriet Thompson, daughter of John and Mary McConnell Thompson, died Feb. 27, 1886; age 5 years 7 days.
Jos. H. Thompson, Jr., son of Jos. H. and Ella Thompson, died June 6, 1891.
Ella Vaughn Thompson, died June 13, 1896, daughter of Michael Vaughn and wife of Jos. H. Thompson.

Mary Hamilton Thompson, wife of John Thompson, Sr., and daughter of Jos. D. Hamilton and Sarah Morgan Hamilton, died June 23, 1901.

John Thompson, son of John and Mary Hamilton Thompson, died at Glen Leven, Sept. 25, 1919.

Jos. H. Thompson, son of John and Mary Hamilton Thompson, died March 18, 1917, on a railway train near Atlanta, Ga.

Samuel H. Orr, son of Samuel and Adeline Holt Orr and husband of Mary Hamilton Thompson, died Dec. 31, 1920. Funeral services at Glen Leven, Jan. 1, 1921.

John Thompson, Jr., son of John and Mary McC. Overton Thompson, died at Glen Leven, June 24, 1921.

Mary McConnell Overton, wife of John Thompson, died at Glen Leven, Jan. 15, 1924.

Maxwell Family Bible Record

Sent by Mrs. Samuel Orr, Nashville

Jesse Maxwell, Jr., married Martha A. Claiborne, July 25, 1827.
Mary A. Maxwell, married Thomas B. Claiborne, March 5, 1828.
Elizabeth W. Maxwell, married William H. Phillips, Aug. 19, 1825.
David Maxwell, married Priscilla Rutledge of East Tennessee in 1818.
William Armstrong Maxwell, married Delilah Wilkerson in 1835.
Jesse Maxwell, Jr., married a second wife, Myra T. Rucker, widow, March 4, 1847.

Jesse Maxwell's Children

Ann A. Maxwell, born June 2, 1828.
Mary E. Maxwell, born Sept. 12, 1829.
Harriet V., born Jan. 9, 1832.
Jesse Maxwell III., born Feb. 20, 1845.
Elizabeth James, aged relative of Martha A. Maxwell, born in Brunswick County, Va., March 31, 1781; removed to Tennessee, 1807; came to love at Maxwell Hall in 1833; during the late war moved to Traveler's Rest; died Aug. 28, 188—; age 100 years.
Jesse Maxwell, Sr., born in Lancaster, Pa., 1757.
Annie Armstrong, born in Staunton, Va., July 15, 1760.
David Maxwell, son of Annie and Jesse Maxwell, Sr., born Aug. 19, 1788, in Hawkins County, East Tennessee.
William Armstrong Maxwell II., son of Annie and Jesse Maxwell, Sr., born in Hawkins County, Tenn., Oct., 1792.
Jesse Maxwell, Jr., son of Annie and Jesse Maxwell, born in Hawkins County, April 30, 1796; died Aug. 18, 1856.
Mary Ann Maxwell, daughter of Annie and Jesse Maxwell, born at Maxwell Hall, Middle Tennessee, Jan. 15, 1800.
Elizabeth Washington, daughter of Annie and Jesse Maxwell, born at Maxwell Hall, Tenn., Dec., 1804.
Mrs. Annie A. Maxwell, wife of Jesse Maxwell, Sr., died Jan. 25,

1848, at 5 o'clock a.m.; age 85 years.
Jesse Maxwell, Sr., died at his residence, Maxwell Hall, in Nov., 1821.
Mrs. Martha A. Maxwell, died March 25, 1845.
Jesse Maxwell, died Aug. 17, 1756, 7:30 o'clock Sunday evening.
Jesse Maxwell III., son of Martha A. and Jesse Maxwell, died Aug. 4, 1845, at 7 o'clock a.m.; age 5 months 15 days.
Myra T. Maxwell, second wife of Jesse Maxwell, died at Maxwell Hall Aug. 4, 1863.
Annie Armstrong Maxwell Claiborne, died Oct. 5, 1902.
Harriet Overton Claiborne, died Nov. 10, 1881.
Col. Thomas Claiborne, died April 23, 1911.
John Overton, Sr., died Dec. 12, 1898.
Harriet Virginia Overton, died Feb. 19, 1899.
Robert Lee Overton, died April 10, 1900.
John Overton Dickinson, died Nov. 24, 1910.

MARRIAGE

John Orr and Elizabeth Bayer, Feb. 27, 1932, Nashville, Tenn.

FAMILY RECORD OF ALEXANDER FREEMAN

From Bible owned by Zenobia Freeman (Mrs. T. R. Freeman), Route 6, Murfreesboro, Tenn. Sent by Miss Jetton.

Jeremiah Dial, married to Nancy McDaniel.
Alexander Freeman, married to Anna Dial.
Nancy Harriet Freeman, married George S. Bailey.
Martha Jane Freeman, married William A. Johnson.
Polly Caroline Freeman, married Alic Lingo.
Joseph Henry Freeman, married to Harriet Johnson Dec. 7, 1843.

BIRTHS

Anna Dial, born Sept. 26, 1798.
Alexander Freeman, born Oct. 18, 1789.

CHILDREN

Polly Caroline Freeman, born Oct. 23, 1816.
Nancy Harriet Freeman, born April 17, 1818.
Martha Jane Freeman, born Mar. 11, 1820.
Joseph Henry Freeman, born April 19, 1822.
Christopher A. Freeman, born May 8, 1825.
John Anderson Freeman, born Dec. 5, 1827.
Theophilus Rucker Freeman, born June 1, 1830.
Margarett Melvina Freeman, born Mar. 5, 1833.
Daniel G. Freeman, born May 27, 1835.
George S. Bailey, born June 30, 1813.

Children:
John R. Bailey, born Sept. 13, 1855.
Sarah M. J. Bailey, born Dec. 13, 1857.
Letha C. Bailey, born Jan. 29, 1860.
The twins were born dead May 27, 1862.

Children:
Nancy Ann Johnson, born Mar. 3, 1844.
Joseph C. Johnson, born April 7, 1847.
Newton M. Johnson, born May 10, 1850.
William C. Johnson, born April 7, 1855.

Children:
William Freeman.
Bettie Freeman.
Jimmie Freeman.
Analiza Freeman.
Andrew Freeman.
Fannie Freeman.
Joseph Freeman.
Hattie Freeman.

DEATHS

Jeremiah Dial, died Sept. 22, 1834.
Nancy McDaniel Dial, died Jan., 1849.

John R. Bailey, deceased Nov. 26, 1838.
Edyth Bailey, deceased Oct. 8, 1840.
George S. Bailey, died Oct. 20, 1843, aged 30 years, 3 months, 20 days.
Nancy H. Bailey, died Nov. 23, 1845.

FAMILY RECORD OF THEOPHILUS RUCKER FREEMAN, SR.

MARRIAGES

T. R. Freeman, Sr., and Margaret H. Bingham, married March 31, 1852.
T. R. Freeman, Sr., and Nancy Emily Clark, married March 15, 1866.
T. R. Freeman, Sr., and Rebecca S. Clark, married Dec. 1, 1886.

BIRTHS

T. R. Freeman, Sr., born June 1, 1830.
Margarett H. Freeman, born Feb. 26, 1837.
Four children born:
Joseph E. Freeman, born April 16, 1853.
Mary Ann Freeman, born July 14, 1854.
Daniel S. Freeman, born Aug. 1, 1856.
Robert A. Freeman, born May 9, 1859.
Seven children to second wife:
Margarett H. Freeman, born Mar. 29, 1867.
William Nix Freeman, born June 3, 1868.
Laura Edna Freeman, born Feb. 1, 1871.
John Knox Freeman, born July 10, 1872.
Theophilus Rucker Freeman, born Sept. 1, 1874.
James Harvey Freeman, born Mar. 7, 1877.
Lucy Zenobia Freeman, born May 19, 1879.

DEATHS

Margarett H. Freeman departed this life Nov. 26, 1862, age 31 years, 9 months.
Alexander Freeman departed this life Nov. 29, 1859, age 70 years, 1 month, 11 days.
Anna Dial, wife of Alexander Freeman, departed this life Mar. 4, 1882, age 83 years, 5 months, 7 days.
Nancy E., second wife of T. R. Freeman, Sr., departed this life Mar. 7, 1886.
Rebecca S., third wife of T. R. Freeman, Sr., departed this life Feb. 23, 1899, 11 o'clock, 30 min. p.m., Thursday.
T. R. Freeman, Sr., died July 8, 1916, 7 o'clock a.m., Saturday.
T. R. Freeman, Jr., died June 25, 1933, 9 p.m., Sunday.

MRS. J. W. SANDERS' BIBLE

Sent by Miss Jetton

T. T. Peay, born Feb. 29, 1812.
Daughters by first union:
Mary, born March 6, 1837.
Martha, born Sept. 30, 1839, and married to Dr. T. K. Bostick Sept. 2, 1857.
Nannie, born Oct. 5, 1842, and married T. B. Fultz May 31, 1868.
Daughters by second union:
Paulina, born March 16, 1847.
Alice, born ——— —, ———.
Emma, born Aug. 31, 1855, and married J. W. Paty Dec. 19, 1876.
Tommie, born Aug. 14, 1858, and married W. J. Smith Nov. 2, 1881.
Maggie, born Nov. 21, 1861; married J. W. Sanders May 5, 1886.
Alton, born April 20, 1863; married Alice Tarrant Nov., 1888.
Children of Maggie Peay Sanders and J. W. Sanders:
Herbert, Howell, Sara, Mildred, Aultman, Madaline, Woodie.

Bible of Mrs. C. N. Taylor, near Eagleville. Copied by Mrs. Acklen.

MARRIAGES

C. A. Taylor and M. O. Wood, Dec. 11, 1877.
C. A. Taylor and E. F. McLain, Dec. 2, 1890.

BIRTHS

C. A. Taylor, born Dec. 1, 1850.
M. O. Taylor, born April 18, 1860.
E. F. Taylor, born May 29, 1859.
Annie R. Taylor, born Dec. 18, 1879.
John Washington Taylor, born Oct. 8, 1882.

DEATHS

M. O. Taylor, died June 4, 1888.
C. N. Taylor, died March 24, 1933.

McLAIN CHART

BIRTHS

Judia A. McLain, born Nov. 30, 1802.
John F. Payne, born Nov. 21, 1861.
J. A. McLain, born Jan. 23, 1832.
A. L. McLain, born Oct. 10, 1837.
W. L. McLain, born Sept. 3, 1856.
E. F. McLain, born May 29, 1859.
L. A. McLain, born April 21, 1861.
J. A. McLain, Jr., born Dec. 2, 1866.
E. A. M. McLain, born June 23, 1873.
G. W. McLain, born Dec. 19, 1874.
M. A. McLain, born Dec. 21, 1876.
L. L. McLain, born Nov. 20, 1879.

MARRIAGES

John A. McLain to Adreanah L. Tarpley, Sept. 6, 1855.
C. N. Taylor to Emma F. McLain, Dec. 2, 1890.
G. F. Childress to Ada McLain, Jan. 12, 1898.
Eugene McLain to Cecile Webber, Dec. 5, 1900.

DEATHS

W. L. McLain, Oct. 8, 1861.
L. A. McLain, July 10, 1863.
Margaret Tarpley, June 12, 1875.
Edward Tarpley, Dec. 25, 1876.
G. W. McLain, Oct. 4, 1877.
A. L. McLain, Jan. 24, 1889.
John A. McLain, Jr., June 9, 1897.
John A. McLain, Sr., April 7, 1899.
L. L. McLain, July 14, 1900.

LENOIR FAMILY BIBLE

Bible in the possession of Mrs. Annie Lenoir Cassety, Beulah, Miss. Sent by Lutie C. Jones, Campbell Chapter, D. A. R., Nashville, Tenn.

CHILDREN OF THOMAS AND MOURNING LENOIR

(This list was found in an old "Book of Forms" at Fort Defiance, N. C., home of Gen. William Lenoir, written in his handwriting and dated 1768).
Mourning Lenoir, born May 2, 1709.
Her daughter, Ann, born June 28, 1731.
Her son, Robert, born Mar. 3, 1733.
Her daughter, Betty, born July 19, 1735.
Her daughter, Leah, born Dec. 18, 1737.
Her daughter, Mary, born Sept 30, 1739.
Her son, Thomas, born Aug. 11, 1741.
Her son, Isaac, born Oct. 15, 1743.
Her son, Lewis, born Nov. 25, 1745.
Her son, John, born Nov. 19, 1747.
Her son, William, born May 8, 1751.

BAPTISMAL RECORD

(Taken from Parish Register of old "Bristol Parish," Va.)
Thomas, son of Thomas and Mourning Lenoye, born Aug. 11, 1741; baptized Oct. 18, 1741.
(The spelling an attempt of the clerk or curate to reproduce the French pronunciation.)

Thomas Lenoir, born Aug. 11, 1741.
Martha, his wife, born Jan. 11, 1746.
They were married Sept. 20, 1761.
James Lenoir, born July 2, 1762.

Amelia, born July 10, 1765.
Martha, born Sept. 16, 1767.
Leah, born Oct. 9, 1772.
Thadrick, born April 2, 1775.
Betsy, born 1777.
Lucy, born 1779.
Thomas Lenoir was married to his second wife, March 3, 1783 (Sarah Ransone Gwyn, the widow of Richard Gwyn).
William Lenoir, born June 16, 1785.
Hope, born Jan. 30, 1786.
Amelia Gwyn, daughter of Richard and Patsy Gwyn, born Oct. 29, 1800.
William and Sarah S. Lenoir were married ——— 26, 1815.
Martha Mary Lenoir, their first child, born Sept. 11, 1816; departed this life Dec. 10, 1817.
Margaret James Lenoir, their second child, born Oct. 31, 1822.
Walter Augustus Lenoir, their third child, born Oct. 31, 1822.
Taliaferro James Lenoir, their fourth child, born Jan. 16, 1824.
Frances Courting Lenoir, their fifth child, born Sept. 8, 1837; departed this life Sept. 20, 1828.
Thomas Blanchard Lenoir, their sixth child, born the last day of Nov., 1829.
George William Lenoir, born Oct. 11, 1832.

From Lenoir family burying ground at Fort Defiance, Yadkin Valley, N. C.

Here lies all that is mortal of William Lenoir; born May 8, 1751; died May 6, 1839.
(The matter of inscription was left to his friends and associates in public life. This is their estimate of him—their tribute to his memory):
"In times that tried men's souls he was a genuine Whig. As a Lieutenant under Rutherford and Williams in 1776, and as a Captain under Cleveland at King's Mountain, he proved himself a brave soldier. Although a native of another state, yet North Carolina was proud of him as her adopted son. In her services he filled the several offices of major-general of militia, President of the Senate, first President of the Board of Trustees of the University, for sixty years justice of the peace and chairman of the Court of Common Pleas. In all these high public trusts he was found faithful. In private life he was no less distinguished as an affectionate husband, a kind father and a warm-hearted friend. The traveller will long remember his hospitality and the poor bless him as a benefactor.
"Of such a man it may be truly said that his highest eulogy is the record of his life."

"Sacred to the memory of Ann Lenoir, a patriotic heroine, who died the 9th October, 1833, in the 83rd year of her age. She was the wife of Major General William Lenoir, a Revolutionary Patriot, with whom she lived near sixty-three years in perfect tranquility. For prudence, industry, economy and benevolence none could excel her.
"Let us all strive at God's command
To meet with her at Christ's right hand."
"Her maiden name was Ann Ballard. She was born July 11, 1751, and was two months and five days younger than her husband, whom she married in the year 1771."

Abstracts of Wills

Edgecombe County, North Carolina.

Abstract of Will of Thomas Lenoir I.

Parish of St. Mary's in the prov-

ince of North Carolina.
Name: Thomas Lenoir I.
Date of will, 14th day of May, 1765. Date probated, July Court, 1765.
Legatees mentioned: Wife, Mourning Lenoir.
Sons: Robert, Thomas, Isaac, Lewis, John and William.
Daughters: Ann Westmoreland, Betty Lattimore, Leah Whittaker and Mary Perry.
Executrix: Mourning Lenoir.
Executor: Isaac Lenoir.
Witnesses: James Atkinson, Joshua Pollard.
Recorded in Will Book A, pages 147-149.
Teste: James Hall.

Brunswick County, Virginia.

ABSTRACT OF WILL OF ROBERT LENOIR.

Name: Robert Lenoir.
Date of Will: Oct. 30, 1792; date probated, June 24, 1793.
Executors named: John Wilson, John Peace, James and Joseph Chealy and wife, Winifred Lenoir.
Legatees mentioned: Wife, Winifred Lenoir.
Daughters: Winifred Chealy, Elizabeth James, Ann Lenoir.
Sons: Fisher, Thomas, William, Lewis, Robert C. and John.
Recorded in Will Book No. 5, page 510.
Teste: Willie B. Abernathy, Jan. 4, 1932.

Sumpter District, State of South Carolina.

ABSTRACT OF WILL OF ISAAC LENOIR

Name: Isaac Lenoir.
Date of Will: Aug. 20, 1808; date probated, Nov. 7, 1808.
Executors named: John Barnes, son-in-law; sons, John and Francis.
Legatees mentioned: Martha Lenoir, wife.
Daughters: Mary Barnes, Sarah Thompson, Leah Hall.
Sons: John, Francis B., Isaac and William.
Witnesses: James Howell, John Atkinson, Robert Andrews.
Sworn to and subscribed before me this 7th day of November, 1808.
John Atkinson.

Williamson County, Tennessee.

ABSTRACT OF WILL OF JAMES SHEPPARD

Name: James Sheppard.
Date of Will: Sept. 22, 1828; date probated, Oct. 16, 1828.
Executors named: William C. Sheppard, Ransone Gwyn and Joshua V. Speer.
Legatees mentioned: Wife, Phebe Mastin Sheppard; Elizabeth and Ransone Gwyn, Austin Sheppard, Phebe and Joshua V. Speer, James Sheppard, William C. Sheppard, Martha and Henry Cook.
Witnesses: John H. Holt, James C. Fulton, John Boyd.
Recorded in Will Book, 1825-1830, page 346.
Signed: James Sheppard.

FAMILY BIBLE RECORD OF DR. CLEMENT C. BILLINGSLEA

Copied by Mrs. John Trotwood Moore, member of Campbell Chapter, D. A. R., Nashville, Tennessee.

Clement Billingslea, born April 27, 1794; died July 5, 1870.
Sarah A. Billingslea, born Oct. 29, 1797; died Aug. 16, 1842.

CHILDREN

Wm. Bibb Billingslea, born Mar. 31, 1821; died Dec. 11, 1844.
Mark Lane Billingslea, born Dec. 29, 1822; died July 16, 1847.
Lucy Bolling Billingslea, born Nov. 22, 1824; died Oct. 3, 1847.
James Clement Billingslea, born Dec. 27, 1826; died Dec. 25, 1869.
Sarah Rebecca Billingslea, born Aug. 8, 1828; died July 18, 1843.
Mary White Billingslea, born May 5, 1830; died July 5, 1852.
Emily Adelia Billingslea, born Dec. 27, 1831; died Dec. 14, 1903.

Condy Raquot Billingslea, born Oct. 29, 1833; died Jan. 30, 1851.
Ann Elizabeth Billingslea, born Sept. 2, 1835; born Dec. 19, 1861.
Cora Mark Billingslea, born April 10, 1846; died Sept. 2, 1852.
Lucy Billingslea Foster, born Sept. 11, 1847.
William Billingslea, father of Clement Billingslea, born Mar. 13, 1769; died Oct. 31, 1800.
Sarah Billingslea, mother of Clement Billingslea, born Mar. 16, 1776; died May 21, 1804. (Her maiden name was Sarah Turner).
William Turner Billingslea, son of Wm. and Sarah Billingslea, born Sept. 19, 1798; died Oct. 4, 1812.
Rebecca Billingslea (now Mrs. Moore), sister of Clement Billingslea, born Oct. 30, 1796; died July 12, 1863.
Sarah Foster (now Mrs. Graham), half-sister of Clement Billingslea, born Aug. 17, 1802.
Clement C. Billingslea and Lucy B. Anthony, married Mar. 16, 1816.
Clement C. Billingslea and Sarah A. Lane, married May 13, 1819.
Clement C. Billingslea and Martin Louisa Faulkner, married Mar. 21, 1844.
Clement C. Billingslea and Elizabeth D. Douglas, married Oct. 15, 1851.
Lucy B. Billingslea, wife of Clement C. Billingslea, died May 25, 1818.
Sarah Anthony Billingslea, wife of Clement C. Billingslea, died Aug. 15, 1842.
Martin Louisa Faulkner Billingslea, wife of Clement C. Billingslea, died Nov. 22, 1850. (She was born Aug. 20, 1812.)
Rachel Lane died July 25, 1833.

James Clement Billingslea, M.D., born Dec. 27, 1826.
Mary Ellen (Wooley) Billingslea, born Dec. 21, 1829.

CHILDREN

James Clement Billingslea, Jr., born July 24, 1849; died Mar. 18, 1883.
Condy R. Billingslea, born June 31, 1852; died Dec. 18, 1880.
Willie Billingslea, born Sept. 2, 1854; died May 25, 1864.
Eugene Lane Billingslea, born July 4, 1856; died Dec. 15, 1910.
Lucy Beale Billingslea, born May 19, 1858; died Aug. 11, 1919.
Sarah Matilda Billingslea, born May 23, 1860; died Oct. 25, 1919.
Louis Hallett Billingslea, born Jan. 20, 1862; died Dec. 3, 1926.
Anna Bett Billingslea, born Sept. 7, 1865; died April 9, 1872.
Foster Manly Billingslea, born Dec. 21, 1867; died Aug. 10, 1898.
Joshua Billingslea, born July 19, 1864; died Aug. 13, 1864.
Mary S. White was born Nov. 7, 1786; died Sept. 4, 1853.
Ann Elizabeth Billingslea, daughter of C. C. Billingslea, married John G. Huckabee, April 2, 1856.
John G. Huckabee, died May 30, 1866.
Mary White Billingslea, daughter of C. C. Billingslea, married Dr. Samuel John, of Selma, Alabama. A daughter, Mary B. John, was born Sept. 3, 1851.
Lucy Bolling Billingslea, daughter of C .C. Billingslea, married Prof. Joshua Foster, of Tuscaloosa, Alabama, and left a daughter, Lucy.
Sarah Matilda Billingslea, married July 15, 1878, to J. S. Nerryman; no issue.
Lucy Beale Billingslea, married Nov. 28, 1878, to F. R. Dowell.

CHILDREN

Dr. H. E. Dowell, of St. Louis, Mo.
Earl Dowell, Hermitage, Arkansas.
Foster Manly Billingslea, married Amanda Hays, Oct. 24, 1888.
Issue: Hallette, a son, died 1898.
Louis Hallette Billingslea, married Oct. 29, 1890, to Virginia Eskew.
Issue: Herman, died 1909.
Eugene Lane Billingslea, married Sept. 2, 1894, to Mary E. Watson.
Issue: Lucy E., born Oct. 1, 1895; died Nov. 26, 1911.
Virginia Pearl, born Nov. 28, 1897.
Eugene Louis, Jr., born April 25, 1900.
Arthur Clement, born Dec. 15, 1902.
Eva Lane, born Feb. 12, 1905.

Courtesy Tennessee State Library

THE JACKSON CHURCH

This church was built in 1823 by Andrew Jackson for his beloved wife, Rachel Donelson Jackson. It was here that General Jackson worshipped.

Kenneth Moreau, born Sept. 5, 1907; died Dec. 22, 1907.
Dr. Clement C. Billingslea was born in Washington, Wilkes Co., Ga. His father, William Billingslea, was a pioneer settler in Georgia; his father, James Clement Billingslea moved from Maryland to Georgia in 1773, Wilkes County, later to Jones County, Georgia. The wife of James Clement Billingslea was Mary Smith. Dr. Clement C. Billingslea spent much of the latter part of his life in Marion, Alabama, with the family of his daughter, Emily Adelia (Billingslea), wife of Judge John Moore, parents of John Trotwood Moore.

Family Bible Records

Copied from the family Bible of John Trotwood Moore, by Mrs. John Trotwood Moore, member Campbell Chapter, D. A. R., Nashville, Tenn., March 12, 1932.

Births

John Moore, born Mar. 13, 1829.
Emily Adelia Billingslea, wife of John Moore, born Dec. 27, 1831.
Ann Elizabeth Moore, born Feb. 4, 1852.
Lucy Billingslea Moore, the second daughter of John and Emily Moore, born Aug. 26, 1853.
Wooten Moore, the first son of John and Emily Moore, born June 15, 1855.
Clement Billingslea Moore, the second son of John and Emily Moore, was born Jan. 21, 1857.
John Moore, Jr., the third son of John and Emily Moore, born Aug. 25, 1858. (As an author known as John Trotwood Moore).
Emily Moore, the third daughter of John and Emily Moore, born July 30, 1861.
Elizabeth Tooley Moore, born Aug. 1, 1864, daughter of John and Emily Moore.

Grandchildren of John and Emily Moore

William Gillespie Moore, born Sept. 26, 1888.
Emma Clare Moore, daughter of Wooten and Katie Moore, born Feb. 18, 1890.
John Wooten Moore, son of Wooten and Katie Moore, born Feb. 25, 1892.
Percy Walton Moore, son of Wooten and Katie Moore, born May 26, 1896.
Harold N. Moore, son of Wooten and Katie Moore, born Nov. 8, 1899.
William Allen Moore, son of John and Florence Moore, born Jan. 28, 1896; lived one day.
Merrill Moore, son of John Trotwood and Mary (Daniel) Moore, born Sept. 11, 1903, at Columbia, Tenn.
Helen Lane and Mary Daniel Moore, twins, born at 3:45 and 4:30 p.m., April 11, 1907, in Nashville, Tenn., daughters of John Trotwood and Mary (Daniel) Moore.

Relatives

Mary B. John, born Sept. 3, 1851.
Ethel Mims Jones, born March 1, 1877.
Mary St. John Jones, born March 25, 1878.
William Moore Jones, born Sept. 25, 1881.
John Paul Jones, born June 1, 1888.

Marriages

John Moore and Emily Adelia Billingslea, married Feb. 18, 1851, by the Rev. James H. DeVotie.
Wooten and Katie Gillespie, married Dec. 14, 1887, by the Rev. W. M. Green.
John Moore, Jr., and Florence W. Allen, married Feb. 17, 1885, by the Rev. W. C. Grace.
W. M. Jones and Mary B. John, married Mar. 29, 1876, by Dr. E. Y. Winkler.
John Moore, Jr. (nom de plume, John Trotwood Moore), and Mary

Brown Daniel, married in Nashville, Tenn., June 13, 1900.

GRANDCHILDREN OF JOHN AND EMILY MOORE

Merrill Moore, son of John Trotwood and Mary (Daniel) Moore, married Aug. 14, 1930, in Nashville, Tenn., to Ann Leslie Nichol, daughter of Dr. Adam Gillespie and Bertha (Cheek) Nichol.

Mary Daniel Moore, twin daughter of John Trotwood and Mary (Daniel) Moore, married to Joel Marston Whitney, of Boston, Massachusetts, June 29, 1931, at "Arden Place," Nashville, Tenn.

William Gillespie Moore, son of Wooten and Katie Moore, married Harriet Milligan, in St. Louis, Mo.

John Moore, son of Wooten and Katie Moore, married Mae Wilson, July 29, 1922.

Percy Moore, son of Wooten and Katie Moore, married Flavia Oglesby, Dec., 1919.

Emma Clare Moore, daughter of Wooten and Katie Moore, married George W. Hayes, in Columbia, Tenn.

DEATHS

Ann Elizabeth Moore, first daughter of John and Emily Moore, died March 15, 1853.

Clement Billingslea Moore, died on March 31, 1857.

Elizabeth Tooley Moore, fourth daughter of John and Emily Moore, died Aug. 16, 1865.

Emily Moore, the third daughter of John and Emily Moore, died Jan. 20, 1870.

Emily Adelia Moore, wife of John Moore, died Dec. 14, 1903, 11:15 p.m.

John Moore, died April 27, 1904, at Greensboro, Alabama.

William Allen Moore, son of John and Florence Moore, died Jan. 29, 1896.

Lucy Billingslea Moore, died at Columbia, Tenn., Feb. 9, 1923.

John Trotwood Moore, died at 8 a.m., May 10, 1929, at "Arden Place," Nashville, Tenn.

FAMILY BIBLE RECORDS

MARRIAGES

Henry Clay Daniel to Elizabeth Gillenwaters Brown, Oct. 29, 1868, at the residence of her father, Robert Allison Brown, of Cass County, Missouri, 3 miles northwest of Harrisonville, Mo., at "Wayside Rest."

Issue:

Pearl Daniel, married Jan. 13, 1892, to Austin Heaton Merrill, in Harrisonville, Mo., at the residence of H. Clay Daniel.

Charles Hardin Daniel, married in Galveston, Texas, to Jessie Harriet, Nov. 6, 1900.

Robert Brown Daniel, married in Harrisonville, Mo., to Lilian Boswell, Oct. 20, 1904.

Mary Brown Daniel, married June 13, 1900, in Wesley Hall, Nashville, Tenn., to John Trotwood Moore, of Columbia, Tenn.

H. C. Daniel II, married Effie Ervin, at Harrisonville, Mo.

Elizabeth Daniel, married Dec. 23, 1920, in Liberty, Mo., to William Barnes, of Higginsville, Mo.

Louise Merrill Daniel, married Mar. 23, 1910, in Kansas City, Mo., to Charles Owen Crawford.

MARRIAGES OF GRANDCHILDREN OF H. C. DANIEL

Austin H. Merrill, Jr., married Livinia Shinn, Oct. 29, 19—.

Elizabeth Brown Merrill, married Crawford Duncan Everett, in St. Louis, Mo., Feb. 20, 1923.

Ruth Daniel, married Delmas Given, Jr., Dec. 12, 1922.

Naomi Daniel, married (1st) Andrew Womack, Nov. 14, 1921, in Corpus Christi, Texas; married (2nd) Fred Olson, Oct. 15, 1926.

Merrill Moore and Ann Leslie Nichol, married 5 p.m., Aug. 14, 1930, at Nashville, Tenn.

Helen Lane Moore and Whitefoord Russell Cole, Jr., married Dec. 16, 1933.

Mary Daniel Moore and Joel Marston Whitney, married 4 p.m., June

29, 1931, at "Arden Place," Nashville, Tenn.

CHILDREN OF H. CLAY AND LIZZIE G. (BROWN) DANIEL

Births

Pearl Daniel, born at 5:30 o'clock, Wednesday, p.m., Sept. 1, 1869, at "Wayside Rest."
Charles Hardin Daniel, born at 1 o'clock and 30 min., a.m., Nov. 29, 1871, at "Wayside Rest."
Robert Brown Daniel, born Monday, March 24, 1873, at "Wayside Rest."
Mary Brown Daniel, born Thursday, 12:30 o'clock, midnight, May 17, 1875, Harrisonville, Mo.
Harry C. Daniel, born Tuesday, Jan. 31, 1877, 8 o'clock p.m., in Harrisonville, Mo.
Elizabeth Daniel, born Tuesday, 12 o'clock, noon, June 25, 1879, in Harrisonville, Mo.
William Gillenwaters Daniel, born Sunday, 1 o'clock p.m., Feb. 19, 1882, in Harrisonville, Mo.
Louise Daniel, born Thursday p.m., at 6 o'clock, Jan. 12, 1888, in Harrisonville, Mo.

GRANDCHILDREN OF H. C. AND L. G. DANIEL

Births

Austin H. Merrill, Jr., born March 13, 1893, in Nashville, Tenn.
Elizabeth Brown Merrill, born Aug. 7, 1899, Nashville, Tenn.
Ruth Elizabeth Daniel, born Dec. 23, 1902, in Galveston, Texas.
Naomi Daniel, born June 18, 1904, Galveston, Texas.
Robert Edwin Daniel, born Aug. 19, 1906, in Joplin, Mo.
Infant son, born to R. B. and Lilian Daniel on Jan. 25, 1909; lived 12 days.
Grace Daniel, born Oct. 30, 1911, in Hutchinson, Kansas.
Merrill Moore, born at 6:30 p.m., Sept. 11, 1903, at "Westover," near Columbia, Tenn.
Helen Lane and Mary Daniel Moore, twins, born at 3:45 and 4:30 p.m., April 11, 1907, in Nashville, Tenn.
Frances Ervin Daniel, born Sept. 2, 1904, at Harrisonville, Mo.
Harry C. Daniel III, born Jan. 5, 1911, at Harrisonville, Mo.
Anna Dale Crawford, born Feb. 5, 1911, in Nashville, Tenn.
Elisabeth Waite Crawford, born June 17, 1912, in Nashville, Tenn.
Mary Louise Crawford, born June 9, 1917, Saturday, —— p.m., at Bay St. Louis, Mississippi.
Charles Owen Crawford, Jr., born Oct. 15, 1922, at 12:05 a.m., Monday, at Bay St. Louis, Mississippi.

GREAT-GRANDCHILDREN OF H. C. AND L. G. DANIEL

Births

Patricia Ann Merrill, born April 5, 1918, Goldfield, Nevada; daughter of Austin and Levine Merrill.
Dorothy Womack, born Oct. 16, 1922, 6:20 a.m., Monday, at Corpus Christi, Texas; daughter of Andrew and Naomi Daniel Womack.
Merrill Everett, born Nov. 17, 1925, in St. Louis, Mo., daughter of C. Duncan and Elizabeth Merrill Everett.
Peter Merrill, born Aug. 7, 1928, in San Francisco, Calif., son of Austin and Levine Merrill.
Crawford Duncan Everett, Jr., born May 18, 1930, in St. Louis, Mo., son of C. D. and Elizabeth Merrill Everett.
Adam Gillespie Nichol Moore, born Oct. 21, 1931, 2:30 p.m., in Boston, Mass., son of Merrill and Ann Leslie (Nichol) Moore.

Deaths

Robert Allison Brown, died Sept. 7, 1888, aged 80 years, at Harrisonville, Mo.; buried in family cemetery at "Wayside Rest."
Mary Jane Roddye (Gillenwaters) Brown, died Aug. 28, 1890, aged 71 years, at Harrisonville; buried in family cemetery at "Wayside Rest."
Andrew Broaddus Daniel, died Sept. 30, 1900, aged 87 years, at Vandalia, Mo.; buried in Mexico, Mo.
Matilda (Greenwade) Daniel, died April 15, 1904, aged 83 years, in DeWitt, Arkansas; buried in Mexico, Mo.

Henry Clay Daniel, died Sept. 9, 1925, 1:45 a.m., aged 83 years, in Nashville, Tenn., at "Arden Place;" buried in Mt. Olivet Cemetery.

William Gillenwaters Daniel, died May 29, 1911, Kansas City, Mo., 3 p.m.; buried in family cemetery, "Wayside Rest," near Harrisonville, Mo.

Charles Hardin Daniel, died Nov. 19, 1915, Reno, Nevada; buried Oakland, Cal.

Austin Heaton Merrill, died Aug. 10, 1900, at Tate Springs, Tenn.; buried in Mt. Olivet Cemetery, Nashville.

John Trotwood Moore, died May 10, 1929, Friday, 8 a.m., at "Arden Place," Nashville, Tenn.; buried in Mt. Olivet Cemetery, Nashville.

Family Bible Records

Copied from the Matthews family Bible, of Williamson County, Tennessee, in the possession of the heirs of George L. Matthews, deceased, formerly of Franklin, Tennessee, loaned to the Tennessee State Library by W. K. Matthews, son of George I. Matthews, now of Kobe, Japan.

Copied by Mrs. John Trotwood Moore, Librarian and Archivist, State Library, Nashville, Tennessee, member of Campbell Chapter, D. A. R., Nashville, Tenn., March 10, 1932.

Luke Mathews, born Mar. 15, 1739.

Lucy Mathews, daughter of Richard Fox and Joanna, his wife, born Nov. 28, 1747.

Luke Mathews and Lucy, his wife, married Jan. 26, 1766.

Angelila Mathews, daughter of Luke Mathews and Lucy, his wife, born June 28, 1767.

Hannah Mathews, born Sept. 25, 1768.

Elizabeth Mathews, born May 14, 1772.

Lucy Mathews, born Oct. 27, 1774.

John Mathews, born Mar. 9, 1777.

Luke Mathews, born Aug. 22, 1779.

Isham Mathews, born April 2, 1782.

Nancy Mathews, born Oct. 11, 1785.

Drury Mathews, born Sept. 4, 1788.

Luke Mathews, husband of Lucy Mathews, departed this life April 7, 1788.

Lucy Matthews, wife of Luke Matthews, departed this life Feb. 12, 1831.

(This last entry was made in a different handwriting, and is the first time the name is spelled "Matthews").

Family Bible Records

Copied from the family Bible of William M. Buchanan, placed by his descendants in the Tennessee State Library.

Copied by Mrs. John Trotwood Moore, Librarian and Archivist, State Library, Nashville, Tennessee, member of Campbell Chapter, D. A. R., Nashville, Tenn., March 10, 1932.

Marriages

Sarah Elizabeth Buchanan and John E. Hill, married April 3, 1851.

Thomas Everett Buchanan and Susan Gordon, married April 8, 1856.

Margaret Buchanan and Robert H. Harvey, married Sept. 21, 1859.

Mary Jane Buchanan and J. W. Harvey, Jr., married Oct. 28, 1860.

William Henry Buchanan and Louisa Jane Buchanan, married Aug. 11, 1861.

John E. Buchanan and Mary G. Harvey, married Dec. 21, 1865.
George F. Buchanan and Bettie German, married Sept. 11, 1870.
Margaret Harvey and W. D. Mason, married Oct. 27, 1869.
Mary E. Hill and Samuel P. Hyde, married Dec. 18, 1878.

DEATHS

Susan Buchanan, daughter of Wm. M. and Susan Buchanan, died Nov. 23, 1864, aged 8 years, 4 months.
Ephraim E. Buchanan, died Mar. 30, 1865, aged 13 years, 7 months, 8 days.
Sarah Elizabeth Hill, died Aug. 5, 1870.

Wm. M. Buchanan, died May 31, 1880, aged 71 years, 1 month, 11 days.

Susan E. Harvey, daughter of Robert H. and Margaret Harvey, died Oct. 28, 1864, aged 3 years, 2 months, 10 days.

Robert H. B. Harvey, son of John W. and M. J. Harvey, died Nov. 7, 1862, aged 1 year, 2 months, and 16 days.

Infant daughter of J. W. and M. J. Harvey, died Dec. 22, 1865.

John Bunyan Harvey, died July 29, 1876, aged 7 years, 3 months, 24 days old.

Thomas H. Everett—Record of:

BIRTHS

Thomas H. Everett, born 1782.
Elizabeth Everett, born Dec. 29, 1795.
Sally B. Everett, daughter of Thomas H. and Elizabeth Everett, born Aug. 7, 1811.
Susan Everett, born Aug. 19, 1813.
Elizabeth Everett, born Oct. 18, 1815.
Nancy M. Everett, born Nov. 28, 1817.
Evalina J. Everett, born Sept. 8, 1819.
John B. Everett, born Sept. 21, 1821.
Mary M. Everett, born Aug. 12, 1823.
Lydia R. Everett, born May 27, 1825.
George W. and Benjamin F. Everett, born April 7, 1827.
Thomas H. Everett II, born June 19, 1829.
Zipporah Everett, born July 9, 1831.
Ephraim F. Everett, born Feb. 5, 1834.
Amanda M. F. Everett, born Sept. 19, 1835.
Josephine G. Everett, born Jan. 19, 1838.
Musedora E. Everett, born April 25, 1840.

DEATHS

Thomas H. Everett, died March, 1854.
Thomas H. Everett II, died July 20, 1855.
Sally B. Ridley, died Sept. 17, 1854.
Elizabeth Everett, died May 8, 1875.
Nancy M. Perry, died May 5, 1875.

George F. Buchanan—Record of:

BIRTHS

John Watson Buchanan, born Sept. 27, 1811.
Wm. M. Buchanan, born May 16, 1875.
Ephraim Everett Buchanan, born Dec. 3, 1866.

Susan E. Harvey, born Aug. 18, 1861.

William I. Harvey, born May 20, 1863.

Susan M. Harvey, born Jan. 21, 1867.

Hiram Kilgore Walling's Bible

Record of Mrs. Ida C. Walling, McMinnville

Hiram K. Walling and Mahala Howard, married April 21, 1835.

Alonzo N. Walling and Ida G. Walling, married Nov. 27, 1919.

H. K. Walling and Susan Dorsett, married April 6, 1880.

Felix Grundy Walling and Sarah V. Walden, married June 4, 1874, in White County, Ill; Thomas Stokes, Minister.

Hiram K. Walling, born June 11, 1816.

Mahala Howard, born Dec. 24, 1815.

Mary D. Walling, born July 1, 1836.

Hugh L. Walling, born Jan. 22, 1838.

Felix G. Walling, born Dec. 29, 1839.

Margaret H. Walling, born May 17, 1841.

Amanda C. Walling, born Jan. 19, 1843.

Sarah A. Walling, born Sept. 9, 1844.

Nettie A. Walling, born Nov. 21, 1846.

Millard F. Walling, born Aug. 7, 1850.

Berryman Walling, born July 3, 1814.

Sarah V. Walling, born March 5, 1855.

Hugh L. Walling, born May 2, 1875.

Mary L. Walling, born April 17, 1876.

William S. Walling, born July 17, 1877.

Martha J. Walling, born Nov. 13, 1878.

Mahala Eugenia Walling, born Feb. 6, 1880.

Cora G. Walling, born Oct. 28, 1881.

Robert D. Walling, born Dec. 24, 1882.

Sarah A. Walling, born Oct. 24, 1884.

Nettie May Walling, born April 11, 1886.

Nettie Angeline and Lonnie Emily Walling, born Sept. 6, 1920.

Susan Dorsett, born Dec. 29, 1834.

Alonzo Nelson Walling, born Jan. 27, 1888.

Ida Gay Walling, born Oct. 23, 1887.

Alice Virginia Walling, born Feb. 9, 1889.

Maggie Walling, born July 4, 1868.

James T. Walling, born May 5, 1872.

Deaths

Berryman Walling, died Dec. 18, 1820.

Millard F. Walling, died Aug. 19, 1852.

Hugh Lawson Walling, died May 22, 1857.

Margaret H. Walling, died July 17, 1857.

Mary D. Walling, died July 12, 1890.

Nettie May Walling, died March 11, 1887.

Mary L. Walling, died Sept. 25, 1888.

Sarah V. Walling, died Feb. 9, 1889.

William S. Walling, died Nov. 4, 1898.

Daniel Walling, died March, 1881.

Sarah Nancy Walling, died Nov. 24, 1860.

Mahala Walling, died March 31, 1876.

Hiram Kilgore Walling, died July 14, 1888.

Mary D. Walling (Palmer), died July 12, 1890.

Amanda C. Walling (Harris), died April 26, 1920.

Sarah A. Walling (Whiting), died Nov. 9, 1919.

Felix G. Walling, died April 4, 1913.

David Walling, died Mar. 27, 1923.

Hiram Vard Whiting, died Dec. 15, 1920.

John T. Whiting, died March 28, 1923.

DANIEL WALLING'S BIBLE

Copied from the certified record of Mrs. Ida G. Walling, McMinnville, Tennessee.

Daniel Walling, born July 18, 1792.
Nancy Walling, wife of Daniel Walling, born Sept., 1793.
Hiram Walling, born June 11, 1816.
Malinda Walling, born April 13, 1818.
Matilda Walling, born Sept. 10, 1821.
Marilla Walling, born Oct. 3, 1825.
Harmon Walling, born March 29, 1829.
Mahala Walling, born Feb. 15, 1827.
James H. Walling, born Nov. 6, 1831.

MARRIAGES

Miriam Walling and Mahala Howard, married April 21, 1835.
Malinda Walling and Isom R. Rogers, married April 20, 1838.

DEATHS

Sarah Nancy Walling, died Nov. 24, 1860.

FAMILY RECORDS

Sent by Mrs. A. S. Bowen, State Chairman, Marking Historic Spots, Chattanooga, Tenn.

Bryan McDonald and Mary McCombs, his wife, located at Newcastle, Del., before 1689. In his will, probated in 1707, he centioned the following children:
John, William, James *Bryan, Richard, Annable, Mary (married —— Danger).
Bryan McDonald, Jr., married Catherine Robinson, daughter of James Robinson and his wife, Catherine Howell, and settled in Botetcourt County, Va. In his will probated August, 1757, he mentioned the following children:
Bryan III.
Richard.
Prisla.
Joseph.
Edward (killed by Indians).
James.
Rebecca (married —— Bane).
Catherine (married John Armstrong).
*Mary (married Tobias Smyth).
Mary McDonald, married to Tobias Smyth, son of Ericus Smyth, a Swedish priest, who died in Aug., 1757. After his death she settled at Glade Spring, Va., where she was buried. Their children are as follows:
Rebecca (married —— Crabtree).
Jonas.
Elizabeth or Mary (married —— Kelly).
*Catherine (Elisha MacNew).
Catherine Smyth, married Elisha MacNew, settled near Glade Spring, Va. Their children are as follows:
Nancy (married Joseph Worsham).
Catherine (married John Hockett).
Thomas (married Elizabeth Ivitt).
Rebecca (married William Ivitt, Feb. 23, 1791).
Elish (married Jane Sutton).
*Elizabeth (married Adam Thomas).
William.
Polly (married Daniel Bradley, June 3, 1799).
John (married Sally Althea, May 23, 1797).
George.
Tobias.
Isaac (was literary; wrote manuscript seen by members of younger generations).
Eliabeth MacNew, born April 21, 1797; died June 1, 1855; married Adam Thomas, son of Jacob Thomas and his wife, Louisa Schultz, born April 17, 1794; died Nov. 23, 1866; lived in Sullivan County, Tenn. Their children are as follows:
Louisa, born Feb. 19, 1816; mar-

ried Wm. Wallace, Aug. 16, 1832.
Polly, born Oct. 3, 1817; married John White, Nov. 10, 1842.
William, born Aug. 7, 1819; married Sarah Gross, Aug. 13, 1846.
John, born Aug. 9, 1821; married Minerva West, May 22, 1855; died Aug. 9, 1861.
Adam, born Jan. 9, 1823; married Fannie Eve Hunt, Nov. 24, 1857; died Jan. 26, 1892.
George, born Sept. 18, 1824; died Aug. 1, 1829.
Elizabeth, born July 10, 1826; married John Holt, Nov. 10, 1842.
Elisha, born March 22, 1828; died Aug. 19, 1829.
Margaret, born March 4, 1830; married Asbury K. Cox, Dec. 28, 1852.
Susan, born April 13, 1832; married Chris T. Crow, Aug. 19, 1847, in Dallas, Texas.
Samuel, born July 12, 1834; married Elizabeth Massengill, May 22, 1861; died Sept. 29, 1908.
One son, born June 7, 1836; born dead.
One son, born July 10, 1837; born dead.
*Amanda T., born Jan. 7, 1839; married Thomas West, May 22, 1860; died Aug. 30, 1913.
One son, born Dec. 7, 1840; born dead.
Amanda Thomas, born Jan. 7, 1829; died Aug. 30, 1913; married Rev. Thomas Reed West, born Sept. 3, 1838; died May 2, 1916. Lived at Rutledge and Athens, Tenn.; both buried at Athens. Their children are as follows:
Triphosa, born 1861; died in infancy.
Oscar Lonzo, born 1863; married Lillian Clapp, July 4, 1889; died June 7, 1900.
*Lenora, born Aug. 15, 1867; married Albert Sidney Bowen, Dec. 18, 1891.
George Henry, born Feb. 5, 1869; married Della Ketner, Sept. 18, 1906.
Clyde Thomas, born May 8, 1872; married Nita Eckles.
Victor Reed, born Jan. 5, 1875; married Mae Royce.
Oliphant McNew, born July 4, 1878; married (1) Elizabeth Williams; (2) Esther Patterson.
Lenora West, born Aug. 15, 1867; married Albert Sidney Bowen, Nov. 18, 1891, born June 5, 1863; died March 1, 1923; lived in Jewell, Ga., Chattanooga, Tenn., and Chicamauga, Ga. Their children are as follows:
Lenora West, born Sept. 23, 1892; married James J. Coghlan, Aug. 24, 1920.
Mary Amanda, born Nov. 20, 1895; died June 23, 1896.
Albert Sidney, born June 21, 1898; married Katherine Susan Schaefer, June 15, 1922.
Virginia Lee, born March 6, 1903.
One son, born Nov. 12, 1905; died Jan. 1, 1906.

Tombstone Records from Mahanain Church graveyard:

John McNew, died May 16, 1877; age 50 years 6 months 15 days.
J. G. McNew, born July 1, 1829; died March 25, 1907; age 77 years 8 months 24 days.
Elizabeth McNew, died June 18, 1862; age 63 years.
Thomas B. McNew, died 1856; age 62 years.
Safroney McNew, died 1856; age 33 years.
James McNew, born 1820; died 1857.
Julius McNew, born May 17, 1791; died May 30, 1867.
Geo. E. McNew, born Nov. 17, 1762; died 1846; age 86 years.
Daniel A. McNew, born 1838; died 1847.
Wife of Benjamin Cawood, died Oct. 17, 1823; age 33 years.
Elizabeth Scott, born Oct. 24, 1828; died May, 1847.
Mrs. Sally McNew, wife of James McNew, born Dec. 4, 1801; died May 31, 1859.
(Note: At this Mahanian Church was held the first Methodist Conference.)

Tombstone Records from McNew Family Cemetery, near Abingdon, Va.

Elisha McNew, born Sept. 13, 1788; died Aug. 26, 1854.
Jane McNew, wife of Elisha II., born Aug. 12, 1788; died 1854.
Catherine McNew, wife of Joshua Redwine, born April 26, 1817; died April 16, 1880.
George McNew, born Nov. 23, 1829; died Aug. 1, 1854.

Catherine McNew, born May 2, 1794; died March 5, 1848; daughter of Alexander Eakin.

Granville McNew, born Jan. 11, 1820; died July 24, 1824; son of Elisha and Jane.

George McNew, born March 26, 1806; died May 22, 1883.

Marriages:

James McNew and Mary D. Meadows, married Aug. 8, 1820.

James McNew and Sally Sturgeon, married Feb. 23, 1841.

Harvey Sturgeon and Mary Jane McNew, married Sept. 8, 1853.

William H. Montgomery and Nancy J. McNew, married Nov. 17, 1864.

James McMontgomery and Mary Collings, married Dec. 29, 1903, near Saltville, Washington County.
John Thomas and Susanna Weaver, married Nov. 24, 1801.

W. F. Smyth and Nellie Baker, married Dec., 1889, in Richmond, Va.

Blythe Deems Smyth and Duglas Howard, married June, 1906.

Elizabeth Ethel Smyth and Chas. DeWitt Ellis, married Sept. 29, 1909.

Martha Worley and W. G. Smyth, married Dec. 16, 1874, at Holston, Va.

Mary Anne Smyth and James T. Neilson, married June, 1881.

George W. Smyth and Alice Carter Betts, married Feb. 22, 1892 (his second wife).

John Thomas and Martha Vermillion, married 1843.

Isaac Thomas and Rebecca Bard, married 1817.

Richard West and Jenny Robison, married July 3, 1822.

John Thomas and Sara Ward, married May 13, 1821.

Tyre Thomas and Malinda Balch, married May 9, 1834.

Howell Thomason and Hannah Hoggett, married Jan. 6, 1825.

Nancy Thomason and John Oliphant, married June 17, 1824.

John Thomason and Betty Oliphant, married July 17, 1824.

Edna Thomason and David Grubbs, married Aug. 8, 1820.

Polly Thomason and Jas. Jean, married Oct. 31, 1819.

Elizabeth Thomason and Jas. Stuart, married Sept. 5, 1835.

Thomas Thomason and Caty Stonecifer, married Feb. 23, 1836.

Charles West and Sarah Philipps, married April 23, 1803.

Lucinda West and Alfred Lewis, married Oct. 27, 1831.

Susannah West and Reuben Hutson, married Oct. 27, 1831.

James West and Sarah Johnson, married Oct. 9, 1828.

Edward West and Isabell Rankin, married Aug. 17, 1826.

Ruthy West and B. Smith, married April 11, 1813.

Samuel West and Ann Rankin, married March 16, 1819.

Polly West and Jas. Johnson, married May 4, 1837.

Polly West and George Nease, married March 3, 1828.

Susannah West and Geo. Farner, married June 9, 1837.

Mary West and William Malone, married March 23, 1803.
Nancy West and Michael Myers, married April 25, 1837.
Elizabeth West and John Lindsey, married Sept. 11, 1797.
John Oliphant and Eliz. Hoyal, married Aug. 14, 1819.
James Oliphant and Jane Rankin, married June 6, 1803.
Felix E. Oliphant and Mary Reece, married Aug. 17, 1829.
Betsy Oliphant and William Hoyal, married Oct. 11, 1832 or 34 (?).
Mary Ann Oliphant and Harvey G. Robertson, married Feb. 12, 1836.
Elizabeth Oliphant and Gravenor Marsh, married Sept. 8, 1800.
Sallie Oliphant and Felix Ernest, married May 14, 1802.
Isabell Oliphant and Josua Cannon, married Nov. 11, 1829.
Isabell Oliphant and Geo. Hazelwood, married Nov. 11, 1826.
Felix E. Oliphant and Mary Pierce, married Aug. 17, 1835.
Thomas A. Oliphant and Elizabeth Jones, married March 28, 1823.
Thomas Oliphant and Hannah Morrow, married April 7, 1802.
Hannah Oliphant and William Burton, married Dec. 10, 1812.
Sally Oliphant and Felix Earnest, married May 14, 1808.
Anna Oliphant and Nathaniel Haworth, married May 26, 1806.
Hannah Oliphant and Solomon Beals, married Aug. 4, 1825.
Betsy Oliphant and John Thompson, married July 26, 1829.
Samuel Wear and Sarah Bean, married March 6, 1789.
John Gibson and Sarah Russell, married 1789.
Phillip Stout and Hannah Stanfield, married Oct. 7, 1789.
John Graham and Esther Bowen, married Jan. 2, 1789.
Edward West and Lydia Stanfield, married June 8, 1791.
Samuel Graham and Phoebe Stanfield, married Sept. 5, 1814.
Nathaniel Stanfield and Ann Frouse, married Oct. 30, 1816.
Henry Earnest and Hannah Pitner, married Oct. 28, 1816.
Daniel Bean and Sarah Ross, married Dec. 29, 1789.
Hugh Bean and Elizabeth Hood, married Nov. 3, 1809.
John Bean and Elizabeth Wilson, married March 7, 1797.
William Bean and Margaret McCracken, married Sept. 12, 1791.

Record From Old Bible

Originally owned by Waman Clark; now owned by Mrs. H. J. West, Sparta, Tennessee.

Births

Daniel Clark, born in Shanandrah County, Va., Sept. 23, 1797.
Mourning Hembree Clark, born in Spartanburg District, S. C., Sept. 20, 1800.
Nancy Clark, eldest child of Daniel and Mourning Clark, born in White County, Oct. 16, 1817.
Lourana, born in White County, Dec. 25, 1819.
Waman Clark, born in White County, Tenn., Jan. 20, 1822.
Loucetta Clark, born Sept. 30, 1825.
Daniel W. Young, son of Loucetta Clark and Austin C. Young, born May 4, 1842.
Nancy Young, daughter of Loucetta and Austin Young, born Dec. 6, 1844.
Mark Clark, son of Waman and Elizabeth Lowry Clark, born April 24, 1844.
Nancy Clark, sister of Daniel Clark, born in Shenandoah County, Va., March 7, 1799.

Marriages

Daniel Clark, married Mourning Hembree, July 20, 1815.
Nancy Clark, eldest daughter of Daniel and Mourning Clark, married John Lisk, Feb. 24, 1836.
Loucetta Clark, youngest daughter of Daniel and Mourning Clark, married Austin Clatworthy Young, Nov. 5, 1840.
Waman Clark, only son of Daniel and Mourning Clark, married Elizabeth Lowry, Feb. 28, 1843.
Mark L. Clark, son of Waman and

Elizabeth Clark, married to Mary Gardenhire, Aug. 20, 1868.
Daniel Young, son of Loucetta and Austin C. Young, married Mary Lowry, Jan. 18, 1865.
Nancy, daughter of Loucetta and Austin C. Young, married Dilliard Goodpasture, June 17, 1869.

DEATHS

Thomas Clark, father of Daniel Clark, died in White County, Tenn., Aug., 1809.
Wineford, wife of Thomas Clark, born in Culpepper County, Va.; died in White County, Tenn., March 21, 1850; age 84 years.
Lourana, died Jan. 21, 1839.
Austin C. Young, died Sept. 18, 1873.
Daniel Clark, died in White County, Jan. 29, 1879.
Mourning Clark, wife of Daniel Clark, died in White County, Tenn., April 14, 1876.
Mary Clark, daughter of Thomas and Wineford Clark, died in White County, Tenn., May 5, 1888.

RECORD FROM OLD BIBLE

Bible bought January 20, 1812. Originally owned by Thomas West. now property of J. H. Potter, Sparta, Tenn.

BIRTHS

Thomas West, born Jan. 28, 1760.
Tabitha Dale, his wife, born Aug. 12, 1769.
Children of Thomas and Tabitha Dale, his wife:
Betsey Calling, born June 12, 1792.
John Clemmon, born March 6, 1798.
Mathias Starky, born Sept. 23, 1798.
Jonathan Pickral, born 1801.
Joel Nelson, born May 16, 1803.
Nancy H., born Oct. 9, 1805.
Martha Dale, born July 21, 1808.
Tabitha Miller, born Aug. 15, 1811.
Thos. Wilans, born Nov. 2, 1815.
Stirling Madison Williams, born Dec. 27, 1841.
Gustavus Pitts Williams, born Nov. 6, 1843.
Sarah Amanda Williams, born Aug. 29, 1843.
Elizabeth Frances Williams, born Feb. 19, 1853.
Sampson B. Williams, born April 7, 1802.

MARRIAGES

Thomas West and Tabitha Dale, married Nov. 3, 1791.
Tabitha West, married Sampson B. Williams, Aug. 6, 1840.
John Clemmon West, married Mary Lawrence.

DEATHS

Thomas West, died July 12, 1848, at quarter past 3 o'clock in the evening.
Tabitha West, died March 2, 1849, at five minutes before 3 o'clock in the evening.
Jonathan P. West, died Sept 13, 1823, at half past 10 o'clock in the morning.

FROM DIARY OF REV. JOHN BEARD, CIRCUIT RIDER

Father of James Newton Beard

Diary in the possession of Jeannette Tillotson Acklen.

This book contains several important transactions in my life, viz: number of sermons preached, marriages performed, baptisms, etc. An account of my ministerial career:
I was born Dec. 25, 1800; professed religion Aug. 20, 1820; joined the Cumberland Presbyterian Church in Feb., 1821; joined presbytery as a candidate for the ministry on April 1, 1821; was licensed to preach the gospel as a probationer for the holy ministry April 3, 1823, and was ordained to the whole work of the ministry on April 6, 1826, and having traveled four years and five months as a missionary, was then married to Margaret S. Cloyd on Aug. 30, 1827, by the Rev. David Foster.
I preached the first year after I was licensed, 251 sermons; the second year, 318; the third year, 318, making in the three years, 887. In the fourth year, 304; in the

fifth year, 78, making in the five years, 1,269 sermons. In the sixth year I preached 65 sermons, making in the six years, 1,334. In the seventh year, 123, making in the seven years, 1,457 sermons. In the eighth year, 71; in all, 1,528. In the ninth year, 149; in all, 1,677 sermons. In the tenth year, 157, making 1,834. In the eleventh year, 71, making in all 1,907 sermons. In the twelfth year, 63 sermons, making in the twelve years 1,970 sermons.

The first year after my ordination I baptized 61 children and 29 adults. In the second year, 21 children and 13 adults. In the third year, 4 children and 4 adults. In the fourth year, 14 children and 1 adult. In the fifth year, 3 children and 4 adults. In all, 90 children and 64 adults. In the sixth year 46 children and 11 adults. In the seventh, 13 children and 3 adults. In the eighth year, 11 children and 12 adults, making in the eight years, 160 children and 90 adults. In the ninth year, 3 children and 2 adults; in all, 163 children and 92 adults.

Marriages Performed

Performed the rites of matrimony between John W. Tate and Elizabeth Cloyd, Oct. 11, 1827.
Married Nelson D. Hancock and Margaret Woodrum, Jan. 24, 1828.
Married Gideon Carter and Lydia Case, March 11, 1828.
Married Layton Hunter and Elizabeth Robison, Sept. 29, 1828.
Married Wm. Yandle and Jane Barr, Dec. 10, 1828-9.
Married Alexander Bridges and Elizabeth Rodes, Aug. 18, 1828-9.
Married Robert Elliot and Elizabeth Curry, Sept. 22, 1829.
Married Joseph Roach and Mary D. Barton, Dec. 1, 1829.
Married Edmond Crawford and Elizabeth Smith, Dec. 17, 1829.
Married Theophilus W. Hands and Jane Tilford, Dec. 22, ——.
Married John M. Peyton and Jane H. Donnell, Feb. 25, ——.
Married Henry Devault and Susannah M. Jackson, May 17, ——.
Married John Drumon and Rebecca Ann Brown, Aug. 4, ——.
Married Eli Merrit and Sarah Merrit, Nov. 22, 1830.
Married John W. Sanders and Sarah ———, 1831.
Married Alfred H. Harris and Elizabeth Woodrum, July 21, 1831.
Married Edwin Clemmons and Susannah Woodsum, March 7, 1833.
Married John Hall and Mary Pillow, April 21, 1833.
Married John C. Wilkinson and Emily Ballard, Oct. 21, 1833.
Married Washington Cougill and Violet Hagar, Oct. 23, 1833.
Married Richard D. Curd and Emily E. Hall, Dec. 12, 1833.
Married Parker Sullivan and Mary E. Hamilton, Dec. 31, 1833.
Married Dr. Wm. P. Sale and Agnes F. Watkins, Jan. 9, 1834.
Married Wm. T. Marshall and Lucinda Wright, Jan. 16, 1834.
Married George E. Alexander and Margaret W. Tate, March 6, 1834.
Married Josiah S. Tooly and Sarah N. Cloyd, March 20, 1834.
Married James Caldwell and Louisa Ballard, May 22, 1834.
Married James Drennon and Cyntha Davis, Sept. 18, 1834.
Married James M. Crutchfield and Elizabeth B. Sain, Oct. 9, 1834.
Married Samuel Brown and Nancy McCombs, Oct. 30, 1834.
Married Wm. Bond and Margaret M. Alexander, Dec. 11, 1834.
Married Isaac J. Roach and Matilda Carlone Marshall, Dec. 16, 1834.
Married David E. Wood and Ann B. Brown, March ——.
Married Charles Hall and Polly ———.
Married Hugh Brown and ——— McCarroll, Aug. 20, 1835.
Married Elmore W. Williams and Louisa Bell, Dec. 10, 1835.
Married Calvin Robbins and Susan Wood, March 3, 1836.
Married George W. Hagar and Minerva T. Clements, April 14, 1836.
Married Basel C. Brown and Hannah Rutland, March 16, 1836.
Married Felix R. Gleaves and Nancy M. Davis, June 30, 1836.

Married Ezekiel S. Curry and Rebecca McDaniel, Sept. 28, 1836.
Married Francis C. Newsom and Susan Ridley, Oct. 5, 1836.
Married Samuel Tilford and Katharine Canthran, Oct. 6, 1836.
Married Wm. Gugon and Martha Waldrum, Nov. 24, 1836.
Married Isaac Johnston and —— Tilford, Dec. 1, 1836.
Married Wm. B. Clinton and Mabell A. Beard, Dec. 27, 1836.
Married John W. Harkreder and Sarah Baber, March 2, 1837.
Married Thomas B. Alexander and Elizabeth S. Caldwell, April 13, 1837.
Married Thomas Neil and Mary Beard, May 11, 1837.
Married James N. Yandle and Leonner C. Jones, May 19, 1837.
Married Ezekiel A. Cloyd and Louisa Ann Wilson, June 22, 1837.
Married John Eakart and Jane Hays, Dec. 10, 1837.
Married Wm. Melvin and Tabitha P. Gillespie, Jan. 31, 1838.
Married Wm. M. Taylor and C. F. Taylor, April 26. 1838.
Married Thomas N. Cropper and Tirzah Tilford, Aug. 29, 1838.
Married James N. Douglas and Margaret Rodgers, March 8, 1838.
Married Anchrson F. Roach and Margaret M. Alexander, Nov. 6, 1838.
Married Josiah Smith and Sarah A. F. Williamson, Dec. 11, 1838.
Married Benjamin F. Woodrum and Mary A. Rice, May 21, 1840.
Married Lewis Hugley and Zuritha A. Anderson, Sept. 17, 1840.
Married John W. Cloyd and Sarah Wm. Brooks, Nov. 12, 1840.
Married James A. Moore and Elizabeth R. Ballard, Jan. 13, 1841.
Married Felix R. Gleaves and Nancy T. Huggins, Jan. 14, 1841.
Married Pleasant M. Marcum and Nancy Telford, July 1, 1841.
Thomas N. Williamson and Olivia Connell, Sept. 16, 1841.
Married Thomas Fuqua and Nancy McLanglin, Nov. 4, 1841.
Married John E. Hagar and Emiline Ramsay, Aug. 26, 1841.
Married Josiah C. Bernard and Sarah Watkins, Jan. 11, 1842.
Married Mansfield Ferguson and Malvina McCully, March 17, 1842.
Married Isaac G. Barr and Caroline Huddleston, May 12, 1842.
Married Josiah F. Rucks and Celia D. Pool, May 19, 1842.
Married John W. Creach and Nancy Jane Bell, July 7, 1842.
Married Haman M. Robbins and Mary Jane Rea, July 21, 1842.
Married John S. Shacklett and Louisa Foster, Aug. 11, 1842.
Married Wadkins Hamblin and Sarah F. Cloyd, Nov. 3, 1842.
Married Wm. Baker and Mary Jane Wilson, Dec. 8, 1842.
Married Owen Melvin and Hulda Earhart, Feb. 16, 1843.
Making 68 couples I have married in all.
Married David Chandler and Elizabeth C. Hays, March 2, 1843.
Married James H. Cawthon and Ann Patterson, Aug. 10, 1843.
Married Henry R. Thompson and Almeda S. Pride, July 19, 1843.
Married Wm. H. James and Katherine W. Alexander, Sept. 5, 1843.
Married Robert N. Gleaves and Mary T. Baker, April 11, 1844.
Married Thomas Eahart and Minerva A. Pride, Sept. 11, 1844.
Married Jeptha Clemmons and Frances D. Carver, Oct. 2, 1844.
Married Marcus Lafayette Haley and Elizabeth Jane Huggins, Nov. 7, 1844.
Married James M. Carver and Elenor D. Walker, Dec. 17, 1844.
Married Wm. Jackson and Nancy A. Vanderville, Jan. 8, 1845.
Married Wm. H. Goodwin and Harriet F. Wilkison, Feb. 18, 1845.
Married Moses W. Bettes and Elizabeth B. Hope, April 15, 1845.
Married Alexander Buchanan and Margaret M. Mattock, June 5, 1845.
Married Andrew Melvin and Nancy Melvin, Aug. 25, 1845.
Married Thomas P. Wather and Fereby F. W. Smith, Sept. 10, 1845.
Married Alvin Smith and Hannah Hamilton, Dec. 11, 1845.
Married Robert Foster and Nancy Garrison, Dec. 23, 1845.
Married Robert C. Jackson and Mary Baker, Feb. 1, 1846.
Married George Melvin and Hessey Obriant, Feb. 5, 1846.

Married Wm. W. Wright and Mary Baker, July 29, 1846.
Married James Fowlkes and Nancy Elizabeth Wright, April 1, 1846.
Married Wm. Hagar and Mary Caldwell, Nov. 10, 1846.
Married Addison Buchanan and Sarah M. Fleming, March 9, 1847.
Married Wm. F. Jackson and Elizabeth Wilson, June 23, 1847.
Married Alfred Bass and Sally B. Binkley, Aug. 12, 1847.
Married John C. Foster and Mary Donnel, Sept. 16, 1847.
Married Horrace C. Finney and Elizabeth S. Allexander, March 15, 1848.
Married Carson D. Boren and Mary Hays, Feb. 18, 1849.
Married Joseph E. Roach and Louisa Jane Roach, April 1, 1849.
Married Joseph Meek and Nancy Louisa Latimer, Nov. 13, 1849.
Married Alexander Latimer and Julia Meek, Feb. 21, 1850.
Married Lemuel T. High and Salina Reid, May 18, 1851.
Married John J. Rogers and Margaret J. Mahan, April 13, 1853.
Married Jessie C. Mathis and Nancy A. Seybold, June 13, 1854.
Married John C. Neuton and Sarah H. Mahan, Aug. 31, 1854.
Married Simon Berger and Mary Ann Crow, Nov. 1, 1854.
Married John McDimmitt and Emma M. High, May 15, 1856.
Married William Smes and Lavina Weeks, June 30, 1856.
Married Henry B. Burton and Mary E. Leeper, Sept. 25, 1856.
Married Alexander Dobbins and Louisa Crawford, Oct. 9, 1856.
Married William A. Weaver and Margaret High, March 26, 1857.
Married Mr. T. B. Neil and Miss M. E. Hon, State of Missouri, Cap County, May 1, 1860.
Married Henry Smith and Hannah Sophia Cowler, State of Kansas, Brown County, Sept. 29, 1861.
Married William D. Rippey and Eliza J. Huney, Holt County, Mo., June 5, 1862.
Married Thomas McScarren and Mary Ann Sommers, Kansas, June 22, 1862.
Married William T. Yoakum and Caroline P. Mc Cride, Aug. 25, 1863, Kansas, Atchison County.
Married Dr. W. W. Crook and Miss Miranda H. Hirley, May 26, 1864, Kansas, Ackison County.
Married Mr. James R. Pele and Miss Mary J. Lewis, Sept. 15, 1864.
Married Mr. Marion Thompson and Miss Nancy M. Southard, July 9, 1865.
Married Mr. Robert H. Davis and Mrs. Jane Davis, Sept. 19, 1865.
Married Samuel Armstrong and Miss Sarah Brown, Dec. 26, 1865.
Married Daniel S. Southard and Mary E. Dorrell, May 27, 1866.

Family Bible Belonging to Marienne Richardson of Franklin, Tennessee

Copied by Mrs. Joseph Hayes Acklen.

Births

John G. Sims, son of Walter and Rebecca Sims, born April 8, 1792.
Asenath Hightower, daughter of Richard and Ann Hightower, born April 27, 1796.
Walter H. Sims, their son, born Oct. 16, 1815.
John G. Sims, their son, born May 28, 1818.
Ann Hightower Sims, their daughter, born Jan. 24, 1820.
Boyd McNairy Sims, their son, born July 19, 1822.
Sara A. Ewing Sims, wife of Boyd M. Sims, born July 12, 1826.
Thomas D. Wilson, son of James Wilson, born Dec. 7, 1814.
Walter Sims Wilson, son of Thomas D. and Ann H. Sims Wilson, born Oct. 2, 1837, 10 o'clock a.m.
Sallie Cleveland Sims, wife of Walter H. Sims, born April, 1835.

Marriages

Thomas D. Wilson, son of James Wilson, married Ann Hightower

Sims, daughter of John G. and Asenath Sims, Oct. 27, 1830.
Walter Sims, married Rebecca Green.
Elizabeth Sims, married Philip Scudder.
John G. Sims and Asenath Hightower, married Nov. 10, 1814.
Thomas D. Wilson and Ann H Sims, married Oct. 27, 1836.
Boyd McNairy and Ann Hodgkinson, married Sept. 14, 1809, at 7 o'clock p.m., at the Hill, Phil.
Boyd McNairy Sims and Sarah Ann Ewing, married May 11, 1842.
Walter H. Sims and Miss Sallie Cleveland, married Sept. 22, 1853.
Ann Asenath Sims and Thomas D. Wilson, married Oct. 27, 1830.
Boyd McNairy Sims and Miss Sallie Ann Ewing, married May 11, 1842.
Annie A Sims, daughter of Boyd and Sallie A. Sims, married John W. McFadden, June 30, 1875.
Marienne H. Sims, daughter of Boyd and Sallie A. Sims, married Robert Newton Richardson, Dec. 13, 1871.
John C. Sims, son of Walter and Sallie C. Sims, married Mary Wright, Dec. 19, 1878.
Mrs. Sallie A. Sims, widow of Boyd M. Sims, married Joseph W. Carter, May 12, 1852
William Ewing Carter, their son, married Narsissa Cotman, Nov. 14, 1888.
Joseph W. Carter, their son, married Kate French, July, 1878.
Saidee H. McFadden, daughter of John W. and Annie Sims McFadden, married William Andrew Dale, Oct. 23, 1898.
Sallie A. Sims Carter, married Judge John C. Gaut, Feb., 1875.
Thomas Ewing Carter, married Ethel Thomas, Sept. 21, 1917.
Joseph Cotman Carter, married Mary Stewart, Sept 22, 19—.

Births

Walter S. Wilson, son of Thos. C. Wilson and Ann H. Sims Wilson, born Oct. 2, 1837, at 10 o'clock a.m.
The children born to Walter Sims and Rebecca Green Sims were: Walter B. Sims, John Green Sims, David Sims, Elizabeth Sims, and William Poston Sims.
Elizabeth Scudder, daughter (only child) of Elizabeth Sims and Philip Scudder, born ——.
Annie A. Sims, daughter of Boyd and Sallie Sims, born Sept. 18, 1843.
Marieanne Sims, their daughter, born March 17, 1846.
Addie Franklin Sims, their daughter, born Jan. 3, 1849
John G. Sims, son of Walter H. and Sallie C. Sims, born Nov. 24, 1854.
Carrie C. Sims, their daughter, born May 22, 1857.
Jery Cleveland Sims, their son, born April 23, 1859.
William Ewing Carter, son of Joseph W. and Sallie A. Carter, born March 18, 1854.
Narcissa Cotman, wife of Wm. E. Carter, born Dec. 14, 1865
Joseph W. Carter, their son, born Aug. 12, 1856.
Tom Ewing Carter, son of William and Narcissa Carter, born Sept. 1, 1890.
Joseph Cotman Carter, their son born Aug. 14, 1892.
Will Marian Carter, their son, born April 20, 1902.
Mary Wright Sims, wife of John G. Sims, born Jan. 12, 1856.
John G. Sims, Jr., son of John G. and Mary W Sims, born Oct. 31, 1879.
Walter Hightower Sims, their son, born July 12, 1881.
Elizabeth Harper Sims, their daughter, born March 27, 1883.
Jerimiah Cleveland Sims, their son, born Feb. 3, 1885.
M. Rochester Wright Sims, their son, born Dec. 24, 1887.
Carlton C. Sims, their son, born Sept. 30, 1890.
Lucians Stone Sims, their son, born Jan. 15, 1893.
Saidee H. McFadden, daughter of John W. and Annie Sims McFadden, born Jan 5, 1879.
Joseph W. Carter, son of Joseph W. and Kate French Carter, born April 29, 1879.
Mary Clayton Carter, their daughter, born 1881.

John Gaut Carter, their son, born March, 1883.
Willie Ewing Carter, their daughter, born April, 1885.
Horace Richardson Carter, their son, born Aug. 7, 1886.
Elizabeth Carter, their daughter, born 1889.
Sarah Carter, their daughter, born Jan., 1892.
William Andrew Dale, son of William A. and Saidee McFadden Dale, born Oct. 28, 1899.
Ethel Thomas Carter, daughter of Thomas Ewing and Ethel Carter, born Dec. 15, 1918

DEATHS

John Green Sims, died Aug. 22, 1824, in Nashville, Davidson County, Tenn.
Ann H. Wilson, died Nov. 27, 1837, 7 o'clock p.m., in Texas.
Walter Sims, died 1820.
Ann Hightower Wilson, died Nov. 27, 1837, at 7 o'clock p.m., in Texas.
Walter Sims Wilson, died Feb. 24, 1839, at 5 o'clock a.m , in Texas.
Asenath Sims, died Nov. 23, 1839, in Nashville, Tenn.
Jno. G. Sims, Jr., died July 16, 1844, in Nashville, Tenn.
Boyd McNairy Sims, died April 4, 1850, in Williamson County.
Walter H. Sims, died July 2, 1882, in Wartrace, Tenn.
Perry Cleveland Sims, died Sept., 1860, in Wartrace, Tenn.
Addie Franklin Sims, died Dec., 1849, in Williamson County, Tenn.
Sallie Cleveland Sims, died May 19, 1862, in Wartrace, Tenn.
Annie Sims McFadden, died July 19, 1893, in Nashville, Tenn
Joseph W. Carter, Jr., died Aug., 1891, in Nashville, Tenn.
Kate French Carter, died 1892, in Atlanta, Ga.
Mary Clayton Carter, died 1882, in Atlanta, Ga.
John Gant Carter, died 1884, in Atlanta, Ga.
Elizabeth Carter, died 1889, in Nashville, Tenn.
Sarah Carter, died Jan., 1892, in Nashville, Tenn.
Saidee H. McFadden Dale, died Jan. 21, 1900, in Columbia, Tenn.
William Andrew Dale, died April 7, 1900, was laid to rest beside his lovely young mother, Saidee McF. Dale, on Sunday evening in Rose Hill Cemetery, Columbia, Tenn.
John W McFadden, died 1920.
Walter Hightower Sims, son of John G. and Mary Wright Sims, died April 17, 1882.
Elizabeth Harper Sims, daughter of John G. and Mary Wright Sims, died Sept. 30, 1884.
Sallie A. Sims Gaut, died Aug. 21, 1912, in her 86th year, at the home of her daughter, Marienne Richardson.
Robt. Newton Richardson, husband of Marienne Sims, died Nov. 30, 1915, in his 75th year, at their home in Franklin, Tenn.
William E. Carter, died Sept. 25, 1916, at his home in South Pittsburg, Tenn.
Joseph W. Carter, son of Joseph W. and Kate French Carter, died Oct. 7, 1920, at Navy Hospital, Fort Syon, Colo.; was in U. S. Marines sixteen years.
Carrie C. Sims, died in a hospital in Philadelphia, 1925.

MARRIAGE

Horace Richardson Carter and Bessie Post, married Sept. 6, 1916, in Marshall, Texas.

BIRTHS

Horace R. Carter, born in Nashville, Tenn., Aug. 7, 1886.
Bessie Post, his wife, born Aug. 18, 1897.
Katherine Isobell, their daughter, born Aug 14, 1917.
Ewing Marian, their daughter, born Jan. 1, 1920.
Horace R., Jr., their son, born Feb. 23, 1923.
Joe Tyler, their son, born Sept. 12, 1925.

BIBLE OF JOHN BOYD

Bible now in the possession of Mrs. Count Boyd, of Nashville, Tennessee.

These are the children of John Boyd, who came from Fairfax County, Va., with the Donelson Party.

BIRTHS

Milly Boyd, born Jan. 26, 1769.
John Boyd, born Oct. 26, 1771.
Sally Boyd, born Sept. 21, 1773.
John A. Boyd, born Aug. 4, 1775.
Harrison Boyd, born March 24, 1777.
Richard Boyd, born April 15, 1780.
Nancy Boyd, born May 21, 1784.
George W. Boyd, born Feb. 3, 1786.
William L. Boyd, born Jan. 15, 1788.
James R. Boyd, born June 14, 1790.

DEATHS

John Boyd, died April 5, 1805.
Sally Boyd, died May 26, 1803.
John Anderson Boyd, died Jan. 29, 1789.
Milly Boyd, died while on board en route to Nashville with Donelson party, was shot and killed by an Indian, 1778.
A boy, born dead, March 21, 1783.
Irma R. Boyd, died Aug. 16, 1802 (no record of her birth).
Harrison Boyd, died March 1, 1818.

MARRIAGE

George W. Boyd, married Elizabeth Vaughn (have no record of the other marriages).

BIRTHS

Children of George W. and Elizabeth Vaughn Boyd were:
Susan Boyd, born March 20, 1815.
James R. Boyd, born April 14, 1817.
Marisp Boyd and Felix G. Boyd, twins, born Oct. 21, 1819.
G. Washington Boyd, Jr., born May 3, 1821.
Sary Ann Boyd, born Oct. 3, 1822.
William L. Boyd, born Feb. 17, 1825.
Elizabeth Jane Boyd, born June 15, 1828.

DEATHS

James R. Boyd, died Oct. 15, 1819.
Marisp Boyd, died Jan. 28, 1820.
Felix G. Boyd, died June 24, 1820.
George Washington Boyd, Jr., died Sept. 16, 1821.
George Washington Boyd, Sr., died March 1, 1830.
Elizabeth Boyd, died April 19, 1853.
Elizabeth Jane Boyd, died April 13, 1854.

MARRIAGES

Susan Boyd, married Alexander Lowe, Jan. 8, 1831.
Sary Ann Boyd, married Winfield Scatt Watson, March 4, 1841.
William L. Boyd, married Tennessee Coleman, May 7, 1845.

BIRTHS

Children of William L. and Tennessee Coleman Boyd:
Margaret Sarah Cheney Boyd, born Feb. 17, 1846.
George Washington Boyd, born Aug. 25, 1848.
Thomas Boyd, Gilbert Boyd, William L. Boyd.
Count Reynolds Boyd, born June 27, 1857.

DEATHS

Margaret Boyd Fletcher.
George Washington Boyd, died Oct. 6, 1825.
Thomas Boyd, Gilbert Boyd, William L. Boyd.
Count Reynolds Boyd, died May 30, 1900.
Minnie Brainard Boyd, wife of Count Reynolds Boyd, died Nov. 23, 1898.
Mary Wick Boyd, wife of Geo. Washington Boyd, died Oct. 10, 1915.
George W. Boyd, Jr., son of George W. and Mary Wick Boyd, died Feb. 8, 1917.
Tennessee Coleman Boyd, daughter of C. R. and Ninnie Brainard Boyd, died July 6, 1887.

MARRIAGES

Margaret Boyd, married A. A. Fletcher.
George Washington Boyd, married Mary Felicia Wick, 1872.

Count Reynolds Boyd, married Ninnie Salome Brainard, 1883.
Count Reynolds, son of G. W. and Mary Wick Boyd, married Mary Brainard Boyd, 1904.
Count Reynolds Boyd, Jr., married Margaret Odell Spotswood, 1927.

Births

George W. Boyd and Mary Wick Boyd had the following children:
George W. Boyd, Jr., born Sept. 24, 1873.
Count Reynolds Boyd, born May 23, 1879.
Count Reynolds and Ninnie Brainard Boyd had the following children:
Mary Brainard Boyd, born Nov. 13, 1884.
Tennessee Coleman Boyd, born Feb. 28, 1887.
Countess Salome Boyd, born Aug., 1890; died in less than one hour after birth.
Count Reynolds and Mary Brainard Boyd had the following children:
Count Reynolds Boyd, Jr., born May 25, 1905.
Elna Salome Boyd, born Feb. 1, 1910.
Mary Brainard Boyd II., born March 6, 1923.
Count Reynolds, Jr., and Odell Spotswood Boyd have one son:
Count Reynolds Boyd III., born Aug. 5, 1928.

Hinton Records

Births

Jeremiah Hinton, born Feb. 22, 1774.
Elizabeth Hinton, born June 14, 1776.
John I. Hinton, born Aug. 28, 1798.
William M. Hinton, born Dec. 7, 1799.
Elizabeth A. Hinton, born Dec. 7, 1803.
Ninerva Ione Hinton, born —— 1, 1804.
Harrison B. Hinton, born May 7, 1806.
Christopher Hinton, born April, 1808.
Sarah Ann Hinton, born July 22, 1811.
Martha P. Hinton, born April 27, 1804.

Deaths

Minerva Ione Hinton, died May 30, 1805.
Nancy Young, died Dec. 14, 1821.
Jeremiah Hinton, died March 31, 1833.
Sarah Boyd Hinton, died Jan. 25, 1844.
Elizabeth Hinton McGavock, died May 1, 1861.
William M. Hinton, died Aug. 26, 1854.
John J. Hinton, died June 1, 1861.
Sarah Hinton Williamson, died Sept. 2, 1863.
Christopher C. Hinton, died Feb. 10, 1879.

Marriages

William M. Hinton, married July 4, 1820.
John J. Hinton, married March 5, 1822.
Elizabeth A. B. Hinton, married Nov. 6, 1823.
Sarah Ann Hinton, married July 16, 1829.
H. B. Hinton, married July 20, 1831.
Sarah A. Hinton, married Sept. 20, 1849 (married a Tolbot).
C. P. Burton and Ruth G. Tolbot, married Nov. 3, 1853.
John B. Tolbot and E. H. Williamson, married Jan. 24, 1855.
C. R. Mayson and Mary E. Tolbot, married Jan. 25, 1855.

Disconnected Hinton Records

Ruth G. Tolbot, born Aug. 4, 1830.
John B. Tolbot, born May 18, 1832.
Mary Elizabeth Tolbot, born Feb. 5, 1834.
George T. Burton, son of C. R. and R. G. Burton, born Nov. 9, 1854.
Chas. P. Burton, son of C. R. and R. G. Burton, born June 5, 1856.

Bible of Joshua S. Ensey, found in the Curio Shop of C. L. Hooberry, Nashville, Tenn. Copied by Mrs. Acklen.

FATHER

Joshua L. Ensey, his Book, born May 15, 1816, in Virginia, Amhusk County; raised in Tennessee; bought this book Jan. 12, 1851; he is the son of William and Delphy Ensey and the husband of Mary Spray; we married Jan. 3, 1850.

MOTHER

Mary was born June 3, 1820.

BIRTHS

William J. Ensey, son of Joshua L. and Mary Ensey, born Sept. 28, 1850.

James Elijah Ensey, born July 10, 1852.

Benona Robinson Ensey, born Nov. 20, 1854.

Henery P. Pilale Ensey, born Oct. 13, 1856.

Jane Y. Cordely Ensey, born Dec. 17, 1858.

Delpha L. Martha Ensey, born July 10, 1861.

William Gren Ensey, son of W. F. Ensey and Menurvy Ensey, born Feb. 3, 1878.

DEATHS

—— Joshuway Ensey, died Sept. 16, 1868.

Mary Ensey, died Dec. 7, 1890.

Infant daughter of Joshua L. Ensey and Mary Ensey, born Dec. 17, 1853; died Dec. 18, 1853, without name.

BUCHANAN FAMILY BIBLE RECORD

History of the Buchanan Family, written by Henry Buchanan, owned and lent by Mrs. Roy Rascoe, Nashville, Tenn. Copied by Mrs. Acklen.

Capt George Ridley, born near Guilford Court House, N. C., Jan. 11, 1739; married Betsy Weatherford, 1760; married Sally Vincent May 23, 1776. In his first marriage was father of four sons and four daughters, viz: Beverly, John, William and George; Betsy, Patsy, Sallie and Letty; second marriage was father of six sons and two daughters, viz: Vincent, Thomas, Moses, James, Henry and Samuel, and Abbagil and Winneford.

He moved to Nashville in 1780; located three miles south of Nashville on the Fishing Ford Road, now the Nolensville Pike, and remained there till his death, Nov. 29, 1835; age 96 years. He had the coffin in which he was buried made ten years before his death, and kept it in an adjoining room. He was a member of Rev. James Whitsitt's church, located on Mill Creek, and known as Mill Creek Church, which was organized Saturday, April 15, 1797, with a code of profession which has never undergone any change, and to this day has existed 82 years, April 15, 1879.

Maj. John Buchanan I., was born at Harrisburg, Pa, Jan. 12, 1759, and married Margaret Kenedy in 1786, having one son who was born May 15, 1787. After the death of Margaret, his wife, he again married, to Sarah Ridley, the daughter of Capt. Geo. Ridley, in 1791. The celebrated battle against Buchanan's Station was on the night of Sept. 30, 1792. Commencement of firing began at 12 o'clock and lasted two hours. George Buchanan was born eleven days after this memorable battle. The first wedding ever entered into in the City of Nashville, Tenn., was in the summer of 1779, between Cornelius Riddle and Jane Mulherin. Dr. Felix Robertson was the "first born" white child in the City of Nashville, Jan. 11, 1781.

Maj. John Buchanan moved to Nashville, Tenn., Dec., 1778. After a stay of four years he moved to

Mill Creek, four miles from the city, where he lived the remainder of his days. His body now lies interred near his old residence in his family burying ground.
The following records will show the various branches of families eminating from him down to this date, Feb. 22, 1855:
Maj. John Buchanan I's record:

BIRTHS

Maj. John Buchanan I., born Jan. 12, 1759.
Sarah Buchanan I., born Nov. 28, 1774.
John Buchanan II., born May 15, 1787 (first marriage).
George Buchanan, born Oct. 11, 1792.
Alexander Buchanan, born March 22, 1794.
Elizabeth Buchanan, born Dec. 29, 1795.
Samuel Buchanan, born Aug. 27, 1797.
William Buchanan, born Jan. 12, 1800.
Jane Trindle Buchanan, born March 23, 1802.
James Bryant Buchanan, born March 10, 1804.
Moses Ridley Buchanan, born April 4, 1806.
Sarah Vincent Buchanan, born Dec. 31, 1807.
Charles Bingly Buchanan, born Oct. 28, 1809.
Richard Gregory Buchanan, born Nov. 3, 1811.
Henry Ridley Buchanan, born Nov. 8, 1814.
Nancy Mulherin Newman Buchanan, born July 31, 1818.
John Buchanan II. is the son of John and Margaret Buchanan, in his first marriage, the others are of John and Sarah Buchanan.

MARRIAGES

Maj. John Buchanan's record of Marriages:
Maj. John Buchanan and Margaret Kenedy, married 1786.
Maj. John Buchanan and Sarah Ridley, married 1791.
John Buchanan II. and Margaret Sample, married Sept. 19, 1805.
Alex Buchanan and Mary Ridley, married.
Elizabeth Buchanan and Thos. H. Everett, married Nov. 1, 1810.
William Buchanan and Jane E. Hogan, married Dec. 8, 1818.
Jane T. Buchanan and George Goodwin, married Oct. 2, 1817.
Jas. B. Buchanan and Letty Roberts, married May 2, 1827.
Moses R. Buchanan and Sarah V. Ridley, married July 16, 1827.
Sarah V. Buchanan and Jas. B. Williams, married Oct. 21, 1824.
Richard G. Buchanan married Martha A. Murphey.
Nancy M. N. Buchanan and Jackson Smith, married March 7, 1834.
Nancy M. N. Smith and Henry Bridges, married (second marriage), March 1, 1866.

DEATHS

Maj. John Buchanan's record of deaths:
Maj. John Buchanan I., died Nov. 7, 1832.
Sarah Buchanan, died Nov. 23, 1831.
John Buchanan II., died June 29, 1834.
Alx Buchanan, died April 8, 1836.
George Buchanan, died Feb. 22, 1816.
Samuel Buchanan, died Feb. 20, 1816.
William Buchanan, died Jan. 21, 1849.
Jane T. Goodwin, died May 6, 1837.
Chas. B. Buchanan, died April 16, 1836.
James B. Buchanan, died July 6, 1862, Sunday, 5 o'clock a.m.
Sarah V. Williams, died April 10, 1866, Tuesday, 3 o'clock a.m.
Nancy M. N. Bridges, died July 13, 1873, Sunday, 6 o'clock a.m.
Elizabeth Everett, died May 8, 1875, Saturday, 12:40 o'clock p.m.
Richard G. Buchanan, drowned at Memphis, never found.
Moses R. Buchanan, died May 29, 1887, Sunday, 1:45 a.m.

BIRTHS

John Buchanan II's record of births:
John S. Buchanan, born April 6, 1806.

Peggy Ann Buchanan, born Dec. 5, 1807.
William M. Buchanan, born April 20, 1809.
Samuel Buchanan, born Nov. 20, 1810.
Sarah Buchanan, born March 20, 1812.
Elizabeth Buchanan, born Aug. 1, 1815.
Robert S. Buchanan, born Feb. 3, 1818.
Mary B. Buchanan, born July 17, 1820.
Thomas Buchanan, born Jan. 21, 1823.

MARRIAGES

John Buchanan II's record of marriages:
John S. Buchanan, married Elizabeth A. Vaughan, Nov. 1, 1827.
Peggy Ann Buchanan, married Smith Sample, Feb. 24, 1825.
William S. Buchanan, married Susan Everett, Jan. 26, 1832.
Sarah Buchanan, married Daniel J. Sample, 1830.
Sarah Buchanan, married Mr. Stone.
Elizabeth Buchanan, married Rev. Lemuel H. Bethell.
Robert S. Buchanan, married Harriet S. Bateman, Feb. 8, 1838.
Mary B. Buchanan, married Geo. Goodwin.
Thomas Buchanan, married Rebecca J. Shannon, Nov. 5, 1846.

DEATHS

John Buchanan II's record of deaths:
John Buchanan II., died June 29, 1834.
John S. Buchanan.
Samuel Buchanan.
Margaret Buchanan, wife of John Buchanan II, died 1860.
William M. Buchanan, died May 31, 1880.
Robert S. Buchanan.
Elizabeth Bethell.

BIRTHS

Alexander Buchanan's record of births:
Sarah B. Buchanan, born Jan. 31, 1820.
John R. Buchanan, born April 2, 1822.
Jane T. Buchanan, born Oct. 31, 1824.
Mary Ann E. Buchanan, born Sept. 1, 1826.
Elizabeth B. Buchanan, born Feb. 28, 1829.
George Buchanan, born April 2, 1831.
Alx Boosy Buchanan, born May 8, 1833.
Henrietta M. Buchanan, born Aug. 12, 1835.

MARRIAGES

Alexander Buchanan's record of marriages:
Sarah B. Buchanan and Anderson B. Joice, married Oct. 3, 1840.
Jane T. Buchanan and Rev. Tom W. Haynes, married Nov. 3, 1840.
Elizabeth B. Buchanan and Dr. Chas. T. Love, married Sept. 12, 1848.
John R. Buchanan and Nancy E. Hays, married Oct. 31.
Alx Boosy Buchanan and Louisa A. Buchanan, married July 13, 1854.
Henretta M. Buchanan and Thos. Shilcut, married Feb. 14, 1858.
Mary Ann E. Buchanan and Alfred Green, married July 21, 1842.
George Buchanan and Ann Patterson, married Nov. 21, 1855.
Mary T. Buchanan (Alx's widow), married Everett Owen.

DEATHS

Alexander Buchanan's record of deaths:
Jane T. Haynes, died July 27, 1843.
Sarah B. Joyce, died July 21, 1845.
John R. Buchanan parted with his wife and left this country in 1854.
Mary T. Owen, formerly the wife of Alx Buchanan, died Sept. 27, 1845.
Ann Green, died 1877.
Henretta Shilcut.
Mary Ann E. Green.

BIRTHS

Elizabeth Everett's record of births:
Sarah B. Everett, born Aug. 7, 1811.
Susan Everett, born Aug. 19, 1813.
Elizabeth Everett, born Oct. 18, 1815.

Nancy Mulherin Everett, born Nov. 28, 1817.
Evelina Jane Everett, born Sept. 8, 1819.
John Buchanan Everett, born Sept. 21, 1821.
Mary M. Everett, born Aug. 12, 1823.
Lydia Ridley Everett, born May 27, 1825.
Geo. Washington Everett, born April 7, 1827.
Benj. Franklin Everett, born April 7, 1827.
Thomas H. Everett II., born June 19, 1829.
Zipporah Everett, born July 9, 1831.
Amanda M. F. Everett, born Sept. 19, 1835.
Josaphine Green Everett, born Jan. 19, 1838.
Musadora Ellen Everett, born April 25, 1840.
Ephraim Foster Everett, born Feb. 5, 1834.

MARRIAGES

Sarah B. Everett and Hance H. Ridley, married June 9, 1830.
Susan Everett and William M. Buchanan, married Jan. 26, 1832.
Elizabeth Everett and Lewis Lindsay, married June 27, 1841.
Nancy M. Everett and William S. Perry, married Nov. 14, 1843.
Mary M. Everett and Richard D. Harwood, married Dec. 20, 1842.
John B. Everett and Elizabeth M. Hunt, married Jan. 21, 1846.
Evelina J. Everett and Elmo G. Rowe, married May 27, 1849.
Benj. F. Everett and Mary Jane Jetton, married May 6, 1852.
Josaphine G. Everett and Jno. W. Murray, married Feb. 16, 1854.
Ephraim F. Everett and Ellen J. Douglas, married Nov. 17, 1857.
Lydia R. Everett and Jas. A. Harwood, married Feb. 2, 1858.
Amanda M. Everett and James S. Cannon, married June 18, 1868.
Musadora Ellen Everett and Cephas Harwood, married Oct. 1, 1872.
Geo. W. Everett and Lavenia Hillsman, married Nov. 30, 1870.
Geo. W. Everett and Bettie Thomas married May 13, 1880.

DEATHS

Elizabeth Everett's record of deaths:
Sarah B. Ridley, died Sept. 17, 1834.
Thos. H. Everett II., died July 20, 1835.
Thos. H. Everett I., died March 29, 1854, at 8:10 o'clock a.m.
Benj. F. Everett was wounded at the Battle of Franklin Nov. 30, 1864, and died Dec. 2, 1864.
Elizabeth Everett, Sr., died May 8, 1875, Saturday at 12:40 o'clock p.m.
Nancy M. Perry, died May 5, 1875, at 1:42 p.m.
Lavenia Everett, Dr. G. W. Everett's first wife and daughter of Rev. Mat Hillsman.
Dr. Geo. W. Everett, died Jan. 11, 1889, at 6:10 p.m.
Susan Buchanan, died April 12, 1892.
Elizabeth Lindsay, died Feb. 23, 1893, at 3 p.m.
Zipporah Everett, died Aug. 28, 1893, at 2:45 a.m.
Eva G. Rowe, died May 17, 1911.
Lydia R. Harwood, died June 7, 1911.
Ellen M. Harwood, died Aug. 7, 1912.
Ephraim F. Everett, died Oct., 1909.

FAMILY RECORD

William Buchanan's family record:

BIRTHS

Alexander Buchanan, born Oct. 25, 1819.
Jno Anthony Buchanan, born Dec. 17, 1820.

DEATHS

Alexander, died March 16, 1820.

MARRIAGES

Jane T. Goodwin's record of marriages:
Mary Ann Goodwin and Green Berry Goodwin.
George B. Goodwin and Martha Barns.
Wm. W. Goodwin and Harriet F. Wilkerson, Feb. 18, 1845 (first marriage).
Jno. B. Goodwin and Theodocia Thompson, Feb. 19, 1845.

Jno. B. Goodwin and Sarah Ann Mabry, March 21, 1860 (second marriage).
Wm. H. Goodwin and Mrs. Patterson, July 6, 1868 (second marriage).

DEATH

Jane T. Goodwin's record of death:
Geo. Goodwin, Jane's husband, died Nov. 1, 1836.

JAMES B. BUCHANAN RECORD OF BIRTHS

Alexander Buchanan, March 7, 1828.
Mary Jane Buchanan, July 22, 1829.
Sally Buchanan, Jan. 8, 1831.
Nancy M. N. Buchanan, Aug. 7, 1836.
Jno. Henry Buchanan, Feb. 1, 1833.
Caroline E. L. Buchanan, Oct. 31, 1838.
Adah Buchanan, Dec. 25, 1842.
Jas. Buchanan II., Jan. 1, 1844.
Geo. W. Buchanan, July 10, 1850.
Margaret Buchanan, 1840.
Letty Buchanan (Jas. B.'s wife), Sept. 27, 1804.

MARRIAGES

James B. Buchanan's record of marriages:
Alexander Buchanan and Louisa East, March 16, 1853.
Nancy M. N. Buchanan and Felix G. Ross, Sept. 7, 1853.
Jno. H. Buchanan and Margaret Petway, April 11, 1855.
Caroline E. L. Buchanan and Jno. A. Ewing, July 8, 1856.
James Buchanan II. and Corah Duncan.
Caroline E. L. Ewing and Hays Buchanan (second marriage).
Adah Buchanan and Andrew Payne.

DEATHS

James B. Buchanan's record of deaths:
Mary Jane Buchanan, Sept. 8, 1838.
Margaret Buchanan, 1840.
Sally Buchanan.
James B. Buchanan, Sunday, July 6, 1862, at 5 a.m.
Letty Buchanan, Wednesday, April 4, 1866, at 6 p.m.
Nancy Ross.

BIRTHS

Moses R. Buchanan's record of births:
Sarah Ann Buchanan, July 22, 1828.
Mary Jane Buchanan, Aug. 30, 1830.
James Ridley Buchanan, Dec. 21, 1831.
Elizabeth C. Buchanan, Feb. 20, 1834.
Jno. Alx. Buchanan, Dec. 16, 1835.
Catharine Buchanan, Sept. 7, 1837.
Tennessee Louisa Buchanan, Jan. 22, 1839.
Geo. T. R. C. Buchanan, Aug. 30, 1841.
Samuel Jones R. Buchanan, Feb. 21, 1843.
Moses R. Buchanan, May 1, 1845.
Hance H. R. Buchanan, April 1, 1847.
Henri Sarah O. Buchanan, June 20, 1849.
Nancy A. S. Buchanan, April 26, 1852.
Virginia Loftin Buchanan, Nov. 29, 1854.

MARRIAGES

Moses R. Buchanan's record of marriages:
Sarah Ann Buchanan and Thos. J. Mabry, Aug. 30, 1846 (first marriage).
Mary Jane Buchanan and Timothy D. Sample, Aug. 30, 1846.
Tennessee L. Buchanan and Robert R. Coldwell, April 3, 1856.
Catherine E. Buchanan and Jas. M. Mitchell, Sept. 7, 1857.
Sarah Ann Mabry and Jno. B. Goodwin, March 21, 1860 (second marriage).
Jno. Alx. Buchanan and Micky Ann Ridley March 21, 1860.
Geo. T. R. C. Buchanan and Sally Gooch.
Saml. J. Buchanan and Dorah Duncan.
Moses R. Buchanan, Jr., and Minnie Vestell.
Henri S. O. Buchanan and Robert Mullen.
Nancy A. S. Buchanan and Andrew Vaughan.
Virginia Loftin Buchanan and William Vaughn, May 19, 1881.

DEATH

Moses R. Buchanan's record of death:
Moses R. Buchanan, died in Williamson, Tenn., at Andrew Vaughn's, Monday, May 30, 1887.

BIRTHS

Sarah V. Williams' record of births:
Amanda M. Williams, Aug. 23, 1825.
Augustus H. Williams, Oct. 18, 1826.
Amanda M. F. Williams, March 21, 1828.
Eugene B. Williams, Dec. 16, 1829.
Hortense B. Williams, May 12, 1831.
Sidney A. Williams, April 7, 1833.
Araminta D. Williams, Jan. 5, 1835.
Oscar F. Williams, Aug. 10, 1836.
Victoria Williams, Aug. 27, 1840.
Alexena Williams, March 25, 1842.
Mortimer Williams, Sept. 17, 1843.
Victoria B. Williams, March 8, 1846.
Estella Williams, June 9, 1851.

MARRIAGES

Sarah V. Williams' record of marriages:
Augustus H. Williams and Caroline Wright.
Alexena Williams and Wallace Evans.
Mortimer Williams and Syntha Jerman.
A. M. F. Williams and Hilas Traylor.

DEATHS

Sarah V. Williams' record of deaths:
Amanda Williams, April 15, 1827.
Victoria Williams, Sept. 19, 1844.
Eugene B. Williams, June 15, 1853.
Sidney A. Williams, Jan. 19, 1855.
Sarah V. Williams, April 10, 1866, Tuesday, 3 p.m.
Estella Williams, 1888.
Alexena Evans.

BIRTHS

Richard G. Buchanan's record of births:
Louisa Buchanan, Ellen Buchanan, Leonidas Buchanan.

MARRIAGES

Richard G. Buchanan's record of marriages:
Louisa and Alx. B. Buchanan.
Ellen and Charles Walden.

BIRTHS

Nancy M. N. Smith's record of births:
Jno. Charles Smith, Dec. 5, 1834.
Wm. Madison Smith, Aug. 30, 1836.
Jas. Buchanan Smith, March 25, 1838.
Francisco Templemore Smith, Sept. 30, 1839.
Ann Lettitia Jane Smith, May 22, 1841.
Bartholenew Jackson Smith, July 21, 1843.
Wm. Brown Smith, April 5, 1845.
Sarah Elizabeth Smith, June 21, 1846.
Mary Louise Melville Smith, June 21, 1846.
Jackson Woods Smith, Feb. 5, 1848.
Jno. L. Smith, March 3, 1854.
Thomas E. Smith, Feb. 20, 1856.

FAMILY RECORD

Jackson Wood Smith's family record:
Fannie Mable Smith, born Sept. 26, 1872.
Lillian Claire Smith, born Dec. 15, 1874.
Maggie Warmuth Smith, born April 24, 1877.
Jackson Watkins Smith, born Nov. 7, 1881.

MARRIAGES

James B. Smith and Martha Davis, Dec. 17, 1856.
Ann L. J. Smith and Thomas Beaty, Feb. 14, 1860.
Nancy N. M. B. Smith and Henry Bridges, March 1, 1866.
Jack Wood Smith and Watkin Vorters, Feb. 7, 1871.
Thos. E. Smith and Jennie Vorters.

DEATHS

Nancy M. N. Smith's record of deaths:
Jno. Charles Smith, Sept. 20, 1835.
Wm. Madison Smith, Sept. 30, 1837.

Francisco Templemore Smith, June 9, 1842.
Sarah Elizabeth Smith, June 24, 1846.
Mary Louise Melville Smith, June 27, 1847.
Jackson Smith, Sr., Feb. 17, 1861.
Bartholemew Jackson Smith, Sept. 21, 1861, in the army.
William Brown Smith, Oct. 21, 1861, in the army.
James Buchanan Smith, in the army.

BIRTHS

John S. Buchanan III's, son of John II, record of births:
John Buchanan, 1828.
William S. Buchanan, Nov. 1, 1830.
Mary M. Buchanan, March 27, 1832.
Thomas Buchanan, Nov. 30, 1833.
John Henry Buchanan, June 12, 1835.

MARRIAGES

John S. Buchanan III's, son of John S. Buchanan II, record of marriages:
Mary M. Buchanan and W. Fields.
Jno. Henry Buchanan and L. Goodwin.

DEATHS

John S. Buchanan III's, son of John II, record of deaths:
John Buchanan, 1832.
William S. Buchanan, killed.

BIRTHS

Peggy Ann Sample's, daughter of John II, record of births:
John B. Sample, April 17, 1826.
Sarah Ann E. Sample, Aug. 17, 1828.
Daniel J. Sample, April 26, 1830.
Margaret B. Sample, Aug. 23, 1832.
Susan J. Sample, Nov. 21, 1834.
Thornton S. Sample, Sept. 21, 1836.
Missouri E. Sample, Nov. 19, 1839.
Mary M. Sample, April 9, 1842.
Calodonia R. Sample, Dec. 7, 1844.

MARRIAGES

Peggy Ann Sample's, daughter of John II, record of marriages:
Sarah Ann E. Sample and H. Lester, Nov. 13, 1845.
Margaret B. Sample and Jno. Turner.
Susan J. Sample and Alfred Rutherford.
Missouri E. Sample and George Shannon, Dec. 19, 1859.
Mary W. Sample and Orville Watkins.
Danl. Sample.

DEATH

Peggy Ann Sample's, daughter of John II, record of deaths:
Thornton S. Sample, died July 24, 1851.

BIRTHS

William M. Buchanan's, son of John II, record of births:
Thos. Everett Buchanan, March 31, 1833.
Sarah E. Buchanan, Jan. 31, 1835.
Margaret Buchanan, July 22, 1837.
Mary Jane Buchanan, Sept. 18, 1839.
William Henry Buchanan, Oct. 24, 1841.
Evelina F. Buchanan, May 23, 1844.
John E. Buchanan, Jan. 23, 1846.
George F. Buchanan, Aug. 24, 1848.
Ephraim E. Buchanan, July 22, 1851.
Charles B. Buchanan, Nov. 5, 1853.
Susan Buchanan, July 23, 1856.

MARRIAGES

William M. Buchanan's, son of John II, record of marriages:
Sarah E. Buchanan and John E. Hill, April 3, 1851.
Thomas E. Buchanan and Susan Goodwin, March, 1856.
Margaret Buchanan and Robert Harvy, Oct., 1859.
Mary Jane Buchanan and Jno. W. Harvy, Oct. 28, 1860.
William Henry Buchanan and Louisa J. Buchanan.
Margaret Harvy and Lafayett Mason (second marriage).
John Buchanan and Mary Harvy.
George F. Buchanan and Elizabeth German.
Evelina F. Buchanan and Dr. —— Winstead, Nov. 4, 1885.

DEATHS

William M. Buchanan's, son of John II, record of deaths:

Susan Buchanan, Jr.; Ephraim E. Buchanan; Sarah E. Hill.
William Henry Buchanan, Sr., May, 1879.
William M. Buchanan, Sr., May 31, 1880.
Mrs. Susan Buchanan, April 12, 1892.

MARRIAGES

Elizabeth Bethell's, daughter of John II, record of marriages:
Palmyra Bethell and Dr. Conner.
Mary Bethell and Jno. Eagleton.
Margaret Bethell and Dr. Tatum.
Indiana Bethell and Jno. Covington.
Lydia Bethell and James Kennedy.
Tom Bethell and Mortimore M'Knight.
Tennessee Bethell and Jno. Rushing.

BIRTHS

Robert S. Buchanan's, son of John II, record of births.
John Buchanan, Nov. 24, 1838.
Enoch B. Buchanan, Aug. 9, 1840.
Thomas Buchanan, Oct. 8, 1842.
Robert S. Buchanan, Oct. 13, 1844.
William Henry Buchanan, Nov. 5, 1846.
Margaret Ann Buchanan, Dec. 23, 1847.
Daniel B. C. Buchanan, Dec. 25, 1849.
Martha V. Buchanan, Dec. 23, 1851.
Elizabeth Buchanan, Oct. 8, 1853.

DEATHS

Robert S. Buchanan's, son of John II, deaths:
William Henry Buchanan, 1846.
At this page, on a loose sheet, are the following names:

DEATHS

Mrs. Era G. Rowe, May 17, 1911.
Mrs. Lydia Harwood, June 7, 1911.
Mrs. Ellen M. Harwood, Aug. 7, 1912.
Cephas Harwood, Sept. 20, 1912.

BIRTHS

Mary B. Goodwin's record of births:
Susan Goodwin, Louisa Goodwin, Elizabeth Goodwin.

MARRIAGES

Mary B. Goodwin's record of marriages:
Susan Goodwin and Thomas E. Buchanan.
Louisa Goodwin and (1) John H. Buchanan; (2) William H. Buchanan.
Elizabeth Goodwin and (1) Ivy; (2) Wade; (3) Wilson.

BIRTHS

Thomas Buchanan's, son of John II, record of births:
John P. Buchanan, Oct. 24, 1847.
Mary Margaret Buchanan, July 20, 1849.
Susan Ann Buchanan, Sept. 12, 1851.
Sarah Buchanan.
John Price Buchanan was Governor of Tennessee, 1891 and 1892.

DEATH

Thomas Buchanan's, son of John II, record of death:
Sarah Buchanan.

BIRTHS

Sarah B. Ridley's, daughter of Elizabeth Everett, record of births:
S. Ann Elizabeth Ridley, Jan. 9, 1832.
Evelina Jane Ridley, Jan. 18, 1834.

MARRIAGES

S. Ann Elizabeth Ridley and John Fitzgerald, Jan. 27, 1852.
Evelina Jane Ridley and Charles Currin, Feb. 1, 1855.

DEATH

Evelina J. Currin, Dec. 15, 1883.

BIRTHS

Elizabeth Lindsay,'s daughter of Elizabeth Everett, record of births:
Rev. Lewis Lindsay, Sr., Dec. 6, 1806.
Thomas H. Lindsay, June 9, 1842.
Benj. F. Lindsay, Sept. 1, 1843.
George W. Lindsay, Oct. 21, 1845.
Evelina Jane E. Lindsay, May 27, 1848.
Zipporah E. S. Lindsay, Dec. 24, 1853.

DEATHS

Thomas H. Lindsay, Sept. 17, 1842.
Evelina J. E. Lindsay, June 1, 1852.
Benj. F. Lindsay, Sept. 23, 1863, in Confederate Army.

Rev. Lewis Lindsay, Sr., Aug. 5, 1877.
Elizabeth Lindsay, Sr., Feb. 23, 1893.

BIRTHS

Nancy M. Perry's, daughter of Elizabeth Everett, record of births:
Thomas H. Perry, Aug. 29, 1844.
William L. Perry, Jan. 15, 1847.
Elizabeth C. Perry, July 16, 1848.
Evelina J. Perry, May 24, 1851.
Charles Perry, Edward Everett Perry.

MARRIAGE

E. J. Perry and Dr. M. D. L. F. Jordan.

DEATHS

Thomas H. Perry, Dec. 20, 1844.
William L. Perry, Feb. 15, 1847.

BIRTHS

Mary M. Harwood's, daughter of Elizabeth Everett, record of births:
Richard D. Harwood, Sr., April 17, 1817.
James Harvy Harwood, June 5, 1845.
Sarah E. A. Harwood, Aug. 8, 1847.
Lydia E. Harwood, Oct. 28, 1849.
Thomas E. Harwood, Aug. 5, 1852.
Emma Harwood, Feb. 7, 1855.
Richard D. Harwood, Aug. 31, 1857.
Everett Harwood, April 8, 1860.
Josephine Harwood, Aug. 11, 1862.
Benjamin Frankland Harwood, April 7, 1865.
Infant son, born Nov. 5, 1843; died Nov. 10, 1843.

BIRTHS

Benj. F. Everett's, son of Elizabeth Everett, record of births:
Henry Buchanan Everett, May 30, 1853, 11 a.m.
Olivia Everett.
Geo. Washington Everett.

DEATHS

B. F. Everett's record of deaths:
B. F. Everett was wounded Nov. 30, 1864, in the Battle at Franklin, Tenn., and died Dec. 2, 1864.
Henry B. Everett, Olivia Everett.

BIRTHS

Lydia R. Harwood's, daughter of Elizabeth Everett, record of births:
Ephraim Harwood, born July 29, 1861; died July 1, 1880.

BIRTHS

Ephraim F. Everett's, son of Elizabeth Everett, record of births:
Douglas Everett, Feb. 15, 1859.
Thomas H. Everett, Dec. 14, 1860.

BIRTHS

Josephine G. Murray's, daughter of Elizabeth Everett, record of births:
Jno. W. Murray, Nov. 10, 1828.
Cora Ella Murray, Jan. 3, 1856.
Eugene Murray, Dec. 30, 1859.
Fanny Wilson Murray, Dec. 1, 1863.
Glenn Murray, April 8, 1866.
Hugh Murray, Aug. 31, 1868.

DEATH

Cora Ella Murray, Thursday night, Oct. 15, 1857, 10 o'clock.

BIRTHS

Sarah Ann Elizabeth Fitzgerald's, granddaughter of Elizabeth Everett, record of births:
Charles Houston Fitzgerald, March 15, 1853.
Martha Ann Fitzgerald, March 8, 1855.

FAMILY RECORD

Evelina Jane Currin, granddaughter of Elizabeth Everett.
Thomas E. Buchanan, son of William M. Buchanan and grandson of John Buchanan II, also grandson of Elizabeth Everett, his parents being cousins.

MARRIAGE

Thomas E. Buchanan and Susan Goodwin, March, 1856.

BIRTHS

Sarah Elizabeth Hill's, daughter of William M. Buchanan, record of births:
William Hill, John Hill, Mary Hill, Thomas Hill.

MARRIAGES

Mary Hill and Perkins Hide.
William Hill.
John Hill and Fanny Carothers.

DEATH

Thomas Hill.

BIRTHS

Margaret Harvy's, daughter of W. M. Buchanan, record of births:
Susan Harvy, William Harvy.

DEATH

Susan Harvy.

BIRTHS

Mary Jane Harvy's, daughter of W. M. Buchanan, record of births:
Robert Hester Harvy.

William Henry Buchanan, son of Wm. M. Buchanan.
Sarah Ann E. Lester's, daughter of Peggy Ann Sample, record of births:
Henry Smith Lester, Nov. 11, 1846.
John S. Lester, July 3, 1849.
William W. Lester, July 29, 1851.

BIRTHS

Mary Ann Goodwin's, daughter of Jane T. Goodwin, record of births:
Susan Goodwin, Louise Goodwin, Elizabeth Goodwin.

George B. Goodwin, son of Jane T. Goodwin.
Sarah B. Morton, daughter of Jane T. Goodwin.
William K. Goodwin, son of Jane T. Goodwin.

BIRTHS

Sarah Jane Trindle Goodwin, Oct. 4, 1850.
George M. Goodwin, July 23, 1852.
Lydia Ann, June 30, 1854.

BIRTHS

John B. Goodwin's, son of Jane T. Goodwin, and Leodocia's children:
Mary Jane Trindle Goodwin, April 2, 1847.
Sarah Ann Elizabeth Goodwin, April 5, 1849.
Margaret Letticia Goodwin, May 28, 1850.
George Moses Goodwin, July 7, 1852.
Tennessee Louisa Goodwin, Feb. 25, 1854.
Corah Morton Goodwin, Aug. 20, 1855.
Baby without name, April 30, 1857.
Catharine Theodocia, June 18, 1858.
The above are children of the first marriage.
Sarah Ann's children:
John B. Goodwin II, 1861 (by second marriage).
Henry Morgan, Robert Lee, William Hughes, Jo Davis.

DEATHS

Theodocia Goodwin, John's first wife, died Oct. 25, 1859.
Mary Jane Trindle Goodwin, 186—.
Corah Morton Goodwin, Aug. 6, 1856.
Baby without name, May 6, 1857.

BIRTHS

Mary A. E. Green's, daughter of Alx. Buchanan, record of births:
Medora Green, Alexander Green, Cornelia Green, Sherwood Green.

BIRTHS

Elizabeth B. Love's, daughter of Alx. Buchanan, record of births:
Alonzo Francisco Love, July 11, 1849.
Landon B. Love, Jan. 26, 1851.
Oscar May Green Love, May 23, 1852.
Emma E. Love, April 23, 1854.
Temple E. Love, March 21, 1857.
Charles Y. Love and Elizabeth B. Love, twins, born April 9, 1859; both died June 29, 1861.
Brodie E. Love, March 15, 1862.
Jennie Love, Nov. 26, 1864.

John R. Buchanan, son of Alx. Buchanan.
Sarah P. Joice, daughter of Alx. Buchanan.
Jane T. Haines', daughter of Alx. Buchanan, record of birth:
Mary Jane Haines II, born Dec. 2, 1842.

Alexander Boose Buchanan, son of Alx. Buchanan.
"Old Grandfather" (Capt. George Ridley) was born in Virginia, according to his traditional account, about the year 1739. He died Nov. 29, 1835, and in count was 96 years of age, but his wife and children contended that he had lost eleven years in his count during a severe spell of sickness and if they are correct, the old sire must have been

108 years old at his death and consequently born about 1727.
He was married twice, first to Elizabeth Weatherford, and had four sons and four daughters:

BIRTHS

Beverly Ridley, July 23, 1762.
George Ridley, Jan. 11, 1764.
John Ridley, June 5, 1765.
William Ridley, Feb. 2, 1767.
Patsy Ridley, March 13, 1770.
Betsy Ridley, Feb. 13, 1772.
Sally Ridley, Nov. 28, 1773.
Letty Ridley, Nov. 24, 1776.
His second marriage was to Sally Vincent, who had six sons and two daughters:
Vincent Ridley, June 26, 1778.
Thomas Ridley, Feb. 16, 1780.
Moses Ridley June 6, 1782.
James Ridley, May 24, 1784.
Abby Ridley, April 26, 1786.
Winney Ridley, Feb. 7, 1789.
Samuel Jones Ridley, Oct. 1, 1791.
Henry Ridley, May 29, 1794.

Elizabeth Weatherford's birth, marriage and death are unknown.
Sally Vincent, second wife, was born May 23, 1754; died March 20, 1836.
Some of his children claim his birth place was in Virginia, and he claimed Guilford Court House in North Carolina as his place of birth.
Mary Jane Buchanan, daughter of William M. and Susan Buchanan, married Jno. W. Harvey, Jr., Oct. 28, 1860, with the following list of children.
Robert H. Harvey, dead; Susan E. Harvey; Susan Harvey, dead; S. Mildred Harvey; John Bunyan Harvey, dead; Nancy Evey Harvey; Mary M. Harvey; Willie May Harvey; Andrew B. Harvey; Lillian Harvey; William M. B. Harvey, dead; Thomas E. Harvey.
H. Mortimer Williams, the son of Sarah V. Williams, was born Sept. 17, 1843, and married Cynthia C. German, with the following list of children:
Sallie Emma Williams, born July 17, 1869.
Lizzie McEwan Williams, born June 19, 1871.
Mary Estell Williams, born Feb. 19, 1873.
Carrie Augusta Williams, born Aug. 24, 1874.
Infant, born Nov. 1, 1876; died Nov. 3.
Oscar F. Williams, born Jan. 9, 1878.
Eugenia Williams, born June 2, 1880.
Minnie Myrtle Williams, born Sept. 16, 1882.
Agness Gertrude Williams, born Dec. 20, 1884.
John B. Everett was born Sept. 21, 1821, and married Elizabeth M. Hunt, Jan. 21, 1846, with the following list of children:
Thomas Hunt Everett, Tuesday, Dec. 1, 1846.
William Francis Everett, Friday, Dec. 7, 1849.
John Buchanan Everett, Monday, Dec. 9, 1850.
Emma Everett, Wednesday, March 15, 1854.
Charles Henry, Thursday, July 5, 1855.
Infant girl, Tuesday, May 5, 1857.
Frank Everett, Thursday, April 1, 1858.
Edward Topp Everett, Friday, Sept. 23, 1859.
Infant girl, Wednesday, Dec. 18, 1861.
Martha Elizabeth Everett, Friday, Oct. 17, 1862.
Henry Sheffield Everett, Sunday, May 20, 1866.
George Everett, Monday, Feb. 17, 1868.
Infant girl, Tuesday, Dec. 10, 1872.
Thomas H. Hunt Everett married Mary Newson with the following list of children:

BIRTHS

John B. Everett II, Sunday, Nov. 25, 1876.
Albert Dake Everett, May 19, 1881.
Earnest Everett, March 18, 1883.

DEATHS

William Francis Everett, Jan. 30, 1850.
John Buchanan Everett, March 15, 1857.

Emma Everett, Oct. 1, 1854.
Charles Henry Everett, Sept. 1, 1892.
Infant girl, May 5, 1857.
Frank Everett, June 4, 1858.
Edward Topp Everett, Nov. 25, 1864.
Infant girl, Dec. 18, 1861.
Martha Elizabeth Everett, June 8, 1865.
George Everett, July 1, 1868.
Infant girl, Dec. 10, 1872.
Rev. George Vincent Ridley, son of Col. Moses Ridley, residence in Warrensburg, Mo., married Miss Emma Cannon, with the following list of children:
Mary Kate Ridley married Mr. Baker of Kansas and is the mother of several children.
Louisa Ridley, married Mr. Ward, Kansas City, and is the mother of four children.
Almira Ridley, married Mr. Jo Stewart, Warrensburg, Mo.
Joanna Ridley, married Mr. Barr.
Cyrus Ridley, Warrensburg, Mo.
Rev. Geo. W. Ridley, died in Kansas City, Oct. 21, 1892.

Additional data on Buchanan family in a record book kept by H. R. Buchanan.

From family Bibles owned by Miss Fannie Blackman Batey, Rutherford County, Tenn.

Miss Evelina Buchanan, married Dr. Winstead of Williamson County, Nov. 4, 1885, at her brother-in-law's, Jno. W. Harvey.
Mrs. Evelina "Puss" Curran, died Dec. 15, 1883.
Miss Lizzie Cannon and Hick Davis, married Oct. 26, 1886.
Miss May Jordan and Earnest Dixon, married Jan. 7, 1890, and on May 21, 1891, their first baby came in excellent order to gladden the heart of his grandfather, Dr. M. D. L. Jordan.
George Buchanan and the young widow, Mrs. Rosanna Stephens, married; she then had one small son, Dec. 4, 1889.
Mrs. Blanche Brower, daughter of Mrs. Jacky Ann Roberts, died Sept. 22, 1888, leaving her infant girl only 3 hours old; 19 months afterwards it took its flight heavenward to join its mother.
Mrs. Corrah Ingram, the daughter of Thomas and Susan Buchanan of Gibson County, Tenn., died Dec. 28, 1888, and William (familiarly called him Billy) died in June following his mother; he was 12 years old.
W. M. Fuqua, married Bettie Gleaves, daughter of Jno. Bell Gleaves, March 20, 1889.
Mrs. Molly Buchanan (Johnnie's wife,) died Sunday evening at 4 o'clock at her home in Franklin, Tenn., Jan. 26, 1890.
William D. Baker, Esq., died at Watertown, in Wilson County, at his son's, Dr. Howell Baker, Jan. 28, 1890.
Mrs. Ida Donnell, daughter of Jack Bond, died Feb. 11, 1892; May 22, 1891, gave birth to a son, who died some days before its mother.
Gussie Shaw and Robert Rucker, married April 24, 1890.
Miss Mattie Bond, Jack Bond's daughter, married, June 14, 1893, a widower with three children; his name is ——— Seldon.
Elmore C. Rowe took to his bed Saturday, May 24, 1890, and died Aug. 1, 1890.
Mrs. Bettie Roop, died April 7, 1891; her little baby died May 17, 1891.
Henry Evans, died June 24, 1891.
Sammie Caldwall and Thomas T. Parkes, married Nov. 4, 1890.
Tuesday, March 15, 1892, fell a big snow and on Wednesday night another, 18 inches deep in the street.
Miss Eva Bowman and Jack Greer, married Sunday morning, April 10, 1892.
George Valkenburg, died Aug. 13, 1891.
Mrs. James K. Polk, died Aug. 14, 1891.
Mrs. Harriet Jenkins, died April 16, 1893.
Mrs. Susan Buchanan, died at her son-in-law's, J. W. Harvey, resi-

dence, April 12, 1892; she was aged 78 years 7 months 24 days.

Mrs. Elizabeth Lindsay, died at Leeville, Wilson County, Tenn., at the house of her daughter, Mrs. E. Z. Pendleton, Feb. 23, 1893, and was buried in the graveyard at Leeville. Her grandfather, Maj. Jno. Buchanan, years ago, gave the ground for a church, school house and a public burying ground.

Harry Everett (Ephraim's son), died Tuesday, March 14, 1893, at his father's home near Columbia. Harry was in his 23rd year.

Mrs. Mary Hyde, Perk Hyde's wife, Jno. and Liz. Hill's daughter and granddaughter of William M. and Susan Buchanan, died July 12, 1893.

Mrs. Micha Buchanan, Jno. R. Buchanan's wife, died Jan. 9, 1891.

Frank Parks, died Friday night, Feb. 25, 1892.

Dr. M. D. L. Jordan moved to Nashville from Milan, June 10, 1890.

Mrs. Gardner, mother of Rev. C. H. Gardner, died in Knoxville, buried in Mt. Olivet, Jan. 28, 1892; she died at the residence of her son-in-law, Rev. Mr. Grace.

"Old" Aunt Betty Roby, died July 2, 1892, in her 73rd year.

"Old" Aunt Clark, died March 10, 1893; on July 11 she would have been 85 years of age.

From Family Bibles owned by Miss Fannie Blackman Batey, Rutherford County. Copied by Miss Batey; sent by Miss Jetton.

John Buchanan I, married Jane Trindle Russell. To this union 4 sons were born:

Samuel Buchanan, John Buchanan, Andrew Buchanan, James Buchanan.

Maj. John Buchanan, born Jan. 12, 1759; died Nov. 6, 1832; married first to Margaret Kennedy. John III was the only child born to this union. He married second to Sarah Ridley, born Nov. 24, 1774; died Nov. 23, 1831. To this union 13 children were born:

George Buchanan, born Oct. 11, 1792; died Feb. 22, 1816; not married.

Alexander Buchanan, born March 22, 1794; died April 18, 1836; married Mary Ridley.

Elizabeth Buchanan, born Dec. 29, 1795; died 1874; married Thomas H. Everett.

Samuel Buchanan, born Aug. 27, 1797; died Feb. 20, 1836; not married.

William Buchanan, born Jan. 12, 1800; died ———; married Jane Hogan.

Jane T. Buchanan, born March 23, 1802; died May 6, 1837; married George Goodwin.

James B. Buchanan, born March 10, 1804; died July 6. 1862; married Letty Roberts.

Moses R. Buchanan, born April 4, 1806; died ———; married Sallie Ridley.

Sarah V. Buchanan, born Dec. 31, 1807; died April 10, 1866; married James B. Williams.

Charlie B. Buchanan, born Oct. 28, 1809; died April 13, 1836; not married.

Richard G. Buchanan, born Nov. 3, 1811; died ———; married Martha Murphy.

Henry R. Buchanan, born Nov. 8, 1814; died ———; not married.

Nancy Mulherin Buchanan, born July 31, 1818; died July 18, 1873; married first to Jackson Smith; second, to Henry Bridges.

Nancy Mulherin Buchanan, born July 31, 1818; died July 18, 1873; married Jackson Smith, and to this union twelve children were born:

John C. Buchanan Smith, born Dec. 5, 1834; died Sept. 20, 1835.

William Madison Smith, born Aug. 30, 1836; died Sept. 30, 1837.

James Buchanan Smith, born March 25, 1838; was killed in Dalton, Ga., May 8, 1861 (Civil War); married Martha Davis.

Francisco Templemore Smith, born Sept. 30, 1839; died June 9, 1842.

Ann Letitia Jane Smith, born May 22, 1841; died April 30, 1905; married Thomas J. Batey.

Bartholomew Jackson Smith (Batty), born July 21, 1843; died

Sept. 21, 1861 (Civil War); not married.
William H. Brown Smith (Brown), born April 5, 1845; died Oct. 1, 1861 (Civil War); not married.
Mary Louisa Melville and Sara Elizabeth, twins, born June 21, 1846; Sara Elizabeth died June 24, 1846, and Mary Louisa Melville died June 27, 1847.
Jackson Woods Smith, born Feb. 5, 1848; died Feb. 17, 1906; married Mary Watkins Vawter.
John L. Smith, born March 3, 1854; died in Tampa, Fla., about 1927; not married.
Thomas Everett Smith, born Feb. 20, 1856; married Jennie Vawter; still living.
Ann Letitia Jane Smith, born May 22, 1841; died April 30, 1905; married Thomas J. Batey. To this union six children were born:
Nancy Eviline Batey, born April 12, 1861; living; married David Mitchel Peebles.
Minnie Batey, born May 17, 1863; died Oct. 27, 1894; married Charlie Beesley.
Jackson S. Batey, born Aug. 22, 1865; living; married Minnie Beesley.
Frank Batey, born Aug. 13, 1867; living; married Annie Ross.
Effie Lee Batey, born July 24, 1870; living; married James Smith.
John Charles Batey, born June 5, 1872; living; married Mary A. Blackman.
John Charles Batey and Mary A. Blackman's children:
Bessie Lee Batey, married G. W. Haynes.
Fannie Blackman Batey, not married.
John L. Batey, not married.
John Charles Batey, Jr., not married.
Thomas Alfred Batey (Al), not married.

Buchanan's Station, a Pioneer Fort

The deeds of heroism and chivalry of the daring and ambitious spirits from Virginia and the Carolinas, the pioneer builders of a future state, are unsurpassed. The unexplored territory, stretching from the Cumberland Mountains on the east to the "Father of Waters" on the west, lies on the happiest line of latitude and longitude, girdling the globe. Upon it nature bestowed some of her richest blessings: a mild climate, where summer pours out her flood of sunshine and shower—wild fruits and berries in prodigal profusion—beautiful hills, fertile valleys and virgin forests. The many small streams, tumbling down the mountains, winding their way along the valleys to the Tennessee or Cumberland, abound in fish. Wide expanses of rich pasture land lured all sorts of wild game, such as bears, deer, buffalo and turkey. It was the favored hunting ground of the Creeks, Cherokees and Shawnees. Tales of the wonders of this region brought back by brave hunters and trappers fired the restless souls of those pioneers with a desire for greater adventures.

In the year 1772, a few of these adventurers crossed the Alleghany Mountains and settled in the beautiful valley of the Watauga, in what is now East Tennessee. About half way between the Cumberland Mountains and the Mississippi River lies the central basin, the blue grass section. Its beautiful fluted valleys, surrounded by the highland rim, form one of the most fertile, picturesque and enchanting regions nature ever produced. One of Tennessee's most beloved writers called it "the dimple of the universe." Learning of the great resources of this valley, through which the Cumberland flows, some of the Watauga settlers determined to press forward in spite of the perils of the wilderness and the savage Indians.

There was no more eventful occasion in the life of the nation than this expedition in the year 1779 of Gen. James Robertson and Col. John Donaldson from the Watauga Valley to the new settlement on the Cumberland. The parties of Donaldson and Robertson and two small ones conducted by Capt. Rains and Maj. John Buchanan, father and son, met at the French Lick, where Nashville now stands, in the early spring of 1780. Less than five hundred souls, of whom one hundred and fifty were all that were able to bear arms, constituted the entire colony of the Cumberland Valley. "These pioneer settlers were considered intruders, and a war of extermination was waged upon them by the Indians for fifteen years. Every settler became an armed occupant who held his life and his fort or block-house only by the strength of his arm." (Ellet's The Women of the Revolution.)

Four miles east of Fort Nashborough was an inviting scope of country, through which a small creek found its way to the Cumberland River, not far distant. It was on the east bank of this stream, later known as Mill Creek, because its waters furnished the power for the first grist mill in the community, that Maj. John Buchanan built a fort, which bore his name. The spot was a natural fortification: a bluff of rock rising perpendicular from the creek some thirty or forty feet high, so as to make it impregnable from an enemy approaching from the west. Stretching out in an eastwardly direction was a wide expanse of level land, from which the approach was protected by stockade and block-house. The creek makes a bend around the bluff which added much to its defense. It was a picturesque place for a home as well as a fort, the natural beauties of which still exist. A large spring under the bluff, whose sparkling waters once cooled the lips of the tribal hunter and quenched the thirst of the hardy pioneer, flows ever anon.

The gray limestone bluff, with the waters of the little creek flowing lazily by, stands today a monument to the daring deeds of noble souls, who blazed the way for this civilization we enjoy, as it stood sentinel for them one hundred and fifty years ago.

Maj. John Buchanan's family had originally emigrated from Lancaster, Pa. He had come with his father in 1779 from South Carolina, where he had been a soldier under Col. Pickens. He was married in 1786 to Margaret Kennedy, who died in the year 1789. To this union one child, John, was born.

On account of his great bravery and fearlessness in continuous warfare with the Indians, Major Buchanan had become the terror of the savages as well as the pride of Cumberland Valley. It is said that he was even dressed in buckskin from head to foot, equipped with rifle and powder horn, ready for a scouting expedition when he courted Sarah Ridley (better known as Sally), who lived in a fort, two miles distant.

Sarah, the daughter of Capt. George Ridley, one of the sturdy pioneers who sought homes in the Watauga Valley in 1772, was born in a rough block-house in December, 1773, one of the first, if not the first-born daughter of Tennessee. When only 6 years of age, she made that eventful trip with her father in Col. Donaldson's party down the Tennessee River and up the Cumberland—suffering privations and terrors untold. These early years of hardships and harrowing experiences amid Indian warfare strengthened her character and created in her that fearless and dauntless spirit that so well fitted her as mistress of Buchanan's Station. Her bravery and resourcefulness during these stressing times carved for her a name in history as one of the most outstanding women of her time.

Within the space of thirty miles around Nashville were about a dozen forts. Having no schools or churches, the only social intercourse was an occasional visit. Few women would dare venture forth without a male escort, but Sarah, noted for fearlessness, would visit the other forts, a distance of two or three miles.

Returning from one of these trips with Susan Everett, late in the afternoon, a party of Indians with rifles appeared directly in their path. Impulsive, quick-thinking Sarah, whispering to her relative to do as she did, immediately assumed the position of a man on horse back, waved her bonnet in the air and yelled as she galloped past the Indians, "Clear the track, you d——d red skins!" The Indians, thinking that they were men at the head of a charging body of troopers, fled in dismay. On account of her excellent horsemanship, she was called "the fast rider of Mill Creek."

At the age of 18 she was married to Maj. John Buchanan in the year 1791. To this union thirteen children were born.

The Indian warfare continued—these sturdy pioneers worked with guns by their side. Their daily life was fraught with danger. Sarah's brother-in-law, Samuel Buchanan, was attacked by Indians, who scalped and killed him while he was plowing in a near-by field.

One day, while the men of the fort were away, two horse-thieves appeared and demanded two of the Major's finest horses. Pretending to agree to their demands, she led them to the stable, but as they reached the door, she suddenly drew a large hunting-knife from under her apron and dared them to enter. Notwithstanding their threats, she held her ground, and they finally left without the horses.

Happy in their work of home-making, even though beset with perils of the red men, the colony gradually grew larger and stronger. In the year 1792, the population of the Cumberland Valley, principally around Nashville, was seven thousand. Of these about one thousand were men of arms. Many efforts had been made to establish peace between the settlers of Tennessee and the red men of the forest. It was thought in May, 1792, that amicable relations had been established and less care was taken in guarding the forts and the mounted rangers were dismissed. But the crafty Indians, professing friendship and pretending to be reconciled to peace, were busy preparing for an attack under the leadership of Colonel Watts.

Some of the settlers had considered it unwise to disperse the soldiers at such a crisis and among these was Major Buchanan. His station, being four miles east of Nashville, on the farther side of Mill Creek, was the outpost toward the Indians and necessarily exposed to the first assault. Having only about a dozen men living in his station, he asked several courageous young men to spend several days with him. He told no one but his wife of his fears.

On Sunday, about midnight, Sept. 30, 1792, the attack was made on Buchanan's Station. The stockade had been repaired, but its force consisted of only twenty gunmen besides Buchanan—James Bryant, Thos. Wilcox, Jacob Castleman, Abraham Castleman, James O'Connor, James Mulherrin, Thos. McCrory, Morris Shane, Wm. Kennedy, Robin Kennedy, George Findleston, Samuel Blair, Charles Herd, Sampson Williams, Samuel McMurry, Robin Turnbull, Robin Hood, Thos. Lattimer, Robin Thompson and Joe Duratt, the last named being a half-breed, but a friend of the whites. (Merritt's History of Tennessee.)

The Indian army consisted of 280 warriors—197 Cherokees and 83 Creeks. Shawnees living at Running Water were numbered with the Cherokees. (American Historical Magazine, Vol. II, page 80.) The whole was under the command of Col. John Watts.

When the Indians were close enough to hear the lowing of the cows at Buchanan's Station, they halted for consultation. Watts wanted to advance and fall upon Nashville, but

Talotiskee, of the Creek division, insisted on destroying Buchanan's Station. After much argument they attacked the station at midnight.

The approach of the Indians was disclosed by the running of the cattle and they were discovered and fired upon when within ten yards of the gate. Thirty balls passed through a single port hole of the "overjutting," and lodged in the roof, within the circumference of a hat. The Indians were never more than ten yards from the block-house and large numbers tried to fire the lower walls. A young chief, Chiachatella, ascended the roof with a torch but was shot down and killed. The Creek Chief Talotiskee and the Shawnee's Warrior of Running Water were also killed. Colonel Watts fell pierced through both thighs with a rifle ball and was carried away on a stretcher. Several other warriors were wounded and later died. Toward morning the Indians withdraw. No casualties on the side of the besieged. (Moore's Tennessee, the Volunteer State.)

Major Buchanan's policy during the battle was to leave the impression that the fort contained a large garrison. He had his men fire often, and occasionally in volleys. The women held men's caps to the empty port holes to deceive the Indians as to the number of men. But alas! the bullets gave out. But Mrs. Buchanan, resourceful as usual, with Nancy Mulherrin, Mrs. Shane and others, moulded 300 bullets out of pewter plates and spoons. She also gave the tired soldiers brandy and cheered them continuously. In order to keep up a show of good spirits, the men frequently cried out to the Indians, "Shoot bullets, you squaws! Why don't you put powder in your guns?" This was understood, for Watts and many others spoke good English and they replied, daring them to come out and fight like men.

Mrs. Buchanan gave an Irish man named O'Connor an old blunderbuss and told him to shoot. He pulled the trigger when the rest fired three or four times, having it reloaded every time, and when he pulled the trigger again he landed under the bed.

This was the first formidable invasion of the Cumberland Valley and its tide was rolled back as much by the presence of mind and heroic firmness of Sarah Buchanan and Nancy Mulherrin as by the rifles of their husbands and friends. The fame of the gallant defense went abroad and the young wife of Major Buchanan was celebrated as the greatest heroine of the West. (Ellet's The Women of the Revolution.)

This victory saved the settlement but it was many years later before its inhabitants were safe from the terrors of the tomahawk and the scalping knife.

It is said that Henry Buchanan and his sister, children of Major John and Sarah, were in the woods alone one day, when they were attacked by Indians, scalped and left unconscious. They recovered, but afterward had to wear wigs.

Situated only a short distance north of the old home lies the family graveyard. Many graves have long since been erased by time. For instance, it is known that the bodies of Archibald Buchanan, cousin of John, and his wife, Agnes Bowen, were removed from the garden of the "Old Blue Brick" on Stewart's Ferry Road by their son, James, when the homestead was sold, and both placed in the same grave in the Buchanan graveyard. However, no trace can be found of same.

A few markers still remain and bear the following inscriptions:

In memory of John Buchanan, died Nov. 7, 1832; age 74 years 9 months 25 days.

In memory of Sarah Buchanan, died Nov. 23, 1831; age 57 years 11 months 23 days.

Martha Buchanan, died Sept. 15, 1840; age 28 years; graves of 3 infants of Martha Buchanan.

In memory of George Buchanan, died Feb. 22, 1816; age 23 years 7 months 11 days.

In memory of Samuel Buchanan, died Feb. 20 (tombstone crumbled here, date missing); age 18 years.

Sacred to memory of Elizabeth Ridley, born 1794; died May 25, 1810; age 16 years.

Janet Alexandretta, wife of T. W. Haynes, died June 7, 1843; age 18 years 8 months 8 days.

Alexander Buchanan, born March 22, 1794; died April 9, 1836; age 42 years 18 days.

Robert McFarland, born March 30, 1795; died Jan. 16, 1823 or '28 (figures indistinct).

Sacred to the memory of Mrs. Winifred, consort of R. P. McFarland, born Oct., 1793; died April, 1863; age 69 years 6 months.

T. H. Williams, born Aug. 23, 1826; died Jan. 7, 1878.

This old pioneer fort and surrounding acreage located on Elm Hill Pike, four miles from Nashville, is now known as the Seamen A. Knapp Demonstration Farm of the Peabody College for Teachers in Nashville, Tenn.

Mrs. Berry D. Shriver.

Ezell Lane, Route 7, Nashville, Tenn.

Family Record

From Bible of Elijah Hughes and his son, Richard Ellis Hughes. Sent by Mrs. J. Hughes Darden.

Elijah Hughes, born Sept. 8, 1770.

Frances Hughes, his wife, born ———.

Mary Anna Bella Hughes, daughter of Elijah and Frances Hughes, born Jan. 2, 1801.

Elizabeth Hannah Hughes, born June 13, 1804.

Richard Ellis Hughes, born Sept. 25, 1805.

Jesse Hamilton Hughes, born April 12, 1807.

Richard E. Hughes, married Amanda M. Oursler, March 1, 1832.

Amanda, his wife, born Aug. 28, 1813.

BIRTHS

Elizabeth Hannah Hughes, married Simon Peter, Aug. 28, 1822.
Mary Francis Peter, daughter of E. H. Peter, born June 28, 1823.
Isabella Ann Peter, born June 6, 1825.
Elizabeth Hughes Peter, born Feb. 4, 1827.
John Coke Peter, born Dec. 20, 1829.
Richard H. Peter, born March 14, 1831.
Elijah Hughes, married in Baltimore County, Md., to Fanny Daugharday, Feb. 14, 1799.
Mary Anna Bella Hughes, married Benjamin Whitehead, July 1, 1819.
Henry Cartwright Whitehead, son of Benjamin and Mary A. B. Whitehead, born June 19, 1820.
Sterling Hamilton Whitehead, born Feb. 23, 1822.
John Thomas Whitehead, born Jan. 12, 1825.
Emily Francis Whitehead, born Feb. 13, 1829.
Josiah Niblett Whitehead, born Dec. 20, 1830.
George Hamilton Hughes, son of Richard and Amanda Hughes, born April 14, 1833.
Emily Elizabeth Hughes, born April 16, 1838.
Ellen Udorah Hughes, born Jan. 1, 1840.

DEATHS

Elijah Hughes, died April 11, 1828, in the 57th year of his age.
George Hamilton Hughes, died July 1, 1833.
Frances Hughes, my mother, died March 1, 1834.
Jesse H. Hughes, married Mary L. Buckner, June 16, 1835.
Hellen Oursler, died April 22, 1839.
Ellen Frances Hughes, died June 16, 1839; age 1 years 1 month.
The property of Elijah Hughes, bought April 20, 1803, in Baltimore City; price, eleven dollars.
Minnie Hughes, married G. M. Fizer, Dec. 2, 1875.
Emily Hughes, married Dr. C. H. Lockert, March 20, 1855.

FAMILY RECORD

Family record of Ellis Hughes and Hannah Yarnell, his wife. This copy from the Bible of Jeremiah Hughes was taken Nov., 1889, by E. H. Lockert while in Annapolis, Md., visiting his daughter, Hannah Ann Gray.

Ellis Hughes, born March 17, 1739; died Oct. 6, 1785, in his 46th year.
Hannah Yarnell, born Jan. 1, 1747; died April 1, 1816.
They were married at Reading, Pa., Jan. 1, 1764.
She was left a widow over thirty years.
Of this marriage there were ten children—five sons and five daughters:
Phebe, born Friday, March 8, 1865.
Ann, born Nov. 7, 1766; died at Baltimore, Nov. 15, 1793.
Annabella, born Sept. 7, 1768.
Mrs. Annabella Little, died at Baltimore, Feb. 20, 1815.
Elijah Hughes, born Saturday, Sept. 8, 1770; died April 11, 1828, in his 58th year.
Mary Hughes, born Saturday, Sept. 11, 1772; Mary Fowler, died in Annapolis, June 26, 1840.
Jesse Hughes, born Wednesday, July 26, 1775; died May 14, 1790, in his 15th year.
Thomas Hughes, born Jan. 23, 1777; moved from Baltimore West in 1797.
Eleanor, born Friday, Nov. 25, 1778; lived and died in Baltimore.
Gideon Hughes, born Sabbath eve, about 6 o'clock, June 24, 1781.
Jeremiah Hughes, born Saturday, Jan. 21, 1783; died in Baltimore, Nov. 27, 1848; age 66 years.

FAMILY RECORD

Family of R. E. Hughes and Amanda Oursler, his wife. Sent by Mrs. J. Hughes Darden.

George Hamilton Hughes, born April 14, 1833; died July 1, 1833.

Emily Elizabeth Hughes, born Aug. 25, 1835.

Ellen Frances Hughes, born April 16, 1838; died Jan. 16, 1839.

Ellen Eudora Hughes, born Jan. 1, 1840; died June 25, 19—.

Mary Louisa Hughes, born June 16, 1842; died.

Sarah Frances Hughes, born Oct. 1, 1842; died.

George W. Taylor Hughes, born Feb. 22, 1847; died.

Richard Oursler Hughes, born Dec. 3, 1849; died third Sunday in Aug., 1853.

Amelia Amanda Hughes, born Oct. 28, 1851.

R. E. Hughes, born Sept. 25, 1805; died Jan. 24, 1855.

Amanda Oursler Hughes, born Aug. 28, 1813; died Jan. 15, 1891.

MARRIAGES

Emily Hughes, married Charles H. Lockert, March 20, 1855.

Ellen Hughes, married Andrew Jackson Allensworth, June 25, 1857.

Mary Hughes, married William H. Darden, May 21, 1872.

Sarah Hughes, married Andrew Bentley, Aug. 15, 1867.

George Hughes, married Louelia Valeria Hughes (sister of Andrew), June 3, 1869.

Amelia Hughes, married George M. Fizer, Dec. 2, 1875.

DEATHS

Dr. C. H. Lockert, died Nov. 4, 1865.

Andrew W. Bentley, died.

William H. Darden, died June 22, 1889.

George M. Fizer, died Jan. 16, 1911.

Louelia Valeria Hughes, died April 18, 1925; age 81 years 10 months.

FAMILY RECORD

Family record from the Bible of John Catlett Allensworth and Amelia Pollard Carter, of Christian County, Ky.

MARRIAGES

John C. Allensworth, married Amelia P. Carter, Aug. 27, 1829.

Wm. M. Sullivan, married Lucinda B. Allensworth, by Elder M. B. Ferguson, Dec. 17, 1850.

A. J. Allensworth, married Joanna B. Fauntleroy, by Rev. I Bennett. March 2, 1854.

A. J. Allensworth, married Ellen E. Hughes, by Rev. J. W. Cullom, June 25, 1857.

Eliza Emily Allensworth, married Joseph Settle, Oct. 4.

Mary D. Allensworth, married James Reeks, Wednesday, Nov. 3, 1869.

Amelia Catlett Allensworth, married Isaac Johnson, Nov. 3, 1869.

Lucinda B. Sullivan, married Charles W. Ransom, Nov. 8, 1860.

Sue Ella Allensworth, married George T. Price, Wednesday, Dec. 15, 1875.

BIRTHS

John Catlett Allensworth, born March 30, 1805.

Amelia Pollard Allensworth, born Nov. 22, 1812.

Lucinda B. Allensworth, born Jan. 26, 1831.

Andrew Jackson Allensworth, born Feb. 13, 1833.

Eliza Emily Allensworth, born May 25, 1839.

Mary Elizabeth Allensworth, born May 22, 1840.

Jessee F. Allensworth, born July 2, 1842.

Mary Daniel Allensworth, born Aug. 22,, 1844.

Amelia Catlett Allensworth, born Feb. 10, 1847.

DEATHS

Elizabeth Allensworth, died May, 1840.
Joanna B. Allensworth, died March 12, 1855.
Amelia P. Allensworth, died Jan. 11, 1873, at 12:25 in the morning; funeral preached by Elder Charles Day, from I Thes. 8th chapter, 13th verse, to end of chapter.
Allie, son of I. O. and A. Catlett Johnson, died Jan. 22, at 12:24 p.m.
John C. Allensworth, died Jan. 16, 1879.
Lucy B. Ransom, died June 1, 1890.
A. J. Allensworth, died Nov. 5, 1891.

FAMILY RECORD

Records from Bible of James Young, who died at Bagdad, Jackson County, Tenn. Bible now owned by Sam M. Young, Dixon Springs.

Sent by Mrs. Rhea Garrett, Dixon Springs.

DEATHS

Sampson W. Young, died Oct. 19, 1819.
Addaville A. White, alias A. A. Young, died Oct. 7, 1831.
Addison H. Young, died March 4, 1832.
Harriet A. Myers, alias H. A. Young, died Feb., 1850.
Eliza C. Coker, alias E. C. Young, died July 28, 1853.
Elizabeth M. Sutton, alias E. M. Young, died Oct., 1854.
James Young, died Aug. 2, 1860.
Wm. M. Young, died Oct. 13, 1862.
Elizabeth Young, died Nov. 24, 1871.
Aletha E. Slaughter, died Oct., 1878.

BIRTHS

James Young, born Sept. 8, 1788.
Elizabeth Young, born July 27, 1788.
William M. Young, born Oct. 23, 1807.
Nancy H. Young, born Dec. 28, 1808.
Addaville A. Young, born May 8, 1810.
Addison H. Young, born July 8, 1811.
Thomas R. Young, born May 12, 1813.
Eliza C. Young, born Jan. 31, 1815.
Elizabeth M. Young, born Aug. 21, 1816.
Sampson W. Young, born Oct. 13, 1818.
Sally A. Young, born Nov. 12, 1820.
Harriet A. Young, born April 16, 1823.
Oliver F. Young, born Jan. 4, 1825.
Aletha E. Young, born Dec. 15, 1826.

FAMILY RECORD

Records of Wilson Yandell Martin. Bible now owned by Sam M. Young, Dixon Springs, Tenn.

Inscription of fly leaf reads:

This Bible is presented to Mr. and Mrs. Wilson Y. Martin, of Smith County, Tenn., by Howard Lodge No. 13, of the Independent Order of Odd-Fellows, Gallatin, Sumner County, Tenn, as a tribute of its gratitude for their kind attention to our deceased brother, Gustavus C. Newton, of Mystic Lodge No. 19, Mystic, Connecticut, who departed this life at their residence, Jan. 14, 1847.

MARRIAGES

First generation:
William Martin and Franky Ferris, married July 29, 1790.

Betsey Martin and Henry Brooks, married June 28, 1811.
Joseph A. Martin and Nancy Hord, married Nov. 22, 1815.
Sally Martin and Thomas T. Young, married July 31, 1817.
George W. Martin and Judith Bradley, married March 8, 1820.
Brice F. Martin and S. Cayce, married April 14, 1825.
William L. Martin and Emily Allcorn, married Sept. 3, 1828.
Second generation:
Wilson Y. Martin and Mary B. Bridgewater, married Nov. 21, 1833.
Third generation:
Nannie E. Martin and James Howard Young, married July 14, 1859.
Fourth generation:
Sam M. Young and Elisabeth A. Wright, married Nov. 3, 1886, in church; reception at "Stony Lonesome."
Laura Gaston Young, married Rhea Edward Garrett, June 1, 1916, by Elder E. A. Elam, at garden twilight; roses and jasmine in bloom.—E. A. Y.
Wm. Martin Young, married Agnes M. Garrett, June 12, 1918.

BIRTHS

First generation:
William Martin, born Nov. 26, 1765.
Franky Ferriss, wife of the said William, born June 30.
Joseph A. Martin, born July 2, 1792.
Betsey Martin, born Aug. 13, 1794.
George W. Martin, born Dec. 8, 1796.
Sally Martin, born Dec. 8, 1798.
Brice F. Martin, born Oct. 15, 1800.
Jacob B. Martin, born Nov. 6, 1802.
William L. Martin, born Sept. 23, 1804.
Thomas J. Martin, born Nov. 25, 1806.
Second generation:
Wilson Y. Martin, born Dec. 23, 1810.
Norval D. Martin, born Nov. 14, 1814.
Third generation:
Nannie E. Martin, daughter of Wilson Y. and Mary B. Martin, born Dec. 21, 1834.
Fourth generation:
Sam Martin Young, son of Nannie E. and James Howard Young, born May 29, 1861.
Laura Gaston Young, daughter of Elisabeth and Sam Young, born Aug. 6, 1887, at "Stony Lonesome."
Fifth generation.
Wm. Martin Young, son of Sam M. and Elisabeth A. Young, born Sept. 4, 1892.
Sam M. Young Garrett, son of Rhea E. and Laura Gaston Garrett, born Feb. 2, 1919.
William Martin Young, son of William Martin and Agnes Garrett Young, born May 12, 1920.

DEATHS

Jacob B. Martin, died Oct. 31, 1822.
Mrs. Frances Martin, died July 27, 1831.
Thomas J. Martin, died July 18, 1833.
Mrs. Betsey Brooks, died Sept. 12, 1834.
Norval D. Martin, died Feb., 1837.
Brice F. Martin, died Dec. 18, 1843.
Col. William Martin, died Nov. 4, 1846.
William L. Martin, died Feb. 5, 1865.
George W. Martin, died Oct. 10, 1867.
Wilson Y. Martin, died March 25, 1868.
Mary B. Martin, died Dec. 10, 1876; cancer.
Mary M. Young, died Dec. 18, 1880; lungs.
Nannie E. Young, died Jan. 18, 1889; lungs.
James Howard Young, died Dec. 3, 1895; cerebral hemorrhage.
Wm. Martin Young, son of Elisabeth A. and Sam M. Young, died June 5, 1924; lobar pneumonia.

Family Record

From inscriptions in Bible of Chesley Bridgwater of Smith County, Tenn., sent to my father, Sam Young, by John Bridgwater of Riddleton, Tenn., who now owns the Bible.

Births

Chesley Bridgwater, Sr., born March 26, 1781.
Nancy Bridgwater, born July 29, 1785.
Martha A. Bridgwater, born June 19, 1805.
Ann Bridgwater, born Oct. 15, 1806.
Sally Bridgwater, born March 13, 1808.
Mary B. Bridgwater, born May 7, 1810.
Elizabeth Bridgwater, born June 1, 1812.
Nancy S. Bridgwater, born Nov. 24, 1814.
Samuel C. Bridgwater, born Aug. 8, 1816.
Lucy J. Bridgwater, born April 9, 1819.
Richard Bridgwater, born Jan. 26, 1821.
Emily C. Bridgwater, born Sept. 10, 1822.
Harriett Bridgwater, born March 18, 1824.
Chesley Bridgwater, born March 4, 1826.
John Chambers Bridgwater, born March 19, 1828.

Marriages

Thomas Phelps and Ann Bridgwater, married Jan. 6, 1825.
Walter C. Allen and Nancy S. Bridgwater, married Oct. 25, 1831.
Wilson Y. Martin and Mary B. Bridgwater, married Nov. 21, 1833.
Jacob S. Johnson and Elizabeth Bridgwater, married Oct. 25, 1837.
Samuel C. Bridgwater and Amelia H. Moores, married July 15, 1841.
James High and Sally Bridgwater, married Oct. 31, 1842.
Thomas C. Cryer and Emily C. Bridgwater, married Feb. 12, 1846.
John C. Bridgwater and Mary F. Vaughn, married Jan. 1, 1852.
Richard A. Bridgwater and Ann M. Seay, married Dec. 19, 1853.

Deaths

Chesley Bridgwater, Sr., died April 1, 1846.
Nancy Bridgwater, Sr., died March 23, 1849.
Martha A. Bridgwater, died Jan. 23, 1821.
Sally High, died Nov. 1, 1846.
Harriett B. Bridgwater, died Oct. 6, 1845.
Ann Smith, formerly Phelps, died Oct. 10, 1860.
Chesley W. Bridgwater, died Jan. 21, 1862.
Mary B. Bridgwater, died Dec. 10, 1876.
John C. Bridgwater, died July 24, 1864.
Nancy Allen, died July 1, 1865.
Chesley C. Cryer, born March 4, 1847; died Jan. 8, 1867.
Elizabeth Luster, formerly Johnson, died Jan. 13, 1869.
Samuel C. Bridgwater, died Jan. 13, 1869.
Lucy Jane Bridgwater, died Jan. 2, 1896.
Richard A. Bridgwater, died Sept. 3, 1875.
Emily C. Martin, died Jan. 24, 1876.

Marriages

Geo. T. Wright and Sarah H. Burton, married, 1815.
R. C. Wright and Bettie Burford.
John R. Wright and Nancy Bradley, 1857.
Eliza Wright and Lewis H. Ward, Oct. 18, 1859.
Sydney S. Wright and Jas. S. Dyer, Oct. 24, 1860.

Births

George T. Wright, Feb. 27, 1787.
Sarah H. Wright, June 12, 1800.
Frances Ann Wright, Sept. 19, 1816.
Romulus C. Wright, March 12, 1818.
Nancy S. S. Wright, March 6, 1820.
George D. Wright, April 3, 1822.
Robert L. Wright, Nov. 5, 1823.

Sarah H. Wright, Aug. 25, 1825.
Josephus Wright, March 15, 1827.
Green Wright, May 1, 1831.
Mary M. Wright, May 4, 1833.
John R. Wright, March 6, 1835.
Eliza J. Wright, Jan. 3, 1837.
William C. N. B. Wright, June 24, 1840.
Moscow L. Wright, Dec. 14, 1842.

DEATHS

Francis Ann Wright, Dec. 25, 1817.
George D. Wright, July, 1824.
Mary M. Wright, Aug. 24, 1834.
Sarah H. Wright, Aug. 1, 1841.
R. L. Wright, Sept. 10, 1845.
George T. Wright, Aug. 25, 1847.
Sarah H. Wright, Aug. 24, 1856.
Green Wright, Sept. 13, 1861, at Camp Trousdale.
William Wright, killed in Virginia at Bulls Gap, Nov., 1864.
Romulus C. Wright, July 15, 1892.
Nancy Sydney Dyer, 1898.
Harriet Wright Lowe, 1900.
John R. Wright.
Eliza Wright Jenkins.
Moscow L. Wright, July 19, 1924.
Milly was born Jan. 11, 1853.

These inscriptions are from the Bible of George and Sarah Wright of Smith County, Tenn. Bible published at Cooperstown, N. Y., 1837, and now in the possession of Mrs. Moscow Wright, Hartsville, Tenn.

FAMILY RECORD

Copy of a copy made by Mrs. Wm. M. Young of the records of the Bible of Wm. D. and Sally Amanda (Martin) Garrett of Dixon Springs, Smith County, now owned by Sam Cornwall, Hartsville, Tenn.

BIRTHS

William D. Garrett, Sept. 2, 17—.
Sally A. Garrett, Aug. 15, 1790.
Jane Ann Garrett, May 6, 1812.
Elizabeth James Garrett, March 2, 1814.
Mary Barthurst Garrett, Feb. 9, 1816.
William Archer Garrett, Feb. 8, 1818.
John Y. Garrett, May 3, 1820.
Samuel W. Garrett, Feb. 7, 1822.
James Paschal Garrett, April 30, 1824.
Martha T. Garrett, July 17, 1826.
Sally M. Garrett, Jan. 10, 1829.
Frances Tabb Garrett, April 25, 1831.
Louisa D. Garrett, July 2, 1834.

DEATHS

John Y. Garrett, April 29, 1822.
Jane Ann Garrett, May 19, 1842.
William D. Garrett, March 14, 1860.
Sally A. Garrett, Feb. 6, 1873.
James P. Garrett, Feb. 16, 1895.
Sally M. Cornwell, July 21, 1809.

MARRIAGES

Elisabeth J. Dillon, married July, 1842.

William D. Garrett and Sally A. Martin, April 13, 1811.

Jane A. Garrett and Marshall Leftwich, Dec. 11, 1839.

Elizabeth J. Garrett and Thomas J. Maddox, Feb. 5, 1837.

Mary B. Garrett and Elijah Miller, Jan. 19, 1842.

Wm. A. Garrett and Mary Ann Payne, Dec. 23, 1841.

Samuel W. Garrett and Sarah Payne, July 7, 1843.

Martha T. Garrett and Wm. J. Payne, Aug. 13, 1843.

Frances T. Garrett and James B. Haynie, Dec. 22, 1847.

James P. Garrett and Caran Payne, Aug. 10, 1848.

Sally M. Garrett and Fushhe Cornwell, Dec. 25, 1851.

Louisa D. Garrett and Wm. Hudson Porter, July 27, 1855.

Porter Bible

The early inscriptions in this Bible were written by Esther Settle, daughter of Capt. Edward Settle, early settler of Smith County, Tenn., from Fauquier County, Va., by the way of North Carolina.

Copy made by Mrs. Wm. M. Young, now owned by Mrs. Josie Porter Kemp Dean, Carthage, Tenn.

Marriages

Calvert and Esther Porter, Tuesday, Feb. 24, 1824.
Elizabeth Porter and A. Russel, Jan. 31, 1843.
Josier Sloan and Mary Ann Porter, Feb. 26, 1846.
James Garrett and Susannah E. Porter, Thursday, Feb. 24, 1853.
John T. Estes and Matilda E. Porter, Thursday, Jan. 26, 1854.
William K. Porter and Louisa D. Garrett, Thursday, July 25, 1855.
Thomas C. Porter and Lucy C. Taylor, Wednesday, May 13, 1857.
Edward S. Porter and Aura J. Wuhles, June 5, 1862.
C. T. Nunley and Sallie S. Porter, Dec. 25, 1884.
C. L. Porter and Lucy West, June 26, 1892.
H. E. Kemp and Josie Porter, Oct. 19, 1910.
Herod Porter and Estelle Kemp, Sept. 16, 1914.

Births

Calvert Porter, Sept. 19, 1801.
Esther S. Porter, Jan. 25, 1800.
Elizabeth Jane Porter, Saturday, April 2, 1825.
Mary Ann Porter, Wednesday, May 2, 1827.
William Kendall Porter, Sunday, Jan. 4, 1829.
Matilda Esther Porter, Wednesday, Sept. 7, 1831.
Thomas C. Porter, Wednesday, Dec. 19, 1833.
Emily Susannah Porter, Monday, March 7, 1836.
Edward S. Porter, Saturday, Sept. 15, 1838.
Sarah Porter, Thursday, June 17, 1841.

Deaths

Calvert Porter, Sept. 12, 1867.
William K. Porter, Aug. 19, 1874.
Matilda E. Estes, May 5, 1875.
Esther S. Porter, Oct. 21, 1875.
Edward Settle, July 23, 1839.
Elizabeth Settle, July 29, 1840.
Sarah Herod, Feb. 24, 1839.
Susannah Sloan, Oct. 8, 1835.
Rachel Porter, Feb. 22, 1839.

Family Record

Jas. Young's Bible records.

Births

James Howard Young, Dec. 29, 1828.
Byrd S. Young, April 18, 1831.

Marriages

James Young and Elizabeth (Draper), Nov. 27, 1806.
Addaville A. Young, Oct. 15, 1827.
William M. Young, Aug., 1830.
Nancy H. Young, Jan. 20, 1831.
Thomas R. Young, Nov., 1834.
Elizabeth M. Young, Nov., 1834.
Eliza C. Young, Oct., 1838.
Sally A. Young, Dec. 10, 1839.
Harriet A. Young, Aug., 1841.
Aletha E. Young, Dec. 26, 1844.
Oliver F. Young, Oct., 1849.
James H. Young and Nancy E. Martin, July 14, 1859.
Byrd S. Young, Oct. 30, 1856.

Items copied from two-column extra Lincoln Journal, Fayetteville, Tenn., July 7, 1854. Miss Clara Earle, Clarksville, Ark., has it; sent to her ancestor by David Buchanan for his information. Items by Mrs. W. P. Bouton, Lebanon, Tenn., 1933.

"Are only able to issue an extra after two weeks; may not be able to get out paper next week. We took refuge from the epidemic (Cholera) on the highlands of Pea Ridge, a place more famous for hospitality of its people, pure and limpid water, refreshing and invigorating atmosphere than for fertility of soil or value of produc- Are only able to issue an extra tion.

List of Deaths—White Persons

"Mrs. Mary Steele, age 41; Mr. N. F. Neil, 36; Mr. A. L. Miller, 20; Miss Martha Winn, 32; Mr. Samuel Edmondson, 27; infant of same, 8 months; Mr. B. W. D. Carty, 54; Mrs. D. S. Hobbs, 35; son of same, 14; Mrs. W. M. Smith, 28; Kate, daughter of Dr. M'Nelly, 9; Mrs. Eunice B. Shull, 50; Mrs. Jones, 25; infant of same; J. R. Chilcoat's child, 1; Mrs. Rowland's daughter, near town; Mrs. T. Whitaker, Mulbery; Mrs. Dr. Woods, Boon's Hill; Dr. Martin, Norris Creek; Hugh Hamilton, near Boon's Hill; James Caldwell.

"Died at the residence of his brother, in this county on 24th inst., George Cunningham, Esq., Clerk of the County Court of Lincoln County.

In this county, on the 25th inst., of flux, Mrs. Jane Stephens, wife of Mr. Wm. Stephens.

On the 27th inst., Mrs. Wheeler, wife of Capt. Wheeler, disease not known.

On the 1st inst., of disease of the liver, Mrs. Nancy Walker, wife of Smith Walker, Esq.

On the 1st inst., Nannie, infant daughter of Cornelius Allen, age 10 months.

On the 3rd inst., of flux, a child of Pascal R. Andrews.

On the 4th inst., Mrs. Mason, wife of Mr. J. Mason, disease not known.

Married

On Tuesday evening, the 4th inst., at the residence of Joseph S. Clark, Esq., by W. Pryor, Esq., Mr. James B. Carty, of this place, to Miss Bettie Elliott, of Huntsville, Ala.

A Freak of Nature

On the 25th inst., Mr. Abraham Washborn, of this place, was presented, by his better half, with three fine daughters, two of whom are living and doing well.

County Court well attended; forty Justices present. Col. Eli L. Hodge elected to fill vacancy by death of George Cunningham.

Records from the Bible of Ransford McGregor and Elizabeth B. Alford (first wife) and Isabella S. Henderson (second wife). Copied from the McGregor Bible now in the possession of Miss Sallie Tilghman, niece of Ransford McGregor, Mt. Juliet, Tennessee.

Marriages

Ransford McGregor son of Flowers and Mary McGregor, married Aug. 14, 1832, to Elizabeth B., daughter of William and Sarah Alford.

Ransford McGregor, son of Flowers and Mary McGregor, and Isabella S. Henderson, daughter of James and Margaret Henderson, married Aug. 20, 1834.

Births

Ransford McGregor, Nov. 11, 1801.
Elizabeth B. McGregor, March 16, 1815.

Elizabeth McGregor, June 11, 1837.
Isabella H. McGregor, Sept. 8, 1807.

James A. McGregor, Sept. 21, 1837.
Mary Flowers McGregor, Oct. 21, 1835.

John L. McGregor, July 5, 1839.
Violet E. McGregor, Feb. 16, 1842.
Joseph D. McGregor, April 16, 1843.
William Albert McGregor, July 16, 1845.
Ransford P. McGregor, Jan. 1, 1848.

DEATHS

Elizabeth B. McGregor, June 18, 1833.
Elizabeth McGregor, June, 1833.
Isabella H. McGregor, Aug. 16, 1849.
William Albert McGregor, March 17, 1874.

Sent in by (Miss) Mary Elizabeth White, 2106 Twenty-first Ave., South, Nashville, Tenn.

2006 Warnock St.,
Philadelphia.
Dec. 18, 1883.

Mr. Richard White.
Dear Sir:

In the course of my enquiries in the Straughn branch of the Buckman family, I learn that you are a son of Dr. Jacob Straughn White of Foxtown, Madison County, Ky.

Of that family I have the names of eleven children; no dates nor the name of the mother.

I desire your aid in obtaining as complete a list and history of the family as practicable, with the view of publication, as soon as the patronage inducements are sufficient to meet the expenses of getting it out. I have some quite interesting biolographical sketches of several of the Illinois pioneers of the Straughn family, but of John White, who married Hannah Straughn, I have nothing but the fact of his marriage and the names of his children.

Hannah Straughn was born 1756, 5th month, 8th day, at Quakertown, Pa., of Jacob and Christiana Strawn. They migrated to the Redstone County (Fayette County, Pa.) sometime near or during the Revolution and married John White, it is believed, while at Redstone.

Whatever information you can give me respecting the family will be thankfully received.

Very respectfully yours,
E. D. Buckman, M.D.

COPY OF DATA FROM MARCUS FAMILY BIBLE
Given by Mrs. Albert Akers.

MARRIAGES

William E. Marcus and Sarah F. Marcus, married Thursday, March 19, 1815.

BIRTHS

Zachry Young Lockhart, born Aug. 31, 1852.
Sarah Lockhart, born Aug. 5, 1854.
Thittns Ick, born Nov. 22, 1857.
Marcus Lockhart, born Nov. 30, 1859.
Charles Tennet, born Feb. 13, 1861.
Mag Lou Lockhart, born June 7, 1864.

Elizabeth Hollinger, daughter of William and Sarah Marcus, born Wednesday, June 26, 1816.

John Hix, son of William and Sarah Marcus, born Saturday, April 11, 1818.

William Griffin, son of William and Sarah Marcus, born Friday, Aug. 4, 1820.

Martha Ann Rogers, daughter of William and Sarah Marcus, born Wednesday, March 19, 1823.

Milton McDaner, son of William and Sarah Marcus, born Friday, July 9, 1824.

Amanda Hentietta Thomas, daughter of William and Sarah Marcus, born Saturday, Feb. 11, 1826.

Rebecca Jane, daughter of William and Sarah Marcus, born May 20, 1828.

Susan Harriet, daughter of William and Sarah Marcus, born Aug. 22, 1830.

Martin Van Buren, son of William and Sarah Marcus, born Wednesday, March 14, 1832.

DEATHS

Martha E. R. Williams, died March 13, 1864.
John Hix, son of William and Sarah Marcus, died Thursday, Sept. 2, 1819.
William Griffin Marcus, died Nov. 19, 1863.
Mrs. Sarah F. Marcus, died Dec. 20, 1867.

OTHER DATA

From Marcus family burying ground:
Mrs. Sarah F. Marcus, born May 4, 1798; died Dec. 20, 1867.
Mr. William E. Marcus, born in Washington County, Ga., July 1, 1792; died in Troup County, Ga., Jan., 1850, in the 58th year of his age; son of John and Hannah Marcus.
Mrs. Elizabeth H. (Hollinger Marcus) Sledge, born June 26, 1816; died Sept. 27, 1883.
Miss Rebecca A. Sledge, born Aug. 21, 1832; died March 14, 1892.
John W. Sledge, born Feb. 12, 1838; died Aug. 11, 1881.
Latter part of above my ancestress and two relatives of my great-grandmother, Elix., oldest child of William and S. F. Marcus, sister of Mrs. Frost.

FAMILY RECORD

This data was furnished by Mrs. W. Henderson Barton from an old Bible in her family and copied by Mrs. J. F. Draughon, Chairman of Genealogical Research, and credited to Cumberland Chapter, D. A. R., Nashville, Tenn.

William Lester, son of William Lester and Elizabeth, his wife, was born Sunday, Oct. 3, 1761.
Susanna Fields, daughter of Mary Fields, born Dec. 15, Sunday, 1765.
Chloe Faris, daughter of Joseph Faris and Mary, his wife, born May 7, 1772.
William Lester and Susanna Fields were married Sept. 17, 1780, and she died Sept. 20, 1791.
William Lester and Chloe Faris, married Sept. 10, 1795, and she died Oct. 23, 1796.
Elizabeth Echols, daughter of Henry Dillon and Mary, his wife, born March 5, 1765.
William Lester and Elizabeth Echols, married Sept. 30, 1798, and she died Dec. 12, Sunday, 1802.

BIRTHS

Nancy Webb, daughter of Edmund Webb and Nancy, his wife, born Jan. 16, 1781.
William Lester and Nancy Webb, married March 18, 1803.
Joshua Lester, son of William Lester and Susanna, his wife, born Sept. 6, Thursday, 1781.
Presley Lester, son of William Lester and Susanna, his wife, born Feb. 9, Sunday, 1783.
William Lester, son of William Lester and Susanna, his wife, born May 20, Sunday, 1785.
Vincent Lester, son of William Lester and Susanna, his wife, born July 3, Thursday, 1787.
John Lester, son of William Lester and Susanna, his wife, born March 3, Wednesday, 1790.
Thomas Lester, son of William Lester and Susanna, his wife, born March 22, Friday, 1793.
Faris Lester, son of William Lester and Chloe, his wife, born Oct. 19, Wednesday, 1796, and died March, 1797.
James Smith Lester, son of William Lester and Elizabeth, his wife, born April 21, Saturday, 1799.

Henry D. Lester, son of William Lester and Elizabeth, his wife, born May 18, Sunday, 1800.

Daniel Webb Lester, son of William Lester and Elizabeth, his wife, born March 17, 1812.

Susanna Webb Lester, daughter of William Lester and Nancy, his wife, born Jan. 7, Saturday, 1804.
Chloe Faris Lester, daughter of William Lester and Nancy, his wife, born April 4, Thursday, 1805.

Edmund Webb Lester, son of William Lester and Nancy, his wife, born Dec. 23, Tuesday, 1805.
Elizabeth Ann Dillon Lester, daughter of William Lester and Nancy, his wife, born July 4, Monday, 1808.
Manson Bolton Lester, son of William Lester and Nancy, his wife, born Feb. 22, Thursday, 1810.
Nancy Webb Lester, daughter of William Lester and Nancy, his wife, born Aug. 18, Sunday, 1811.
Mary Ann Marshall Lester, daughter of William Lester and Nancy, his wife, born Sept. 3, Friday, 1813.
George Washington Lester, son of William Lester and Nancy, his wife, born Aug. 20, Sunday, 1815.
Martha Ann Custis Lester, daughter of William Lester and Nancy, his wife, born March 20, Sunday, 1817.

BIRTHS

Lucy Ann Dillon Lester, daughter of William Lester and Nancy, his wife, born April 22, Wednesday, 1818.
Sally McAllister Lester, daughter of William Lester and Nancy, his wife, born Sept. 21, Thursday, 1820 .
Martha Ann Dunn, daughter of John Dunn and Nancy W. Dunn, born April 18, 1834.
Mary Jane Dunn, daughter of John Dunn and Nancy W. Dunn, his wife, born Feb. 1, 1836.
John F. Dunn and Nancy W. Lester, married April 18, 1833.
James S. Lester, died Dec. 1, 1878.
Thomas Lester and Olivia Pierce, married Sept. 4, 1820.
John Lester, son of William Lester, died in 1836; age 46 years.
Joshua Lester, son of William Lester and Susan, his wife, died Feb. 8, 1844; age 62 years.
Thomas Lester, son of William Lester, died Aug. 30, 1835; age 42 years.

BIRTHS

Lucy Dillon, daughter of Henry Dillon and Mary, his wife, born Oct. 8, 1782.
Joshua Lester and Lucy Dillon, married Jan. 13, Thursday, 1803.
William D. Lester, son of Joshua Lester and Lucy, his wife, born June 16, Saturday, 1804.
Polly Smith Lester, daughter of Joshua Lester and Lucy, his wife, born Saturday, March 29, 1807.
Susanna Fields Lester, daughter of Joshua Lester and Lucy, his wife, born Sunday, Jan. 8, 1809.
Vincent Lester, son of Joshua Lester and Lucy, his wife, born Thursday, Sept. 20, 1811.
Nancy Lester, daughter of Joshua Lester and Lucy, his wife, born Thursday, Dec. 9, 1813.
Henry Dillon Lester, son of Joshua Lester and Lucy, his wife, born Monday, June 17, 1810.
Presley Smith Lester, son of Joshua Lester and Lucy, his wife, born Tuesday, Dec. 29, 1816.
Joshua Lester, son of Joshua Lester and Lucy, his wife, born Nov. 21, 1821.
Lucy Dillon Lester, daughter to Joshua Lester and Lucy, his wife, born Tuesday, June 29, 1824.
Anderson Webb and Susanna W. Lester, married Nov. 8, 1821.
William Golding Webb, son of Anderson Webb and Susanna, his wife, born Dec. 21, 1822.
George Washington Webb, son of Anderson Webb and Susanna, his wife, born July 7, 1824.
James Foster Webb, son of Anderson Webb and Susanna, his wife, born April 22, 1826.
Edmund Lester Webb, son of Anderson Webb and Susanna, his wife, born Dec. 21, 1827.
W. R. Hammon, born Sept. 18, 1847; married Miss Deel Snider, Dec. 28, 1875.
Manson B. Lester, died 1852.
Elizabeth Thompson, died 1869.
Abner Jennings and Chloe Farris Lester, married Oct. 16, 1828.
William Carroll Jennings, son of Abner Jennings and Chloe F., his wife, born July 11, 1829.
Mary Ann White Jennings, daughter of Abner Jennings and Chloe Farris, his wife, born Saturday, Feb. 19, 1831.
Jesse Thomas Jennings, son of Abner Jennings and Chloe F., his wife, born Dec. 10, 1832.

Courtesy of M. L. Lewis, Carnegie Library

Davidson County Courthouse, built in 1859-1863.
Francis Strickland, son of William Strickland, who built the State Capitol, was the architect.

Nancy A. Jennings, daughter of Abner Jennings and Chloe Farris, his wife, born July 5, 1834.

Nancy A. Jennings, daughter of Abner Jennings and Chloe Farris, his wife, died July 9, 1834.

James S. L. Jennings, son of Abner Jennings and Chloe Farris, his wife, born June 16, 1835.

Edmund W. Lester and Elizabeth Jennings, married Dec. 15, 1829.

Emmialine Frances Lester, daughter of Edmund and Elizabeth, born Sept. 17, 1830.

Elizabeth Lester, died Jan. 10, 1832.

E. W. Lester and America Warson, married Jan. 28, 1836.

William Abner Lester, son of Edmund and America, born Jan. 16, 1837.

William Lester, Sr., died June 3, Friday, 1842; age 80 years 9 months.

Lucy Ann Dillon Summers, died Aug. 14, 1842, Sunday, at 5 o'clock; age 24 years 3 months 23 days.

Nancy Lester, died Aug. 15, 1859; age 72 years 7 months 5 days.

Will of John Hope

Sent by Mrs. W. O. Ogden

John Hope's last will and testament, May 23, 1804, said will being of record in the County of Davidson, State of Tennessee.

The legatees under the will are his wife, Anne, and the following children, namely: Adam, William, Frances, Agnes, Mary. A bequest is also made to my brother, Adam Hope's son, John.

I do hereby revoke and annul all former wills and testaments made by me and do declare this my last will and testament in full force and virtue, and I further constitute and appoint my trusty and well beloved brother, Adam Hope, and my son, Adam Hope, both of the county and State aforesaid, executors, and my beloved wife, Anne, executrix; and I hereby authorize and impower them to execute this, my last will and testament, and to perform all things therein mentioned as my will and desire.

Signed, sealed and declared this 23rd day of October, 1804, in the presence of D. Frazor, Joseph Walker and Benj. Canon.

This last will and testament, above recited, being exhibited in court for probate, April session, 1805, and was duly proven to be the act and deed of the said John Hope.

A codicil was annexed to the will regarding a bequest to his son, Adam, on December 22, 1804, and signed in the presence of T. B. Craighead, William Crawford and John Walker.

This codicil annexed to the above will was proven by the oaths of William Crawford and John Walker to be the act and deed of the said John Hope, deceased, and the executors therein named qualified as such.

John Walker and Ann Barnett, married Aug. 20, 1765.

Births of Their Children

Alexander Walker, June 30, 1766.
Jane Walker, March 8, 1768.
William Walker, Oct. 11, 1769.
Abraham Walker, Feb. 20, 1773.
Joseph Walker, Nov. 20, 1775.
John Walker, Sept. 20, 1777.
James Walker, Sept. 3, 1779.
Ann Walker, March 16, 1782.
Matthew Patton Walker, Aug. 16, 1787.
Rebekah Walker, Aug. 19, 1791.

Matthew Patton Walker and Agnes Hope, married March 18, 1807.

Births of Their Children

John Hope Walker, Jan. 27, 1808.
Ann Brevard Walker, Dec. 1, 1809.
Matthew Alexander Walker, Nov. 8, 1811.
Mary Frances Walker, Nov. 9, 1813.
William Shelton Walker, Nov. 13, 1815.
John Adams Walker, Feb. 12, 1818.
Abram Joseph Walker, Nov. 24, 1819.

Agnes Rebekah Walker, March 21, 1822.

Malvina Tennessee Walker, Jan. 7, 1824.

Katrina Matilda Walker, Oct. 8, 1825.

Amanda Parilir Walker, —— 1, 1827.

Adeline Sibella Walker, May 24, 1829.

Andrew Jackson Walker and Mailssa Constantia Walker, Feb. 5, 1833.

Will

John Walker's last will and recorded May 19, 1818, said will being of record in the County of Davidson, State of Tennessee.

The legatees under the will are his son-in-law, Charles Miller, his son, Matthew Patton Walker, also the will bequeaths unto my sons, Alexander Walker, Abrm. Walker, Joseph Walker's heirs, John Walker, James Walker and Ancy Enochs and Rebecca Andrews, my daughters, an equal division of all my other property.

I do hereby nominate and appoint my sons, Alexander Walker, Abraham Walker and James Walker, my executors of this, my last will and testament, hereby revoking all former will and wills by me heretofore made.

In testimony whereof I have hereunto set my hand and affixed my seal the 17th day of March, in the year of our Lord 1816, signed, sealed and delivered in the presence of us: James A. Cobbs, Langham Scruggs. John Walker (seal).

James Garrard's Family Record

James Garrard, son of Col. William Garrard and Mary Lewis, his wife, was born in Stafford County, Va., Jan. 14, 1749. It is found that he served as Colonel in the State Militia of Stafford County during the Revolutionary struggle, and while in that service was elected to the Virginia Legislature, where he was a staunch supporter of the bill to establish universal religious liberty. He was thus distinguished by his fellow citizens in being elected to the State Assembly, and receiving military appointments.

In 1783 he moved to Kentucky and settled in Bourbon County, on Stoner Creek, where, in 1786, he built his residence, which has always been known as "Mount Lebanon." The records of the land office of Kentucky show that he entered large tracts of land.

He was a member of the conventions held in Danville, Ky., in May, 1785, in Aug., 1785, in 1787, and 1788. He was also a member of the convention held in Danville in 1792, which formed the Constitution of Kentucky, and was several times a Representative in the Legislature.

In 1796 he was elected Governor of Kentucky, serving until 1800, when he was again elected under the new Constitution.

Garrard County, Ky., was formed in 1796, and was named in honor of James Garrard, then Governor of the State.

Gov. Garrard was re-elected Governor in 1800, the only instance, as already quoted, of a man's filling two successive terms as Governor.

Gov. Garrard had united with the Baptist Church in Virginia, and had his membership at Hartwood Church, situated about twelve miles from Fredericksburg. After his settlement in Kentucky, he was ordained to the ministry, and was for a time pastor of the church of Cooper's Run.

On Dec. 20, 1769, in Stafford County, Va., Gov. Garrad married Elizabeth Mountjoy, of Overwharton Parish, Stafford County. One of her brothers, Col. John Mountjoy, married a sister of Gov. Garrard, and in their branch of the family some data of the Mountjoys is given.

The following data was taken from the monument of Col. James Garrard and furnished by Mrs. J. R. Robinson, who is one of his descendants. Copied by Mrs. Draughon.

This marble consecrates the spot on which repose the mortal remains of Col. James Garrard, and records a brief memorial of his virtues and of his worth. He was born in the Colony of Virginia, on the 14th day of January, 1749. On attaining the age of manhood, he participated with the patriots on the day in the dangers and privations incident to the glorious contest which terminated in the independence and happiness of our country. Endeared to his family, to his friends and to society by the practice of the social virtues of husband, father, friend and neighbor; honored by his country by frequent calls to represent her dearest interests in her Legislative councils; and finally by two elections to fill the chair of the Chief Magistrate of the State, a trust of the highest confidence and deepest interest to a free community of virtuous men, possessing equal rights and governed by equal laws; a trust which, for eight successive years, he fulfilled with that energy, vigor and impartiality which, tempered with Christian spirit of God-like mercy and charity for the fraility of man, is but calculated to perpetuate the inestimable blessings of government and the happiness of man. An administration which received its best reward below, the approbation of a grateful and enlightened country, by whose voice, expressed by a resolution of its General Assembly in December, 1822, this monument of departed worth and grateful sense of public service was erected and is inscribed. He departed this life on the 19th day of January, 1822, as he had lived, a sincere Christian, firm, constant and sincere in his own religious sentiments, tolerant for those who differed from him; reposing in the mercy of God and the merits of his Redeemer, his hopes of a glorious and happy immortality.

(Reference book: Governor Garrard, of Kentucky, His Descendents and Relatives, by Anna Russell Des Cognets.)

Family Record

Family record of Captain John Snoddy.

Capt. John Snoddy, born in Ireland in 1720; not known when he came to this country, but lived and died in Washington County, Va. He married Agnes Glasgo in 1741 at Philadelphia, Pa. He had two sons, Thomas and Wm. G. He died in 1784.

John Snoddy served as Captain of the Militia of Washington County, Va., 1777-1780. He was directed to administer the oath of allegiance to the State, to the males of his Company, Aug., 1777. He served under Col. Wm. Campbell in the Battle of Kings Mountain. He was also Justice of the Peace and Dedimus of Washington County, Va.

Family Record

Family record of the Carter family, taken from an old Bible published in 1814.

Marriages

J. M. Carter and F. A. Killebrew, Nov. 7, 1841.

R. S. Chilton and Willie Carter, Dec. 20, 1866.

H. F. Moore and F. R. Carter, Dec. 18, 1872.

John W. Carter and Jennie Holloway, Dec. 18, 1884.

*Mary Brandon, born Nov. 11, 1749; §died Sept., 1834, in Tennessee. (See Brandon family record.)
William Alexander served in the Revolutionary War, from Rowan County, N. C. For his service in the Revolution, see U. S. Pension Records, Claim No. S-361, Commissioner of Pensions, Washington, D. C.
William Alexander also served as a "Member of the Committee of Safety for Rowan County, N. C., Sept. 20, 1775."
Reference for this service: Wheeler's History of North Carolina, Vol. 2, pp. 368-69.

*See record in Bible now in possession of the son of Judge William Hall, deceased, Wm. Hall V.
†See copy of William and Elizabeth (Watkins) Cunningham's Bible record, now in possession of Mrs. Elizabeth Alexander (Wright) Young.
‡See inscription on tomb in Cunningham - Saunders - Alexander graveyard on Rome Road, near Dixon Springs, Tenn.
§See inscriptions on tomb in William Alexander graveyard, on land originally granted to William Alexander for Revolutionary services, at Hartsville, Trousdale (formerly Sumner) County, Tenn.

Brandon Family Record

The Brandon family was originally from England, where for many centuries they played a conspicuous part in public affairs, as every reader of English history knows. In America they first settled in Pennsylvania, from thence to Rowan County, N. C.
Mary Brandon, born Nov. 11, 1749; died Sept., 1834; married Jan. 21, 1769, to William Alexander, born Dec. 25, 1746, died Aug. 4, 1830.
She was a daughter of Richard Brandon, died (will dated April 16, 1770, probated 1790, Rowan County, N. C., filed in Will Book C, at page 14); married Margaret Locke.
Richard Brandon was a son of *John Brandon; married Elizabeth ——.

*See Brandon data following.
†See Locke data following.

John Brandon was a Justice of the Peace for Anson County, N. C. (from which Rowan was formed), April 11, 1749, and April 1, 1751.
Reference for service as Justice of Anson County, N. C.: North Carolina Colonial Records, Vol. 4, pp. 951-1243.
John Brandon was a member of the Assembly for Rowan County, N. C., 1746-47-1754, taking his seat at the thirteenth session.
Reference for service in Assembly: North Carolina Manual, 1913, p. 381. Also North Carolina Colonial Records.
The following is from Rumple's History of Rowan County, N. C., pp. 281, 283:

*Brandon Family

"In 1752, John Brandon obtained a grant of 630 acres of land from Earl Granville, upon waters of Grant's Creek.
"John Brandon appears among the Justices who presided over our County Courts in the year 1753, along with Walter Carruth, Alexander Cathey, Alexander Osborne, John Brevard and others."
From a deed dated 1753, we learn that John Brandon's wife's name was Elizabeth.
John Brandon had three sons, namely:
Richard Brandon (see copy of his will, dated April 16, 1770, probated 1790, naming daughter, Mary, and grandson, Richard Alexander). (Copy of this will follows. "Mary" is Mary Brandon Alexander, mother of "Richard.")
William Brandon.
John Brandon, Jr.
Richard Brandon, married Marga-

ret Locke, the sister of Gen. Matthew Locke. The children of Richard Brandon and Margaret Locke were:
(These names taken from will of R. Brandon, filed in Will Book C, p. 14, Rowan County, N. C., Records, and witnessed by Will Cathey, John Johnston and Marlan Martin. See following page.)
Col. John Brandon, Mary (Alexander); Matthew Brandon, Ottis, and Elizabeth Brandon, married Francis McCorkle.

LOCKE FAMILY RECORD

From North Carolina Booklet, Vol. X., No. 1, p. 13.
†The first of this once large, influential and patriotic family in Rowan County came from the north of Ireland to America in the Seventeenth Century and settled in Lancaster County, Pa. Tradition says that the head of his family was Sir George Locke. He married Mrs. Richard B. Brandon, a lady of distinguished parentage. From Lancaster County, Pa., the three brothers, Matthew, Francis, George, and his sister, Margaret, came to North Carolina and settled in Rowan County. The Lockes were of English descent, originally from London.
From Rowan County, N. C., Marriage Bonds:
William Alexander, to Mary Brandon, Jan. 21, 1769. Witnesses: William Alexander, John Dunn.

WILL

Will of Richard Brandon, filed in Will Book C, p. 14, Rowan County, N. C., Records

In the name of God. Amen.
I, Richard Brandon, of the County of Rowan, and State of North Carolina, being in a sick and low condition of body but of perfect sound mind, memory and judgment (blessed be God for his mercies), and calling to mind the mortality of my body and that it is appointed for all men once to die, do make and ordain this, my last will and testament, in manner and form following, that is to say: First, I will that all my lawful debts be paid and my funeral expenses discharged. Also I give and bequeath to my son, John, my bay mare. Also I give and bequeath to my daughter, Mary, five pounds. Also I give and bequeath to my grandson, Richard Alexander, my silver buckles. Also I give and bequeath to my daughter, Elizabeth, one rigged cow and one yellow cow. Also I give and bequeath to my daughter, Attis, one negro man, Sam, and my negro woman, Sarah, and my saddle. Also I give and devise to my son, Matthew, the tract of land on which I now live, containing two hundred and forty acres with all the improvements and appertanencies thereunto appertainned and belonging to him, the said Matthew Brandon, and his heirs, and to their only proper use and behoof forever. Also I give and bequeath to my son, Matthew, my negro boy, Andy, and my roan horse and all and every of my personal estate, goods, and chattels of every kind, not already mentioned or bequeathed, and I will that my negroes, Sam and Sarah, and my bay mare above mentioned remain to the use of my son, Matthew, until the present crop in which he is now engaged be finished. And lastly, I do hereby constitute and appoint my beloved sons, John and Matthew, executors in trust of this my last will and testament. In witness whereof, I have hereunto set my seal the 16th day of Aprile, in the year of our Lord 1770.
Richard Brandon, his mark (seal).
Signed, sealed, published and declared by the said Richard Bran-

don as his last will and testament before us who were present at the signing and sealing of the same.

Will Cathey, John Johnston, Marlan Martin.

DOAKS OF VIRGINIA

Samuel, David, John, Robert and Thankful Doak, children of James and Elizabeth Doak, emigrated from North Ireland and settled in East Nottingham Township, Chester County, Pa.

Thankful Doak was born on ship coming over. There was a severe storm at sea and her parents, so glad to land safely, named her Thankful. Exact date of landing has not been found—about 1704. She married John Finley.

John Doak moved to North Carolina, married. His daughter, Thankful, baptized June 30, 1743, married Major William Hall and became mother of William Hall, born 1775, 'seventh Governor of Tennessee. He married Mary B. Alexander. Oldest daughter, Mary Hall, married Capt. John Morgan.

Samuel Doak married in Chester County, Pa., Jane Mitchell, and moved to Augusta County, Va., where he died between Nov. 5, 1771, date of will, and May 19, 1772, will proven. (Chalkley's Augusta County Records, Vol. 3, p. 123), in which he mentions his brother-in-law, John Finley, to advise executors of his will. He was the father of Rev. Samuel Doak, Presbyterian minister, founder of Washington College, Tenn., who married Esther Houston Montgomery.

Samuel Doak, married Jane Mitchell, in Pennsylvania. Issue:

John Dqak, born ——.

David Doak, baptized Dec. 9, 1740.

Elizabeth Doak, baptized May 14, 1747; married Nathaniel Hall, son of William and Janet Hall.

Rev. Samuel Doak, born 1749; died Dec. 12, 1830; married, first, Esther Houston Montgomery, who died in 1807, by whom he had eight children; married, second, Margaret Houston McEwen.

Issue by first marriage:

Julia Doak, born Aug, 10, 1776.

John Whitfield Doak, born Oct. 10, 1778; married Jane Alexander.

Samuel Witherspoon Doak, born March 24, 1795; died 1864; married March 3, 1808, Sarah Houston McEwen, born June 17, 1792; died 1864. Sarah Houston McEwen was the daughter of Margaret Houston McEwen, the second wife of Rev. Samuel Doak.

HALL FAMILY RECORD

The Hall family is one of the most distinguished in Tennessee and North Carolina records. Several members of this family made the supreme sacrifice in the endeavor to open the new country which we now call Tennessee. One son of the family became a Governor of Tennessee and many served in the Revolution.

It has been difficult to follow the early history of the family as some historians have confused the history of the Major William Hall family with that of Robert Hall, who was an early settler and a prominent citizen of Pennsylvania. Major William Hall was, however, a son of Richard Hall, who was born in Ireland and emigrated to Virginia.

RICHARD HALL

Richard Hall, born in Ireland, emigrated to Virginia. He served in Virginia in 1751 in the French and Indian War and in 1771 in the Militia in North Carolina. He is said to have had eleven children, but the record preserved in the family Bible of one descendant gives the names of four children only. They were:

William Hall, Richard Hall, Jr., John Hall and Sarah Hall.

The Virginia State census from 1782 to 1785 gives his residence in Fluvanna County.

Major William Hall was born in Virginia about 1740. He married Thankful Doak, also of a Virginia family, some members of which removed to North Carolina. Major William Hall and Thankful Doak lived in Surry Co., N. C., for several years before the Revolution. Major Hall was appointed Major of Surry County Militia by the Provincial Congress of North Carolina Sept. 9, 1775. This is a Colonial Record. He was member of the Provincial Congress from Surry County, 1776. He was a member of the Committee of Safety, Sept. 20, 1775, and Dec. 18, 1776. In 1779 he sold his possessions in Surry County and removed to what is now upper East Tennessee and was then New River, Virginia, settling at a place called Hall's Bottom. He lived on this place for five years, when he received, for military service during the Revolution a grant of land in Sumner County, Tenn., and removed to that county in 1784. His oldest son, James Hall, was killed by Indians shortly after the arrival of the family in Sumner County. Major William Hall and another son, Richard Hall, were killed by Indians Aug. 6, 1786. The husband of his daughter, Mary Hall, Capt. John Morgan's father and brother were killed. Other members of the family barely escaped with their lives and the record is one of the most heroic and sacrificing in Tennessee's history. Major William Hall was pierced by thirteen wounds when he was killed and scalped; his two youngest children, Prudence and John, escaped; William, Jr., the future Governor, escaped after fighting desperately, and the mother, Thankful Doak Hall, escaped in a strange manner. She was riding a large and powerful horse at the time of the attack and, frightened by the noise and fighting, he ran a mile with her, thus saving her life. At the time of the attack the family were enroute from their home to the fort for protection. They had gone only half a mile from their house when the massacre took place.

Reference for the foregoing statements: For appointment as Major, 1775, North Carolina Records, Vol. X, page 206; for service in Provincial Congress, North Carolina Records, Vol. X, page 931; for service on Committee of Safety, North Carolina Records, Vol. V, page 974, Vol. X, page 251; for death at hands of Indians, Ramsey's Annals, page 394, 463, also History of Sumner County Tenn., and statement of Governor William Hall, son of Major William Hall.

The children of Major William Hall and Thankful Doak Hall were:

Mary Hall, married Captain John Morgan.

James Hall, killed by Indians 1785; the first white person killed in what is now Middle Tennessee.

Richard Hall, killed by Indians when his father was killed, Aug. 5, 1786.

Sarah Hall, married Andrew Lynum and James Anderson.

William Hall, married Mary Alexander, and was Governor of Tennessee; born 1773.

John Hall and Prudence Hall.

Thankful Hall II, married Charles Morgan.

(These names may not be given in exact order of birth).

Family Record of James Morgan

Sent by Mrs. George Harsh, 1902 Union Avenue, Memphis, Tenn.

James Morgan and his wife, Jane, with their children, Margaret, John, Evan and James, natives of Nantmeal, Radnorshire, Wales, set sail for this country in 1691. Both parents died at sea and were buried in a Maryland port at the head of the Bay of Bohemia. All of the children settled in Chester County, Penn., and James and Evan became distinguished clergymen. John purchased a farm near "Morgan's Corner" in Radnor township, now Delaware County. I do not know that this John is my ancestor, but the John Morgan which I can positively identify as my ancestor was related to Gen. Daniel Morgan and had seven sons and five daughters. His sons were John, Charles, Joseph, Isaac, James, William and Armstead. His daughters were Charity, Phoebe, Ailsie, Mary and Susan. This son, *John*, was Capt. John Morgan, who married Mary Hall, daughter of Maj. William Hall and Thankful Doak Hall. He and family moved to Sumner County in 1784 with his father-in-law, Major Hall. He had married Mary before leaving North Carolina. He built his fort on an eminence in the vicinity of Rogana on lands since owned by Dr. Jesse Johnson. Some of the logs of which the fort was constructed are now in the wall of a barn on this farm. Capt. Morgan's father, "Squire John Morgan," came with him and was killed by an Indian warrior under the hill. The Indian rushed upon him and sank his tommy-hawk deeply into his brain, where it was left, being too tightly wedged into the skull to be withdrawn. Capt. John's brother, Armstead, a fine young man and very popular with the settlers, was killed from ambush at Southwest Pass, while piloting a party of emigrants from Knoxville. Capt. John Morgan or Capt. Charles Morgan, husband of Thankful Hall, was wounded by the Indians at the time Major Hall and his son, Richard, were killed. His son, James, had been killed shortly before this.

The children of Capt. John Morgan and Mary Hall Morgan are:
Nancy, married James Bright.
Patsy, married George Gillespie; lived near Franklin, Tenn.
Malinda, married Francis Porterfield, of Fayetteville, afterwards of Nashville.
Susan, married Dr. Davis.
Polly, married James Fulton.
Thankful, married John Cage, son of Maj. William Cage and Elizabeth Douglass Cage, of Sumner County.
These daughters were said to be quite handsome and sensible. His sons were: Hiram, John H., Dan (who died young), and Charles, a prominent citizen of Sumner County. Capt. Morgan's eldest daughter, Nancy's husband, James Bright, was a surveyor of Kentucky, but settled at Fayetteville, Lincoln County, Tenn. Capt. Morgan left Sumner County and settled at Mulberry, near Fayetteville. He died in 1820 as reported by one of his descendants, although "Historic Sumner County," by Cisco, reports his death in the 1830's. He was buried in his garden at Mulberry. On the breaking out of the Creek War, Capt. Morgan raised a company of mounted troops and joined Gen. Jackson at the rendezvous at Huntsville, Ala. "He was a large, handsome man, with noble features and gray hair that hung down on his shoulders, and when he rode through Fayetteville at the head of his company, his appearance and the occasion was never forgotten by those who witnessed it, and is one of the traditions of the town." He was well advanced in years, but he said: "A man should never get too old to fight the British and Indians." His wife, Mary Hall Morgan, had black eyes that flashed at the mention of either, but could one expect differently of her whose father (Maj. William Hall) and two brothers (James and Richard), father-in-law (Esquire John Morgan), two brothers-in-law (Charles and Armstead Morgan), were all killed by Indians? Mary Hall Morgan died in 1850, about 90 years of age, at the home of her daughter, Polly, and her husband, Col. James Fulton, in Fayetteville, and was buried in the old Fayetteville Cemetery at the Presbyterian Church.

Douglass Family Record

Sent by Mrs. George Harsh, 1902 Union Avenue, Memphis, Tenn.

The Douglass family of which Elizabeth Douglass, the first wife of Major William Cage, was a member, was also prominent and distinguished. They also lived in Virginia, moving to North Carolina, Chatham County, and thence to that part of what is now Sullivan County, Tennessee. Elizabeth Douglass was the daughter of Col. Edward Douglass, who was born in Fauquier County, Virginia, about 1720. He married Sarah George about 1740. He served in the Revolution in North Carolina. Reference for service: North Carolina Colonial Records, Volume 22, page 204. After living in Sullivan County for a short time he took up a land grant in what is now Sumner Co., Tenn., for military service. Before Sumner County was erected he, and the other early settlers, resided in Davidson County, and he was one of the first two lawyers in the County. When Sumner County was erected his land was in that county and he became immediately a leading citizen. He was appointed a member of the first county court. He was elected to the North Carolina Convention of 1788, representing Sumner County. He was a member of the first Tennessee Constitutional Convention, 1796, representing Sumner County.

He married about the year 1740, Sarah George, of Virginia. Their seven sons and the husbands of their two daughters were in the Revolution, which is a remarkable record—ten members of one family, including himself, all in the Revolution.

Their children were:

John Douglass, killed by Indians during the Revolution.

William Douglass, married Peggy Stroud.

Elizabeth Douglass, married Major William Cage, as his first wife.

Elmore Douglass, married Mary Gibson.

Ezekial Douglass, married Mary Gibson.

Sally Douglass, married Thomas Blakemore.

Edward Douglass, Jr., married Elizabeth Howard.

Reuben Douglass, married Elizabeth Edwards.

James Douglass, married Catherine Collier.

Cage Family Record

Sent by Mrs. George Harsh, 1902 Union Avenue, Memphis, Tenn.

The Cage family was one of the earliest in Virginia, Edward Cage being established in James City County, Virginia, by 1625. The family had emigrated from England where they bore arms and where they intermarried with many prominent families, Bacon, Culpeper and others. It was evidently association with these families that caused the emigration to Virginia.

William Cage, widower, of Millgate, married Dec. 2, 1937, in London, Joane, daughter of Thomas Culpeper. Joane was born Aug. 16, 1607. The will of John (Lord) Culpeper mentions William Cage, husband of Joane as "my brother-in-law, Mr. William Cage."

However, an earlier marriage in London between the Cages and Culpepers is that of Sir William Cage to Ciceley, daughter of Sir Cheney Culpeper, and it was no doubt a descendant of this marriage, Edward Cage, who came first to Virginia.

The family was noble and bore arms. The Cage coat-of-arms is described: Per pale gules and azure; a saltire or. Crest: A stag trippant erm, attired or; charged on the shoulder with an annulet gules.

After emigrating to Virginia, the Cages carried on the name, but there were never many of the family, only an occasional member appearing in the records through some service. Benjamin Cage served in the French and Indian War, 1758, and I imagine he is the father of Major William Cage, the distinguished North Carolina-Tennessee Revolutionary soldier, who was born in Virginia in 1745. Though I have not been able to find documentary proof, I have no doubt Major William Cage is the direct descendant of Edward Cage, the emigrant to Virginia in 1625, and the son of Benjamin Cage, the Colonial soldier.

MAJOR WILLIAM CAGE

Major William Cage, born in Virginia, 1745, moved to Chatham County, N. C., before the Revolution. He was prominent and popular, and when the Revolution began he was appointed Major and was chiefly active in suppressing Tories under the notorious Col. David Fanning. For reference to his service as Major, see North Carolina Colonial Records, Vol. 22, page 575. It is said that he was taken prisoner at one time and remained for some time a prisoner of the British. I think this was at the siege of Charleston. After the Revolution he moved from Chatham County, N. C., to what was then Sullivan County, Virginia, or North Carolina, the boundary line being for a long time a matter of dispute, where as before he became a leading citizen. He was a delegate to the North Carolina House of Commons from Sullivan County in 1783, his associate being Col. Abraham Bledsoe; he was elected to the next session when his associate was David Looney.

When the question of session from North Carolina was agitated and the State of Franklin was proposed he first opposed it, but later became a warm supporter of the State of Franklin and as usual a leader in affairs. He was elected to the Franklin legislature from Sullivan County and was elected Speaker of the Lower House. He was later elected first Treasurer of the State of Franklin.

In 1785 when the State of Franklin seemed lost, he moved probably because of his friendship with the Bledsoes, to Davidson County and Sumner County, where he received a military land grant, and where, as usual, he immediately took an active part in all affairs. Gov. Blount of the Territorial Government appointed him Sheriff of Sumner County and he served from 1790 to 1796, when he was succeeded by his son. Major Cage died at his home, Sumner County, March 12, 1811. His tombstone relates that he served in the Revolution.

He married twice, both wives coming of patriotic and distinguished ancestry. His first wife was Elizabeth Douglass, daughter of Col. Edward Douglass and Sarah George Douglass. Major Cage's second wife was Anne Morgan.

By his first marriage Major Cage had ten children, namely:

Priscilla Cage, married William Hale.

Wilson Cage, married Polly Dillard.

Reuben Cage, married Polly Morgan.

William Cage, Jr., married Fannie Street.

Sally Cage, married Jack Carr.

James Cage, died unmarried.

Edward Cage, married Elizabeth Jarrett.

John Cage, married Thankful Morgan.

Lofton Cage, married ——— Gillespie.

Jesse Cage, married Polly Gillespie.

By his second wife, Anne Morgan, Major Cage had six children:

Richard Cage (no information).

Harry Cage, married Catherine Stewart of Mississippi.

Albert Cage (no information).

Elizabeth Cage, married Harman Hays; parents of the celebrated Col. Jack Hays of the Texas Rangers.

Patsy Cage, married Thomas Morton.

Robert Cage, married Lucy Hunley, of Wilson County, Tenn.

The eldest of the children of Major William Cage, Priscilla Cage, married while still in Sullivan County, William Hale, who belonged to a prominent family. He was a son of Nicholas Hale, a soldier of the Revolution, whose will is on file in Jonesboro, Tenn. In Nicholas Hale's will he mentions his son, William. He also mentions a daughter, Elizabeth Cage, but I have not been able to prove by records the Christian name of Elizabeth's husband and his relation to the large family of children of Major William Cage. He was probably a nephew of Major William Cage.

William Cage of Cage's Bend

By Douglas Anderson

Sent by Mrs. George Harsh, 1902 Union Avenue, Memphis, Tenn.

In response to the urgent requests of congress that states which claimed western lands should cede them "as a further means of extinguishing the debt and establishing the harmony of the United States," the North Carolina legislature early in 1784 ceded certain of her western lands upon certain conditions. One was that congress should accept the lands within one year. By a subsequent act, passed during the same session, North Carolina declared that it would retain its sovereignty over the territory ceded until the cession should be accepted by congress.

In August, 1784, a convention composed of delegates from the counties of Washington, Sullivan and Greene, met at Jonesborough, "empowered to adopt such a course as should appear wise" with respect to their newly created situation.

In November, 1784, North Carolina repealed the cession act. But before the news of this repeal reached the people across the mountain they had elected delegates to another convention. In the face of this repealing act this convention met at Jonesborough Dec. 14, 1784, and created, as far as it was within their power to do so, the state of Franklin, named in honor of Benjamin Franklin.

North Carolina reasserted her jurisdiction over the territory, and for several years thereafter the conflict raged between the parent state and her rebellious offspring. The "Franks" were divided over the issues involved. This made matters worse for the advocates of independence. Petitions, memorials, speeches, addresses and letters followed each other in diplomatic succession, while physical force was not an unknown factor in the struggle.

While sparring with her mother state and some of her own truant sons, the state of Franklin also made repeated efforts to obtain the intercession of Congress in its behalf. Old Ben, himself, was besought to draw the lightning of congressional approval down his kite string. Doubtless the promoters of the new state had in mind his powers as a magician when they honored him in naming the state.

Old News That's New

As my purpose here is to make public the recent discovery that Major William Cage, of Cage's Bend, was one of the leading spirits in the effort to establish the new state of Franklin, it is proper that I should first give an idea of what that movement was.

When the late J. G. Cisco wrote his "Historic Sumner County," published in 1909, he included, it seems, all the information that he could get from members of the Cage family about the Cage family. If Cisco could have learned from any of the descendants of William Cage of Cage's Bend, or from my other source, that this ancestor of all the Sumner County Cages had been instrumental in establishing the state of Franklin, it may be safely assumed that he would have mentioned so interesting and important a fact. He does not mention it; from which, it is a reasonable conclusion that this fact was unknown to any of Major Cage's descendants or to any one else in this section. Cisco makes it appear that Major Cage came to Sumner County directly from Virginia; he does not mention Major Cage's long period of residence in North Carolina.

Lost Traditions

It is not remarkable that all knowledge of Major Cage's connection with the state of Franklin should have been lost to his posterity when the state itself is referred to as "the lost state."

In his brief sketch of Franklin, Haywood refers several times to "William Cage" and Ramsey follows suit. They do not tell what became of "William Cage" after Franklin fell.

Haywood's history, printed in 1823, is not a book that appeals to the average reader—in fact, it is very tiresome; and without an index is about as useful as an ax without a handle. For many years before the second edition was printed, also without an index (1891), only three copies were known to be in existence—so Col. John Allison told me; and one of these he rode a long distance across the mountains to buy at $25.

Ramsey's Annals is a bulky, unattractive volume (published in 1860, during the war excitement), with no more drawing power among "the people" than Haywood's history. It never had much of a circulation here, and can rarely be found except in some public library, or that of some person who is specially interested in Tennessee history. And these are very few—and always have been few.

Traditions frequently fall on unsympathetic ears, and the chain is broken.

Members of families scatter from Dan to Beersheba, as members of the Cage family did, and traditions are lost in this way.

From one or all of these causes, or some other cause that cannot be surmised, it has been left to Judge Samuel C. Williams, formerly of the Supreme Court of Tennessee, now a resident of Atlanta, Ga., to identify "William Cage" of Franklin as Maj. William Cage of Cage's Bend.

Also, it may be remarked, the author of "The Lost State of Franklin" gives more facts about Maj. William Cage, in other respects, than Cisco gives, upon the authority of the Cage family.

Leader In Franklin

Major Cage was one of the delegates from Sullivan County to the convention of Dec. 14, 1784, held at Jonesborough. Although he voted against independence "at this time," he suffered nothing by being in the minority. He was elected Speaker of the House of Commons of the first Assembly, which met in March, 1785. At the same session he was elected State Treasurer.

Williams publishes an answer to a letter received by Governor Sevier from Governor Martin of North Carolina. The letter was "formulated by the Assembly" and is signed by Major Cage and Landon Carter, Speaker of the Senate.

Another address from the Assembly to Congress praying for acceptance of the secession act and the admission of Franklin as a state is likewise signed by Speakers Cage and Carter.

MEMBER OF CONVENTION

In May, 1787, a convention was held at Greeneville to consider the final adoption of the Constitution promulgated at the place in November, 1785. There is no complete record of the members of the convention of 1785. Possibly Major Cage was a member. He was a member of the convention of 1787, which adopted a Constitution. Before this convention adjourned William Cocke proposed a resolution favoring holding an election for members of the North Carolina Legislature on the same day that North Carolina should hold an election for this purpose in Franklin. The idea was that by this means the "Franks" could elect men favorable to a separation from North Carolina; in which event a sufficient number of members of the North Carolina Assembly would grant the separation.

On this motion Major Cage was reported at the time to have spoken in substance as follows:

"Colonel Cage was of the opinion that if we did not hold the sham election proposed under the authority of North Carolina, thereby to get friends to represent us in that Assembly, we should never bring about a reconciliation; and as a friend to peace as well as a faithful friend to the state of Franklin, he heartily wished that the motion now in question might be carried; thus, with their own weapons, we should prove victorious over our enemy."

WILLIAMS' SKETCH

Judge Williams prints a sketch of Major Cage, which is here copied, with the author's permission:

"William Cage was born in Virginia in 1745. He removed to Chatham County, N. C., and served for a time as Major in the Revolutionary Army. His chief service was against the Tories under the noted Col. David Fanning. He seems to have been a prisoner of the Tories for a short time. He removed after the war to Sullivan County, N. C. That county sent him as one of its delegates to the House of Commons of the North Carolina Legislature of 1783, his associate being Col. Abraham Bledsoe. He was returned the succeeding session, along with David Looney. He voted against the first secession act; but became one of the moving spirits in organizing the new state of Franklin. He was elected Speaker of the Lower House of the first Assembly, and was the first Treasurer of the State.

"In 1785 he removed to Sumner County, probably influenced to do so by the Bledsoes. When the territorial government was organized he was appointed by *Governor* Blount sheriff of Sumner County, and by successive appointments he served until 1796, when he was succeeded by James Cage. Another son, Harry Cage, removed to Mississippi, where he became Supreme Judge and Congressman.

"William Cage died at his home in Cage's Bend (of Cumberland River), March, 1811."

CONFLICT OF DEATHS

There is a conflict of dates in Judge Williams' book with respect to Major Cage, due, doubtless, to the statement made by Cisco that Major Cage moved to Sumner County in 1785. Such oversights will happen in the best regulated families. A contemporaneous account of the convention of 1787 shows that Major Cage was still a resident of Franklin. He moved to Sumner County in 1790 or before; for he was first appointed sheriff by Governor Blount in the year named. During his last term as sheriff (as appears from Cisco) he was also collector of taxes. The records in the register's office of Sumner County may indicate, without showing positively, when Major Cage moved to Sumner County.

Major Cage's tombstone bears this inscription:

"William Cage, a Major in the

Revolutionary War, died March 12, 1811."

It was one of my duties, as a boy, to keep the stock fenced out of the old Cage graveyard where Major Cage is buried. The brick walls were then in good condition, but the gate had long before disappeared. The brick walls are now rapidly decaying and the inscriptions on the tombstones are almost illegible.

The Sons of the American Revolution are putting up monuments to mark the resting places of Revolutionary soldiers. I respectfully call their attention to the condition of the grave of one who was not only an officer in the Revolutionary Army, but (as has only recently been made known) a participant in one of the most notable struggles in American history.

In a future article I will have more to say of Major Cage, and the Cage family and homestead; for be it known that I am not yet through with Cage's Bend.

Ancestors of Thankful Barry Harsh (Mrs. George Harsh), of Watauga Chapter, D. A. R., 1902 Union Ave., Memphis, Tenn.

Inscriptions on the tombs of Col. Edward Douglas, his wife, Sarah George Douglas, also their daughter, Elizabeth Douglas Cage, and her husband, Maj. Wm. Cage. These graves are in the old Cage cemetery at the old Cage home which was owned and occupied by Maj. Cage from the time that he came to Sumner County (then Davidson) until his death.

Edward Douglas, born 1713; died 1773.

Sarah Douglas, born 1714; died 1777. Wife of E. Douglas.

Elizabeth Cage, died July 1772, age 38 years.

Wm. Cage, died March 12, 1811, age 66 years. A major in the Revolutionary war.

Wm. Alexander, born Dec. 25, 1746; died Aug., 1830.

See inscription on tomb in Wm. Alexander graveyard on land originally granted Wm. Alexander for Revolutionary services located near Hartsville in Trousdale County (formerly Sumner County), Tenn. Wm. Alexander married Mary Brandon in Rowan County, N. C., Jan. 21, 1769.

Mary Brandon, born Nov. 11, 1749; died Sept., 1834.

See Bible records of Judge Wm. Hall of Gallatin, Tenn., and Mrs. Sam Young, Dixon Springs, Tenn. The graves of Maj. Wm. Hall and Thankful Doak Hall are on the old Hall homestead near Castalian Springs, Tenn., and are marked by stones of the limestone rock quarried on the place. This land was granted to Maj. Hall for Revolutionary services. There are no inscriptions on these stones, but this record was kept by the late Judge Wm. Hall of Gallatin, Tenn., who was the great-great-grandson of Maj. Hall and Thankful Doak Hall.

Capt. John Morgan, who married Mary, the eldest daughter of Maj. Wm. Hall and Thankful Doak Hall, before leaving North Carolina, moved with the Halls to Sumner County, but later settled in Mulberry near Fayetteville, Tenn. Capt. Morgan died in the 30's and was buried near Mulberry. His wife, Mary Hall Morgan, survived him until 1850 and was buried in the old cemetery at Fayetteville, where their grandson, Gen. John Morgan Bright, lived.

John Cage, son of Maj. Wm. and Elizabeth Douglas Cage, married Thankful Morgan, daughter of Capt. John and Mary Hall Morgan. Mary Priscilla Cage, daughter of John and Thankful Morgan Cage, married David Barry; their son, David F. Barry, married Lutie Chenault; their daughter, Thankful Barry, married George Harsh, attorney of Memphis, Tenn.

Jane Alexander, daughter of Wm. and Mary Brandon Alexander, married Redmond Barry; David Barry, their son, married Mary Priscilla Cage; their son, David F. Barry, of Gallatin, Tenn. (deceased), married Lutie Chenault; their daughter, Thankful Barry, married George Harsh, attorney of Memphis, Tenn.

MAST AND CABLE GENEALOGY

Copied from Adam Mast's Bible which bears date of February 12th, 1814. Sent by Mrs. W. M. Vaught.

Adam Mast, son of Joseph and Eve (Bowers) Mast, born in Randolph County, N. C., March 6, 1884; died Oct. 18, 1857.
Elizabeth Cable, daughter of Gasper (Casper) Cable and Elizabeth Cable, born in County of Randolph near Huwarre, N. C., March 15, 1785.
Adam and Elizabeth, aforesaid, were married by Esquire Thornton, of Little Doe River, at her aforesaid father's, in Roan's Creek Settlement, Turnpike Road, Carter County, Tenn., March 26, 1807.

THEIR OFFSPRING:

Joseph Mast, Jr., born on Cove Creek in Ashe County, N. C., May 7, 1808; died April 1, 1862.
Mary Mast, born in same place, Aug. 28, 1809; died Aug., 1876.
Elizabeth Mast, Jr., born on the same waters, May 29, 1811; died March, 1853.
Eve Mast, Jr., born in same place, June 20, 1813; died June 11, 1891.
Susannah Mast, born May 5, 1817; died Aug. 19, 1881.
Jacob Mast, born Jan. 12, 1819; died Oct. 29, 1880.
Nancy Mast, born Aug. 20, 1822; died Nov. 29, 1908.

BIRTHS

Joseph C. Mast, May 10, 1808.
Celia Mast, Jan., 1801.
James Hamilton Mast, Aug. 17, 1833.
J. S. Mast, March 12, 1836.
Lou J. Mast, Jan. 20, 1838.
D. B. Mast, Dec. 10, 1841.
W. C. Mast, Dec. 8, 1843.
V. B. Mast, Dec. 8, 1843.
J. J. Mast, May 20, 1846.
John S. Vaught, June 11, 1810.
Rebecca Vaught, Jan. 4, 1813.
Eliza B. Vaught Mast, Nov. 21, 1835.
J. D. S. Mast, Aug. 27, 1857.
J. N. Mast, Oct. 13, 1859.
R. W. G. Mast, Aug. 24, 1862.
S. Danford Mast, May 15, 1871.
W. A. Mast, April 2, 1877.

DEATHS

Joseph C. Mast, March, 1862.
Celia Mast, July 30, 1887.
John S. Vaught, May 18, 1885.
Rebecca Vaught, April 28, 1853.
James H. Mast, July 5, 1912.
Eliza B. Mast, Feb. 9, 1917.

MARRIAGES

James H. Mast and Eliza B. Vaught, Sept. 4, 1856.
This is all the record of the Masts and Vaughts that the old Bible contains, copied just as it is.

DUGGER RECORDS

From the papers in the Revolutionary War pension claim, W-7062, it appears that John Dugger was born in 1749 in Surry County, Va.
While residing in Dinwiddie County, Va., he enlisted and served six weeks as a private in Captain Peterson Goodwin's Company, Colonel Banister's Regiment in the Virginia Troops, dates not stated. About a year later he served six or seven weeks under Captain Dickson and Colonel Edward Pegrim in the Virginia Troops.
While residing in Brunswick County, Va., he enlisted in the fall of 1780 and served more than three months in Captain William Lucas' Company, Colonel Robert Mumford's Regiment, and was in the Battle of Guilford.
He was allowed pension on his application executed Aug. 21, 1832, while a resident of Sumner County, Tenn. He died March 23, 1834.
Soldier, married Nov. 4, 1771, Francis (her maiden name is not stated). She was allowed pension on her application executed April

27, 1838, while a resident of Sumner County, Tenn.; age 88 years.

Leonard, their second child, born Nov. 4, 1773, and Flood, their seventh child, was born Jan. 20, 1788.

Leonard Dugger, married Rhodia (maiden name not given), Jan. 12, 1791.

Their children were:

Jarrot, born Feb. 8, 1792; married August 25, 1811, Polly W. Adams.

Wesley, born April 30, 1893; married July 15, 1816, Letty (?).

Polly, born Dec. 14, 1795.

Betsey and John, twins, born Nov. 14, 1797.

Leonard Dugger, married Elizabeth Taylor, Jan. 12, 1801. She was born in 1773. Their daughter, Nancy, was born Sept. 5, 1801; married John Johnson, Aug. 27, 1818; died July 10, 1820.

Leonard Johnson, son of Nancy and John Johnson, born Sept. 24, 1819. Leonard Dugger, son of Jarrot and Polly Dugger, born Sept. 12, 1815. William Ferguson Dugger, son of Jarrot and Polly Dugger, born April 4, 1817.

Will of Leonard Shoun

From records of County Court Clerk of Johnson County. Sent by Mrs. W. M. Vaught, Elizabethton.

In the name of God. Amen. I, Leonard Shoun, of the County of Johnson and State of Tennessee, being of sound and perfect mind and memory, blessed be God, do this 6th day of December, in the year of our Lord 1841, do make and publish this as my last will and testament, thereby revoking and making void all other wills by me at any time made.

First, I direct that my funeral expenses and all of my debts be paid as soon after my death as possible out of any moneys that I may die possessed of or may first come into the hands of my executors.

Secondly, I give and bequeth to my beloved wife, Barbary, to have and enjoy peaceable during her natural life, then to be disposed of as hereafter mentioned, the brick house, kitchen, barn and all other outhouses, all lands here where I now live, and all entries of lands that I now own, and all the negroes that I now own, together with their increase, and all the cash that may be on hand, and all the debts that may be owing, and all the farming tools and smith tools of every description, and all other property of every description except such as I have herein bequethed to my other heirs. I hereby empower my beloved wife, Barbary, to sell either one or all of the negroes if she may wish to do so by first calling on my executors to aid and assist in such sale or sales of said negroes, and all the ground and products of every description that may be on said farm must remain on it for the use and comforts of my beloved wife, Barbary.

Thirdly, I give and bequeth to my two younger sons, David H. and Elihu, to have peaceable and full possession of all my lands above named after the death of my beloved wife, Barbary, and not before, viz: David H. must have possession of the brick house and kitchen for the first ten years, Elihu to have possession of all my buildings at the Cross Roads for the same length of time, then change possession and continue to change every ten years during life, and all farming and smith tools of every kind to be equally divided between D. H. and Elihu and one wagon and gearing and one truck wagon to equally belong to them both and all the kitchen furniture to be equally divided between them, and David H. to have one Chiney Press and one Secretary, and Elihu to have one bureau and one desk and one clock and each one to have one bedstead and furniture to the same, one cow and calf and six sheep, and one sow and pigs, and killing hogs, what my executors my think sufficient for one year's support.

Fourthly, I give and bequeth to my daughter, Susannah, two bedsteads with their furniture to the same, one small and one large spinningwheel, one bureau, known by the Hyatt bureau, one horse, best saddle and bridle, to be worth between eighty and one hundred dollars, two cows and calves or cows with calf, and twenty dollars worth of cupboard and kitchen furniture.

Fifth, I give and bequeth to my grandson, James L., the son of my daughter, Catharine, one good horse, saddle and bridle, worth between eighty and one hundred dollars, and all his wearing clothes, one new Sunday suit, worth not less than fifty dollars.

Sixth, all the remainder of my property, both real and personal of every description that is not herein named must be sold at the proper time by my executors for cash on six or twelve months as they may think best, and to be divided amongst my lawful heirs as follows, viz: My executors must make an equal division of all the proceeds of the sale or sales after first paying all lawful expenses, except my daughters, Elizabeth, Catharine, Susannah, Louisa Leah (deceased), daughter, Elizabeth, to have one hundred dollars, but if she should become a widow before the distribution of said estate, then she must have one additional hundred dollars, and her husband to have his notes I now hold on him. Daughter Catharine's equal part must be divided equally between her and her daughter, Elizabeth, and her son, James L.; Susannah's equal part must be divided one-half to her and her other half to be divided equally between her two children; and daughter, Louisa Leah (deceased), her equal share must be equally divided among her three children, except my children should raise and school those three orphan children; if so, they must have fifty dollars out of it for each orphan child so raised and schooled.

Lastly, I give and bequeth to my son-in-law, John N. Maddox, one dollar, to be paid out of the proceeds of my estate.

I do hereby nominate and appoint my three sons, viz: John G., Andrew and Isaac, my executors. In witness, I do, to this, my last will and testament, set my hand and seal this 6th day of December, A. D. 1841.

Leonard Shoun, his mark (seal).

Witness: M. M. Wagner, Alex. C. D. Smith.

Genealogical account of births marriages and deaths of Leonard Shoun and family:

Leonard Shoun, born in Loudon County, Va., Nov. 10, 1773.

Barbara (Schlemp) Slimp, his wife, born on Holston Waters, Washington County, Va., May 3, 1775.

Leonard Shoun and Barbara Slimp, married in the same place where she was born, Aug. 14, 1792.

Leonard Shoun's offspring, born in Carter County, Tenn. (now Johnson County):

John Shoun, born June 28, 1793; wife, Susie Baker.

Mary Shoun, born Dec. 5, 1794; husband, Peter Parkee.

Elizabeth Shoun, born Feb. 27, 1796; husband, James Spears.

Andrew Shoun, born Sept. 3, 1797; first wife, Hilly Campbell; second wife, Betsey Powell.

Isaac Shoun, born Feb. 17, 1798; wife, Polly Wills.

Frederick Shoun, born March 20, 1800; wife, Sallie Burkett of North Carolina.

William Shoun, born June 8, 1801; first wife, Jane Brown; second

wife, Mrs. Katy Heaton Goodwin.
Joseph Shoun, born Feb. 27, 1803; wife, Polly Wills.
Catherine or Caty Shoun, born Nov. 6, 1804; husband, Rufus Moore.
Rachel Shoun, born June 3, 1806; husband, David Wagner.
Sarah Shoun, born April 22, 1808; husband, Green Moore.
Nancy Shoun, born Jan. 4, 1811; husband, Peter Phillips.
Rebecca Shoun, born June 4, 1813; husband, John S. Vaught.
Leah Shoun, born July 2, 1815.
David Henderson Shoun, born Jan. 9, 1817; wife, Sarah Baker.
Susanna Shoun, born Jan. 31, 1819; husband, Andrew Wagner.
Elihu Shoun, born Nov. 11, 1820; wife, Mary Hardin.
(Note: Barbara Slemp's father was Simeon Slemp; her mother was Mary Mitz (Slemp), mother of Barbara Shoun; died April 20, 1826; age 84 years. Their children were John, Michael, Jacob and Barbara, and others.)

Dugger Records

Sent by Mrs. W. M. Vaught, Elizabethton.

Children, as known, of Julius Dugger, Sr., and wife:
William, born 1750.
Julius, Jr., born 1760.
Mary, married, first, Lawson Goodwin; second, Jacob Smith.
Julius Dugger, Sr., had two brothers. Ben settled at Brushy Fork, N. C. Five generations of his descendants are buried in Brushy Fork Burying Ground. David settled in Kentucky.

Julius Dugger, Jr., born Sept. 9, 1760.
His wife, Mary Hall, formerly of Rockbridge County, Va., married 1779.
Mary Hall Dugger, died March, 1838.
Julius Dugger, died July, 1838.
Children of Julius Dugger, Jr., and Mary Hall Dugger:
John Dugger, Sr., born Oct. 1, 1780, Wilkes County, N. C., where Wilkesboro is located; died Aug. 2, 1869. His wife, Mary Engle, born Dec. 22, 1785; died Feb. 7, 1869.
Nancy Dugger, born Oct. 31, 1782; husband, James George.
William Dugger, born Sept. 7, 1784; died unmarried, Jan. 13, 1875.
Abel Dugger, born Dec. 29, 1786; wife, Jennie Jenkins.
Julius Dugger, born 1787; died 1792.
Elizabeth Dugger, born 1789; died Jan. 10, 1850; husband, Elisha Rainbolt, married 1817.
Charlotte Dugger, born Nov. 6, 1791; husband, Thomas Anderson.
Margaret (Peggy) Dugger, born May 22, 1798; died April 20, 1876; unmarried.
Polly or Mary Dugger, born Aug. 18, 1800; died Sept. 13, 1875; husband, Michael Pierce, died March 4, 1876.

Mary Engle Dugger was a daughter of Mr. and Mrs. George Engle. Her mother was a Sturm and her brother was Jacob Sturm, born in Hagerstown, Md., Dec. 6, 1774, her mother being an older sister. Jacob died April 13, 1834, at Blountville, Tenn.
Jacob Sturm was register of deeds for historic Sulivan County for many years. Jacob Sturm was the only county officer who saved the records pertaining to his office when the court house was destroyed by fire during a battle of Civil War days.

Record of John Dugger, Sr.'s, family and wife, Mary Engle, formerly of Virginia. He was the son of Julius Dugger, Jr., who was born Sept. 9, 1760, and whose wife was Mary Hall, formerly of Rockbridge County, Va. Julius Dugger, Jr., was the son of Julius Dugger, Sr., or Julius C. Dugger, the pioneer of the Watauga Settlement. (Julius C., according to Ramsey.)

Record of John Dugger, Sr.'s, family, eldest son of Julius Dugger and wife, Mary Hall Dugger, of Rockbridge County, Va.

John Dugger, Sr., was born Oct. 1, 1780, in Wilkes County, N. C., where Wilkesboro is now located, and came with his parents when he was 1 year of age to Dugger's Ferry (now Fish Springs), where they made their home. He died Aug. 2, 1869.

He was married to Miss Mary Engle, Feb. 26, 1801, by John Sands, Esq., in a house near where Shupe's Mill is located at Butler, Tenn.

Mary Engle, wife of John Dugger, Sr., born Dec. 22, 1785; died Feb. 2, 1869.

THEIR CHILDREN

Elizabeth Dugger, born April 22, 1802; died March 17, 1842; unmarried.

Julius Dugger, twin, born Feb. 9, 1803; died May, 1803.

Geo. Dugger, twin, born Feb. 9, 1803; died Sept., 1803.

John Dugger, Jr., born Aug. 23, 1804; died Feb. 10, 1894; wife, Rhoda Cable, born Oct. 10, 1809.

Samuel Dugger, born Jan. 16, 1806; died June 12, 1890; wife, Hannah Potter.

William B. Dugger, born March 14, 1807; died Aug. 19, 1881; wife, Elizabeth Holtsclaw.

Abel N. Dugger, born Dec. 24, 1808; died Aug. 25, 1849; wife, Loranie Holtsclaw.

Hiram Dugger, born Sept. 6, 1810; wife, Zanie Nolan.

Jacob Dugger, born March 10, 1812; wife, Mary Brown.

Benjamin C. Dugger (a resident of Georgia), born Dec. 7, 1813; wife, Mrs. Taylor.

Charlotte Dugger, born Oct. 15, 1815; died June 29, 1906; husband, Claiborn Cable.

Peter Engle Dugger, born Nov. 22, 1817; died Dec. 23, 1898; wife, Elizabeth Cable.

Joseph Dugger, born Feb. 13, 1818; died March 1, 1896; wife, first, Polly Step; second, Eliza Campbell.

Mary Dugger, born Jan. 10, 1832 (record very dim); husband, Thomas Whitehead.

James B. Dugger, born April 27, 1821; died Oct. 5, 1861, killed by soldier; wife, Rebecca Vines.

Nancy Dugger, born July 29, 1825; died Dec. 16, 1909; husband, Thomas Anderson.

Margaret Jenkins Dugger, born Dec. 17, 1826; died Nov. 16, 1850; husband, Harrison Gregg.

Solomon Quincy Dugger, born April 25, 1828; died Aug. 12, 1910; wife, first, Jane Vines; second, Mack Mary King.

Emily Dugger, born Sept. 2, 1830; died March 2, 1912; husband, Elijah Bunting.

Mildred Dugger, born June 21, 1833; husband, John Anderson.

(Note: Tradition—Julius Dugger, Sr., or Julius C. Dugger, and wife returned to Virginia in their old age to visit relatives. There they died and were buried probably with children and other relatives.)

CHILDREN

Children of Julius, Sr., or Julius C., as far as known:

William, born 1750 (Revolutionary War).

Julius, Jr., born 1760 (Revolutionary War).

Mary; husband, first, Lawson Goodwin; second, Jacob Smith.

Julius is buried at Fish Springs.

Ben is buried at Brushy Fork, N. C.

Mary is buried at Fish Springs.

Julius Dugger, Sr., or Julius C., had two brothers, David and Ben, and a sister, Mary.

WILL OF WILLIAM DUGGER

From the records of County Court Clerk of Carter County. Sent by Mrs. W. M. Vaught, Elizabethton.

In the name of God. Amen. I, William Dugger, Sr., in East Tennessee, Carter County, calling to mind that it is appointed for all men once to die, I do constitute and ordain this, my last will and testament, and desire that it may be received of all people as such. First, I give and bequeath my soul to God that gave it and my body to the grave to be buried at the discretion of my friends. And as for my worldly good and possessions, I give in the following manner: First, I give and bequeath to my daughter, Anna Willson, five dollars; I give and bequeath to my son, Mark Dugger, five dollars; I give and bequeath to my son, James Dugger, five dollars; I give and bequeath to my son, Julius Dugger, five dollars; I give and bequeath to my daughter, Elizabeth, and my daughter, Levina Vanhuss, and to my son, Thomas Dugger, and to my daughter, Rhoda Pierce, and to my daughter, Martha, and to my daughter, Rosamond Morton, an equal share of my tract of land lying in Carter County, East Tennessee, on Watauga, where Mathias Vanhuss and Anderson Pierce now live. I give and bequeath to my daughter, Nancy, and to my daughter, Sabre Morgan, an equal part in my tract of land where my son, Thomas Dugger, now lives, containing one hundred and fifty acres. I give and bequeath to my wife, Anna, possession of all the tract of land I now live on with all the farm and orchard and buildings, during her natural life, and at her death William, David and Tarlton, my three sons, shall have an equal share of it and of the entry joining it. And as for all the flocks and herds and household furniture that remains at the death of my wife, shall be divided amongst my three sons, namely, William, David and Tarlton, and my two daughters, Nancy and Sabre, equally. And I do constitute and ordain my son, William Dugger, and my son, Tarlton Dugger, the sole executors of this, my last will and testament, in witness whereof I have hereunto set my hand and seal this 10th day of April, 1839.

Now in my right senses, William Dugger.

Interlined before signed.

Test.: Jas. Morgan, Wyatt Griffith.

I have written the above will and feel sure that the man that made it was at that time in his right senses. Jas. Morgan.

Brothers and Sister

William, born 1750.

Julius, born 1760.

Mary D. G. Sniule.

Last Will and Testament of William Dugger

From the records of County Court Clerk of Johnson County. Sent by Mrs. W. M. Vaught, Elizabethton.

In the name of God. Amen.

I, William Dugger, of the County of Johnson and State of Tennessee, being of sound mind and memory and considering of this frail and transitary life, do, therefore, make and ordain, publish and declare this to be my last will and testament.

That first, after all my lawful debts are paid and discharged, the residue of my estate, real and personal, I give and bequeath and dispose of as follows:

To the male and female, two tracts of land known as the Forge land, together with the forge and half of the saw-mill, first tract, two thousand acres of land, more or less, adjoining the lands of Ezekiel Smith and others. Second tract of land, one thousand acres of land, more or less, adjoining the lands of Daniel Baker and others. All the above-named lands, iron works and saw-mills I bequeath to the heirs of John Dugger, deceased, to John Dugger, Sr., Benjamin Dugger, Jacob F. Dugger, Hiram Dugger, Joseph Dugger, Sr., Peter E. Dugger, Solomon Q. Dugger and Wm. B. Dugger, Samuel Dugger,

Charlotte Cable, Mary Whitehead, Emanuel Bunton, Nancy Anderson. These are the heirs which I give and bequeath the above described land, premises to be equally divided and to dispose of as they may see fit. Furthermore, I give and bequeath to my beloved niece, Nancy J. Cowan, daughter of Charlotte Anderson and wife of Thomas Cowan, my hope plantation, which is three hundred and fifty acres of land, more or less, with the exceptions of forty acres of land out of the above-named tract of land with the buildings thereon to her and to her heirs and her children and her children's heirs forever. And I furthermore give and bequeath to Mary C. Bogle, daughter of Charlotte Anderson, deceased. I give and bequeath to her and her heirs twenty-five acres of land, a part of my farm lying on the north side of Roan's Creek opposite Ezekiel Smith's, where Washington Bowman and others now live. The above described lot of land she is at liberty to dispose of as she may see fit. I furthermore give and bequeath to my beloved sister, Mary Pierce, and her heirs, fifty acres of land lying on Roan's Creek, opposite Ezekiel Smith, which is at liberty to dispose of as she may see fit. And to the heirs of my beloved brother, Abel Dugger, deceased, fifty acres of land out of the above-named tract of land lying on the north side of Roan's Creek, opposite Ezekiel Smith's, which they are at liberty to dispose of as they may see fit. Furthermore, I give to the heirs of my beloved sister, Nancy George, deceased, and wife of James J. George, deceased, fifty acres of land lying on the north side of Roan's Creek, opposite Ezekiel Smith's, which they are at liberty to dispose of as they may see fit. Furthermore, I give to the heirs of my beloved sister, Elizabeth Rainbolt, deceased, wife of Elisha Rainbolt, deceased, lying on the north side of Roan's Creek, opposite Ezekiel Smith's, which they are at liberty to dispose of as they may see fit. The last six above-named heirs are to have their lands out of which is known as the Roan's Creek farm, lying on the north side of Roan's Creek, opposite Ezekiel Smith's, where Washington Bowman and others now live. The above-described lots of land are taken out of four hundred acre tract of land, be it the same, more or less. And I furthermore give and bequeath all my claim and interest in and to the estate of my father, Julius Dugger, deceased. To my two sisters, Margaret Dugger and Mary Pierce, and I also empower my executor, J. D. Pierce, to make titles to all the lands I have sold to my sister, Margaret Dugger, on the south side of the Watauga River, opposite where Margaret Dugger now lives. I know to be properly understood I reserve one hundred and twenty-five acres of land out of my farm lying on the north side of Roan's Creek, opposite Ezekiel Smith's, including the first mill and water navigation, power and building thereon, where Washington Bowman now lives. The last six above-named heirs are to have their lots outside of the 125 acres of land, which I reserve to do as I please with hereafter, and to be more properly understood, they are to have fifty acres of land apiece, with this exception, Mary C. Bogle is to only have twenty-five acres of land if there be that amount after my own one hundred twenty-five acres of land is taken out. I furthermore desire and request my niece, Nancy J. Cowan, to let my colored woman, Anna George or alias Anna Dugger, to have a room or house to put her household property in or let her stay in the house with her as they may agree on by giving Anna her choice. I furthermore request that she have a garden spot and land to maintain herself on. Otherwise, see that she is maintained her lifetime out of the proceeds of the farm and after Anna's death all the above privilege to go back to Nancy J. Cowan and her heirs forever. Furthermore, I want it to be properly understood that iron ore is on the land that I bequeath to Nancy J. Cowan and her heirs is to go to the use of the forge, known as Dugger's Forge, and what other minerals, be it what it may, must be equally divided among all my above-named brothers and sisters. And I furthermore give to the heirs of John Dugger, deceased, the Baker Iron Ore Bank, to be equally divided among themselves. I furthermore want my executors to pay over out of my estate to Nancy Rainbolt ten dollars which I feel myself indebted to her for waiting on me when I had the smallpox. I furthermore bind my executors to pay out of my estate my burial and funeral expenses if there be any. I give, bequeath and desire all the rest, residue and remainder of my real and personal estate to my above-named brothers and sisters, to be equally divided, share and share alike.

Likewise, I make, constitute my nephew, Julius D. Pierce, and my brother-in-law, Thomas Anderson, to executors of my last will and testament, hereby revoking all former wills by me made.

In witness to hereof I have hereunto subscribed my name and affixed my seal the 5th day of October, in the year of our Lord 1872. William Dugger.

The above written instrument was subscribed by the said William Dugger in our presence and acknowledged by him to each of us and at the same time published and declared the above instrument so subscribed to be his last will and testament, and we, as the testators, request and in his presence have signed our names as witness hereunto and written opposite our names our respective places of residence.

S. P. Sorrells, Johnson County, Tenn.

I. F. McQueen, Johnson County, Tenn.

Stout Records

David Stout and Elizabeth Howard were married July 14, 1818.

Births

Samuel Stout, April 11, 1819.
Nancy Stout, Nov. 3, 1820.
Alfred Stout, Aug. 20, 1823.
Barbary Stout, Nov. 27, 1825.
Sarah Stout, June 12, 1828.
Godfrey Daniel Stout, May 2, 1830.
George W. Stout, May 27, 1833.
Mary Stout, Dec. 23, 1836.
Dicy Stout, Jan. 17, 1840.
Elizabeth Stout, Aug. 25, 1843.
David D. Stout, Nov. 6, 1790.
Abraham Stout, Jan. 20, 1871.
Elizabeth Stout, May 12, 1843.
Eliza Matilda Stout, May 12, 1868.

Deaths

Godfrey D. Stout, March 2, 1900.
David D. Stout, April 11, 1888.
Eliza Matilda Stout, Dec. 15, 1893.
Susan Garland, May 21, 1905.
Dicy Garland, Nov. 20, 1925.

Births

J. Walter Leo Crosswhite, Nov. 26, 1893.

James Morgan, April 26, 1760, in Maryland, Baltimore County, and chiefly raised between Salsborough and Hillsborough. Certified Feb. 10, 1839.

Widow's certificate of David D. Stout is No. 34988. David was a son of Catherine and Godfrey Stout. His first wife was Elizabeth Howard; second wife, Anne Martin. David Stout died April 11, 1888; age 97 years 5 months 5 days.

Jeremiah Campbell's Last Will and Testament

Exhibited in open court and admitted to probate the 6th day of November, 1843.

I, Jeremiah Campbell, do make and publish this as my last will and testament, hereby revoking and making void all other wills by me at any time made. First, I direct that my funeral expenses and all my debts be paid as soon after my death as possible, out of any moneys I may die possessed of, or may first come into the hands of my executor. Secondly, I give and bequeath to Nathaniel T. Campbell, my negro boy, Joel, aged 5 or 6 years, and also the first child that Amanda may bring forth hereafter, and no more thereafter, and also one of two young horses in the woods at this time. Thirdly, I give and bequeath to Andrew I. Campbell my negro woman, Amanda, and her child, Eliza Ann, and also two head of horses, and one wide horned cow, and one red cow, and also two red barrows and one spaid sow. Also my household furniture; also one big pot and oven, except one bureau, which belongs to Nathaniel T. Campbell, and also my crop now growing, to wit: wheat, rye, oats, corn and buckwheat. Lastly, I do hereby nominate and appoint Nathaniel T. Campbell my executor. In witness whereof I do, to this my will, set my hand and seal, this 11th day of August, A. D. 1843. Jeremiah Campbell.

Signed, sealed and published in our presence, and we have subscribed our names hereto in the presence of the testator. This 11th day of August, 1843.

Benjamin Dyer, Alexander Lacey.

Will of John Vaught

From the records of County Court Clerk of Carter County. Sent by Mrs. W. M. Vaught, Elizabethton.

In the name of God. Amen. I, John Vaught, of Carter County, State of Tennessee, being sick and weak in body, but of sound mind and disposing memory, for which I thank God, and calling to mind uncertainty of human life and being desirous to dispose of all such worldly estate as it hath pleased God to bless me with.

Item: I do will and bequeath to my beloved wife, Esther, all the household furniture for her benefit during her lifetime, and at her death to be equally divided between our two daughters, Elizabeth Heaton and Barbara Howard, also I leave and bequeath to my wife two negroes, Joseph and Rachel, for her use and benefit during her life, and at her death to be equally divided among our three children; also leave my wife her choice of our horse and mare, three milk cows, her choice of my stock, six head of sheep, the whole of the hogs and the remainder of my stock to be sold and equally divided among my three children. I also leave and bequeath to my wife the full benefits of the third part that is or may be raised on the plantation where I now live, that is of all kinds of grain and hay for her use, and at her disposal, also the house I now live in during her life, and likewise I leave her one-third part of my money after paying all just debts.

Item: I leave and bequeath to my son, Josop, the plantation where I now live and all lands belonging to me. I also leave him four negroes, Jean, Bishop, Elijah and Moses. I leave my son the mills by him paying his mother the third of the profits if she requires it during her life. I also leave my son my smith tools.

Item: I leave my daughter, Elizabeth Heaton, one-third part of my money after paying all just debts.

Item: I leave my daughter, Barbara Howard, one-third part of my money after paying all just debts.

Item: I leave my wife the benefit of the barn and all out-houses at her disposal and for her use.

Item: I desire my son, Joseph, to pay all my just debts out of my money and collect and settle my affairs.

I hereby revoke all my other or former wills or testaments by me

heretofore made.
In witness whereof I have hereunto set my hand and affixed my seal, this 6th day of June, in the year of our Lord, 1806. John Vaught (seal).

Signed, sealed and delivered as and for the last will and testament of the above John Vaught, in presence of us.
Mathias Wagner, Jurat, Tapley Wilson, Jurat (his mark).

Will of Isaac Lincoln

From the records of County Court Clerk of Carter County. Sent by Mrs. W. M. Vaught, Elizabethton.

In the name of God. Amen. I, Isaac Lincoln, of the County of Carter and State of Tennessee, being sick and weak of body, but of sound mind and disposing memory, for which I thank God, and calling to mind the uncertainty of human life, being desirous to dispose of all such worldly substance as it has pleased God to help me with.
I give, devise and bequeath the same in manner following, that is to say:
First, I desire that all my just debts and funeral expenses be paid out of my perishable property by my executor hereinafter named.
Second, after the payment of my debts and funeral expenses, I give, devise and bequeath to my wife, Mary Lincoln, all my real and personal estate to dispose of as she may think proper.
Third, and lastly, I do hereby constitute and appoint my wife, Mary Lincoln, my sole executrix of this, my last will and testament, hereby revoking all other or former wills or testaments by me heretofore made.

In witness whereof I have hereunto set my hand and seal this 22nd day of April, in the year of our Lord 1816.

Signed, sealed, published and declared to be the last will and testament of the above-named Isaac Lincoln, in the presence of us, who at his request and in his presence have hereunto subscribed our names as witnesses to the same.

George W. Carter, Godfrey Carriger, Daniel Stover, Christian Carriger.

Isaac Lincoln (seal).

Will of Mary Lincoln

From the records of County Court Clerk of Carter County. Sent by Mrs. W. M. Vaught, Elizabethton.

I, Mary Lincoln, of the County of Carter and State of Tennessee, being of sound mind and memory, though weak of body, and being anxious to dispose of such worldly property as my Creator has blessed me with, do hereby make, ordain and establish this as my last will and testament. I give my soul to God who created it, hoping that he will receive and bless me in a world of happiness hereafter; and when I shall have departed this life, I desire that my executor hereinafter named shall give my body a decent and Christian burial.
First, I will give, devise and bequeath to Campbell Crow, the lower plantation, it being the one on which he now lives, adjoining the lands of Alfred M. Carter on the west, and south of John Carriger on the east. Second, I will give and bequeath to Phoebe Crow, wife of Campbell Crow, my negro girl, Margaret, and her four children, to win: Lucy, Mina, Martin and Mahala. Third, I will give, devise and bequeath the hereditaments and appurtenances to the same belonging, the said plantation supposed to be composed of two different parcels and adjoining John

Carriger's home plantation and believed also to adjoin the land of Alfred M. Carter on the south and bounded on the east and north by Watauga River, I give the said plantation to the said William Stover to have, hold and enjoy during his life and at his death to descend to his heirs. Fourth, I will give and bequeath to William Stover the following negroes, to wit: Patsey, a negro girl, and her two children, Cynthia and Landon, also negro woman, Jane, and her two children, Sam and Tom, also negro woman, Mary, and her six children, to wit: Elizabeth, Campbell, Margaret, Charlotte, Delphy and Bill, also Caesar and Lucy, whom I desire the said William Stover to permit to remain during their lives on the plantation which I have herebefore bequeathed to him. It is my will that the said Stover, so long as the said Caesar and Lucy continue to live shall clothe and support them. I also give and bequeath to the said William Stover three other negroes, to wit: George, Phoebe and Eliza, children of Lucy, whom I wish the said William Stover to permit to remain on the home plantation that they may take care of the aforesaid negroes, Caesar and Lucy, during their lives. I also give and bequeath the following other negroes to the said William Stover, to wit: Esther and her seven children; that is to say, Louise, Violet, Juda, Lucinda, Mary, Lewis and Phoebe. I also give and bequeath to the said William Stover two other negroes, to wit: William and Isaac, children of Lucy.

Fifth, I also will give, devise and bequeath to the said William Stover all my horses, cattle, hogs and sheep, my wagon, all my farming utensils, my household and kitchen furniture, and all the debts, dues and demands which may be owing to me at the time of my decease.

Sixth, I also will give and bequeath to Campbell Crow, my interest in any crop which he may have attended for himself upon my land, or which he may be attending for himself upon my land at the time of my decease.

Seventh, I also will give and bequeath to William Stover all the grain of every description, which I own at the time of my death.

Eighth, I will give, devise and bequeath to Christian Carriger, Sr., the following negroes, to wit: negro woman, Letty, and five of her children, to wit: Chrisby, Tennessee, Mardecia, Nathaniel, and also said Letty's youngest child.

Ninth, I will give, devise and bequeath to Mary Lincoln Carriger, daughter of Christian Carriger, Sr., two negro girls, children of Letty, to wit: Sarah Seraphina, and Ann.

Tenth, I will give, devise and bequeath to William Stover all other real and personal estate not hereinbefore specifically named, of which I may be possessed or the owner of at the time of my decease.

Eleventh, I require the said William Stover out of the estate herein bequeathed to him, to pay and discharge all of the honest debts or claims which I may be owing or which may be against me at the time of my death.

Lastly, I do hereby constitute, nominate and appoint the said William Stover the executor of this, my last will and testament, and it is my will that the said William Stover be not required to give any security for the discharge of his duties as executor of this, my last will and testament.

In testimony whereof I have hereunto set my hand and seal this 17th day of April, in the year of our Lord 1834.

Mary Lincoln, her mark (seal).

Signed, sealed, acknowledged in presence of us.

Thos. A. A. R. Nelson, J.; A. M. Carter, J.; A. W. Taylor.

Will of Obed Hull

From the records of County Court Clerk of Carter County. Sent by Mrs. W. M. Vaught, Elizabethton.

I, Obed Hull, do make and publish this as my last will and testament, hereby revoking and making void all wills by me at any time made. First, I direct that my funeral expenses and all my debts be paid as soon after my death as possible out of my personal estate that I fetched with me from Sullivan County, exclusively.
Secondly, I will give back to my wife, Margaret, and her two daughters, Ruth and Ann Hatcher, all the property that she had with the increase of the same when I married her; thereby, I will to my son, Frances Marin Hull, one feather bed and half of the bedding that I fetched with me from Sullivan County, and one large cherry chest and one rifle gun that is at Groces Gun Smith Shop in Sullivan County, and my riding saddle and my interest in ——— that John Powell has for collection off of R. White for forty-five dollars, and all the book accounts that I have coming to me in Sullivan County and the running gears of a three-horse wagon and a bond that I hold on W. S. Cross for the payment of three hundred dollars and upwards for a piece of land.
Fourthly, I will to my wife, Margaret, and daughter, Martha Hull, all my personal property of every kind and description that I now have in Carter County, excepting my windmill and sheep which is to go to my wife exclusively for her own use.
In witness whereof I do to this, my will, set my hand and seal this, the 3rd day of April, 1847.
Obed Hull (seal).
Signed, sealed and published in our presence and we have subscribed our names hereto in the presence of the testator this 3rd day of April, 1847.
James M. Smith, John N. Ellis.
State of Tennessee, Carter County.
June term, June 7, 1847, then was the within will on exhibit, read and proven in open court by James M. Smith and John N. Ellis, the subscribing witnesses thereto witness.
James L. Bradley, Clerk of said Court, June 7, 1847.
Test.: J. L. Bradley, Clerk.

Kercher (Carriger) Records

Sent by Mrs. W. M. Vaught, Elizabethton.

Gotfrey (Godfrey), born March 7, 1732.
Johan (John), born Feb. 28, 1761.
John Michael, born April 26, 1764.
Johan Lenhart.
Gotfried, born May 13, 1769.
Elizabeth, born May 12, 1771.
Johan Henrick (Henry), born Feb. 26, 1774.
Christian, born July 28, 1779.
(Translated by Mrs. Weager of Sacramento, Calif.)
Godfrey Carriger, Sr., died Oct. 8, 1811.
Gotfried Kercher, born March 7, 1732.
Johan Nicholas Kercher, born Feb. 28, 1761.
Johan Michael Kercher, born April 26, 1764.
Johan Lenhart Kercher, born Jan. 3, 1766.
Gotfried Kercher, born May 13, 1769.
Elizabeth Kercher, born May 12, 1771.
Johan Henrich Kercher, born Feb. 26, 1774.
Johan Kercher, born Feb. 24, 1777.
Christian Kercher, born July 28, 1779.
(Translated by Mr. Kirbach of Vallejo, Calif. The original record written in German was taken to California by Christian Carriger descendants in 1846. Mrs.

Evelyn Nelson Tufts, a descendant of Christian Carriger, had this translated by two different German scholars and was sent to me under date of May 5, 1914.)

—

Walnut Grove, March 8, 1835.
Dear Sister: Upon application of John Stover to me for the record of our common father, Godfrey Carriger, of the ages of us, his children, I cheerfully sent to you, but I must assure you that it would have given me more pleasure to have handed this to you myself at my home.
Respectfully, your brother, Christian Carriger.

To Elizabeth Nave.
Godfrey Carriger, Sr., was born March 7, 1732; died Oct. 8, 1811.
John Nichlos Carriger, born Feb. 28, 1761.
John Michael Carriger, born April 26, 1764.
John Leonard Carriger, born Jan. 3, 1767.
Godfrey Carriger, born May 13, 1769.
Elizabeth Carriger, born Feb. 14, 1771.
John Henry Carriger, born Feb. 26, 1774.
John Carriger, born Feb. 14, 1777.
Christian Carriger, born July 28, 1779.

Two deeds recorded in Book 7, pages 191-194, at Reading, Pennsylvania:

Godfrey Kercher and Margaret, his wife, for the sum of 4,000, lawful money of Pennsylvania, to Jacob Morgan, the younger, mentions Philip Banson's land, land late belonging to James Boone, etc., containing 100 acres and allowance of 6 acres for rent, roads, highways, part of 262 acres, 67 perches, by warrant March 5, 1750, surveyed to Robert Levers of Philadelphia, who by deed Dec. 21, 1753, granted to David Barnes of Philadelphia, for whose debts land was sold by Henry Christ, High Sheriff, to Philip Bansom, Aug. 13, 1761, who sold it to Godfrey Kercher.
(German) Godfried Kercher.
Margaret Kercher.
Michael Lindemuth.
Ludwig Herring.
Recorded March 18, 1780.
Henry Christ, Recorder.
Book 7, Page 194.

Deed made Sept. 9, 1779, between Godgrey Kercher of Brunswig Township, Berke County, and Margaret, his wife, of the one part and Jacob Morgan, the younger, of Reading, Berke County: Sold for 8,000, lawful money of Pennsylvania; messuage, saw-mill and four several tracts of land in Brunswig Township. (1) One at mouth of Mahoning Creek, bounded, south, River Schuylkill; west, land surveyed for George Boone; north, James Boone's land; northeast, Francis Paroinis land; east, by hill of vacant land, containing 500 acres.
Surveyed by virtue of warrant granted in 1752 to a certain Burgoon Bird, who by deed Sept. 14, 1754, granted to Peter Conrad in fee, who by deed thereon, endorsed May 22, 1762, granted to John, Isaiah and Isaac Willits and Ellis Hughes, which said John and Isaac Willits and Ellis Hughes, by deed, 28th day of 8th month, 1764, did release their right unto Isaiah Willits, who, by indenture, Aug. 29, 1765, granted 400 acres thereof unto Godfrey Kercher and afterwards granted the overplus 100 acres, by indenture, March 25, 1768, unto James McNail in fee, who, by deed, Nov. 22, 1768, granted overplus unto Godfrey Kercher.

(2) One other of them adjoining the said last mentioned tract and land of James Boone on Mahoning Creek containing 125 acres, surveyed or intended to be surveyed by warrant dated June 1, 1751, unto Francis Parvin, who by indenture, 3rd day, 9th month, 1762, granted to John, Isaiah and Isaac Willits and Ellis Hughes, who by

deed, 28th day, 8th month, 1764, Isaiah and Isaac Willits and Ellis Hughes released same to John Willits, who, dying, seized thereof and also of other 50 acres, next herein mentioned, granted by will Feb. 25, 1765, directed executors to sell land. Ellis Hughes and Isaac Willits by deed, April 13, 1771, granted to Godfrey Kercher.

(3) One other, adjoining last mentioned 125 acres, containing 50 acres, intended to be surveyed to John Willits (application No. 257), bearing date Aug. 5, 1765, sold to Godfrey Kercher.

(4) Other adjoining Charles Berger and Rudolph Kendle, about three miles from Schuylkill River, containing 50 acres, granted by warrant, March 13, 1752, to George Gardner, who by deed, July 22, 1752, granted to Michael Fisher, who, June 15, 1762, granted to James Boone, who by deed, June 4, 1774, granted to Godfrey Kercher.

Godfrey Kercher (Godfried Kercher, in German).

Margaret Kercher.

Witnesses: Michael Lindemuth, Ludwig Herring.

Recorded March 10, 1780. Henry Christ, Recorder.

Book 7, Page 191-194, Reading, Pa.

Letter concerning genealogy of the Carriger (Kercher) family:

Berlin, S. O. 33, March 8, 1927.
Bevernstrasse.

His Highness, Baron Von dem Husche, Aix-la-Chapelle, Alfonsstrasse 17.

Dear Sir: The family in question can be only that of Karcher, from Kaiserslautern, an extremely energetic family which I took up several times in connection with other genealogies. It is in close relation to the Rochlings, von Gienath, Rettig, etc., and appears also as branches in the book revised by me, the "Kpf Geschl Buch" (next in that of Starks). A special genealogy does not exist so far. Karcher or Kercher (Mediaeval Karrigers) were called at Kaiserslautern the coachman who formed a corporation. The family rose from a low situation and had later a distinguished name in manufacturing (cloth and iron).

The firm of Karcher is mentioned there already in 1746. Later on this name appeared as alderman and was often mentioned in connection with the position of burgomasters. At the end of the French period the family rose high. It emigrated partly, for instance, to Saarbrucken.

The conditions at Kaiserslautern were at that time, 1784, very poor and they became worse during the revolution. Many people emigrated, some to Pennsylvania. Pennsylvania had from 1,683 on very close relations with the Platinate, and Germantown was a pure German city. I published numerous articles on these questions. If your acquaintance wants the exact date, fundamental researches must be made on the spot. The family belonged to the Reformed Church, as is shown by the existing church books from 1703 on. The missing information must be completed from the documents of the city. I had found several things concerning this family also in the Speier Archives and would be glad to make abstracts as far as the material is available here. A detailed research would be worth while as it concerns a very interesting and typical family and I often regret that nobody was interested in it. On this occasion I found in another book of genealogy (Oehlert) which appeared as a private edition about the director, P. H. Karcher, who introduced in the Platinate the manufacture of Siamose, at the end of the Eighteenth Century. I have sent you also some pamphlets in which you will find this family mentioned. As I said above, the question is not of a complete and full genealogy.

In case of a desire to undertake the research, I could do this on the occasion of my next visit here.

Always ready to serve you, I remain, respectfully, (signed) E. L. Antz.

Letter concerning genealogy of the Carriger (Kercher) family:

Sobernheim, March 19, 1927.
Dr. Betzler.
My Dear Baron: The researches on the origin of Michael Karcher will probably not be easy to make as the name was at that time very common in the Platinate and its territory was large. It was over 8,000 sq. km., while the present Platinate is only 6,000 sq. km. The Kurpfalz, the principality of Simmern, Valdenz, Lautern and the duchy of Zweibrucken belong to it. I know the name especially from Saarbrucken, which, of course, had never belonged to the Platinate. There exists also a Karcher Street. I know here a family Karcher from Genheim near Kreuznach and Stromberg, small farmers. In the vicinity there are the Stromberg iron works. Genheim belonged in 1738 to the Kurpfalz, district of Kreuznach. It is possible that the emigrant came from Genheim, but it is also possible that he was from many other places of the Platinate. Karcher or Kercher means "mediaeval word," Karrner, that is coachman. This occupation was, owing to the numerous communications lines of Central Germany with the west, Paris, Metz and Trier, very widespread. Genheim is close to the old Roman road, Bingen-Trier.
To obtain more information, I consider the following necessary: A complete copy of the ships register of the sailing ship "Friendship." We must suppose that some other people from the same village or neighborhood, ones of the Platinate, emigrated at the same time. Better information about the place may exist as far as the others are concerned. We could probably establish the place of the origin more easily by using those names.
A finding out by the mentioning of the names of Karcher or Kercher in the former Platinate based on the records of losses during the World War. According to my experience, the records give almost complete information on the names of the present time. An examination of the directories will be incomplete as the population of the country is not mentioned there. These inquiries could be made without great expenses by the aid of the Central Information Office at Spandau. In the places where the name exists at the present time the church books should be examined.
Finally, the following printed sources, which, of course, are not at my disposal, can be taken into consideration: F. Kapp History of the German Immigration to America, Leipzig, 1868; Nebenius, History of the Platinate, Heidelberg, 1874. Some facts on the origin of the emigrants might be found there.
Some information on the Kercher family could probably be obtained also from the well-known Rhine Sowing Co., Raab, Karcher and Co. (Rheinschlepprhedrei Raab, Karcher & Co.)
After you have a copy of the ship's register I will be glad to make further inquiries or help you in making researches at Genheim or other places of the Kurpflaz and Simmern as well as in the Central Information. I hope that I was of a little service to you and am sorry that I could not help more. I will inform you in other information on the name is known to me.
With excellent respect, Dr. Betzler, District Court Adviser.
P. S.: As I know from other emigrants, of course from a later period of time, documents with the mark on the day of the arrival of the ship and places in Germany

where from the emigrants arrive, are served in America. Perhaps some information on the origin, if the name could be obtained also from the first place of settlement in Pennsylvania.

WILL OF MARGARET CARRIGER

From the records of County Court Clerk of Carter County. Sent by Mrs. W. M. Vaught, Elizabethton.

I, Margaret Carriger, being in feeble health, but of sound mind, do this day make and ordain this my last will and testament.
First, I request that all the debts which I may be owing at the time of my death and also all my funeral expenses shall be paid out of my money which I may have on hand or may be due me at my death.
Secondly, I give and bequeath to my son, James P. Carriger, my black woman, Delphy, a slave, and my mare, Pet, and my buggy, and also all my household and kitchen furniture and my loom.
Thirdly, I give and bequeath to my son, George M. Carriger, twenty-five dollars.
Fourthly, I give and bequeath to my daughters-in-law, Martha M. Carriger and Isabella P. Carriger, all the gears and stays belonging to my loom, to be equally divided between them.
Fifthly, I give and bequeath to my granddaughter, Margaret I. E. Carriger, my small table.
Sixthly, I give and bequeath to my son, Elliott Carriger, all the residue of my estate of every manner and kind after satisfying the foregoing bequeaths and paying the expenses of executing this will.
Sevently, I appoint my sons, James P. Carriger and Christian E. Carriger, executors of this, my last will and testament.
In testamony whereof I have hereunto set my hand and affixed my seal, this 8th day of August, 1854.
Margaret Carriger, her mark (seal).
Witnesses: G. T. Magee, Thomas Nave.

DEED OF GIFT

From the records of County Court Clerk of Carter County. Sent by Mrs. W. M. Vaught, Elizabethton.

This indenture made the 13th of January, in the year of our Lord 1795, between Godfrey Carriger, Sr., of the County of Washington and Territory of the United States, south of the River Ohio, of the one part, and Godfrey Carriger, Jr., his son, of the county and territory aforesaid, of the other part.
Witnesseth: The said Godfrey Carriger, Sr., as well for and in consideration of the natural love and affection which he hath and beareth unto the said Godfrey Carriger, Jr., his son, as also for the better maintenance and preferment of the said Godfrey Carriger, Jr., hath given, granted, aliened, enfeoffed and confirmed, and by these presents doth give, grant, alien, enfeoff and confirm unto the said Godfrey Carriger, Jr., and his heirs a certain piece or parcel of land situate, lying and being in the County Washington and territory aforesaid, bounded as follows, viz:
Beginning at the mouth of Stony Creek at white walnut running north one hundred and fifty poles up Stony Creek to a poplar; thence East two hundred and forty poles to a black oak on the top of a hill, thence South two hundred and twenty-five poles to a stake on the line of that tract of land whereon said Godfrey Carriger, Senior, lives on; thence West

one hundred and ninety poles to the south of Sugar Creek; thence North thirty poles to a thorn bush; thence North twenty-five degrees West fourteen poles to a sycamore; thence North forty degrees West twenty-four poles to a large sycamore; thence North sixty-three degrees West, twenty-nine poles to the beginning corner, including the improvements, containing three hundred and twenty-two acres and all houses, buildings, orchards, ways, waters, water courses, profits, commodities, hereditaments and appurtenances whatsoever to the said premises hereby granted or any part thereof belonging or in any wise appertaining, and the reversion and reversions, remainder and remainders, rents, issues and profits thereof, and also all estate, right, title, interest, use, trust, property, claim and demand of him, the said Godfrey Carriger, Senior, of, in and to the said premises, and all deeds, evidences, and writings touching or in any wise concerning the same; *To Have and to Hold* the lands hereby conveyed, and all and singular other the premises hereby given and granted and every part and parcel thereof, with their and every of their appurtenances unto the Godfrey Carriger, Junior, his heirs and assigns forever, to the only proper use and behoof of him, the said Godfrey Carriger, Junior, and of his heirs and assigns forever.

And the said Godfrey Carriger, Senior, doth, for himself, his heirs, executors and administrators, promise, covenant and agree to and with the said Godfrey Carriger, Junior, his heirs, executors and administrators, that he, the said Godfrey Carriger, Senior, will warrant and forever defend the aforesaid tract of land against the claims of all and all manner of persons whatsoever to him the said Godfrey Carriger, Junior, his heirs and assigns forever; and that he, the said Godfrey Carriger, Junior, and his heirs shall forever peaceably and quietly enjoy, possess and occupy the aforementioned tract of land without the least hindrance or molestation of any person or persons whatsoever.

In witness whereof, the said Godfrey Carriger, Senior, hath hereunto set his hand and seal the day and year first above written.

GODFREY KERCHER (Seal).

Signed, sealed and delivered in presence of William Ward and Pharoah Cobb (his mark).

Washington County, February term, 1795.

This deed was duly proven in Court. Let it be registered.

Test.: Jas. Sevier, Clk.

Washington County, March 16th, 1795. Registered in Book F, page 78.

Wm. Stephenson, Clk.

Endorsed on back:

Deed of Gift—Godfrey Carriger, Senior, to Godfrey Carriger, Jun., his son—322 Acres Land.

LAST WILL AND TESTAMENT OF GODFREY CARRIGER, SR.

From the records of County Court Clerk of Carter County. Sent by Mrs. W. M. Vaught, Elizabethton.

In the name of God, Amen:

I, Godfrey Carriger, Senior, of the County of Carter, in the State of Tennessee, being weak and frail of body, but of perfect and sound mind and memory, do make, publish and declare this my last will and testament in manner and form following, that is to say:

First: I give and bequeath to my son, Nicholas Carriger, the plantation whereon he now lives on Stoney Creek, for which I have heretofore executed to him a deed of conveyance; also give and bequeath to my said son, Nicholas, one negro wench named Sall and her child "Will" and the increase of the said Sall. I also give and bequeath to my said son Nicholas, the sum of two thousand and thirty-three dollars and thirty-three

cents to him and his forever.
Secondly: I give and bequeath unto Godfrey Carriger, Polly Carriger, Anny Carriger and Betsey Carriger, heirs and heiresses of Michael Carriger, deceased, the sum of two thousand five hundred and sixty-six dollars and sixty-six cents.
Thirdly: I give and bequeath to my son Godfrey Carriger, the plantation whereon he now lives for which I have heretofore executed him a deed of gift. I also give and bequeath to my said son, Godfrey, the sum of ——— thousand nine hundred and five dollars and thirty-three cents, to him and his heirs forever.
Fourthly: I give and bequeath to my son-in-law, John Nave, the plantation whereon he used to live, for which I have heretofore made to him a deed of conveyance. I also give and bequeath to my said son-in-law, John Nave, one negro girl named Berry. I also give and bequeath to my said son-in-law, John Nave, the sum of one thousand nine hundred and eighty-three dollars and sixty-six cents, to him and his heirs forever.
Fifthly: I give and bequeath to my son, John Carriger, one tract of land containing two hundred and fifty acres, known by the name of the Sugar Holly tract; also one tract of land containing six hundred and forty acres, known by the name of the Blue Spring tract; also one other tract of land lying and situated on the south side of Watauga River below and adjoining Isaac Lincoln's, which land I bought from William Cocks. I also give and bequeath unto my said son, John Carriger, the sum of one thousand and three hundred and twenty dollars, to him and his heirs forever, for the two aforesaid tracts of land of eight hundred and ninety acres, I have heretofore executed a deed of gift to the said John Carriger.
Sixthly: I give and beqeath to my son Christian Carriger, the plantation whereon I now live, including all the improvements thereon. I also give and bequeath unto my said son, Christian Carriger, one other tract of land known by the name of Linchas place, to him and his heirs forever. I also give and bequeath to my said son, Christian Carriger, an entry or claim of land which I have to an Island in Wataugah including a fish trap in a sluice of said river, to him and his heirs forever. My further will is that all the rest and residue of my estate, as well real as personal, of which I may be possessed at the time of my death (after paying and satisfying all and every of the foregoing legatees and bequeaths) be sold and the money arriving from such sales be divided among the legatees hereinbefore mentioned, share and share alike, except that the heirs of Michael Carriger have but one share to be divided among them.
Lastly, I hereby nominate, constitute and appoint my sons, Godfrey Carriger and Christian Carriger, executors of this last will and testament whereof I, Godfrey Carriger, Senior, have hereunto set my seal the sixteenth day of January, in the year of our Lord, one thousand eight hundred and eight.
Signed, sealed, published, pronounced and declared by the said Godfrey Carriger, Senior, to be his last will and testament in the presence of us who, in the presence of the testator, and in the presence of each other, hereunto signed our names as witnesses.

GODFREY KERCHER (Seal).

Geo. Duffield, Jurat.
William Campbell.
William Bridges, Jurat.
Robert Crow.
This 30th of March, 1808.

Last Will and Testament of John Dugger

From the records of County Court Clerk of Carter County. Sent by Mrs. W. M. Vaught, Elizabethton.

Last Will and Testament of John Dugger, deceased:

1. I, John Dugger, Senior, desire that here after my death bury me in plain and decent form.

2. I give my soul to God who gave it to me.

3. I desire that my sons that are alive shall have one equal share of my part in the forge and sawmill. I desire that my oldest son, John Dugger, Junior, shall have 105 acres of land including the place where Soloman Younce now lives, and to join Esquire Morgan Swift's which is that much more than the rest of his brothers gets of the Forge lands. The rest of his brothers get minerals except he shall have equal share of all the rest of the Iron Works land.

4. I desire that my daughter, Mildred Anderson, shall have an equal share in my part of the sawmill with her brothers.

5. I desire that my son, Samuel Dugger, shall have one hundred acres of land where he now lives on, and an equal share in the Forge land and sawmill, mines and minerals excepted.

6. I desire that my son, William B. Dugger, have the land he now lives on. It is thought to be one hundred acres more or less, and an equal share in the Forge and sawmill and Forge land mines and minerals excepted.

7. I desire that my son, Joseph Dugger, shall have the land he now lives on. The minerals of iron ore to be divided with his brothers if they want to work in the Forge and sawmill. I desire them to sell to some of their brothers. I desire that Jacob F. Dugger have an equal share in my Forge and Iron Works lands and sawmill. I desire that my son, Hiram Dugger, shall have a piece of land on the Chestnut land on the Chestnut Ridge, thought to be one hundred and twenty acres, more or less, adjoining the flat of Dugger Branch, and an equal share in my Forge and sawmill and Forge land with his brothers that has a part in said Forge land, only his brother, John Dugger, has two shares in the Forge land, the mines and minerals excepted for me and my heirs.

8. I desire that my son, Benjamin C. Dugger, shall have one hundred acres of land at the foot of Stone Mountain and Baker's Gap Road, and joins Thomas Ward's land, mines and minerals excepted. I desire that my son, B. C. Dugger, shall have an equal share with his brothers in my Forge and sawmill and Forge land, only John Dugger, Jr., he has two shares of mines and minerals excepted for me and my heirs.

9. I desire that Joseph Dugger shall have an equal share with his brothers in my part of the Forge and sawmill and an equal part in my share of the Forge land with the rest of his brothers, only his brother, John, he has two shares in the Forge land, mines and minerals excepted for my use and the use of my heirs.

10. I desire that Soloman Quince Dugger, my youngest son, have the land I sold him for his part of my land. I also desire that he shall have equal share in my Forge and sawmill and Forge lands with the rest of his brothers, only his brother, John Dugger, shares in the Forge lands, mines and minerals excepted for me and my heirs.

11. I desire that my son, Peter E. Dugger, shall have the land I sold to him and he paid me for the same. I also desire that he, Peter E. Dugger, shall have an equal share with the rest of his brothers in my part of the Forge and Forge lands and sawmill, and his brother, John, has two shares in the Forge lands, mines and minerals excepted for me and my heirs.

12. I, John Dugger, Senior, desire

that my daughter, Charlotte Cable, wife of Claiborn Cable, shall have one hundred acres of land known by the name of the Flat Springs land, lying in Watauga County, North Carolina, it being a two hundred acre tract of land, being granted to me by the State of North Carolina. I also desire that my daughter, Emmily Bunton, wife of Elijah Bunton, have the other half of said Flat Spring land to be equally divided by them and a line made through said land with the courses and distances, and they shall have deeds for it, mines and minerals excepted for my use.

13. I desire that my daughter, Nancy Anderson, wife of Thomas Anderson, shall have first choice of two hundred acres of land in a thousand acre tract which joins a thousand acre tract of iron works land on Dry Run. I also desire that my daughter, Nancy Anderson, have thirty-three acres of land that joins in the upper end of the land that Samuel Dugger lived on and joins Elijah Bunton's land, mines and minerals excepted for my use.

14. I desire that my daughter, Mary Whitehead, wife of Thomas Whitehead, have two hundred acres of land in a thousand acre tract of land that joins a thousand acre tract of land on the East end. Joins the land that Esquire Dougherty used to own on Dry Run, joins the foot of the Iron Mountain and Baker's Gap Road, mines and minerals excepted for me and my heirs.

15. I desire that my grandson, George W. Dugger, and Elizabeth Angeline Dugger and Nancy Goddy, wife of Charlie Goddy, and Martha Green have one hundred acres of land, each of them in the thousand acre tract—joins the foot of Stone Mountain in part along the Baker's Gap Road, mines and minerals excepted for my own use.

16. I desire that my grandson, Hiram Gregg, have one bed and bedding.

17. I desire that my son-in-law, Harrison Gregg, shall have if he find a good vein of lead on any of my lands only the fifty acres of mine, and William Dugger shall have fifty dollars worth of minerals or the value of it when smelted.

18. I desire that my daughter, Mildred Anderson, and John Anderson have the place where I now live on and has sold it to Mildred and John Anderson, her husband, for $400.00, and they are to take good care of me and my property, feed and clothe me all the rest of my life time, and on the above conditions the house and one hundred acres of land shall be their's; otherwise they must pay me one thousand dollars or give my house and land and make me a title to it and all will be right.

19. I desire that Col. Kerk have privilege to work my lead mine if he cares to do it soon, and if he finds metal let him melt it and give what is right of the metal.

20. I desire that S. Quince Dugger and Peter E. Dugger and Joseph Dugger, my sons, shall make settlement with their brothers and sisters and all others that have lawful claims.

21. I desire that my well beloved brother, William Dugger, help my heirs in their settlement and keep them at peace if he can, and that Peter and Joseph and S. Quince Dugger pay him for his trouble out of my estate.

22. I desire that my son, S. Quince Dugger, have power of attorney or a general letter of attorney to do my business as I am not able to see to it myself. I hope you will see to it faithfully and honestly and take an oath to do it without fear or favor and honestly. This June, 2nd day, 1869.

23. I desire that my children all meet together and settle with each other in love and peace. I desire my son, Solomon Quince Dugger, to write to them soon after my death as he can and set a time for them to meet here.

24. I desire that John Anderson and Mildred Anderson, if I die before I sell what little stock and

property I have, to let it be sold or divided among themselves. The scraps of land that I have not divided you may divide or sell for money to help in paying my debts, etc.
25. I hereby revoke all former wills made in witness whereof I have set my hand and affixed my seal this 8th day of June, 1869.
JOHN DUGGER, SEN.

Signed, sealed and delivered in the presence of us who have hereunto subscribed our names in the presence of the testator.
Test:
Benjiman D. Cable.
William Dugger, Sen.
A true copy of John Dugger's will.
R. E. BERRY, *Clerk*,
County Court.

WILL OF JACOB SMITH

From the records of County Court Clerk of Carter County. Sent by Mrs. W. M. Vaught, Elizabethton.

State of Tennessee, Carter County: I, Jacob Smith, of the County and State aforesaid, being of sound mind, do make this my last will and testament, in the name of God, Amen: I will and bequeath to my beloved wife, Mary Smith, the land where I now live on and one tract adjoining the same, and all my household furniture of every description and all my stock of every kind, and four negroes, namely, Reuben, Susanah, Minton and James, during her natural life, and then at her decease the said negroes to be my son, Daniel Smith's, the balance of all to be equally divided between my two sons, Daniel and Ezekiel Smith.
I will and bequeath to my oldest son, Daniel Smith, that tract of land where he now lives, and two adjoining tracts also.
I will and bequeath to my son, Ezekiel Smith, that tract of land where he now lives on, and two negroes, Nathaniel and Justice.
I will and bequeath to my daughter, Selah George, ten dollars.
I will and bequeath to my step-son, Lawson Goodwin, my black-smith tools.
I will and bequeath to my step-daughter, Nancy Vaught, fifty dollars at her mother's death to be paid in property.
I will and bequeath to my grand-daughter, Selah Smith, her bed and furniture, mare and cow which she claims.
I also will and bequeath to my beloved wife, Mary Smith, my wagon and all farming tools. In the presence of us, I have hereunto set my hand and affixed my seal on this the 7th day of October, in the year of our Lord 1822.
N. B.—I do hereby dominate and appoint my trusty friends, Daniel Smith and Ezekiel Smith, executors.
Day and date above written.
JACOB SMITH.
Lawson White.
Thomas Barry.

LAST WILL AND TESTAMENT OF EDWARD SMITH

From the records of County Court Clerk of Carter County. Sent by Mrs. W. M. Vaught, Elizabethton.

In the name of God, Amen, I, Edward Smith, of the State of Tennessee and County of Carter, farmer, being in perfect health of body, and of perfect mind and memory, thanks be given to God, calling unto mind the mortality of my body and knowing that it is appointed for all men once to die, do make and ordain this my last will and testament, that is to say, principally first of all, I give and recommend my soul in the hands of the Almighty God that gave it, and my body I recommend to the earth to be buried in a decent Christian manner at the discretion of my Executors, nothing doubting but at the General Resurrection I shall receive the same again by the Mighty Hand of God, and as touching such worldly estate wherewith it has pleased God to bless me in this life, I give, demise, bequeath and dispose of the same in the following manner:

First, I direct that my executors hereafter named do sell my negro man, Tom, and three mares, to-wit: a sorrel mare, a gray filly and a sorrel filly, to pay such debts as I may be justly owing at my death, and the surplus from such sale, if any, to be paid to my four sons, Nicholas, Jacob, William and Daniel, to be equally divided amongst them and their heirs.

Secondly, I give and bequeath to my beloved wife, Catherine, all my stock of horses, only the three mares above excepted, together with all my stock of cows, hogs, sheep and bees, with all my household furniture and farming utensils of every kind, also my wagon and gear, also my plantation whereon I now live for and during her natural life; also my negro woman, Agnes, and her child, and their increase for and during her natural life, and then to go to my youngest daughter, Nancy, and her heirs forever; and further I do direct that the land at my said wife's death to descend to my four sons, to-wit: Nicholas, Jacob, William and Daniel Smith, to be equally divided amongst them and their heirs forever, they paying fifty pounds, ten shillings, current money into the hands of my executors within one year after my said wife's death, which sum of fifty pounds, ten shillings, I direct my said Executors to pay to my daughters hereafter named and their heirs and the heirs of John Smith, deceased, in the following manner, that is to say, to my daughter, Catherine Peeveyhouse, or her heirs, ten pounds; also to my daughter, Sarah Bowman, or her heirs, ten pounds; also to my daughter, Margaret Gabert, or her heirs, ten pounds; also to my daughter, Susannah Campbell, or her heirs, ten pounds; also to the heirs of my daughter, Mary Smith, the sum of five shillings; also to the heirs of my daughter, Elizabeth Dunkin, five shillings; also to the heirs of my son, John Smith, deceased, the sum of ten pounds, which said several sums above mentioned and to the use of the person above named and their heirs forever, which is all I do intend for them to have of my estate; furthermore, it is my will and pleasure that my son, Daniel Smith, and his heirs, have fifty acres of land or whatever quantity there may be on that side of Watauga River where the said Daniel now lives, it being part of the tract which I now live on and that my said wife, Catherine, is only to have such land in her lifetime as is on the side of the river which I am now living on, and further it is to be understood that the land named to be divided amongst my four sons and their heirs is only to extend to that part of my land which lies on the south side of Watauga River and the balance of said tract of land which lies on the north side, I give and devise to my son, Daniel Smith, and his heirs forever.

Furthermore, I do ordain, constitute and appoint my said wife, Catherine, Executrix, and my son, Daniel Smith, and Julius Dugger, Esquires, Executors, of this my last will and testament, and do hereby revoke, disallow, and disannul all and every will by me heretofore made, and I do declare this to be my only last will and testament.

In testimony of which I have hereunto set my hand and affixed my seal this 11th day of February, one thousand eight hundred and seven.

Signed, sealed and declared in the presence of us.

EDWARD SMITH (Seal).

Matthias Wagoner, Jurat.

John Heaton, Jurat.

Acknowledged before us this 15th of April, one thousand eight hundred and seven.
Nathaniel Taylor.
Godfrey Carriger.
William Boyd.

WILL OF CASPER CABEL

Sent by Mrs. W. M. Vaught, Elizabethton.

In the name of God. Amen. I, Casper Cable of Carter County and State of Tennessee, farmer, being in perfect health of body and of perfect mind and memory, thanks be unto God, calling unto mind the mortality of my body and knowing that it is appointed for all men once to die, do make and ordain this, my last will and testament, that is to say principally and first of all I give and recommend my soul unto the hand of Almighty God that gave it, and my body recommended to the earth to be buried in decent Christian burial, at the discretion of my executors, nothing doubting but at the general resurrection I shall receive the same again by the mighty power of God. And as touching such worldly estate wherewith it has pleased God to bless me in this life, I give, demise and dispose of the same in the following manner and form. First, I give and bequeth to my dearly beloved wife, Elizabeth, a double feather bed and two good milk cows, one pot to cook in, and to stay and have the command in my household estate, and one pewter dish and one basin, four plates, one-half dozen spoons, and to continue in the situation where she now is during her widowhood. And, if at my decease or after, if a horse there is one to spare out of the estate. And my son, Benjamin Cabel, to have fifty acres of land off of the lower end of my land; and Joseph Cabel, my son, to have the old plantation, fifty acres there; and Daniel, my son, to have, with Coonrad Cabel, fifty acres of land, more including the big spring. And for them that holds the land to pay to the rest of my sons in proportion to the value of the land as an equal divide in good property. And the rest of my household furniture to be equally divided with my sons and daughters. And every son a horse creter and one cow; and the daughters each a double feather bed and two cows. And the remainder of the stock to be divided among the whole of them and any other property.

All this I give to my wife and children, and constitute and make and ordain Jacob Cabel and John Baker my sole executors of this, my last will and testament, and singular my land, mesuages and tenements them freely to be possessed and by them to be enjoyed, and I do hereby utterly disallow, revoke and disannul every other former testaments, wills, legacies, bequeths and executors by me in anywise before named willed and bequeth. To ratifying and confirming this and no other to be my last will and testament, in witness whereof I have hereunto set my hand and seal this 24th of December, in the year of our Lord 1807.

Signed, sealed and published.
Casper Cabel (seal).

Pronounced and declared as his last will and testament.

John Graves, John Dugger, John Asher.

Records from the Bible of Paulding and Martha Terrell Anderson, now in the possession of Mrs. Rutledge Smith, Lebanon Road, Nashville, Tenn.

BIRTHS

Paulding Anderson, born Nov. 2, 1803.
Martha T. Anderson, born Dec. 5, 1804.
——— Anderson, born Nov. 23, 1821.
Patrick Henry Anderson, born June 24, 1823.
Jesse Hord Anderson, born Jan. 27, 1826.
Paulding Francis Anderson, born Sept. 27, 1828.
Rufus Dixon Anderson, born July 31, 1831.
Martha Anderson, born April 22, 1834.
Joseph Anderson, born July 2, 1836.
James Monroe Anderson, born May 1818, 1838.
Eudora Anderson, born Jan. 8, 1841.
DeWitt Anderson, born May 2, 1843.
Anthony Wayne Anderson, born Oct. 14, 1845.
Sally Erskine Anderson, born Nov. 20, 1847.
Churchwell A. Robinson, born July 14, 1853.
John McGregor, born May 6, 1858.
Patsie Hord McGregor, born March 4, 1860.
Andrew McGregor, born Nov. 8, 1861.
Paul Britton McGregor, born Jan. 23, 1866.
Leonora McGregor, born Friday morning, Feb. 16, 1868.
Temple Harris McGregor, born Thursday morning, May 12, 1870.
Eudorah Anderson McGregor, born Tuesday night, Oct. 22, 1872.
Frankie Graeme McGregor, born Monday at 9 o'clock, March 1, 1875.
Sally Ashe McGregor, born April 23, 1877.
Frank Anderson McGregor, born Oct. 9, 1879.
The twins, M. and D. McGregor, Nov. 28, 1881.

MARRIAGES

Paulding Anderson and his wife, Martha T. Anderson, were married May 24, 1820.

P. F. Anderson and his wife, Mary McGregor, married Aug., 1841.

J. H. Anderson and his wife, Martha Mottley, married June 24, 1851.

Dora Anderson and Andrew McGregor, married Oct. 29, 1856.

Sam S. Ashe and Sally Erskine Anderson, married May 23, 1866.

Graeme McGregor and Rutledge Smith, married May 14, 1896, at Lebanon.

Albert P. Smith and "Muff" Mace, married July 9, 1921, Lebanon.

McGregor Smith and Elizabeth Wilson, married Nov. 19, 1924, in Nashville, Tenn.

Eudora Anderson Smith and Malcolm R. Williams, married Sept. 12, 1928, in Nashville.

DEATHS

Mrs. Sarah Anderson, died June 12, 1832.
Rebecca Anderson, died Sept. 23, 1835.
Martha Anderson, died June 18, 1838.
Francis Anderson, Jr., died July 25, 1838.
Louisa Anderson, died Aug. 9, 1822.
Francis Anderson, Sr., died June 25, 1842.
Anthony Wayne Anderson, died Aug. 21, 1846.
Joseph Anderson, died Dec. 23, 1862.
Mrs. Martha T. Anderson, died April 17, 1861.
Joseph T. Anderson, died Dec. 23, 1862.
Patrick Henry Anderson, died Sept. 28, 1867.
Jesse Hord Anderson, died Aug. 8, 1866.
Jesse Hord Anderson, Jr., died Sept. 18, 1866.

Chloe, wife of DeWitt Anderson, died Dec. 5, 1870.
Paulding Anderson, Sr., died Manday evening, Feb. 13, 1882.
Baby McGregor, died Saturday night, Feb. 5, 1882.
My Little Pet M——, died Sept. 1, 1858.
Paulding F. Anderson, died Sept. 12, 1878.
Rufus B. Anderson, died July, 1878.
James Monroe Anderson, died June 28, 1882.
John McGregor, died Friday, Oct. 7, 1887.

Records from the Bible of Captain Walton Smith and Marian R. Black Smith, now in the possession of Major Rutledge Smith, Lebanon Road, Nashville, Tennessee.

Marriages

John Puckett, born Feb. 26, 1764, in Botetourt County, Va., and Rhoda Lida, born 1784, of White County, Tenn., married on Dec. 25, 1809.

The above are the parents of Matilda Puckett, who married T. J. Smith. They were the parents of Walton Smith. Record of John Puckett, found in Bureau of Pensions. He died Sept. 4, 1844.
Walton Smith and Marion R. Black, married in the town of Monroe, Walton County, Ga., May 19, 1864.

Rutledge Smith and Graeme McGregor, married in Lebanon, Wilson County, Tenn., May 14, 1896.
Elva Cecil Smith and C. H. Tholman, married in Cookeville, Tenn., May 2, 1899.

Births

Walton Smith, born April 23, 1837, in DeKalb County, Tenn., died March 8, 1903, in Cookeville, Putnam County, Tenn.

Rutledge Smith, born Aug. 1, 1870, in the southwest corner of Putnam County, Tenn.

Elva Cecil Smith, born in Cookeville, Putnam County, Tenn., June 11, 1841.

Marian R. Black, wife of Walton Smith, was born in Charleston, S. C., Jan. 14, 1841.

Deaths

Mrs. Margaret A. Black, born in Charleston, S. C., May 1, 1812, died in Cookeville, Putnam County, Tenn., Jan. 21, 1894.
Mrs. Marion Richardson Smith, wife of Walton Smith, born in Charleston, S. C., Jan. 14, 1841; married to Walton Smith in Monroe, Walton County, Ga., May 19, 1864; died in Cookeville, Putnam County, Tenn., of heart failure, April 19, 1894. She lived and died a true and humble Christian and is now safe and happy in the realms of bliss and eternal glory.
Thomas E. England, died May 21, 1843, age 26 years.
John Ferguson, died Sept. 16, 1843, age 16 years 5 months.
John P. Black, died Oct. 6, 1845, at Savannah, Ga., age 27 years 6 months.
Alexander England, died Oct. 9, 1849, age 78 years 11 months 4 days.
Catharine C. Graham, died Dec. 25, 1857.
Dr. Wm. C. Graham, died Feb. 2, 1853.
George C. Graham, died June 27, 1862.
Elizabeth England, died March 9, 1857.
Mrs. Margaret England Black was the daughter of Elexander England, above. She was born in Charleston, S. C., in 1812, died in Putnam County, Tenn., Jan. 21, 1894.

Records from the Bible of John McGregor and Milbry Donelson McGregor.

Marriages

John McGregor and Milbry Donelson, married Feb. 10, 1825.

Flowers McGregor and Frances E. Roane, married March 22, 1849.

Andrew McGregor and Eudora Anderson, married Oct. 29, 1856.

A. J. Donelson, Jr., and Catherine J. Nelson, married Oct. 13, 1835.

Rutledge Smith and Graeme McGregor, married May 14, 1896.

Albert P. Smith and "Muff" Mace, married July 19, 1921.

McGregor Smith and Elizabeth Wilson, married Nov. 12, 1924.

Dolly Smith and Malcolm R. Williams, married Sept. 12, 1928.

Births

John McGregor, born Aug. 29, 1794.

Milbry Donelson, wife of John McGregor, born July 27, 1806.

Martha Malvina McGregor, daughter of John and Milbry McGregor, born Dec. 4, 1825.

Mary Ann McGregor, daughter of John and Milbry Donelson, born May, 1827.

Flowers McGregor, son of John and Milbry McGregor, born Wednesday morning at 4 o'clock, Dec. 17, 1828.

A. J. Donelson, born March 14, 1815.

Donelson McGregor, son of John and Milbry McGregor, born Nov. 6, 1830, Friday morning, 4 o'clock.

Andrew McGregor, son of John and Milbry McGregor, born 6 o'clock Monday morning, Aug. 13, 1832.

Milbry McGregor, daughter of John and Milbry McGregor, born Nov. 22, 1835.

Eudora Anderson, wife of Andrew McGregor, born Jan. 8, 1841.

Catherine J. Donelson, daughter of Andrew and Catherine J. Donelson, born Oct. 6, 1836.

Deaths

John McGregor, age 42, died July 4, 1835.

Milbry McGregor, wife of John McGregor, age 30, died Jan. 2, 1836.

Donelson McGregor, son of John and Milbry McGregor, killed at Murfreesboro, Dec. 31, 1862. He was Colonel of First Arkansas Infantry; was put on Roll of Honor (at ——— Mound) for gallantry on that occasion. Loved by the men with whom he had associated.

Catherine J. Donelson, wife of A. J. Donelson, Jr., age 18, died Oct. 27, 1837.

Copied from Bible of Elizabeth Jane Wilson, now in the possession of William B. Neely, Brookeville, Maryland. Sent in by (Miss) Mary Elizabeth White, 2106 Twenty-first Ave., South, Nashville, Tenn.

W. M. Neely, born July 15, 1843.

Malissa Ann Wilson, born Oct. 31, 1847.

Martha Shook Wilson, born Dec. 2, 1849.

W. M. Neely and Malissa Ann Wilson, married Sept. 16, 1868.

Isaac Shook Wilson and Elyzabeth Jane Sheffield, married Nov. 26, 1846.

Isaac Shook Wilson, born March 13, 1827.

Elizabeth J. Wilson, born April 16, 1830.

W. F. Neely, born Nov. 7, 1804; married to Elyzabeth Blackwell, March, 1832. (The initial "W" in the name "W. F. Neely," also date 1804, are very indistinct. Suppose this date is 1804 instead of 1814.)

Elyzabeth Blackwell, born Feb. 13, 1813.

Copied from the family Bible of Mrs. T. A. Boyd (Martha Shook Wilson), Route 3, Box 157, Nashville, Tenn., by (Miss) Mary Elizabeth White, 2106 Twenty-first Ave., South, Nashville, Tenn. This Bible was printed in 1730.

BIRTHS

John Boyd, July 1, 1769.
Rebecca Boyd, Jan. 1, 1772.
Aaron Boyd, Dec. 29, 1794.
Nancy Boyd, March 27, 1797.
Elizabeth Boyd, April 28, 1799.
David R. Boyd, March 30, 1802.
Mary Boyd, Sept. 10, 1805.
Sarah Boyd, May 24, 1807.
Jos. B. Boyd, May 5, 1810.
Mariam Boyd, April 11, 1813.
Mary E. Bibb, April 27, 1821.

MARRIAGES

John Dixon and Elizabeth Boyd, married July 7, 1816.
Aaron Boyd and Mary Britton, married July 10, 1817.
Asa Tillman and Mary Boyd, married Sept. 14, 1824.
David R. Boyd and Trecy Coleman, married Sept. 22, 1824.
Jos. B. Boyd and Susan Camden, married July 19, 1831.
Elisha A. Patton and Sarah Boyd, married March 27, 1832.
Henry Bibb and Nancy Boyd, married Feb. 17, 1820.
John H. Robinson and Mariam Boyd, married Nov. 1, 1837.
Aaron Boyd and Sarah Edmiston, married Nov. 16, 1848.

DEATHS

John Boyd, May 12, 1831.
Nancy Bibb, July 29, 1821.
David R. Boyd, Aug. 17, 1835.
Mary E. Bibb, Sept. 14, 1836.
May M. Boyd, Sept. 8, 1837.
Rebecca Boyd, Feb. 5, 1854.

Copied from the family Bible of Mrs. T. A. Boyd (Martha Shook Wilson), Route 3, Box 157, Nashville, Tenn., by (Miss) Mary Elizabeth White, 2106 Twenty-first Ave., South, Nashville, Tenn.

BIRTHS

Malissa Ann Wilson Neely, born Oct. 31, 1847, died Jan. 3, 1885. Married William M. Neely, Sept. 16, 1868.
Cleopatra Texanna Wilson Ezell, daughter of J. M. and Charity M. Wilson, born Dec. 13, 1844, died Oct. 19, 1882. Married James B. Ezell, Aug. 20, 1865.
Martha Martins Sheffield, born Aug. 24, 1805, died April 28, 1883.
Miss Patra Davis, daughter of Giv Davis of Bedford County, born March 10, 1859, died Jan. 3, ——. (do not know date).

Tom Aaron Marble Boyd, July 25, 1844.
Martha Shook Wilson, Dec. 2, 1849.
William W. Boyd, Feb. 8, 1868.
Anna Lizzie Boyd, Jan. 14, 1869.
Sallie Malisa Boyd, Aug. 4, 1871.
Joseph Shook Boyd, Nov. 21, 1873.
John Marble Boyd, Sept. 16, 1876.
Nannie Blans Boyd, Nov. 24, 1879.
Thos. Albert Boyd, Nov. 16, 1881.
Earnest Lee Boyd, June 23, 1883.
Ada Sue Boyd, Jan. 16, 1886.
Lynn Boyd, Aug. 29, 1888.
Claude Boyd, Feb. 23, 1891.
Joe Boyd Ezell, May 21, 1897.

MARRIAGES

Thos. Aaron Marble Boyd and Martha Shook Wilson, married Dec. 20, 1866.
W. M. Hardison and Lizzie A. Boyd, married Sept. 14, 1886.
Dr. A. G. Dickson and Sallie M. Boyd, married April 23, 1890.
E. M. Ezell and Nannie B. Boyd, married March 22, 1896.
Joe Shook Boyd and Norma Ambrose, married Nov. 21, 1900.
L. M. Crawford and Nannie Boyd Ezell, married Jan. 28, 1901.
Ernest L. Boyd and Fannie Bowen, married Jan. 11, 1905.
Lynn C. Boyd and Mary L. Stammer, married Dec. 31, 1912.
Claude S. Boyd and Emma H. Smith, married June 4, 1919.

FAMILY HISTORY

Isaac Shook Wilson, born March 13, 1827; died Sept. 28, 1851.

Elizabeth J. Wilson, born April 10, 1830; died Aug. 18, 1861.
Malissa Ann Wilson, born Oct. 31, 1867; died Jan. 3, 1885.
The above names are Mother, Father, and Sister of Martha Shook Boyd.
J. B. Boyd, born May 5, 1810; died June 21, 1897; married July 19, 1831.
Susan W. Boyd, born July 27, 1809; died March 8, 1885.
Rebecca F. Boyd, born May 31, 1833; married to E. T. Williams, Nov. 1, 1869; died Sept. 12, 1884.
Sallie C. Boyd, born April 11, 1838; married T. J. Wilson, March 4, 1857.
John C. Boyd, born March 5, 1841; married Mollie Logan, Aug., 1864.
E. M. Ezell, born Jan., 1873; died July 22, 1899.

DEATHS

William Wilson Boyd, Feb. 15, 1868; 2 weeks old.
Thos. Albert Boyd, Sept. 6, 1882.
John Marble Boyd, Sept. 13, 1882.
Lizzie B. Hardison, Oct. 5, 1916.
Sallie M. Dickson Ramsey, Nov. 28, 1826.
Thos. A. M. Boyd, Oct. 28, 1917.

Bibles (2) owned by Joseph Ballanfant, of Culleoka. Copied by James Horton Davis for Captain Wm. Lytle Chapter.

Sent by Miss Jetton.

MARRIAGES

Joseph Ballanfant, eldest son of John Ballanfant, a native of France, and Sally Turner, fifth daughter of James Turner, were married by the Rev. Garner Nawnnico in Williamson County, Tenn., April 22, 1819.

BIRTHS

Joseph Ballanfant, born in Hallifax County, Va., Nov. 14, 1790.
Sally Turner, wife of the said Joseph, born in Caswell County, N. C., Aug. 7, 1801.
John Ballanfant, son of the said Joseph and Sally, born in Williamson County, Tenn., March 7, 1820.

DEATHS

Joseph Ballanfant, died Nov. 9, 1869, in his 79th year.
Sally Ballanfant, wife of Joseph Ballanfant, died April 18, 1876, in her 75th year.

BIRTHS

John Ballanfant, born March 7, 1820.
Eliza Easter Turner, wife of John Ballanfant, born Feb. 17, 1827.
Josiah Turner Ballanfant, oldest son of John and Eliza Ballanfant, born Oct. 1, 1845.
James Webb Ballanfant, born Dec. 23, 1846.
Sarah Ballanfant, born March 17, 1848.
Susan Mary, born Nov. 6, 1849.
Wm. Evans, born March 11, 1853.
Alace Mebane, born Dec. 13, 1854.
John Ballanfant, Jr., born Sept. 2, 1856.
Jonathan Hunt Ballanfant, born Sept. 13, 1858.
Madersen Frierson Ballanfant, born March 6, 1861.
Martha Booker Ballanfant, born May 11, 1863.
Lucy Ballanfant, born Feb. 9, 1865.
Eva Ballanfant, born Dec. 15, 1867.

MARRIAGES

John Ballanfant and Eliza E. Turner, married Oct. 2, 1844, in Hillsboro, N. C., by the Rev. Robert Burevill.
Josiah P. Ballanfant and Sallie Turner, married Nov. 28, 1871, in Mooresville, Marshall County, Tenn., by the Rev. William McKenzie.
W. Pike Cockrill and Sallie Ballanfant, married Feb. 1, 1872, in Culleoka, Tenn., by W. H. Hughes.
Henry A. Martin and Susan M. Ballanfant, married at Culleoka, Tenn.
Wm. E. Ballanfant and Callie Fleming, married Nov. 17, 1875,

in Maury County, Tenn., by the Rev. Wm. Stoddard.
W. P. Taylor and Eliza T. Ballanfant, married Aug. 30, 1875, in Culleoka, Tenn., by the Rev. Mr. Taylor.
J. Hunt Ballanfant and Ida Wilsford, married Nov. 8, 1878, by the Rev. Orman at Culleoka.

DEATHS

James Webb Ballanfant, died Nov. 10, 1861; age 15 years.
Lucy Ballanfant, died June 9, 1865; age 4 months.
Joseph Ballanfant, died Nov. 9, 1869; age 79 years.
Sarah Ballanfant, died April 10, 1876.
John Ballanfant, Sr., died March 4, 1900, three days of being 80 years of age. His grandparents were all in the Revolutionary War. His father, Joseph Ballanfant, was in the War of 1812, stationed at Norfork, Va. His grandfather on his mother's side was in the Fight at Guilford Court House and was wounded and died after the war in Williamson County, Tenn.

Eliza E. Ballanfant, died July 15, 1903; age 76 years 5 months 2 days. Her grandparents were in the Revolutionary War. Her grandfather, Jas. Turner, was in the Battle of Guilford Court House. His grandfather, Theophelus Evans, was one of the signers of the Declaration of Independence and fought in Cumberland County, N. C., in 1875 and the fight on Allamance River in 1871.

Madersen Friersen Ballanfant, died Jan. 26, 1815.

Sallie Cockrill, died July 1, 1913.

CROCKETT AND NELSON BIBLES

Family Bibles owned by Miss Stella Nelson, 221 Oak St., Murfreesboro, Tenn. Copied by Rebekah Jetton for Capt. Wm. Lytle Chapter, Sept. 18, 1933.

BIRTHS

Overton Washington Crockett, born Feb. 14, 1791.
Evelina Augusta Smith, born July 8, 1800.
John Anthony Crockett, born Aug. 11, 1817.
William Granville Crockett, born Dec. 25, 1818.
Anne Maria Crockett, born Oct. 22, 1820.
America Maria Crockett, born Jan. 20, 1822.
Overton Washington Crockett, born Feb. 4, 182—.
Allen Battle Crockett, born Aug. 6, 1830.
Robert Payne Crockett, born April 29, 1835.
Kitty Buckner Crockett, born Sept. 1, 1839.

MARRIAGES

Overton W. Crockett and Evelina A. Smith, married Nov. 25, 1815.
John Anthony Crockett and Margaret K. Ransom, married Sept. 4, 1839.
Dandridge Madison Crockett and Lucetta E. Harrison, married March 9, 1843.
William Granville Crockett and Elizabeth J. Jarratt, married Dec. 28, 1843.
Overton Washington Crockett and Elizabeth Caroline Ransom, married (date not recorded).
Allen Battle Crockett and Louisa Hall, married April 17, 1851.

BIRTHS AND DEATHS

Dandridge M. Crockett, born May 16, 1823.
Lucetta E. Harrison, born July 15, 1825.
William Coleman Crockett, born Oct. 14, 1841 or 45.
Overton Washington Crockett, born Dec. 25, 1848.
Allen Batey Crockett, born Feb. 2, 1851; died Oct. 3, 1927.
Dandridge Madison Crockett, born Feb. 4, 1853.
John Dromgoole Crockett, born Nov. 29, 1855.

Pinkney Boyd Crockett, born May 22, 185—.
Ella Belle Crockett, born Aug. 11, 1860.
Fanny Lou Crockett, born Aug. 22, in Alabama, 1864.
John Dromgoole Crockett, died Sept. 2, 1857.
Samuel Crockett, born Nov. 11, 1866 or 65.
Rebecca Harrison Crockett, born Aug. 6, 1871.
Mrs. Lucetta H. Crockett, died Jan. 18, 1901.
Ella Belle Crockett, died Oct. 17, 1887.
Dandridge M. Crockett, died May 11, 1902.
Mrs. Fannie L. Johns, died June 12, 1906.

MARRIAGES

Dandridge M. Crockett and Lucetta E. Harrison, married March 9, 1843.
William C. Crockett and Sallie Lawrence, married Dec. 5, 1807.
U. W. Crockett and Alice Crockett, married Dec. 24, 1808.
Fannie L. Crockett and H. P. Johns, married Oct. 17, 1888.
D. M. Crockett, Jr., and Ada Lowe, married Dec., 1883.
P. B. Crockett and Sallie E. Crockett, married Dec. 6, 188—.
Ross C. Nelson and Hattie Crockett, married Sept. 7, 1902.
H. P. Johns and Lula Crockett, married Oct. 28, 1906.

FUNERAL NOTICES IN BIBLE

Henry Hudson Norman, born July 4, 1839; died Sept. 6, 1906.

BIRTHS

Joe C. Nelson, born May 31, 1811.
Martha L. (or D.) Nelson, born Feb. 13, 1816.
Elizabeth P. Nelson, born Aug. 16, 1835.
Pettis W. Nelson, born Nov. 16, 1837.
Logan J. Nelson, born Oct. 7, 1839.
Susan H. Nelson, born Nov. 18, 1841.
Amanda J. Nelson, born Feb. 24, 1844.
Ephriam F. Nelson, born Aug. 24, 1846.
John P. Nelson, born Aug. 28, 1848.
Jos. G. Nelson, born Jan. 23, 1851.
Sarah F. Nelson, born Dec. 7, 1854.
Martha L. Nelson, born April 14, 1856.

MARRIAGES

Jos. C. Nelson, married Martha L. Norman Nov. 6, 1834.
Logan J. Nelson, married Hattie A. Campbell Oct. 9, 1866.
Logan J. Nelson, married Hattie E. Morgan Feb. 25, 1890.
Ross Campbell, married Hattie Crockett Sept. 7, 1902.

BIRTHS

Logan J. Nelson, born Oct. 7, 1839.
Hattie A. Nelson, wife of L. J. Nelson, born April 13, 1847.
Ross C. Nelson, born July 17, 1870.
Stella B. Nelson, born Aug. 7, 1876.
Jos. W. Nelson, born March 7, 1879.
Wm. G. Nelson, born April 21, 1881.
Hattie E. Morgan, second wife of L. J. Nelson, born Aug. 12, 1849.
Johnnie Morgan Nelson, son of W. J. Nelson and H. M. Nelson, born March 26, 1891.
Sons of Hattie and Ross C. Nelson:
Joel Crockett Nelson, born March 22, 1904.
Edwin Ross Nelson, born Jan. 25, 1906.
James Overton Nelson, born Dec. 11, 1907.
Samuel Madison Nelson, born May 8, 1913.

DEATHS

Hattie A. Nelson, wife of L. J. Nelson, died May 28, 1881.
Jos. W. Nelson, son of Hattie A. and L. J. Nelson, died July 20, 1879.
Wm. G. Nelson, son of Hattie A. and L. J. Nelson, died Aug. 16, 1881.
Edwin Ross Nelson, died June 18, 1906.
Hattie E. Nelson, wife of L. J. Nelson, died June 12, 1908.
Joel Crockett, died Sept. 17, 1918.
Logan Joel Nelson, died May 1, 1915.

Sarah F. Nelson McGrew, died July 7, 1902.

BIRTHS

Joel Nelson, the son ———, born Nov. —, ——.

Nancy, their second ——— the 5th, 1806.

Barzer ———, born Feb. —, ——.

Fourth child was born ———.

James C. Nelson ——— May 31, 1811.

Child was born ———.

Elender L. Nelson ———, Sept. 1, 18—.

Records sent by Miss Sallie Jacobs.

BIRTHS

John Walden, born March 10, 1789, in McLenburg, C. N. Via.

Lucy E. Walden, born June 23, 1800.

L. C. Walden, born Aug. 17, 1824.

John E. Walden, born April 20, 1826.

Sam N. Walden, born Aug. 14, 1829.

L. A. F. Walden, born Aug. 27, 1839.

Lucy Elizabeth Trigg, born Jan. 17, 1857.

Kate Walden Trigg, born July 15, 1859.

John Walden Trigg, born July 7, 1862.

Lizzie B. Trigg, born July 7, 1871.

Martha Jane Wadley, born Oct. 2, 1849.

Sallie C. Wadley, born Dec. 10, 1852.

Albert B. Wadley, born April 17, 1864.

John W. Wadley, born Feb. 12, 1826.

F. L. Jacobs, born Dec. 23, 1846.

Belle Wigdon Jacobs, born June 30, 1850.

Clara Belle Jacobs, born Sept. 19, 1884.

DEATHS

John Walden, died Oct. 4, 1871.

John E. Walden, died Jan. 12, 1848.

L. C. Walden, died June 5, 1850.

John Etter, died Feb. 19, 1851.

S. W. Walden, died July 29, 1861.

Lucy E. Walden, died Nov. 26, 1852.

Lucy A. Trigg, died March 18, 1875.

Sallie Higdon, died Feb. 3, 1879.

John S. Bishop, died July, 1878.

Mrs. Cyrena Shepard, died Dec. 19, 1880.

Mrs. Mary Elrod, wife of John Elrod, died June 30, 1887.

John W. Wadley, died April 11, 1891.

Elizabeth Wadley, died May 17, 1892.

Mrs. Belle Jacobs, wife of F. L. Jacobs, died Nov. 16, 1927.

F. L. Jacobs, died Aug. 23, 1933.

Clara Belle Jacobs, died Dec. 28, 1904.

MARRIAGES

John W. Walden and Elizabeth Bishop, married April 18, 1855.

John W. Wadley and Elizabeth Bishop, married March 27, 1874.

F. L. Jacobs and Belle Higdon Jacobs, married Dec. 23, 1883.

CATHERINA BOLTZEN STAUT'S RECORD IN HER BOOK

(Records sent by Mrs. Wm. Vaught)

English Translations From the German Record recorded in A German Prayer and Sermon Book, Published in 1785: Recorded on Inside Front Cover:

Let me be and remain for you my dear God and Lord, nothing will drive me away from you, maintain me in your wisdom, Lord let me abide in you through all Eternity and give me constancy.

Catherina Stauten born Boltzen has received this book from

her parents Anno Domoni 1790 September 2nd.

Recorded on the inside Front Fly Leaf:

Catherina Stauten born Boltzen, was born in the year 1755, the 21st of March, in the county of Shenandoah, Virginia. Her father is Johann Peter Boltzen and her mother Maria Elishabetha Boltzen, born Mintzin.

The parents are donating this book to their daughter for her memory and to remind her that she shall remember her parents and shall pray incessently to God and shall remember also that she has been baptised, also that she will not betray and will not abandon the truths of God and so that she will not come into wrong doing, for you should have all your life long God before your eyes and in your heart, and you shall be ware yourself not to agree to any sin or act against the commands of God.

Recorded on a Fly Leaf at the beginning of a second section of the book:

Catherina Stauten born Boltzen got married with her husband Daniel Stauten in the year 1772, the 3rd of March.

Note: The above was translated by Dr. Martin Wadewitz, Chief Chemist of the American Glanzstoff Corporation, Elizabethton, Tennessee, August 23, 1933. Dr. Wadewitz is a native of Germany.

Will Book 1—Page 27.

Will of Godfrey Daniel Stout, Sen.

State of Tennessee,

Johnson County.

Know all men by these present, that I, Godfrey Daniel Stout, Sen., being of sound mind and memory do make this my last will and testament, to wit:

Unto my beloved son, George Peter Stout, I give and bequeath one dollar and unto my beloved son, Daniel Stout, I give and bequeath one dollar and unto my beloved son, John Stout, I give and bequeath one dollar and to my beloved son, Henry Stout, I give and bequeath one dollar and unto my beloved son, Abram Stout, one dollar and unto my beloved son, David D. Stout, one dollar and unto my son, Thomas Stout's Heirs, one dollar and unto my beloved son-in-law, John Potter, one dollar, and unto my beloved son-in-law, Nicholas Grindstaff, one dollar, and unto my beloved son-in-law, Joseph Robinson, one dollar; unto my beloved daughter, Catherine Stout, one dollar.

And I do hereby make and appoint my son, John Stout, my executor of this, my last will and testament.

Signed, Sealed and Acknowledged in presence of us September 26, 1843. Godfrey Daniel Stout.

Rufus Moore

John H. Stout

David H. Stout

Courtesy of Dr. W. A. Provine

Davidson County Courthouse. From an old print in the Tennessee Historical Society.
Built about 1830. Burned April 13, 1856, between two and three o'clock.

John Stout, Executor of Godfrey Daniel Stout, Deceased.
State of Tennessee
Johnson County
County Court, April term 1846

Whereas, it appears to the Court here, that Godfrey Daniel Stout, late of said County, is dead and hath made his will and testament in writing in which he has appointed John Stout his executor to the same, which will hath been exhibited into Court and proved as the law directs.

It is therefore ordered by the Court that letters, testamentary of all and singular, the goods and chattels, rights and credits of said deceased issue to the said John Stout, he having been qualified according to law.

These are therefore to empower you, the said John Stout, to enter into and upon all and singular the goods and chattels, right and credits of the said Godfrey Daniel Stout deceased and the same into your possession, taken wherever the same may be found and a true and perfect inventory to make and return in our next term of County Court and the just debts of the said Godfrey Daniel Stout deceased to pay and also try pay and deliver all the legacies contained and specified in said will and testament, as far as the said goods, chattels and rights and credits will thereto extend and the law charges.

Witness whereof I, Alfred T. Wilson, Clerk of our said Court, do hereunto subscribe my name and affix the seal of my office in the Town of Taylorsville, the 6th day of April A. D., 1846.

Family Record of Godfrey Daniel Stout, Sr., and Wife, Catherina Boltzen Stout

Godfrey Daniel Stout (or Captain Daniel Stout, Revolutionary War, Pennsylvania) (Tradition says that he was 96 at the time of his death, 1846; still another tradition that he was older).

Catherina Boltzen Stout was born March 21, 1755, in Shenandoah County, Virginia.

Records show that the above parties were married March 3, 1772.

Children of this marriage:

George Peter Stout, born ...., wife, Elizabeth Potter.

Daniel Stout, born August 9, 1781, wife ....

John Stout, born December 16, 1783; wife, Sallie Grindstaff.

Henry Stout, born May 25, 179—; first wife, ... Done; second wife, Kizzie Gentrey (?).

Abraham Carter Stout, born July 23, 1791; wife, ...

David D. Stout, born November 11, 1790; wife, Elizabeth Howard; second wife, Anne Martin.

Thomas Stout, born October 2, ...; wife, ...
Mollie Stout, born ....; husband, John Potter, II.
Mary Stout, born ....; husband, Nicholas Grindstaff.
Mary Stout, born July 8, 1787; husband, Joseph Robinson.
Catherine Stout, born ....

(One tradition says that she died unmarried; another says she was married. The Bible record of Daniel Stout's family is written in English.

Note: Some of the records are too dim to be deciphered; this accounts for the many blanks; too dim to be read with a magnifying glass.

Captain Daniel or Godfrey Daniel Stout of the Revolutionary War was, according to family tradition, of German descent and came from Pennsylvania through the Shenandoah Valley to Sullivan County, Tennessee, and settled on the left bank of the Holston River near the mouth of Jacobs Creek; spring on right bank (a Mr. Dogget lives at the same place now). The house was still standing up to a few years ago. (Date of writing, 1933.)

On the Register's Books in Carter County deeds are executed by Godfrey Daniel or Daniel Stout, conveying land to his sons and sons-in-law.

He and his wife, Catherina, are buried in a country cemetery in a community known as "Little Doe." The cemetery is now called the Asa Shoun Cemetery.

COPY

In Reply Refer to 3-1865,
Rev. and 1812
Wars Section.

DEPARTMENT OF THE INTERIOR

BUREAU OF PENSIONS

WASHINGTON

March 20, 1924.

Mrs. W. M. Vaught,
Elizabethton, Tenn.
Madam:

I have to advise you that from the papers in the War of 1812 pension claim, Widow Certificate 34988, it appears that David or David D. Stout, son of Catherine and Godfrey Stout, enlisted in Elizabethton, Carter County, Tennessee, September 13, 1814, and served in Captain Henry Hunter's Company of Tennessee

Militia, in October, 1814, at Ross' Landing; while lifting heavy wagons he was ruptured and later contracted pleurisy; he served until May 3, 1815.

He was allowed pension on account of disability resulting from said disease from September 19, 1855, at which time he was a resident of Johnson County, Tennessee, and he died there April 11, 1888; age, ninety-seven years, five months and five days.

Soldier married Elizabeth Howard, who died June 19, 1857, and he married March 20, 1870, in Johnson County, Tennessee, Anne or Anna Martin; she was allowed pension on her application executed April 18, 1888, while a resident of Johnson County, Tennessee; age, sixty years. She died about January, 1906.

Respectfully,
Washington Gardner, Commissioner.

MICHAEL SLIMP FAMILY RECORD

Michael Slimp was born Feb. 8, 1773.
Nancy Slimp, his wife, was born April 9, 1790.
Elizabeth Rasor was born Mar. 17, 1804.
John Slimp, son of Michael and Nancy Slimp, was born Nov. 6, 1809.
Daniel Slimp was born June 22, 1811.
Alfred Slimp was born April 16, 1813.
David Slimp was born Mar. 4, 1816.
Sarah Slimp was born Sept. 18, 1818.
Mary Slimp was born Oct. 8, 1820.
Elizabeth Slimp was born Feb. 22, 1823.
Frederick Slimp was born Nov. 26, 1824.
Andrew B. Slimp was born June 5, 1827.
Martin Slimp, son of Michael and Nancy Slimp, was born Mar. 28, 1830.
Susana Slimp was born June 1, 1832.
Louisa Slimp was born Feb. 7, 1838.

Deaths

Michael Slimp died Mar. 6, 1846.
Nancy Slimp, his wife, died June 17, 1876.
Alfred Slimp died May 15, 1878.
Andrew B. Slimp died July, 1861.

GENEALOGICAL REGISTER OF BIRTHS, MARRIAGES, AND DEATHS OF JAMES AND ELIZABETH HALL AND THEIR FAMILY

Taken at his home on the banks of Watauga River one-half mile from Holston River in Washington County, Tennessee, on this Tuesday, October 6, 1818.

Nathaniel Hall married Elizabeth Doak.
James, son of Nathaniel and Elizabeth Hall, was born in Rockbridge County, Virginia, on the North Fork of James River, New Virginia, on Feb. 25, 1776.
Elizabeth Biddle, daughter of Thomas and Sallie Biddle, was born in North Chucky River, a water then called Big Limestone, in Washington County, Tennessee, Dec. 15, 1783.
James Hall and Elizabeth Biddle were married by Samuel Doak, a Presbyterian minister, in Jonesboro and its vicinity at her father's home on Nolachucky River, Washington County, Tenn., Nov. 13, 1800.

Their Offspring

Sallie Hall, born Oct. 13, 1801; married William King.
John Hall, born July 17, 1803; died while young.

Thomas Hall, born June 1, 1804; married his cousin, Peggy Hall.
Jane Hall, born Mar. 16, 1806; married Mr. Baird.
Nathaniel Hall, born Nov. 18, 1807; married Rachel Nelson; moved to Ohio.
Samuel Doak Hall, born Sept. 8, 1809; married Janet Stephens.
Nancy Hall, born May 20, 1811; married Mr. Odell.
Polly Hall, born Feb. 19, 1813; married Amos Holoway.
Elizabeth Hall, born Jan. 9, 1815; died young.
Peggy Hall, born June 6, 1817; died young—drowned.
Lucinda Hall, born June 15, 1819; married Edward Hodge.
James Hall, born Sept. 13, 1821; married Elizabeth Snyder.
William Hall, born June 15, 1823; died young.
Eliza Ann Hall, born June 9, 1826; died young.
Edman Hall, born Feb. 2, 1828.

FAMILY RECORD—GEORGE BROWN

George Brown was born in the year of our Lord, 1784, April 12, in the State of Virginia, Rockingham County, on a river known by name of Shenandoah and remained there until about twelve years old, then moved from there to old Virginia, Albermarle County, and remained there until nineteen years of age, then moved from there to North Carolina, Wilkes County, and remained there about three years and then married Sarah Roberts by Abraham Kilby, a Methodist preacher, it being in the year of our Lord, 1806, May 1, and remained there until the year 1813, then moved to the State of Tennessee, Carter County, then volunteered into Capt. Coles Company on the 18th of October, 1813, and served a three months term in Col. Mear's Regiment against the Creek Indians and received his discharge in Carter County at Fish Springs in the year of 1814, January 18.

Wife and Children

Sarah Brown, wife, born June 13, 1787.
William Shoun and Jane Brown married in the year of 1825, Sept. 1.
John Grindstaff and Elizabeth Brown were married July 6, 1828.
John Grindstaff, born Feb. 15, 1810.
Elizabeth Grindstaff, born Jan. 1, 1811.
George W. Grindstaff, born Aug. 22, 1830.
William N. Grindstaff, born June 13, 1834.
David Grindstaff, born July 7, 1837.
Sarah E. Grindstaff, born Feb. 26, 1841.
Isaac Grindstaff, born Feb. 17, 1844.
Alexander S. Grindstaff, born Dec. 28, 1845.
Eliza J. Grindstaff, born July 13, 1848.
Mary E. Grindstaff, born Nov. 23, 1851.

Deaths

Sarah Brown, died Mar. 20, 1869.
George Brown, died Oct. 27, 1873.

BIBLE RECORDS

Sent by Miss Mary Elizabeth White, Nashville.

W. M. Neely was born July 15, A. D., 1843.
Malissa Ann Wilson was born Oct. 31, A. D., 1847.
Martha Shook Wilson was born Dec. 2, 1849.
W. M. Neely and Malissa Ann Wilson married Sept. 16, 1868.

Isaac Shook Wilson and Elyzabeth Jane Sheffield married in the year of our Lord, Nov. 26, 1846.
Isaac Shook Wilson was born Mar. 13, A. D., 1827.
Elizabeth J. Wilson, April 16, A. D., 1830.
W. F. Neely was born Nov. 7, 1804, A. D., and married to Elyzabeth Blackwell Mar., A. D., 1832. (The initial "W" in the name "W. F. Neely," also date 1804, are very indistinct. Suppose this date is 1804 instead of 1814.)
Elyzabeth Blackwell was born Feb. 13, 1813.
Note: Copied from Bible of Elizabeth Jane Wilson now in the possession of William B. Neely, Brookeville, Maryland.

BIRTHS

John Boyd, July 1, 1769.
Rebecca Boyd, Jan. 1, 1772.
Aaron Boyd, Dec. 29, 1794.
Nancy Boyd, Mar. 27, 1797.
Elizabeth Boyd, April 28, 1799.
David R. Boyd, Mar. 30, 1802.
Mary Boyd, Sept. 10, 1805.
Sarah Boyd, May 24, 1807.
Jos. B. Boyd, May 5, 1810.
Mariam Boyd, April 11, 1813.
Mary E. Bibb, April 27, 1821.

MARRIAGES

John Dixon and Elizabeth Boyd, July 7, 1816.
Aaron Boyd and Mary Britton, July 10, 1817.
Asa Tillman and Mary Boyd, Sept. 14, 1824.
David R. Boyd and Trecy Coleman, Sept. 22, 1824.
Jos. B. Boyd and Susan Camden, July 19, 1831.
Elisha A. Patton and Sarah Boyd, Mar. 27, 1832.
Henry Bibb and Nancy Boyd, Feb. 17, 1820.
John H. Robinson and Mariam Boyd, Nov. 1, 1837.
Aaron Boyd and Sarah Edmiston, Nov. 16, 1848.

DEATHS

John Boyd, May 12, 1831.
Nancy Bibb, July 29, 1821.
David R. Boyd, Aug. 17, 1835.
Mary E. Bibb, Sept. 14, 1836.
May M. Boyd, Sept. 8, 1837.
Rebecca Boyd, Feb. 5, 1854.
Note: Copied from the Family Bible of Mrs. T. A. Boyd (Martha Shook Wilson), Route 3, Box 157, Nashville, Tenn., by (Miss) Mary Elizabeth White, 2106 21st Avenue, South, Nashville, Tenn. This Bible was printed in 1730.
Malissa Ann Wilson Neely, born October 31, 1847; died, Jan. 3, 1885; married William M. Neely, Sept. 16, 1868.
Cleopatra Texanna Wilson Ezell, daughter of J. M. and Charity M. Wilson, born Dec. 13, 1844; died October 19, 1882; married James B. Ezell, Aug. 20, 1865.
Martha Martins Sheffield, born Aug. 24, 1805; died, April 28, 1883.
Miss Patra Davis, daughter of Giv Davis of Bedford County, born Mar. 10, 1859; died, Jan. 3, ... (do not know date).

BIRTHS

Tom Aaron Marble Boyd, July 25, 1844.
Martha Shook Wilson, Dec. 2, 1849.
William W. Boyd, Feb. 8, 1868.
Anna Lizzie Boyd, Jan. 14, 1869.
Sallie Malisa Boyd, Aug. 4, 1871.
Joseph Shook Boyd, Nov. 21, 1873.
John Marble Boyd, Sept. 16, 1876.
Nannie Blane Boyd, Nov. 24, 1879.
Thos. Albert Boyd, Nov. 16, 1881.
Earnest Lee Boyd, June 23, 1883.
Ada Sue Boyd, Jan. 16, 1886.
Lynn Boyd, Aug. 29, 1888.
Claude Boyd, Feb. 23, 1891.
Joe Boyd Ezell, May 21, 1897.

MARRIAGES

Thos. Aaron Marble Boyd and Martha Shook Wilson, Dec. 20, 1866.
W. M. Hardison and Lizzie A. Boyd, Sept. 14, 1886.
Dr. A. G. Dickson and Sallie M. Boyd, April 23, 1890.
E. M. Ezell and Nannie B. Boyd, Mar. 22, 1896.
Joe Shook Boyd and Norma Ambrose, Nov. 21, 1900.
L. M. Crawford and Nannie Boyd Ezell, Jan. 28, 1901.
Ernest L. Boyd and Fannie Bowen, Jan. 11, 1905.
Lynn C. Boyd and Mary L. Stammer, Dec. 31, 1912.

Claude S. Boyd and Emma H. Smith, June 4, 1919.

FAMILY HISTORY

Isaac Shook Wilson, born Mar. 13, 1827; died, Sept. 28, 1851.
Elizabeth J. Wilson, born April 10, 1830; died Aug. 18, 1861.
Malissa Ann Wilson, born Oct. 31, 1867; died, Jan. 3, 1885.
The above names are mother, father, and sister of Martha Shook Boyd.
J. B. Boyd, born May 5, 1810; died, June 21, 1897; married July 19, 1831.
Susan W. Boyd, born July 27, 1809; died, Mar. 8, 1885; married July 19, 1831.
Rebecca F. Boyd, born May 31, 1833; married to E. T. Williams, Nov. 1, 1869; died Sept. 12, 1884.
Sallie C. Boyd, born April 11, 1838; married T. J. Wilson Mar. 4, 1857.
John C. Boyd, born Mar. 5, 1841; married Mollie Logan, Aug., 1864.
E. M. Ezell, born Jan., 1873; died, July 22, 1899.

DEATHS

William Wilson Boyd, Feb. 15, 1868 (2 weeks old).
Thos. Albert Boyd, Sept. 6, 1882.
John Marble Boyd, Sept. 13, 1882.
Lizzie B. Hardison, Oct. 5, 1916.
Sallie M. Dickson Ramsey, Nov. 28, 1926.
Thos. A. M. Boyd, Oct. 28, 1917.
Note: Copied from the family Bible of Mrs. T. A. Boyd (Martha Shook Wilson), Route 3, Box 157, Nashville, Tenn., by (Miss) Mary Elizabeth White, 2106 21st Avenue, South, Nashville, Tenn.

BIBLE RECORDS

Copied from Bible of Mattie White Lindsey by Robert Jamison. This Bible was destroyed by fire in 1916.

Sent by Mary Elizabeth White, 2106 Twenty-first Ave., South, Nashville, Tenn.

George Calloway, born Jan. 12, 1748; married to Amelia Calloway, May 18, 1770.
John Patrick, born March 17, 1776.
John Patrick, died Sept. 23, 1824.
Eliza Patrick, died March 24, 1819.
George C. Patrick was listed in Winchester defeat at River Rasin in Canada on Jan 22, 1813.
Isaac Patrick, died Aug. 5, 1823.
George Calloway, married to Amelia, his wife, May 8, 1770.
Betsy Calloway, born Sept. 21, 1771; married John Patrick.
George Calloway, died Dec. 2, 1772.
Amelia Calloway, died April 7, 1773.
John Patrick and Eliza Calloway married Dec. 2, 1787.
Amelia Patrick, born Sept. 17, 1788 (Wednesday); married Thos. Howard.
Isaac Patrick, born Oct. 23 (Saturday), 1790; married Miss Penn, grandfather was William Penn.
George Patrick, born Oct. 3, 1792 (Wednesday); unmarried—lost at River Rasin.
Alexander Patrick, born Nov. 14, 1794 (Friday); married ——— White, from Richmond, Ky.
John Patrick, born Jan. 26, 1797 (Thursday); married Matilda Calloway.
Mary Patrick, born Dec. 15, 1799 (Sunday); married Uncle Cornelius Homan.
Eliza Patrick, born June 10, 1802 (Thursday); married David Decherd.
Anne Patrick, born March 25, 1805 (Monday); Anne Davidson, grandmother.
Thomas Patrick, born May 9, 1808 (Monday); unmarried.
William Patrick, born May 28, 1811 (Thursday).
James Patrick, born July 26, 1814 (Tuesday); Presbyterian preacher, lawyer, lived in Grand Gulf, Miss.

ABSTRACTS OF THE WILL OF THOMAS HARRY

Of the township of Pennsbury, County of Chester, State of Pennsylvania.

I give and devise unto my two sons, Amos Harry and Isaac Harry, all the plantation of land I live on in the township of Pennsbury, they to pay the following legacies:

To my sons, Evan Harry and Jacob Harry, and daughters, Mary Hollingsworth, Hannah Walter, Betsey Harlen, and Sarah Vernon, the sum of one hundred dollars each. My daughter, Lidia Walker, the sum of five dollars; grandson, Samuel Harry, son of my daughter Lidia Walker, the sum of ninety-five dollars. My daughter, Rachel, the sum of six hundred dollars. I give and bequeath unto my son, Amos Harry, the sum of four hundred dollars to be paid from my personal estate. To my daughter, Rachel, one hundred dollars worth of my household and kitchen furniture of her own choice. To my two sons, Amos and Isaac, all the residue of my estate to be equally divided between them. My two sons, Amos and Isaac to be executors of this my last will and testament.

I hereunto set my hand and seal the twelfth day of the eighth month in the year of our Lord, 1824.

Wills in possession of Julia Elizabeth Sprint Ferguson, descendant.

JOHN NASH READ'S WILL

Sent by Miss Rebekah Jetton

In the name of God, Amen. I, John Nash Read, of the County of Rutherford and State of Tennessee, being sound in mind, but weak and sickly in body, do appoint, constitute and make this my last will and testament; hereby revoking all others by me heretofore made. In the first place I recommend my soul to Almighty God from whom it came, confiding in his mercy and goodness, and that my body at my decease be decently interred without any ostentation or parade.

Item 2nd. I will and direct that my executors hereinafter to be named pay all my just debts which are but few.

Item 3rd. I give to my beloved wife, Mary, formerly Mary Barksdale, the plantation whereon I now live, known by the name of the grove, including all that is fenced in, except so much as is included in a deed made to my son, Thomas H. Read, during her life, subject to disposition hereafter to be named. I also give her Jerry and his wife, Polly, and her infant Caswell, and Sucky, during her life. Likewise I give specifically to my wife, Mary, one Negro man Joe and $1,000, my clock, peer glass, china press, sugar chest, tin safe, one ox cart, one yoke of oxen, four cows and calves, ten sheep, fifteen hogs, two horses, three beds, bedsteads and furniture of her own choosing, subject to her discretion without control, two folding tables, and twelve chairs.

Item 4th. I give unto my daughter, Harry Anne Read, one Negro girl named Polina and increase to be enjoyed and disposed of at her discretion, and I give my daughter, Harry Anne, one bed, bedstead and furniture, and it is my wish that she should remain and live with my wife and be supported out of my estate during her life.

Item 5th. In the event that the dividend from my estate to each legatee amounts to more than $2,700 which is the amount I have advanced to my son Clement, deceased, I will and direct that his heirs shall come in for an equal portion of the surplus above the last mentioned sum, but should the dividend fall below it, I direct my executors, hereinafter to be appointed, shall not call upon them to refund any part of the advance which my said son Clement has already received, unless he should have a medical account against me.

Item 7th. Should the dividend of each legatee of my estate amount to more than $1,700, which is the amount I have advanced to my son John H., I direct that he shall come in for an equal portion of the excess over and above the last mentioned sum, but should the dividend fall below it, it is my will and desire that my son John H. shall not be required to refund any part of the advance he has already received, unless he has a medical account against me.

Item 8th. It is my will and desire that when Randolph Barksdale, who married my daughter, Mary H. Read, shall draw his dividend from my estate the sum $1,000 advanced (as per receipt) shall be considered a part of said dividend.

Item 9th. It is my will that when my son Sion shall draw his dividend from my estate, the sum of $1,000 (as per receipt) shall be considered a part of his dividend.

Item 10th. I give unto my son, Thomas H. Read, one tract of land containing 60 acres (as per deed), estimated at $420, one Negro girl named Betsy, rated at $350, one Negro boy named Dennis, rated at $220, one bed and furniture at $20, making the sum of $1,020 (as per receipt), shall be considered a part of said dividend.

Item 11th. I direct that the legacies left my sons, Francis Nash Read and James Allen Read, by John Night, deceased, of Virginia, their grandfather who had promised it to me, in his lifetime, shall be considered as a part of the dividend they are entitled to from my estate.

Item 12th. I direct that my two old Negroes, Jack and Aggy, remain and live with my beloved wife, and that they draw from the estate the sum of $15 annually for their support.

Item 13th. I direct that each of my children, except my said daughter, Harry Anne, as they marry or come of age shall draw the sum of $1,000 in money or property to that amount.

Item 14th. I direct that my executors, hereafter to be named or appointed, shall sell any part of my real estate or Negroes not already disposed of whenever they think the interest of the estate requires it, and the faithful performance and carrying into effect the above will and disposition of property. I do appoint my son-in-law, Randolph Barksdale, my son Thomas H. Read, and my wife Mary, my executors to this my last will and testament.

N. B. The words "the legacies left" in the 11th item interlined before signed, likewise the word "think" in the 14th item, signed, sealed and published this 15th of November, 1825.

John Nash Read.

Witnesses:

Peter Le Grand,
David Robinson,
Nathaniel Barksdale,
A. H. Harris.

John R. Laughlin, Clk.

Recorded 24th February, 1826.

(Taken from Book 6, pages 179, 180, 181; to be found in the County Court Clerk's Office, Murfreesboro, Rutherford County, Tennessee.)

BENJAMIN LIDDON

Sent by Miss Jetton

Benjamin Liddon was born near Wilmington, North Carolina, and served in a North Carolina Regiment, 1771-1773; died, 1815.

"Benjamin Liddon served his country in the American Revolution and for special service for his country was awarded two grants of land, one for 144 acres and one for 250 on Stones River, Rutherford County, Tennessee." From the Archives of State in Wilmington District, New Hanover County, N. C. Benjamin Liddon married Sarah Rutledge, widow of Alveam Ivey, also a soldier in the War of Independence. She had two Ivey children, Anne Gilbert and Thomas R.

A few years after the War the Liddons moved to Tennessee and occupied the land that lay along Stones River on which was a fine spring, known as "Liddon Spring."

Benjamin Liddon and Sarah Rutledge had three children: Wm. Abram, married Mary White Davis; Sarah Jane, married Stephen Owen; Benjamin Franklin, married Mary Ann Hooper Merrill. About 1880 the three families moved to Alabama and Mississippi.

A tablet to Benjamin Liddon was dedicated several years ago by the Col. Hardy Murfree Chapter, D. A. R. The tablet was placed near Liddon's Spring on the Shelbyville Road.

REV. LORENZA DOW OVERALL

Columbia, Sept. 3, 1834.

Messrs. Editors:

It becomes my painful duty to announce to you the death of our beloved brother, Rev. L. D. Overall. He died in this town on the 28th ult. at eight o'clock P. M. of bilious fever, at the home of P. Nelson, Esq., etc. . . . Brother Overall was born July 18, 1803; was convicted of his lost estate at Windrows camp meeting, 1821, in that great revival under the Rev. Sterling C. Brown (now in heaven), whose giant soul scattered salvation, through his indefatigable labors, all over these lands.

Young L. D. Overall, after traveling to this place on foot, about 20 miles, was then and there literally struck to the ground under conviction, and for two whole days and nights neither ate nor slept, crying for mercy.

From this meeting he went home with a bleeding heart, still inquiring, "What must I do to be saved?" About two weeks after, with fifteen of his unconverted associates, he left home for a Cumberland Presbyterian camp meeting, eight miles from Murfreesboro, at which place he with fourteen of his companions obtained the pearl of great price. It was not long before our young brother was moved by the Holy Spirit to call sinners to repentance. It was like fire shut up in his bones; nor could he rest until he broke from the scenes of his boyhood. With the silver trumpet of the gospel he mounted the walls of Zion and filled it with the sound of salvation. . . .

With these feelings and exercises, Young Overall entered upon his ministerial life at the age of 20. He was licensed to preach at the District Conference for Nashville District held in this place in 1823. It is worthy of remark that here he commenced and here he closed his ministerial labors and perhaps was not in columbia more than a dozen times in the interim, etc. . . . T. M.

"History of Methodism in Tennessee," John B. McFerrin. Vol. III, page 98.

Catherine Young Brown, the youngest child of John Brown and Rebecca Young, was born in Nashville, September 19, 1829. She was married December 23, 1851, to Edward William Morgan, and died October 30, 1891. The youngest of her six children was Natalie Morgan, born June 12, 1866, and married on September 18, 1888, to William Francis Theobald. Her only child is Catharine Theobald, born November 26, 1891, and married on September 11, 1919, to Frank W. Ridley of Smyrna. Her oldest child is Natalie Morgan Ridley, born June 21, 1920; also William Hibbett Ridley, born May 4, 1922, and Edith Claire Ridley, born April 8, 1927.

ANCESTORS OF MRS. JOSEPHINE JONES WEAKLEY

Sent by Miss Jetton

My Father's ancestors: Col. Richard Calloway, born about 1722, was killed by Indians near Boonsborough, Ky., in March, 1780, during the Revolutionary War. The Indians carried his scalp to Ohio, their camp. He had peculiar long, gray hair. A friend named Jackson, a prisoner, recognized his scalp. It is said that the Indians, after scalping him, stripped him, mutilated his body and rolled it in the mud. His remains were interred at Boonsborough, Ky.

Frances Calloway: Col. Richard's daughter was born in 1763. She married Capt. John Holder. Their daughter, Lydia Holder, married Thomas G. Jones. Lydia Holder Jones was born about 1788. Her husband, Thomas, came from what is now Augusta County, Virginia. This couple settled in Bourbon County, Ky. They had three children: Thomas, Caleb Holder (our father), and one girl, Mary Frances.

Caleb Holder Jones married Eliza Morrow Hume who was born in Nashville about 1812. They were married about 1835. They had six children: Henry Clay, who died in infancy, Thomas, Edgar, Caleb Holder, Rachel Jackson, Ruth, and Josephine.

Caleb Holder Jones, Sr., was in the Mexican War. He enlisted as private on July 7, 1847, and served as private in Company B, 1st Batln., Louisiana Volunteer Infantry. He died in service on November 4, 1847, at Pueblo, Mexico.

Eliza Morrow Hume Jones died in Nashville May 11, 1857.

Edgar Jones married Susan Cheatham December 4, 1866; Caleb H. Jones married Lizzie Fortson of Kentucky, June, 1861; Rachel and C. F. Weakley married June 24, 1862; Ruth and Rev. W. L. Rosser married July 6, 1869; and Josephine and Samuel Morford Weakley married October 15, 1873.

Josephine Jones Weakley and Samuel Morford Weakley had seven children. Their names are as follows: Evelina Morford, born August 29, 1874; Samuel Hickman, born January 2, 1877; Julia House, born April 21, 1879; Mamie E., born September 7,

1881; Robert, born February 21, 1884; Ray, born August 4, 1886; Ferman Morford, born October 5, 1889.

Samuel M. Weakley, born September 7, 1837, near Smyrna, Tenn; died, February 22, 1908, at his home four miles from Smyrna.

Josephine Jones was born February 26, 1847, in Nashville, Tenn.

Weakley

Col. Robert Weakley, 1st, came from Wicklon County, Ireland, sometime before the Revolutionary War and settled a while in Pennsylvania. He brought three sons. His son William settled in Pennsylvania. Samuel went to Ohio. Robert, about ten years of age, went with his father to Virginia. This Robert, 2nd, married Eleanor Stewart. They had six or seven children: William, Robert, Samuel Davis, Thomas, Mary, and Martha.

Col. Robert Weakley, 3rd, in his 16th year was in the Revolutionary War. Our grandfather was in the battle of King's Mountain and in the hard-fought battle of Guilford Courthouse. Shortly after the war he was in North Carolina with a relative, General Rutherford, studying and surveying between 1782 and 1784. He came to Davidson County near Nashville. That time of the year he could not survey so he taught school at Tulon Station. After coming of age he was appointed County Surveyor and Justice of Peace. He settled on Whites Creek. Later he bought a place east of Nashville and named it for his wife who was before her marriage Jane Locke. The place was called Lockland. Col. Weakley was a member of Congress which met in Washington, D. C., November, 1809. He married Jane Locke of Rowen County, North Carolina.

General Matthew Locke, father of Mrs. Robert Weakley, 3rd, was one of the first settlers of Rowen County, N. C. He was born in 1730. He was a patriot and an early and devoted friend of liberty and rights of the people. In 1771 he was selected by the people to receive the lawful fees of sheriff. In 1775 he was a member of the Colonial Assembly. In 1776 he was a member of the Provincial Congress which met in Philadelphia November 12th and planned the Constitution. He was married twice—first wife a daughter of Richard Brandon. General Locke and his wife had twelve children. Their daughter married Robert Locke Weakley. This couple had four children. Their names were: Mary, born July 12, 1792, married Gen. John Brahan; Narcisses, married Major John P. Hickman; Robert Locke married Evelina Belmont Morford; Jane Baird married Major John Lucian Brown.

Morford Family

Zebulin Morford, a native of Wales, was born in 1722 and died October 25, 1794. He married Susan Barton of England who was born September 24, 1727, and died January 15, 1812. They came to America and settled in Cranberry, New Jersey, and raised a large family. Their son, Zebulin, Jr., was born March 29, 1759. He married Mary Denton, born Dec. 5, 1765. Their daughter, Evelina Belmont, was born January 30, 1804, died March, 1882. She married Robert Locke Weakley, 4th (born 1801 ....). This couple had ten children. Robert, born in 1823, January 2, died a bachelor. Mary Jane, born August 29, 1825, married Rev. Jesse W. Hume in 1845, first; later she married Dr. J. W. Davis in 1850. Susan Narcisses, born July 4, 1828; she married T. B. Trigg. Matthew Locke (bachelor). Harriett married Isaac Brunson. Hickmon Bryor, born November 5, 1833, married Lucy Muse. Charles Furman, born November, 1835, married Rachel Jackson Jones, born September 16, 1842. Samuel Morford Weakley, born September 9, 1837, married Josephine Jones October 15, 1873. Evie Belmont, born in 1843, married Lyceryas Nelson.

JOSIAH MARTIN

Sent by Miss Jetton

Dates of Appointment or Enlistment	Service Length	Rank	Officers under Whom He Served Captain	Colonel	State
Spring, 1780	1 month	Private	Barber		N. Car.
About June, 1780	4 months	Private	Barber	Graham	
Late in 1780	3 months	Private	Thos. White		
Spring, 1781	3 months	Private	Isaac White		
Fall, 1781	3 months	Lieutenant	Isaac White	Smith	

Battles engaged in: In skirmish near Buffington Iron Works in 1780 and accidentally wounded by spear in hands of comrade; in battle of Cowpens. Residence of soldier at enlistment: Lincoln County, N. C. Born February, 1757, in a county adjacent to Cumberland County, Pa. He died September 17, 1835. Date of application for pension, October 1, 1832. Claim allowed. Residence at date of application for pension, Rutherford County, Tenn.

He married in Mecklenburg County, N. C., May 28, 1783, Mary, daughter of Robert McClary. She was allowed a pension on her claim executed April 3, 1845, while 80 years old and a resident of Rutherford County.

Children: Abigail, born March 28, 1784; William, born December 8, 1786; Hannah, born October 20, 1790; Robert, born November, 1793; Clarissa, born August, 1796; Marilla, born September 29, 1799; Mary McDowell, born November 16, 1806; Matilda, born February 15, 1808.

Record of McGowan Family, Compiled by C. M. Stockard,

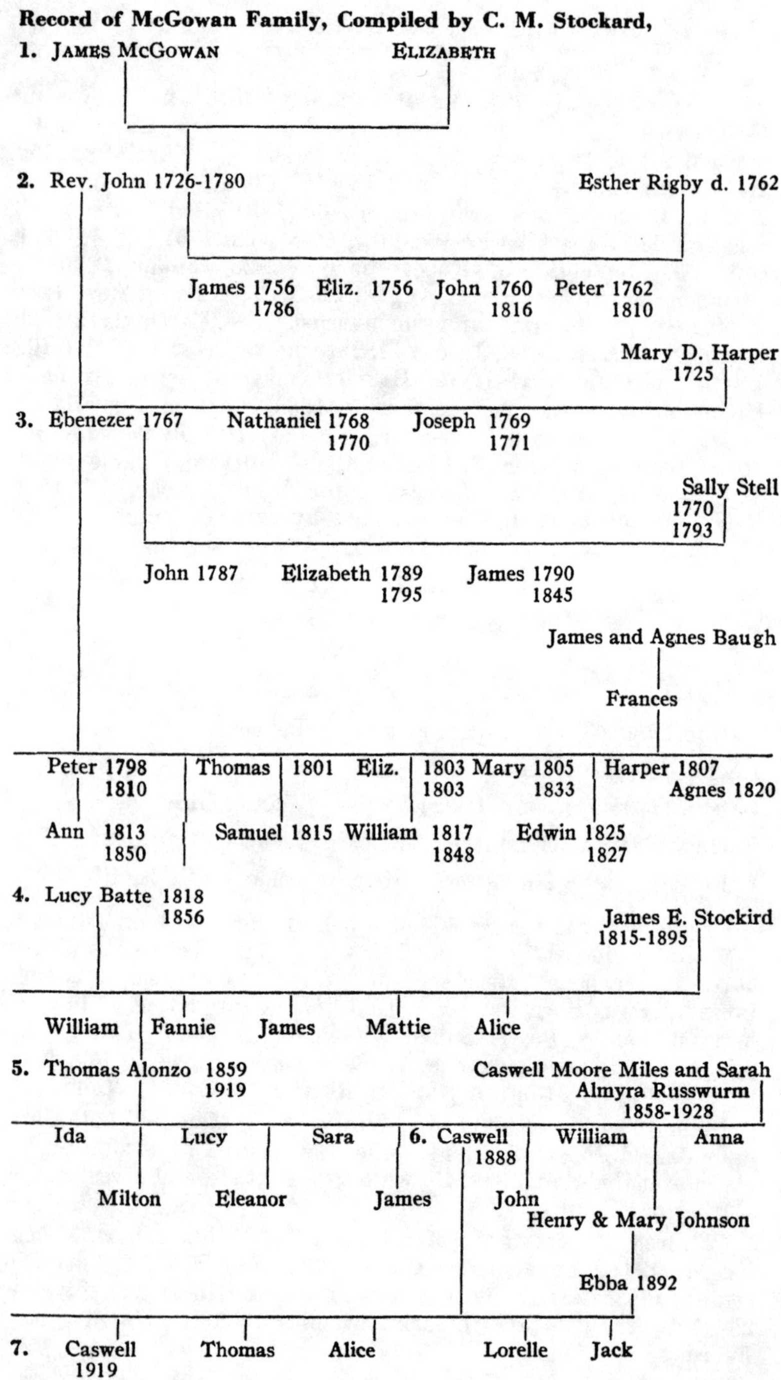

Seven generations compiled from family records by Mrs. C. M. Stockard, October, 1932.

(Data by Mary E. Baker, a descendant, Knoxville, Tenn. Grave is in Old Cannon Cemetery, near Smyrna; road almost inassessible. There is a tombstone with name and dates of birth and death only. This I was told by a Murfreesboro descendant.)

MEMORANDA FOUND IN VIRGINIA D. BYRN'S BIBLE

Copied by Rebekah Jetton

Temperance Herbert married John Herbert and to them were born Joe Herbert, Richard M. Herbert, Sarah Jane Herbert, John G. (Green?) Herbert, Julia A. Herbert.

Rebecca Hunt married E. H. Jones; two children, Gershom H. Jones, Fannie G. Hunt.

Green Hunt married Fannie Watkins; had four children, Ownet Hunt, Joe Hunt, Jim Hunt, Fanny G. Hunt.

William Hunt married Elizabeth A. Ogilvie; had three children, William, John, and Elizabeth.

Enoch Hunt married Lucy Bailey; had no children to live.

Sarah C. Hunt married W. B. Byrn; had six children.

Joe Hunt died young.

Mary Hunt died young.

MRS. JOHN C. HOOPER'S FAMILY BIBLE

Records Copied by Rebekah Jetton

John Clark, Sr., born Dec. 17, 1781.
Elizabeth Bowman, consort of John Clark, born Jan. 3, 1784.
E. M. Clark, born Nov. 9, 1805.
Samuel B. Clark, born Sept. 29, 1807.
Margaret A. Clark, born Oct. 7, 1809.
Terzah A. Clark, born Oct. 7, 1809.
Mary C. Clark, born Sept. 11, 1811.
John N. Clark, born Jan. 25, 1814.
Nancy A. Clark, born July 26, 1816.
Eleanor M. Clark, born Dec. 29, 1818.
Isabella J. Clark, born Mar. 21, 1821.
William A. Clark, born Sept. 1, 1823.
Adaline Clark, born Oct. 15, 1827.
John Clark and Elizabeth Bowman married Oct. 24, 1804.
Married the 17th of May, 1860, Isabella Jane Clark to Lemuel Ransom.
Mr. Lemuel Ransom died the 4th of June, 1869; age, 71 years.
Polly Caroline Clark, born Sept. 9, 18—.

————————————

——————, 1814.

————————————

——————, July 26, 1816.

Eleanor Malica Clark, born Dec. 29, 1818.

Isabella Jane Clark, born Mar. 18, 1821.

John N. Clark and Caroline McFadden were married Jan. 12, 1837.

John N. Clark was born Jan. 25, 1814.

Caroline McFadden was born Sept. 3, 1818.

Samuel Houston Clark, born Nov. 24, A. D., 1837.

James Newton Clark, born May 15, A. D., 1842.

Holly Ann Elizabeth Clark, born Aug. 9, A. D., 1844.

Mary Jane Louisa Clark, born Dec. 29, A. D., 1846.

William John Clark, born Feb. 10, A. D., 1849.

Finis Erastus Clark, born Oct. 2, A. D., 1851.

Ida Eldora Clark, born, Dec. 11, 1853.

Cora Adaline Clark, born Mar. 4, 1856.

Holly Ann Elizabeth Clark departed this life Sept. 11, A. D., 1845; age, 13 months and 2 days.

Samuel Houston Clark departed this life Jan. 11, A. D., 1851; age, 13 years, 1 month, and 17 days.

William John Clark departed this life Mar. 8, 1853; age, 4 years and 25 days.

James N. Clark was killed at the battle of Shiloh April 6, A. D., 1862;

age, 19 years, 10 months, and 21 days.
Elizabeth Clark died Aug. 28, 1853.
John Clark, Sr., died Aug. 23, 1857.
Adaline Clark died April 15, 1835.
Margaret A. Clark died Mar. 6, 1849.
Terzah A. Clark died Oct. 4, 1853.
Nancy A. Love died April 2, 1856.
Eleanor M. Tucker died Aug. 1, 1867.
William A. Clark died April 21, 1868.
Mr. Lemuel Ransom died Oct., 1883.
Lemuel B. Clark died Oct. 17, 1883.
Isabella Jane Ransom died Oct. 7, 1891; age, 70.

MEMORANDA IN ALLIE BYRN LEDBETTER'S BIBLE

James D. Richardson's father was named John W. Richardson; his father was James Richardson and mother Mary Watkins.

James D. Richardson's mother's name was Augusta Starnes; her father was Daniel Starnes and mother Harriet Russell.

Alabama Pippen's father's name was Eldred Pippen; her mother, Hicksy High.

MEMORANDA IN VIRGINIA DARE BYRN'S BIBLE

Sketch by William Leslie Talley (deceased). Typed at his office, Stahlman Building. Copied by Rebekah Jetton.

Enoch Hunt married Miss Lorrance, a German girl, in New York. They moved either to New Hampshire or to Massachusetts, and later to North Carolina, settling on the Roanoke River; they had seven sons and three daughters. In the year 1795 two sons, Noah and Gershom, and the three daughters moved to Tennessee. After two years residence in Tennessee, Noah Hunt moved to the Blue Grass region of Kentucky. One of the daughters, Margaret, married Ezra Jones of Rutherford County, Tenn.; one, ——————, married Henry Warren of Williamson County, Tenn.; and one married Mr. Orten.

Gershom Hunt married Sarah Orten of Virginia. They had eight children:

Temperance Powell Hunt, born, 1800.
Rebecca Frances Hunt, born, 1803.
Green W. Hunt, born, 1806.
Josephus Hunt, born, 1809.
Mary F. Hunt, born, 1812.
William Carroll Hunt, born, 1815.
Enoch J. Hunt, born, 1818.
Sarah Caroline Hunt, born, 1824.

Gershom Hunt was born in Roanoke County, N. C., July 10, 1765, and died in Williamson County, Tenn., Nov. 16, 1838; age, 73 years.

Sarah Orten Hunt was born in Virginia in 1781, and died in Williamson County, Tenn., Aug. ——, 1849; age, 68.

Temperance Powell Hunt, born ——, 1800, and died Oct. 4, 1875; age, 75 years.

She married John B. Herbert in 18—.

Rebecca Frances Hunt, born Oct. 3, 1803, and died May 19, 1856; age, 52 years.

She married Enoch Hunt Jones of Rutherford County, Tenn., in Oct., 1839.

Green W. Hunt was born in ——, 1806, and died ———, 1847; age, 41 years.

William Carroll Hunt, born Nov. 30, 1815, and died May 11, 1860; age, 44 years. He married Elizabeth Ogilvie of Davidson County, Tenn., ———, 1837.

Enoch J. Hunt was born Feb. 24, 1818, and died Jan. 26, 1851; age, 33 years. He married Lucy V. Bailey, who died in 1849, one week later than his mother, Sarah Orten Hunt.

Sarah Caroline Hunt was born December 20, 1824, and died June 25, 1886; age, 62 years. She married William B. Byrn of Rutherford County, Tenn., Jan. 26, 1843.

RANSOM LINE

Ransom and Jarratt Bibles copied by Mrs. J. Moore King and Evelyn King Miller (Mrs. H. Grady Miller) for Rebekah Jetton, Chairman of Historical Research, Capt. Wm. Lytle Chapter, Murfreesboro.

1. Generation: Peter Ransom, born in 1620, Elizabeth City County, Virginia. He was a member of Virginia House of Burgesses in 1652. He was a large landowner.

2. Generation: James Ransom, son of Peter Ransom, was a member of the Virginia House of Burgesses, 1690-93-97. He was a vestryman in Kingston Parrish, Episcopal Church. He belonged to the Colonial Militia with Mathew Page and Peter Beverly.

3. Generation: James Ransom, II. He married Amy Davis of Isle-of-Wight County, Virginia. She was the daughter of William Davis. They had eleven children, six girls and five boys:

Richard Payne married Kezziah Portis.
James died unmarried; served in Revolutionary War.
Clevions and Samuel, both married and reared families; lived and died in North Carolina.
Davis died unmarried; served in Revolutionary War.
Mary married Warren Warren.
Elizabeth married William Harrison.
Nancy married Niles Nelms.
Sallie married David Whitehead.
Priscilla married Green Andrews.
Amy married William Davis.

4. Generation: Captain Richard Payne Ransom, son of James and Amy D. Ransom, was born in Isle-of-Wight County, Virginia, in 1752. He was a Revolutionary soldier, first private, then lieutenant, then captain. He was captured at Giles Defeat in South Carolina August 16, 1780. He heard that the pioneers were to be sent to England and he fled with ten other soldiers, lived on raw corn for eleven days and lay covered with mud for two days. After the Revolution he moved to North Carolina and settled in Halifax County; married Kezziah Portis, daughter of Job Portis, in 1784. He had eleven children:

Robert married Mary Harris.
Benjamine C. married Sarah Jarratt.
Athelston married Elizabeth Clark.
William died unmarried.
Alfred married Sally Snell.
Lemuel married Jane Comer.
Henry D. married Priscilla Manor.
John married Elizabeth Bowman.
Richard married Elizabeth Snell.
Polly married Milton Birdwell.

Sarah married Joe Mallard.

5. Generation: Benjamine Clevious Ransom, son of Captain Richard Payne and Kezziah Portis Ransom, born in 1787, Halifax County, North Carolina. He married Sarah Jarratt. In 1810 he moved to Rutherford County, Tennessee, and settled on Salem Road. They had eleven children, ten boys and one girl:

William King married Sarah Wilson.
John C. died unmarried.
Elizabeth married Thompson.
Thompson died unmarried.
Benjamine married, first, Frances Jordan; second, Margaret Fuggett; third, Elizabeth Slater.
Gideon died unmarried.
Whitnal married Martha Williams.
D. J. moved to Texas.
Thomas died unmarried.
Medicus married, first, Temperance Peck; second, Julia H. Lillard.
Joseph married, first, Virginia Williams; second, Mary McClellan.

6. Generation: Dr. Medicus Ransom, son of Benjamine Clevious and Sarah J. Ransom, born in Rutherford County, Tennessee. He was educated in Europe, eminent physician and surgeon. He was on Gen. Forrest's staff during a part of the Civil War. He died December 31, 1891. He was first married to Temperance Peck, daughter of John and Temperance Crawford Peck. His second wife was Julia Lillard, daughter of William and Delia Blackman Lillard. The children of first union were:

Lorena Peck married Giles Harding.
Walter Peck married Edith Adkins.
Jessie Amanda married William Ewing Chadwell.
Carrie Elizabeth married William E. Hudson.
Birdie Temperance married James Moore King.

The children of the second union were:

William Lillard, died when young.
Delia Sally married Charles Gannaway.
Med.
Julia Mae married Hugh McVeigh Craig.

7. Generation: Lorena Peck Ransom, daughter of Dr. Medicus and Temperance P. Ransom, married Giles S. Harding. They had four children. She died February 18, 1932. The children are: Jesse, Lalla Mae, Med, and Giles.

7. Generation: Walter Peck Ransom, son of Dr. Medicus and Temperance Peck Ransom, married Edith Adkins of West Tennessee. A daughter, Lorena, who married Terry Johnson.

7. Generation: Jessie Amanda Ransom, daughter of Dr. Medicus

and Temperance Peck Ransom, married William Ewing Chadwell. No children.

7. Generation: Carrie Elizabeth Ransom, daughter of Dr. Medicus and Temperance Peck Ransom, married William E. Hudson. The children are:

Helene married Tom Jones.
Temperance married Sam Chester.
William.
James.

7. Generation: Birdie Temperance Ransom, daughter of Dr. Medicus and Temperance Peck Ransom, married James Moore King. The children are:

Louise married F. C. Griffith.
Mary Frances married Garnett Stith Andrews.
Evelyn Ransom married Henry Grady Miller.
Madelyn Peck, born Feb. 27, 1905; died, Oct. 16, 1916.
James Moore.

7. Generation: Delia Sally Ransom, daughter of Dr. Medicus and Julia Lillard Ransom, married Charles Gannaway. Their children are:

Julia married Jesse Thomas.
Janice.
Elizabeth married Joris McDonald White.
Virginia Ann married—

7. Generation: Med Ransom, son of Dr. Medicus and Julia Lillard Ransom.

7. Generation: Julia Mae Ransom, daughter of Dr. Medicus and Julia Lillard Ransom, married Hugh McVeigh Craig.

8. Generation: Lalla Mae Harding, daughter of Giles and Lorena Ransom Harding, married, first, Eugene Hunter, second, Frank E. Mudge. One son by first union: Eugene Harding Hunter.

8. Generation: Med Harding, son of Giles and Lorena Ransom Harding.

8. Generation: Lorena Ransom, daughter of Walter P. and Edith Adkins Ransom, married Terry Johnson. They have one daughter, Terry Edith.

8. Generation: Helene Hudson, daughter of William E. and Carrie Ransom Hudson, married Tom Jones. Their children are: Tom, Jr., Helene, William Johnathan (died in infancy).

8. Generation: Temperance Hudson, daughter of William E. and Carrie Ransom Hudson, married Sam Chester. Their children are: Temperance, Caroline Elizabeth, and Sam.

8. Generation: William Hudson, son of William E. and Carrie Ransom Hudson.

8. Generation: James Hudson, son of William E. and Carrie Ransom Hudson.

8. Generation: Louise King, daughter of James Moore and Birdie Ransom King, married F. C. Griffith. A son, Frank Colville.

8. Generation: Mary Frances King, daughter of James Moore and Birdie Ransom King, married Garnett Stith Andrews. One daughter: Mary Frances.

8. Generation: Evelyn Ransom King, daughter of James Moore and Birdie Ransom King, married Henry Grady Miller.

8. Generation: James Moore King, son of James Moore and Birdie Ransom King.

8. Generation: Julia Gannaway, daughter of Charles and Delia Ransom Gannaway, married Jesse Thomas.

8. Generation: Janice Gannaway, daughter of Charles and Delia Ransom Gannaway.

8. Generation: Delia Elizabeth Gannaway, daughter of Charles and Delia Ransom Gannaway, married Joris McDonald White. Their children are: Betty, Joris.

8. Generation: Virginia Ann married. Has a son.

8. Generation: Julia Lillard Craig, daughter of Hugh McVeigh and Julia Mae Ransom Craig.

FAMILY BIBLE OF W. B. BYRN AND SARAH HUNT

Willed to Ida Lee Byrn Evans (Mrs. E. J. Evans) by the late C. H. Byrn. Copied by Rebekah Jetton.

W. B. Byrn of Rutherford County, Tenn., and Sarah C. Hunt of Williamson County, Tenn., on 26th of Jan., 1843, at Mrs. S. Hunts, by Rev. R. W. Janary.

Births of Wm. B. Byrn's children:
William M. Byrn, July 22, 1845.
Rufus G. Byrn, June 26, 1847.
Mary Francis Byrn, May 19, 1849.
James F. Byrn, June 15, 1851.
Sarah V. Byrn, Oct. 15, 1853.
Charley H. Byrn, Feb. 8, 1856.

Wm. M. Byrn's children: Arthur Byrn, Etter Byrn, Iner Byrn, Mark W., Delia.

Rufus G. Byrn's children: Charley H., Byrn, Jr., Daisy L. Byrn, Cardie H. Byrn, Roy G. Byrn.

Mary Frances' children: Owen Freas, Wm. H. Freas.

J. F. Byrn's children: W. B. Byrn, Jr., born June 6, 1878; Erwin Byrn, born April 17, 1880; first one born Jan. 22, 1877.

Mary Freas Byrn, born Aug. 25, 1883; James Finley Byrn, born Jan. 8, 1885; Jesse V. Byrn, born Nov. 13, 1886.

S. V. Talley's children: Leslie Talley, born Aug. 30, 1881.

Marriages

W. B. Byrn and S. C. Hunt, Jan. 26, 1843.
W. M. Byrn and D. Dougherty, Nov. 24, 1869.
Mary F. Byrn and S. H. Freas, Dec. 28, 1871.
R. G. and Fanny Martin, Jan. 14, 1875.
James F. Byrn and Jimmy Blackman, May 5, 1875.
Sarah V. Byrn and Leslie W. Talley, Sept. 28, 1877.
Sarah V. Talley and Harris B. Northcut, April 24, 1884.
C. H. Byrn and Alle Richardson, Dec. 26, 1889.
Wm. Henry Freas and Gertie Hill, Nov. 4, 1902.
Daisy Byrn and Rufus Edwin Jarman, Oct. 25, 1906.
Carrie Byrn and Ivan Bass, Sept. 23, 1913.
Will Byrn and Lucy Lee Swope, Aug. 25, 1910.

Charlie Byrn and Elizabeth Durham, June 5, 1918.
Lucile Byrn and Clyde Reagor, June 24, 1919.
Mary Byrn and Harry Alexander, Oct. 16, 1909.
Delia Byrn and Rufus Williamson, Dec. 28, 1909.
Ina Byrn and Charlie Blankenship, Dec., 1899.
Annie Mary Byrn and Earl Roberts, Nov. 20, 1923.
Allie Byrn and William C. Ledbetter, Oct. 19, 1926.
Ida Lee Byrn and E. J. Evans, Nov. 6, 1929.

DEATHS

W. B. Byrn, Aug. 4, 1883.
Sarah C. Byrn, June 20, 1886.
Mary F. Freas, July 3, 1890.
Leslie W. Talley, Jan. 31, 1881.
Harris B. Northcutt, May 1, 1890.
James F. Byrn, Dec. 3, 1903.
D. Byrn, wife of Wm. Byrn, ———.
Ina Byrn Blankenship, April, 1900.
Rufus Green Byrn, Dec. 5, 1914.
Sarah Byrn, daughter of C. H., and Allie Byrn, died Aug. 9, 1914.
Wm. Leslie Talley, Nov. 9, 1920.
Harry O. Alexander, July 2, 1928.
C. H. Byrn, Dec. 24, 1929.
Mrs. Wm. Byrn, July 4, 1930.
Jesse Byrn, Feb. 22, 1929.
Children of C. H. Byrn and Allie R. Byrn:
Sarah, born Dec. 16, 1890.
Charley Richardson Byrn, Aug. 16, 1893.
Lucile, July 27, 1896.
Annie Mary, Feb. 13, 1900.
Allie Richardson Byrn, June 24, 1903.
Ida Lee Byrn, July 21, 1906.
Virginia Dare Byrn, May 24, 1910.
Charles Richardson Byrn, son of C. R. Byrn and Elizabeth Durham Byrn, was born Nov. 14, 1920.
Ann Byrn, daughter of Earl and Annie M. B. Roberts, born Mar. 26, 1927.
James Daniel, son of Earl and Annie M. B. Roberts, born July 30, 1928.
William Ledbetter, son of Wm. Ledbetter and Allie Byrn Ledbetter, born June 30, 1929.

(ALLIE'S BIBLE) RICHARDSON FAMILY BIBLE

Willed to Allie Byrn Ledbetter (Mrs. Wm. L.) by her father, C. H. Byrn. Copied by Rebekah Jetton.

James Daniel Richardson and Alabama Rebecca Pippen were married in Greene County, Ala., at the residence of John P. Rice on Wednesday evening, Jan. 18, 1865.
Children: Annie Augusta, born Tuesday, Nov. 21, 1865; Ida Lee, born Friday, May 3, 1867; Allie Sue, born Saturday, Nov. 6, 1869; John Watkins, born Friday, April 27, 1872; James Daniel, born, Monday, Jan. 4, 1875.
John Watkins died Nov., 1873.
James D. Richardson died July 24, 1914.
Mrs. James D. Richardson (Alabama Rebecca Pippin) died May 23, 1927.
Annie Augusta married Thursday, April 6, 1888, to Thomas G. Garrett.
Allie Sue married Thursday, Dec. 26, 1889, to Charles H. Byrn.
James Daniel married in Columbia, Tenn., Thursday, Nov. 20, 1901, to Miss Mina McLemore.

VIRGINIA D. BYRN BIBLE

Willed to her by her father, C. H. Byrn. Copied by Rebekah Jetton.

James Byrn and Rebecca Word was married April 2, 1807.
James Leech and Elizabeth Byrn were married Nov. 11, 1829.
James Wilson and Sintha Byrn were married Dec. 9, 1830.
R. Bumpas married Jan. 25, 1837.
Brogan married Oct. 12, 1837.

John C. Byrn and Ginet Ketchen married June 12, 1838.
Jany Byrn and Wm. Alsop were married 12th month, 1840.
October 13, 1842, Dimet Jinnings and ——— Byrn married.
Wm. Byrn and Sarah Hunt married Jan. 26, 1842.
James H. Byrn and Sarah E. McKnight were married 20th day of Feb., 1845.
L. R. Jennings and Rebecca G. Byrn were married 28th of Feb., 1850.
Elizabeth Leech departed this life Feb. 16, 1876.
James Leech departed this life Aug. 7, 1835.

BIRTHS

James Byrn, June 27, 1775.
Rebecca Word, Feb. 16, 1784.
Rozin Byrn, May 7, 1808.
Betsey Byrn, Sept. 17, 1809.
Wm. B. Byrn, Feb. 27, 1811.
Gintha Byrn, Feb. 4, 1813.
John C. Byrn, April 1, 1815.
Fanny Byrn, Aug. 1, 1819.
Pollyan Byrn, July 11, 1822.
Jas. H. Byrn, June 11, 1824.
Lafatte Byrn, Sept. 4, 1826.
Rebecca Elizabeth Byrn, Mar., 1829.
Rebeccann Leech, Dec. 4, 1831.
H. B. Leech, Aug. 25, 1834.
Tip Alsup, Feb. 19, 1841.
Mary Elizabeth Alsop, Jan. 9, 1847.
——————— Alsop, July 6, 1843.

DEATHS

A. R. Byrn, Dec. 14, 1820; age, 41.
May Byrn, Jan. 29, 1822; age, 78.
James Leech, Aug. 7, 1835.
James Byrn, Sept. 4, 1848.
Rebecca Byrn, May 21, 1865.
Polly McAdo, July 5, 1860.
Rezin Byrn, Jan., 1876.
Elizabeth Leech, Feb. 6, 1876.
J. H. Byrn, 1876.
Xanthus Baxter, Aug. 21, 1876.
Polly Ann Jennings, July 17, 1898.
Dimit Jennings, June 26, 1897.
Wm. B. Byrn, Aug. 4, 1883.
Sarah C. Byrn, June 24, 1886.
Benjamin Franklin Knox, May 24, 1911. He was confined to the house 17 years.
At the death of Nancy B. Knox this Bible is to be given to C. H. Byrn.
Signed, B. F. Knox.
July 19, 1895.

Mary F. Freas, July 3, 1890.
Dr. Jas. F. Byrn, Dec. 1, 1903.
R. G. Byrn, Dec. 5, 1914.
Wm. B. Byrn, Aug. 4, 1883.
Sarah C. Byrn, wife of Wm. B., June 20, 1886.
Weslie W. Talley, Jan. 31, 1881.
H. B Northcut, May 1, 1890.
Rhidelia Byrn, wife of Wm. Byrn.
Ina Byrn Blankenship, 1900.

NEGROES

Vilet, born Oct. 3, 1801.
Dolerson, June 12, 1807.
Anna, May 9, 1819.
George, Sept. 11, 1821.
Charles, Dec. 8, 1827.
Joe, Nov. 16, 1835.
Rachel, Oct. 13, 1836.
Linday, June 11, 1837.
Dartherly, July 21, 1839.
Mary Fanny, May 2, 1839.
John of Any, June 17, 1841.
Monroe of Anna, Feb. 22, 1843.
Frankey of Anna, April 6, 1845.
Hannar of Anny, Aug. 15, 1847.
Prince of Emoline, June 2, 1842.
Picy, Sept. 1, 1844.
Daniel died Mar. 21, 1830.
Rachel died Mar. 25, 1843.

GOODLOE RECORDS

Given to Rebekah Jetton by Hallam Goodloe of Nashville

George Goodloe, born, 1639; died, 1710, the first in America, came from Aspul, Lancashire, England. His wife, Mary.

II. Generation. Henry Goodloe, died, 1748 or 49; wife, Elizabeth. Middlesex and Spotsylvania, Va.

III. Generation. Robert Goodloe, born, 1711; died, 1790; wife, Elizabeth Guinca, Spotsylvania County, Va.

Their children: John Goodloe; his wife, Elizabeth Hoskins; large family, now in Virginia. Robert Goodloe, born, 1744; died, 1801; married first Priscilla Johnson; second, Sarah Castle; came to Tennessee, Rutherford County.

Children of George Goodloe and Priscilla Johnson: George Goodloe, lost sight of. Robert Goodloe, born, 1774; died, 1844; wife, Elizabeth Hallum. Henry Goodloe, born, 17—; died, 1864; wife, Rebecca Wright.* Mary Goodloe; husband, Stephens, in DeKalb County. John Goodloe, and Aquilla, died, 1840.

Child of George Goodloe and Sarah Castle: Sym Bluford Goodloe; family still in Virginia.

Children of Robert Goodloe and Elizabeth Hallum: Henry Goodloe, born, 1812; died, 1877; wife, Mirian Barton. Aquilla Johnson Goodloe, born, 1810; died, 1865, in West Tennessee where he moved in 1849.

Children of Henry Goodloe and Rebecca Wright: Cynthia Goodloe, married Henry Orr, moved to Texas. Robert Goodloe; wife, Ozina Stokes; moved to Alabama in 1839 or 40. Rebecca Goodloe, married Lewis Jetton. Theodocia Goodloe, married W. W. Nance; died at Alamo, Tenn. Newton Cannon Goodloe, who moved to Alabama and has descendants around Mobile and Demopolis.

Children of Henry Goodloe and Mirian Barton: Bennett R. Goodloe and sister Altamina Hare—her son is David Hare.

Child of Aquilla Johnson Goodloe: Caswell A. Goodloe, born, 1838; died, 1916, at Alamo, Tenn. His child: Hallum Wood Goodloe of Nashville, Tenn.

Child of Theodocia Goodloe and W. W. Nance: P. B. Nance, and his child, Booker Nance, who is now at Alamo.

*Spelled Rebekah in our Bibles, just one Rebekah Thompson, 1752.

LYTLE RECORDS—BELONGING TO ANN TAYLOR LYTLE

Copied by Mrs. Charles Youree and Mrs. Edward Jordan. Sent by Miss Rebekah Jetton.

William F. Lytle, Sr., son of Robert and Sarah Lytle, Feb. 17, 1755-Sept. 4, 1829; age, 74 years, 6 months, 18 days.

Ann Taylor Lytle, daughter of John and Sarah Taylor, and wife of William F. Lytle, Feb. 17, 1770-Nov. 7. 1825; age, 55 years, 8 months, 21 days.

John M. Tilford, born in Lusien County, Va., Sept. 18, 1783; died in Rutherford County, Tenn., April 13, 1860.

Ann T. Lytle, daughter of William F. and Ann T. Lytle, and wife of John M. Tilford, born in Orange County, N. C., Jan. 18, 1795; died in spring of 1878; age, about 83 years.

James M. Tilford, Aug. 10, 1812-Jan. 5, 1848; died in Macon, Ga.

William Lytle Tilford, April 1, 1814-Aug. 29, 1815.

Sarah Tilford, Oct. 30, 1817-July, 2, 1862.

Lucilla Tilford, Aug. 21, 1820-Aug. 5, 1842.

Thomas White Tilford, April 9, 1823-Sept. 23, 1823.
Jane F. Tilford, Aug. 22, 1824-Sept. 30, 1867.
William H. Tilford, Feb. 8, 1827-Aug. 2, 1872; died in Birmingham, Ala.
Henry Wm. Tilford, Oct. 8, 1830-Dec. 16, 1874; age, 44 years.
Mary Ellen Tilford, Jan. 2, 1833-May 5, 1875.

MARRIAGES

John M. Tilford to Ann Taylor Lytle, Oct. 24, 1811.
Sarah Tilford to David Ramsey, Jan. 3, 1844.
William H. Tilford to Elizabeth Vantreece, April 2, 1845.
Jane F. Tilford to Henderson McGowan, Oct. 28, 1845.
H. W. Tilford to Eliza Jane Ivie, Jan. 27, 1859.
Mary Ellen Tilford to R. McFarlin, Jan. 2, 1860.
The following notations were made by John M. Tilford:
John Tilford, my father, was born Oct. 10, 1752; died, age 83 years.
Peggy Tilford, my mother, was born Jan. 28, 1762; died, age 85 years.
My father's father was from Ireland. My father's mother was from Germany. My mother's father and mother were among the first settlers of Virginia.

NEGROES BORN IN SERVICE OF JOHN M. AND ANN LYTLE TILFORD

Elsey, 1805.
Stephen, Feb. 25, 1814.
Avery, Oct. 23, 1820.
Indy, Mar., 1823.
Washby (Amy's son), May 3, 1839.
Angeline, Oct. 8, 1840.
Monroe (Judy's son), Oct. 8, 1846.
Zachary Taylor, Aug. 10, 1847.
Caesar (Judy's son), Mar. 27, 1854.
Isiac (Judy's son), July 24, 1855.
Francis, Dec. 6, 1857.
Mary Grace (Caesar's and Judy's daughter), June 10, 1860.

SEARCY FAMILY BIBLE

Owned by Mrs. Sarah Searcy Tompkins. Copied by Rebekah Jetton.

MARRIAGES

William W. Searcy to Elizabeth Harris of Warren County, N. C., Jan. 22, 1797.
William W. Searcy to Sarah Morton of Rutherford County, Tenn., Sept. 18, 1806.
William W. Searcy to Sarah Campbell, May 6, 1838.

BIRTHS

Robert M. Searcy, April 6, 1818.
A. B. Fisher, Dec. 20, 1820, A. D.
William W. Searcy, Jan. 1, 1769.
Sarah Morton, his wife, Mar. 30, 1783.
Isham G. Searcy, Oct. 20, 1797.
William W. Searcy, July 4, 1809.
Lucy W. Searcy, Aug. 4, 1802.
James Morton Searcy, Mar. 15, 1808.
Catherine Morton Searcy, Oct. 26, 1809.
Anderson Searcy, Sept. 12, 1811.
John Searcy, Feb. 21, 1814.
Sarah M. Searcy, May 23, 1816.
Robert W. Searcy, April 6, 1818.
Tabitha Searcy, July 10, 1820.
Judy Searcy, Feb. 19, 1824.
Lafayette Searcy, April 8, 1827.
William W. Searcy, son of John W. and Ann Searcy, Oct. 25, 1840.

DEATHS

Elizabeth Searcy, wife and consort of William W. Searcy, Sept. 22, 1804, in the 25th year of her age.
James Morton Searcy, Aug., 1809, in the 2nd year of his age.
Sarah M. Searcy, wife and consort of William W. Searcy, April 29, 1832, in the 49th year of her age.
Sarah M. Battle, Oct. 3, 1835, in the 20th year of her age.
Isham G. Searcy, July 24, 1841, in the 44th year of his age.
John W. Searcy, Sept. 18, 1843, in the 29th year of his age.
Ann Searcy, wife of John W. Searcy, Sept. 1, 1843.
Catherine W. Yandell, wife and con-

sort of Doctor Wm. M. Yandell, Sept. 12, 1843, in the 34th year of her age.
James T. Richardson, Tuesday morning, Sept., 1846.
William W. Searcy, Jan. 8, 1846, in the 27th year of his age.
Anderson Searcy, son of Wm. W. and Sarah, April 3, 1847, in the 36th year of his age.
Tabitha Batey, consort of Benjamin Batey, and daughter of Wm. W. and Sarah Searcy, May 31, 1849, in the 29th year of her age.
Robert W. Searcy, son of Wm. W. and Sarah, Jan. 24, 1851.
Layfayett Searcy, son of Wm. W. and Sarah Searcy, Mar. 15, 1852, in the 26th year of his age.
Lucy W. Randolph, consort of Beverly Randolph, Dec. 30, 1891.
W. W. Searcy, son of W. W. Searcy and Elizabeth Searcy, 1880, in the 80th year of his age.

RECORDS FROM BIBLE IN POSSESSION OF REBEKAH JETTON

Copied by Rebekah Jetton

Edward Scott, His Book, 1709.
John Ware, his hand and pen.
Washington Ware.
Henry Ware, his hand and pen; God save King George and all his men.

Births

Paullina Jordan, 17—.
Jane Ware, 1723.
Jane Jordan, Mar. 2, 1721.
John Ware, Nov. 4, 1731.
Jonath Ware, Mar. 22, 1733.
Judith Ware, Sept. 25, 1735.
Henry Ware, Feb. 14, 1737.
Elizabeth Ware, Feb., 1739.
Elizabeth Ware, Oct. 30, 1741.
John Ware, 1727-1781; age, 54 years.
John Ware's Book, June 6, 1808.
Archbishop Parker's translation first printed in 1568. King James Bible in 1613.
"Imprinted at London by Robert Barker, printer to the Kings most excellent Maiejtie. Cumptivilegio Regiae Maieftatis, Anno, 1611, Maieftatis.

FRIERSON

Copied from a Frierson Bible owned by Harry Walton Frierson, Columbia, by James Horton Davis. Sent by Miss Jetton.

From the Bible of William Frierson, the emigrant.
William Frierson married.
They had **six children:**
1. John.
2. James.
A. William.
4. Thomas.
5. Robert.
6. Agnes.

I. John Frierson married Margaret Smith. They had six children:
A. William.
B. Joshua.
C. Robert.
D. Jabez.
E. George.

B. Joshua Frierson, Nov. 25, 1755-Jan. 26, 1817; married Oct. 15, 1805, Elizabeth Bingham, June 5, 1775-Dec. 26, 1830. They had three children:
Aa. Joshua Bunyan Frierson, Sept. 9, 1806-Feb. 3, 1876.
Ab. John James Frierson, Sept. 16, 1808-Aug. 17, 1827.
Ac. Samuel Doddridge Frierson. Feb. 16, 1811-Feb. 3, 1860.

Ac. Samuel Doddridge Frierson married, July 21, 1831, Martha Wilson, who died Jan. 31, 1879. They had thirteen children:
Aca. Margaret Elizabeth Frierson, born April 24, 1832.
Acb. Mary Emeline Frierson, June 10, 1833-Dec. 13, 1893.
Acc. Francis LeGarde Frierson, June 24, 1834-April 7, 1914.
Acd. Joshua James Frierson, Dec. 22, 1835-Sept. 24, 1898.

Ace. Martha Ann Frierson, Jan. 1, 1837-Oct. 7, 1887.
Acf. Hester Brown Frierson, Feb. 26, 1838-Mar. 8, 1908.
Acg. John Henry Frierson, Nov. 5, 1839-July 3, 1923.
Ach. Henrietta Isabelle Frierson, May 26, 1841-Oct. 12, 1921.
Aci. Samuel Wilson Frierson, July 19, 1842-Nov. 22, 1895.
Acj. Susan Adaline Frierson, Mar. 17, 1844-July 17, 1899.
Ack. William Newell Frierson, Aug. 17, 1845-Sept. 21, 1854.
Acl. David Doddridge Frierson, Aug. 27, 1847-Oct. 5, 1854.
Acm. Madison Squires Frierson, born Mar. 17, 1849.
Acg. John Henry Frierson married, Oct. 25, 1876, Sallie Brown, July 4, 1853-May 26, 1913. Their only child was: Acga. Harry Walton Frierson, born Nov. 4, 1878.
Acga. Harry Walton Frierson married, May 12, 1913, Annie Steen, born June 12, 1893. Their children are:
Acgaa. Annie Frances Frierson, born Feb. 26, 1914.
Acgab. Harry Walton Frierson, Jr., born Jan. 9, 1917.
Acgac. Sara Jane Frierson, born Feb. 18, 1918.

WILLIAM LYTLE

By Ethel Benedict J. Lytle (Mrs. Richard R.), Moores Mills, New York

William Lytle, born February 17, 1755; died, September 4, 1829. Captain of 4th Regiment, North Carolina Line, an original member of the North Carolina Society of the Cincinnati, was* universally beloved for his honesty, firmness and integrity of his character. He was the third son of Robert Lytle (born, 1729; died, 1774) and his wife Sarah Mebane. This Robert Lytle was one of the three brothers (John, William, and Robert) of Scotch descent (Robert went to North Carolina, William to Kentucky and Ohio, John remained in Pennsylvania) who migrated from Ulster County, Ireland, and landed at New Castle, Delaware, in 1718-1720, and settled in Lancaster County, Pa. There Captain Lytle was born. We next hear of his father as Justice of the Peace at Hillsboro, Orange County, North Carolina, in 1771.

Captain William at twenty-one years of age entered the service as lieutenant, Sixth Regiment, April 16, 1776; became captain January 28, 1779; transferred to First, January, 1781, and to the Fourth in 1782. He served to the close of the war with his older brother, Lt.-Col. Archibald Lytle, and they both became original members of the Society of the Cincinnati at its formation in Hillsboro, October, 1783. They were with Washington at the battle of Germantown in October, 1777, in which General Nash was killed. The blood-stained sash on which General Nash was borne from the field of battle is now in the possession of Dr. Richard Ridgely Lytle's son, who is a great-grandson of Capt. Wm. Lytle.

*See tombstone, Murfreesboro, Tenn.

In 1798 Captain Wm. Lytle gave power of attorney to his *"trusty friends, Absalom Tatom, William Norwood, and Catlet Campbell" to dispose of all his property and settle any debts on the eve of his departure for Tennessee. This deed of trust is dated October 3rd, 1798, at Hillsborough, North Carolina.

Two land warrants were issued on March 12, 1784, by Col, Archibald Lytle, brother of Capt. William Lytle. One was for 4640 acres on the main fork of Stones River, and the other for 2560 acres on the Big Harpeth (on record at Rutherford County Courthouse, Murfreesboro, Tenn.). One of these grants, the first of 4640 acres, is the original body of land from which 60 acres were given with the reservation of one lot on the public square, by Capt. William Lytle for the founding of Murfreesboro, which Capt. William Lytle also stipulated should be so named in honor of his life-long friend, Maj. Hardy Murfree of the North Carolina Continental Line. This large tract of land had come to Capt. Wm. Lytle from his brother, Col. Archibald Lytle, at his death. The deed for the founding of Murfreesboro is dated 1811.

Capt. Lytle is buried on the homestead at Murfreesboro, Tenn.

There are some very interesting papers, eighty-six (86) in all, which were in the possession of Dr. Lytle and which revealed a great amount of historical interest to the period about Capt. Lytle's life—mostly centered at or near Hillsborough, N. C., between the years 1773-1836. These old documents are now in the keeping of the Southern Collection, University of North Carolina at Chapel Hill. There are nineteen tax receipts, between 1792 and 1812. These are on the property grants around Murfreesboro, Tenn. We find many muster rolls—one of Capt. Lytle's Company, July, 1781, and one also for the month of February, 1779. Also, list of deserters from North Carolina Brigade, including Capt. Lytle's Company. To this there is no date. Another, "Inspection Return of Capt. Lytle's Company 31 July, 1781, under Command of Lieut-Col. John Baptist Ashe, men and officers, accoutrements and clothing." Also, a muster roll, 7th Co. 1st and 2nd Carolina Battalions: "Rool and muster of Capt. Wm. Lytle's Co. of foot in the North Carolina Brigade comm'd by Lieut.-Col. Murfree from the 1st of Jan. to the 1st of April, 1782."

There are many personal letters to Capt. Lytle—one from John Nichols in Nashville, May 8, 1793, sent to Hillsborough, N. C. The contents of this are concerning Isaac Bledsoe, a very devoted friend and servant of Capt. William, who was scalped by the Indians in April, 1793. A letter from Isaac Bledsoe of January, 1792, speaks of taking charge of Capt. Lytle's landed business, his

*Original document in *Southern Collection*, University of North Carolina, Chapel Hill, N. C.

personal service and affection for Capt. Lytle. In a letter from Alexander Mebane dated April 25, 1794, there is an interesting note at the end, written in Capt. Lytle's handwriting in regard to France. In this collection there are also numerous indentures and receipts. Among the latter is one of a very few samples of Capt. Lytle's handwriting. This was written June, 1795.

In speaking of the emigration to this country of the Lytles, it is interesting to note the reasons for their coming from Ireland, and the cause of their presence there. Large colonies of Scotch-Irish Presbyterians left Ireland in 1718, '20, '26, and '37 and landed in New Castle, Delaware, with Penn, and settled in Lancaster County, Pa. Donegal Springs Church was the first church organized by the Scotch-Irish in Lancaster County in 1720. Rev. Adam Boyd, the first secretary of the North Carolina Society of the Cincinnati, was also pastor of Pequa Church, second oldest church, organized in 1722, Salisbury Township, Lancaster County, Pa. No doubt Capt. William Lytle was born here, as he and Adam Boyd were fellow members of the North Carolina Society at the same time in 1783. In 1755, the year he was born in Pennsylvania, large numbers moved to North Carolina; among them, Adam Boyd and the Lytles. They disseminated on all occasions their views of the relation between civil magistrates and the church, their hatred of oppression and of England. They quickly displayed an aptitude for settlement, for public office, and for fighting when it was necessary. They were the most important formative influences in Colonial Society and life and antagonistic to the British Government. After the Revolution of 1688 in England, Scotch migration set in strongly for Ulster, North Ireland, over 50,000. Under James I six counties in Ulster escheated to the crown, and were settled by Scotch Presbyterians. Hence the Lytles in Ulster. Persecuted under Queen Anne, 1700-1714, both in religious matters and in trade, they refused to submit to oppression and began their exodus to the land of freedom.

(This sketch was compiled for the most part by Dr. Richard R. Lytle, born in Murfreesboro in 1852 and grandson of Capt. Wm. Lytle.)

A TENNESSEE PIONEER, NATHANIEL OVERALL (1758-1835)

By Nadine Webb Overall

Perhaps not one person out of a thousand today realizes or visualizes the life of our pioneer ancestors in Tennessee scarcely a century ago. Yet dry documents and yellowed court records may sometimes serve to bring us face to face with this past of ours, forgotten all too soon.

A reminder of this kind was an old deed, "Deed No. 45, State of Tennessee, County of Rutherford," dated October 22, 1804, which was recently discovered. By this deed Joseph Dickson transferred to Nathaniel Overall "100 acres of land on Bushnell's Creek, the waters of the east fork of Stone's River," for the sum of $50.00. A dry legal document, but it brought to mind again the life of one of Tennessee's pioneers, Nathaniel Overall, whose story is typical of his times.

The family from which Nathaniel Overall was sprung was Saxon in origin and seems to have two main characteristics as suggested by the family name, the coat-of-arms, and the motto. "Overall," in Saxon, meant "the family who dwells in the hall by the shore of the sea"; the sea inspired a spirit of wanderlust; they came from the Danish peninsula to England, and early from England to America. The helmeted head and mailed fist, with the Norman-French motto, "Tant que je puis," were indicative of the fighting, hard-working folk whose individual daily efforts seems to have been "to the limit of my ability."

In England the family became best known in church history, for the intellectual ability and militant common sense of Bishop John Overall (1560-1619), Regius Professor of Theology at Cambridge, later dean of St. Paul's, London, and bishop of Coventry and Lichfield, and of Norwich, successively. He was one of the 47 translators of the King James' Version of the Bible. Bishop Overall had two brothers, William and Nathaniel; and the three names, John, William, and Nathaniel, have been transmitted without interruption in most Overall families since 1560.

In 1637 Nathaniel Overall sailed from Kent to the Virginia Colony. William Overall, the great-great-great-grandfather of our Nathaniel Overall, bought 990 acres of land in Westmoreland County, Virginia, in 1661 and 1665. Another Nathaniel Overall did service as a Virginia trooper from Prince William County in 1756.

The subject of our sketch was the son of John Overall and Maria Christiana Froman, who were married in Frederick County, Va., in 1753. Five of their seven children gradually left Virginia and came to North Carolina, then to the Watauga Settlement, and finally to Nashville (then Nashborough). Capt. William Overall, the oldest of the family, came first; later he was chosen by James Robertson as one of the eight men who should set out with him from Watauga on his first trip of exploration to the Cumberland country.

Ramsay, in his *Annals of Tennessee*, under the entry of 1779, says: "Nearly ten years had now elapsed since the germ of a civilized community has been planted in Upper East Tennessee. . . . In the early spring of 1779 a colony of gallant adventurers from the parent hive at Watauga crossed the Cumberland Mountains, penetrated the intervening wilds, and pitched their tents near the French Lick, and planted a field of corn where the city of Nashville now stands. . . . These pioneers were Capt. James Robertson, George Freeland, Wm. Neely, Edward Swanson, James Hanly, Mark Robertson, Zachariah White, and Wm. Overall. A Negro fellow also accompanied them. . . After the crop was made, Overall, White, and Swanson were left to keep the buffaloes out of the unenclosed fields of corn while the rest of the party returned for their families."

Among these men who returned with Robertson in the fall of 1779 was Nathaniel Overall. Both he and William, his brother, signed the Articles of Agreement, or Compact of Government, of the Cumberland settlers at Nashborough, May the first, 1780.

Another historian eloquently remarks of that crucial second year of the new settlement: "Within the next few months the settlers on the Cumberland were to be tried to the utmost. The river overflowed upon the bottoms and destroyed their corn. Thirty-nine of their number perished from the rifle or the tomahawk of the Indian. Their ammunition ran low. Starvation stared them in the face. Some of the less courageous deserted and fled. Only one hundred and thirty-four answered to the roll call in November, 1780; but these were Spartans, every man of them, and Robertson was as brave a leader as Leonidas."

In spite of all these disasters, however, the two Overall brothers were joined not long afterward by another brother, Robert, and by their sisters, Mary and Nancy. William and Nathaniel were soon married to two sisters, Susannah and Anne Thomas; Nancy Overall became the wife of Joshua Thomas, a brother from the same family; Mary Overall was married to Thomas Espey.

Only a short time later (1783) Robert Overall and Joshua Thomas, while on a journey from the Bluff to Kentucky for supplies, were ambushed and killed by the Indians. The Overall sisters were Quakers—the religion inherited from their grandparents, Paul and Elizabeth Heidt (Hite) Froman—and they did not believe in warfare; but from thenceforth they were among the hardest workers at Fort Nashborough in keeping the guns loaded, or reloaded, and constantly ready for service.

Another tragedy overshadowed the members of the Overall family at Nashborough in 1793: "On January 22, 1793, The Bench, or Bob Benge, the most daring and crafty of the Chickamauga bushwhackers, and Double Head (beyond question the most cruel and bloodthirsty Indian in the Cherokee nation) fell in with a party of traders at Dripping Spring, on the trace from Cumberland to Kentucky, killed Capt. William Overall and Mr. Burnett, took nine horses loaded with goods and whiskey, and made their escape. . . . It was reported that they cut and carried off the flesh from Capt. Wm. Overall's bones." (American State Papers, Indian Affairs, I, 436 ff.) "Double Head cut the flesh from Capt. Wm. Overall's bones and carried his scalp and that of his companion to the Cherokee nation, and had war dances over them at Lookout Mountain, Willstown, and Turnip Mountain, his party having been enlisted from all these settlements."

Historians agree that it was because of Wm. Overall's effective work as a spy for the colonists that the Indians "cut the flesh from his bones."

The devotion of the Overall brothers and sisters to each other was proverbial in the settlement; Nathaniel had lost his two brothers and a brother-in-law; but indulgence in personal grief had no place in the life of the pioneer. The five children of William, as well as his own brood of five, and the widowed Nancy Thomas, all had to be cared for. The settlement must succeed.

Time went on. Another ten years passed by. The Indians now seemed subdued, and Nashborough began to flourish. Perhaps life became too tame there for the seasoned warriors. At any rate, one day in September, 1804, Nathaniel Overall went on another scouting trip; this time he discovered the wild beauty of the country along Bushnell's Creek, "the waters of the east fork of Stone's River," in Rutherford County. The Indian fighter now became a pioneer in land deals and colonization in the new county of Rutherford; and he built the first house with glass windows, and the first built with manufactured nails, in the eastern part of that section. According to the county records he was concerned in seventeen different real estate transfers between 1804 and 1835, the year of his death; and at various times he owned about two thousand acres of land in that county. From Governor Willie Blount he received two grants of 100 acres in 1814; he bought from Andrew Jackson 640 acres, and from John Donelson another 640 acres; and various amounts from other men. His astuteness and success in business deals is shown by such facts as these: In 1804 he bought 100 acres from Joseph Dickson for $50.00; in 1808 he sold the same tract to David Moore for $400.00; in 1816 H. C. Bradford sold to him 300 acres for $1,050.00; ten years later Overall received $1,000.00 for only 118 acres of the same land, sold to Richard J. Floyd.

His close friendship with Andrew Jackson is recorded in such incidents as the following: Robert Overall (1785-1863), the second son of Nathaniel, had none of the spiritual meekness of his three brothers, who were Methodist ministers—a religious fervor transmitted through their Quaker mother—but, on the other hand, he did have all the fiery courage and keen business ability of his father. Radical differences of personal opinion were popularly settled by the fist in those days in Tennessee, and young Robert's fistic ability became well known. On one occasion he defeated his able opponent so thoroughly that he was sued for his success. Andrew Jackson heard of the incident, offered his services as Robert's lawyer, and when he had won the case refused to take one cent of father Nathaniel's money in payment. His professional services, he said, were given gladly for friendship's sake.

Nathaniel's three sons who became pioneer Methodist preachers and "circuit riders" in Tennessee were: Lorenzo Dow, Abraham, and Nace. Lorenzo Dow, at the age of twenty-seven, was pastor of McKendree Church in Nashville. His brilliant promise was cut off by death just after his thirty-first birthday. Again, a dry court record reveals an unsuspected story of the carefully hidden heart throbs of a rugged old Indian fighter of the early days. "Deed No. 282, County of Rutherford, State of Tennessee, September 1, 1826. Nathaniel Overall to Lorenzo Dow Overall: In consideration of the natural love and affection which the said Nathaniel Overall hath and beareth unto the said Lorenzo Dow Overall, and also for the better maintainance, support, and livelihood of him, the said Nathaniel Overall hath given to him 185 acres of land on a branch of Bradley's Creek, the waters of the east fork of Stones River."

On the 1280-acre tract of land owned by Nathaniel, through the influence of his wife and children, one of the county's early centers of religion, called Overall's Camp Ground," was located. There, in 1831, was built a church which still stands and still bears the name of "Overall's Church." The deed still records the names of the first trustees: "Robert Overall, Nace Overall, Abraham Overall, Richard Floyd, and Wm. Ramsey, Sr."

But in the background one sees the aged Nathaniel and Anne Thomas Overall standing hand in hand, quietly smiling upon another result of their matter-of-fact, pioneer labors.

VAUGHN RECORDS

Sent by Mary Robertson

Births

Julia Ann Vaughn, April 30, 1858.
John Floyd Poff, Nov. 14, 1861.
George Kelley Poff, Jan. 15, 1881.
Myrtle M. Poff, April 28, 1883.
Add Carmel Poff, Mar. 31, 1885.
Maud Eunice Poff, May 24, 1888.
Floy Elizabeth Poff, Jan. 20, 1894.
John Alfred Poff, Sept. 4, 1896.
Gladys Virginia Poff, Sept. 29, 1904.

Marriages

Julia Ann Vaughn to J. F. Poff, Nov. 19, 1879.

Maud Eunice Poff to Bunyan Read, Jan. 17, 1905.

George Kelley Poff to Emma Gowin, Mar. 25, 1905.

Floy Elizabeth Poff to John Howard Preston, Feb. 10, 1911.

Myrtle Matilda Poff to Albert B. Miller, Dec. 28, 1910.
Add C. Poff to Berl Gereldean Griffin.
Gladys Virginia Poff to Frank Herbert Miller, Nov. 4, 1921.

BIRTHS OF THE GRANDCHILDREN

John Lawrence Vaughn, Aug. 2, 1895.
Raymond Douglas Preston, Sept. 8, 1912.
Julia Clarice Miller, Mar. 15, 1912.
Jack Keneth Poff, Mar. 20, 1912.
James Howard Preston, Aug. 6, 1914.
Albert B. Miller, Jr., June 1, 1914.
Harold Kelly Miller, April 22, 1916.
Christine Elizabeth Preston, Mar. 16, 1916.
May Frances Preston, May 6, 1918.
Morris Leslie Miller, June 1, 1918.
Charles Lawrence Preston, Feb. 10, 1921.
Julia Ann Miller, Aug. 18, 1921.
Virginia Louise Miller, June 21, 1922—Wednesday.
Jewell Katherine Preston, July 28, 1922—Friday.
Dorothy Poff Preston, Dec. 13, 1923.
Margurite Ann Preston, Mar. 16, 1926.
Marjorie Jane Miller, Sept. 30, 1925—Wednesday.
Herbert Poff Miller, Dec. 17, 1927—Saturday.
Robert Lester Preston, Feb. 9, 1925.
Everlyn Marie Preston, July 4, 1927.
Henry Curtiss Preston, Nov. 25, 1928.
James Lawrence Miller, Dec. 10, 1929.

DEATHS

Maud Eunice Poff Read, Sept. 28, 1806.
John Alfred Poff, fireman, U. S. N. Lost on U. S. S. Cyclops, Mar. 14, 1918.

JONES FAMILY RECORD

Sent by Mary Robertson

BIRTHS

William Jones, Mar. 16, 1786.
Isabel Jones, April 5, 1790.
Albert Jones, Mar. 6, 1810.
John Jones, Mar. 8, 1813.
Andrew Jones, Sept. 21, 1814.
Robert Jones, Dec. 28, 1815.
Peggy Ann Jones, Dec. 21, 1810.
William Ewin Jones, April 15, 1821.
Enoch J. Jones, Mar. 10, 1824.
Samuel P. Jones, Oct. 7, 1826.

Thomas Thorn was born June 16, 1842; was married to Margaret A. Jones Nov. 5, 1858. Her age would have been twenty the 21st of Dec.

Wm. T. Thorn was born Nov. 6, 1839.
Mother Jones departed this life Jan. 5, 1831; age, 61 years.

Sarah Smith departed this life Mar. 6, 1848, in her sixty-second year of her life.

CANNON RECORDS

MARRIAGES

James S. Cannon and Angerona Jones, Oct. 6, 1858.
James S. Cannon and Amanda M. Everett, June 18, 1868.
Sinnie Cannon and John F. Tucker, July 14, 1880.
Elizabeth Cannon and Hick W. Davis, Oct 26, 1886.
James E. Cannon and Chloe A. Wilber, July 16, 1894.

BIRTHS

Joseph Cannon, Sept. 5, 1859.
Malinda Cannon, Dec. 9, 1861.
Infant son of J. S. and A. M. Cannon, July 16, 1869.
Elizabeth Cannon, Aug. 30, 1870.
James Everett Cannon, May 18, 1873.
Margaret Jane Cannon, April 15, 1876.

GRANDCHILDREN

Everett B. Tucker, April 12, 1881.
Gray C. Tucker, June 30, 1882.
Eleanor Tucker, May, ——.
Limmie Tucker, Feb. 14, 1890.
John Hick Tucker, May 30, 1895.
James Cannon Tucker, Oct., 1897.
Emma Cannon Davis, July 30, 1887.

DEATHS

Angerona C. Cannon, Jan. 1, 1867.
Infant son of J. S. and A. W. Cannon, Aug. 13, 1869.
James S. Cannon, Oct. 14, 1880.
Joseph E. Cannon, Jan. 30, 1886.
Infant daughter of Hick W. and Elizabeth Davis, Sept. 3, 1889.
Gracy C. Tucker, Dec. 11, 1891.

The Cannon Graveyard was given to the community for a public burying ground by Grandfather Joseph Cannon. His wife was Polly Cannon, originally spelled Canon, as you will see on some of the tombstones in the old burying ground. No one seems to know Father Cannon's birth date.

RIDLEY FAMILY—SMYRNA

Sent by Mary Robertson

MARRIAGES

Washington Green Ridley and Mary Jane Calton, Oct. 10, 1849.
Knox Ridley and Sallie E. Crockett, Nov. 18, 1874.
Louisa J. Ridley and W. P. Crawford, Dec. 21, 1882.
Janie Ridley and Samuel Trigg Weakley, Mar. 6, 1907.
James Anthony Ridley and Mima Easley Hibbett, Oct. 26, 1909.
Lula Ridley and Charles E. Kelton, Dec. 28, 1911.
William Crawford Ridley and Mary Emma Young, Oct. 16, 1913.
Sallie Ridley and Epps E. Matthews, Feb. 14, 1918.
Frank White Ridley and Catherine Theobold, Sept. 11, 1919.
Allen Thurman Ridley and Frances Louise Jarratt, April 28, 1920.
Octavia Ridley and Aubry D. Jarratt, Feb. 14, 1821.

BIRTHS

W. G. Ridley, Nov. 21, 1823.
Mary Jane, wife of W. G. Ridley, Oct. 15, 1824.
Knox Ridley, son of W. G. and Mary Jane Ridley, Feb. 28, 1851—at 5 o'clock in the morning.
Lewis Ridley, Feb. 22, 1856.
Louesa Josephine Ridley, Dec. 9, 1860.
Moses Ridley, June 6, 1782.
Katherine C. Ridley, Mar. 11, 1793.
Mary Ellen Ridley, Aug. 8, 1875.
James A. Ridley, Feb. 8, 1877.
Roberta Ridley, Aug. 30, 1878.
W. G. Ridley, Jr., May 18, 1880.
Janie Ridley, June 23, 1882.
Lula Ridley, Sept. 3, 1884.
Wm. Crawford Ridley, Dec. 24, 1887.
Allen Thurman Ridley, June 10, 1892.
Sallie Ridley, Aug. 19, 1894.
Ella Ridley, Feb. 14, 1897.
Octavia Ridley, Jan. 22, 1900.
Hannah, Feb. 12, 1853.
Milton David, Jan. 17, 1861.

DEATHS

Katharine C. Ridley, Nov. 11, 1841.
Sarah B. Newsom, Sept. 20, 1852.
Moses Ridley, Mar. 20, 1854.
John E. Carlton, June 22, 1863.
Mary Jane Ridley, May 29, 1876.
W. Green Ridley, April 5, 1862.
Mary Ellen Ridley, Oct, 2, 1879.
Ella Ridley, Oct., 1897.
Janie Ridley Weakley, July 27, 1914.
Sallie Crockett Ridley, Dec. 4, 1927.

CANON FAMILY BIBLE RECORD

(Property of Mrs. James Cannon, Smyrna)

BROTHERS AND SISTERS OF JOSEPH CANON

James Canon was born Aug. 9, 1762.
John Canon was born Aug. 9, 1760.
Rachel Canon was born Aug. 9, 1769.
Theophilus A. Canon was born Sept. 14, 1771.
Ruth Canon was born June 28, 1773.
Arrominty Canon was born Nov. 22, 1775.
Joseph Canon was born Oct. 17, 1777.
Peggy Canon was born July 14, 1783.
Joseph Canon and Polly Canon were

married Aug. 19, 1803.
Joseph Canon was born Oct. 17, 1777.
Joseph Canon died Oct. 14, 1857.
Polly Canon was born Dec. 8, 1783.
Mary Canon died Aug. 12, 1853.
Theophilus A. Canon was born Feb. 18, 1805, about 11 o'clock at night.
Theophilus A. Canon died Sept. 13, 1824.
Alanson Canon was born Oct. 13, 1806.
Lydia Adaline Canon was born Mar. 31, 1808.
Cyrus Canon was born Mar. 7, 1810.
Cyrus Canon died Sept. 14, 1833.
Emma Canon was born April 22, 1812.
Polly Canon was born June 3, 1815.
Polly Canon died Aug. 19, 1822.
James Canon was born April 26, 1827.
Margret Jane Canon was born May 4, 1819.
Rachel Lucinda Canon was Born July 15, 1821.
Rachel L. Canon died Aug. 20, 1825.
John Martin Canon was born April 27, 1824.
John M. Canon died May 20, 1830.
Theophilus Alexander Canon was born April 3, 1826.
Theophilus A. Canon died Sept. 8, 1829.

VAUGHAN

Typed by Mary Robertson

John Vaughan the 2nd, and the last born son of William Vaughan the 2nd, and Elizabeth Fielder Vaughan, was born at what is now called Spring Valley on Knobfork, in Grayson County, Va. He was born on the old Vaughan homestead on Sept. 16, 1816, and died there on March 17, 1883. He was married three times and raised three sets of children. His first marriage was to Julia Ann Rhudy, sister of the late William Rhudy and of Aunt Jemima Cornett, all of Elk Creek, Grayson County, Va., Jan. 23, 1837, and the following named children were born to them:

Stephen Freel, July 30, 1839-April 30, 1844.
William Harrison, April 15, 1841-1867.
Lieut. James Commel, Nov. 15, 1842-1920.
Alex Comett, Oct. 7, 1844-Sept. 19, 1864. (Lost his life in the Civil War in a battle near Winchester, Va., in the year 1864.
Lewis Clark, April 5, 1847-Sept. 4, 1856.
Alfred Augustus, April 15, 1849-Jan. 10, 1852.
His second marriage was on Dec. 16, 1849, to Matilda Bedwell, daughter of the late Rev. Wilson Bedwell of near Independence, Grayson County, Va., and the following are the children born to them:
Lilburn Johnson, born Sept., 1850. (Married Canzada Hines and is living at Spring Valley, Grayson County, Va.)
Malinda Elizabeth, Nov. 2, 1851-Mar. 22, 1903.
Charles Croskett, born May 27, 1853 (date lost).
George Currnen, born July 2, 1854. (Married Laura Elizabeth Fulton Lyons and is living at 5527 Townsend Avenue, Detroit, Mich.)
Rosomond Caroline, born Aug. 3, 1856. (Married William Hines and is living at Spring Valley, Grayson County, Va.)
Julia Ann, born April 30, 1858. (Married John Floyd Poff and is living at Murfreesboro, Tenn.)
Martha Jane, born Dec. 11, 1859. (Married Dallas Byrd and is living at Frios, Grayson County, Va.)
Stephen Clark, Dec. 25, 1861-July 6, 1877.

Alfred Crockett, born June 28, 1865. (Married Mary Crofford and is living at Pulaski City, Va.)

His third marriage was on Oct. 21, 1870, to Martha Ham, and the following named children were born to them:

Charlie Winton, July 30, 1871-Nov. 6, 1928.

William Alexandrew, April 12, 1874-Jan. 15, 1896.

Mary Mallie, born Aug. 15, 1876. (Married Samuel J. Hale and is living at Whitney, Oregon.)

He having been the husband of three wives and the father of eighteen children, departed his life as above stated on Mar. 17, 1883.

The foregoing records obtained and preserved by his son, George C. Vaughan, now living at 5527 Townsend Avenue, Detroit, Mich.

EDMUND RANDOLPH READ

Submitted by James Horton Davis

Back during the years of 1835-36 there took place in Texas a struggle that in a few years led to one of our major conflicts for territorial rights. It was at this time that the Texas Rebellion took place.

These two years were filled with repeated atrocities on the part of the Mexican army under Santa Anna. The particular one of these outrages that deals with our subject was the massacre of Goliad. This incident was one of the worst charges against the military ethics of Santa Anna.

A few days before March 27, 1836, a small group of men, under the leadership of Captain Fannin, were made, under false pretenses, to surrender to the Mexican General Urrea. This General promised Fannin the release of his soldiers and the privilege to return to their homes. They were instead taken to a church in the town of Goliad and imprisoned there. On Palm Sunday, March 27, 1836, as the people of the town were going to early Mass, the imprisoned soldiers were taken from the church, having their full equipment with them, and made to walk a short distance outside the town. At this point they were told to kneel down. One of the Americans, from this order, guessed the intentions of the Mexicans, so he shouted, "They are going to kill us!" At this the guards fired into the group. During the confusion that followed some of the Americans escaped. Among these few was Edmund Read.

Due to the inaccuracy of early records of the wars, the name of Edmund Read is not given on the list of Fannin's men who escaped. A few years ago one of the Nashville papers printed an account of another soldier who escaped. It was only this year that one of the later Reads revealed the facts concerning Edmund Read.

Our subject was the great-grandson of Clement Read, important in the early history of the Virginia colony. He was the son of John Nash Read, the progenitor of the Tennessee branch of the Reads. This John Nash Read settled in Rutherford County and established his estate, calling it Templeton Grove. Edmund's father ran away from home and joined General Greene's army when only a boy, fighting at Guilford Courthouse, Cowpens, and other engagements. So it was only natural that Edmund should run away and join the fight for Texan rights.

Family tradition has it that Edmund Read, when the small group of soldiers were fired into, fell to the ground as if he too had been shot. He remained thus until night, at which time he crawled to the home of a Mexican woman who gave him food. He made his way a few days later, by foot, towards Tennessee. After what seemed an eternity of walking he at last reached the home of friends in Nashville, they in turn notified John Nash Read, and he drove his carriage to Nashville and brought back his son.

Due to the effects of the war on his health, he died in only a few years. It is fitting and proper therefore that his name be added to those who laid down their lives for their country.

BEESLEY FAMILY BIBLE

Sent by Miss Mary Lou Beesley

Susan Jane Preston Ridout was born Jan. 4, 1818; married Christopher Beesley Dec. 17, 1835. Children:
John Beesley.
William Beesley.
Martha C. Beesley.
Mary E. Beesley.
George Beesley born Mar. 14, 1846; died Nov. 22, 1920.
Durant Beesley.
Louisa Rachel Beesley, born April 13; died, Jan.
Christopher C. Covington, born Dec. 13, 1828.
Jesse Covington, born April 24, 1831.
C. Louisa Covington, born Oct. 25, 1833.

Deaths

Solomon Beesley, Feb. 27, 1862.
Mary Ann Jenkins. Jan. 19, 1864.
Louisa Covington, Nov. 18, 1866.
Catharine A. Traylor, Dec. 12, 1866.
Needham Beesley. Oct. 20, 1865.
Louisa Hollowell, Sept. 4, 1869.
Casandra Beesley, Sept. 27, 1873.
Durant Beesley, Nov. 1874.
Christopher Beesley. Mar. 10, 1879.
Rachel Beesley, July 12, 1877.

Marriages

Solomon Beesley and Casandra Acklin, April, 1799.
Jesse Covington and Lavisa Beesley, Oct. 24, 1816.
Durant Beesley and Harriet Blackman, Dec., 1823.
Needham Beesley and Louisa Black, Feb. 15. 1832.
Joseph Hollowell and Louisa Beesley, Feb. 16, 1832.
Christopher Beesley and Susan Jane Preston Ridout, Dec. 17, 1835.
James Jenkins and Mary A. Beesley, Nov., 1839.
Hilas F. Traylor and Katherine A. Beesley, Feb. 14, 1846.

Births

Emily M. Beesley, Aug. 31, 1825, daughter of Durant Beesley and Harriet, his wife.
Tabitha J. Beesley, Oct. 19, 1827.
James M. Beesley, Oct. 20, 1830.
Mariah M. Beesley, Dec. 21, 1833.
Thomas J. Beesley, Mar. 2, 1836.
Needham Beesley, June 16, 1838.
Susan C. Beesley. Dec. 23, 1841.
Ben F. Beesley, Nov. 19, 1844.
Minerva Covington, daughter of Jesse Covington and Lavisa Beesley, his wife, Oct. 20, 1817.
Eldridge Covington. July 20. 1821.
Ambrouse B. Covington, Mar. 18, 1823.

Katherine R. Covington, Dec. 20, 1825.
Solomon Beesley, son of John Beesley, June 15, 1777.
Casandra Acklin, his wife, May 28, 1782.
Solomon Beesley and Casandra Acklin married April, 1799.
Rachel Beesley, daughter of Solomon Beesley and Casandra, his wife, April 6, 1800.
Lavisa Beesley, Oct. 24, 1801.
Durant Beesley, May 13, 1803.
Christopher Beesley, July 19, 1804.
Needham Beesley, Aug. 20, 1804.
Louisa Beesley, Nov. 16, 1812.
Mary Ann Beesley, Oct. 20, 1818.
Katherine Beesley, April 27, 1820.
Christopher Beesley.
Katherine Susan Beesley, Mar. 28, 1855-Mar. 13, 1933.
Solomon Beesley.
Lavisa Beesley.
Charley Acklin Beesley.
Christopher Beesley, son of Solomon and Cassandra Beesley, was born July 19, 1804, in Rutherford County, Tenn.; died Mar. 10, 1879.
Susan Jane Preston Ridout, daughter of William and Martha L. Ridout, was born Jan. 4, 1818, in Brunswick, County, Va.; died Jan. 13, 1909.
Christopher Beesley and Susan Jane Preston Ridout were married Dec. 17, 1835.
To this union were born the following children:
William Beesley, Dec. 23, 1838-Dec. 27, 1921.
John Beesley, Sept. 3, 1840-July 3, 1891.
Martha Cassandra Beesley, May 11, 1842-Nov.. 1922.
Mary E. Beesley, June 24, 1844-Feb. 18, 1907.
George Beesley, Mar. 14, 1846-Nov. 22, 1920.
Durant Beesley, Nov. 2, 1847.
Louisa Beesley, April 13, 1851- Jan. 7, 1928.
Christopher Beesley, Mar. 20, 1853-Jan. 4, 1901.
Susan Katherine Beesley, Mar. 29, 1855-Mar. 13, 1933.
Solomon Beesley, July 18, 1856-Feb. 22, 1903.
Lavia E. Beesley, Mar. 1, 1858-Jan. 20, 1893.
Charles Acklin Beesley, Aug. 7, 1860-May 8, 1919.

Marriages of These Children

William Beesley to Alice G. Elliott, May 29, 1866.

John Beesley to Mattie A. Job, Dec. 12, 1866.

R. H. Dudley to Mary E. Beesley, April 9, 1868.

George Beesley to Adeline Jordan, Oct. 15, 1872.

Durant Beesley to Willie A. Elliott, Aug. 30, 1870.

Christopher Beesley, Jr., to Bettie O. Pope, Nov. 7, 1876.

Thomas H. Williamson to Susan Katherine Beesley, Nov. 7, 1876.

Solomon Beesley to Betty S. Harvey, Oct. 15, 1886.

John Beesley to Mary E. Matthews, Jan. 30, 1884.

Lavisa E. Beesley to William A. Mathews, June 20, 1888.

George Beesley to Maggie Ransom, April 9, 1885.

Charles A. Beesley to Minnie E. Batey, Nov. 1, 1882.

Louisa R. Beesley to G. H. Crocket, Sept. 11, 1888.

Martha C. Beesley to James M. Brooks, Sept. 18, 1889.

Charles A. Beesley to Mary L. Hall, Nov. 28, 1900.

BATEY BIBLE

Copied by Mary Robertson, Smyrna

Marriages

Benjamin Batey to Evalina Amanda Morton, Dec. 7, 1824.

Benjamin Batey to Mrs. Tabitha Jetton, Mar. 5, 1844.

John Bass Batey to Mary Richardson Batey, May 6, 1868.

Births

Benjamin Batey, July 31, 1801
Evalina A. Batey, Aug. 31, 1807.

James Morton Batey, June 1, 1826.
William B. Batey, Oct. 16, 1828.
Francis M. Batey, May 26, 1831.
Evalina A. Batey, Mar. 9, 1834.
Thomas Jefferson Batey, May 12, 1836.
John Bass Batey, Mar. 24, 1839.
Mary Richardson Batey, Oct. 23, 1846.
Annie May Batey, May 19, 1869.
John Richardson Batey, July 29, 1873.
James Benjamin Batey, Jan. 21, 1877.
Augusta Batey, Jan. 5, 1881.

SECOND WIFE AND CHILDREN

Tabitha Jetton Batey, July 11, 1820.
Robert Searcy Batey, Feb. 13, 1845.
Benjamin Batey, Jr., July 4, 1846.
Zachary Taylor Batey, Nov. 18, 1848.

DEATHS

Benjamin Batey, Sr., Aug. 29, 1872.
Evalina A. Batey, Sept. 16, 1840.
Francis M. Batey, Oct. 4, 1836.
Robert Searcy Batey, Aug. 26, 1845.
James M. Batey, Aug. 23, 1856.
Mary Richardson Batey, Nov. 8, 1916.
John Bass Batey, Nov. 30, 1923.
John R. Batey, Jan. 15, 1923.
Augusta Batey, Sept. 28, 1881.

JOHN HILL BIBLE

Copied by Mary Robertson

BIRTHS

Green Hill, Nov. 20, 1714.
Grace Burnett Hill, April 26, 1721.
Henry Hill, Feb. 12, 1840.
Green Hill, Nov. 3, 1741.
Hannah Hill, Aug. 24, 1745.
Bennett Hill, Dec. 7, 1747.
William Hill, Feb. 20, 1750.
Mary Hill, May 11, 1754.
Sarah Hill, April 27, 1756.
Temperance Hill, Feb. 10, 1761.
Elizabeth Hill, July 26, 1763.
Jordan Hill, Oct. 17, 1864.
Hannah Hill, May 28, 1766.
Nancy Hill, Jan. 25, 1768.
Martha Hill, Oct. 7, 1769.
Richard Hill, Sept. 14, 1771.
Green Hill, May 5, 1774.
Lucy Hill, July 20, 1776.
John Hill, Nov. 23, 1778.
Thomas Hill, Sept. 5, 1781.
Sally Hill, Dec. 11, 1783.
May Seawell Hill, Oct. 1, 1786.
William Hill, 1781.
Joshua Cannon Hill, Aug. 10, 1795.
John Hill, son of Thomas and Elizabeth Hill, Mar. 17, 1804.
Margaret P. G. G. Roulhac, daughter of Francis and Margaret Roulhac, April 10, 1808.
Margaret Elizabeth, daughter of John and Margaret Hill, Aug. 16, 1834.
Francis Roulhac, son of John and Margaret Hill, Nov. 26, 1835.
John Roulhac Hill, son of John and Margaret Hill, Sept. 24, 1837.
George William Roulhac Hill, son of John and Margaret Hill, June 8, 1839.
Thomas Roulhac, son of John and Margaret Hill, Jan. 21, 1841.
Eleanor Jane Roulhac, daughter of John and Margaret Hill, Aug. 21, 1842.
John Roulhac Hill, son of John and Margaret Hill, Mar. 6, 1844.
Mary Frances Roulhac, daughter of John and Margaret Hill, Oct. 26, 1845.
Margaret Gray Roulhac, daughter of John and Margaret Hill, Oct. 31, 1846.
Martha Elizabeth Roulhac, daughter of John and Margaret Hill, Oct. 8, 1850.
J. R., son of J. R. and C. C. Hill, Aug. 23, 1867.
Jack, son of E. R. and A. G. Fanning, June 11, 1868.
Edward, son of J. W. O. and M. F. R. Douglass, June 20, 1869.
Margaret Roulhac, daughter of J. R. and C. C. Hill, Aug. 15, 1869.
John H. Fanning, son of E. R. and A. G. Fanning, Mar. 15, 1872.
George W. R., son of Thomas and Margaret Hill, Sept. 27, 1872.
Pattie R., daughter of J. R. and C. C. Hill, Oct. 27, 1872.

Joe Roulhac, son of Thomas R. and Margaret R. Hill, Dec. 2, 1873.
Emily R., daughter of Thomas and Margaret Hill, Aug. 26, 1875.
Margaret Eleanor Roulhac, daughter of Thomas and Margaret Hill, Oct. 16, 1876.
John Hill, son of Thomas R. and Margaret R. Hill, April, 1876.
T. R., Jr., son of T. R. and M. R. Hill, Mar. 9, 1881.
Francis R. Hill, son of Thomas and Margaret, Aug. 25, 1885.
Mary R., daughter of T. R. and M. R. Hill, Jan. 25, 1884.
Eleanor G. R. Hill, daughter of T. R. and M. R. Hill, Sept. 20, 1886.
S. G. Fanning, son of W. A. and Pattie R. Francis, Dec. 1, 1886.
Jouett R. Hill, son of T. R. and Margaret R. Hill, Aug. 8, 1888.
Mildred Frances Owen, daughter of J. N. and Emily Owen, Aug. 12, 1902.
James Thomas Hill, son of George and Nannie Hill, Sept. 10, 1905.
Anna Margaret Hill, daughter of George and Nannie Hill, April 10, 1908.
George Roulhac, son of George and Nannie Hill, July 20, 1913.
Sue Margaret Owen, daughter of J. E. Owen and Margaret Owen, July 31, 1914.
Thomas Roulhac, Jr., son of T. R. and Kathleen Hill, Feb. 9, 1917.
Mary N. Hill, daughter of T. R. and Kathleen Hill, Oct. 7, 1918.
Margaret R. Hill, daughter of T. R. and Kathleen Hill, Oct. 7, 1918.
Mary Brown Hill, daughter of Jouett and Annie Hill, Dec. 26, 1916.
Kathleen C. Hill, daughter of T. R. and Kathleen Hill, July 7, 1921.
John Richardson Hill, son of T. R. and Kathleen Hill, Feb. 8, 1924.
Emily Jane Young, daughter of F. B. and Mildred Young, June 29, 1924.
Margaret R. Owen, daughter of J. N. and Eleanor Owen, Jan. 17, 1925.
Francis T. Hill, son of T. R. and Kathleen Hill, Aug. 28, 1926.

Marriages

John Hill and Margaret P. G. G. Roulhac, Oct. 28, 1833.
John R. Hill and C. C. Townsend, Feb. 9, 1865.
E. R. Hill and A. J. Fanning, Aug. 19, 1867.
M. R. Hill and J. W. Douglas, May 5, 1868.
Thomas R. Hill and Margaret A. Anderson, Dec. 8, 1871.
Pattie R. Hill and W. A. Fanning.
Joe N. Owen and Emily R. Hill Oct. 3, 1899.
George R. Hill, Jr., and Nannie P. Hales, Nov. 24, 1904.
John Hill and Opal Snead, 1912.
J. E. Owen and Margaret Hill, 1912.
Thomas R. Hill and Kathleen Charlton, Oct. 14, 1914.
Jouett R. Hill and Annie Louise Brown, Mar. 4, 1915.
J. N. and Eleanor Hill, Oct. 4, 1921.
Mildred Frances Owen, Sept., 1923.

Deaths

Margaret Elizabeth, daughter of John and Margaret Hill, Dec. 13, 1834, at 2 o'clock P. M.
Francis Roulhac, son of John and Margaret Hill, June 28, 1838, at 10 o'clock A. M.
Joe Roulhac Hill, son of John and Margaret Hill, Mar. 6, 1844.
Margaret Gray R. Hill, daughter of John and Margaret Hill, June 13, 1855.
John Hill, son of Thomas and Elizabeth Hill, Feb. 28, 1873.
Margaret R. G. G. R. Hill, daughter of Francis and Margaret Hill, Sept. 8, 1884.
Pattie R. Fanning, daughter of J. and M. P. G. R. Hill, Jan. 3, 1887.
J. R., son of J. R. and C. C. Hill, Nov. 1, 1867.
Jack, son of E. R. and A. J. Fanning, Aug. 27, 1867.
A. J. Fanning, son of W. A. and Pattie R. Fanning, Nov. 29, 1887.
Tolbert, son of A. J. and E. R. Fanning, Nov. 29, 1906.
Eleanor R. Fanning, daughter of John and Margaret Hill, Dec. 2, 1909.
Margaret Roulhac Hill, daughter of Joseph and Jane Roulhac, June 12, 1915.
Thomas R. Hill, son of John and Margaret Hill, Jan. 15, 1916.
Emily Hill Owen, daughter of Thomas and Margaret Hill, July 19, 1917.

"America Presenting at the Altar of Liberty Her Illustrious Sons." Toile de Jouy, property of Mrs. Susie Mentlo Anderson, Gallatin, Tenn. Inherited through several generations from her Revolutionary ancestor, William Alexander, who is buried near Hartsville, Tenn. The bedspread is made of chintz imported from Joury, France. These prints, in several patriotic designs, were very popular as household decorations just after the Revolution, but the originals are now scarce. Mrs. Anderson's grandmother quilted the bedspread to homespun cloth in order to preserve the fabric.

Francis Hill, son of Thomas R. and Margaret Hill, June 29, 1919.
George William Hill, son of John and Margaret Hill, Dec. 3, 1924.
George R. Hill, son of Thomas and Margaret Hill, Jan. 24, 1925.
Thomas R. Hill, son of Thomas and Margaret Hill, Dec. 31, 1927.

JARRATT

What therefore God hath joined together let not man put asunder.
This is to certify that Wm. B. Jarratt of Smyrna, Tenn., and Miss Fannie P. Dudley of Nashville, Tenn., were united by me in holy matrimony at Nashville, Tenn., on the 5th day of December in the year of our Lord, 1876. In presence of a number of witnesses.

(Signed) Felix R. Hill.

Therefore shall a man leave his father and his mother and shall cleave unto his wife and they shall be one flesh.—Genesis 2:24.

Births

Wm. B. Jarratt, June 29, 1850.
Fannie P. Jarratt, April 15, 1856.
Houston Dudley Jarratt, Nov. 7, 1877.
Daisy Irene Jarratt, Dec. 8, 1879.
Willie B. Jarratt, Feb. 9, 1886.
Fannie Louisa Jarratt, Aug. 9, 1894.

Marriages

"What therefore God hath joined together, let not man put asunder."
Daisy Irene Jarratt and William Vawter Smith, Oct. 23, 1907.
Willie B. Jarratt and Samuel Morton McMurray, Dec. 30, 1909.
Fannie Louisa Jarratt and Allan Thurman Ridley, April 28, 1920.

Deaths

William Benjamin Jarratt, Nov. 26, 1896.
Houston Dudley Jarratt, Feb. 1, 1910.
Fannie P. Jarratt, Mar. 12, 1933.

TILFORD RECORDS

Copied by Mrs. E. L. Jordan, Rutherford County

Marriages

John M. Tilford to Nancy Lytle, Oct. 24, 1811.
David Ramsy to Sarah Tilford, Jan., 1844.
William H. Tilford to Elizabeth L. Vantriece, April 2, 1845.
Henderson McGowan to Jane F. Tilford, Oct. 28, 1845.
Henry William Tilford to Eliza Jane Ibie, Jan. 27, 1859.
Eliza Jane Ibie Tilford born Jan. 27, 1830.
Wells Floyd Tilford born Dec. 29, 1859.
John M. Tilford and Thomas E. Tilford born Mar. 9, 1862.
Willie Edgar Tilford, born June 17, 1866.
Lucille Tilford, born Oct., 1868.
Henry Hershel Tilford, born Oct. 5, 1873.
Thomas Edmond Tilford to Mollie Isabella Abernathy, Nov. 16, 1890.
Willie Edgar Tilford to Alnora Dillon, Feb. 24, 1897.
Lucilla Tilford to William B. Drake, Nov. 1893.
Henry Hershel Tilford to Mamie Cary.
Charles I. Youree to Virginia Tilford, Thursday, July 19, 1922.
Edward Lealand Jordan to Evelyn Tilford, Jan. 8, 1925.

Births

John M. Tilford, Sept. 18, 1783.
Nancy Lytle Tilford, his wife, Jan. 18, 1795.
James MacCowan Tilford, Aug. 10, 1812.
William Lytle Tilford, April 1, 1814.
Margaret Ann Tilford, Feb. 15, 1816.
Sarah Tilford, Dec. 30, 1817.
Lucilla Stanley Tilford, Aug. 21, 1820.
Thomas White Tilford, April 7, 1823.
Jane Foster Tilford, Aug. 22, 1825.

William Hume Tilford, Feb. 8, 1827.
Henry William Tilford, Oct. 18, 1830.
Mary Ellen Tilford, Jan. 2, 1833.
Born to Charles D. Youree and Virginia Tilford Youree:
Ann Nora Youree, May 4, 1925.
Charles David Youree, Sept. 4, 1928.
Born to Edward Lealand Jordan and Evelyn Tilford Jordan:
Nancy Perkins Jordan, Oct. 21, 1925.
Edward Lealand Jordan, Sept. 25, 1926.
Evelyn Tilford Jordan, Oct. 2, 1927.
Richard Munford Jordan, Aug. 31, 1929.
Born to Willie Edgar Tilford and Alnora Dillon Tilford:
Willie Virginia Tilford, Feb. 10, 1898.
Edgar Talmage Tilford, Dec. 1, 1899.
Sara Estelle Tilford, Oct. 31, 1902.
Eliza Evelyn Tilford, Aug. 22, 1904.
Bessie Lucille Tilford, Jan. 11, 1906.
Mary Alnora Tilford, Aug. 1, 1910.

NEWSOM RECORDS

Sent by Frances Pamelia Newsom Allen

Mrs. Alice Elizabeth Hill Newsom was born November 17, 1853, near Antioch, Tenn. She was a direct descendant of the first settlers in the vicinity of Nashville. Her great-great-grandmother was among those captured by Indians in a raid on the settlement, and after being held prisoner for some length of time was finally given her freedom through an exchange of prisoners, a number of Indian prisoners being exchanged for white people whom the Indians were holding. The exchange took place in Washington, D. C., and she rode horseback from Washington to her home in Tennessee. Upon her arrival home, romance, it seems, decided to add another chapter to her life, and as she alighted from her horse she met for the first time the man who later became her husband. His name was Thompson. To this union were born children that also were to play an important part in Tennessee history. One granddaughter married a Mr. Cockrell, and it was he who gave the spring and an acre of ground to the City of Nashville, this being now a part of Centennial Park. Another granddaughter married a Mr. Davis, who was related to Jefferson Davis, president of the Confederacy.

Mrs. Newsom's grandmother, Mrs. Pamelia Collinsworth Davis, owned the property adjacent to the railroad during the Civil War and when a train carrying Union soldiers was wrecked near her place it was she who requested that the dead Union soldiers be buried in the burial plot on her plantation instead of their being buried in an embankment as was suggested by those in charge. Mrs. Davis, while a true Southern woman, was so admired by the Federals that they placed a special guard at her home and neither she nor her property was ever molested. One of the survivors of the above mentioned railroad wreck was located years later by Mrs. Laura Davis Hill who was the late Mrs. Newsom's mother; he was living in Ohio at the time she heard from him. Mrs. Newsom was a little girl during the Civil War and could tell many interesting stories of those trying days. During her early girlhood she became a member of the M. E. Church. She was married to A. G. Newsom October 17, 1871. She has four living children and three dead.

As she lived, so she died,
Ever faithful, kind, and true;
God called her to her heavenly home,
There to begin her sweet life anew.

HOWSE RECORDS

Copied from family Bible by Mrs. Lula Howse Rucker, Nashville Road, Rutherford County.

Claiborne Howse was born Oct. 6, 1774, in Burnswick County, Va.

Mary Ledbetter, afterwards Mary Howse, was born in Burnswick County, Va., Mar. 15, 1782.

John C. Howse, son of Claiborne Howse and Mary Howse, was born July 15, 1817.

Claiborne Howse died Sept. 27, 1851, at the age of 76 years, 11 months, and 21 days.

Mary Howse, wife of Claiborne Howse, died in Rutherford County, Tenn., in Sept., 1821; age, 39 years and 6 months.

John C. Howse died April 18, 1855, at the age of 37 years, 9 months.

Mary A. Howse, daughter of John C. Howse, was born Oct. 16, 1851, and died Nov. 30, 1928.

Johnie M. Howse, daughter of John C. Howse, was born July 13, 1853, and died Feb. 23, 1870.

Louise H. Howse was born Feb. 28, 1855.

BACHUS BIBLE RECORDS

Copied by Mrs. W. P. Bouton, Lebanon, Tenn. James H. Bachus Bible in possession of great-grandddaughter, Mrs. Harry Johnson, Leeville, Tenn.

Births

James H. Bachus, Mar. 1, 1812.
Martha W. Bachus, Jan. 20, 1813.
Lueasy J. Bachus, July 28, 1838.
Indana A. Bachus, Dec. 10, 1840.
Larken E. Bachus, Jan. 7, 1842.
Mary S. Bachus, May 21, 1843.
William L. Bachus, Mar. 8, 1846.
Emely A. L. Bachus, Aug. 24, 1848.
James M. Bachus, Dec. 12, 1851.
Martha A. D. Bachus, June 9, 1854.

Marriages

James H. Bachus and Martha W. Echols, July 6, 1837.

James H. Bachus and Jane B. Martin, Jan. 15, 1865.

Deaths

Martha W. Bachus, Jan. 6, 1860.

James H. Bachus, Oct. 30, 1895.

Jane B. Bachus, wife of James H. Bachus, Jan. 1, 1896.

Indana A. Bachus, daughter of James H. and Martha W. Bachus, Dec. 25, 1841.

Larken E. Bachus, son of James H. and Martha W. Bachus, Jan. 17, 1842.

Emely A. L. Bachus, daughter of James H. and Martha W. Bachus, May 20, 1853.

William L. Bachus, son of James H. and Martha W. Bachus, Dec. 14, 1861.

Mary S. Watson, daughter of James H. and Martha W. Bachus, and wife of T. A. Watson, Nov. 13, 1878.

Martha A. Golden, daughter of James H. and Martha W. Bachus,

and wife of T. R. Golden, Jan. 11, 1908.
Mary Echols, wife of Larken Echols and mother of Martha W. Bachus, Aug. 13, 1859.
Lueasy J. Hame, daughter of James H. and Martha W. Bachus, Nov. 30, 1866.

LAWRENCE BIBLE RECORDS

Copied by Mrs. W. P. Bouton, Lebanon, Tenn. Joseph Lawrence Bible in possession of grandson, Monroe Wiley Lawrence, Murfreesboro, Tenn.

Births

Joseph Lawrence, Aug. 25, 1786.
Joannah T. Lawrence, July 4, 1799.
John M. Lawrence, June 13, 1816.
Thomas H. Lawrence, Mar. 18, 1818.
William H. Lawrence, June 2, 1820.
Ann E. Lawrence, April 2, 1822.
Joseph P. Lawrence, June, 1825.
Margaret Hannah Lawrence, Mar. 28, 1850.
Josephine Lawrence, April 16, 1852.
John Wilson Lawrence, Sept. 4, 1854.
Fannie Matilda Lawrence, Feb. 22, 1857.
Cora Elizabeth Lawrence, May 16, 1868.
Monroe Wiley Lawrence, Feb. 15, 1864.
John Baird, Dec. 20, 1805.
Margaret M. Thacker Baird, Dec. 3, 1809.
Elizabeth A. Baird, Feb. 16, 1829.
John Larkin Baird, Dec. 1, 1831.
Charles W. Baird, Oct. 16, 1834.
Wiley M. Baird, May 5, 1840.

Marriages

Joseph P. Lawrence and Elizabeth A. Baird, Mar. 26, 1848.

Deaths

John Baird, Aug. 26, 1876.
Margaret M. Baird, May 23, 1841.
Elizabeth A. Lawrence, Mar. 30, 1889.
Joseph P. Lawrence, Dec. 3, 1899.
Charlie W. Baird, Oct. 5, 1872.
John Larkin Baird, Mar. 1, 1862.
Joseph Lawrence, Oct. 20, 1840.
Joannah T. Lawrence, Oct. 23, 1853.

CLEMMONS BIBLE RECORDS

Copied by Mrs. W. P. Bouton, Lebanon, Tenn. Nancy Bomar Clemmons Bible in her possession on Murfreesboro Pike, Wilson County, Tenn.

Births

James Lee Clemmons, Nov. 3, 1835.
Nancy Ferguson Bomar, July 18, 1837.
John Randolph Bomar, Jan. 3, 1836.
Mary B. Bomer, July 28, 1830.
Sarah Ann Elizabeth Bomar, April 21, 1834.
Nancy Jane Bomar, June 3, 1856.
Lucy Isabelle Bomar, Mar. 30, 1860.
John Patrick Bomar, Jan. 17, 1863.

Marriages

James Lee Clemmons and Nancy Ferguson Bomar, June 5, 1855.
John R. Bomar and Mary B. Bomar, Oct. 1, 1856.

Deaths

James Lee Clemmons, July 28, 1917.
John Bomar, June 11, 1840, in the State of Illinois.
Nannie Bomar, wife of John Bomar, Feb. 15, 1842.
John R. Bomar, Nov. 30, 1862.
Mary B. Bomar, Nov. 4, 1895.
Lucy Isabelle Bomar, July 15, 1861.

SKEAN BIBLE RECORDS

Copied by Mrs. W. P. Bouton, Lebanon, Tenn. Martin Skean Bible in possession of great-grandson, Claude Collier, Lebanon, Tenn., R. F. D.

Births

Martin Skean, June 5, 1813, A. D.
Maranda J. Skean, Sept. 7, 1838.
Elizabeth T. Skean, Aug. 27, 1839.
William P. Skean, April 28, 1841.
Lucy J. Skean, Feb. 16, 1843.
Wilson H. Skean, Aug. 16, 1844.
Martha D. Skean, Oct. 3, 1846.
Marcus P. Skean, Mar. 10, 1849.
Robert W. Skean, Aug. 11, 1852.

Marriages

Martin Skean and Marinda J. Hearn, June 24, 1837.
Lucy J. Skean and William F. Hancock, Sept. 24, 1860.
Joseph E. Lane and Elizabeth T. Skean, Feb. 1, 1866.

Deaths

Wilson H. Skean, Sept., 1845; age, 13 months.
Martin Skean, June 23, 1880; age, 67 years, 18 days.
Maranda J. Skean, Oct. 7, 1882; age, 69 years, 1 month.
Martha D. Hearn, Feb. 22, 1872.
Lucy J. Hancock, Jan. 7, 1881.

RIGGAN BIBLE RECORDS

Copied by Mrs. W. P. Bouton, Lebanon, Tenn. Samuel H. Riggan Bible in possession of Mrs. Will Riggan, Leeville, Wilson County, Tenn.

Births

Samuel H. Riggan, Sept. 11, 1803.
Martha Ann Riggan, Nov. 30, 1812.
Children:
Benjamin Calvin Riggan, Oct. 22, 1833.
William Henry Riggan, May 19, 1835.
Amanda Louise Riggan, Nov. 12, 1836.
James Madison Riggan, Oct. 17, 1838.
Daniel Newton Riggan, Nov. 25, 1840.
Livonia Touson Riggan, Dec. 12, 1842.
Fredonia Elizabeth Riggan, Aug. 17, 1845.
Martha Ann Riggan, Dec. 8, 1847.
Margaret C. Thompson Riggan, May 17, 1838.
Samuel H. Riggan, son of J. M. and M. C. Riggan, Dec. 1, 1859.
Jefferson Davis Riggan, April 14, 1861.
Mary Ann Riggan, Aug. 28, 1862.
Amanda Louise Riggan, Mar. 5, 1864.
James Newton Riggan, July 22, 1865.
Martha Odelia Riggan, Nov. 25, 1867.
Willie Ozburn Riggan, Oct. 10, 1868.
Corrah Riggan, April 25, 1870.
Burkitt Ferrell Riggan, Oct. 14, 1871.
Charlie Wesley Riggan, Aug. 20, 1873.
Clarence Wynn Riggan, Mar. 8, 1876.
Daisy L. Riggan, Jan. 20, 1878.
Margaret F. Riggan, June 9, 1881.

Marriages

James M. Riggan and Margaret C. Thompson, Jan. 12, 1889.

Deaths

James H. Riggan, July 14, 1848.
Martha Ann Riggan, Mar. 31, 1850.
Martha Ann Riggan, daughter of J. H. and M. A. Riggan, Oct. 22, 1848.
Samuel H. Riggan, son of J. H. and M. A. Riggan, Dec. 24, 1889.
Amanda Louise Riggan, Oct. 6, 1865.
James Newton Riggan, Aug. 15, 1865.
Corrah Riggan, May 2, 1870.
Jefferson Davis Riggan, Oct. 25, 1885.
Margaret C. Riggan, Oct. 26, 1906.
J. M. Riggan, Oct. 30, 1915.

HISTORY OF MT. ZION CHURCH FOR 100 YEARS 1832-1932

Located between Humboldt and Medina, West Tennessee. Sent by Miss Sarah V. Clement, Jackson.

Possibly no one character has been more to the uplift of early pioneer days than the faithful Methodist preacher, the "Circuit Rider." No doubt our beloved Mt. Zion was organized by some of these vanguards of our church one hundred years ago, 1832. We failed to find a record of the name of the first pastor. We know he lived in Trenton and rode horseback to his appointments.

What was his name? I do not know his name.

I only know he heard God's call and came and brought all he loved across the sea to live and work for God and me.

The land where our church now stands and the original part of our cemetery was a gift from Robert Shane, who was born in Down County, Ireland. Came to America in the early part of the eighteenth century and is beloved in our cemetery, and whose great-great-grandson, Cecil Hemphill, is a member of Medina Methodist Church.

The deed stated that it was given for church school and burial purposes. We have gathered some of the charter members names: Thomas E. Hale and wife, Hardy Jackson and wife, Hardy Shelton, Some Shane, Tommy Walker, Sam Cole and wife, Johnnie Umstead, and John Green. These members have long since joined the choir invisible and some are resting across the road. Who can estimate the influence of these pious ancestors of ours?

The first church was built of logs on the right side of the driveway in the cemetery. It was heated by a fireplace and lighted by homemade tallow candles. The only music was the grand old church hymns, lined out by the pastor and often led by Olive Cole.

This log house after the Civil War was replaced by a frame building on the same location and in after years a two-story frame building was erected on this side of the road for church and school and was also used as a Masonic Hall. The present building was begun in 1903 during the pastorate of Brother Stratten and completed the following year. It was dedicated October 23, 1904. The dedicatory sermon was preached by Dr. J. W. Blackard. Two children were baptized just before the sermon, Frank Blackmon, now a steward of this church, and William R. Cole, grandson of Sam Cole, a charter member.

MARRIAGE RECORDS OF KNOX COUNTY, TENNESSEE

These records were published in the *Tennessee Historical Magazine* in 1920 and are reproduced here by permission of Miss Kate White who gave them to Mrs. Acklen for publication and Dr. W. A. Provine, Editor of the Magazine.

Note by Editor of the Magazine which accompanied the first publication:

"The following valuable data of marriage license register of Knox County, Tennessee, is the fruitage of the indefatigable labors of Miss Kate White of Knoxville, Tennessee. The list here compiled by years and alphabetically has been culled from enumerable loose papers and records in the archives of the county courthouse. Much patience was required in the attempt to decipher much of the damaged manuscript sources, hence many question marks appear indicating uncertainty. It is probable that these records as here printed may be corrected by data in the hands of many of the families whose names appear in the list; the Magazine will be glad to publish such corrections in future issue."

1792

Anderson, John, to Rachel Roberts; Dec. 28, 1792.
Brown, Wm., to Fannie Lidwell.
Hamilton, Robert, to Jean Hannah; Aug. 30, 1792. C. McClung.
Johnson (or Johnston), Carven, to Patty Lowe; Dec. 21, 1792.
McClung, Charles, to Margaret White; Oct. 8, 1792(?).
McNutt, George, to Catherine McKean; Nov. 5, 1792.
Ritchie, Joseph, to Nancy Rhea; Nov. 6, 1792.
Stockton, James, to Lidetha Pruitt; 1792(?).
Vaughn, Reuben, to Mary Warren; Oct. 4, 1792 (or 1793). Attest: Ramsey.

1793

Boyd, Robert, to Margaret Meek; April 3, 1793.
Caldwell, Samuel, to Rachel Ewing; Jan. 28.
Callum, John, to Cathrine Low; Nov. 1.
Cunningham, Isaac, to Margaret Hannah; April 23.
Cusick, Joseph, to Jean Blackburn; Jan. 31.
Douglass, William, to Elizabeth Martin; Dec. 23.
Finley, John, to Margaret Kerr; Nov. 13.
Goulston, John, to Margaret Low; Feb. 5, 1793 (W. Blount, Gov.).
Gum, Norton, to Sallie Clampit; Mar. 23.
Fermault, John, to Margaret Kerr; 1793 (?).
Kennedy, Sampson, to Sarah Edwards; Jan., 1793 (?).
Kerr, William, to Anne Brooke (or Brooks); Sept. 8.
McCullough, James, to Susanna Henderson; Jan. 20.
McMullen, William, to Mary Doak; July 25, 1793 (?).
Mansfield, Nicholas, to Eliza Looney; Oct. 30.
Maybory, John, to Eliza Brock; Sept. 23, 1793 (?).
Miller, Hugh, to Mary Good; Aug. 27.
Miller, Peter, to Peggy Simpson; May 20.
Montgomery, Humphrey, to Mary Walker; April 1.
Richey, Abel, to Ann Dixon; Oct. 11. Or Ritchie, Able, to Ann Dickson.
Ritchie, Thomas, to Rosannah Fermault; Oct. 9.
Robertson, Willoughby, to Polly Brock; Sept. 3.
Sears, John to Nancy Brock; Mar. 1, 1793 (?).
Stephenson, William, to Gene Hamilton; April 17.
Sloan, William, to Margaret McKee; May 20, 1793 (?).
Stover, Nelson, to Margaret McTeer; May 6, 1793 (?).
Stockton, Davis, to Agnes Miller; Aug. 27.
Stone, Henry, to Patrenis Southerlain.
Tedford, Joseph, to Mary McNutt; Feb. 11.
Telfour, George, to Jean Hannah, April 3.

Tiner, Lewis, to Tabby Cook; Sept. 7, 1793 (X).
Vance, Samuel, to Mary Blackburn; Jan. 30.

1794

Birden, Wm., to Eleanor Hutson; Jan. 27.
Bryan, John, to Esther Anderson; Sept. 10.
Bryan, William, to Jenny Gillespie; May 9.
Byrd, Amos, to Anne Gillespie; Jan. 21. (Chas. McClung.) (W. Blount, Gov. Tr. of the U. S., south of the Ohio, Knox County.)
Byrd, Stephen, to Polly Gillespie; April 1.
Caldwell, David, to Elizabeth Kelley; May 5.
Callison, James, to Annie Gillespie; Jan. 21.
Carrick, Samuel, to Annie McClelland; Jan. 27.
Clark, Isaac, to Nancy Bounds; Aug. 6.
Cowan, John, to Polly Kirkum (?); Mar. 24.
Cunningham, Moses, to Mary Simpson; June 3.
Cunningham, James, to Susan Craig; April 24.
Evans, David, to Margaret Blackburn; June 6.
Furgason, James, to Mary Cheesman; July 8.
Ferguson, James, to Nancy Churchman; July 8 (?) (Which is correct?)
Hale, Luke, to Mary Key; Aug. 4.
Hayes, Theophlus, to Polly Morgan; Sept. 16, 1794 (?).
Heslit, William, Jr., to Elizabeth Jack; Jan. 28.
Henderson, William, to Susannah Gillespie; May 29.
Houston, Robert, to Margaret Davis; Mar. 24 (or 20).
Huffaker, Jacob, to Pegg Bodken; Feb. 8.
Huges, Theoples, to Peggy Morgan; Sept. 16, 1794 (?).
McClelland, John, to Polly Wallace; May 13.
McNutt, James, to Eliza Gillespie; Jan. 15, 1794 (?).
McNutt, James, to Eliza Gillespie; Feb. 16, 1794 (?).
Milikan, Thomas, to Priscilla Brock; Jan. 7, 1795 (?).
Moore, David, to Mary McNair; June 10, 1794 (?).
Mynatt, John, to Libell Linville; Jan. 28.
Raulston, George, to Elizabeth Gilliam; May 1.
Sheilds, John, to Hannah Evans; June 10.
Somerville, John, to Elizabeth Chisholm; May 20.
Stephenson, William, to Jean Hamilton; April 17.
Swan, Samuel, to Jean Gambell; June 5.

1795

Davis, Samuel, to Peggy Page; Dec. 30, 1795 (or 98?). Attest: A. White.

1796

Alexander, Nicholas, to Annie Smith; Dec. 31.
Alexander, William, to Martha Haslet; Oct. 20.
Bates, John, to Didamy (?) Bohannon; Dec. 20.
Bower, John, to Jane Crawford; Dec. 28.
Brassfield, Thomas, to Mary Davis; Dec. 25.
Childers, James (X), to Susannah Thompson; Nov. 15.
Conway, Charles, to Elizabeth Robertson; Oct. 19, 1796. Attest: Hu Lawson White, Chas. Conway, David Robertson.
Eldridge, John, to Sarah Gilliland; Dec. 2.
Gallaher, John, to Sally Hardin; 1796.
McDonald, Edward, to Nancy Smith; Nov. 22.
McIntire, James, to Margaret Henderson; Oct. 17.
McNutt, George, to Gene Anderson; 1797 (?).
Mason, Dan, to Mary Gilliland; May, 1796.
Matthews, William, to Mary Taylor; Nov. 10.
Pickel, William, to Rachel Haslet; Oct. 21.
Wilson, Isaac, to Sarah Shook; Nov. 28.

1797

Adams, William, to Nancy Frazier; Feb. 28.
Anderson, Andrew, to Margaret Roberts; Dec. 11.

Anderson, David, to Ruth Kew; April 10.
Armstrong, Robert, to Polly Crane.
Baker, Henry, to India Alt; Feb. 13.
Beales, William, to Rachel Pierce; Mar. 12.
Bishop, Jacob, to Anne Gammon.
Bray, James, to Rachel Smith; April 20.
Brumit, William, to Rebecca Simpson; Sept. 16, 1797 (?).
Cooper, John, to Lucy Graves; Nov. 1.
Dale, Alex, to Sue Harris; Dec. 30.
Davidson, Nathaniel, to Sallie Hanna; April 27.
Davis, Francis, to Eleanor Lyons; April 20.
Dawdy, John, to Polly Moss; Sept. 28.
Fisher, Archibald, to Elizabeth Sharp; Dec. 11.
Flynn, Hezekiah, to Elizabeth Capps; July 25.
Forest, Robert, to Polly Bishop; Dec. 7.
Frost, John, to Polly Sartain; May 29.
Fox, Enoch, to Peggy Dale; Jan. 9.
Gibbs, John, to Sallie Hardin; Aug. 4.
Gallaher, John, to Sallie Hardin; Dec. 11.
Gragg, Harmon, to Susanna Smelless; June 20.
Halfacre, Jacob, to Pegg Bodkin; Feb. 4.
Harlason, Paul, to Mary Fuller; Dec. 8.
Harmon, Joseph, to Margaret Hess; Oct. 5.
Harp, Willie (x), to Sarah Rice.
Harrison, Joseph, to Margaret Hess; Oct. 5.
Human, Basel, to Winifred Gillum; Jan. 28.
Ingram, George, to Nancy Crane; Mar. 5.
Jackson, John, to Martha White; Jan. 31.
Julien, Hohn, to Sarah Altradge; Mar. 4.
Keen, John, to Rosanna Brady; Sept. 29.
Kimberlin, Jacob, to Sarah Hines; Mar. 6.
Lanskuin (?) ——, to Hannah McCoy; Oct. 12.
Lowry, Andrew, to Catharine Conn; Dec. 20.
Lyons, Thomas, to Frances Irwin; Aug. 9. On outside has Margaret Irwin.
McCloud, Andrew, to Malinda Golliway; Aug. 23.
McNanee, William, to Polly Witt; Nov. 28.
Mason, David, to Mary Gilliland; Mar. 5.
Miller, Samuel, to Rebeccah Givins; Feb. 21.
Montgomery, Samuel, to Magdalena Shook; July 19.
Moore, Joseph, to Anne Horne (or Howell?); July 29.
Morgan, Goan, to Mallinda Nevilles; Dec. 27.
Morrow, William, to Nancy Mebane; Aug. 6.
Neilly, Robert, to Nancy Overstreet; Dec. 29.
Osburn, Charles, to Sarah Newman; Dec. 28.
Pate, John, to Fannie Hubbs; Dec. 8.
Richmond, Alexander, to Prudence Stockton; Dec. 18.
Robertson, David, to Nancy Guthrie—Jan. 21.
Robertson, James, to Sarah Black; July 1.
Robertson, Stephen, to Sally Curtain; Oct. 4.
Robinson, John, to Peggy Owens; Sept. 13.
Ross, Samuel, to Catherine Hill; Jan. 9.
Russell, William, to Elizabeth Weatherton; Aug. 11.
Sander, Isaac (x), to Frances Frost; Dec. 26, 1797—H. L. White.
Sartain (?), David, to Henrietta Stanley; Sept. 15.
Sartain, David (x), to Henretita Harley; Sept. 18.
Scaggs, Charles, to Patsy Bashurs; Jan. 4.
Sharkey, Patrick, to Polly Rhodes; Aug. 17.
Shields, John, to Hannah Evans; July 10, 1797. Attest: H. L. White.
Snodgrass, William, to Rachel White; Mar. 1.

Standiford, Israel, to Phoebe Frost; Dec. 30.
Stanton, John, to Dicie Oliver; Aug. 20.
Sutherland, David, to Margaret Gregg; April 25, 1797 (?).
Stout, Ephraim, to Jean Smith; Nov. 29.
Terry, Tip, to Hannah McNain (?); Mar. 31, 1797 (?).
Trout, John, to Polly Sartain; May 29.
Wear, John, to Elizabeth McClellan; Feb. 14.

1798

Barnes, Thomas, to Alice Buchanan; June 21.
Bray, Hugh, to Elizabeth Hawry; May 23.
Casteel, David, to Sarah Mitchell; May 3.
Cunningham, David, to Jane Cunningham; May 30.
Davis, James, to Nancy Golding; Oct. 7.
DeArmond, John, to Nellie Moore; Sept. 26.
Dunlap, Moses, to Mary Robertson (Robinson?); Aug. 8.
Eldridge, Nath, to Rebecca Davis; May 12.
Fermault, Thomas, to Polly Matlock; May 28.
Galbraith, Thomas, to Sophia Mowry; Aug. 20.
Grayson, Joseph, to Pattie Braizealle; Dec. 10.
Hare, David, to Hannah Fisher; Sept. 27.
Harris, John, to Elizabeth ———; July 5, 1798 (1790?).
Henderson, Robert, to Jean Hackett; Nov. 20.
Henderson, Squire, to Polly Hackworth; Nov. 24.
Hitchcock, William, to Nancy Rhea; Mar. 5.
Hogshead, William, to A. Kirkpatrick; Jan. 9.
Irwin, John, to Nancy Adamson; June 15.
Jenkins, Anson, to Catherine Davis; May 11.
Latham, Lewis, to Laviney Chainey; Feb. 5.
Latin (?), Patrick, to Mary Neil; Feb. 13.
Lowe, John, to Lydia Reid; May 23.
Loyd, William, to Mary Anna Stearns; June 29.
McKinley, James, to Margot Barnett; Aug. 7.
Mitchell, Alexander, to Nancy Casteel; June 5.
Price, Martin, to Barbara Tillman; Nov. 16.
Rainey, John, to E. Stuart; Dec. 21.
Rawlings, James, to Sarah Ritchey; July 4.
Riley, Samuel, to Sarah Smith; Dec. 11.
Ritchie, Alexander, to E. McMullen; Sept. 12.
Scott, James, to Sarah Johnson; June 7.
Searcey, Richard, to Elizabeth Carlisle; Sept. 24.
Sidwell, Isaac, to Elizabeth Conn; Jan. 27.
Sidwell, Joseph, to Margaret Hutchison; Sept. 15.
Strickler, Joseph, to Mary Carpenter; Jan. 7.
Sutler, Abraham, to Sarah Rhea; May 1.

1799

Barclay, Felix, to Price Brock; Jan. 17.
Bounds, Francis, to Anny White; Jan. 18.
Bowman, Jonah, to Betsy Cavett; Jan. 15.
Brown, Jeremiah, to Mollie Menceley; Nov. 26.
Bukinstaff, Henry, to Peggie Hannah; June 8.
Chapman, Arch, to Mattie Hart; Sept. 19.
Crawford, Joseph, to Betsy Brock; April 10.
Crozier, John, to Hannah Barton; Jan. 2.
Davis, John, to Elizabeth Johnson; Feb. 1.
Farmer, John, to Sarah Farmer; Nov. 12.
Ferell, Enoch, to Nancy Nevill; Feb. 5.
Fleming, Samuel, to Peggy Taylor; Dec. 2.
Foster, Alexander, to Pasty Plumbly; Nov. 29.
Frost, Thomas, to Martha Naville; Oct. 18.

Hardin, Joseph, to Fanny Douglass; Jan. 6.
Hany (?), Monday, to Kittie Carpenter; Nov. 29.
Heavner, James, to Mary Blizzard; Nov. 26.
How, Stephen, to Juanita Menifee; Dec. 23.
Huges, John, to Polly Nelson; Sept. 15.
Hutson, John, to Polly Keith; Sept. 29.
Jent (?), Josiah, to Polly Sullins; Aug. 31.
Johnson, Elijah, to Betsy Collier; Feb. 18.
Johnson, August, to Mary Scarborough; Oct. 16.
Johnson, James, to Ann Ballway; June 18.
Kath, Micajah, to Millie Hickey; Feb. 14.
Kennedy, Martin, to Eliza Ebler; Dec. 16.
McNutt, ———, to Jean Anderson; Oct. 10, 1799 (?).
Mansfield, Fames, to Peggy Parker; July 1.
Miller, Martin, to Liveney Mansfield; July 30.
Mills, Hugh, to Polly Moffitt; Feb. 26.
Morrow, Robert, to Nancy Dobson; Jan. 22.
Nicayah, Kath, to Millie Hickey; Feb. 14.
Nosidikely, Daniel, to Mary Higgins; Jan. 8.
Price, Martin, to Barbara Tillman; Nov. 16.
Redmond, Martin, to Sarah Clark; May 2.
Reid, James, to Malinda Fuannulart; June 19.
Roberts, Nathan, to Abigale Bishop; Nov. 10.
Roach, Jesse, to Sally Cobb; May 6.
Ruth, James, to Rebecca Gower; July 6.
Scott, Edward, to Sarah C. Harris; Jan. 17.
Scott, Samuel, to Betsy Lowe; Dec. 3.
Sharp, Daniel, to Jean Howard; April 3.
Smith, Alexander, to Catherine Lowe; June 20.
Stogar, John, to Polly Sheafor; May 25.
Sullens, Richard, to Agnes Farmer; July 8.
Thompson, William, to Nancy Miller; Mar. 28.
Vance, John, to Martha Davidson; Mar. 4.
Vanhoosir, Isaac, to Polly Poor; Feb. 1.
Young, John, to Polly Smith; Mar. 5.

1800

Adams, Alexander, to Barbara Foust; Dec. 8.
Bales, Kaleb, to Anne Smith; Mar. 19.
Basher, Bazil, to Peggy Horton; July 31.
Bowman, John, to Peggy Jack; April 21.
Boomer, Peter, to Rebeccah Farmer; Mar. 7.
Branon, John, to Donah Scott; Sept. 17.
Brent, William, to Patty Chisolm; Nov. 4.
Brooks, Sam (?), to Catherine Doyle; —— 13, 1800.
Butler, Valentine, to Polly Gideon (Gedion?); Sept. 26.
Campbell, David, to Mary Hamilton Campbell; May 14.
Davis, John, to Matty Minecly (?); Nov. 25.
Hackworth, Nichodemus, to Mary England; Nov. 5.
Lester, John, to Polly Crozer (?); Dec. 30.
McAlister, Joseph, to Margaret Stirling; June 17.
Maxwell, John, to Lucy Smith; April 18.
Perkins, John, to Mary Thomas; June 14.
Pew, George, to Margaret Anderson; Mar. 29.
Terry, John, to Elizabeth Crain; Dec. 3.
Thornhill, Armstead, to Rachel Johnson; Oct. 1.
Tunnell, John, to Ann Weatherington; Dec. 8.
White, Charles, to Jenny Rhea; May 2.

1801

Anderson, Samuel, to Benthing Lowe; April 3.

Botkin, Hugh, to Rachel Keener; Mar. 17.
Bowmer, Peter, to Mary Beman; June 10.
Brown, Thomas, to Jane McElwee; Feb. 16.
Carpenter, Thomas, to Mary Ann Shook; June 13, 1801 (or 7?).
Carter, William, to Charity Baker; Mar. 25.
Craven, Benjamin, to Jenny Shelton; Jan. 12.
Crawford, William, to Sally Terry; Dec. 7.
Harless, George, to Margaret McGruff; Mar. 6.
Hobbs, Sammy, to Nancy Holt; Mar. 3.
McFarlan, George, to Nancy Golden; April 20, 1801 (or 7?).
McNair, David, to Delilah Vann; Dec. 30.
Mason, Nathaniel, to Phoebe Brashears; July 9.
Matthews, Britton, to Patsy Browder; Sept. 26, 1801. Signed, Mathis.
Meek, Thomas, to Nancy Bowen; Mar. 23.
Terry, Stephen, to Isbel Netherlin (?); Nov. 5.
Whitechurch, William, to Elizabeth Howel; June 20.
Whiteman, William, to Jean Simms; Mar. 2.

1802

Anderson, Isaac, to Florence McCampbell; Oct. 16.
Taylor, Thomas, to El —— Ferrill; Mar. 23.
Tharp, Daniel, to Catharine Henson; Dec. 20.

1803

Christian, George, to Eliza McCormack; June 1.
Craighead, Thomas, to Polly Gillespie; Dec. 23.
George, Solomon, to Peggy Crawford; Sept. 12.
Lee, Abraham, to Jane Burrows; Nov. 16.
Tenor, Jacob, to Esther Gibson; June 22.
Treadway, John, to Polly Haynes; June 6.

1804

Brewer, Oliver, to Polly Henderson; Jan. 10.
Buckley, William, to Polly Henneman; Jan. 25.
Cox, George, to Rachel Moffet; July 4.
Cunningham, Samuel N., to Jean Flannagan; Jan. 15, 1804 (or 6?).
England, Aaron, to Nancy McCampbell; Aug. 27.
Epps, Edward, to Sallie Cross; Aug. 27.
Nelson, Mathis, to Parsey Cannon; Feb. 1.
Park, James, to Sophia Grady; Feb. 21.
Wilson, James, to Ann Cozby; Mar. 2.

1805

Bell, Thomas, to Elener Tillery; Jan. 22.
Bowen, Abner, to Jenny Thompson; Nov. 27.
Carter, Peter, to Sally Medly; Oct. 12.
Casedy, Reuben, to Rachel McCoy; Oct. 14.
Childers, Robert, to Polly Lucas.
Conner, William, to Sally Case; Dec. 30.
Courtney, Jonathan, to Mary Goan (or Goadns?); Oct. 15.
Coxe, John, to Peggy Hamilton; Oct. 30.
Turpin, Martin, to Elizabeth Russell; Oct. 28.

1806

Barnett, William, to Rosannah Kirkum; Nov. 3.
Cameron, Alexander, to Margaret Cameron; Feb. 5.
Cowan, William Wallace, to Polly Flennikin; Mar. 1.
Currier, James, to Anne Stockton; Mar. 9.
McClelland, Wm., to Eliza C. Sevier; Aug. 9. (Daughter of John Sevier.)
Overstreet, Wm., to Polly Sevier; Sept. 17. (Daughter of John Sevier.)
Simms, Eli, to Rachel Townsend; 1806.
Smith, Elias B., to Jenny Malloon (Malone?); Sept. 4.
White, Jesse, to Mary Manifer; June 28.
Wright, John, to Crissy Smith; Sept. 6.

1807

Carmichael, Pumrey, to Nancy Bell; Nov. 6.
Carthy, Andrew, to Suky Mitchell; July 13.
Cleveland, John, to Mary Martin; May 3.
Close, William, to Elizabeth Herron; Nov. 19, 1807. Signed by William Close and Abner Witt.
Cochran, Absolom, to Mary Stringfield; Mar. 10.
Coker, Joel, to Susan McCampbell; June 9.
Cox, Samuel, to Margaret Crippen; Dec. 9.
Cruise, Hardeman, to Esther Maney; April 11.
Palmer, Robert, to Jane Rorick; Mar. 11.
Scarborough, Elijah, to Molly Adams; Dec. 27.
Senton, Matthew, to Nancy Ellis; Nov. 4.
Shell, George, to Patsy Haynes; Nov. 27.
Stamper, David, to Kazie Keick; June 23.
Tarwater, Jacob, to Peggy Dozier; May 25.
Taylor, Henry, to Molly Nosler; July 11.
Thornton, John, to Nancy Alexander; Aug. 24.
Trout, John, to Mary Kerr; Aug. 24.
Witt, Thomas, to Polly Wright; Dec. 19.
Wood, Isaac, to Nelly Holt; Aug. 6.

1808

———, Reuben, to Barbara Barger; Dec. 12.
Casteel, Abednego, to Agnes Hensly; April 26.
Childress, James, to Polly Ayres; Nov. 7.
Coker, Warren, to Polly Cunningham; Sept. 28.
Cozby, John, to Abigal McBee; Aug. 10.
Crippen, James, to Patsey Hall; Mar. 28.
May, William, to Elizabeth Murray (or Luttrell?); Feb. 22.
Sargent, John, to Rebecca Crane; ——— 13, 1808.
Shook, Harmon, to Margaret Mcmillan; Feb. 16.
Skidmore, John, to Polly, daughter of William Bell; Nov. 7.
Smith, Moses, to Jemima Hunter; May 28.
Smith, Reuben, to Barbara Bargar; Dec. 12.
Smith, William, to Suky White; Jan. 28.
Spain, Thomas B., to Jane Mayes; April 15.
Stephenson, Robert, to Hettie Sterling; Nov. 18.
Tillery, Samuel, to Annie Paul; May 9.
Toomy, Ambrose, to Lucy Walker; Jan. 13.
Williams, John, to Margaret Caldwell; May 26.
Williams, John, to Artimessa Millikan; July 16.

1809

Ashley, Thomas M., to Elizabeth Shelton; Nov. 2.
Ault, John, to Peggy Hastings; Nov. 22.
Baldwin, William, to Betsy Luttrell; Mar. 25.
Bell, James S., to Jenny Bell; Nov. 21.
Bond, William, to Elizabeth Keller; 1809.
Campbell, James, to Peggy Ramsey; Sept. 20.
Carter, Joel, to Hannah Stockton; Nov. 6.
Chapman, Thomas, to Patsey Jones; 1809.
Childress, Mitchell, to Frances Dowell; Sept. 28.
Claiborne, Ephram, to Polly Brown; Dec. 20.
Cox, Lewis, to Emily Holt; Nov. 9.
Crippen, John, to Elizabeth Allen (?); Dec. 28.
Cruze, Elison, to Sally Gillespie; Aug. 3.
Davis, Levey, to Cynthia Hurdle; Mar. 23.
Galloway, Charles, to Nelly Hinds; July 12.
Garner, John, to Polly Conk; Mar. 28.
Levey, Davis, to Cynthia Hurdle; Mar. 23.
McAuley, Edward, to Esther Martin; May 30.
McDonnell, John, to Sallie Whitson; Jan. 12.

McMillan, William, to Elizabeth Reed; Jan. 4.
Meek, Henry (?), to Betsy McCloud; Aug. 22.
Moffett, Hamilton, to Nancy Smith; Mar. 8.
Morrow, Alexander, to Rosannah Spence; Dec. 2.
Park, William, to Jane Crozier Armstrong; Nov. 22.
Sanburg, Reason (or Sambury?), to Rodey Dunnedee; Aug. 31.
Sawyers, John, to Nancy Shell; June 27.
Skinner, William, to Elizabeth Aidman; Aug. 15.
Tarwater, Frederick, to Sally Reid; Oct. 12.
Tarwater, Tewalt (or Tenalt?), to Polly Eddington; June 22.
Taylor, John, to Amelia A. King; May 29.
Tipton, Isaac, to Fanny White; Oct. 12.
Wells, Stephen, to Hannah Eddington; Dec. 28.
Willis, Daniel, to Volley Haley (?); Jan. 21.
Wright, Thomas, to Susannah Pickle; Aug. 11.

1810

Abel, Francis, to Barbara Harner; May 25.
Alexander, John, to Frances Ross (or Koss?); Oct. 23.
Ault, Thomas, to Peggy Baker; July 9.
Barr, John, to Elizabeth Cronk; Jan. 11.
Bilderbach, Jacob, to Polly Probst; Mar. 26.
Carithers, John, to Elizabeth Clark; April 18.
Carrell, Simon M., to Sarah Dougherty; Dec. 26.
Chapman, Miles, to Nancy Burk; Jan. 24.
Childress, Stephen, to Sally Hall; June 10.
Coalman, Daniel, to Mary Chumbley; Nov. 2.
Coats, David, to Jency Lee; Dec. 2.
Cox, James, to Betsy Gammon; Oct. 8.
Cullen, John, to Rachel Craighead; May 30.
Cunningham, John, to Rosannah Shinpoch; Nov. 16.
Givens, James, to Easter Hutchason; Mar. 19.
Howard, Thomas, to Peggy Price (or Pines?); July 9.
Howard, John, to Nancy Howard; Jan. 21.
Murphy, John, to Patsy Gillam; Dec. 31.
Taylor, William, to Stacy West; Oct. 15.
Tindell, Robert, to Peggy McLain; Jan. 18.
Wear, George, to Ann Mynatt; Mar. 27.
York, Aron, to Nancy Rogers; Apr. 13.

1811

Ault, Jacob, to Sally Griffin; Feb. 3.
Barnett, Robert, to Elizabeth Porter; April 16.
Campbell, Isaac, to Mary Ann Fristoe; June 8.
Campbell, Robert, to Betsy Gamble; Aug. 26.
Carter, Richard, to Elizabeth Lonas; Jan. 17.
Cobb, James, to Sallie Harper; May 7.
Day, John, to Polly Ford; Aug. 20.
Dearmond, John, to Annie Burnett; June 4.
Dunnington, Gustine, to Priscilla Linn; June 15.
Franklin, William, to Sallie McMillan; Mar. 11.
Galbreath, Joseph, to Polly Fleming; Aug. 20.
Galloway, Joseph, to Sallie Williams; April 4.
Given, William G., to Sallie Mayberry; June 9.
Harmon, Phillip, to Kitty Viken (?); Sept. 14.
Hawkins, Daniel, to Polly Cook; Feb. 19.
Hinds, James, to Sally Payne (?); Sept. 24.
Hodges, William C., to Mary Douglass; Oct. 7.
Hood, Thomas, to Fanny Simmons; Dec. 18.
Jones, Isaac, to Polly McCaleb; Aug. 5.
Jones, John, to Rebecca Gallaher; April 16.

Kean, Jacob, to Rebecca Mason; Mar. 4.
Kyle, William M., to Betsy White; May 20.
McCarty, James, to Hannah Mansfield; Feb. 5.
Malone, Richard, to Lucy Litt; Feb. 27.
Mann, Peter, to Nellie McDonnell; June 4.
Massey, Thomas, to Jenny Blackwell; April 9.
Meek, Alexander, to Nancy Douglas; Jan. 29.
Miltibarger, Jacob, to Peggy Trout; Feb. 23.
Morton, Simon, to Lucy Sanderson.
Newman, John, to Mary Crow; May, 1811.
O'Neill, John, to Polly Waggoner; Mar. 30.
Osburn, William, to Marony Edwards; Oct., 1811.
Parker, Jesse, to Betsy Copeland; Feb. 5.
Price, Edward, to Sallie Spain; Nov. 5.
Reagan, Peter, to Nancy Cunningham; Oct. 27.
Reid, Thomas, to Elly Burnett; Aug. 15.
Robinson, Nathaniel, to Margaret Lyons; Oct. 22.
Rutherford, John, to Margaret Tunnell; Mar. 1.
Seiton, James, to Eliza Lowe; Sept. 5.
Sharp, James B., to Lockey M. Peterson.
Shelton, Hall, to Elizabeth Mayberry; Jan. 15.
Shipley, Christopher, to Betsy Rutherford; April 2.
Shupock, John, to Polly Crowder; Jan. 10.
Smith, Joseph, to Peggy McCloud; June 26.
Stone, John, to Patsy Summers; Dec. 20.
Strong, Joseph C., to Jane Kain; May 22.
Wear, Samuel, to Sally White; Sept. 26.
Welch, Peter, to Nancy Giddian; May 25.
White, Absolem, to Betsy Reed; Jan. 24.
Wright, Lindsey, to Cynthia Cavitt; Mar. 5.
Wrinkle, Andrew, to Nancy Burnett; Dec. 24.

1812

Albright, Christopher, to Patsy Walker; Jan. 6.
Beard, William, to Mollie Wiseman; May 23 (or Nearmour—25).
Brockus, John, to Sophia Dewitt; Oct. 30, 1812.
Buckhart, Joseph, to Sallie Lumpkin; Aug. 11.
Campbell, John, to Jane Reed; June 4.
Carrick, Addison, to Rebeccah Gamble; Nov. 5.
Clair, Henry, to Nancy Dunlap; Jan. 25.
Coats, Thomas, to Alsey Lee; July 21.
Cox, Jesse, to Feasiby (?) Leahy; July 13.
Davis, Robert, to Sarah Doyle; Oct. 8.
Dodd, John, to Sallie Leek; Feb. 12.
Dodd, Richard, to Elizabeth Dodd; June 25.
Etter, George, to Eve Karnes (Carnes); Mar. 31.
Everetts, Theo, to Peggy Edmonson; Dec. 6.
Ferguson, Joel, to Susannah Stockton; June 2.
Firman, Joshua, to Peggy Council; May 27.
Fleming, David, to Lydia Shelton; Sept. 1.
George, Travis (or George Travis), to Elizabeth Miller; Jan.
Hawkins, Gilbert, to Elizabeth Delaney; Sept. 20.
Harnet, John, to Rebecca Wolff; Nov. 9.
Hargus, Solomon, to Sarah Agnes Shoul; Jan. 30.
Hassel, R. M., to Polly Hardin; Jan. 29.
Hayes, Martin, to Sallie January; April 24.
Hinds, Simon, to Elizabeth Lockard; Feb. 11.
Hines, Joseph, to Susanna Hawkins; June 9.
Hudiburg, Louis, to Dorcas Kelso; Jan. 1.
Johnson, George, to Barbara Husstler; Oct. 28.

Johnston, Jonathan, to Patsy Hinds; Dec. 23.
Kime, Matthias, to Rachel Ross; Feb. 10.
Kirkpatrick, John, to Peggy Brown; Sept. 7.
Kusken (?), Pascal, to Martha Stevenson; Aug. 5.
Luttrell, L., to P. Gibbs; Feb. 11.
McNutt, James, to Polly Fleming; Dec. 23.
Montgomery, James, to Hally Lowe; Jan. 1.
Moore, Andrew, to Rebecca Hollis; Aug. 26.
Murrian, Peter, to Pricy Bartlett; June 5.
Moses, George, to Sarah Bledsoe; Sept. 7.
Nelson, James, to ———; July 7.
Newberry, Thomas, to Polly Payton; Dec. 24.
Norman, William, to Nancy King; Aug. 31.
Ore (?), Joseph, to Margaret Gillespie; Dec. 16.
Reed, Jacob, to Esther Hollis; Aug. 6.
Ruskin, Pascal, to Martha Stephenson; Aug. 5.
Tarwater, William, to Judah Childress; July 23.
Warrick, Western, to Fannie Walker; Jan. 6.
Wright, Obidiah, to Malindy Jones; April 30.

1813

Adams, Robert, to Charlott Montgomery; Jan. 19.
Adkins, Lewis, to Elizabeth George; July 8.
Admonson, David, to Mary Ann Roberts; Nov. 2.
Childress, James, to Locky Johnson; Jan. 26.
Clark, James, to Nancy McCampbell; Jan. 19.
Clark, William, to Nancy White; Nov. 11.
Cline, John, to Polly Meltebarger (?); Mar. 13.
Conn (?), Alexander, to Rebecca Hutchinson.
Copeland, Abdrew, to Elizabeth Bell; Dec. 21.
Cruse, William, to Lucy Childress; April 19.
Dale, Abner, to Jane McDonnel; Feb. 24.
Doyall (Doyle), Isaac, to Jane Capshaw; Dec. 24.
Dozier, Danul, to Jude Maxey; Aug. 25.
Eblin, Samuel, to Martha Young; Feb. 4.
Elliott, William John, to Sophia Pearson; Nov. 29.
England, Elijah, to Eliza Scott; April 7.
Ferguson, William, to Fannie Bowman; April 22.
Flenniken, John, to Sally Cottrelle; July 1.
Flowers, Thomas, to Nancy Brunk; Nov. 25.
Fristo, Markham, to Catherine Grove; Jan. 16.
Gier, Benj., to Betsy Williams; —.
Grantham, John, to Susannah Branham; Nov. 11.
Hall, David, to Rebecca Wilkerson; Feb. 10.
Hall, John, to Susanna Yarnell; Dec. 27.
Harmon, Jacob, to Polly Wright; Feb 1.
Harwick, William, to Mary Hope; May 5.
Howell, Elijah, to Jude Maxey; Aug. 24.
Hynds, Byron, to Betsy Childress; Oct. 2.
Jackson, Baalim (?), to Patsy Bradford; June 19.
Jones, Abner, to Sarah Griffin; July 27.
Kerby, Richard, to Temperance Grant; April 24.
Kilingsworth, Reuben, to Anne McClain; April 16.
Kirkpatrick, Robert, to Rachel Bayless.
Mclocky (McClosky), John, to Matty Benton; May 15.
McCollough, Henry, to Mary Thompson.
McMillan, Alexander, to Susannah Watt; Jan. 18.
McSherry, William, to Elizabeth Peterson; July 21.
Manly, Wilson, to Vin Gammon; Jan. 5.
Meek, Daniel, to Betsy L. Campbell; Mar. 8.

Norris, Reuben, to Catherine Morris; May 25.
Parsons, Enock, to Kitty Kean; Sept. 7.
Reagan, Willie, to Patsy Campbell; Dec. 28.
Robinson, Thomas, to Peggy Broadway; Dec. 23.
Roberts, John, to Eliza Brown; Dec. 27.
Scaggs, Solomon, to Ruth McDaniel; April 19.
Scott, Arthur, to Elizabeth Nance; Dec. 23.
Shipe, Adam, to Frances Carter; Dec. 25.
Simpson, John, to Frances Maybury; Aug. 5.
Smith, Michael, to Polly McCloud; Sept. 9.
Stout, Moses, to Margaret Dodson; April 24.
Tays, Robert, to Elizabeth Buckalew; Dec. 7.
Tillry, Richard M., to Rebecca Cole; Mar. 2.
Tillery, Sampson, to Catharine Yoast; Dec. 22.

1814

Baker, Thomas W., to Esther McMillan; Oct 3.
Booth, Zachariah, to Mary Massengill; May 12.
Clark, John, to Catey Moats; Mar. 14.
Davis, Charles, to Catherine Overton; May 30.
Davis, George, to Cynthia Dearmond; Sept. 13.
Dobbins, Cornelius, to Polly Smith; June 16.
Eaton, Campbell, to Jeanett Paul; May 13.
Edington, Phillip, to Betsey Hall; Feb. 12.
Evans, William, to Nancy Johnson; July 6.
Gammon, Henry, Jr., to Polly Stephenson; Mar. 28.
Gatewood, Ignatius, to Polly Pruit; Oct. 14.
Graves, Henry, to Betsy Ann Grills; Aug. 30.
Haney, Sam, to Polly Brooks; June 30.
Hines, Isaac, to Polly Carless; May 17.
Johnson, William, to Kittie Fairchilds; Feb. 26.
Kirkpatrick, Martin, to Annie Bayless; Jan. 25.
Kyle, John, to Catherine Risedon; June 19.
Love, Samuel C., to Nancy Counsell (?); May, 1814.
Lowe, John, to Betsy Scott; June 16.
McCaleb, Andrew, to Ann Boyd; Oct. 8.
McFarland, William, to Mary McNutt; Sept. 14.
McMillan, Andrew, to Peggy Reagan; Aug. 11.
Malcom, George, to Ann Gillespie; Aug. 15.
Martin, Samuel, to Patsy Love; Feb. 24.
Meek, Joseph, to Rebecca Sawyer; Mar. 22.
Monday, Jobe R., to Sarah Smith; Oct., 1814.
Owens, John K., to Peggy Walker; Mar. 12.
Reid, Thomas, to Elizabeth Council; June 27.
Renfro, Stephen, to Eleanor Christer; Nov. 3.
Roberts, Abram, to Nancy Ballins; Oct. 1.
Roberts, James, to Mahala Evrett; June 16.
Russell, Andrew, to Elizabeth Birdwell; Mar. 14.
Rutherford, Edward, to Polly Harkinson; June 16.
Seymore, James, to Peggy Kelly; April 11.
Sitlu, Philip, to Anny Necnesananha (?); Oct. 22.
Spradlin, William, to Mackey Knox; Feb. 19.
Thompson, James, to Nancy Renfro; Mar. 3.
Thompson, Isaac, to Polly Peler; July 4.
Thompson, William, to Mary Boyd; Dec. 17.
Tipton, Jacob, to Hanna Watson; Sept. 6.
Walker, George, to Betsy Wear; Feb. 25.
Washington, George, to Catherine Tobler; July 7.
Wells, George, to Jane Murphy; July 8.

White, Benjamin, to Mary Callaway; Nov. 26.
Wilson, William, to Elizabeth Davenport; Jan. 22.

1815

Abel, Peter, to Any Ward; Feb., 1815.
Allen, William, to Margaret Ault; Feb. 16.
Anderson, William, to Sophia Davis; Jan. 6.
Ault, Jacob, to Sarah Hannah; Mar. 15.
Bagwell, Allen, to Sarah Lancaster; Oct. 14.
Birdwell, George, to Eliza (?) Russell; July 31.
Blankenship, Reuben, to Jane Couch; Dec. 20.
Bucallo, William, to Eleanor Holt; Dec. 16.
Capps, Solomon, to ——— Smith; Sept. 18.
Cathcart, Daniel, to Rodea Anderson; April 28.
Cate, Jesse, to Rachel Pynor; Aug. 8.
Chavis, James, to Catherine Chavis; Mar. 14.
Chesney, John, to Sarah Scaggs; Nov. 3.
Childress, Mitchell, to Rachel Hendrix; Mar. 1.
Cole, Caleb, to Polly Wright; Mar. 16.
Cox, John, to Alice Gammon; —— 16, 1815.
Davis, David, to Betsy Tays; Oct. 2.
Davis, Lewis, to Nancy McHenry; Jan. 11.
Dowell, Coleby, to Sally Elliott; Nov. 14.
Eaton, William, to Isabella Gillespie; July 22.
England, John, to Mary Scott; Dec. 25.
Evans, Harris, to Aurelia Lewis.
Falkner, William, to Nancy Talent; April 3.
Galbraith, John, to Naads (?) Edington; Dec. 25.
Gambel, William, to Polly Russell; Oct., 1815.
Garner, Abner, to Margaret Hardin; Oct. 25.
Garrison, John, to Polly Hubbs; Oct. 4.
Gillespie, S., to Nancy Ward; Aug. 14 (Isaac on outside).
Gilmore, Thomas, to Anne Wilson; Dec. 31.
Grayson, Ben, to Nancy Regney (?); May 29.
Hamilton, William, to Polly Breedlove; Mar. 1.
Hammen, Isaac, to Mary Underwood; Dec. 8.
Haney, Samuel, to Polly Brooks; June 20, 1815; married by Thomas H. Nelson, Pres. Ch.
Hayes, Alexander, to Catherine McNutt; Sept. 16.
Henderson, Thatch, to Sally Nipper; Dec. 20.
Hilton, Henry, to Rachel Quinn; Dec. 28.
Hill, Martin, to Polly Hansard; Feb. 12.
Jackson, Solomon, to Rebecca Hembree; April 3.
Johnstone, Samuel, to Elizabeth Stevenson; Jan. 17.
Kain, William, to Any Bledsoe; July 21.
Keyhill, Richard, to Elizabeth Groves; Mar. 21, 1815?
Lenning, Isaac, to Polly Leek; June 20.
Lones, Jacob, to Jane Hickey; July 5.
Lyon, Nathan, to Betsy Coxe; July 31.
McCampbell, Solomon-Peggy Dowler; Nov. 28, 1815. Is this wrong? Did Peggy Dowler marry a Campbell?
McLemore, ——, to Sally Fowler; Sept. 20.
McMillan, Thomas, to Sara Ragan; Jan. 12.
Morris, William, to Elizabeth Morris; Sept. 4.
Morrow, John, to Ann J. Jones; June 26.
Newman, Henry, to Priscilla Plumtz; Dec. 20, 1815. McMinn: Gov.
Ore, Marcus, to Susannah Carpenter; Oct. 14.
Peterson, Joseph, to Mary Rutherford; May 24.
Reed, Abram, to Nancy Murry; Sept. 17.
Rhea, Robert G., to Peggy Majors; Feb. 27.

Rodgers, Thomas, to Anne Patton; April 3.
Rogers, James, to Betsy Bond; Dec. 27.
Shell (?), John, to Nancy Pursely; Dec. 4.
Shelton, Edward, to Polly Cutechem; May 24, 1815 (?).
Taylor, Thomas, to Sarah Brown; July 3.
Thatch, Henderson, to Sally Nipper; Dec. 20.
Underwood, George, to Elizabeth Hinds; Sept., 1815.
Williams, Robert, to Elizabeth Clayton; Sept. 28.
Wray, Robert G., to Peggy Majors; Feb. 27.

1816

Aikenson, James, to Patience Gallihor; June 27.
Beall, Samuel, to Hanna Luttrell; Oct. 20, 1816.
Hutchinson, S. Beall; David Ramsey (?).
Coats, David, to Jincy Lee; Dec. 24.
Douglass, Thomas, to Betsy Bryan; Feb. 20.
Dunham, Thomas, to Sarah Jones; May 18.
David Roane.
Edmondson, John, to Sarah Grayson; Aug. 13.
Edminson, Sterling, to Rebecca Taylor; July 27.
Elliott, Samuel, to Jane Manly; April 16.
Ellis, John, to Sarah Clapp; Sept. 14.
Ferguson, Robert, to Patsy Stansberry; Nov. 7.
Fryar, James, to Betsy Hill; Dec. 17.
Galloway, Jesse, to Nancy Caldwell; July 29.
Gooding, James, to Jane Hardin; April 13.
Grabell, Jack, to Elizabeth Shipe; Mar. 4.
Hicks, Richard N. K., to Lucinda Elliott; May 20.
Hill, Martin, to Polly Hansard; Feb. 12.
Hood, Luke, to Elizabeth McCavern; Feb. 25.
Houston, William, to Margaret Swan; Sept. 23.
Howell, William S., to Myse Maness; Feb. 15.
Ingram, Aaron, to Anne Evans; Aug. 14.
Jacobs, Solomon D., to Susan Young; Jan. 4.
Johnson, Jonah, to Priscilla Gallahor; Feb. 21.
Low, David, to Elizabeth Abel; Nov. 15.
Low, Jacob, to Betsy Rodgers; Feb. 13.
McCall, William, to Rachel Ragan; Oct. 17.
McCampbell, William A., to Mary L. Anderson; Nov. 11.
McCloud, John, to Mary Koontz; Oct. 7.
McComb, James, to Betsy Lewis; Sept. 26.
McGhee, Alexander, to Anne M. Emerson; Jan. 11.
McNally, William, to Easter Hope; July 11.
McVey, John, to Malinda Quarley; Aug. 25.
Montgomery, John McKee, to Mary Dunlap; Sept. 30.
Mowery, Moses, to Nancy Clapp; Dec. 17.
Murphy, Abediah, to Mary Berry; Mar. 18.
Nelson, John, to Lucinda Payne; Mar. 26.
Paul, William, to Rebecca Caruthers; Aug. 27.
Rhea, James, to Elizabeth Cabin; Feb. 13.
Rhea, John, to Betsy White; April 22.
Richerson, Brice, to Temperance Davis; Oct. 23.
Roberts, John, to Eleanor Gilmer; Aug. 20.
Rodgers, William, to Mahalie Low; Aug. 13.
Rutherford, James, to Nancy Owens; Feb. 3.
Scaggs, James, to Nancy Majors; July 20, 1816. Signed: Pleasant Miller.
Shook, John, to Catherine Wilson; Aug. 7.
Van Dyke, John H., to Phoebe Martin; Feb. 27, 1816. Signed: Samuel Martin.
Vitner, David, to Ruth Sparks; Dec. 3, 1816. Signed: Hugh Brown.

Ward, Leonard, to Peggy M. Greene; —— 4, 1816.
Williams, John, to Rhoda Morgan; Jan. 1.
Wolf, James, to Barbara Hasley; Mar. 25.
Williams, John D., to Sarah Ward; Oct. 20.
Woods, James, to Polly Bradley; Nov. 30.

1817

Alexander, William, to Elizabeth; Oct. 17.
Atkinson, Jesse, to Patsy Goodman; Jan. 26.
Baldwin, Moses, to Killingsworth; Feb. 6.
Baldwin, Moses, to Margaret Kahoe; June 2, 1817. Same as Keogh or Keough?
Barnes, John, to Mary Coker; Feb. 25.
Beasley, Abraham, to Barbara Danewood; Aug. 5.
Blakely, John, to Lavinia Brown; June 6.
Byerley, David, to Mary Johnson; Nov. 22.
Carter, William, to Susan Ferguson; May 20.
Chapman, Isaiah, to Polly Crabb; Mar. 5.
Clapp, David, to Sarah Rutherford; —— 25, 1817.
Coker, Willie, to Eliza Taylor; Feb. 1, 1817.
Dale, James, to Nancy McDonald; Aug. 30.
Danewood, Isaac, to Sally Norris; Oct. 7.
Davis, Jesse, to Elizabeth Hill; Jan. 6.
Dickey, James M., to Polly Douglas; Nov. 1.
Early, Alexander, to Leamy Moore; June 13.
Elkins, Joseph, to Patsy Whitecotton; Oct. 7.
Everett, William C., to Polly Gillespie; Sept. 30.
Gains, Robert, to Nancy Price; Dec. 10.
Gammon, Dozier, to Lavinia V. Turbivill; Oct. 13.
Gentry, Martin, to Sally Mitchell; Oct. 6.
Geron, Isaac, to Anne Hawkins; Nov. 18.
Goddard, Thornton, to Polly Cunningham; Feb. 3.
Graves, David, to Polly Holloway; Sept. 13.
Green, Abner, to Rebecca Johnson; Jan. 2.
Harmon, Adam, to Polly Housong; Nov. 13.
Hawkins, John, to Malinda Hinds; Feb. 8.
Henderson, William, to Matilda King; Dec. 11.
Hill, Anderson, to Rachel Bridwell; May 14.
Hodges, William, to Rebecca Calaway; Feb. 15.
Huddleston, Jacob, to Polly Litnager; Nov. 12.
Jarnagin, Thomas, to Winty Bledsoe; Nov. 17.
Johnson, Elijah, to Polly Childress; Jan. 13. Married by Jeremiah King.
Johnston, Benjamin, to Nancy Kiltner; Nov. 22.
Karns, John, to Sally Gammon; Aug. 20.
Keger, Matthew, to (?); —— 23, 1817.
Kidd, Horatio, to Mary Anne Kidd; Oct. 23.
King, Thomas, to Elizabeth Keehill; July 19.
King, William, to Eliza Anderson.
King, William Y., to Peggy Lavimore; June 19.
Kissinger, Jacob, to Polly Nausler; Mar. 11.
Laben, Benjamin, to Milly Tindell; Sept. 30.
Lee, Samuel, to Polly York; Jan. 16.
Lee, William, to Barbara Moats; Nov. 28.
Legg, Wesley, to Christian Price; May 17.
Lister, Reuben, to Sally Cole; Nov. 20.
Low, Aguila, to Nancy Lewis; Feb. 20.
Lucas, William, to Sally Tindell.
McCartney, William, to Betsy Ferguson; Nov. 22.
McClellan, Samuel, to Eliza Sterling; July 25.
McClellan, William, to Peggy Sterling; April 8.
McCloud, James, to Polly McCloud; Sept. 26.

McCulloch, James, to Jane Swan; Nov. 11.
McNutt, John, to Martha Jack; April 14.
Martin, George, to Jane English; Dec. 9.
Massey, Abel, to Judith Farmer; Aug. 7.
Miller, Robert G., to Sophy; Aug. 21.
Mode, James, to Polly Randall; Aug. 19.
More, Levi, to Nancy Shilhouse; Nov. 15.
Mynatt, William, to Nellie Reed; Oct. 29.
Newman, Hiram, to Hannah Yarnell; June 10.
Norwood, Nicholas, to Rachel Meek; Sept. 11.
Patrick, James, to Katy Gibbs; Aug. 9.
Peterson, Aaron S., to Sally Howell; Mar. 5.
Pickle, William, to Polly Swader (?); Oct. 18.
Rentfroe, Larkin, to Elizabeth White; July 24.
Roberts, Amos, to Sallie Wing; June 19.
Roper, William, to Elizabeth Brown; June 26.
Routh, Isaac, to Sallie Roberts; Oct. 20.
Rowland, Thomas, to Mary Dunn; Aug. 14.
Scarbough, Elijah, to Mallie Adams; Dec. 27.
Shelton, Skirving, to Peggy Roberts; May 16.
Smith, Isaac, to Venus Ramsey; Mar. 29.
Stringfield, Richard, to Christian Garrett; Mar. 11.
Taylor, Samuel, to Rebecca Jones.
Troops (?), Henry, to Sally Payne; Nov. 27.
Walker, Daly, to Drusilla Epps; Aug. 23.
White, T., to Elizabeth Hendson (?); July 13.
Widimer, William, to Betsy Bayless; Nov. 6.
Wiott, Henry, to Susannah Foster; July 11.
Wilson, Ignatius, to Jane C. King; Dec. 1.
Yarnell, Saniel, to Polly Scott; Jan. 7.

1818

Abel, John B., to Rosanna Johnson; Aug. 25.
Alexander, Ephraim, to Lucy Parry (Perry?); Feb. 10.
Anderson, Jim, to Anne Ford; Nov. 30.
Armstrong, John, to Patsy McClain; Mar. 3.
Ault, John, to Amanda Hainey; Sept. 19.
Baker, Charles, to Margaret Lowe; Dec. 18.
Bedsolt, Daniel, to Molly Martin; April 16.
Bell, Joseph, to Betsy Widener; Nov. 21.
Blang, George, to Margaret Bell; Nov. 4.
Braden, Jesse, to Lila Vickers; Aug. 28.
Bradley, John, to Milinda Dowell; Feb. 17.
Brashier, Isaac, to Elizabeth Wilson; Oct. 6.
Bray, James, to Mary Martin; Feb. 5.
Britt, Thomas, to Sally McCloud; June 13.
Brown, Francis, to Betsy Browning; Dec. 29.
Brown, Joshua, to Frances Blakely; Sept. 27.
Bryan, William, to Hester Walker; Aug. 6.
Capp, Caleb, to Peggy Hood; July 18.
Carroll, Wily, to Clarenda P——; May 29.
Dale, Abner, to Jane McDaniel; April 19.
Davis, Alexander, to Anny Courtney; April 1.
Duffield, James, to Katty Whurly; Oct. 7.
Farmon (?), Thomas, to Betsy Swaddley; Oct. 15.
Floyd, Jesse, to Betsy Williams; Sept. 17.
Ford, Benjamin, to Rachel Steel; Oct. 20.
Formmalt, John, to Nancy Council; Jan. 29.
Fortner, George, to Polly Lewis; Mar. 12.

French, George, to Betsy Houser; July 31.
Frost, Sam, to Nancy Childress; Dec. 29.
Gentry, Isaac, to Elizabeth Lewis; Sept. 23.
Green, William, to Eliza Coats McGilton; Jan. 29.
Hall, Obadiah, to Sarah Bayles; April 29.
Harris, Meredith, to Charlotte Tobler (?); Sept. 1.
Haswell, Benjamin, to Frankey ———; Feb. 16.
Hawkins, Wesley, to Patsy Foster; May 23.
Henderson, Isaac, to Jane Ledgerwood; Aug. 6.
Hoffman, Daniel, to Sally Quarles; Dec. 11.
Houser, Daniel, to Katy French; Mar. 30.
Housong, John, to Rosanna Rule; Dec. 10.
Hubbs, William, to Betsy Rutherford; Oct. 1.
Human, James, to Sarah Hopper; Jan. 22.
Hunter, John, to Phoebe Douglass; Jan. 26.
Kain, Solomon, to Jane Lyon; June 13.
Killingsworth, Thomas, to Jane Hickey; Jan. 12.
Kitts, Andrew, to Nancy McBride; Dec. 17.
Lea, Pryor, to Miriah Kennedy; Oct. 6.
Lett, Armbrose, to Lois Couch; Aug. 17.
Lewis, William, to Rhody Higdon; Mar. 12.
Lindsay, John, to Elizabeth Bishop; April 9.
Lones, Jesse, to Martha Daniel; Nov. 10.
Love, Samuel, to Charlotte Bell; May 16.
McBride, John, to Susan Cline; Dec. 2.
McCaleb, Samuel, to Jane Smith; May 5.
McClain, David, to Malinda Yarnell; Dec. 29.
McClain, James, to Polly Yarnell; Feb. 3.
McConnell, Thomas, to Catherine Haven; June 25.
McKee, Robert, to Jane Brooks; Mar. 11.
McMillan, James, to Alice Houston; Jan. 1.
McMunn, William, to Nancy Crawford; Sept. 1.
McNutt, George A., to Malinda Houston; May 21.
Majors, William, to Susannah Scaggs; Mar. 16.
Martin, James, to Becke Ledinger; Sept. 24.
Massey, Hugh, to Anne Murphy; Aug. 1.
Medlock, Nich, to Katy McCall; April 7.
Miller, Pleasant, to Rachel Cox; Feb. 16.
Morrow, William M., to Milly Bishop; Oct. 23.
Moses, Solomon, to Mary Anne Foust; Feb. 26.
Nipp, Adam, to Catherine Graybill; Dec. 1.
Owens, Abraham, to Lucy Rolen; April 13.
Owens, John, to Sarah Gibbs.
Parker, Jesse, to Rhody Alary (or Rhody may be surname); May 12.
Parr, William, to Betsy Mettibarger; Oct. 10.
Peterson, William, to Jane Kelly; Dec. 9.
Pickle, Jonahan, to B—— Cunningham; June 22.
Rhodes, Lewis, to Nancy Fry; April 28.
Richison, John, to Rhody Luttrell.
Roberts, James, to Elizabeth Luttrell.
Roberts, Jozadak, to Mary Luttrell; Oct. 22.
Russell, John, to Sally Sewell; Nov. 26.
Stephenson, Robert, to Eunice Meade; April 13.
Summers, Johnston, to Sally Williams; Nov. 18.
Thompson, Harvey, to Nancy McCampbell; May 21.
Thompson, Samuel, to Elizabeth Brock; May 13.
Thuerritz (?), John, to Tabitha Clayton; July 29.
Vance, Samuel, to Elizabeth Brock; May 13.
Watson, William, to Sarah Houk; June 23.

Wheeler, John, to Sarah Sanders; April 2.
Witt, James, to Libby Reed; April 20.

1819

—Umpler, James (?), to Susanna Guinn; Jan. 11.
Armstrong, Aaron, to Elizabeth Bounds; Feb. 3.
Barnwell, Robert H., to Jane Barnwell; Oct. 7.
Benny, William, to Sally Simpson; Mar. 17.
Berry, William, to Ruthy White; Sept. 25.
Bradley, Archilles, to Nancy Dowell; June 3.
Caldwell, James A., to Mary McCampbell; Mar. 11.
Carson, John, to Cynthia Spilman; Aug. 4.
Carter, Amos, to Nancy Luttrell; Mar. 11.
Chapman, John L., to Eleanor Warnick; Feb. 17.
Childress, Richard, to Cecka White; May 21.
Clapp, Boston, to Polly Tenneyhill; April 15.
Coker, James, to Polly McGammon; Jan. 29.
Conner, Samuel, to Patsy Hickey; Jan. 12.
Courtney, Samuel, to Susan Luttrell; July 5.
Cox, Jonathan, to Mary An Golliher; Oct. 25.
Crew, Pleasant, to Margaret Layton; June 7.
Cruse, Walter, to Louisa Tucker; Feb. 5.
Davis, Robert, to Betsy Halsey; Mar. 17.
DeArmond, Elisha, to Sally Johnson; Dec. 15.
Dennis, William, to Ruth Pettie; Feb. 29.
Dockett, William, to Katty Longwith; July 10.
Dunlap, William, to Betsy Swaggerty; Sept. 17.
Evans, William, to Mary Evans; Mar. 30.
Evans, Joseph, to Hilda Hoggett; Aug. 10.
Ewing, Samuel, to Sarah Steel; Mar. 17.
Everett, Sylomess, to Mary Douglass; Aug. 18.
Fiske, Harland, to Jane Campbell; July 27.
Forman, John, to Jane Swadley; July 27 (or Fannon).
Fulton, William, to Peggy Sample; Aug. 2.
George, Parnick, to Polly McPhenin (?); Dec. 1.
Gibbs, John, to Susanna George; June 19.
Gillespie, Robert, to Mary G. King; June 16.
Gilmore, John, to Betsy Ferguson; June 20.
Glass, Harvey, to Rebecca Paul; Mar. 2.
Glass, Lewis, to Sally Simpson; Oct. 19.
Gound, John, to Betsy Low; Dec. 15.
Graves, Adney, to Betsy Miller; July 5.
Green, Samuel, to Patsy Ferguson; Oct. 4.
Hackney, Charles, to Elizabeth Levi; May 18.
Hainey, Archibald, to Catherine Brown; Oct. 2.
Harmon (Hamer?), Daniel, to Polly McColough; April 12.
Hansard, John, to Nancy Hansford; April 18.
Harbison, Please, to Polly Graves; Feb. 10.
Hazelwood, Benjamin, to Mary Reed; Jan. 1.
Hickey, Cornelius, to Catherine Keith; July 6.
Hickey, Joseph, to Abigal Julian; Nov. 9.
Hill, Harry M., to Mary Fizzard; Aug. 28.
Hill, John, to Sally H. Davis; Mar. 30.
Hindman, Thomas C., to Polly Holt; Jan. 27.
Horton, Daniel, to Polly Needham; Aug. 25.
Howard, James, to Lucy Chumley; Mar. 27.
Howard, Thomas, to Polly Lumpkin; Sept. 15.
Hurdle, Thurman, to Sally Nelson; Oct. 13.
Jackson, Uriah, to Dolly Martin; July 27.

Jarnagon, Spencer, to Clarissa Montgomery; Dec. 13.
Jett, John, to Elizabeth Con; Nov. 25.
Johnston, Benjamin, to Jeneva Eddington; Dec. 9.
Johnston, Joseph, to Betsy Crew; Nov. 25.
Kelly, Walthan, to Nancy Lones; Jan. 10.
Kidd, James, to Frankie Childress; Jan. 6.
King, Solomon H., to Nancy Lammon (or Larwood?); Feb. 6.
Leek, James, to Mary Dowler; Jan. 16.
Lincoln, Mordacai, to Sophia Heiskell; April 15.
Lones, Henry, to Bethena Whitman; Dec. 13.
Low, John, to Jane Mowrey; Jan. 4.
McCampbell, James, to Betsy Ingram; Mar. 30.
McKean, Aaron, to Caty Houser; Sept. 25.
McKean, Edward, to Elizabeth Mapes (or Epps); Aug. 3.
McKeehen, A————, 1819.
Michaels, Frederick, to Polly Bowman; Mar. 24.
Monday, Thomas, to Elizabeth Meeks; Dec. 14.
Morrow, George, to Nancy Carter; April 7.
Mowry, Lewis, to Betsy Lisbee; Mar. 3.
Mowrey, Samuel, to Jane McCloud; Mar. 11.
Murphy, Archibald, to Polly Monday; Nov. 12.
Nelson, Winchester, to Sally Bright; July 26.
Newman, John, to Dolly Lewis.
Owen, John, to Dobby Bumwott; Oct. 24.
Pamler, Robert, to Mary Green; Oct. 4.
Pow, James, to Anne Beal; Oct. 25.
Rhoady, John, to Polly Conn; Dec. 28.
Roberts, William, to Martha Sample; Mar. 4.
Rodgers, Andrew, to Sally Kirkland; Aug. 24.
Rodgers, John, to Rebecca Patton; Dec. 25.
Russell, Reuben, to Docay Oans; Sept. 7.
Sherwood, Benjamin, to Rachel Everett; Nov. 25.
Sampler, James, to Sussannah Guin; Jan. 11.
Shipe, Henry, to Deborah Scaggs; Oct. 4.
Snodgress, Elijah, to Peggy Smith; Mar. 13.
Shoeky (?), John, to Polly Hainey; Aug. 2.
Shuler, Abner, to Nancy Burnett; Sept. 22.
Smith, John, to Mariah Christia; Aug. 2.
Smith, William M., to Elizabeth Gardner; July 24.
Vance, Joseph, to Eliza Green; Dec. 29.
Walker, Daniel, to Mary Carpenter; Feb. 11.
Webb, Thomas, to Betsy Corkbund (?); Oct. 18.
Wiley, Moses, to Alice Gardener; June 14.
Wilkerson, Obadiah, to Rachel Clayton; July 24.

1820

Arthur, James, to Hannah Houser; Sept. 20.
Ayres, Jesse, to Elizabeth Reed; Nov. 3.
Badgett, James, to Susan Harris; Nov. 23.
Bayles, Isaac, to Susannah Sumter; July 15.
Bell, James, to Nancy Stephenson; Jan. 13.
Bookout, John M., to Peggy Guin; June 12.
Boyd, Alexander, to Catherine Starnes; Aug. 21.
Butler, William D., to Elizabeth Cabett; Feb. 4.
Butten, Edward, to Nancy Holt; May 13.
Calfee, Henry, to Tabitha Hazlewood; Aug. 23.
Clark, Jones P., to Susannah M. Cony; June 27.
Comstock, Jasper W., to Nancy Keys; July 27.
Conn (?), Henry, to Elizabeth Guinn; Oct. 2.
Courtney, William, to Rachel McClure; Dec. 20.

Davis, John, to Nancy Johnson; July 22.
Dickson, John, to Margaret Wills; Sept. 25.
Doughty, Benjamin, to Polly Kiness; Sept. 20.
Douglass, Alex, to Rhoda Ruth; Nov. 13.
Dunlop, Nathaniel, to Miss Polly Montgomery; Mar. 11.
England, Alfred, to Bershiba Walker; Nov. 11.
Everett, Aquilla, to Sarah Thompson; July 1.
Galbraith, Joseph, to Abgail Strickland; Mar. 14.
Galbraith, Joseph, to Betsy Love; April 26.
Gallaher, Alexander, to Jane Carter; June 2.
George, Travis, to Elizabeth Johnson; April 14.
Gillespie, Abraham, to Peggy Paul; Aug. 10.
Goddard, John, to Anne Campbell; Jan. 25.
Grizzle, Henry, to Susan Jones; Nov. 4.
Hawkins, Levi, to Elizabeth Guin; Oct. 17.
Hicklin, George, to Margaret Roberts; Aug. 14.
Hunter, James, to Fanny McCloud; Dec. 2.
Johnson, Lorenzo, to Katy Hunter; Jan. 17.
Johnston, Elliott, to Susan Luttrell; Aug. 1.
Kime, Lewis, to Sarah Short; June 21.
King, James B., to Isabella McNeil; Feb. 25.
Kirkland, George W., to Louisa Alexander; Aug. 30.
Larew, Francis, to Nancy A. Young; Oct. 19.
Long, John, to Betsy Parker; Dec. 2.
Loudenmulk, William, to Betsy Wilhite; Feb. 17.
Lyle, Samuel, to Susan McDonald; Jan. 30.
Lyons, Washington, to Patty Lyons; July 3.
McIntosh, Donald, to Margery Campbell; Feb. 1.
Martin, Samuel, to Sally Ragan; Oct. 2.
Mason, Winsor, to Mariah Lane; April 1.
Mayberry, James, to Lucretia Ross; Sept. 13.
Mayberry, Joseph A., to Alsie Scott; Dec. 4.
Mitchell, Jesse, to Rachel Gentry; Mar. 6.
Moats, John, to H—— Huffstutler; Dec. 15.
Monday, Fandy, to Polly Wood; Sept. 5.
Naill, John, to Polly Benkly; Jan. 19.
Newman, Jacob, to Keziah Hathcock; Dec. 5.
Overton, John, to Mary May; July 28.
Patterson, William, to Esther Rutherford; June 13.
Paul, Eddy, to Eleanor Cole; Mar. 23.
Price, John, to Betsy King; April 19.
Ragan, Eli, to Charlotte Ayres; Jan. 4.
Ramsey, Francis A., to Margaret Humes, April 13.
Robert, Andrew, to Jean Kelley; Oct. 5.
Robinson, James, to Mary Dardis; Aug. 3.
Russell, William, to Jane Lowe; May 30.
Rutherford, William, to Elizabeth; Feb. 15.
Scott, Harden S., to Patsy Larew; Mar. 28.
Sensabaugh, Jacob, to Nancy Thompson; Jan. 24.
Smith, Bannister, to Sarah Coker; Dec. 2.
Smith, John, to Rachel Mulvaney; April 4.
Swan, John, to Jane H. Swan (?); Sept. 13.
Sword, Phillip, to Nancy Cheatham; Jan. 21.
Sylar, Peter, to Polly Arnold; Dec. 16.
Wagener, Peter, to Polly M. Smith; June 20.
Walker, Reuben, to Betsy Gallaher; Dec. 22.
White, Abraham D., to Elizabeth Douglass; Feb. 24.
Whittle, John, to Polly Karns; Aug. 29.

Wilson, John, to Betsy Campbell; July 28.

1821

Adkinson, Peter, to Harriet Sharp; Sept. 11.
Aldridge, William, to Patsy McClellan; Nov. 12.
Allison, William, to Sally McKinney; Aug. 20.
Adamson, Isaac, to Jane Underwood; July 28.
Badgett, James, to Mary Ann Moore; Sept. 8.
Barton, Isaac, to Charity Barker; April 10.
Bayles, Israel, to Betsy Sumter; Nov. 23.
Brooks, John, to Mary Armstrong; Jan. 8.
Brown, Frances, to Polly Bice; Dec. 6.
Burnett, Lemuel, to Jane Fisher; June 6.
Carter, Winston, to Susannah Luttrell; June 15.
Cliburn, Lasley, to Cynthia Hopper; Oct. 27.
Cole, Benjamin, to Polly Walker; Mar. 21.
Cooley, Joshua, to Nancy Maney; Dec. 26.
Cottrell, Thomas, to Lydia Cheesman; Dec. 27.
Cruse, Walter, to Nancy Walker; April 13.
Cunningham, Samuel, to Eleanor F. Houston; Oct. 25.
Debusk, David B., to Jerusha E. Rudder; Dec. 28.
Dozier, Peter, to Rebecca Haines; Aug. 25.
Early, Benjamin, to Polly Lilburn; Jan. 8.
Edmondson, Samuel, to Rebecca Hicks; Dec. 2.
Findley, John, to Patty Pean (?); Dec. 8.
Fulton, Thomas, to Polly Wills; Jan. 25.
Galbraith, James, to Charity Mayberry; Dec. 25.
Hackworth, Austin, to Betsy Rehry (?); Oct. 24.
Hamilton, Joseph, to Elizabeth Moore (or Moon); Jan. 23.
Hardin, Martin, to Mariah Taylor; Oct. 10.
Harris, Joseph, to Julia Shull; Nov. 7.
Harris, Nathan, to Rebecca Gibbs; Oct. 27.
Hawkins, Silas, to Nancy Cruze; Dec. 24.
Hazen, William, to Hannah Walker; June 2.
Hester, Hwen (?), to Polly Creswell; Mar. 11.
Hewlin, James, to Sally Crew; Dec. 4.
Hicks, James, to Sally Couch; Oct. 20.
Hill, William, to Julia Anne Wright; Oct. 18.
Johnson, Andrew, to Catherine Stephenson; Sept. 28.
Jordan, John, to Nellie Goundy; July 17.
Kesslinger, Matthew, to Sally Con; Dec. 24.
Killingsworth, William, to Matilda McClure; Mar. 30.
King, Thomas, to Mary Hagan; May 17.
Knox, James, to C—— Bond; Oct. 20.
Lee, Thomas J., to Maty Talbert; Sept. 27.
Looney, Benjamin, to Jane Caldwell; Mar. 18.
Lumpkin, Richard, to Rebecca Juslin; Dec. 19.
Lyles, Wilson, to Betsy Pritchet; Feb. 6.
McCabe, Starkey, to Elizabeth Murphy; May 29.
McCarroll, Joseph G. M., to Jane Henson; July 10.
McCloud, Alexander, to Dice Baker; Aug. 13.
Olinger, George, to Mary Forganson; May 14.
Oliver, Henry, to Peggy Stokes; Aug. 28.
Parker, Nelson, to Margaret Kelly; Nov. 28.
Patrick, James, to Betty Lewis; June 2.
Payne, Edmond, to Jane Wrinkle; June 20.
Peterson, Israel, to Jane McBride; Dec. 4.
Ramsey, James G. M., to Margaret B. Crozier; Mar. 1.
Rody, Alexander, to Dicey Johnson; Mar. 29.

Simpson, John, to Rachel Fete; Sept. 28.
Smith, Beverly, to Lucinda Killen; Nov. 17.
Sterit, James, to Polly Lyon; Dec. 24.
Sterling, John, to Sally Anderson; Aug. 16.
Stowell, John, to Margaret Armstrong; Mar. 17.
Tinker, William, to Margaret Robinson; Oct. 31.
Underwood, John, to Susan Guinn; April 3.
Wallace, John, to Rebecca Norton; Sept. 7.
Weaver, Walter, to Elizabeth Martin; Oct. 27.
White, John, to Caty McNutt; Dec. 31.
Williams, Joshua L., to Judith Roberts; Mar. 24.
Yenell, Solomon, to Sally Hubbs; Oct. 3.
Young, John, to Ruthy Cruze; Jan. 1.

1822

Agnus, Samuel, to Keziah Roberts; Nov. 30.
Allison, David, to Isabell McConnell; Sept. 12.
Badgett, James, to Fanny Williams; Oct. 5.
Baker, Solomon, to Susanna Bayles; Nov. 25.
Baker, William, to Sarah Howser; Dec. 16.
Bayles, John, to Lucinda Whitecotton; Mar. 2.
Boyd, Joseph, to Peggy Kilburn; Feb. 22.
Boyd, William, to Eliza Reynolds; Sept. 4.
Bright, Elias R., to Deborah Hawkins; Oct. 4.
Brown, Elisha, to Jane Booker; April 17.
Brown, James, to Margaret Fraker; Feb. 12.
Campbell, James, to Patty Hazelwood; Oct. 5.
Campbell, John, to Mary Cowan; May 23.
Carpenter, William, to Isabella McCloud; Feb. 18.
Cheser, Dennis, to Betsy Ault; Feb. 28.
Chumlee, Claiborne, to Elizabeth Cabit; Sept. 20.
Clap, Adam, to Rebecca Roberts; Sept. 17.
Cloud, Levi, to Peggy Courtney (?); Oct. 29.
Coleman, James, to Sally Hickey; May 1.
Couch, David, to Elizabeth Reed; June 13.
Courtney, John, to Nanny Robinson; Oct. 29.
Foster, Isaac, to Mary Gibbs; Mar. 16.
Frost, Joel, to Susannah Tindell; Dec. 9.
Fry, Rhodes, to Betsy Doyle; April 17.
Gilstrop, Israel, to Larky Davis; Mar. 22.
Hackney, Jacob, to Sarah Fisher; May 20.
Hackney, Jacob, to Sarah Fisher; June 4.
Haden, Franics, to Mary Lyons; July 23.
Hall, James, to Elizabeth Pensley; June 24.
Hansard, Archilus, to Nancy Lewis; Dec. 24.
Heavers (?), William, to Elizabeth Shell; Jan. 8.
Henson, William, to Ferbia Cottrell; Aug. 29.
Hinkle, Phillip, to Rachel Smith; July 13.
Houser, Jacob, to Betsy Anderson; Aug. 29.
Ingram, Samuel, to Polly Gillam; July 24.
Jones, Francie K., to Polly Forkner; Feb. 26.
Kelley, Samuel, to Catherine Formalt; Jan. 24.
Keys, Henry, to Rebecca Lyons; Oct. 31.
King, S. V. R., to Mary Anne Walker; Dec. 2.
Kunn (Green or Know or Yrun), Peter, to Nancy Rector; April 1.
Love, Samuel, to Polly Smith; July 9.
McNaim (?), to Mary Shutz; July 12.
Martin, Samuel, to Patsy Stewart; April 17.
Maupine, Morgan G., to Elizabeth Callen; May 28.

Milliken, Elisha, to Mary Clayton; Sept. 23.
Mitleberger, John, to Sally Caig; Feb. 12.
Mounger, Jethro W., to Elizabeth Galliher; Oct. 23.
Mulvany, Jacob, to Nancy Low; Mar. 25.
Murray, Rena, to Annie Elliott; Aug. 6.
Mynatt, James, to Nancy Parker; Aug. 5.
Newman, Edmond, to Margaret Bowman; Feb. 2.
Nickerson, Frederick, to Catherine Howell; Dec. 16.
Norris, Alfred, to Tabitha Bledsoe; Nov. 14.
Ogg, Peter, to Eliza Dowell; April 15.
Smith, Robert, to Eliza Sterling; Sept. 3.
Ramsey, Reynolds, to Anne Roan; July 17.
Ransom, John, to Betsy Luttrell; Nov. 14.
Reagan, David, to Betsy Catheum; Sept. 11.
Reed, Joseph, to Bessie Breese; Dec. 12.
Rody, William, to Martha Childress; Jan. 15.
Reynolds, John M., to Jane McHaffie; April 11.
Rohr, Philip, to Margaret Formalt; Dec. 26.
Routh, James, to John Lovelass; Dec. 24.
Sheretz, John, to Georgia Walker; Sept. 2.
Smith, Charles J., to Betsy Simpson; Aug. 21.
Smith, John, to Henrietta Counsell; Feb. 4.
Smith, William, to Polly Goodman; Dec. 4.
Snow, Archibald, to Nancy Griffin; Aug. 10.
Swaggerty, Stokley D., to Polly Guinn; Dec. 20.
Tobler, George W., to Peggy Henshaw; May 13.
Thompson, James, to Dinah Bitchbord; July 25.
Ubank, John, to Pasty Walker; Aug. 24.
Walker, Richard, to Susan Thomas; April 9.
Wheeler, Sevier, to Sally Johnston; Mar. 28.
Wilhite, George, to Nancy Gunn (Guin?); July 2.
Woods, Mason, to Elizabeth Cole; Oct. 14.

1823

Abel, Moses, to Betsy McHenry; July, 1823.
Anderson, John, to Sallie Dunham; May 15.
Armstrong, Addison W., to Nancy McMillian; Mar. 21.
Bell, James L., to Nancy Conner; April 28.
Bell, Robert, to Malinda Scott; Feb. 20.
Boaz, Obediah, to Prudence King; Nov. 18.
Bowman, Samuel, to Betsy Hippenstall; Dec. 31.
Butler, Jacob M., to Sarah Hardin; Nov. 17.
Campbell, David, to Jane Smith; Nov. 29.
Cartul (?), Elijah, to Sally Fairchild; Aug. 30.
Cheasman, George, to Malinda Mayfield; April 2.
Clift, William, to Nancy Brooks; April 15.
Crew, David, to Polly Smith; Oct. 4.
Cunningham, James, to Peggy Anderson; Sept. 30.
Davis, Edmond, to Mary Ann Marthena Lefevre (?); May 7.
Davis, William, to Betsy Hunter; Feb. 10.
Doyle, David, to Sally Houser; May 3.
Edmondson, John B., to Polly Crawford; May 7.
Eldridge, Stephen, to Milly Walker; Dec. 18.
Elliott, Isaac, to Fireby Williams; May 29.
Fout, David D., to Dorcas M. King; Oct. 7.
Gusling (?), Joseph, to Betsy Keys; Jan. 9.
Hammond, Jesse, to Lilah Underwood; Jan. 18.
Hanalson, William, to Catherine Wills; Mar. 31.
Hanes, Jordan L., to Letty Conn; Mar. 5.
Harmon, John, to Milly Honsong; Dec. 22.

Hill, Lewis, to Rachel Birdwell; July 18.
Hood, Aaron, to Nancy Hensey; May 28.
Hunter, John, to Elizabeth McMillan; Dec. 23.
Israel, Isom, to Neety Parr; Mar. 28.
Jett, William, to Ailsy Norman; Nov. 3.
Keith, Andrew, to Martha Mitchell; April 16.
Kennedy, Lucas, to Mary Kain; July 15.
Kimbrough, John, to Mary L. Hasen; Oct. 15.
Lewis, Loren R., to Levina Roddy; Feb. 25.
Lones, Joseph, to Nancy Cavett; Dec. 14.
Lyon (or Lyhow), David, to Milly Head; Jan. 29.
McCampbell, James, to Jane Boyd; Mar. 27.
McMillan, James, to Nancy Kennedy; Dec. 30.
McNamy (or McNanny), Jahn, to Rachel Smith; June 16.
Morgan, John, to Judy Quails; Aug. 28.
Morrow, Charles, to Sally Davis; Dec. 18.
Murphy (or Morphee), Silas, to Matilda Clayton; Nov. 11.
Murray, Eli, to Phoebe Hawthorn; May 15.
Norwood, John, to Mary ———; June 21.
Overton, John, to Anne Parr; April 21.
Patton, William, to Jane Cunningham; June 11.
Reagan, John, to Rebecka Moore; Oct. 30.
Rector, Washington, to Nancy Kirkpatrick; Jan. 12.
Rentfrow, James, to Sally Yost; Dec. 22.
Rogers, Thomas, to Cynthia Campbell; June 19.
Rutherford, John, to Betsy McAffrey; Feb. 18.
Short, Adam, to Polly Pratt; Jan. 22.
Smith, Robert, to Phebe Clap; Nov. 25.
Smith, Samuel, Jr., to Oney Kearns; Aug. 12.
Smith, William, to Nancy Burnett; Feb. 22.
Spears, Leven (?), to Anna Waddell; June 12.
Stanton, Washington, to Sarah Hood; Mar. 7.
Starky, Samuel, to Maria Bennett; Jan. 27.
Stephenson, James, to Margaret Brooks; Mar. 12.
Stowell, Ales, to Maria Stephenson; Oct. 16.
Warmack, Isaac, to Nancy Lonas; Jan. 4.
Watkins, Richard, to Martha Caldwell; Mar. 4.
Wert, Josheph, to Catherine Gardner; Nov. 13.
Williams, Berry, to Lucretia Hill; Mar. 22.
Wilmoth, William, to Margaret Kirkland; June 29.

1824

Bails, Asher, to Sally Kind; July 22.
Bell, William W., to Susan Low (or Love); Feb. 13.
Bryan, Thomas H., to Patsy Manifold (?); Nov. 27.
Byerly, Jacob, to Sally Brown; Nov. 2.
Cassaday, Richard, to Mary Walker; Sept 7.
Cox, Moses, to Polly Conners; Oct. 21.
Cunningham, Andrew, to Elizabeth Anderson; Nov. 11.
Doyle, William, to Catharine Thomas; Nov. 25.
Drain, John, to Sarah Henderson; Dec. 5.
Dunlap, Auterson (?), to Betsy McBride; Jan. 10.
Foust, David, to Hanna Clap; July 29.
Gault, John, to Patsy Murphy; Feb. 4.
Hackworth, Samuel, to Polly Hall; June 16.
Halfacre, Jacob, to Peggy Bodkin; Feb. 1.
Hawkins, Edward, to Elizabeth Skaggs; Feb. 28.
Hawkins, George, to Matilda Flakner; April 7.
Henderson, John, to Peggy Ann Antry; Nov. 9.

Henderson, John, to Ann Carr; Dec. 22.
Hill, Marvel, to Milly Con; Mar. 15.
Hines, Joseph, to Mary A. Grimes; Dec. 16.
Hinds, —— (Sam?), to Fanny Ann Reynolds; Dec. 23.
How, Jacob, to Elizabeth Sensebaugh; April 23.
Johnson, Lillerbury, to Edg George; April 5.
Love, Thomas B., to Susan Smith; Feb. 21.
McBath, Alexander, to Peggy McCall; Dec. 30.
McCaughorn, John, to Margaret Ann Gray; July 7.
McClure, Samuel, to Sally G. Love; Sept. 22.
McMillan, Charles, to Rosanah Hunter; Feb. 24.
Miller, Mark L., to Mary Ann Jane Pinkson; Dec. 15.
Rector (?), Benjamin, to Lilly Shell; Oct. 14.
Richardson, Alexander W., to Elizabeth Gibbs; May 22.
Rodgers, David, to Lumina Jackson; Mar. 29.
Scott, William A., to Mary Ann Odel; Feb. 12.
Shields, Robert, to Prudence Boyd; April 29.
Smith, Alexander, to Peggy Galliher; Feb. 28.
Spears, James, to Sophy Ragsdale; Dec. 25.
Sterrit, David, to Bethia H. King; Jan. 8.
Swann, Robert M., to Ann Aurelia Ramsey; Dec. 15.
Thompson, Joseph, to Sally Legg; Feb. 12.
Weaver, William, to Patsy Zand (?); Mar. 7.
White, Thomas, to Margaret Smith; Nov. 11.

1825

Chrisman, Isaac, Jr., to Isabella Pursley; Oct. 27.
Crawford, Thomas, to Maria Harris; Sept. 20.
Dunn, John, to Mahala McClure; July 25.
Humphreys, Alexander, to Nancy Bond; Nov. 5.
McLemore, William to Betsy Luttrell; Feb. 16.
Walker, Jesse, to Rebecka Greer; Sept. 23.
Williams, Jason, to Nancy Cottrell; Dec. 15.

1826

Ballinger, James, to Anne Dow; Oct. 25.
Bayless, Samuel, to Nanny Lister; Mar. 9.
Benson, Matt, to Hannah Smult (?) Aug. 1.
Chiles, Micajah, to Elizabeth Wilkens; July 29.
Coker, John, to Sally Ferguson; Dec. 16.
Crank, James, to Nancy George; Jan. 17.
Cunningham, Jesse, to Betsy Newman (?); July 18.
Doyle, Isaac, to Peggy Campbell; Dec. 14.
Drain, John, to Sallie Henderson; Dec. 5.
Fleming, Washington L. (or S.), to Ruth Brown; April 21.
Horne, George, to Amanda Luttrell; Oct. 11.
Houston, Walter, to Jane Cunningham; Mar. 15.
Howser, Jonathan, to Polly Harmon; Aug. 15.
Taylor, Al——, to Nancy Simpson; July 26.
Thompson, James, to Frances Yarnell; Oct. 26.
Watkins, Samuel, to Lucy Birely; Mar. 15.
Webb, George, to Nancy Calloway; Sept. 18.

1827

Catham, Edmond, to Betsy Longwutt (?); Aug. 16.
Clark, Hugh M., to Mary Smith; Mar. 5.
Dyer, William, to Polly McDaniel; Jan. 8.
Honnycut, Henry, to Dice Israel; May 30.
Luttrell, Robert H., to Harriet Monday; Dec. 27.
McCall, John, to Mary Ann Rentfro; Jan. 2.
McCormack, Samuel, to Merica Burnett; Mar. 14.
Simpson, William, to Susan Luttrell; April, 1827.

Webber (or Wibbed), William W.; Oct. 26.

1828

Allen, John, to Sophia Almander (?); Feb. 14.
Ayles, William Porter (?), to Lucinda Chambers; Dec. 17.
Brooks, Joseph A., to Margaret A. McMillan; Sept. 9.
Brown, Edward, to Joanna Hill; Jan. 25.
Campbell, John S., to Nancy Smith; Feb. 2.
Cobb, Melton, to Jane H. Dickey; Sept. 11.
Cox, Elisha, to Melinda Coker; April 1.
Craig, James W., to Rebecca Lowe; Feb. 9.
Hair, James, to Elizabeth J. McCampbell; Jan. 8.
Hood, Isaac, to Elizabeth Casteel; Jan. 31.
Larew, Ransom R., to Sallie Crawford; July 3.
Luttrell, Jackson, to Sally Fisher; Oct. 23.
McMillan, Andrew, to Mary Littleford (?); May 8.
Roddy, Moses, to Hetty Looney; Feb. 22.
Watt, Joseph, to Jane Luttrell; June 9.
Wood, Joseph, to Gilly Munday; Aug. 16.

1829

Bearden, John, to Caroline O. Dell; Sept. 14.
Bowen, John W., to Polly Carter; Mar. 30.
Bowman (?), Carter, to Frances Badgett; Dec. 15.
Campbell, John, to Elizabeth Armstrong; June 29.
Cash, Shadrack, to Elizabeth Shink (?); April 7.
Chapman, John, to Ellen Legg; Jan. 30.
Clibourn, John, to Sarah Lusby; July 23.
Conley, Richard, to Rosannah Stout; Jan. 26.
Crank, Jesse, to Eliza George; Jan. 30.
Hansard, William, to Rachel Graham; June 12.
Murphy, Alexander, to Margaret Johnston; June 20. Witness: Hugh A. Murphy.
Solomon, Ale—(?), to Maria W. Luttrell; Dec. 29.
Walker, Barkley, to Peggy Anne Douglas; Dec. 7.
West, John, to Jenny West; Sept. 10.
Williams, Benjamin, to Nancy Israel; Dec. 8 (?).

1830

Anderson, Samuel, to Elizabeth Kirby; April 1.
Anthony, John D., to Mary Ann Douty; Mar. 27.
Baker, John, to Ellen Graves; July 28.
Bishop, Lewis, to Susan Mynatt; Sept. 23.
Braden, William, to Julia Ann McHaffie; Sept. 20.
Fraker, Michael, to Winifred Gillam; Aug. 26. Witness: John Murphy.
Luttrell, Hugh, to Amelia Rutherford; Dec. 9.
Neathing, Samuel, to Mahala Coker; Dec. 21.
Wilkerson, John, to Tabitha Harris; Feb. 18.
Wilson, Francis, to Betsy, daughter of Matt Thompson; Oct. 16.

1831

Luttrell, Hugh, to Ruth Graves; April 10.
Luttrell, James, to Dicie Murphy; Nov. 28.
Mathis, James J., to Sarah R. Foust; June 1.
Mynatt, William, to Elizabeth Bishop; Aug. 23.
Thornton, James A., to Amelia A. McMillan; Aug. 19.
Willis, Hardin, to Maud Cooper; Jan. 25.

1832

Christy, William T., to Ellen T. Morgan; July 11.
Cummings, Uriah, to Tabitha Smith; Dec. 24.
Fink, George, to Nancy Smith; Dec. 24.
Heathcoat, Alan (?), to Isabelle McMillan; June 28.
Luttrell, Richard, to Jany Mynatt; Dec. 3.

Murphy, Richard S., to Mariah J. King; Jan. 11.
Paxton (?), James W., to Patsy Campbell; Nov. 27.
Williams Jeremiah, to Minnie Chiles; May 3.

1833

Arnold, Oliver, to Hannah Melton; Sept. 28.
Blackburn, Alexander, to Hariet Campbell; Dec. 12.
Chinn, Richard M., to Sarah Ann Cruse; Nov. 23.
Coffman, James, to Sarah Chumbley; May 23.
Crawford, Adam, to Cathrina Scott; Jan. 18.
Currier, James, to Sarah Bearden; July 14.
Goddard, John, to Martha Johnson (?); 1833.
Harbison, Joseph A. M., to Leona Crippin; April 13.
Like, Jacob, to Rebecca Pratt; May 25.
Miller, Thomas H., to Elizabeth Carr; June 16.
Trout, Isaac, to Nancy Luttrell; Sept. 17.
Willson, Thomas, to Nancy Bummitt; July 3.
Woods, John A., to Sally Kirkpatrick; Dec. 18.

1834

Cloud, Reuben, to Elizabeth Stout; July 15.
DeArmond, William, to Jane Campbell; Dec. 16.
Williams, Alexander, to Sally McClure; Mar. 27.

1835

Alexander, Josephus, to Cynthia Roberts; April 10.
Anderson, Alexander, to Lettie McCammon; Dec. 21.
Anderson, William J., to Mary Childress; Dec. 24.
Been, Andrew, to Cynthia Pedigo; Nov. 25.
Bird, Thomas, to Malvina Goins; April 11.
Bright, John, Jr., to Susan Pugh; Aug. 13.
Brown, William, to Mary Ann Lyle; Nov. 3.
Chenowith, George W., to Nancy Minton; Aug. 25.
Cork, Gunsbery (?), to Phebe Olinger; Mar. 11.
Covington, Daniel, to Marcissus Kitman (or Pitman?); May 7.
Cuthbert, W. B., to Lucy Carlos; Oct. 9.
Davidson, Samuel, to Elizabeth Russell; June 10.
Drake, John, to Fannie Danewood; Aug. 27.
Dunkin, Stephen, to Margaret Been; April 14.
Edington, Nicholas, to Patience Dwight; —— 12, 1835.
Ferguson, Andrew, to Catherine Zackery; Oct. 17.
Frazier, Samuel W., to Lydia Julian; Mar. 7.
Gamble, Robert, to Anne Younell (?); Aug. 18.
George, Samuel, to Eliza Harris; Sept. 21.
Goddard, Samuel M., to Harriet Lones; Aug. 20.
Graves, Henry, to Sarah Danewood; Sept. 12.
Griffin, Benjamin, to Sarah Culson; Nov. 17.
Hair, Larkin, to Cynthia Miller; Sept. 1.
Harben, Aaron, to Dicey Adkins; Aug. 30.
Hinsn, William, to Margaret Devault; Sept. 17.
Hood, Daniel R., to M. J. L. Swan; Feb. 20.
Johnson, Nathan, to Cynthia Miles; Jan. 28.
Johnson, Stephen, to Mary Ann Hillsman; Aug. 13.
Johnson, William D., to Eliza Hinton; Nov. 2.
Joroulman, R. D., to Maria W. Caldwell; Feb. 26.
King, John F., to Elizabeth Wells; Sept. 3.
Lucas, Robert, to Nancy Con; Sept. 12.
Luttrell, Hugh F., to Eliza Bounds; Mar. 7.
McCall, Duncan, to Mary Beckley; June 20.
McCollum, Daniel, to Nancy Ayers; Dec. 30.
McMillan, Jackson, to Avey Cates; Sept. 26.

McPhetridge, C. A., to Eliza Livy (or Lucy?); Mar. 11.
Major, John, to Mary Gault; June 27.
Manson, William, to Nancy Long; Dec. 9.
Maxwell, John, to Levina Moon; Dec. 10.
Meek, Adam C., to Sarah Douglas; Dec. 1.
Menton, Preston, to Elizabeth McCalish; Mar. 28.
Monday, Joshua E., to Sarah E. Little; Jan. 27.
Morley, William E., to Nancy Gamble; July 16.
Mourfield, Daniel A., to Rebecca Lucy; Aug. 10.
Mowrey, Jackson, to Sarah Coffin; Aug. 7.
Multeburger, William, to Sarah Forest; Jan. 6.
Murphy, Hugh I., to Rebecca Ford; Feb. 9.
Mynott, Joseph, to Nanie Lindell; Jan. 5.
Mynott, Rufus, to Elizabeth Hillsman; June 2.
Nance, Leonard C., to Nancy Tipton; Jan. 20.
Parham, Thomas Daniel, to Catherine Rudder; Sept. 24.
Perry, John, to Alvina Madris; Aug. 3.
Perry, Robert, to Margaret M. Campbell; Oct. 2.
Pickett, John, to Martha Howell; June 25.
Prior, Lewis, to Lucy Cruse; July 30.
Pryor, John, to Ann Trigg; July 7.
Ried, Jacob, to Elizabeth McCall; Dec. 9.
Robertson, Samuel, to Elizabeth Hanna; April 21.
Russell, John P., to Mary Ann Smith; May 14.
Sartin, Clark, to Sarah Anderson; May 7.
Scruggins, Josiah, to Martha Harvey; Sept. 28.
Sheretz, William, to Sarah Miller; Dec. 31.
Simpson, William, to Jane —— Davis; Feb. 3.
Singleton, John W., to Fanny Badgett; May 19.
Smith, John H., to Catherine Low; Mar. 23.
Smith, James H., to Susan Major; Oct. 1.
Smith, Jesse R., to Rebecca Bond; Dec. 30.
Smith, William H., to Martha L. Anderson; Dec. 30.
Walsh, Francis, to Elisa Calvert; Aug. 28.
Webster, Sanders, to Sarah Stanton; Sept. 5.

1836

Adair, Alexander, to Sarah A. McThompson; Feb. 1.
Ayres, Joseph, to Lottie Shelton; Aug. 23.
Bell, Robert, to Mary Wood; Jan. 12.
Blang, P. L., to Sarah A. Bell; Jan. 8.
Brittingham, James, to Louiza Bayer; Nov. 21.
Burkhart, Peter, to Anna Gillum; Aug. 10.
Byrd, Nathaniel, to Mary Lea; Nov. 7.
Clown, George, to Nancy McIntosh; Dec. 27.
Dunn, William, to Sarah Cummings; Jan. 5.
Eleson, Joseph, to Elizabeth Simpson; Mar. 12.
Eleson, John C., to Polly Wall; Aug. 29.
Elliott, William, to Lucinda K. Anderson; June 15.
Fisher, Emslay, to Sarah McNutt; Feb. 25.
Fitzgerald, George W., to Betsy Practon; April 29.
Fortner, David, to Melinda Barnes; Aug. 27.
Fisher, George, to Eliza Cable; July 22.
Foust, John, to Lucy Shinaberry; Aug. 31.
Frits, Isaac, to Franky Fortner; April 11.
Gillespie, Frank, to Elizabeth Simpson; July 11.
Haines, Clinton, to Margaret Henry; Feb. 1.
Hall, M. S., to Adalina McCampbell; Jan. 20.
Hansard, Calvin B., to Hannah Ailor; Sept. 8.

Harris, Samuel, to Elizabeth Mynatt; Nov. 25.
Hawkins, Abraham, to Anora Sherrodd; May 30.
Hood, Payton, to Catherine Davis; July 4.
Huffaker, George, to Nancy Lones; Dec. 10.
Hunter, Robert, to Jane Thompson; Mar. 26.
Jett, Jefferson, to Sarah Webb; May 28.
Johnson, Laborn, to Saroh Ann Brown; Jan. 30.
Johnson, Stephen, to Nancy Hillman; June 19.
Jones, John, to Matilda Holt; Feb. 16.
Jones, John, to Nancy Buckhart; Nov. 7.
King, Benjamin, to Priscilla Cates; Feb. 29.
Kirkpatrick, Robert, to Melinda Hartley; Nov. 4.
Lacey, Jacob, to Catherine Boyd; Aug. 4 (or 1863?).
Lamon, Henry, to Elizabeth Ann Kennedy; Aug. 12.
Lea, John, to Rebecca Coats; July 30.
Lithgo, William, to Malvinvilla Stouts; June 20.
Little, Adam, to Mary Campbell; Mar. 5.
Lones, George W., to Elizabeth Watkins; Sept. 28.
Lyles, Lewis, to Loy Rourk; Sept. 7.
McHaffie, John, to Sarah Sherwood; Mar. 16.
McTorff, John, to Mary Ann Price; Mar. 19.
Matlock, John, to Sarah Holoway; Dec. 24.
Monday, Charles, to Biddy Livly; Feb. 21.
Moon, Elija, to Mary Beadley; May 18.
Moon, Joshua, to Isabella Dunn; Mar. 24.
Moore, William C., to Eliza Eddington; Dec. 19.
Nelson, Charles W., to Cynthia Hilburt; Nov. 14.
Nelson, David, to Charlotte Lones; Jan. 30.
Nelson, Henry M., to Mahala Kidd; Nov. 16.
Nelson, James, to Mary Lones; Sept. 17.
Osborn, Holland, to Martha Nelson; Nov. 29.
Perry, James, to Elizabeth Hudson; Sept. 11.
Powell, Benjamin, to Patsy Buffaton; Sept. 10.
Rice, William N., to Margaret Rice; Oct. 5.
Riggins, Lloyd, to Ruth Ann Israel; Jan. 10.
Roberts, Charles, to Charlotte Mitchell; July 5.
Rudd, Joel, to Sarah Camp; April 6.
Rule, George, to Mary Ann Capps; Nov. 17.
Rutherford, Houston, to Maggie Mitebarger; Dec. 7.
Seguine, Roby, to Nancy Mourfield; Oct. 24.
Shannon, Wesley, to Susan Davis; Jan. 30.
Shelby, Elija, to Margaret Somdrumulk (?); Jan. 20.
Sherrod, Philip, to Elizabeth McMillan; Dec. 20.
Simpson, Joseph, to Margaret Coke; Jan. 4.
Smith, Andrew, to Sarah Richards; Jan. 8.
Smith, John, to Rutha Murphy; June 16.
Statten, Thomas, to Elizabeth Kennedy; Nov. 30.
Willis, Luke, to Patsy Ann Lisby; June 20.

1837

Anderson, Henry G., to Drusilla McCampbell; Mar. 6.
Atkins, Charles W., to Mary Henry; July 8.
Ault, Andrew J., to Mary Rutherford; Sept. 15.
Bean, John I., to Sarah Carroll; July 26.
Bowen, William R., to Matilda Sprinkly; Dec. 27.
Caldwell, Robert, to Elizabeth Clapp; Oct. 30.
Carson, William, to Ann McCallum; Jan. 15.
Chapman, Charles P., to Mary B. Thompson; Mar. 4.
Chastin, George, to Betsy Lisby; Mar. 10.
Chinn, Reuben, to Lottie Eddington; Feb. 16.

Clark, William, to Susan Clark; Jan. 3.
Con, Joseph, to Deliton Hay; Dec. 15.
Crawford, Barnes, to Amanda Lorin (?); Dec. 4.
Evans, Robert C., to Elizabeth Sherrod; Aug. 29.
Elledge, Isaac, to Jane Morrow; Sept. 15.
Fleming, Thomas W., to Catherine Walland; Dec. 27.
Ford, William, to Margaret Tarwater; Jan. 16.
Formalt, Adam, to Mary McAffrey; May 11.
Franklin, John, to Anne Luster; April 15.
Futril, Etheldred, to ——— Martin; Sept. 17, 1837 (?).
Futril, Etheldred, to Sarah Nicholmus; Sept. 18, 1837 (?).
Goldson, William, to Margaret Smith; April 14.
Graves, William, to Mahala Graves; Oct. 3.
Henderson, Andrew, to Mary Campbell; Aug. 26.
Henderson, William, to Mary Golden; Oct. 21.
Hinson, Bichard, to Evelina Cowan; Oct. 12.
Hoasu, Joseph, to Polly Ann Buchford; Nov. 11.
Hood, Lewas, to Nancy Robey; Oct. 7.
Howell, William S., to Minerva Cruze; Jan. 11.
Hufferman, Ellet, to Nancy Bund; Jan. 11.
Israel, Lewis, to Tilda Webb; Jan. 25.
Jackson, Hugh, to Huldah Wilson; Aug. 14.
Jacobs, J. B., to Patsy Ann Cozart; May 17.
Johnson, Frederick, to Dorothe Ledgerwood; Sept. 1837.
Karnes, Henry, to Charlotte McLain; Mar. 22.
Karnes, Henry, to Jamima Conners; Sept. 21.
Kidd, Edmund, to Melinda Griffin; Oct. 20.
King, John, to Polly Mills; Nov. 25.
King, Matthew, to Naunduch Ford (?); Oct. 17.
Koons, George, to Sallie Ezell; Feb. 25.
Lee, Duncan, to Olivia Nance; Feb. 13.
Like, Anderson, to Sophia Roberts; April 15.
Lisby, James, to Mahala Harris; Dec. 27.
Little, Christopher, to Mary L. McCampbell; Nov. 15.
Lones, George, to Rebecca Johnson; Dec. 7.
Lucy, Thomas, to Mary McDaniel; July 27.
McCann, Hugh, to Margaret Ann Price; Aug. 17.
McClure, Charles A., to Elizabeth L. Keith; April 25.
McKinley, Samuel, to Peggy Mitchell; April 11.
McLain, Joseph, to Margaret Anne Shocky; Mar. 17.
Mabring, John, to Betsy Smith; May 22.
Massey, Jacob, to Ann Lou Graves; July 26.
Medaris, Wilson F., to Evalina Young; Dec. 13.
Mikel, Wesley, to Margaret Gaddis; July 7.
Mitchell, Thomas, to Rosana Smith; April 6.
Mourfield, Wesley, to Margory Thompson; Oct. 27.
Murphy, Thomas, to Sarah Luttrell; Oct. 25.
Nance, James M., to Elizabeth Litow; Dec. 27.
Neal, William, to Elizabeth Smith; May 4.
Nicholson, Frederick, to Anne Barker; May, 1837.
Oliver, John, to Malinda B. Cobb; Oct. 12.
Palmer, William, to Jane Smith; Feb. 10.
Perham, William F., to Nellie Ann Taylor; Mar. 24.
Pearson, Thomas, to Elizabeth Hashbarger; June 22.
Perry, Allen, to Eliza Ann Con; Mar. 28.
Petty, William, to Agnes Con; Oct. 26.
Pilant, Robert, to Susannah Ruth; Dec. 2.
Pratt, David, to Sarah Mitchell; Nov. 2.

Pratt, James, to Rebecca Cunningham; Nov. 21.
Reed, Thomas, to Martha L. Cobb; Mar. 6.
Reynolds, Martin L., to Polly Nestor; April 17.
Robey, John C., to Lavinia Knave (?); Aug. 7.
Rose, John, to Eliza Wrinkle; May 25.
Roth, William, to Sallie Hanney; Feb. 9.
Scarburg, John, to Anna G. Hollingsworth; Mar. 7.
Shelby, Elija, to Amanda Lane (?); Aug. 21.
Shipes, Nelson, to Nancy Johnson; Nov. 28.
Smith, John N., to Sarah Nicholson; Jan. 4.
Smith, William, to Judith Lane; Nov. 30.
Thomas, Jacob, to Sarah Barnett; April 27.
Thompson, Lewis R., to Ann Maria Hickey; June 28.
Temple, Pleasant L., to Mary I. Galbraith; June 23.
Turner, Alexander, to Hannah Sterling; Sept. 9.
Watkins, James K., to Mary McMillan; Dec. 16.

MARRIAGE RECORDS OF DICKSON COUNTY, TENNESSEE, FROM 1838 TO 1849

Copied from the original book. Ex. means date and by whom executed; M. G. means minister of the Gospel; J. P. means Justice of the Peace.

1838

Jan. 9—Henry Southerland to Elizabeth McCollom.
Jan. 11—Benj'n Bowman to Wineford Walker.
  Ex. by David Gray, M. G.
Jan. 20—James Rop (Ross?) to Edy Wyatt.
  Ex. Jan. 21 by L. Russell.
Jan. 23—Thomas M. Caldwell to Elizabeth W. Bell.
  Ex. Jan. 25 by Jesse Edwards, M. G.
Jan. 27—Aaron J. Tarnish to Rebecca C. Dickson
  Ex. Feb. 1, by Jesse Edwards.
Jan. 29—John H. Wright to Mary Martin.
  Ex. Feb. 1, by L. Russell, J. P.
Jan. 30—Lincoln M. McCloudon to Carolina Reynolds.
  Ex. Jan. 30, by Tho. Imogin, J. P.
Feb. 1—William R. Raney to Susana C. Iamogin.
  Ex. Feb. 1, James Daniel, J. P.
Feb. 9—Richard Murphy to Mary E. Sewes.
  Ex. Feb. 11, James Daniel, J. P.
Feb. 12—A. D. Crochran to Nancey Bowen.
  Ex. Feb. 17, L. Russell, J. P.
Feb. 12—Wm. E. Ellis to Mary Ann Ellis.
Feb. 19—John R. Jones to Rebecca Russell.
  Ex. Feb. 22, K. Myatt, J. P.
Feb. 19—John Bone to Parmelia Darrow.
  Ex. Feb. 20, Wm. McMurry, J. P.
Feb. 24—Ervin T. Swift to Matilda Walker.
  Ex. March 12, M. W. Gray, M. G.
March 5—U. Burns to Margaret Foster.
March 8—A. J. Myatt to Emaline Oakley.
  Ex. March 8, L. Russell, J. P.
March 10—John W. Ragon to Lellicia Tycer.
  Ex. by John Eubank, J. P.
March 13—James Lee to Gerland Christer.
  Ex. March 15, John Larkins, J. P.
March 14—Howell A. Davidson to Sarah Davidson.
  Ex. Mar. 15, L. Russell, J. P.
March 29—Jerimiah Gray to Polly Ragon.
  Ex. April 1, K. Myatt, J. P.
April 14—Mark Harris to Martha Gentry.
  Ex. April 19, M. B. Stuart, J. P.

April 28—Daniel M. Jones to Mary Dunuegan.
Ex. Apr. , by Henry Govdnick, Esq.

June 2—John Turner to Sarah C. Parrish.
Ex. June 14, A. I. W. Turner, J. P.

June 4—Judge Jackson to Mary E. Rooker.
Ex. June 5, M. W. Gray, M. G.

June 7—Samuel Buggs to Lucy Sweaney.
Ex. June 8, Henry Govdnick, Esq.

June 16—Tryor H. Smith, to Tasolu D. Christian.
Ex. June 17, H. W. Turner, J. P.

June 20—Wm. Creach to Sarah White.
Ex. June, John Eubank, J. P.

June 25—John Austin to Penslope Creach.
Ex. June 27, M. B. Stuart, J. P.

June 26—Wm. A. Steele to Susanah Stone.
Ex. June 28, Willie Miller.

June 27—Richmond Brazzell to Any Evans.
Ex. June 28, Henry Govdnick, Esq.

July 3—Wm. C. Glen to Elizabeth Walker.
Ex.

July 17—William Russell to Faletha Gunn.
Ex. July 18, Henry Govdnick, Esq.

July 19—Jesse Eastes to Margaret Marsh.
Ex. July 19, Henry Govdnick, Esq.

July 19—Joseph Chrisman to Margaret Northern.
Ex. July 19, Jas. Daniel, J. P.

July 24—Bennett C. Duke to Martha Jones.
Ex. July 25, D. S. Ford, J. P.

August 30—Stanford Dunnegan to Alcy Dunnegan.
Ex. Aug. 30, L. Russell, J. P.

Sept. 10—Benjamin Sims to Kizziah C. Hunter.
Ex. Sept. 16, W. Hand, J. P.

Sept. 14—Elijah F. Pendergrass to Hannah Sears.
Ex. Sept. 16, William White, J. P.

Sept. 14—J. M. Miller to Catharine Douglas.

Sept. 18—Solomon George to Ferobe Holland.
Ex. Sept. 30, D. Gray, M. G.

Sept. 18—James Hunter to Sarah Jones.
Ex. Sept. 20, Henry J. Binkly, J. P.

Oct. 2—William N. Gunn to Mary Ann Puckett.
Ex. Oct. 8, by Henry Goodrick, J. P.

Oct. 9—Thomas I. Kelly to Eliza J. Hardwicke.
Ex. Oct. 9, Rev. James Marchall.

Oct. 9—Clayton T. Hall to Martha S. White.

Oct. 10—Thomas M. Reynolds to Durina Slayden.
Ex. Oct. 16, H. W. Turner, J. P.

Oct. 12—John M. Bibb to Caroline Johnson.
Ex. Oct. 11, Empson Bishop.

Oct. 15—Joshua Clarkston to Delila Hand.
Ex. June 16, D. S. Ford.

Oct. 18—Daniel Cathey to Mary Goodwin.
Ex. Oct. 18, Henry Goodrich, J. P.

Oct. 18—Francis E. Fowler to Jane Robinson.

Oct. 20—Joseph Nesbitt to Caroline Jane Burns.
Ex. by M. Berry, M. G.

Nov. 1—William J. Spradlin to Lucretia Blockley.

Nov. 3—William King to Rebecca Tatom.
Ex. Nov. 4, D. Womack, J. P.

Nov. 8—William D. Reynolds to Elizabeth Jane Walker.

Nov. 19—Hiram Morgan to Sally Stuart.
Ex. Nov. 20, Henry J. Binkly, J. P.

Nov. 21—Jesse Wall to Mary J. Hightower.
Ex. Nov. 29, William McMurry, J. P.

Nov. 23—A. C. Gunn to Louiza C. Tucker.
Ex. Nov. 25, John Larkins, J. P.

Nov. 25—Albert N. Joslin to

Dec. 24—Thomas Petty to Rebecca Ann Adcock.
Ex. by David Gray, M. G.

Dec. 1—John W. Hudson to Mary Tilly.

Dec. 24—Jesse Coleman to Pricilla L. Perry.
Ex. Dec. 24, L. Russell, J. P.

Dec. 28—William Fleet to Sally Edwards.
Ex. Dec. 28, Jas. Daniel, J. P.

Dec. 28—Washington Isby to Margaret Smith.
Ex. M. Berry, M. G.

1839

Jan. 2—Benjamin F. McCaslin to Luvena Tidwell.
Ex. Jan. 3, 1839, William White, J. P.

Jan. 4—Lewis Evans to Rachael Brazzell.

Jan. 8—Thomas H. Hinson to Catherine Ellis.

Jan. 31—Washington Winns to Matilda Vineyard.

Feb. 2—William Adkinson to Mary Ann Jane Mills.

Feb. 11—Jacob Petty to Nancy Bibb.

Feb. 16—David Record to Elizabeth Sanderson.
Ex. Feb. 21, M. B. Stuart, J. P.

Feb. 23—Gilbert Marsh to Dolly Cathey.

March 8—Joseph S. Slayden to Julia Ann Shelton.
Ex. Apr. 11, by William McMurry.

March 12—John Holland to Mary Myatt.
Ex. March 14, K. Myatt, J. P.

March 16—Robert S. Nesbitt to Martha E. Ragon.
Ex. by M. Berry, M. G.

March 19—Lorenso Burpo to Arena Lewis.
Ex. H. W. Turner, J. P.

March 20—Benjamin R. Craig to Mary G. Lewis.
Ex. H. W. Turner, J. P.

March 30—Madison Dunnegan to Manervia Dodson.
Ex. March 30, L. Russell, J. P.

May 2—James McDurmit to Olif Harris.
Ex. Mary 2, D. S. Ford, J. P.

May 23—Edward McCormack to Mariah Link.
Ex. May 23, John Eubank, J. P.

June 8—John Welch to Elizabeth Luther.
Ex. June 9, John McCaslin, J. P.

June 21—William Johnson to Susan Richardson.
Ex. June 23, Rev. Jas. T. Morris.

July 5—Henry White to Martha Parker.
Ex. July 11, D. S. Ford, J. P.

July 10—Lewis D. Collins to Sally Ann Hickerson.
Ex. July 14, John Eubank, J. P.

July 17—Jackson Brazzell to Sarah Tatom.

July 17—Fanning Yates to Elizabeth Murrell.
Ex. July 25, K. Myatt.

July 31—Job P. Doty to Sarah R. Ford.
Ex. Aug. 4, W. Hand, J. P.

Aug. 9—John H. Jones to Finett B. Jabes.
Ex. Aug. 22, I. C. Blankenship.

Aug. 15—Feliso Robertson to Sarah Hunter.
Ex. Aug. 16, H. J. Binkly, J. P.

Aug. 18—Frank Mulhemis to Susan Oliver.

Aug. 19—John C. West to Lueslia Blockly.

Aug. 21—G. G. Paschall to Mary Ann Toler.
Ex. Aug 25, John Eubank, J. P.

Aug. 24—Absalom Massie to Milberry Matlock.

Aug. 27—William Lee to Syntha Jordan.
Ex. H. W. Turner, J. P.

Sept. 10—Joseph Price to Elizabeth Rose.
Ex. Sept. 12, John McCaslin, J. P.

Sept. 19—Miles Long to Sophia Heard.

Sept. 28—Moses Tidwell to Nancy McCaslin.
Ex. D. Gray.

Sept. 28—B. F. Larkins to Emily I. Bowen.

Sept. 28—John G. Hill to Caroline Scott.
Ex. Oct. 3, James Daniel, J. P.

Sept. 29—James M. Albright to Margaret S. Halliburton.
Ex. Sept. 29, Thos. Janiagin, J. P.

Oct. 1—George L. Smith to Mary Larkins.

Oct. 4—George Russell to Lucinda Mathews.

Oct. 5—James Gould to Martha W. Farrar.
Ex. Oct. 6, H. J. Binkly, J. P.

Oct. 11—Willie I. Gunter to Martha Jones.
Ex. Oct. 11, Cornelius Grimes, J. P.

Oct. 19—James Bagett to Nancy Davis.
Ex. Oct. 21, 1840, Benjamin Darrow.

Oct. 21—George Russell to Lucinda Mathews.
Ex. Oct. 21, Cornelius Grimes, J. P.

Oct. 23—Henry Hall to Sarah Ferrell.
Ex. Oct. 23, H. W. Joslin, M. G.

Nov. 9—Burgess Wall to Nancy Harvey.
Ex. May, 1840, Jordan Moore, M. G.

Nov. 14—John L. Martin to Minerva J. Hobbs.

Nov. 21—Drury Seals to Susan Oliver.
Ex. Nov. 21, John Larkins, J. P.

Dec. 5—John Corlew to Susan Leech

Dec. 5—James Brown to Sellers.
Ex. Dec. 5, Wm. White, J. P.

Dec. 7—Isaac Hunter to Nancy Dane.
Ex. Dec. 10, Joseph Morris, J. P.

Dec. 9—James C. Balthrope to Mary Russell.
Ex. Dec. 17, Jas. Daniel, J. P.

Dec. 24—Joseph Larkins to Emily Martin.

Dec. 28—John Burgess to Phebee Watkins.
Ex. W. B. Dotson, J. P., Dec. 29.

1840

Jan. 2—Thomas Gilbert to Elizabeth D. Collier.

Jan. 11—James M. Baker to Caroline Goodrich.
Ex. Feb. 14, Thomas Janiagin, J. P.

Jan. 11—William Phillips to Elender Hogins.
Ex. D. Gray.

Jan. 11—Edward M. Rogers to Lucy L. Halliburton.
Ex. by H. W. Turner, J. P.

Jan. 14—Kinderick Myatt to Sinthy Loftis.

Jan. 15—Robert Leftrick to Emeline Arnold.

Jan. 20—Thomas Kames to Martha Hall.

Jan. 24—William M. Mitchell to Surrena Speight.

Jan. 29—James H. O'Kelly to Louisa Myatt.
Ex. Jan. 30, L. Russell, J. P.

Feb. 7—George Parnell to Harriet Price.
Ex. Feb. 7, John McCaslin, J. P.

Feb. 8—John W. Green to Nancy Rye.
Ex. Feb. 16, Thomas Janiagin, J. P.

Feb. 25—Wesley Jackson to Parthenia Cook.
Ex. by John Eubank.

March 2—George Dunnevin to Anna Waldin.
Ex. March 3.

March 14—John M. Biter to Jennette March.
Ex. by John Eubank, J. P.

March 16—John A. Weakly to Anna Wall.
Ex. March 19, by William Hand, J. P.

March 19—James A. Nesbitt to Nancy Long.
Ex. by John Eubank.

March 26—John E. Ellis to Harriet Henson.
Ex. March 31, Willie Miller, J. P.

April 4—James D. Hudson to Winnefred M. Lane.
Ex. by M. Berry, M. G.

March 31—Judge W. Crocket to Polly Wall.
Ex. April 2, W. Hand, J. P.

April 2—Thomas Murphy to Sarah Barter.
Ex. April 3, John Eubank.

April 18—John Rye to Mary Jane Davidson.
Ex. April 20, Reuben Chadion.

April 20—Henry M. Hutton to Anna Drummonds.

April 20—Joseph Done to Caroline E. F. Fowler.

April 25—Hamilton Parks to Rebecca Etherley.

May 16—John G. Crumpler to Elizabeth Caldwell.
May 21—Cullin Price to Pemelia Ann Reece.
Ex. May 21, John McCaslin, J. P.
May 27—Martin H. Cobbler to Mary Ann Smith.
Ex. May 28, Jesse Edwards, M. G.

June 20—Willis Jackson to Mary Hightower.
Ex. by John Eubank.

June 22—Benjamin Hay to Huldy Tidwell.
Ex. June 24, E. Bishop.

June 24—Minor Bibb to Lydia Pryor.
Ex. June 25, M. B. Stuart, J. P.

July 4—Andrew Price to Dorothy Fletcher.
Ex. July 5, 1841, John McCaslin, J. P.

July 15—Benajah Gentry to Jane Gentry.
Ex. July 19, M. B. Stuart, J. P.

July 23—James C. Hambrick to Mary Fussell.
July 27—James Tatom to Anne Tatom.
Ex. July 30, Jas. C. Pullen, J. P.

July 30—Vernon F. Bibb to Elizabeth Bibb.
Ex. July 30, Empson Bishop.

Aug. 5—Drury Chappell to Rebecca Henry.
Ex. Aug. 5, William White, J. P.

Aug. 5—William Bell to Elizabeth Grimes.
Ex. Aug. 6, R. Chadion.

Aug. 5—Robert S. B. Gunn to Dolly Gunn.
Ex. Aug. 11, Jas. C. Pullen, J. P.

Aug. 5—William Cane to Mary James.
Ex. Aug. 6, W. Hand, J. P.

Aug. 31—Wesley Williams to Nancy Dickson.
Ex. Sept. 1, Rev. Benjamin Rawls.

Sept. 3—Walter C. Gentry to Nancy Gentry.
Ex. Sept. 3, Marcus B. Stuart, J. P.

Sept. 17—Jesse Walton to Elizabeth Hagwood.
Ex. Sept. 8, William Hand, J. P.

Sept. 28—John H. Shelton to Sophia Patterson.
Oct. 6—James W. Hunter to Elizabeth Anne Rooker.
Oct. 18—Jarrett N. Langford to Lytha Sanders.
Ex. Oct. 18, 1840.

Oct. 14—Joseph Fulfer to Amanda Durin.
Oct. 20—Henderson Prokter to Charlotte Spicer.
Ex. Oct. 21, C. Grymes, J. P.

Oct. 20—George B. Lewis to Sarah M. Fly.
Ex. Oct. 29, James Daniel, J. P.

Oct. 29—Benjamin Rye to Mary Anne Valentine.
Ex. Oct. 29, James Daniel, J. P.

Oct. 31—Elijah Davidson to Mary Hudson.
Ex. Oct. 1, K. Myatt, J. P.

Nov. 7—Epps Jackson to Sarah M. Eleazer.
Ex. David Gray, M. G., Nov. 8.

Nov. 17—Robert L. Dunaway to Eveline Allen.
Nov. 21—Allen Halliburton to Susan Rainey.
Dec. 5—Manoah Parrott to Cassander Nicholds.
Ex. Dec. 10, Jas. Daniel, J. P.

Dec. 14—Joseph F. White to Jane Nalls.
Ex. Dec. 15, Panon Bishop.

Dec. 21—John James to Phoebe Price.
Ex. Dec. 22, J. Binkly, J. P.

Dec. 21—Mark Garton to Jensey Tidwell.
Ex. Dec. 22, M. B. Stuart, J. P.
Dec. 22—Martin Cathey to Louisa Creech.
Ex. Dec. 23, L. Russell, J. P.

Dec. 24—Nepolian F. Wilkins to Mary Anne Steele.
Ex. by John Eubank, J. P.

1841

Jan. 1—William Luke to Emeline Hickerson.
Ex. by John Eubank, J. P.

Jan. 9—William M. England to Luviea Higgenbotthum.
Ex. by John Eubank, J. P.

Jan. 10—James Daughtery to Luvina White.

Jan. 11—Albert Hunter to Sarah Crews.
Ex. Jan. 14, William Hand, J. P.

Jan. 19—Owen Monroe to Caroline Sweeny.
Ex. Jan. 20, H. J. Binkly, J. P.

Jan. 30—William Spears to Menerva Hudson.
Ex. Jan. 31, K. Myatt, J. P.

Feb. 2—Thomas Wiseman to Stacy Bishop.
Ex. Feb. 4, Jas. Daniel, J. P.

Feb. 2—David W. Adcock to Martha Anne Crow.
Ex. Feb. 3, J. Pendergrass, J. P.

Feb. 4—Robert Layne to Sarah Paschall.

Feb. 9—Elisha L. Lloyd to Angeline Bown.
Ex. Feb. 14, 1841.

Feb. 11—William B. Rawles to Mary T. Raworph.

Feb. 15—George W. Bruce to Lydia Dunnegan.
Ex. Feb. 16, 1841.

Feb. 17—James M. Davidson to Sarah Jane Luther.
Ex. Feb. 28, K. Myatt, J. P.

Feb. 18—Albert G. Sweeny to Kisiah Murrell.
Ex. Feb. 19, G. W. Tatom, J. P.

March 1—Thomas Steele to Mary Stone.

March 11—Blount Dunnegan to Parthena Dunnegan.
Ex. March 11, L. Russell, J. P.

March 16—Anthony G. Lewis to Nancy Hawkins.
Ex. March 18, W. R. Hicks, J. P.

March 17—William Hand to Nancy Hunter.
Ex. March 18, William Garrett, J. P.

March 20—Thomas Smith to Malinda Matlock.
Ex. by John Eubank, J. P.

March 22—James McEnnerie to Dicy Crumpler.
Ex. March 23, George F. Raworth, J. P.

March 26—James Jones to Elizabeth Brown.

March 26—James N. Hunter to Elizabeth Rooker.
Ex. April 4, George F. Raworth, J. P.

April 1—Moses Sears to Lucretia Pendegrass.
Ex. April 3, J. Pendergrass, J. P.

April 13—Jerry Miah Bateman to Nancy Morris.
Ex. April 13, I. Hill, J. P.

April 14—Edward S. Young to Sarah A. Irby.
Ex. John Eubank, J. P.

April 16—David Wizenhunt to Elizabeth Brown.
Ex. April, 1841, George F. Raworth, J. P.

April 21—Henry Cole to Frances Johnson.

April 29—Andrew Monk to Cynthie Haley.
Ex. April 29, L. Russell, J. P.

May 4—Henry Whizenhunt to Elizabeth Barnett.
Ex. May 16, George F. Raworth, J. P.

May 18—John Anderson to Polly Hagewood.
Ex. May 18, William Garrett, J. P.

June 5—Memory England to Malinda Hedge.
Ex. June 6, Joel Erranton, J. P.

June 13—William McCoin to Anna Jones.
Ex. June 14, Jas. Daniel, J. P.

June 16—Elida Burns to Lucy Cogh.
Ex. June 17, Benjamin Darrow.

July 27—Joshua Y. Knight to Elizabeth Anne Parish.
Ex. July 29, W. R. Hicks, J. P.

July 27—George Scott to Elizabeth Jane Richardson.
Ex. July 28, H. J. Binkly, J. P.

Aug. 3—Thomas M. Wheeler to Louiza Tycer.

Aug. 17—John C. Ashworth to Nancy Cornett.
Ex. Aug. 17, John Eubank, J. P.

Aug. 23—Washington G. L. Buttrey to Mary Lampley.
Ex. Aug. 26, I. Hill, J. P.

Aug. 24—Alexander Southerland to Julia Anne Wilkins.
Ex. Aug. 24, John Eubank, J. P.

Aug. 30—Thomas Jones to Amanda M. Carter.
Ex. Sept. 9, Marcus B. Stuart, J. P.

Aug. 31—Eli Ashworth to Cyrena Hickerson.
Ex. Aug. 31, John Eubank, J. P.

Sept. 9—Ramsey Linsey to Elizabeth Gafford.
Ex. Sept. 12, William Garrett, J. P.

Oct. 2—John D. Halliburton to Julia Anne Parrott.
Ex. Oct. 3, James Daniel, J. P.

Oct. 4—John White to Eliza R. Jackson.
Ex. Oct. 5, Geo. F. Raworth, J. P.

Oct. 11—Oliver McMenn to Elizabeth Redden.
License returned by Oliver McMenn and states that the same was not executed, that the girl backed out from the engagement June 22, 1842.

Oct. 15—James Davidson to Kisiah Davis.
Ex. Oct. 21, M. B. Stuart, J. P.

Oct. 21—James Hudgins to Jane Nesbitt.
Ex. Oct. 21, William Garrett, J. P.

Oct. 25—Henry B. H. Williams to Jane E. Coleman.
Ex. by M. Berry, M. G.

Oct. 28—John Marsh to Lucy Goodwin.
Ex. Oct. 28, G. W. Tatom, J. P.

Oct. 30—Alford Dillihay to Mary Newman.
Ex. Nov. 5, James Daniel, J. P.

Nov. 3—James W. Richardson to Nancy Powers.
Ex. Nov. 4, G. W. Tatom, J. P.

Nov. 6—Neil W. Byrne to Martha Anne Norman.
Ex. Nov. 7, James Daniel, J. P.

Nov. 24—Tolbert Slayden to Louiza Shelton.

Nov. 24—Harvey Nesbitt to Mary V. Hall.

Dec. 2—William Goodwin to Arena Puckett.
Ex. Oct. 2, G. W. Tatom, J. P.

Dec. 4—Calvin S. Batson to Eveline Ellis.
Ex. Dec. 9, Rev. William Guthrie.

Dec. 15—Ebenezar Larkins to Elizabeth A. Dickson.
Ex. Dec. 16, W. R. Hicks, J. P.

Dec. 15—James R. Kemble to Rebecca C. Tidwell.
Ex. Dec. 16, K. Myatt, J. P.

Dec. 15—Robert H. Weakley to Elizabeth Weakley.

Dec. 16—J. W. Green to Mary E. Ragan.
Ex. Dec. 24, W. R. Hicks, J. P.

1842

Jan. 12—James McNeely to Cassander Rye.

Jan. 15—Simpson A. Norman to Elizabeth Vanhook.
Ex. Jan. 20, Jas. Daniel, J. P.

Jan. 22—Andrew J. Griffin to Anna Welker.
Ex. Jan. 23, Jordan Moore.

Jan. 27—N. M. Hall to Martha J. Cunningham.
Ex. Jan. 27, M. B. Stuart, J. P.

Feb. 1—Joseph Brown to Nancy Southerland.
Ex. Feb. 1, W. Hand, J. P.

Feb. 4—Richard Fowler to Victoria Vanhook.
Ex. Feb. 7, James Daniel, J. P.

Feb. 11—Allen Brazzell to Nancy Baker.
Ex. Feb. 13, James W. Lloyd, J. P.

Feb. 17—Thomas Shelton to Eliza T. Bumpass.
Ex. Feb. 17, G. W. Tatom, J. P.

Feb. 17—John A. Baker to Eliza Walker.
Ex. February, 1842, by John Eubank, J. P.

Feb. 18—Robert T. Williams to Martha T. Kephart.
Ex. Feb. 24, Caleb Rooker, L. D.

Feb. 18—Warren Hale to Rhoda Hickerson.
Ex. George W. Tatom, J. P.

Feb. 21—John Forsythe to Eliza Fane.
Ex. Feb. 25, W. Hand, J. P.

Feb. 23—Sharp Dunnegan to Jane Dunnegan.
Ex. Feb. 23, G. W. Tatom.

Feb. 26—William Simpson to Emeline Speight.

March 26—Robert H. Weakley to Elizabeth Weakley.
Ex. April 6, W. Hand, J. P.

March 27—Joab Hardin to Menerva J. Leech.
Ex. last of March or first of April, George Eubank.

April 11—William M. Ellis to George Anne West.
Ex. April 12, Jesse Edwards, M. G.

April 22—A. A. C. Rogers to Eliza Anne Brown.
Ex. May 1, John McNobs, M. G.

May 7—James T. White to Nancy F. Richardson.
Ex. May 8, H. J. Binkly, J. P.

May 21—Mathew L. Gentry to Eliza Gentry.
June 4—Duvean L. Matlock to M. Phipps.
June 10—Daniel S. Mosley to Frances Holland.
Ex. June 12, John A. Petty, J. P.

July 21—James Johnston to Sarah Carr.
Ex. July 21, John Brown, J. P.

Aug. 6—William Auglin to Susannah Hay.
Aug. 24—James Ethridge to Margaret McLain.
Sept. 14—David Weynick to Malinda Dickson.
Ex. Sept. 14, James G. Hinson, J. P.

Sept. 23—John W. Coleman to Elizabeth Gray.
Ex. Sept. 23, I. C. Pullen, J. P.

Sept. 29—Henry A. Bibb to Milberry Masseye.
Ex. Sept. 29, John Eubank, J. P.

Oct. 12—James M. Swift to Rebecca McMurry.
Ex. Oct. 13, J. Moore.

Oct. 13—John Miller to Sarah Jones.
Ex. Oct. 13, John Brown, J. P.

Oct. 19—William B. Simmons to Rebecca M. Clelland.
Ex.

Oct. 26—Benjamin Link to Martha Caroline Gafford.
Ex. Oct. 27, William Garret, J. P.

Oct. 27—Elisha Bell to Sarah E. Collier.
Ex. Oct. 27, Rev. Uriah Smith.

Nov. 17—Andrew Jackson Brin to Mary Jane Boyd.
Ex. Nov. 22, James C. Hinson, J. P.

Nov. 17—William H. Thompson to Mary Anne Oliver.
Ex.

Nov. 22—John Crow to Mary Tidwell.
Ex. Nov. 22, John Brown, J. P.

Nov. 27—John M. Boyd to Nancy Anne Clay.
Ex. Nov. 29, John McCaslin, J. P.

Dec. 10—William M. Larkins to Elizabeth Sanders.
Ex. Dec. 11, Allen Nesbitt, J. P.

Dec. 15—Hudson I. Richardson to Rena Hicks.
Ex. Dec. 15, John Eubank, J. P.

Dec. 15—William D. Bateman to Parthenia H. Blunt.
Ex. Dec. 15, James Daniel, J. P.

Dec. 22—Johnie M. Shelton to Martha Lewis.
Ex. Dec. 20, Ruben Chadowen.

Dec. 23—Henry D. Jones to Sarah M. Paschall.
Ex. Dec. 25, William Garrett, J. P.

Dec. 26—Albert G. Shelton to Rachel Lewis.
Ex. Jan. 3, 1843.

Dec. 24—George Coon to Nancy Wallace.
Ex. Dec. 25, 1842.

Dec. 29—George W. Oakley to Artierrecon Dicks.
Ex. Dec. 29, John Eubank, J. P.

Dec. 29—William Good to Edney Durard.
Dec. 31—William O'Kelly to Elizabeth Pinegar.
Ex. Jan. 1, 1843, James Lloyd, J. P.

1843

Jan. 4—Jesse Newman to Ellinor Bishop.
Ex. Jan. 7, James G. Hudson, J. P.

Jan. 5—Robert Halliburton to Lucretia Tilly.
Ex. Jan. 5, 1843.

Jan. 5—Randell Mills to Louisa Moore.
Ex. June 10, 1843, W. H. Johnson.

Jan. 17—Ellington Carroll to Sarah E. Danile.
Ex. Jan. 28, W. Hand, J. P.

Jan. 30—Gafford Lovell to Elizabeth Petty.
Ex. Feb. 6, John A. Petty, J. P.

Feb. 3—Martin Pinegar to Eliza Lee.
Ex. Feb. 5, John A. Petty, J. P.

Feb. 4—Richard Murphy to Araminta Burgess.
Ex. Feb. 7, James Daniel, J. P.

Feb. 8—Benjamin Stoves to Mary Jane Napier.

Feb. 15—Robert Dillihay to Sarah Anne Self.
Ex. Feb. 16, James Daniel, J. P.

Feb. 18—Richard Hartzog to Susanah C. Vanlandingham.
Ex. Feb. 19, I. Porter, J. P.

March 3—Stanford Dunnegan to Caroline Lloyd.
Ex. March 5, L. Russell, J. P.

March 4—J. D. Woodward to Mary Anne Kephart.
Ex. March 5, Caleb Rooker, L. D.

March 12—John Mickle to Sarah C. Smith.
Ex. March 12, John Eubank, J. P.

March 13—Mathew Morgan to Eliza Anne Harris.
Ex. March 15, William Hand, J. P.

March 14—John Matlock to Mary A. Mallory.
Ex. March 14, John Eubank, J. P.

March 14—Albert G. Wilson to Sarah S. Hogan.
Ex. March 16, L. Russell, J. P.

March 18—Britton Harris to Mary Mitchell.
Ex. March 27, H. J. Binkly, J. P.

James Blackwell to Lucy Wallace.
Ex. March 28, William Adkins.

April 18—Hugh McClerkin to Isabella McMahan.
Ex. April 18, James Daniel, J. P.

April 20—Joseph Shelton to Susan Rice.
Ex. April 20, R. P. Halliburton, J. P.

April 22—James E. England to Nancy Willy.
Ex. April 23, A. Nesbitt, J. P.

April 28—John Castleman to Lurana Lankford.
Ex. April 30, J. Porter, J. P.

June 5—Hugh Deprest to Mary Amanda Vanlandingham.
Ex. June 8, J. Porter, J. P.

June 7—Yen Lewis to Didamy Watson.
Ex. June 7, Jas. Daniel, J. P.

June 10—William Watson to Elizabeth Gorin.

June 15—Agustine Reeves to Aurena Spicer.
Ex. June 15, Samuel Tate, J. P.

Aug. 4—Andrew I. Waynick to Mary Hill.
Ex. Aug. 23, R. P. Halliburton, J. P.

Aug. 24—Samuel Heath to Julia Anne McCormack.
Ex. Aug. 24, Allen Nesbitt, J. P.

Samuel Whitsitt to Henrietta E. Trotter.
Executed.

Eamuel Boughter to Sarah M. West.
Ex., Jesse Edwards, Min.

Moses A. Sutton to Emeline M. Hall.
Ex. Sept. 5, John Eubank, J. P.

Samuel Hedge to Sarah Gunn.
Ex. Sept. 5, Samuel Tate, J. P.

John T. Lampley to Harriett Lankford.
Ex. Sept., 1843, J. Porter, J. P.

Sept. 20—Marvell M. Petty to Nancy Castleman.
Ex. Sept. 21, John Brown, J. P.

Sept. 21—Thomas N. Williams to Mary A. Norman.
Ex. Sept. 21, Burham A. Price.

Oct. 17—Wilie B. Joslin to Martha Mitchell.
Ex. Oct. 19, H. Parks.

Oct. 28—Franklin Robertson to Frances M. Dalton.

Nov. 8—W. R. Taylor to Charlotty Flannery.
Ex. Nov. 9, J. W. Hedge, J. P.

Nov. 15—Edward Smith to Anne Miscon.
Ex. Nov. 18, Jas. Daniel, J. P.

Nov. 15—John McLole to Mary Anne Williams.
Ex. Nov. 16, B. Darrow, M. C.

Nov. 18—Richard A. Estes to Caroline Tatom.
Ex. Nov. 19, James W. Lloyd, J. P.

Dec. 2—William Caldwell to Martha Joslin.

Dec. 5—Isaac Giffin to Mary I. Hambrick.
Ex. Dec. 7, Allen Nesbitt, J. P.

Dec. 17—George Turner to Edna Lewis.
Ex. Dec. 17, James G. Hinson, J. P.

Dec. 19—Alford Elliott to Tennessee Smith.
Ex. Dec. 19, Allen Nesbitt, J. P.

Dec. 20—Felix Badger to Amanda Eleazer.
Ex. Dec., 1843, E. Hanks, M. G.

Dec. 25—Henry Coleman to Frances Burns.
Ex Dec. 26, M. Berry, M. G.

Dec. 26—Robert T. Clay to Sarah Edwards.

Dec. 30—John Hayes to Susan McCaslin.
Ex. Dec. 31, John Brown, J. P.

1844

Jan. 4—Thomas Patterson to Delila Holly.
Ex. Jan. 4, James G. Hinson, J. P.

Jan. 5—William H. Hendricks to Lucinda Tilly.
Ex. Jan. 5, Thomas Palmer, J. P.

Jan. 6—John B. Evans to Letticia B. Christian.
Ex. Jan. 6, Thomas Palmer, J. P.

Jan. 16—Mansel Tidwell to Nancy White.
Ex. Jan. 17, John Brown, J. P.

Jan. 18—Benjamin Darrow to Mary Murphy.
Ex. Jan. 21, William Adkins, J. P.

Jan. 19—Waid Hampton to Lucinda Baily.
Ex. Jan. 21, William Hand, J. P.

Jan. 25—Aaron Pinson to Elizabeth Mitchell.

Feb. 17—Ezekeel N. Parrish to Elizabeth Self.
Ex. Feb. 18, James G. Hinson, J. P.

Feb. 22—John S. Whitsitt to Rizbah Waynick.
Ex. Feb. 23, R. P. Halliburton, J. P.

Feb. 22—Bartlet A. O'Kelly to Eliza A. Willy.
Ex. Feb. 12, L. Russell, J. P.

Feb. 29—F. F. V. Schmittoq to Lavina C. Crews.
Ex. Feb. 29, William Adkins, J. P.

March 12—Isaac Hill to Susan Newman.

March 14—Thomas Hammons to Lavena Anderson.
Ex. March 15, John Brown, J. P.

March 16—Mathew L. Gentry to Nancy I. Richardson.

March 19—Silas Thompson to Anne Gentry.
Ex. March. 20, John Brown, J. P.

March 24—Henry Newman to Eliza Parrish.
Ex. March 24, James Daniel, J. P.

April 2—R. N. Q. Hunt to Mary Jane Jackson.
Ex. by John Eubank, J. P.

April 6—W. H. Horner to Susan Tatom.
Ex. April 7, James Thedford, J. P.

April 27—Benjamin N. Tatom to Sarah Dotson.
Ex. April 28, Silas Murry, J. P.

April 30—Thomas M. Richardson to Mary H. Williams.

April 18—Elijah Marsh to Polly Harris.
Ex. April 18, J. C. Angelin, J. P.

June 18—Solmon Ridings to Sarah Homer.
Ex. June 20, L. Russell, J. P.

June 25—James Reynolds to Lucy R. Hayes.
Ex. June 25, Thomas Palmer, J. P.

June 26—Paul Duvauh to Martha Durard.
Ex. June 27, Allen Nesbitt, J. P.

June 29—Robert Dolton to Mary A. Cook.

July 1—Portan Pruit to Martha Mosley.
Ex. Aug. 3, J. C. Anglin, J. P.

July 4—Monroe G. Dotson to Sarah E. Brewer.
Ex. July 4, A. Nesbitt, J. P.

July 13—Jesse H. Bryan to Sarah Myatt.
Ex. July 17, David Gray, M. G.

July 16—George W. Scott to Elizabeth Speight.
Ex. July 17, H. J. Binkly, J. P.

July 18—Joseph H. Chester to Mary White.
Ex. July 19, John Brown, J. P.

July 23—James W. Cook to Cymphy A. Walker.
Ex. J. Eubank, J. P.

July 30—A. B. J. Turner to Nancy M. Shelton.

Aug. 16—Samuel Cathy to Lucinda Edwards.

Aug. 21—Henry Bullion to Sarah Hambrick.
Ex. Aug. 22, Samuel Tate, J. P.

Aug. 29—Thomas Stark to Rebecca Grymes.
Ex. Aug. 29, William Garrett, J. P.

Sept. 3—Jesse G. Holland to Frances C. Hudson.
Ex. Sept. 8, David Gray, M. G.

Sept. 8 — Wiley Davis to Nancy Crow.
Ex. Sept. 9, Empson Bishop, M. G.

Sept. 12—James Blackwell to Cintha Bleadsoe.
Ex. Sept. 12, Benjamin Darrow, M. G.

Oct. 7—Ceborn Puckett to Nancy Goodwin.
Ex. Oct. 7, Samuel Tate, magistrate return gives Nancy Robbs instead of Goodwin, name on license.

Oct. 21—Moses H. Jones to Sarah E. James.
Ex. Oct. 21, Thomas Payne, J. P.

Nov. 4—William C. Lampley to Elizabeth White.
Ex. Nov. 7, J. Porter, J. P.

Nov. 7—William H. Wells to Avery Haley.
Ex. Nov., 1844, David Gray, M. G.

Nov. 14—Hugh McClerkin to Susan Self.
Ex. by James Daniel, J. P.

Nov. 18—William Carroll to Caphorme Williams.
Ex. Nov. 19, C. Rooker, L. E. M. E. Church.

Nov. 18—Jesse Adkock to Dolly M. Adcock.
Ex., David Gray, M. G.

Nov. 19—Edward T. Southerland to Helena Anne Taschal.
Ex. Nov. 19, William Garrett, J. P.

Nov. 21—James G. Jackson to Susan Eleazer.
Ex. Nov. 21, J. C. Pullen, J. P.

Nov. 26—James B. Stokes to Elizabeth J. Eavans.
Ex. Nov. 28, H. W. Turner, M. G.

Nov. 27—A. F. Nesbitt to Nancy Anne Dillihay.
Ex. Nov. 28, James Daniel, J. P.

Dec. 3—John M. Wiley to Marthena Frasher.
Ex. Dec. 5, David Gray, M. G.

Dec. 14—David G. Dotson to Elizabeth Hudson.
Ex. Dec. 18, Silas Murry, J. P.

Dec. 17—William Marsh to Nancy Sullivan.

Dec. 17—Thomas Brown to Jane Gentry.
Ex. Dec. 19, J. Porter, J. P.

1845

Jan. 5—William Bell to Sarah B. Bell.
Ex. Jan. 5, Jess Edwards, M. G.

Jan. 8—William Adcock to Sarah Thedford.
Ex. Jan. 8, Samuel Tate, J. P.

Jan. 9—Thomas L. Holt to Flora A. Kyle.
Ex. Jan. 9, 1845.

Jan. 13—William M. Finley to Elizabeth West.

Jan. 15—Jeremiah Smith to Elizabeth Bone.

Jan. 18—Selson Whitaker to Nancy Briggs.
Ex. Jan. 19, Samuel Tate, J. P.

Jan. 22—Elbert I. Hicks to Mariah C. Huston.

Jan. 18—Daniel Glass to Rachael King.
Ex. Jan., 1845.

Feb. 19—Joshua Petty to Fatha Kimbrough.
Ex. Feb. 19, L. Russell, J. P.

June 6—W. H. Evans to Catherine Boyd.
Ex. June 6, O. L. V. Schmittou, J. P.

June 21—George Russell to Nancy Hampton.

July 17—William Hall to Nancy Carroll.
Ex. C. Rooker, L. E. M. E. Church, July 17, 1845.
July 17—H. D. Bails to May A. Grimes.
July 23—Henry R. Johnson to Martha J. Beck.
July 31—Pullen A. Dudley to Lucyanah Graham.
Sept. 15—William T. Patterson to Milly Comer.
Sept. 20—Humphries Halliburton to Mary E. Humphries.
Sept. 22—Joseph Parker to Jamima Lankford.
Oct. 18—Zachriah Batson to Arabella Turner.
Feb. 26—Isaah King to Nancy Williams.
Ex. Feb. 26, J. C. Anglin, J. P.
Feb. 27—James Brown to Mary Link.
Ex. Feb. 27, John Eubank, J. P.
March 10—Jesse Rives to Anny England.
Ex. March 13, Samuel Tate, J. P.
April 7—Jasper R. Ferguson to George Anne Ellis.
April 8—John Walker to Anne Coleman.
Ex. Apr. 8, Allison Akin.
April 19—Joseph Burgess to Rebecca Maham.
Ex. Apr. 21, J. C. Pullen, J. P.
April 30—George M. Evans to Lucinda Brazzell.
Ex. May 1, James Thedford, J. P.
May 12—William L. Baker to Lucinda J. Johnson.
Ex. May 15, William Hand, J. P.
May 28—Noah Cross to Nancy Van Rutledge.
Ex. May 29, J. W. Hedge, J. P.
Oct. 20—David Sellers to Margaret Brown.
Oct. 30—Wilson I. Mathis to Sarah E. Roberts.
Nov. 5—Hiram Sears to Parthena Glass.
Nov. 8—Thomas Jones to Sarah C. Admans.
Ex. Nov. 7, James Daniel, J. P.
Nov. 9—Willis W. Spears to Susan Mosely.
Ex. Nov. 9, J. C. Angelin.
Nov. 24—John K. Boyce to Martha A. Bowen.
Ex. Nov. 25, John W. Ogden, M. G.
Nov. 24—N. A. D. Bryant to Susan E. Joslin.
Nov. 25—Micajah Blackwell to Rebecca Crayne.
Nov. 29—Barney Wallance to Susan Holly.
Dec. 9—Granville Carter to Martha Jones.
Dec. 16—Alford H. Douglas to Marilla Wiles.
Ex. Dec. 18, 1846, C. Rooker, L. E.
Dec. 7—Jefferson Fowler to Elizah Banhook.
Ex. Dec. 7, Silas Murry, J. P.
Dec. 16—Richard Caroland to Louisa Chapman.
Dec. 18—John Harris to Mary A. Baker.
Ex. Dec. 18, Samuel Tate, J. P.
Dec. 19—Mathew J. Smith to Martha A. P. Berry.
Dec. 22—Robert Nolin to Kissiah Sears.
Ex. Dec. 23, John Brown, J. P.
Dec. 25—Millington M. Petty to Cyntha Myatt.
Ex. Dec. 25, David Gray, M. G.
Dec. 16—Thomas Owens to Tennessee A. Sharich.
Ex. Dec. 18, William Garrett, J. P.
Dec. 26—Druary Williams to Elizabeth Russell.
Ex. Dec. 29, David Gray, M. G.
Dec. 27—Thomas Murrell to Elizah Austin.
Ex. Dec. 28, Samuel Tate, J. P.
Dec. 29—John T. Patterson to Anney Newell.
Dec. 29—N. P. Hagewood to Mary J. Carroll.
Ex. Jan. 8, 1846, E. Bishop, M. G.

1846

Jan. 2—Jeremiah Bull to Mary E. Horn.
Ex. Jan. 6, E. Bishop, M. G.
Jan. 2—I. B. Taylor to Cecelia McCarver.
Executed.
Jan. 2—William Davidson to Patsey Luther.
Ex. Jan. 4, J. C. Anglin, J. P.

Jan. 7—Michael Berry to Nancy A. S. Nesbitt.
Ex. by L. R. Dennis, M. G.

Jan. 8—Allen G. Crow to Nancy Adcock.
Ex. Jan. 8, J. C. Pullen, J. P.

Jan. 10—Giles J. Oliver to Nancy C. Evans.
Ex. Jan. 11, E. Bishop, M. G.

Jan. 12—Nathaniel L. Duff to Elizabeth Jane Sullivan.

Jan. 20—John W. Rhea to Sarah Myatt.
Executed.

Feb. 2—Carroll Greer to Martha A. Pendergrass.

Feb. 4—John B. Dickson to Nancy L. Binkly.
Ex. Feb. 5, J. Moore, M. G.

Feb. 23—George Chrisman to Malinda Smith.

March 6—Gabrael R. Petty to Elizabeth Wells.

March 10—Charles Halliburton to Nancy Ragon.
Ex. March 11, J. G. Hinson, J. P.

March 18—James Kimbrough to Nancy Chappell.

April 6—John H. Owens to Nancy B. Gamble.
Ex. April 8, J. Moore, M. G.

April 9—W. A. James to Mary I. Collier.

April 11—David Walls to Martha Christy.

April 20—Benjamin Waynix to Elizabeth Fleet.
Ex. April 23, James Daniel, J. P.

April 20—M. H. Meek to Arlamisa Davidson.
Ex. April 21, J. C. Anglin, J. P.

April 25—Anderson Tate to Mary Luther.
Ex. April 26, J. C. Anglin, J. P.

May 11—George W. Suggs to Martha Reynolds.
Ex. May 12, Edward Holly, J. P.

May 15—Benjamin B. Dunnegan to Elizabeth Adcock.

May 16—Moses Rhodes to Sarah A. Adcock.
Ex. May 17, J. C. Pullen, J. P.

May 19—David Jones to Elizabeth J. Daniel.
Ex. May 20, E. Bishop, M. G.

May 21—Thorton Perry to Mahala Leathers.
Ex. May 24, L. Russell, J. P.

May 23—Druary C. Jones to Pricilla Appleton.

May 27—John T. Patterson to Olive C. Webster.
Ex. May 27, Edward Holley, J. P.

June 27—John G. Parrish to Stacy Wiseman.

June 27—Hopkins Lloyd to Elizabeth Hughs.

June 29—John Jones to Eliza Whatly.

July 13—Henry Paschal to Catherine Link.
Ex. May 28, W. B. Rawles, J. B.

Aug. 1—James W. Evans to Rhoda Willy.

Aug. 2—James B. Hayes to Malinda Gunn.

Aug. 3—John Welker to Elizabeth S. Lathan.

Aug. 10—John Bishop to Jane Morgan.

Aug. 22—Reuben Brown to Marguerite Cathey.

Sept. 2—William M. Patterson to Mary A. Lane.

Sept. 3—Jacob S. Law to Sarah I. Whatley.

Sept. 11—Henry King to Sary Brown.

Sept. 16—Caber Dien to Martha Gunter.

Sept. 20—A. A. Fussell to Menerva Dunnegan.

Sept. 22—William R. V. Schmittou to Martha Tilly.

Sept. 30—Marton Garton to Catherine Carter.

Oct. 6—Joel D. Everatt to Nancy A. Smith.

Oct. 12—John B. Shelton to Mary Jennings.

Oct. 21—Wayne Vanleer to Mary E. Mills.

Oct 22—St. George Pentecost to Paralee Davis.

Oct. 26—John Edwards to Marjah Annah Pentecost.

Nov. 5—James C. Hambrick to Elizabeth Hickerson.

Nov. 9—Newton Dodson to Nancy Sugg.

Nov. 16—Jesse Hagewood to Sarah L. Bryson.

Nov. 20—Daniel W. Anderson to Lucy A. Tilley
Nov. 26—Lewis L. Petty to Mannas Dunnegan.
Dec. 2—William S. Latham to Cardin P. Hill.
Dec. 4—Benjamin F. Wills to Mary J. Clemmons.
Dec. 7—G. W. Gunn to Ritha Brazzell.
Frederick Hughs to Margaret Bouldin.
Dec. 20—Edward D. Holly to Antinella Lewis.
Dec. 21—James R. Rye to Jane A. Burgie.
Washington Hunter to Charlotte Duke.
Dec. 25—J. Daniel to Phebie Anne Cooksey.
Allton Myatt to Mary Sugg.
Dec. 31—George Hambrick to Margaret Hickerson.

1847

Jan. 21—William Humphries to Arrabella Halliburton.
Jan. 7—William Gray to Margaret Dunnegan.
Jan. 7—Mathew I. Hayle to Rebecca Bone.
Jan. 10—Gideon Davis to Lucy J. Clardy.
Jan. 11—W. W. Walker to Mary Willy.
Jan. 12—Thomas W. Halliburton to Martha E. Ragon.
Jan. 12—John B. Austin to Fredonia Walker.
Jan. 14—John W. Fussell to Mary Harmond.
Jan. 26—Isaac Hall to Angelin Flannery.
Jan. 27—Ezekeel Jordon to Rachael Seal.
Feb. 1—Manley J. Pendergrass to Mary Tidwell.
Feb. 13—John Robbins to Mary E. Norris.
Feb. 17—William Hand to Lillicia Hunter.
Feb. 22—George Ragon to Sarah I. Robertson.
Feb. 22—William D. Balthrope to Dilly A. E. Slayden.
Feb. 24—William T. Weakley to Sarah J. Speight.
Feb. 24—Robert Caroland to Elizabeth Everett.
March 15—Charles Warren to M. M. Smith.
March 31—Jesse Edwards to Elizabeth Smith.
April 6—Wesley Holland to Nancy Yates.
April 13—William Etheredge to Mary Underwood.
May 5—Samuel D. Bowen to Mary A. Jackson.
John Bethel to Martha Ethredge.
June 3—John Ellison to Eliza Brown.
June 23—Mathew P. Hall to Sarah C. Jackson.
Ex. C. Rooker, June 30, 1847.
June 24, Geo. C. Brown to Lucinda V. Austin.
July 15—William Sanders to Susan Martin.
June 26—Ira Castelman to Indiana Sears.
July 19—James Hudson to Nancy Tate.
July 27—James Lewis to Susan Parrott.
Ex. July 27, James G. Hinson, J.P.
Aug. 18—Hartwell Sinks to Elizabeth Russell.
Sept. 4—James Carter to Susanah Morris.
Sept. 14—W. P. Ryan to Elizabeth Galaway.
Sept. 14—John C. Weaver to Caroline Lampley.
Sept. 16—Benjamin W. Swift to Olive Sinks.
Sept. 22—Perry A. Cephart to Christiana M. Charlton.
Ex. Sept. 23, C. Rooker, L. E. Meth, C.
Sept. 30—John R. Cathey to Rebecca Spicer.
Oct. 7—Isaac Anderson to Martha Glass.
Oct. 13—G. W. Gray to Elizabeth J. Jones
Oct. 16—Elias Sanders to Mary Hedge.
Oct. 18—William Petty to Susan Deshazer.
Oct. 25—Benjamin W. Weems to Mary Vineyard.
Nov. 11—Senard A. Waynick to Elizabeth I. Baily.
Ex. Nov. 11, James G. Hinson, J. P.
Nov. 19—Henry A. Petty to Lucinda Gentry.
Ex. John Brown, J. P.

1848

Jan. 3—Issah King to Rebeccah King.
Ex. Jan. 3, J. C. Anglin, J.P.

Feb. 2—Samuel A. Bibb to Martha Carr.
Ex. by John Brown, J. P.

Feb. 2—John Porter to Zilpha Tidwell.
Ex. by John Brown, J. P.

Feb. 23—John R. Brown to Sarah N. Harris.
Ex. Feb. 23, W. B. Ross, J. P.

March 2—Jaccob Myers to Martha A. Eddes.
Ex. March 2, John Brown, J. P.

March 2—William P. Lankford to M. Davidson.
Ex. March 2, John Brown, J. P.

July 5—Cyrus Chichester to Jane Mallory.
Ex. July 5, Allen Nesbitt, J. P.

July 13—John R. Vanhook to Harriet A. Coleman.
Ex. July 13, Jas. Daniel, J. P.

Sept. 20—Wilson M. Sarrett to Catherine Miller.
Ex., Samuel Tate, J. P.

Sept. 21—James Stringfellow to Susan Carroll.
Ex. Sept. 21, William Johnson, J. P.

Oct. 8—John Carson to Hester A. Palmer.
Ex. Oct. 8, I. Hardin, J. P.

Nov. 9—Andrew Cunningham to Bedy White.
Ex. Nov. 9, John Brown, J. P.

1849

Mar. 22—John G. Reynolds to Frances Hand.
Ex. J. P. Paschall, J. P.

May 1—William Beard to Paralee Clark.
Ex. May 1, C. Grymes, J. P.

May 3—W. A. Wagoner to Elizabeth Ellis.
Ex. May 3, J. T. Wagoner.

1847

Dec. 9—James M. McCollom to Sarah A. Sanders.
Ex. Dec. 9, 1847, Samuel Tate, J. P.

Dec. 13—Thomas Flannery to Nancy Thedford.
Ex. Dec. 13, Samuel Tate, J. P.

Dec. 15—James B. Rooker to Jane A. Williams.
Ex. Dec. 15, W. B. Ross, J. P.

Dec. 16—George W. C. Lovell to Elizabeth A. Hunter.
Ex. Dec. 16, W. B. Ross, J. P.

Dec. 16—W. A. Johnson to Sarah Jame McCollom.
Ex. Dec. 16, Samuel Tate, J. P.

Dec. 30—E. M. Potts to Rebecca Meger.
Ex. Dec. 30, James Thedford, J. P.

Dec. 30—Issah Bagett to Harriett A. Suggs.
Ex. Dec. 30, R. P. Halliburton, J. P.

1848

Jan. 9—Anner King to Elizabeth Dunnegan.
Ex. Jan. 9, L. Russell, J. P.

Jan. 24—Lewis Hedge to Elizabeth S. Petty.
Ex. Jan. 24, L. Gunn, J. P.

Jan. 27—Hugh Burns to Sarah Jordan.
Ex. Jan. 27, O. L. V. Schmittou, J. P.

Feb. 3—John Hughs to Rebecca Dunaway.
Ex. Feb. 3, James Daniel, J. P.

Feb. 6—James Staley to Elizabeth Hudgins.
Ex. Feb. 6, Allen Nesbitt.

Mar. 5—John H. Caldwell to Donna M. Christian.
Ex. Mar. 5, Allen Nesbitt, J. P.

Mar. 12—Thomas Ladd to R. Jane Baker.
Ex. Mar. 12, David Gray.

Mar. 22—Thomas Clark to Elizabeth Hampton.
Ex. Mar. 22, William Garrett, J. P.

Mar. 24—Jesse Steeley to Aney Jordan.
Ex. Mar. 24, R. P. Halliburton, J. P.

April 13—Thomas Alsbrook to Tennessee Owens.
Ex. April 13, C. Grymes, J. P.

April 13—James H. Hall to Louisiana T. Richardson.
Ex. April 16, J. T. Paschall, J. P.

April 27—Issach Halley to Rosannah Gray.
Ex. April 27, G. W. Tatom, J. P.

April 27—James Ellis to Abba Proctor.
Ex. April 27, C. Grymes, J. P.

May 3—J. G. Marshall to Mary T. Mosley.
Ex. May 3, C. Rooker, L. E.

May 18—John D. Woodward to Hannah E. Brown.
Ex. May 18, J. S. Paschall, J. P.

June 18—Benjamin F. Larkins to Martha Willy.
Ex. June 18, W. S. Coleman, J. P.

June 30—John B. Walton to Nancy Jordan.
Ex. June 30, O. L. V. Schmittou, J. P.

July 2—Solomon McCauly to Elizabeth C. Paschall.
Ex. July 2, C. Grymes, J. P.

July 8—G. W. Choate to Mary Jane Gibbs.
Ex. July, 1848, William Hill, J. P.

July 13—George T. Harris to Lucinda A. Walker.
Ex. July 13, J. Paschall, J. P.

July 13—Simon Deloach to Ginnett Biter.
Ex. July 13, W. S. Coleman, J. P.

July 13—L. S. Paschall to Martha F. Duke.
July 13, C. Grymes, J. P.

July 23—Edward Caldwell to Elizabeth J. Durard.
Ex. July 23, J. Hardin, J. P.

July 30—Harvey Dunaway to Treas Bateman.
Ex. July 30, O. L. V. Schmittou, J. P.

Aug. 1—John M. Stringfellow to Sarah Jane Carroll.
Ex. Aug. 1, William Johnson, J. P.

Aug. 3—Joshia Proctor to Martha Owens.
Ex. Aug. 3, C. Grymes, J. P.

Aug. 6—W. G. Estis to Margaret Austin.
Ex. Aug. 6, A. V. Hicks, J. P.

Aug. 14—Benjamin I. Mosier to Martha Jordan.
Ex. Aug. 14, O. L. V. Schmittou, J. P.

Aug. 24—James James to Palitha N. Walker.
Ex. Aug. 28, A. V. Hicks, J. P.

Aug. 31—A. B. Stoud to Mary Jane McLaughlin.
Ex. Aug. 31, J. Paschall, J. P.

Sept. 3—James B. Stokes to Harriett A. Potts.
Ex. Sept. 3, O. L. V. Schmittou, J. P.

Sept. 7—William Underwood to Nancy Dunaway.
Ex. Sept. 7, James Daniel, J. P.

Sept. 25—John Hampton to E. A. Buchanan.
Ex. Sept. 25, C. Grymes, J. P.

Oct. 8—Thorton Hendricks to Amanda M. Smith.
Ex. Oct. 8, J. Hardin, J. P.

Oct. 8—William C. Dotson to Nancy E. Hudson.
Ex. Oct. 8, William Hill.

Oct. 26—W. D. Mitchell to Martha E. Darrow.
Ex. Oct. 26, O. L. V. Schmittou, J. P.

State of Tennessee,
Dickson County.

I, Lillian Williams, of Charlotte, Dickson County, Tennessee, do certify that I transcribed the foregoing marriage records of Dickson County, Tennessee, from the original Book of Marriages from 1838 to 1849, as the same appears in the office of the County Court Clerk of Dickson County, and the foregoing is a true copy of same.

LILLIAN WILLIAMS,
Stenographer.

Sworn to and subscribed before me, this 7th day of June, 1933.

My commission expires Feb. 28, 1934.

W. M. LEED, *N. P.*

Marriage Bonds—Lebanon, Wilson County, Tennessee
By Mrs. W. P. Bouton

1802

Name	Test.	Surety
Sept. 16—John W. Baker	John Allcorn	John W. Baker
Polly Boleman		Benj. Baker
Nov. 4—Lynsey Martin		Lynsey Martin
Nancy Haley		Joseph Stacey

1805

Name	Test.	Surety
Dec. 30—John Winset	John Allcorn	John Winset
Jenny Jones		Lewis Wilson

1806

Name	Test.	Surety
Christopher Koonce	John Allcorn	Christopher Koonce
Ann Small		Amos Small
Elisha Brown	John Allcorn	Elisha Brown
Polly Allin		Jesse Cage
Isaac Jonston		Isaac Jonston
Prisilla Arnton		Charlie W. Abnten
Jan. 3—Elijah Gwyn	John Allcorn	Elijah Gwyn
Sarah Idlett		John Rice
Jan. 6—John Phillips		John Phillips
Elizabeth Scott		John Phillips
Jan. 11—Daniel Walls		Daniel Walls
Rebecca Butt		David Fields
Jan. 18—John Fergeson	A. Harris	John Fergerson
Patsey Harris		Eli Wearrell
Jan. 19—Vachel Blalock	John Allcorn	Vachel Blalock
Latsey Chapple		Alsey Elkin
Jan. 21—John Scobey	John Allcorn	John Scobey
Ann Spears		T. Bradley
Jan. 25—George Ross	John Allcorn	George Ross
Lydia Dickings		Allen Ross
Jan. 27—Amos Small		Amos Small
Polly Koonce		Christopher Koonce
Jan. 31—Hardy Peneel	John Allcorn	Hardy Peneel
Lucy Patterson		John Fonville
Feb. 9—William Holebrooks	John Allcorn	William Holebrooks
Sarah Davis		Arthur Davis
Feb. 3—Thomas Dill	John Allcorn	Thomas Dill
Agness Hopson		John Harpole
Feb. 18—James Johnson	John Allcorn	James Johnson
Elizabeth Nixon		Samuel Johnson
Feb. 18—Julius Alford		Julius Alford
Ann Hays		Harmon Hays
Feb. 24—Phillip Anderson	John Allcorn	Phillip Anderson
Polly Macnatt		Leven Macnatt
Feb. 24—Leven Macnatt	John Allcorn	Leven Macnatt
Nancy Smith		Phillip Anderson

Name	Test.	Surety
Mar. 15—Elijah Jones Patsey Browning	John Allcorn	Elijah Jones David Hocks
Mar. 24—Anthony Copland Nancy Craig		Anthony Copland David Craig
Apr. 3—George Lockmiller Polly Porter	J. Allcorn	George Lockmiller Samuel Caple
Apr. 5—Isham Wynne Sally Eckels	Ben Winford	Isham Wynne Jesse Cage
Apr. 10—George Brown Polly Thompson	John Allcorn	George Brown Terry Williams
Apr. 11—Samuel Dickings Polly Clampet		Samuel Dickings Henry Truet
May 3—Amos Winsett Polly Phillips	John Allcorn	Amos Winsett John Winsett
May 20—Sam Stockard Polly Thomas Flood	John Allcorn	John Stockard Thomas Flood
May 20—Phillip Hintson Elizabeth Tucker		Phillip Hintson John Impson
May 20—Peter Cotton Lebenah Tucker	John Allcorn	Peter Cotton Jeremiah Tucker
May 26—John Gwine Jenny Berry	John Allcorn	John A. Gwine John Bradley
June 6—Edward James Margret Thomas		Edward James John Winsett
June 15—John Pankey Peggy Smith		John Pankey George Hallum
June 23—John Powell Sally Boothe	John Allcorn	John Powell David Boothe
June 30—Jesse Cunningham Rosey Beasley		Jesse Cunningham Dillard Beasley
July 3—John Echols Judith Compton	John Allcorn	John Echols William Allen
July 5—Stephen Lankford Lear Herrod	John Allcorn	Stephen Lankford Samuel Herrod
July 7—John B. Bedford Ruth Brown	John Allcorn	John B. Bedford J. Criply
July 8—Noah Kelly Hannah Hicks	John Allcorn	Noah Kelly Richard Hicks
July 17—Thomas Wooldridge Jennie Bradley	John Allcorn	Thomas Wooldridge Thomas Bradley
July 18—Garland Tedwell Susannah Magness	John Allcorn	Garland Tedwell James Higdon
July 21—Benjamin Alexander Sarah Cloyd	John Allcorn	Benjamin Alexander Samuel Hogg
July 23—Joseph Dixson Polly Clack		Joseph Dixson Spencer Bevins
July 26—Joseph Jadwin Mary Vanhooser	John Allcorn	Joseph Jadwin Isaac Bartlett
Aug. 4—Andrew Hays Susannah Enoch	John Allcorn	Andrew Hays Campbell Hays
Aug. 7—Wyall Bettis Milly Powers	John Allcorn	Wyatt Bettis John Bettis

	Name	Test.	Surety
Aug. 11—	Robert Boyd Elizabeth Gardner	John Allcorn	Robert Boyd John Boyd
Aug. 11—	Patrick Youree Respey Chapman	John Allcorn	Silas Chapman
Aug. 11—	Alexander Steele Lucy Compton	John Allcorn	Alexander Steele James Steele
Aug. 25—	Levi Holland Nancy Siddle	John Allcorn	Levi Holland Aaron Anglin
Aug. 27—	Anthony Winston Sally Ann Watson	John Allcorn	A. Winston Joel James
Aug. 27—	John Afflack Nancy Taylor	John Allcorn	John Afflack David McMurray
Aug. 27—	Hugh McCoy Caty Wilson	John Allcorn	Hugh McCoy John McCoy
Aug. 28—	George Allin Sally Johnson	John Allcorn	George Allin Soloman Harpole
Sept. 2—	Hugh McElyea Polly McElyea	John Allcorn	Hugh McElyea William Donaldson
Sept. 2—	Peter Walker Drucilla Hendrick		Peter Walker John Smith
Sept. 6—	Andrew Morrison Jane Robertson		Andrew Morrison Moses M. Robertson
Sept. 12—	Edward Brown Sally Bandy		Edward Brown Ruth Bandy
Sept. 22—	Avery Brown Sarah Marlow	John Allcorn	Avery Brown Richard Marlow
Sept. 23—	Donald McMicole Betsey Bradley		Donald McMicole John Patton
Oct. 9—	Kenedy Bay Fannie Barnett		Keneda Bay John Gray
Oct. 21—	Stephen Hopkins Polly Adamson	John Allcorn	Stephen Hopkins George Price
Nov. 3—	Samuel Gibson Sally Browing	John Allcorn	Samuel Gibson Joshua Gibson
Nov. 10—	Richard Hancock Mary Cooper		Richard Hancock John Fuston
Nov. 14—	William Holland Fannie Still		William Holland Richard Holland
Nov. 18—	Geo. Allen Brough Mirah Bone	John Allcorn	George A. Brough William Bone
Nov. 19—	Benjamin Winford Elizabeth Babb	John Allcorn	Ben Winford Thomas Wilson
Dec. 4—	James Smith Christian Devault	John Allcorn	James Smith Peter Devault
Dec. 15—	Thomas Sisson Alsey Munday	John Allcorn	Thomas Sisson Quick John
Dec. 21—	Samuel Thomas Bailory Pitner	John Allcorn	Samuel Thomas, Sr. Samuel Thomas, Jr.
Dec. 22—	Lai Lact Rebecca Williamson	John Allcorn	Cathan Clampitt
Dec. 22—	Thomas Clifton Letty Rogers	John Allcorn	Thomas Clifton Jno. Tucker

Name	Test.	Surety
Dec. 22—James Newby Sally Batley	John Allcorn	James Newbey John Hallum
Dec. 26—Charles B. Smith Elly Hutson		Charles B. Smith William Scott
Aug. 30—Levi Lannom Rachel Gibson	John Allcorn	Levi Lannom Samuel Gibson
June 16—James Elliott Polly Carlock	John Allcorn	James Elliott John Quesenberry
	1807	
Jan. 22—John Gray Fanny Die	John Allcorn	John Gray John Brady
Jan. 14—James Broadaway Elizabeth Forbes	Jesse Cage	Genry Forbes
Jan. 10—John Bettis Sally Bradley	John Allcorn	John Bettis Hugh Bradley
Jan. 10—Joshua Barnes Nancy Reiff	John Allcorn	Joshua Barnes Henry Reiff
Jan. 4—Jacob Baring Ann Ray	John Allcorn	Jacob Baring Samuel Ray
Jan. 7—Richard Ramsey Patsey Bloodworth	John Allcorn	Richard Ramsey Wm. Bloodworth
Jan. 23—Moses Carter Polly Davidson	Jesse Cage	Moses Carter John Brown
Jan. 24—Thomas Bowen Lucy Drew	John Allcorn	Thomas Bowen William Drew
Jan. 24—John Smith Polly Warmack		John Smith William Warmack
Jan. 26—Lary Epps Elizabeth Craton	John Allcorn	Lary Epps John Bradley
Jan. 30—James D. Walker Nancy Davis	John Allcorn	James D. Walker Arthur Davis
Feb. 1—Adam Barns Polly Leonard		Adam Barns Joshua Barns
Feb. 9—John Braddock Nelly Leonard		John Braddock Richard Penny
Feb. 16—John Wilkinson Elizabeth Thomas		John Wilkinson Rodham Allen
Feb. 14—Stephen Barton Ellenora Baird		Stephen Barton Zebulon Baird
Feb. 21—Buster Alford Mary Bryant	John Allcorn	Buster Alford Archibus Bryant
Feb. 25—John Mooney Lydie Burns		John Mooney Thomas Patterson
Mar. 9—William Webb Rachel Godfrey		William Webb Burtis Alford
Mar. 14—William Anderson Nancy Greenwood		William Anderson Mirco Anderson
Mar. 20—James Carruth Sally Williams	John Allcorn	James Carruth
Mar. 21—John Jennings Fanny Word	Jesse Cage	John Jennings James Cross

Name	Test.	Surety
Mar. 23—James Byrns	John Allcorn	James Byrns
Rebeca Ward		Jetton Thomas
Mar. 30—Edward Bruce	John Allcorn	Edward Bruce
Nelly Burns		John Burns
April 4—Joshua Anderson	John Allcorn	Joshua Anderson
Sally Patton		Thomas Poteat
April 10—David London		Daniel Sanders
Polly Parten		John B. Walker
June 2—William Thompson		William Thompson
Rebecca Wilson		John Lewis
June 13—John Morris	John Allcorn	John Morris
Nancy Walls		Ranyon Stroud
July 13—John Keeling		John Keeling
Polly Manning		Thomas Bradley
July 15—William Smith	John Allcorn	
Suckey Hail		
July 22—Ezekiel Lindsey	John Allcorn	Ezakiel Lindsey
Elizabeth McNeeley		William McNeeley
July 28—Samuel Dickings	Jesse Cage	Samuel Dickings
Nancy Heflin	John Allcorn	Jacob McDermit
Aug. 1—Henry Howel	John Allcorn	Henry Howel
Polly Eagan		William Eagan
Aug. 2—Hartwell Keeling	Jesse Cage	Hartwell Keeling
Nancy Guinnes		John Wilkerson
Aug. 6—Samuel Thomas		Samuel Thomas
Ann Eatherly		Moses Odum
Aug. 6—Johnathan Biles		Johnathan Biles
Polly Barnit		John B. Barnit
Aug. 7—Dread Bass		Dread Bass
Nancy Brean		Jacob McDermit
Aug. 11—Middleton Bell		Middleton Bell
Rebecah Gibson		William Gibson
Aug. 13—James Anderson		James Anderson
Elizabeth Chapman		John Crawford
Aug. 22—John Hallem		John Hallem
Polly Davis		Arthur Davis
Aug. 26—John Ashford		John Ashford
Jinsey King		Wiley Elkin
Aug. 27—John Whitson		John Whitson
Nancy Keeling		John House
Sept. 4—Simeon Wherry		Simeon Wherry
Ann Scypert		Thomas Bradley
Sept. 13—James Gray		James Gray
Patsy Denton		Edward W. Vaughan
Sept. 23—John Barnet		John Barnet
Polly McAdow		Jenny McAdow
Oct. 8—William Milligan	John Allcorn	Wm. Milligan
Nelly Mechee		Samuel Elliott
Oct. 8—John Rice		
Nancy Ramsey		
Oct. 8—Abner Stuart	John Allcorn	Abner Stuart
Nancy Gray		James Gray

Name	Test.	Surety
Oct. 8—David Burton Ann Davis		David Burton Ebenezer Drakes
Oct. 10—Samuel Smith Polly Roach	Jesse Cage	Samuel Smith William Smith
Nov. 14—Zebulom Baird Clevy Hunt	John Allcorn	Zeb Baird John Searcy
Dec. 8—John Nicks Anna Richards		John Nicks Robert Alexander
Dec. 14—Thomas Smith Sarah Mouditk		Thomas Smith Samuel Smith
Dec. 17—Joseph Johnson Nancy Brown		Joe Johnson Jesse Cage
Oct.—Daniel Forbes Elizabeth Horn	Jesse Cage	Daniel L. Forbes Johns*****———
James Elliott Polly Carlock		

1808

Name	Test.	Surety
Jan. 6—Willsher Bandy Nancy Johnson		Willsher Bandy Jesse Cage
Jan. 9—Dabney Tatum Polly Whitson		Dabney Tatum
Jan. 18—Milbrey Hearn Hestey Mickle	John Allcorn	Milbrey Hearn Josiac Vanhooser
Jan. 20—Joel Swindle Nancy Hudson	Jesse Cage	Joel Swindle Samuel Harris
Jan. 23—Grissam Movies Sarah Bradberry	John Allcorn	Grissam Moves Jesse Cage
Feb. 17—Humphrey Donalson Sally Kelly	John Allcorn	Humphrey Donalson Obediah Woolwine
Feb. 23—Tarver Spradley Susan Showers		Tarver Spradley Samuel Carter
Mar. 1—Bennajah Gray Elenor Warmack	John Allcorn	Bennajah Gray John Roach
Mar. 12—Luke Tippit Jeney Cooksey	John Allcorn	Luke Tippit Henry Carson
Mar. 14—John Davis Polly McAlpin		Jesse Holt
April—Baswell West Rebecca Lewis	John Allcorn	Baswell West Thomas Drennon
April 6—Micajah Hollis Fanny Hodges	John Allcorn	Micajah Hollis Jeremiah Hodge
April 21—William Hartgroves Jane Greenwood		William Hartgroves Benj. Williams
April 25—John Green Nancy Myrick	John Allcorn	John Green Walter Myrick
June 2—Robert Bogle Sally Brison		Robert Bogle Thomas Luck
June 3—Duke Wortham Betsey Norton		Duke Wortham
June 7—William Adamson Demorris Bledsoe	John Allcorn	William Adamson George Pue

Name	Test.	Surety
June 21—Jonathan Hunt Hannah Hendricks	John Allcorn	Jonathan Hunt William Pratt
June 27—Joshua Brown Prudence McAllen		Joshua Brown Solimon George
Dec. 31—James Crator Jenny Warmack	John Allcorn	James Crator Rich Dishell
Aug. 17—James Cropper Peggy Poviance		James Cropper John Poviance
Aug. 19—William Parmer Polly Bond	Jesse Cage	William Parmer John Bond
Aug. 29—Thomas Smith Susannah Hill		Thomas Smith James Anderson
Sept. 2—Hezekiel Cartwright Elizabeth Maholland	John Allcorn	Hugh Cartwright M. W. Cartwright
Sept. 29—John Clemment Jane Pullin	John Allcorn	John Clemment Samuel Barton
Oct. 15—Thomas Telford Elizabeth Chawning	John Allcorn	Thomas Telford Samuel Telford
Oct. 15—John Bond Sarah Cummings		John Bond James Bond
Nov. 2—John Campbell Pheby Casady		John Campbell Samuel Barton
Nov. 5—Graham Jackson Betsey Smith	Jesse Cage	Graham Jackson William Caple
Nov. 5—Jeremiah Hodges Peggy Brown	John Allcorn	Jeremiah Hodges Thomas Leach
Nov. 6—Robert Harris Elizabeth McCowen	John Allcorn	Robert Harris Isham Webb
Nov. 7—John Fakes Mary Edwards		John Fakes Robert Edwards
Nov. 9—Stephen Williams Cinthy Rogers	John Allcorn	Stephen Williams George Rogers
Nov. 21—Henry Coke Elizabeth Tipton	John Allcorn	Henry Coke Joshua Tipton
	1809	
Jan. 6—Richard Mount Polly Martin	Jesse Cage	Richard Mount John Pirtle
Jan. 20—Rhaford Rutland Sally Cawthon	John Allcorn	Rhaford Rutland John G. Graves
Jan. 21—Thomas S. Smith Margret Cannon		Thomas S. Smith Samuel Cannon
Feb. 1—Joshua Anderson Peggy H. Thomas	John Allcorn	Joshua Anderson Henry Thomas
Feb. 3—George Telford Elizabeth Relbreath	Jesse Cage	George Telford Gilbert Cribby
Feb. 13—John Baker Genny Bearding		John Baker John Powell
Feb. 21—Spencer Edwards Sally Wilson		Spencer Edwards B. Howard
Feb. 25—Sion Bass Polly Perry	John Allcorn	Sion Bass Richardson Perry

Name		Test.	Surety
Feb. 25—George Whitson	Polly Meridith		Thomas Bradley
Mar. 1--William Pitts	Elizabeth Johnson	John Allcorn	William Pitts Arin Riddle
Mar. 9—John Robertson	Elizabeth Williamson		John Robertson John Williamson
Mar. 6—Phillip Smart	Rebbecca George	John Allcorn	Phillip Smart Clark Blalock
Mar. 20—George Martin	Patsey Dillard	John Allcorn	George W. Martin Sion Hogg
Mar. 22—Joseph Hubbard	Susannah Wamack	John Allcorn	Joseph Hubbard Richard Wamack
Mar. 25—Soloman Bell	Nancy Jacobs		Soloman Bell Andrew Baird
Mar. 27—Samuel Vick	Drucilla Neil	John Allcorn	Samuel Vick David Heflin
Mar. 27—Nathaniel Wade	Polly Melton	John Allcorn	Nathaniel Wade Aaron Lambeth
Mar. 29—William Porterfield	Myrandy Young		William Porterfield Joseph Young
April 1—Andrew Morrison	Lyda Alexander	John Allcorn	Andrew Morrison Ezekiel Alexander
Apr. 1—James E. Davis	Polly Taylor		James E. Davis James Hudson
April 19—John Rieff	Hannah Ross	John Allcorn	John Rieff Samuel Bryant
April 27—Daniel McCoy	Jane ?		Daniel McCoy John Hamilton
May 8—Lewis McCartney			Lewis McCartney
May 23—Gabrial Anderson	Polly Scaret		Gabrial Anderson J. Anderson
June 3—William Cartwright	Patsey Fuller		Wm. Cartwright William Draper
June 17—Isham Johnson	Sally Carrell	John Allcorn	Isham Johnson
June 20—John Leech	Jensey Stuart	John Allcorn	John Leech James Stuart
June 21—James Drennon	Fanny Devault	John Allcorn	James Drennon Mathew Devault
June 30—John Woodall	Polly Collins	John Allcorn	John Woodall
July 6—John Marshall	Ann Donelson		John Marshall William Marshall
July 25—Richard Talley	Sally Taylor	John Allcorn	Richard Talley Mathew Talley
Aug. 21—Samuel Cannon	Polly Alexander		Robert Alexander
Aug. 22—Isaac Thomas	Nancy Jones		Isaac Thomas John Winsett

Name	Test.	Surety
Aug. 26—Josiah Impson Polly Smith	John Allcorn	Josiah Impson J. Bradley
Sept. 1—John Anglin Elizabeth Carver	John Allcorn	John Anglin Aaron Anglin
Sept. 2—Robert Morrison Edy Sharpe	John Allcorn	Robert Morrison William Campbell
Sept. 6—Richardson Carr Mily Sawyers	John Allcorn	Richardson Carr Thomas Carr
Sept. 7—Benjamin Castleman Polly McFarland		Benjamin Castleman Samuel Merridith
Sept. 13—Joseph Knox Jane Crocket	John Allcorn	Joseph Knox Andy Crocket
Sept. 20—Alexander Marrs Martha Donnell	John Allcorn	Alexander Marrs Robert Donnell
Sept. 23—Bryant Ward Polly Wynne	John Allcorn	Bryant Ward Hardy Hunter
Sept. 25—William Marshall Milly Hargis		William Marshall Samuel Moore
Sept. 26—Archibald Sherrill Elizabeth Anderson	John Allcorn	Archibald Sherrill Gabrial Chandler
Sept. 27—Jonathan Eatherly Jenny Thompson		Jonathan Eatherly Warren Eatherly
Sept. 30—Eli Donnell Peggy Logue	John Allcorn	Eli Donnell Robert Donnell
Oct. 1—Isham F. Davis Rachel S. Hays		I. F. Davis Samuel Merredith
Oct. 2—John McKnight Margret Alexander		John McKnight Andrew Alexandrew
Oct. 3—Jerremiah Taylor Milly Mitchell	Jesse Cage	Jerremiah Taylor T. Bradley
Oct. 5—John Martin Patsy Lane	John Allcorn	John Martin Aaron Lane
Oct. 12—John Berry Elizabeth Campbell		John Berry John A. Givens
Oct. 12—William Tolbert Jane Parks		William Tolbert Samuel Tolbert
Nov. 3—Robert Campbell Tilly Stuart		Robert Campbell Joseph Kirkpatrick
Nov. 7—John Jones Frances Knight	John Allcorn	John Jones William Mount
Nov. 11—David Barret Jemima Allen	John Allcorn	David Barret Jamison Bandy
Nov. 18—Abraham Whitson Rutha Brown	John Allcorn	Abraham Whitson Dabney Tatum
Nov. 20—Joseph Wally Jensey Thaxton		Joseph Walley Richard Potts
Dec. 4—Thomas Carver Margaret Donelson	John Allcorn	Thomas Carver Humphrey Donelson
Dec. 10—Roland Gipson Betsey Rather		Roland W. Gipson James Rather
Dec. 11—Jesse Bloodworth Narcissa Gibson		Jesse Bloodworth Wm. Bloodworth

Name	Test.	Surety
Dec. 16—John Brown Rachel Lomax	John Allcorn	John Brown Jonathan Pickett
Dec. 21—Jas. Horton Rebecca White		Jas. Horton Robert Ross.
Dec. 25—Parron Bandy Lytia Rice		Parron Bandy Ransom George
Dec. 28—Zachariah Hardridge Peggy Dodds		Zachariah Hardridge John Patterson
Feb. 29—Simon Adamson Susannah Hopkins		Simon Adamson Stephen Hopkins
No date—Tillman Betty Sally Carr	Samuel Meredith	Tillman Betty Richardson Carr
No date—John M. Garrison Patsey Cannon	John Allcorn	John M. Garrison Samuel Cannon
	1810	
Jan. 4—William Mann Frances Turner	John Allcorn	William Mann Samuel Meredith
Jan. 8—David Johnson Elizabeth Walker	John Allcorn	David Johnson James Higdon
Jan. 8—John Walker Nancy Nelson	John Allcorn	John Walker James Higdon
Jan. 15—David Gibson Prudy Bloodworth	John Allcorn	David Gibson John Barber
Jan. 24—Nathaniel Brown Sally Scott	John Allcorn	Nathaniel Brown Thomas Donnell
Jan. 24—Stephen Smart Kindness Shorter		Stephen Smart Atsey Elkin
Jan. 25—Justis Rulmon Ruth Standford	John Allcorn	Justis Ruleman Abner Morrison
Jan. 27—John Donnell Elizabeth Davidson		John Donnell Jesse Donnell
Jan. 29—Obediah Woodrum Dolley Bradberry	Samuel Meredith	Obediah Woodrum John Bradberry
Jan. 29—Edward Lawrence Delilah Woodward		Edward Lawrence Joshua Harris
Jan. 30—Gabrial Chandler Jensey Thomas		Gabrial Chandler Samuel Sherrill
Feb. 1—William Williams Nancy Brown	John Allcorn	W. Williams John Tudora
Feb. 6—Andrew Creswell Anna Brown	Edmund Crutcher	Andrew Creswell William Halbrook
Feb. 7—John Harris Sally Cartwright	Samuel Merrets	John Harris Samuel Cartwright
Feb. 10—David W. Breedlove Nancy Breedlove	John Allcorn	David W. Breedlove Martin Breedlove
Feb. 21—Francis Woodward Jensey Brannon		Francis Woodward Boswell Pearcy
Feb. 27—James Dickings Mary McWhirter	Edmund Crutcher	James Dickings George McWhirter
Mar. 2—James Hicks Lobithia Standeford	John Allcorn	James Hicks Noah Kelley

Name	Test.	Surety
Mar. 8—John Travillian Mary Carson		John Travillian John McNeely
Mar. 8—John McNeely Belinda W. Carson		John McNeely John Travillian
Mar. 13—James George Sibetha Eslick	John Allcorn	James George Isaac B. Eslick
Mar. 14—Leeroy Bradley Sally McSpadden	Samuel Meridith	Leroy Bradley John McSpadden
Mar. 17—Josiah Jackson Nancy Clampit	John Allcorn	Josiah Jackson James Clampit
Mar. 17—Jeremiah Hendricks Nancy Farmer		Jeremiah Hendricks Thomas Wilson
Mar. 20—Samuel Cartwright Letty Moore	Samuel Meridith	Samuel Cartwright John Harris
Mar. 27—Samuel Scott Amy Donnell		Samuel Scott John Foster
Mar. 27—John Thompson Peggy Wilson	John Allcorn	John Thompson Ezekiel Cloyd
Apr. 4—James W. Hearne Mary Godphry	Edmund Crutcher	James W. Hearne James Godphry
Apr. 7—William Hollandworth Jensey Walker	John Allcorn	Wm. Hollandworth James Hollandworth
April 16—Merrel Elkins Thankful Maddox		Merrel Elkins Jacob Castleman
April 19—Miles Gray Rhody Harkins	John Allcorn	Miles Gray Jorday Bass
April 29—Gabrial Higdon Rebecca Davis		Gabrail Higdon Alex Higdon
April 30—Isaac B. Eslick Jencey George		Isaac B. Eslick Joseph Sharp
May 4—Daniel Baker Sally Woodward	John Allcorn	Daniel Baker Benja Baker
May 10—John Galloway Sally Barret		John Galloway Andrew Robertson
May 14—George Donnell Armela Shanks	Edward Crutcher	George Donnell Abel Williams
June 2—William Young Hannah Bridges	John Allcorn	William Young Beverly Young
June 11—John Hubbard Elizabeth Jennings	Edward Crutcher	John Hubbard Presley Lester
July 17—Tryry Laine Nancy Ligon		Tryry Laine John Martin
July 21—Cornelious Joiner Suckey Cary	Edmund Crutcher	Cornelious Joiner Moses Adams
July 21—Richarson Perry Frankey Joiner	Edmund Crutcher	Richarson Perry Moses Adams
Aug. 11—Moses Sterrett Sarah Witherspoon	John Allcorn	Moses Sterrett Galley Swann
Aug. 14—John Seabalt Mahaly Kelly	John Allcorn	John Seabalt Abner Wasson
Aug. 18—James Shorter Margret Smith	John Allcorn	Janes Shorter Ralph Smith

Name		Test.	Surety
Sept. 4—Thomas McCartney	Sarah Lowery		Thomas McCartney Archibald Davis
Sept. 5—Charles Henry	Nancy Cutrell	John Allcorn	Charles Henry Aron Spring
Sept. 18—John Martin	Rebecca Davis		John Martin James E. Davis
Oct. 1—Thomas Bormer	Polly Granade		Thomas Bormer James S. Rawlings
Oct. 8—Ezekiel Alexander	Polly Cooper	T. Bradley	Ezekiel Alexander Abraham Cooper
Oct. 13—Rezon Byrn	Frances Craddock		Rezon Byrn James Byrn
Nov. 8—Jesse Bowers	Nancy Mann		Jesse Bowers T. Bradley
Nov. 27—Benjamin Ferrell	Polly M. Davis	H. L. Douglas	Benj. Ferrell Benjamin Hobson
Nov. 30—John Harris	Catharine Baker	John Allcorn	John Harris Harry Smith
Dec. 5—Henry Dameron	Sally Wright	Edmund Crutcher	Henry Dameron Ebenezer Gilbert
Dec. 11—William Dunn	Elizabeth Bradey		William Dunn John Dunn
Dec. 13—Robert Anderson	Nancy Sands	John Allcorn	Robert Anderson John Roberts
Dec. 19—William Stacey	Polly Sherrill	H. L. Douglas	William Stacey Bradford Howard
Dec. 25—Samuel Alsup	Elizabeth Jennings	John Allcorn	Sam Alsup Arthur Harris
Dec. 31—William Nicks	Sally Pugh	John Allcorn	William Nicks Thomas Bradley
		1811	
Feb. 16—James Tipton	Polly Gray	John Allcorn	James Tipton Thomas Ford
Aug. 21—Robert Shannon	Rachel Osment		Robert Shannon James Steed
Dec. 28—William Lewis	Casandy Knight		William Lewis Reuban Allen
Dec. 10—Green Williams	Sally Reiff		Green Williams Harvey Reiff
Oct. 22—Nathaniel Thomas	Nancy Talley		Nathaniel Thomas Pleasant Talley
July 10—Sampson Allen	Polly Somers		Simpson Allen William Maxwell
Oct. 9—Bass Webb	Elizabeth Moore		Bass Webb Thomas Watson
Jan. 23—Stephen Medlock	Sarah Tucker		Stephen Medlock Littleberry Medlock
July 19—John Smith	Hannah Canon		John Smith Samuel Canon
Mar. 6—Aaron Spring	Rachel O'Neal		Aaron Spring Charles Henry

Name	Test.	Surety
April 16—Nathaniel Davis	John Allcorn	Nathaniel Davis
Elizabeth McFarland		John Davis
Aug. 27—Thomas W. Porter-field		Thomas W.Porterfield
Cinthea Ireland		David Ireland
Jan. 14—Samuel Irwin		Samuel Irwin
Jency Howell		Henry Howell
Oct. 19—Andrew Thompson		Andrew Thompson
Anna Betta Kelley		Isaac Williams
May 11—Pitts Chandler		Pitts Chandler
Pernelia Henderson		Wm. Moss
Feb. 7—Joseph Orondaff	H. L. Douglas	Joseph Orondaff
Nelly Harlen		Tom Bradley
June 8—John Wheeler		John Wheeler
Anne Clark		Albin J. Dearing
Mar. 16—John Cartwright		John Cartwright
Polly Dillard		Robert W. P'Pool
July 10—Hugh Henry	H. L. Douglas	Hugh Henry
Phebe Oneal		Charles
Mar. 27—John Blurton		John Blurton
Sally McMennaway		Ebenezar Donelson
Feb. 23—Robert Irwin	John Allcorn	Robert Irwin
Mary Luch ?		John Luch—?
Evered Parker		Evered Parker
Nancy Johnson		John Bryan
Feb. 26—Thomas Bogle	John Allcorn	Thomas Bogle
Rachel Brison		Joseph Brison
Oct. 7—David Barton	John Allcorn	David Barton
Sarah Borum		Richard Borum
Oct. 12—Samuel Bettis	John Allcorn	Sam'l Bettis
Achaza Chapman		Will Bettis
Kenneth Bethoson		Kenneth Bethoson
Delilah Ragsdale		Richard Ragsdale
Mar. 23—Bernard Carter		Bernard Carter
Betsy Benthal		Dan Benthal
Jan. 21—James Mays		James Mays
Polly Tucker		James Murmett
Dec. 4—James Laceter	John Allcorn	James Laceter
Susannah Allen Cetchern		Jacob Laceter
James Crawford		James Crawford
Amy Thrower		William Crawford
May 30—John W. McSpaden	John Allcorn	John W. McSpaden
Rachel Brady		Collin C. Stoneman
Feb. 13—Morris G. Burton	Edmund Crutcher	Morris G. Burton
Polly Reading		Lewis Reading
Sept. 14—John W. White	John Allcorn	John W. White
Susanah Bradley		John Bradley
Jan. 21—Lewis Hancock	John Allcorn	Lewis Hancock
Frances Adams		Abraham Adams
April 16—John Davis	John Allcorn	John Davis
Theodelia Marton		Nathaniel Davis

Name	Test.	Surety
Sept. 10—James Bass Kissiah Rowland		Jones Bass Green Williams
Dec. 14—William Sypert Patsey Dew	John Allcorn	William Sypert Thomas Sypert
Nov. 17—Benjamin Fisher Peggy Crawford	H. L. Douglas	Benjamin Fisher Anderson Fisher
Mar. 16—Robert W. P'Pool Polly Cartwright		Robert W. P'Pool John Cartwright
Aug. 29—Jacob Casselenor Anne Moore		Jacob Casselnor Benjamin Casselnor
Oct. 15—Robert Smith Polly Marshall		Robert Smith William Marshall
Oct. 30—Henry Rogers Sally Graves		Henry Rogers John Ferington
Sept. 25—James Scott Lissa Bane (or Bone)		Jas. Scott William Scott
Feb. 5—Valentine Vanhooser Sally Upchurch		Valentine Vanhooser Joseph Jardwin (?)
June 28—Stephen Cloyd Polly Wilson		Stephen Cloyd Edmund Crutcher
June 4—Mathew East Jinsey McPeak	John Allcorn	Mathew East Aaron Sheron
Jan. 21—Reubin Allin Jemima Lewis	John Allcorn	Reubin Allin William Lewis
Jan. 7—Abraham Adams Nansey Adams	John Allcorn	Abraham Adams William Kennedy
Jan. 19—George McWhorter Patsey Mitchell	John Allcorn	George McWhorter Ishmal Bradshaw
No date—William Adamson Mary Wilson	John Allcorn	Will Adamson Michel Wilson
Oct. 6—Thomas Barton Tabitha Hodges		Thomas Barton Jesse Hodges
Feb. 20—Sam'l R. Anderson Fanny Parish		Sam'l R. Anderson Geo. W. Still
Henry Robertson Polly Lambert	John Allcorn, Clk.	Henry Robertson Jeremiah Taylor
Jan. 1—Richard B. McCorkle Ibby Campbell	John Allcorn	Richard B. McCorkle Thomas Hobbs
Jan. 16—Eddins Chandler Huldy Sherrool	John Allcorn	Eddins Chandler Sam'l Meredith
May 11—Randal Carter Polly Johnson		Randal Carter Harrison Eakin
June 17—Beuriah Bateman Sally Magness	John Allcorn	Beuriah Bateman Dewey Reeves
Nov. 20—Lamack Whitworth Polly Mitchell	H. L. Douglas	Lanack Whitworth —— Webb
Dec. 23—Benjami Morris Nannie Flowers	John Allcorn	Benjamin Morris Isaac Sanders
Dec. 26—Lewis Clark Patsey Doak		Lewis Clark T. Bradley

NAME	TEST.	SURETY
Aug. 26—James Thomas Nancy McMinn		James Thomas Jacob Thomas
Aug. 1—Isiah Cox Patsey P. Rather		James Rather Isiah Cox
	1812	
Aug. 1—Overton Harlen Betsy Hart	H. L. Douglas	Overton Harlen James Anderson
June 9—John Compton Lucinda Treavilian		John Compton Wm. Harris
June 2—John Rogers Leaty Hanible		John Rogers Wm. Bone
Mar. 2—Robert King Lyda Keeton	John Allcorn	Robert King James Hollingsworth
Feb. 24—John Oneal Dorcas Midget	John Allcorn	John Oneal Joseph Midget
Dec. 5—Byrd Smith Martha McAdow	John Allcorn	Byrd Smith William Brown
Jan. 18—Elijah Armstrong Peggy Higgins	H. L. Douglas	Elijah Armstrong Val Willard
July 4—James McAdow Judith Smith		James McAdow Harris Smith
Jan. 31—James McDaniel Peggy Green	H. L. Douglas	James McDaniel Harvey Young
May 16—John Eagan Margret Wray		John Eagan Luke Wray
Mar. 17—Dempsy Lambuth Hicksy Bettis	John Allcorn	Dempsy Lambuth Samuel Bettis
Mar. 31—Robert Bond Polly Benton		Robert Bond Alexander Carter
May 20—Thomas Knight Rebecah Jones		Thomas Knight Aquilla Knight
Jan. 29—William Terry Betsey Marton	Edmond Crutcher	William Terry T. Martin
Sept. 29—James Cawthon Sally Peak		James Cawthon John Cawthon
July 24—John Caplinger Catharine Harpole	John Allcorn H. L. Douglas	John Caplinger Aron Harpole
April 10—William Jennings Elizabeth Gibson		William Jennings Jesse Jennings
Oct. 1—Brent Blurton Nancy Bass	John Allcorn	Brent Blurton Hunter Blurton
May 13—Patrick Anderson Fanny Chandler	H. L. Douglas	Patrick Anderson Richard Anderson
July 28—Robert Mitchel Agey Moore	John Allcorn	Robert Mitchel Ishmal Bradshaw
June 23—Theodore Ross Peggy Garmany		Theodore Ross Ephram Farr
Nov. 7—James Calhoun Winney Woodward	John Allcorn	Joseph Barton
Oct. 21—Norman McDaniel Mildred Perrywood	H. L. Douglas	Norman McDaniel Samuel Dodd

Name	Test.	Surety
June 23—David Williams Betsey Hoozer	John Allcorn	David Williams Geo. Rogers
Aug. 1—Carter Marlow Gerlates Bryant	Edmund Crutcher	Carter Marlow Richard Marlow
Feb. 22—William Benson Fanny Dodd	John Allcorn	William Benson Moses Pruet
Aug. 26—Lewis Dickins Harriet Ashford	John Allcorn	Lewis Dickens Moses Ashford
Feb. 16—Arden Somers Nancy Tucker	John Allcorn	Arden Somers Cornelius Organ
May 30—Dudley Brown Edness Henderson		Dudly Brown Cornelius Organ
April 20—Dickerson Williams Patsey Allen		Dickerson Williams Valentine Vanhooser
June 14—Henry Blackwell Patsy Brown		Henry Blackwell Moses Brown
Feb. 3—John Blackburn Caty Carver		John Blackburn William Blackburn
April 15—Adam Harpole Polly Bettis	John Allcorn	Adam Harpole George Harpole
Mar. 21—George Smith Ally Martin	John Allcorn	George Smith Joseph Stacy
Feb. 10—James McDaniel Amy B. Vaughn	John Allcorn	James McDaniel Abram Vaughn
No date—James Weir Caty Shaw		James Weir William Steele
Oct. 5—Pleasant Irby Kezia Lamburt	John Allcorn	Pleasant Irby John Irby
William Wood Elizabeth B. Harris		William Wood John Dew
William Kelly Mornaw Keeton	John Allcorn	William Kelly Jas. Hollingsworth
David Smith Priscilla Bennett	John Allcorn	David Smith Joseph Cole
Joseph Hays Susannah Adams	John Allcorn	Joseph Hays John Hays
George Hamilton Doluthea Hamilton		George Hamilton Hugh Bradly
Aug. 29—Robert Wilson Jenny Donall		Robert Wilson Alexander McNeely
Sept. 28—Samuel Realy Cinthia Marler		Samuel Realy Eli Herrel
Isiah Tribble Patience Pemberton	John Allcorn	Isiah Tribble William Johnson
April 2—Luke Kent Polly Mann		Luke Kent Harry Brown
Feb. 22—James Drew Rebecca Brown	John Allcorn	James Drew Moses Brown
Mar. 23—William McHaney Sally Word		William McHaney John Lester
Dec. 24—Thomas Knight Ally Martin		Thomas Knight Charles Warren

Name	Test.	Surety
Wiley Whitley Polly ———	H. L. Douglas	Wiley Whitley Jerauld Lynch
Mar. 3—Lawrence Sypert Polly Lamberth	John Allcorn	Lawrence Sypert Thos. Sypert
July 11—Eli T. Hunt Sarah Webb		Eli T. Hunt Thos. Bradley
Jan. 7—Lewis Howel Polly Jennings	John Allcorn	Lewis Howel Henry Howel
Jan. 7—William Cooper Mary Blaylock	John Allcorn	William Cooper Eli T. Hunt
Joseph Young Peggy Stuart		Joseph D. Young James Stuart
Jan. 21—Aaron Romine Polly Wells	John Allcorn	Aaron Romine Thomas Conyer
Mar. 10—Henry Shelby Hannah Brown	John Allcorn	Henry Shelby Thomas Bradley
Feb. 5—Lewis Reding Elizabeth Johnson		Lewis Reding Isham Johnson
Nov. 2—Smith Belote Nancy Gill		Smith Belote William Gill
Aug. 13—Hugh Bradly Patsey Hunter		Hugh Bradly James Bradly
Mar. 17—William Bettis Minny Lamberth		William Bettis Samuel Bettis
Mar. 14—John C. Tippet Caty Hart	John Allcorn	John Tippet Stephen Barton
Aug. 1—McKinsey Marlow Nancy McMillin	Edmund Crutcher	McKinsey Marlow Richard Marlow
Nov. 27—Harris Smith Nancy Flood		Harris Smith Samuel Kelly
Feb. 11—William Parrish Martha Davis	John Allcorn	William Parrish Berryman Robertson
Mar. 30—John Kimbro Nancy Bearden	John Allcorn	John Kimbro James Mitchel
Oct. 24—Nicholas Edwards Milly Powers	John Allcorn	Nicholas Edwards Daniel Moser
Sept. 10—Lewis Johnson Elly Wright	John Allcorn	Lewis Johnson John Bryan
Mar. 25—William Mount Mary Jones		William Mount Robert Whitton
July 23—William Marshall Catharine Marshall		William Marshall Thomas Bradley
Oct. 15—Shadrick Smith Nancy Howard		Shadrick Smith Lewis Patterson
Feb. 28—Lemuel Brichan Polly Logan	John Allcorn	Lemuel Brichan David Logan
Oct. 2—William Jewell Annie Thomas	H. L. Douglas	William Jewell Jacob Thomas
Jan. 4—Joseph Gray Agness Denton		No witnesses
Jan. 29—Jesse Brinson Susannah Moss		Jesse Brinson Jacob Cook

Name	Test.	Surety
Jan. 3—Michael Robertson Mary Hank		Michael Robertson Sam'l McAdams
Jan. 4—Joseph Humphries Nancy Brown	John Allcorn	Joseph Humphries Edward Brown
Dec. 3—Thomas Patterson Mary Harpole	John Allcorn	Thos. Patterson Wyatt Bettis
Sept. 12—Richard Warmack Agey Smith	Edmund Crutcher	Richard Warmack John Smith
July 25—John Hays Betsey Estes	John Allcorn	Jno. Hays Sam'l Hays
Mar. 21—Martin Frankling Nelly Watson		Martin Frankling Bethlehem Estes
Mar. 30—Alexander Rutledge Nancy Cox		Alexander Rutledge Stephen Barton
Oct. 17—Thomas Robertson Betsey Wooten		Thos. Robertson Thomas McKnight
Aug. 28—Charles Golston Elizabeth Neel		Charles Golston Robert ————
July 7—Isham Quarles Polly Paschal	H. L. Douglas	Isham Quarles Elisha Christian
Nov. 25—Thomas Calleway Alice Griffin		Thomas Calleway James Coats
Aug. 22—William Hancock Neely West	John Allcorn	Wm. Hancock Major Hancock
Nov. 10—John Morrow Sally Hall	John Allcorn	John Morrow Charles Fox
Oct. 14—Joseph Phillips Martha Williams	Edmund Crutcher	Joseph Phillips Abel Williams
Aug. 24—Joseph Bridges Elizabeth Gill	John Allcorn	Joseph Bridges Thomas Bridges
July 15—Robert Johnson Susan Adams		Robert Johnson Isaac McKee
Nov. 17—Henry Wright Sally Endsley	John Allcorn	Henry Wright Hugh Endsley
Sept. 10—Jesse Dickins Polly McDerment		Jesse Dickins Adam Vinyard
Sept. 16—Robert Eason Lidiah Hariss	John Allcorn	Robert Eason Benj. Chapman
Aug. 10—Benjamin Bonner Lucy Locke	John Allcorn	Benjamin Bonner Thomas Locke

1813

Name	Test.	Surety
Dec. 18—John Little Betsey Reynold	Edmund Crutcher	John Little Warren Eatherly
Mar. 10—Niel Smith Betsey Reese	Edmund Crutcher	Niel Smith Richard Smith
Sept. 24—William Jennings Elizabeth Gibson	Edmund Crutcher	William Jennings John Hubbard
Nov. 17—John Bachelor Nancy Clackston		John Bachelor Asa Todd
Nov. 20—James Miligan Elizabeth Blanton	Edmund Crutcher	James Miligan Westley Higgins

Name	Test.	Surety
Oct. 4—Simpson Organ Sina Wilson	Edmund Crutcher	Simpson Organ Koley Organ
Nov. 3—Burwell Kemp Elizabeth Romling		James Dyer Burwell Kemp
July 19—William George Catlincey Hunt	E. Douglas	William George Hardey Hunt
Sept. 30—John Pugh Polly Donelson	Edmund Crutcher	John Pugh W. M. Richards
Nov. 3—Robert Baskin Rachel Ricketts	Edmund Crutcher	Robert Baskin James McKnight
Oct. 25—Dillard Beasley Sally Harris	Edmund Crutcher	Lillard Beasley Thomas Locke
Sept. 20—James Stuart Mary Allen		James Stuart Walter Clopton
Dec. 22—Anderson Freeman Delila Yearnell	Edmund Crutcher	Anderson Freeman Cates Freeman
Dec. 15—James Irwin Elizabeth D. Robb	Edmund Crutcher	James Irwin Will Robb
Jan. 3—William McNeely Grace Shaw	Edmund Crutcher	William McNeely George Ross
Dec. 6—John Cooper Piney Rogers	Edmund Crutcher	John Cooper William Woodward

1814

Name	Test.	Surety
Dec. 28—Brinkley Bridges Nancy McWhirter	John Allcorn	Brinkly Bridges William Young
Mar. 5—James Bates Sally Stephenson	John Allcorn	James Bates James Bradberry
Aug. 15—A. W. Huddleston Elizabeth Lewis		A. W. Huddleston Isaac Winston
Apr. 11—Green Cooke Polly Nicholson		Green Cooke Thomas Bradley
April 20—Nathaniel Parker Polly Thomas	John Allcorn	Nathaniel Parker Willis Bryan
April 25—Thomas Lock Polly Beasley		Thomas Lock Thomas Bonner
April 11—Lewis Shepard Elizabeth Parrish	Edmund Crutcher	Lewis Shepard William Parrish
Nov. 8—Nolley Talbott Rebecah Owens	Edmund Crutcher	Nolley Talbott Jeremiah Owen
Nov. 14—Isaac Griffin Ibby Wiley		Isaac Griffin David Wily
Nov. 17—John Langley Sally Christy	Edmund Crutcher	John Langley Samuel Underhill
Nov. 9—James Smith Patsey Johnston	Edmund Crutcher	James Smith James Braden
Sept. 10—William Reese Livena Scobey		William Reese James Turner
Aug. 22—William Gleeves Polly Wilson		William Gleeves William F. Harris
Aug. 29—Bradford Edwards Jenney Bond		Bradford Edwards Thomas Bond

Name	Test.	Surety
Sept. 12—Hallam Sullivan Polly Osment		Hallam Sullivan James Osment
July 23—Elisha Hodges Milly Ward	John Allcorn	Elisha Hodges Josiah Hodges
Aug. 29—Samuel Crutchfield Nancy Mahaland		Samuel Crutchfield John Cartwright
Jan. 8—Andrew Baird Patsey Hunt	Edmund Crutcher	Andrew Baird David Baird
April 9—Jesse Sullivan Anne Rice	John Allcorn	Jesse Sullivan Hallam Sullivan
Feb. 28—Lewis Land Nancey Bethune	John Allcorn	Lewis Land Richard Ragsdale
Jan. 31—William Bennett Elly Tippet	John Allcorn	Wm. Bennett John C. Johnson
Aug. 9—Richard Lewis Mc- Knight Permelia Woodward		Richard L. McKnight John Thomas
May 10—William McElyea Jenney Sutton	John Allcorn	William McElyea Stephen Barton
May 13—John Cloyd Lettes Alexander		John Cloyd Sam'l Meredith
Mar. 22—Noah Walker Patsey Davis	Edmund Crutcher	Noah Walker Jeremiah Stephens
Oct. 11—Joseph Larwell Selah Hanby		Joseph Laswell Wm. Baskin
Mar. 16—Jeremiah Steven Polly Hallems		Jeremiah Stevens Noah Walker
Mar. 4—James Miller Nancy McPeak	Edmund Crutcher	James Miller Wm. McPeak
Mar. 18—Robert Hight Betsey Harris	Edward Douglas	Robert Hight John L. Bartlett
Feb. 28—John Williams Elizabeth Browning		John Williams Elijah Jones
Nov. 17—John Langley Sally Christy		John Allcorn, Clk. Wilson County
Feb. 25—Eli Allen Elizabeth Lasater		John Allcorn, Clk.
Sept. 3—William Roach Ann Sparrow	John Allcorn	William Roach James Drennon
Dec. 19—William Hall Martha Willard		William Hall James Willard
Dec. 20—Joseph Greenwood Elizabeth ———		Joseph Greenwood A Harris
Sept. 1—Edward Sims Dolly Grubbs		Edward Sims J. H. Dickerson
Mar. 7—James Ewing Nancy Smith		James Ewing Abner Wason
Oct. 1—Lewis Wood Polly Pearcy		Lewis Wood Algen Pearcy
—— 22—Samuel Kelley Polly Cross	H. L. Douglas	Samuel Kelley Elijah Cross

NAME	TEST.	SURETY
Dec. 6—Morris Brewer Sally Shannon		Morris Brewer James Braden
July 7—Isham Quarles Polly Paschal	H. L. Douglas	Isham Quarles Elisha Christian
Aug. 28—Charles Golston Elizabeth Neel		Charles Golston Robert Goodman
	1815	
Feb. 14—Henry B. Maxey Peggy Taylor	John Allcorn	Henry B. Maxey James Davis
April 20—Andrew McDaniel Nancy Harris		Andrew McDaniel James McDaniel
July 31—John Cross Elizabeth West	Edmund Crutcher	John Cross Joshua Anderson
July 22—George D. Summers Polly Jennings		George D. Summers Joel Jennings
Aug. 4—Stephen Drewry Elizabeth Allin	John Allcorn	Stephen Drewry Fredrick Watkins
Aug. 4—Micajah Joiner Patsey Wood		Cornelius Joiner

I, John Jarrett, a minister of the Gospel in the State of Tennessee, do hereby certify that I solemnized the rites of matrimony between Lot Joiner and Polly Jones, the persons herein named, on the 7th Dec., 1815.—John Jarrett.

NAME	TEST.	SURETY
Sept. 18—Joel Jennings Centhia Gibson		Joel Jennings Leonard H. Lewis
Dec. 16—Abel Williams Peggy Massey	John Allcorn	Abel Williams William Phillips
Oct. 9—Solomon Bond Frances Alsup	John Allcorn	Solomon Bond Asap Alsop
Dec. 19—Edward Edwards Nancy Clemmons	W. L. H——?	Edward Edwards Nicholas Edwards
Dec. 21—Thomas Bennett Elizabeth Bond		Thomas Bennett Freeman Madglin
Oct. 9—William Boyd Faithy Lawrence	John Allcorn	Wm. Boyd Alben E. Dearing
Alexander McNeely Fanny Hamilton		Alexander McNeely W. Woodward
July 19—James P. Thompson Mary Gwin		James P. Thompson H. L. Douglas
Oct. 7—James Basford Mary Bradshaw	John Allcorn	James Basford Robert Crary
Oct. 11—William Buchanon Nancy Worthan	Edmund Crutcher	William Buchanan B. W. McWhirter
Oct. 18—Robertson Wright Sally Golston	John Allcorn	Robertson Wright Stephen Sypert
Dec. 20—Samuel Braly Peggy McSpaden	Edmund Crutcher	Samuel Braly Samuel McSpaden
Dec. 18—Thos. C. McSpaden Jane Baker		Thos. C. McSpaden Robert Baker

Name		Test.	Surety
Oct. 21—	Samuel McDaniel Jane McKnight	John Allcorn	Samuel McDaniel James Braden
Oct. 18—	Elijah Wamack Elizabeth Patterson		Elijah Wamack John Campbell
Nov. 6—	Richard Cartwright Anne Waters		Richard Cartwright Wilson T. Waters
Dec. 30—	Thomas Grissom Margery Robertson	L. C. Rease	Thomas Grissom Hilling Peace
Nov. 28—	John Mills Elizabeth Hocker	Edmund Crutcher	John Mills Joseph Swingler
Nov. 4—	James Miller Peggy Henderson	John Allcorn	James Miller Preston Henderson
Sept. 27—	George Small Philpena Jarman		George Small Robert Jarman
Nov. 21—	Henry Radford Caty Crook	Edmund Crutcher	Henry Radford James Crook
Dec. 19—	Henry Rice Nancy Cawthon		Henry Rice John Hannah
Dec. 29—	Geo. Moore Fanny Fuller		George Moore William Draper
Oct. 4—	Thomas Tune Betsey Hickman	Edmund Crutcher	Thomas Tune Joseph Turnham
Dec. 2—	John Motheral Cynthia Farr		John Motheral Allen Smith
Oct. 7—	Arthur McSpaden Hallen Brinson	John Allcorn	Arthur McSpaden John McSpaden
Sept. 27—	Jacob Bennett Ceta Bonds	John Allcorn	Jacob Bennett Thomas Bennett
Oct. 9—	Harrison Harris Priscilla Brown	John Allcorn	Harrison Harris William Bettis
Nov. 9—	George W. Still Polly L. Wynn	Edmund Crutcher	George W. Still James L. Wynn
Oct. 7—	John B. Parker Ellenor Tipton	Wm. Anderson	John B. Parker Edward W. Vaughan
Dec. 20—	Phillip Haas Gracy McNeely		Phillip Haas Christopher Cooper
Oct. 10—	Warren Moore Cleary Babb	John Allcorn	Warren Moore George W. Still
Nov. 30—	Zachariah Davis Elizabeth Hill		Zachariah Davis James Johnson
Dec. 11—	Richard Phelps Patsy Akin	John Allcorn	Richard Phelps Isham Palmer
Dec. 5—	Mason Moore Cealy Caplinger	John Allcorn	Mason Moore Wilson Jenkins
Jan. 31—	James Seal Rebecca Foley	John Allcorn	James Seal John Conegy
Mar. 11—	Joseph Short Biddy Gibson	H. L. Douglas	Joseph Short James Brinson
Aug. 19—	Edward Estes Nancy Lewis	John Allcorn	Edward Estes Martin Franklin
Aug. 3—	Owen Quinley Polly Sullivan		Owen Quinley Stephen W. Byrn

Name	Test.	Surety
July 8—John Whitlock Nancy West	John Allcorn	John Whitlock James Whitlock
July 22—Smidley Lynch Elizabeth Robertson		Smidley Lynch Hezakiah Rhodes
Feb. 14—William Pugh Jenny Donelson		William Pugh David Pugh
Jan. 13—Andrew Finney Nansy Phillips	John Allcorn	David Finney Armstrong Herd
Mar. 6—Abner Wasson Elizabeth Quarles	H. L. Douglas	Abner Wasson A. Dale
Mar. 2—George H. Bullard Elizabeth Spradlen	John Allcorn	George H. Bullard John Harpole
Jan. 2—Josiah Brichun Sally Logan	John Allcorn	Josiah Brichun James Brichun
Mar. 13—Beverly Scurlock Elizabeth Harpole	Edmund Crutcher	Beverly Scurlock George Harpole
Mar. 21—Aquilla Greer Elizabeth Welch	John Allcorn	Aquilla Greer John Johnson.
Feb. 28—William Lawrence Elizabeth Neil		Wm. Lawrence S. Cahoon Reams
Feb. 8—John Boon Cloe Garrison		John Boon William Oakley
July 8—William P. Morris Lucy Maddocks	Edmund Crutcher	William P. Morris Isham Morris
Feb. 23—Henry Akins Sally Still		Henry Akins George W. Still
July 8—Jemison Bandy Elizabeth Taylor		Janison Bandy Silas Freeman
July 27—Richard Ragsdale Margret Mark	John Allcorn	Richard Ragsdale Kennard Bethoon
July 25—Archabald Shannon Matilda Allen	Edmund Crutcher Wm. Overall	Archibald Shannon Joseph Swinglier
Aug. 19—John Roach Polly Kirkpatrick	John Allcorn	John Roach Thomas Kirkpatrick
April 7—Richard Smith Polly Merrett		Richard Smith Absolom Smith
April 8—William Wisener Nancy Hopson	John Allcorn	William Wisener Wm. Tarver
April 25—Littleberry Madlock Phebee Sharp	Edmund Crutcher	Littleberry Madlock William Thomas
April 26—Eli Harris Cinthia Moore		Eli Harris Samuel Harris
April 1—Thomas Williams Elizabeth Williams	John Allcorn	Thomas Williams Henry Smith
Mar. 8—Anset Whitefield Fanny Tisdale	John Allcorn	Anset Whitefield Thomas Blair
Aug. 7—Allen Ross Susannah Proctor		Allen Ross Edmond Proctor
Dec. 21—William Anglen Elizabeth Sheppard	John Allcorn	Wm. Anglen Aaron Anglen
April 22—Seth Hackney Fany Edwards		Seth Hackney Jacob Lasater

Name	Test.	Surety & Minister or Justice of Peace
Feb. 28—Julius Sanders Penney Fields	John Allcorn	Julius Sanders Richard Fields
Jan. 12—Cornelius N. Lewis Polly Figures		C. N. Lewis Edward Dale
Dec. 2—Francis Wynn Susannah Cavis	John Allcorn	Francis Wynn Thomas Bradley
July 31—Peter Sullivan Sally Avary	John Allcorn	Executed by Jacob Sullivan
	1816	
Mar. 28—James Cravens Charity Tait	John Allcorn	John Williamson, J.P.
Nov. 27—Thomas T. Hays Sally Drake	John Allcorn	J. F. Davis, J. P.
Feb. 7—John Flowers Rachel Deloach	John Allcorn	Moore Stepherson
Jan. 22—Benjamin T. Motley Patsey Drake	John Allcorn	Samuel Donnell, J.P.
Dec. 14—Valentine Vanhooser Sally Rowland	John Allcorn	Joseph T. Williams, J. P.
July 25—James Howard Elizabeth Collings	John Allcorn	Joshua Lester, J. P.
Mar. 14—John Phelp Sally Carlin	John Allcorn	Thomas B. Reife, J.P.
July 3—Amos Gibson Jeminiah Collins	John Allcorn	Edmund Crutcher,J.P
Sept. 10—Mercer Morriss Rebecca Wright	John Allcorn	Abner Williams, J. P.
April 12—John Ridgeway Elizabeth Aims	John Allcorn	Abner Hill, Minister Gosp.
Feb. 3—Charles Harrington Visey Johnson	John Allcorn	Abner Hill, Minister Gosp.
Nov. 27—William Modglin Nelly Dukes	John Allcorn	Abner Hill, Minister Gosp.
Sept. 14—Hallan Sullivan Polly Ozment	John Allcorn	L. Sullivan
Aug. 29—James Carruth Polly Donnell	John Allcorn	Samuel Donnell, V. D. M.
Feb. 24—Benton Modglin Patsey Haily	John Allcorn	Abner Hill, Minister Gosp.
Dec. 17—William Hays Jenny Adams	John Allcorn	James Madon, J. P.
Nov. 28—Ebenezer Hearn Elizabeth Foster	John Allcorn	Sam'l Canon, J. P.
April 13—Elijah Parsons Polly Turner	John Allcorn	Executed by James McAdow, Esq.
Sept. 5—Ridley Wynne Fanny Miles	John Allcorn	Executed by John Hannah, J. P.
Feb. 23—Houston Alexander Abby Vernatta	John Allcorn	Abner W. Bone, J. P.
June 6—Custiss Oneal Polly Brooks	John Allcorn	James Davidson,J.P.

NAME	TEST.	Surety and Minister or Justice of Peace
Jan. 4—Drury Hall Sally Thrower	John Allcorn	A. Harris, J. P.
April 16—Joseph Moxley Levina Clemons	John Allcorn	Edward Warren, J. P.
Dec. 8—Solomon Gibson Tempa Modglin	John Allcorn	Abner Hill, Minister Gosp.
July 25—Moses Cunnighan Polly Cropper	John Allcorn	John W. Peyton, J. P.
Jan. 18—David Gibson Purity Bloodworth	John Allcorn	Ransom Gwynne
Aug. 29—Elijah Cherry Jenny Chadock	John Allcorn	Thomas Catroon
Jan. 17—John Guthrie Cloe Babb	John Allcorn	John Jarritt
Nov. 12—John W. Nichols Nancy Anderson	John Allcorn	Ransom Gwynne
Dec. 29—David Bradshaw Tempa Casson	John Allcorn	Alen C. Carruth, J. P.
Aug. 7—Wilson T. Waters Polly Lawrence	John Allcorn	Thomas Durham, Minister Gosp.
Jan. 13—Moses Owen Jenny Reeves	John Allcorn	James McAdow
April 9—Ransom King Addy Rogers	John Allcorn	H. Shelby, J. P.
June 27—Joseph Lawrence Polly Neil	John Allcorn	Thomas Durham, Minister Gosp.
Mar. 11—Robert Tilford Nancy Chawning	John Allcorn	David Foster
Dec. 26—Archibald Ray Lou Ellen Thompson	John Allcorn	William Gray, J.P. J. P.
Jan. 24—Ira Tatum Patsey Eddings	John Allcorn	——— Henderson, J. P.
Oct. 4—David Estes Hannah Jackson	John Allcorn	James McAdow, J. P.
Nov. 24—Wilson Webb Frances Ann Tarp-ley	John Allcorn	John Page
Aug. 4—Owen Quinley Polly Sullivan	John Allcorn	John Sullivan, J. P.
June 25—Henry Moser Elizabeth Oneal	John Allcorn	Abner Hill, Minis-ter
May 16—David Arnold Susannah Bryson	John Allcorn	John Miller, J. P.
July 19—Benjamin Prichard Polly Campbell	John Allcorn	Abner W. Bone, J. P.
Mar. 28—John P. Maddox Polly Jones	John Allcorn	Elijah Moore, Min-ister
Mar. 14—George Sands Cassey Green	John Allcorn	Joseph T. Williams J. P.
June 5—James Dooley Nancy Woodward	John Allcorn	Thomas Calhoun, D. M.

Name	Test.	Surety and Minister or Justice of Peace
Sept. 11—William Reese Levina Scoby	John Allcorn	Thomas Calhoun, D. M.
Jan. 16—Tazwell Mitchell Sally Stuart	John Allcorn	John Bonner, J. P.
Mar. 14—Benjamin Cox Nancy Bean	John Allcorn	Joseph T. Williams, J. P.
Dec. 10—David McKnight Patsey M. McWhirter	John Allcorn	Jesse Alexander, J.P.
Nov. 30—John Mills Elizabeth Hooker	John Allcorn	Ransom Gwynn, J.P.
July 11—Banister Anderson Betsey Anderson	John Allcorn	Joseph T. Williams, J. P.
Nov. 9—George W. Still Polly L. Wynne	John Allcorn	John Jarrett, Preacher
Mar. 14—Edmund Proctor Judith Dill	John Allcorn	John Jarrett, Minister
Sept. 14—William Roach Ann Sparrow	John Allcorn	David Foster
Dec. 10—William Hollinsworth Phebe Owen	John Allcorn	James McAdow, J. P.
Mar. 26—Nathaniel Davis Patsey Bumpass	John Allcorn	Wm. Bumpass, D.D.
May 30—Isham Patterson Peggy Bradley	John Allcorn	Isaac Winston, J. P.
Nov. 3—Enoch Kannedy Nancy Bettis	John Allcorn	Abner Hill, Minister
Mar. 21—Eli Lansden Elizabeth Bone	John Allcorn	Wm. Bumpass
Sept. 5—Abel Hunt Elizabeth F. Bell	John Allcorn	James Richmond, J. P.
Dec. 8—Elisha Dismukes Fany Petty	John Allcorn	Jas. Johnson, J. P.
Mar. 28—Absolon Lasater Elizabeth Rainey	John Allcorn	Isaac Winston, J. P.
April 7—Josiah Brinson Betsy Modglin	John Allcorn	Abner Hill, Minister
Feb. 25—Jacob McDerment Ruby Trusty	John Allcorn	Elijah Maddox
Nov. 7—Butler Arnold Rachel Hudson	John Allcorn	William Gray, J. P.
May 9—Moses Barret Rebecca Fisher	John Allcorn	Ransom Gwynn, J. P.
Nov. 21—John Campbell Mary Dodds	John Allcorn	John W. Peyton, J.P.

1817

Name	Test.	Surety and Minister or Justice of Peace
April 12—Jesse Donnell Sally Croppet		Jesse Donnell John Donnell
Nov. 21—William Jones Polly Florady	John Allcorn	William Jones Benjamin Bright

Name	Test.	Surety
Sept. 16—Sutton Belcher Abigale Ellis	John Allcorn	Sutton Belcher James Ellis
Feb. 5—William Melton Lucinda Wilmath	Henry Cage	William Melton Archibald Melton
Mar. 7—Edmond York Nancy Bass		Edward York James York
Feb. 27—Alexander Stuart Chastain Evans	Edmund Crutcher	Alexander Stuart Joseph Stuart
Oct. 29—Alvis Sellers Jane Cumings	John Allcorn	Alvis Sellars Geo. D. Cumings
Jan. 22—Zachariah Rickets Sally May	John Allcorn	Zachariah Rickets Lanslot Viverett
Sept. 24—Samuel Speed Patsy Archer	John Allcorn	Samuel Speed Jacob Archer
Mar. 19—John W. Greer Rachel Thomas		John W. Greer Samuel Y. Thomas
May 6—Mathias B. Click Nancy Moss		Mathias B. Click Wm. Moss
Jan. 30—Elisha Winter Rhody Campbell	John Allcorn	Elisha Winter William Phillips
July 25—John McAdow Patsy Leech		John McAdow David H. Todd
Jan. 21—Bennett Babb Abegale Guthrie		Bennett Babb Mathew Harris
July 2—William C. Collins Sarah B. Wortham	H. L. Douglas	William Collins Joseph Cocke
Jan. 28—Jacob Hollingsworth Lydia Fuston	John Allcorn	Jacob Hollingsworth James Hollingsworth
Dec. 22—Philip Koonce Polly Fields		Philip Koonce David Fields
Mar. 24—John C. Jones Elizabeth Lane	W. Anderson	John C. Jones Edward Jones
Mar. 26—John McAffry Patsey W. Hunt		John McAffry Hardy H. Leaswell
Sept. 22—George D. Moore Priscilla Horn	John Allcorn	George D. Moore John Hearn
Sept. 24—Daniel Jackson Sally Jackson	John Allcorn	Daniel Jackson James Slate
Aug. 30—John Irby Nancy Harris		John Irby Wm. Steele
Aug. 6—William Patterson Louella Hight	Edmund Crutcher	William Patterson Frank Ricketts
Dec. 16—William Avery Permelia Sparry	Edmund Crutcher	William Avery Peter Sullivan
Dec. 16—Nathan Simpson Polly S. Mitchel	F. C. Crutcher	Nathan Simpson Henry B. McDonald
Aug. 30—Boswell Goodman Mary Bumpass	John Allcorn	Boswell Goodman Robert Smith
Sept. 23—William F. Jones Lucy Warmack	Edmund Crutcher	William F. Jones George H. Bullard
Dec. 3—James Johnson Polly E. Erwin	H. L. Douglas	James Johnson Samuel Calhoun

Name		Test.	Surety
Dec. 29—	Allen Avery Polly Wynne	F. C. Crutcher	Allen Avery John Smith
Sept. 11—	Mathew Horn Martha T. Babb		Mathew Horn Wm. W. Babb
July 26—	William B. Smith Sarah Randolft		William B. Smith George B. Smith
Dec. 6—	Henry Horn Elizabeth Brien	John Allcorn	Henry Horn Richard Hight
Sept. 27—	Absolom Smith Lydia Beard	John Allcorn	John Williamson, J.P.
Oct. 13—	Elisha Simms Ann Clopton		Elisha Simms Joseph Cocke
Oct. 11—	John Davidson Elizabeth Brown	Edmund Crutcher	John Davidson Henry Howell
May 13—	Joseph Moore Lydia Adams		Joseph Moore Elijah Cross
Nov. 9—	Cornelius Organ Kathrine Benthal		Cornelius Organ Elijah Cross
April 28—	Herman Edwards Sally Bond	John Allcorn	Herman Edwards Bradford Edwards
Jan. 9—	Ira E. Eason Dolly Vaughan	John Allcorn	Ira E. Eason James A. Hunter
May 30—	Daniel Mosely Nancy Corder		Daniel Mosely William Talbot
Aug. 3—	John Hogdwood Rhody Pemberton	John Allcorn	John Hogdwood Richard Pemberton
May 13—	Joseph Cloyd Caty Alexander	John Allcorn	Joseph Cloyd Wm. S. Alexander
Jan. 21—	Miller Carter Pheby Phillips		Miller Carter Benjamin Phillips
Jan. 27—	Robert B. Roberts Mary Ann Miller		Robert B. Roberts Thomas Bradly
Oct. 8—	Aaron Romine Polly Conyer	Edmund Crutcher	Aaron Romine Robert Sypert
Sept. 16—	John F. Brown Margret F. Seawell		John F. Brown Mathew Dew
Feb. 13—	James Slate Elizabeth Hallum		James Slate John Hallum
Jan. 12—	Green Tucker Priscilla Williams		Green Tucker Jesse Dew
Mar. 10—	Jonathan Wiley Ruth M. Brown		Jonathan Wiley John B. Brown
Dec. 1—	Sterling Harrison Elizabeth Jones		Sterling Harrison Thomas Edwards
Jan. 2—	Boyd Summers Tobina Jacobs	John Allcorn	Boyd Summers Thomas Bell
Dec. 15—	Tedeceat Tate Ellen Jones		Z. Tate Moses T. Brooks
	John Telford Sally Green		John Tilford Hugh Tilford
	Benjamin Clayton Luckey Quarles		Ben Clayton Edward Clayton

Name	Test.	Surety
Jan. 18—John Ellis Mary Sandford	John Allcorn	John Ellis John Campbell
Jan. 22—William Setter Sally Ray	John Allcorn	William Setter Willis Wray
Jan. 15—Joseph Casky Caty Scobey	John Allcorn	Joseph Caskey Joseph Weir
Mar. 7—Aaron Cluck Marenda Howel		Aaron Cluck Wm. Alsop
Jan. 18—Joseph Eddings Parthena Henderson	John Allcorn	Joseph Eddings Benjamin Tucker
April 19—William Coats Patsey Trasy	John Allcorn	Wm. Coats J. B. Taylor
William Baskins Rebecca Belt	John Allcorn	Wm. Baskins Aaron Gibson
Jan. 8—James Hancock Ann Avery		James Hancock Wm. Avery
Jan. 9—William Wray Ann Wright		Wm. Wray J. W. Wright
Sept. 6—William Willis Rhody Sperry		William Willis George J. Martin
June 19—Elijah Rew Saly A. Brown	Edmund Crutcher	Elijah Rew Stephen Brown
Sept. 2—John E. Warren Sally Jennings		John E. Warren Samuel H. Porterfield
Nov. 2—John Bradberry Bershaba Golston	Edmund Crutcher	John Bradberry Thomas Arrington
Oct. 29—Alvis Sellars Jane Cumings		John Allcorn, C.W.C.
Feb. 26—Green Flowers Mary Sypert		Green Flowers James T. Coats
Oct. 11—Isaac Carver Mary Hugels		Isaac Carver Wm. Carver
Sept. 6—Thomas L. Hill Ann Lansden		Thomas L. Hill Merritt Lansden
Oct. 11—Mils Wood Elizabeth A. Tipton		Mils Wood Elijah Curry
Sept. 27—Absolom Smith Lydia Beard	John Allcorn	Absolom Smith James H. Young
William Chison Patsy Griffin		William Chison John Griffin
May 7—George Webb Nancy Cross		George Webb Woodson Webb
April 2—Nathan Williams Polly Arnold		Nathan Williams John Conyers
Mar. 17—Turner Perry Rhody Goodman	John Allcorn	Turner Perry William Goodman
Aug. 5—Daniel Aston Jane D. Bell		Daniel Aston James Slate
July 16—James Ozment Elizabeth Eddings		James Osment Wm. M. Swain

NAME	TEST.	SURETY
Ephriam G. Harris Isabella H. Miller		Eph'm G. Harris Andrew Foster
June 10—Ezekiel C. Witty Mary Allison		Ezekiel C. Witty Ezekiel A. Sharp
June 19—Eli Edwards Milly Hancock		Eli Edwards Jonathan Dake
Sept. 9—James Turner Kiziah Hunter	John Allcorn	James Turner T. Bradley
Sept. 30—Joseph Patton Ann Patterson	John Allcorn	Joseph Patton Andrew Thompson
June 16—Israel Moore Sally Roach		Isreal Moore Wm. Moore
Dec. 26—John Merritt Nancy Bandy	F. G. Crutcher	John Merritt Miller Carraway
Mar. 26—James M. Hurt Martha Marshall		James M. Hurt Samuel Meredith
Jan. 20—James Oneal Elizabeth Caplinger		James Oneal John W. Carter
Oct. 28—Allen Fuller Nancy Harris	Edmund Crutcher	Allen Fuller Duke W. Harris
Nov. 10—Richard Ramsey Harriet New		Richard Ramsey R. C. Davis
Feb. 4—William Mickie Betsey Flood	F. G. Crutcher	William Mickie John McAdow
Dec. 24—John F. Porter Josaphine Whit- worth		John F. Foshe John Branard
Aug. 19—Harry L. Douglas Zuritha Allcorn	W. A. N. ?	Harry L. Douglas Harry Cage
Dec. 18—Thomas C. Stone Sally Justice		Thomas C. Stone Isaac Easly
Nov. 27—Thomas Taylor Anna Ramsey	Edmund Crutcher	Thomas Taylor James Bowman
May 7—Leaven Rusell Anna Alsup		Leaven Rusel Samuel Meridith
July 12—James Godphrey Frances Rogers	John Allcorn	James Godphrey Josiah Rogers
Dec. 4—William Altman Susannah R. Mitch- ell		Wm. Altman John H. Paskel
Feb. 11—Joseph Hall Rebecca Archer	F. G. Crutcher	Joseph Hall Prescot Mitchel
Dec. 16—Joseph Cocke Sarah W. Winston		Joseph Cocke William C. Collins
Feb. 12—Samuel Parker Maude Shaw	John Allcorn	Samuel Parker Abner Shaw
Sept. 3—William Bilbro Margret McFarland	John Allcorn	Wm. Brilbro John McFarland
April 12—James Braden Betsey M. Merritt	John Allcorn	James Braden Alexander Braden

Name	Test.	Surety
Jan. 21—John Putnar (or Preston) Rachel Bond		John Putnar (or Preston) James Bond
Feb. 21—Moses Mitchel Elenor Hodge		Moses Mitchell George Hodge
Feb. 22—Sion H. Mitchell Elizabeth Cook	John Allcorn	Sion H. Mitchell William Ball
Feb. 25—John Cocke Elizabeth H. Williams	Wm. Anderson	Thomas Cocke Wm. C. Collins
Sept. 2—David Todd Margret Luck	John Allcorn	David Todd O. G. Finley
Aug. 5—Mille Jones Pheby Saterfield	John Allcorn	Mille Jones John P. Maddox
April 26—David Fields Rhody Ferrington		David Fields Ira Gibson
Nov. 15—Richard Penberton Chinca Gillespie	F. G. Crutcher	Richard Penberton Elijah Cross
June 12—George Espey Lucrecy Brown	Edmund Crutcher	George Espey David Brown
Jan. 9—James Bunten Sindy H. Thomas	John Allcorn	James Bunten James Thomas
Jan. 21—Enoch P. Hannah Elizabeth Phillips		E. P. Hannah Elijah Cross
Jan. 27—Robert B. Roberts Mary Ann Miller		Robert B. Roberts Thomas Bradley
Jan. 27—Thomas Ames Elizabeth Aust	Edmund Crutcher	Thomas Ames Elijah Rutledge
Feb. 26—Petterson Burge Elizabeth Palmer		Petterson Burge James Slate
Mar. 1—William Gallady Sarah Cummings	J. A.	William Gallady George Gallady
Mar. 10—Jonathan Wiley Ruth M. Brown		J. W. John Brown
Mar. 12—Moses Starnes Mary Chandler		M. S. Pitts Chandler
Mar. 25—John McMillen Reese Adamson		J. McM. Joseph Addamson
April 26—John Patton Elizabeth Shoras		J. P. William Maxwell
May 29—Haynes Moore Mary Davis		H. M. Solomon Moore
June 13—Edmond Jones Elizabeth Shoras	Edmund Crutcher	E. J. Emanuel Scott
June 21—Mellen Carter Pheby Phillips		M. C. Benj. Phillips
Aug. 6—Benjamin M. Davis Casander Taylor	J. A.	B. D. William H. Moore
Aug. 26—Ezekiel A. Sharp Jane Lansden	H. L. Douglass	E. A. S. Abner Lansden
Aug. 23—Boze Jacobs Nancy Jennings	Harry Cage	B. J. Archibald Campbell

Name		Test.	Surety
Aug. 28—	David M. Tait Elizabeth Clampett	Edmund Crutcher	D. M. T. Nathan Clampett
Aug. 29—	Phillip Smart Abigale Wright	J. A.	P. M. John Somers
Aug. 30—	James Goodrich Patsey Taylor	J. A.	J. G. John A. Taylor
Sept. 9—	Robert Motherall Jane Kirkpatrick	Harry Cage	R. M. Samuel Motherall
Aug. 22—	John Hearn Drucilla L. Bormer	J. A.	J. H. G. D. Moore
Oct. 4—	Phillip Shores Jane Creighton		P. S. Elijah Warmock
Oct. 11—	John Starnes Elizabeth Chandler		J. S. Joseph Singley
Nov. 20—	Wright Hickman Sarah Tucker	J. A.	R. H. Bujain Tucker
Nov. 25—	Thomas Davis Elizabeth Robertson		T. D. John F. Porter
Nov. 29—	William S. New Sally Hancock	J. A.	W. S. Hunt William Shanks
Nov. 29—	Levi Knotts Eliza Young		Levi Knotts Boothe L. Malone
Dec. 1—	Sterling Harrison Elizabeth Jones		S. H. Thomas Edwards
Dec. 10—	Hardy Davenport Martha Bryson	F. G. Crutcher	H. D. Abram Cooper
Dec. 12—	William Chenney Elizabeth Fassey	F. G. Crutcher	W. C. Richard Chenney
Dec. 16—	Jordan Chandler Elizabeth L. Avery	Edmund Crutcher	J. C. William Avery
Dec. 29—	Adam Cowger Kizziah Davis		A. C. Abner Harpole
Dec. 30—	William A. Langston Rebecca Sutton		W. A. L. Rowland Sutton
Dec. 30—	James McDonald Anne L. Moore		J. L. McD. Gabriel Barton

1818

Jan. 3—	James Ellis Rebecca Belcher		J. E. Martin Talley
Jan. 17—	Mosses Harris Sally Dillard	F. G. Crutcher	M. H. John Impson
Jan. 27—	Hansel Trusty Nancy Welch		H. T. Thomas Mitchell
Jan. 29—	Jesse Eagan Nancy Reiff	J. A.	J. E. H. M. Howell
Feb. 2—	Jerremiah Brooks Rachel Spring		J. B. George Swann
Feb. 7—	Reuben Sullivan Polly Climer		R. S. Barnard Sullivan
Feb. 11—	Redding Wright Haily Patterson	J. A.	R. W. Thomas Harrington

Name	Test.	Surety
Feb. 12—Solomon Corder Martha Brown		S. C. Jesse Shaw
Feb. 14—James Bowman Elizabeth Taylor		J. B. Thomas Taylor
Feb. 17—John Cocke Elizabeth Harris		J. C. Leonard B. Sims
Feb. 17—Moses A. Woolen Elizabeth Stokes		M. W. Joshua Woolen
Feb. 18—Anthony Winston Nancy J. Harris		A. W. G. A. Huddleston
Feb. 24—Josiah McGehee Scoty Mitchell		J. McG. A. P. Pool
Mar. 19—John Owen Dalsey Waters	J. A.	J. O. Nolly Talbert
Mar. 19—Wilson Mosley Sally Sands		W. M. Bar Freeman
Mar. 22—Samuel Mosley Mary M. Mosley		S. M. Peter Mosley
Mar. 24—Thomas Breedlove Sally Travelion		T. B. Dewey Bettis
Mar. 24—James Moore Margaret Road	H. L. Douglas	J. M. ——— White
Mar. 30—Thomas Horn Louisa Woollard	J. A.	T. H. Allgood Woollard
April 6—Archibald Wilson Elizabeth Carson		A. W. William H. Wilson
April 8—Sam M. McCorkle Polly Pristly		S. M. McC. H. L. Douglass
April 8—Thomas Marlow Lucy Hall		T. M. Peyton Marlow
April 9—Littleton Benthall Susan Stanley	H. L. Douglass	L. B. Benjamin Stanley
April 27—Anthony Settle Nancy Higgins		A. S. Samuel Settle
April 28—Isaac Green Elizabeth Eagan		I. G. George Brigs
May 5—Jesse Pemberton Ruth Drewry		J. P. Elijah Cross
May 11—Peter Harvell Sally Watkins		P. H. Turner M. Laurence
May 13—Richard W. Ramsey Eliza Miles		R. W. R. James Rice
May 16—William Cox Evelina Reese	McAnderson	W. C. James Turner
May 23—Thomas W. Ellis Caroline Glanton		T. W. E. Richard Bird
May 26—George Cooper Martha Dillard	John Allcorn, C.W.C.	Solemnized on 28th of May, 1818, by John Page
May 26—William Stafford Martha Cartwright		W. S. John Jones

Name	Test.	Surety
May 26—George Cooper Martha Dillard		G. C. James Browing
May 28—Benjamin F. Stevenson Elizabeth Rutland		
June 4—William G. Wood Polly Davis	J. A.	W. G. W. William Sarcy
June 9—William Thomas Elizabeth Hardy	H. L. Douglass	W. T. Edward Jones
June 15—William Dillard Elizabeth Corley		W. D. James Browning
June 18—Nathan Bundy Absilla Johnson	F. G. Crutcher	N. B. Elijah Jones
July 7—Hiram Russell Zilphy Midget	H. L. Douglass	H. R. Nathan Gower
July 7—Anderson Friece Elizabeth Hickman		A. Friece Samuel Hickman
July 7—William Adams Doratha Richardson	H. L. Douglass	W. A. Elisha Dismukes
July 11—Nobles Cannon Annis Chandler	J. A.	N. C. Byrd Guill
July 15—Jonathan Fuston Rebecca Stanley		J. F. Jepha Fuston
July 26—Miler Fuller Charity Seals	J. A.	M. F. James Moore
July 28—James H. Ligon Elizabeth Thompson	H. L. Douglass	J. L. Ozburn Thompson
Aug. 1—Reuben Dial Zilphy Medlin		R. D. Brickle Bridges
Aug. 4—George Waters Polly Clark		G. W. Thomas Phillips
Aug. 6—Benjamin Wilson Charlott Adamson	Edmund Crutcher	B. W. Jesse Adamson
Aug. 25—James M. Sisk Nancy Blair		J. M. S. Hugh Blair
Aug. 27—Jesse Pendergrass Polly Garratt		J. P. John Garratt
Aug. 29—Archibald Allen Matilda Lambert	J. A., Clerk	John W. Peyton, J. P

I do certify that I joined the within Archibald Allen and Matilda Lambert together in the state of matrimony, August 30, 1818.

Name	Test.	Surety
Aug. 29—Archibald Allen Matilda Lambert		A. A. William Hartsfield
Sept. 1—Benjamin Davis Nancy Mitchell	F. G. Crutcher	B. D. Jesse Lysles
Sept. 3—Kader White Betsy Liggon		K. W. Hooker Reese
Sept. 9—John Garratt Ann McWhirter	J. A.	J. G. William Garrett
Sept. 16—William E. McSpadden Margaret Miller	H. L. Douglass	W. E. McS. John N. McS.

Name	Test.	Surety
Sept. 19—Hezekiah Archer	H. L. Douglass	H. A.
Patsey Mitchell		James Nickens
Sept. 22—Edward B. Wheeler		E. B. W.
Elizabeth Young		James Young
Sept. 22—Arden Somers		A. S.
Sally Walker		T. Bradley
Sept. 25—Willis Caraway		W. C.
Susannah Clemons		Sherrod Merrett
Sept. 26—Elisha Brien	H. L. Douglass	E. B.
Elizabeth Johnson		O. G. Finley
Sept. 29—James Mitchell	H. L. Douglass	J. M.
Susan Owen		Richard Locke
Sept. 30—Stephen Brooks		S. B.
Mariah Swiney		Jeremiah Brooks
Oct. 10—James Davis	Edward Crutcher	J. H. D.
Penelope Drake		Thomas Scudder
Oct. 13—John Cox		J. C.
Elizabeth Palmer		John Carlin
Oct. 13—William Carlin		W. C.
Sarah Johnson		John Cox
Oct. 20—Hiram Howard	F. G. Crutcher	H. H.
Cinthia Bennett		Howard Edwards
Oct. 20—Stephen Hamton	Edmund Crutcher	S. H.
Elizabeth Williams		William Sachett
Oct. 19—Allen Smith	Edmund Crutcher	A. S.
Elizabeth Motherall		H. Hobson
Oct. 20—Jose C. Dew	Edmund Crutcher	J. C. D.
Nancy Hunter		M. Dew
Oct. 23—John Campbell	Edmund Crutcher	J. C.
Judah A. Lambert		John Morrow
Oct. 23—Dolphen Bass	Edmund Crutcher	D. B.
Frances Gaddy		Thomas Phillips
Oct. 24—James Seat	J. A.	J. S.
Sally Jones		Jesse Talley
Nov. 5—James Scott		J. S.
Fannie Coe		Jesse Talley
Nov. 10—Joseph Underwood	H. L. Douglass	J. U.
Elizabeth Adamson		Jesse Adamson
Nov. 13—Humphrey Chappell		H. C.
Charity Johnson		John Coe
Nov. 17—James Frazer		J. F.
Hannah Shelby		John L. Wynne
Nov. 17—George A. Evans		G. A. E.
Thussey Hegarty		E. W. Burke
Nov. 21—Mark Joplin		M. J.
Malone Maxwell		John Hancock
Nov. 25—Kendred Tucker	J. A.	K. T.
Darcus King		Joseph Irby
Solemnized Nov. 26, 1818, by Elijah Maddox, Minister Gosp.		
Nov. 27—John Hansberry	J. A.	J. H.
Elizabeth Martin	Certificate Nov. 27, 1818	Good Andrews
Nov. 30—Charles Johnson		Joseph T. Williams
Betsey Barrow		C. J. & Hardy C. Willis

Name	Test.	Surety
Dec. 8—Elisha Bryson Polly Word		E. B. John Leach
Dec. 18—Robert Jening Hannah Word		R. J. Bazel Jacobs
Dec. 21—James Stuart Sarah Smith		J. S. William Gray
Dec. 21—Samuel Dickins Ann Enocks		S. D. James Dickins
Dec. 21—Milton Brittles Winnie Spring		W. B. George L. Swain
Dec. 22—Michael Harris Nancy Talley	H. L. Douglass	M. H. Jesse Talley
Dec. 23—Patrick R. Puckett Martha Cocke		R. R. P. John Bond
Dec. 24—Thomas Proctor Ann Dickins	H. L. Douglass	T. P. Jesse Liles
Dec. 26—Joshua Pedigo Nancy Micher	Edmund Crutcher	J. P. Jeremiah Rewery
	1819	
Jan. 2—William Owens Rebecca Franklin	John Allcorn	
Jan. 28—John Edwards Mary Rich	John Allcorn	By Benj. Cogilman, J. P.
Jan. 28—John Smith Lettie Brown	John Allcorn	By John W. Peyton, J. P.
Jan. 28—Richardson Rowling Polly Neal	John Allcorn	By Jas. T. Williams
Jan. 21—Solomon Kemp Hollon Ray	John Allcorn	By Jas. T. Williams
Jan. 24—Nathaniel Rice Nancy Rice	John Allcorn	By Jas. T. Williams Nathaniel Rice Wilshire Bandy
Jan. 29—James Andrews Elizabeth McDonell		James Andrews Robert Simms
Jan. 7—John T. Goodall Elizabeth Aken	H. L. Douglass	John T. Goodall Thomas Cartwright
Jan. 22—William Goodall Elizabeth Phelps	John Allcorn	William Goodall William Cox
Jan. 3—James Modglin Lucinda Kenedy		James Modglin Edward Burk
Jan. 11—Hugh Martin Elizabeth Lankford		Hugh Martin William Lankford, Father
Jan. 1—William Norman Elizabeth Pursley		William Norman Thomas Knight
Jan. 4—Jesse Clifton Sally Smith	John Allcorn	Jesse Clifton James B. Guthrie
Jan. 9—James Thompson Peggy Williams	Edmund Crutcher	James Thompson Isaac Williams
Jan. 13—Edmund Collins Delsha Drennon		Edmond Collins Henry Belote
Jan. 20—James Wilson Polly Joyner		James Wilson Drewry Joyner

Name	Test.	Surety
Jan. 26—Aaron Anglin	H. L. Douglass	Aaron Anglin
Hannah McGee		Zachariah Hutchings
Jan. 30—Benjamin T. Bell	By Joseph T. Bell,	Benjamin T. Bell
Charlott ———	J. P.	Thomas Cartwright
Feb. 1—John Grigg	John Allcorn, Clk.	John Grigg
Elizabeth Griffin	By Robert Branch	John Wheeler
	J. P.	Edmund Crutcher
Feb. 1—Vincen Cawthon	Edmund Crutcher	Vincen Cawthon
Rasannah Irwin		Thomas Cawthon
Feb. 2—Isaac W. Brook		Isaac W. Brooks
Martha Huddleston		Zedekiah Tate
Feb. 2—James Berry		James Berry
Mary Ann Taylor		Edward Burk
Feb. 8—Stephen Cavley	H. L. Douglass	Stephen Cavley
Patsy Tally		Woodson Layne
Feb. 9—Drury Joyner	H. L. Douglass	Drury Joyner
Polly Wood		Cornelius Joyner
Feb. 11—William Brown	John Allcorn	William Brown
Delila Pate		Sam'l Meredith
Feb. 12—Redding Wright	John Allcorn	
Haity Patterson		
Feb. 12—John Liggon	John Allcorn	John Liggon
Charity Alford		John Thompson
Feb. 12—Joseph Wray	H. L. Douglass	Joseph Wray
Elizabeth Moore		William T. Webb
Feb. 15—Thomas Gains	Edmund Crutcher	Thomas Gains
Lucindy Smith		Michell McDerment
Feb. 17—Silas Freeman	John Allcorn	Silas Freeman
Sally Cook		William W. Babb
Feb. 22—John R. Eatherly	H. L. Douglass	John R. Eatherly
Polly Williams		James Eatherly
Feb. 23—Mathew F. Dew	John Allcorn	Mathew F. Dew
Jane Bradley	By Thomas Calhoun	John L. Wynne
Feb. 25—Azariah Corda	V. D.	Azariah Corda
Viney Shaw	John Allcorn	Hugh Parks
Feb. 25—Abram Prim	John Allcorn	By John Jarrett
Nancy Cook		
Feb. 25—James Nellener	John Allcorn	James Nellums
Nancey Crocker		Thomas Mitchell
Feb. 26—Elliott T. Hollomon	John Allcorn	James Nickins
Rachel Williams		By Abner Williams,
		J. P.
Mar. 1—John F. West	By Thomas Dorman,	John F. West
Polly Lawrence	J. P.	Turner M. Lawrence
Mar. 4—John Woolard	H. L. Douglass	John Woolard
Levina Meagle	By Wm. Settle, J. P.	Simeon Woolard
Mar. 4—Joseph Neal	John Allcorn	
Sally Smith		
Mar. 6—William Babb	By John Jarrett	William Hartsfield
Nancy Ross		Wm. Babb
Mar. 19—James Payne	John Allcorn	James Payne
Elizabeth Williams		James Thompson

Name		Test.	Surety
Mar. 20—John C. Collings	Mahaly Wortham		John C. Collings James Howard
Mar. 20—John Gun	Malinda Bryant	W. Anderson	John Gun John Bryant
Mar. 26—David Bond	Lydia Jones	John Allcorn By John Fakes, J. P.	David Bond Claiborn H. Rhodes
Mar. 27—Shadrick Owens	Aline Dillard	John Allcorn	Shadrick Owens Henry Jacobs
Mar. 30—Mathew Hancock	Elizabeth Mills	John Allcorn By Jacob Sullivan, J. P.	Mathew Hancock A. J. Crawford
April 7—James Smith	Delila Glanton	By William Gray, J. P.	John Smith John Comer
April 8—John Weir	Rebecca Rye	John Allcorn By Wm. Settle, J. P.	John Weir James Weir
April 13—Robert Irwin	Rachel Bogle	J. F. Crutcher	Robert Irwin John Leech
April 22—James Baird	Elizabeth Richmond	John Allcorn By Edward Harris, J.P.	James Baird Thomas Richmond
April 24—William Grier	Polly Ricketts	By Jeremiah Hendricks, J. P.	James Grier Hansel Trusty
April 24—Daniel H. Mabies	Sally Williams		Daniel H. Mabies James Weir
April 25—Seth Hackney	Fanny Edwards	John Allcorn	By Isaac Winston, J. P.
April 29—Thomas Babb	Polly Powel	John Allcorn By John Jarratt	Thomas Babb Thomas Guthrie
April 29—Josiah Kirkpatrick	Nancy Tilford	John Allcorn	By Jacob Browning, J. P.
May 3—Bradford Edwards	Nancy Carraway	John Allcorn	By James Gray, J.P.
May 4—William Shaw	Mary Shaw		William Shaw William Cummins
May 4—Hugh Carlen	Patsey Pemberton	John Allcorn	Hugh Carlen John Pemberton
May 6—Robert Hughes	Sally Harpole	By R. King, J. P.	Robert Hughes Adam Harpole
May 15—Benjamin Rice	Elizabeth Climer	Edmund Crutcher	Benjamin Rice Geralddus Bolton
May 18—William Mays	Sally Mays	By E. Maddox, M.G.	Wm. Mays James McAdams
May 21—William Shaw	Mary Shaw	John Allcorn By James Gray, J.P.	
May 22—John Clampet	Sally Carey		John Clampitt John R. Wilson
May 22—David Cloyd	Nane Wilson		David Cloyd Ozburn Thompson
May 31—Atkinson Johnson	Sally Martin	Edmund Crutcher	Atkinson Johnson James Johnson
June 2—Atkinson Johnson	Sally Martin	John Allcorn	By Wm. Settle, J. P.
June 3—Tolliver Sutton	Ann Melton	John Allcorn	By R. Knight, J. P.

Name	Test.	Surety
June 8—Henry Whitlow	By Joshua Lester	Henry Whitlow
Lucy McHaney		James Lester
June 10—William Jones	John Allcorn	By C. Maddox, M. G.
Polly Jenings		
June 10—Robert Smith	By David Foster, M.G.	Robert Smith
Elizabeth Law		Thomas T. Law
June 10—John Clampitt	J. A.	By John Williamson,
Sally Carey		J. P.
June 12—Solomon Beardon	By John Bonner,	Solomon Beardon
Rebecca Woodrum	J. P.	John Riggs
June 17—Anderson Cox		Anderson Cox
Sally Palmer		Thomas Cox
June 18—Leonard Hatheha-way	John Allcorn	Leonard Hathehaway
		Joseph Anderson
Barthery West		By Jas. Cross, J. P.
June 22—Howel Horn	H. L. Douglass	Howel Horn
Rebecca Stone		William Horn
June 24—Richard Jones	John Allcorn	Richard Jones
Rebecca Martin		Henry Hunt
		By James Gray, J. P.
July 5—William Morton		William Morton
Nancy Walker		R. A. Echols
July 6—Enoch Stiles	H. L. Douglass	Enoch Stiles
Caty McCoy		Samuel Alsop
July 10—Elijah Foster		Elijah Foster
Polly Taylor	By James Cross, J.P.	Littleberry Belcher
July 10—William Shanks		Wm. Shanks
Patsey Wormack		David Phillips
July 19—William Allen	W. Anderson	William Allen
Eliza Marshall		O. G. Finly
July 20—John White		John White
Anne Moore	By John Bonner, J.P.	Jeremiah Moore
July 20—Ishmeal Bradshaw	Edmund Crutcher	Ishmeal Bradshaw
Lucinda McWhirter	By J. P. Williams,	Thomas Mitchell
July 21—David Upchurch	J. P.	David Upchurch
Sally Johnson	By Alex Caruth, J.P.	L. W. Moore
July 23—Charles Horn	W. Anderson	Charles Horn
Rachel Swindle		Wm. Horn
July 24—Robert Scott	John Allcorn	Robert Scott
Nancy Bone		John Morran
Aug. 2—Benjamin Hobson	John Allcorn	Benjamin Hobson
Elizabeth Murry		Thomas Bradley
Aug. 3—James Edwards		James Edwards
Sally Jones		Pettus Ragland
Aug. 3—John H. Southers		John Southers
Polly Seat		Thomas Williams
Aug. 5—Thomas McGriff	John Allcorn	Thomas McGriff
Sally Mitchel		Roland Grisson
Aug. 6—Stephen Deury	John Allcorn	By Isaac Winston,
Elizabeth Allen		J. P.

Name	Test.	Surety
Aug. 6—William W. Hearn Susannah Tarver	John Allcorn	William Hearn James W. Hearn
Aug. 6—Moody P. Harris Susannah Caplin-ger	John Allcorn	Moody P. Harris Henry Chandler
July 7—William Roberts Sally Adams	John Allcorn	By James Cross, J.P.
Aug. 8—Robert Dixon Nancy Adams	John Allcorn	By James Gray, J.P.
Aug. 11—James Edwards Sally Jones	John Allcorn	By ———
Aug. 12—William Phillips Nancy Waters	H. L. Douglass	William Phillips
Aug. 12—John Weir Elizabeth Chandler	John Allcorn	By Wm. Settle, J. P.
Aug. 12—William Brown Mary Johnson	John Allcorn	William Brown James Thomas
Aug. 18—John Shane Nancy Drennon	John Allcorn	By Ransom Gwynn
Aug. 18—John Queshenberry Patsey Major	John Allcorn	By J. Winston, J. P.
Aug. 18—Anthony W. Hud-dleston Elizabeth Lewis	John Allcorn	By J. Winston, J. P.
Aug. 24—Anderson Seat Unicy Mick	John Allcorn By John W. Peyton, J. P.	Anderson Seat Jesse Talley
Aug. 28—Thomas Phillips Sally Lawrence		Thomas Phillips Elijah Cross
Aug. 30—Samuel Justice Hannah S. Cart-wright		Samuel Justice Micheal Yerger
Aug. 31—Thomas Partlow Chloe Hooker	By Jacob Sullivan	Thomas Partlow John Eddins
Sept. 2—Geraldas Link Sally Harrison	John Allcorn	Geraldas Link Norval Douglas By John Page
Sept. 2—William Prim Ann Johnson	John Allcorn	By Jas. T. Williams J. P.
Sept. 7—Stealey Hager Polly Whitley	Edmund Crutcher By John Williams, J. P.	Stealey Hagar W. C. Adams
Sept. 7—Meshaik Carroll Martha Carroll		Meshaik Carroll John Cooper
Sept. 8—Bennett W. Hall Malinda Bradshaw	By James Cross, J.P.	Bennett W. Hall C. — Lewis
Sept. 13—Benjamin Beasley Mary Jackson	John Allcorn	Benjamin Beasley Edward Jackson By Joseph T. Bettis, J. P.
Sept. 16—John Byates Elizabeth Talley	John Allcorn	John Byates Wyatt Beckham
Sept. 20—Ozment Thompson Polly Ann Curd		Ozment Thompson George Williams

Name	Test.	Surety
Sept. 23—Richard Hudson Polly Smith	John Allcorn	By Isaac Winston, J. P.
Sept. 23—Daniel Wilkerson Rebecca Massey		Daniel Wilkerson Littleberry Eatherly
Sept. 29—James Stewart Mary Allen	John Allcorn	By Isaac Winston, J. P.
Sept. 30—William Adams Charlott Ward	John Allcorn	By Joshua W. Mims, J. P.
Oct. 7—James Nettles Tempy Bettes	John Allcorn Ex. by Alexander Caruth	James Nettles Alfred Bettis
Oct. 9—Robert Sweatt Elizabeth Glenn		Robert Sweatt Edward Sweatt
Oct. 13—James Henry Rebecca Mitchell	John Allcorn	James Henry James Mitchell
Oct. 7—John Potts Cynthia Jones	F. G. Crutcher By John Gray, Shff.	James Potts David Bond
Oct. 9—Thomas Atkinson Elizabeth Lambert	John Allcorn	Thomas Atkinson Allen Smith
Oct. 9—Isaac Turnage Patsey Bell	John Allcorn	Executed by Joseph Bell, J. P.
Oct. 10—James Griffin Sally Woodward	John Allcorn	Executed by J. Winston, J. P.
Oct. 20—Allen Powell Anne T. Hutchings	John Allcorn	Allen Powell Stephen Hutchings
Oct. 24—Nicholas Edwards Milly Powers	John Allcorn	
Oct. 26—James Guthrie Teracy McElroy	John Allcorn Executed by	James Guthrie Thomas Guthrie John Jarrett
Oct. 28—William Williams Jane Quarles	John Allcorn	William Williams William Quarles
Oct. 30—John Conyer Susanah Spadlen		John Conyer Cornelius Buck
Nov. 1—George Miller Mary Sellers		George Miller Alford Sellars
Nov. 1—William Davidson Susan Cartwright	Executed by John Peyton, J. P.	Wm. P. Davidson George Swann
Nov. 1—Charles Seay Mary Beard		Charles Seay Mathew Dew
Nov. 2—Thomas Cartwright Patsey Davidson	Executed by Wm. Steele, J. P.	Thomas Cartwright Alexander Braden
Oct. 2—James Woods Elizabeth Morris	John Allcorn	
Nov. 2—Henry Wrye Sally Frout	John Allcorn	Henry Wrye Thomas Edwards
Nov. 2—Robert Boethe Minerva Payne		Robert Boethe William Payne
Nov. 7—James Williamson Lucy Smith	John Allcorn	Executed by John Williamson, J. P.
Nov. 8—Robert Smith Mary Smith		Robert Smith Bernard P. Brown

	Name	Test.	Surety
Nov. 10	Zadock Mulison Polly Talley	Executed by Jas. Cross, J. P.	Zadock Mulison Paton Talley
Nov. 13	John Smith Mickie Hutcherson		John Smith Tom Smith
Nov. 14	William Bailey Sally Talley	H. L. Douglass	William Bailey Paton Talley
Nov. 14	James Queshenberry Elizabeth Edwards	John Allcorn	
Nov. 16	Lemuel Robbins Mary Brown		Lemuel Robbins Wm. Hickman
Nov. 17	Giles H. Glenn Pheby Coe		Giles H. Glenn Thompson Glenn
Nov. 20	Jesse Shaw Mary Pack	John Allcorn	Jesse Shaw Charles Jones
Nov. 20	Mark Jackson Mary Ramsey		Mark Jackson Peterson Burge
Nov. 20	David McKnight Patsy McWhirter		David McKnight Leonard H. Smith
Nov. 25	James Thomas Matilda H. Scobey	John Allcorn	Executed by Wm. Steele, J. P.
Nov. 23	Seaborn Weaks Nancy Johnson	Edmund Crutcher	Seaborn Weaks John Wright
Nov. 24	Robert Bone Polly S. Gwin		Robert Bone Abner W. Lanson
Nov. 25	James H. Young Pheby Woddridge	John Allcorn	Executed by Jas. T. Williams, J.P.
Nov. 25	John Edwards Mary Richmond	H. L. Douglass	John Edwards Bradford Howard
Dec. 2	Henry C. Nichols Elizabeth Hallam	John Allcorn	Henry Nichols L. Moore
Nov. 6	Isham Woods Christana Motsinger	Edmund Crutcher	Isham Woods Thos. Tesnnage
Dec. 7	Archibald Sherrill Agnes Moss		Archibald Sherrell Samuel W. Sherrell
Dec. 7	Josiah Beasley Elizabeth Tarpley		Josiah Beasley Stith T. Tarpley By Joseph T. Bell
Dec. 10	Ira Barber Nancy Leith		Ira Barber John Barber
Dec. 17	Reddick Rutland Milberry Rutland	Executed by J. A. Browning, M. G.	Reddick Rutland John G. Graves
Dec. 18	Andrew Patton Elizabeth Forbes		Andrew Patton Joseph Patton
Dec. 20	Skeen Hancock Nancy Hearn	Executed by B. Branch, J. P.	Skeen Hearn Martin Hancock
Dec. 23	Jesse Goldman Susannah Sullivan		Executed by Jacob Sullivan
Dec. 23	Benjamin Barkley Lydia Reader	John Allcorn	Executed by John Peyton, J. P.
Dec. 23	Henry Mitchell Nancy Graves	Wm. Anderson	Henry Mitchell Benj. Davis

Name	Test.	Surety
Dec. 27—Whitfield Moore Catharine Meredith		White Moore Mathew Dew
Dec. 28—Gabriel Barton Jane Johnson		Gabriel Barton Samuel Calhoun
Dec. 28—James Murry Cassa Yarnell	John Allcorn	James Murry Dandridge Moss
Dec. 28—William Chandler Rachel Shannon	John Allcorn	Wm. Chandler Tobias Henderson
Dec. 28—William Reed Rachel Pentecost	John Allcorn	William Reed Absolom Harris
Dec. 28—John H. Briant Elizabeth Puckett	John Allcorn	
Dec. 28—William Cobb Catharine Jackson	H. L. Douglass	William Cobb Harrison Irby

1808

Name	Test.	Surety
Nov. 7—John Fakes Mary Edwards		J. F. Robert Edwards
Sept. 2—Herzekiel Cartwright Elizabeth Mahol-land	J. A.	Hugh Cartwright M. W. Cartwright
June 3—Duke Worthan Betsey Norton		D. W———
Nov. 21—Henry Coke Elizabeth Tipton	J. A.	H. C. Joshua Tipton
June 27—Joshua Brown Prudence McAllen		J. B. Solinon George
Feb. 17—Humphrey Donalson Sally Kelly	J. A.	H. D. Obediah Woolwine
Mar. 12—Luke Tippit Jenney Cooksey	J. A.	Luke Typet Henry Carson
Jan. 20—Joel Swindle Nancy Hudson	Jesse Cage	Joel S——— Samuel Harris
Oct. 15—John Bond Sarah Cummings		J. B. James B.
June 2—Robert Bogle Sally Brison		R. B. Thomas Luck
Nov. 2—John Campbell Pheby Casady		J. C——— Samuel Barton
Aug. 19—William Parmer Polly Bond	Jesse Cage	William Parmer John Bond
Nov. 5—Graham Jackson Betsey Smith	Jesse Cage	Graham Jackson William Caple
Aug. 29—Thomas Smith Susannah Hill		Thomas Smith James Anderson
Jan. 6—Willsher Bandy Nancy Johnson		Willsher Bandy Jesse Cage
Mar. 14—John Davis Polly McAlpin		Jesse Holt
Oct. 15—Thomas Telford Elizabeth Chawn-ing	J. A.	Thomas Telford Samuel T——

LEBANON COUNTY MARRIAGE BONDS

Copied by Mrs. Acklen and Mrs. Elder

NAMES	SURETY
1820	1820
June 24—Midget Brooks to Rebecca O'Neal	Jeremiah Brooks
Nov. 22—Goldman Pucket to Elizabeth Ellison	John H. Bryan
Oct. 12—Alfred Sherrill to Peggy Sherrill	Zacheriah Tallsner
Dec. 4—John Cook to Anna S. Mathay	Job Mathay
Dec. 7—David Spring to Louisey Jones	Lott Joiner
Dec. 11—David Phillips to Polly Waters	Archamack Bass
Dec. 4—Allen Smith to Frances Woods	Jas. W. Uspion
Dec. 6—James Dyer to Lucy Howe	James Little
Dec. 18—Jas. Gates to Elizabeth Bellow	Jas. Dark
Jan. 19—Alston Morgan to Ann Edwards	Eaton Edwards
Feb. 18—Jesse Berry to Milly Shanks	Geo. Donnell
Jan. 20—John Scoggin to Wincy Pearcy	Jno. Reggs
March 18—Wm. Hutcherson to Jensy Williams	Jas. Smith
Apr. 1—Jno. A. Smith to Nancy McHaney	Jas. L. Lester
June 3—Joseph W. Hinge to Charlotte Heflin	John Manning
Sept. 13—Wm. Brown to Nancy Arnold	Jno. McAdow
Sept. 28—Anthony Gaines to Temple Scott	Thos. Gaines
Apr. 19—Isaac Perryman to Nancy Patterson	Jno. Perryman
Feb. 21—Jno. M. Scott to Jane Bossell	Jeremiah Bailey
March 30—Alfred Bryant to Nancy Hickman	B. T. Matthey
Jan. 12—Shelah Waters to Sarah Clark	David Philips
June 10—Jesse Tally to Margret Wynn	Benj. T. Jones
Aug. 2—Jacob Keaton to Lucinda Fewston	Jeremiah Turner
Oct. 28—Jubal Grant to Nancy Hightower	Jas. Arnold
Sept. 30—Alygood Woollard to Ellender Jones	Wm. L. Lyper
July 14—Jno. Perryman to Polly Arnold	Philip Perriman
July 13—Joseph Williams to Jinney Patterson	Joseph Patton
Jan. 15—Jno. Lasiter to Lucy Edwards	Eli Edwards
Feb. 24—Wm. McKnight to Elizabeth McWherter	Milus McCorkle
March 8—Jas. W. Hodge to Polly Pucket	Wm. Hartsfield
March 10—Zachariah Evans to Cynthia Sweat	Alexander Stuart
Apr. 3—L. D. Crabtree to Winney Medling	Harberd Young
Feb. 3—Jas. Fuston to Elizabeth Adams	John Adams
March 13—Jesse Wright to Mary Young	Jas. M. Young
March 6—Jno. Ricketts to Sarah Alsup	Jacob Cassilman
Nov. 13—Wayne Thomas to Anne Barton	Jno. Blackburn
Nov. 13—Presby Edwards to Mary Sims	Thos. Edwards
Sept. 21—James Dunsmore to Delilah Gowen	Shadrack Gowen
Nov. 28—Taylor Kelly to Cynthia David	Wm. Whitsett
Aug. 8—Robt. Owen to Elizabeth Mieds	Jos. L. Wilson
July 31—John Dortch to Cynthia Walker	Lewis Sutton
Nov. 18—James Chance to Mary Nichols	Henry C. Nichols
Aug. 7—Joseph Barbee to Rachael Compton	Archamac Bass

Names	Surety
Aug. 9--Andrew McHany to Oney Johnson	T. W. Short
Oct. 31—Ransom Ward to Patsy Rogers	Jesse Gibbs
Nov. 10—Wm. Hudson to Sally Tracy	Abner J. C. Dearing
Oct. 24—Joseph N. Leawell to India Nora Leawell	Jno. Wymer
Oct. 4—Henry Leeman to Kesiah Warren	A. Winston
Sept. 4—Abraham Keeton to Jane Hughes	Jno. M. Hall
Nov. 21—Wm. Todd to Elizabeth Steele	George Steel
Feb. 19—Julius Williams to Margaret Cason	Joseph Stacey
Aug. 9—Jno. H. Cawthon to Nancy Rice	Jas. H. Cawthon
March 24—Jno. Smith to Mary Cloyd	Jno. Wilson
Oct. 11—Robert Guthrie to Aseneth Motheral	Allen Smith
June 14—Chas. Harden to Jane Alexander	Wm. S. Alexander
Sept. 19—Wm. Hawkins to Fanny Abernatha	Mark Abanatha
Nov. 6—Jas. Osment to Levena Osment	W. M. Swain
Jan. 15—Ivy Gibson to Sally Aytes	Harvey Robertson
Feb. 8—Hesekiah King to Nancy Hunt	Hardy Hunt
Jan. 25—Sampson Knight to Nancy Robertson	Thos. Knight
March 24—Alexander Foster to Martha Doak	Jas. Foster
Dec. 12—Thos. C. Hoskins to Jane Simpson	Robt. Marshall
Sept. 5—Epenetus Carlock to Nancy Pimberton	Geo. Donnell
Nov. 1—Hazel Butt to Cynthia Hunt	Reuben Webb
Nov. 18—Wm. Hartsfield to Frances H. Anderson	Levi Anderson
Aug. 14—Jas. C. Carruth to Molly C. Davis	Foster G. Crutcher
Oct. 17—Paskel Callico to Janny Wheeler	Jno. Walton
Aug. 20—Wiley Bodin to Nancy Rutchledge	Jno. Stuart
Aug. 21—Wm. H. Buckley to Rebecca Johnson	Oliver C. Johnson
June 13—Jno. A. Criswell to Martha Mays	Alex'nd'r Kirkpatrick
Jan. 31—Wm. Miles to Martha Dwyer	Jno. Massingill
Nov. 13—Byrd Wall to Fanny Johnson	Benj. Wall
Dec. 16—Jno. Leech to Betsy Cooper	Samuel Bryson
March 8—Zachariah Keeton to Margret Walker	Henry Dillon
Jan. 29—Wm. Satterfield to Ann Tally	Thos. Delapp
Feb. 17—Alexander McKnight to Anne Grier	Samuel Grier
Jan. 22—Mark Holleman to Hannah Glen	Benjamin Glen
Dec. 14—Wm. Drennan to Kitty Eddins	Lewis Wright
Oct. 17—Wm. Davis to Elizabeth Webb	Daniel Kelly
July 17—Alexander Periman to Sally Baskins	Allen Periman
Feb. 15—Jas. McCollin to Elizabeth ———	Eli Harris
Aug. 23—John Womack to Milley Webster	Jno. P. Campbell
Feb. 20—Robt. Goodman, Jr., to Martha Richardson	Robt. Goodman, Sr.
Dec. 19—Thos. Standle to Mary Ann Huggins	Joshua Pedigo
March 1—Wm. Chappell to Elizabeth ———	Solomon Walker
Oct. 23—Jno. Travillion to Polly Allison	David Bradshaw
Sept. 20—Jabez Tims to Elizabeth Tims	Allen McVey
Nov. 25—Lemuel Nicholson to Lavena Young	Robt. Young
July 24—Jno. Neely to Jane Brown	Paul Sullivan

Names	Surety
Feb. 14—Phillip Grissim to Sally Spring	B. W. Grissman
Dec. 26—Wm. Whitsitt to Nancy Kelly	Isham Keeton
May 17—Alvin C. Johnson to Hansey H. Buckly	Wm. Cummins
July 13—Jesse Sullivan to Elizabeth Carter	Owen Quinby
July 17—Philip Periman to Hannah Forch	Jno. Periman
July 16—Willie Wray to Eliza Carter	Joshua Gibb
Feb. 6—Jno. D. Atte to Martha Andrews	Wm. Walker, Jr.
Dec. 19—Jas. Sommuns to Anne McFarland	Matthew Dew
	O. G. Finley
Dec. 19—Lemuel Nickings to ——— ———	
Feb. 20—Thos. Hodges to Elizabeth Hodges	Jno. A. Smith
Oct. 10—Jno. Caraway to Narcissa Allen Rogers	Sylvanus Merritt
Sept. 5—Silas M. Williams to Franky Shaw	Jas. L. Haskins
Aug. 26—Thos. C. Scott to Polly Burton	Nathan Reding
Apr. 8—Drummond Wheeler to Caty Reeder	Joseph Phillips
Feb. 25—Payton Marlow to Elizabeth Smith	Richard Marlow
Oct. 16—Richard A. Echols to Abagail M. Brown	Matthew Dew
Oct. 31—Francis Cooper to Ann Thomas	Jas. Reed
Nov. 13—Joseph B. Chance to Nancy Braden	Elijah Chance
Dec. 1—Wm. Sutherland to Polly Hobb	Presley Simpson
Jan. 13—Reuben Davenport to Susan Richardson	Francis Cooper
Dec. 4—Wilson Campbell to Frances Arnold	Richard Harrison
Jan. 19—Zachariah Toliver to Rebecca Sherrill	Norval Douglass
Dec. 23—Jno. S. Foster to Elizabeth Cox	Jno. Cox
Jan. 2—Solomon Sugg to Ira Jacobs	Samuël Booker
Dec. 29—James Burton to Nancy Edwards	Ed. D. Burton
Jan. 5—Melkijah Vaughn to Sarah R. Vaughan	Wm. C. Tisdale
Jan. 26—Littleberry Freeman to Elizabeth Young	Isaiah Paschal
Feb.19—Robert Ellis to Prudence Belcher	Jas. Ellis
Feb. 2—Reese Tipton to Peggy Tipton	Abraham Green
Apr. 22—John Conrod to Catey Morris	Bazel Davis
Dec. 1—Andrew Ward to Sally Rice	Turner Perry
Nov. 23—Hugh Smith to Betsey Roach	Thos. McSpeddin
Dec. 14—Garrett Mansfield to Lydia Sullivan	Reuben Webb
Feb. 10—Alfred McClain to Harriet F. Robinson	Martin Cartmell
Oct. 25—Wm. Alsup to Polly Lane	Asup Alsup
Feb. 10—Thos. Hill to Elizabeth Johnson	Lawrence Sypert
June 8—Jesse Woodcock to Elizabeth M. Williams	Abraham Woodcock
Apr. 5—Robertson Crooks to Selery Eathridge	Chas. Nicholson
May 5—Wm. Chappell to Elizabeth Redding	Nathan Redding
Aug. 31—Abram Murry to Polly Holton	Jno. Murry
Aug. 3—Martin Douglass to Nancy Massey	Jno. Spring
Oct. 17—John Stevenson to Nancy Tristy	Jeremiah McWhorter
Dec. 7—Ebenezer Donelson to Elizabeth Davis	Isham F. Davis
Dec. 1—Edward Trier to Lilly Smith	Jno. Hickman
Oct. 10—Wm. A. Johnson to Lucentia Asby	Jas. Allcorn
Oct. 17—Jno. P. Campbell to ——— Lambut	Jno. Campbell

NAMES	SURETY
July 18—John Dillard to Sarah Jacob	Shadrack Owens
Jan. 25—Jonathan Doak to Isabel Donnell	
Aug. 2—Jno. Sauls to Fany Davenport	Willis Davenport
1821	1821
Aug. 7—Jacob B. Lassiter to Levena B. McMinn	Elihu McMinn
July 21—Green B. Edwards to Martha Howard	Benjamin Cassilman
July 14—Stephen McDaniel to Jane Williams	Alex McDaniel
Aug. 11—Pleasant Markham to Sally Charlton	John Irby
Sept. 12—Littleberry Stevens to Laly Chambers	Archd Wilson
Dec. 29—Lemuel Loyd to ——— ————	Anderson Loyd
Apr. 26—Joshua Bradberry to Susan Wright	Robertson Wright
May 22—Wm. R. Phipp to Elizabeth Cummings	Amos Williams
Aug. 29—John Jennings to Sally Harris	William Jones
July 14—John W. Evans to Catherine Davis	John Allcorn, Clk.
June 29—James S. Tally to Betsey Butler	Spencer W. Tally
Jan. 18—Benj. Stanly (Standley) to Patsey Carter	Littleton Benthal
Jan. 9—Lewis Richards to Sally Dilay	Jacob T. Meshack
Apr. 14—Turner M. Lawrence to Ann Barber	Silas Tarver
Dec. 18—Jonas Livinglay to Martha Curd	Jonas Hale
Aug. 3—Robert Ferguson to Polly Farr	Edmund Jackson
March 14—Reuben Dockings to Rhody Hankins	Jonathan Baker
Dec. 4—Richard Melton to Polly Burdine	Lewis Sutton
July 9—Hughy Revland to Rhoda Jackson	Benjamin Edmonds
Aug. 21—John Ward, Jr., to Elisabeth Hodges	John Ward, Sr.
June 6—George Pemberton to Celah Patterson	Epimitus Carlock
Dec. 22—William Redding to Priscella Knight	Herman Redding
June 5—Richard Ozment to Rebecca Eddins	Jeptha Clemmons
Jan. 30—Lewis Wright to Lempy Eddings	John Drenon
Oct. 6—James Moore to Rebecca Coaper	Mathew Hunt
Aug. 25—Herod Lassiter to Polly Patterson	Joseph McGee
Oct. 13—Marmaduke Mitchener to Barbary Boon	David Beard
Aug. 14—William Blackburn to Lucy Clark	Lewis Blackburn
—— —Levi Donnell to Cynthia Donnell	John F. Doak
March 21—Paton Tally to Rachal Cross	Richard Tally
Aug. 14—John Upchurch to Caty Johnson	Jordan Johnson
July 4—Alexander Thorn to Elizabeth Harrington	Samuel C. Conyer
March 23—David Scoby to Eliza Heflin	Joseph Caskey
Jan. 10—Pryor Tyrell to Elizabeth Collings	Jeremiah Collins
April 12—David Martin to Martha Weir	John Chandler
Feb. 21—David Cole to Diley Pike	Tobias Henderson
March 19—Peter Hollansworth (Wollanswamth) to Polly Miller	James Knight
Sept. 15—George Collings to Nancy Renshaw	Jeremiah Collings
Sept. 22—Dandridge Moss to Sally Richmond	Aaron Churn
Feb. 24—Uriah Sweat to Finetta Phillips	William Phillips

Names	Surety
Dec. 26—Shadrach Moore to Nancy Swaney	Robert Dallis
Dec. 31—George Cato to Eupenia Rife	John R. Rutherford
Sept. 19—Garritt Macey to Lovy Crapper	John Swann
May — —Sampson Couner to Sally Knight	Jas. Hollingsworth
July 25—William Cox to Holland Greer	B. Drake
Sept. 13—Miles Fuller to Nancy Clifton	Anderson Loyd
July 2—Isham F. Davis to Sally Curd	William McGregor
Oct. 22—Philip Howill to Cynthia Willis	William Howill
Aug. 29—Halem Creswell to Elizabeth Johnson	David Brown
March 17—Absolom Ellis to Elender C. Jones	Redding B. Jones
Jan. 19—Burrel Wall to Sally M. Johnson	Benjamin Wall
Jan. 1—Murph Kemp to Ann Baird	Daniel Smith
March 29—Snoden Hickman to Milly Richardson	William Hickman
March 30—Edward White to Rachael Williamson	Littleberry White
Feb. 6—Isiah Swindle to Julian Hickman	Pelidge Swindle
Apr. 19—Daniel Johnson to Sally Gwyn	Matthew Dew
June 9—Joab Sullivan to Cela Barton	Isaac Carver
Apr. 14—Lumsford Bagwell to Rispa Truett	William Tervell
Feb. 20—James Payne to Anne Campbell	James Armstrong
July 26—Peter Sullivan to Polly Tarver	Jacob Sullivan
June 19—Robt. Creedupe (Creedop) to Polly Guylle	Samuel Sperry
Oct. 1—Thomas Merriott to Tempy M. Bennett	Howard Edwards
June 8—James Gaddey to Elizabeth Bass	Archamack Bass
Feb. 15—William Hickman to Equlla Swingle	William Hickman, Sr
Apr. 3—John Cowger to Meecy (Musey) Hill	Walter Carr
March 14—Willie Dockings to Fanny Goodall	Bengjah Cartwright
March 10—Charles Collings to Elizabeth Sanders	Elisha Collings
June 2—Josiah Ely to Jane Lawrence	John Allcorn, Clk.
Apr. 8—Anderson Evans to Mely Stuart	Alex Stuart
Feb. 18—William Peak to Rutha Jones	Sion Duke
Feb. 26—John Walden to Susa Tally	Peter Tally
Aug. 30—John S. Topp to Eliza G. Crutcher	Albert H. Wynne
Feb. 24—John Nichals to Sally Harris	John Springs
Dec. 20—Ryal (Rial) Atkinson to Rebecca Hoak	James Johnson
Feb. 10—Joseph Weir to Lydia Allen	James Weir
Feb. 3—William Webb to Betsey Hull	James Driver
Jan. 19—Samuel Patterson to Jane Smith	David Smith
April 2—Edward Denton to Rebecah Dillard	Thos. Denton
Jan. 3—Joseph Tippit to Ann Ragsdale	Isaac Moore
May 24—John Bradford to Matilda Ray (Wray)	William Robinson
Nov. 14—Annis Douglas to Matilda Corley	James Browning
Nov. 5—Anderson Webb to Susanah Lester	Harry D. Lester
Oct. 10—Samuel Bell to Eliza McCleary Beard	James Mitchell
July 13—Kinsey Prim to (Kinzie) Polly Johnson	Allen Hill
Nov. 30—John Wright to Rebecca Rickets	Benj. Cassleman
Sept. 22—George J. Cain to Chisteaince G. Jones	Geo. Smith, Jr.

NAMES	SURETY
Oct. 24—John Furgasen to Barbary Harpall	Sion Duke
Feb. 14—Enoch Henry to Jane Massey	Joseph Cuteral
Jan. 8—Bird Wall to Christean Kidwell	Robert Johnson
Apr. 2—Thomas Babb to Hicksy Hunt	Henry B. Babb
June 11—Joseph B. Heflin to Emassy Ward	John Neill
Aug. 8—Daniel Dyer to Elizabeth Coapper	Jesse Donnell
July 2—Robert Martin to Fanny Coe	Hugh Canler
—— —Dennis Kelly to Docilia Donnell	Levi Donnell
Oct. 12—John Southern to Polly Davis	James Reid
Dec. 18—Jacob Woodrum to Nancy Miles	John H. Pasley
Oct. 9—Pernal Bennet to Annis Williams	A. H. Wynne
March 12—Lewis Patterson to Sally Jennings	John Hubboard
June 11—John Lankford to Lacey Martin	Littleberry Stevens
Aug. 22—Samuel Bichen to Elizabeth Morriss	Levi Donnell
Oct. 10—Willis Coferld to Maria McDonald	Stephen McDonald
Jan. 27—William Horn to Celia Wollard	Simeon Woolard
Oct. 23—Jesse Lisle to Patsy Gilbert	James Arnold
Dec. 12—James Mitchell to Eliza Reese	John Beard
June 20—Owen C. Dennis to Deborah Green	Isaac Green
Sept. 13—Allen Mitchell to Patsy Glasgow	Jones W. Locke
Jan. 10—Mathew Gibson to Mary Jariman	John Wilson
Jan. 7—Prior Lawrence to Rebecca Haptin	Jesse Pugh
Sept. 10—Thomas W. Ellis to Sally Wright	John Blurton
Nov. 5—James Lowery to Sally Wetherly	John Ozment
June 12—Sherrod Merritt to Tabitha Edwards	John Merritt
Sept. 18—Alfred Mount to Mary Thomas	William Thomas
May 5—William Willeford to Allis Chamberlin	Jeremiah Johnson
Aug. 26—Isaac H. Rutland to Emily Rutland	Rutherford Rutland
Oct. 7—James Stevens to Polly Allen	Reuben Webb
May 22—William R. Phipps to Elizabeth Cummings	John Allcorn, Clk.
Aug. 25—Andrew Gwyn to Esther Rice	Hugh Gwyn
Nov. 10—William Corder to Martha Stone	James Stone
Sept. 12—Archibald Wilson to Cynthia Johnson	Littleberry Stevens
Dec. 18—Thomas Taylor to Polly Garner	J. Garner
Aug. 1—John C. Miller to Peggy Harlin	Richard Hight
May 22—John Wilson to Nancy Koonce	John H. Johnson
May 16—James L. Vawel to Tabitha Scott	John Benson
March 17—Peledge Swingle to Nancy Hickman	Harard Seat
June 15—William Wilkerson to Peggy Kirkpatrick	Robert Campbell
July 11—Lem. Hickman, Jr., to Susannah H. Trice	Samuel Hickman
July 14—John W. Evans to Catharine Davy	Gross Scruggs
Dec. 18—Solomon Caplinger to Martha Massey	Ennis Douglass
March 19—Hardy Youbanks to Nancy Arnold	Thomas Arnold
July 4—Arthur W. Dew to Nancy Hallum	Anderson Cook
Apr. 11—Wallace Caldwell to Abigail Nicholson	Wm. T. Webb
May 31—Mathew Hunt to Elizabeth Moore	James Moore

Names	Surety
May 26—Jonathan Baker to Sally Eagan	Jesse Shaw
Oct. 9—Pernet Bennet to Annis Williams	John Allcorn, Test
Sept. 3, 1813—William Hall to Polly Hall	James Ramsey
July 8, 1836—Thomas Warren to Peggy Williams	Elijah Jennings
Sept. 2, 1813—Josiah Rogers to Patsey McElyea	Levin Mackey
June 24, 1813—Jeremiah Jedwin to Elsey Rogers	David Williams
Sept. 12, 1814—Josiah Rogers to Peggy McElyea	John McElyea
Oct. 10, 1814—James Griffin to Sally Woodward	Bagwell Pearcy
Sept. 12, 1814—Brittain Odum to Reddley Blouston	Jubel Bobbit
Oct. 7, 1814—William Smith to Betsey Gwin	John Roach
Sept. 16, 1814—John Ross to Lucy Barnes	Joshua Barnes
Aug. 13, 1836—Elijah Johns to Delila York	Job S. Haysworth
Jan. 18, 1831—Anthony Hogan to Elizabeth Carlin	Wm. Buchanan
June 9, 1815—Arthur Forbus to Rachel Carruth	Alex C. Carruth
Dec. 18, 1830—James B. Goodwin to Mildred Powell	Geo. W. Martin
July 14, 1813—Moses Brooks to Nancey Tait	David Tate
Sept. 21, 1813—John Foster to Elizabeth Rogers	John Doak
March 26, 1830—Henry R. Cox to Maria Clifton	E. D. Foster
Dec. 17, 1817—John Qualls to Lockey Quarles	Abraham Trigg
Sept. 12, 1814—Solomon Deloach to Rachal Searcy	Claibourn Whitworth
March 25, 1813—John Clopton to Matilda Drake	Jno. W. Ring
May 11, 1814—Murfree Reese to Rebecca Rawland	John Little
June 19, 1830—Jacob Mayo to Polly Driver	John Webb
Jan. 4, 1836—Samuel Hamilton to Jane Harris	McG. Harris
Jan. 18, 1830—Mortimer Waters to Ethalinda Askin	Joseph Gore
April 2, 1822—William Coonrood to Patsey Rogers	James Grissom
July 16, 1813—Elijah Currey to Margaret Law	Robert Tilford
July 16, 1836—Joseph McDonald to Emily Furlong	Joel Algood
Jan. 27, 1836—Charles Coppage to Ann Kennedy	Charles Coppage
Aug. 6, 1836—Theoph. Edwards to Martha Edwards	Joseph Maning
Oct. 3, ——Pearson Garrison to Ellender Baker	John Schoby
Aug. 16, 1815—Wm. L. Smith to Fanny Wooldridge	John Barnard
Jan. 11, 1815—Richard Watkins to Catharine Jones	Edmund Crutcher
June 9, ——Daniel Alexander to Rachel Scott	James Martin
Sept. 20, 1814—Aaron Climer to Rebecca Sullivan	James Ozment
Sept. 14, 1813—Francis R. Smith to Sarah Morgan	Joel Lambeth
Feb. 2, 1822—Nathaniel Sanders to Naomi Summers	John Somers
Mar. 9, 1836—Abraham George to Jemima Gibson	Robt. M. Baskins
Feb. 5, 1836—Joseph Vicke to Mary Jackson	Lemuel Rencher
June 1, 1815—George Marlow to Elizabeth Terry	William Terry
Sept. 29, 1810—Wm. F. Overall to Torry Humble	Nace Overall
Apr. 10, 1860—Sam'l Pemberton to Margaret Dudley	John Foley
Aug. 17, 1830—Ezekiel Bass to Maria Barbee	Elias Barbee
Feb. 18, 1830—James L. Lanwinset to Syntha Firs	Thos. J. Merritt
May 1, '30—Jonathan Hendrixon to Clarisa Lermon	Benjamin Spring
Sept. 7, 1813—Frederick Foster to Sally Broadway	John Broadway

Names	Surety
Jan. 6, '15—Geo. Williamson to Hannah Crutchfield	Thomas Williamson
June 17, 1815—John McFarlin to Sally Bilbrew	John McFarland
Oct. 15, 1836—Thos. P. Hawkins to Eliza K. Scoby.	Answorth H. Howson
Jan. 13, 1836—Adnah Donnell to Elizabeth Donnell	Stephen E. Comer
June 7, 1815—John Johnson to Nancy Young	Littleton Medhen
Dec. 25, 1811—Luke Ray to Elly Daniel	John Eagan
Sept. 21, 1813—Robert Jennings to Polly Word	John Jennings
May 18, 1815—Abraham Jones to Cela Rogers	Jedethan Rogers
Dec. 28, 1814—John Medlin to Susanah Lantin	Jacob B. Lasater
Nov. 3, 1830—William Pemberton to Martha Brooks	Tho. W. Barksdale
Oct. 17, 1836—John B. Bryant to Katharine Waters	Thomas McKee
Sept. 13, '13—Obadiah Merret to Prysilla Clemmons	Samuel Clemmons
Sept. 10, 1813—James Adams to Jenny B. Thomas	James Thomas
Aug. 21, 1815—Jeremiah Russell to Elizabeth Hazlewood	Thos. Hazlewood
Oct. 29, 1814—John Rice to Drucella Parker	Benj. Estes
Oct. 9, 1813—Joshua Dillard to Catharine Quinn	Alex. Chambers
Sept. 13, 1811—Johnson J. Birch to Sally Caldwell	David Caldwell
Feb. 13, 1836—Nicholas Smith to Penelope J. Summac	George Harod
Sept. 2, 1831—Alfred Patton to Lucinda Ray	William P. Allin
Feb. 5, 1831—William Tanner to Jane McCown	Jas. Powell
Apr. 10, 1807—John Brown to Patty Bumpass	William McAdow
Sept. 18, 1830—Samuel Wallace to Nancy Sellar	Richard F. Wasson
Sept. 11, 1830—James M. Boyd to Martha Thomas	David U. Berry
May 17, 1830—James Gibson to Rachel Bowers	Samuel Stone
June 23, '30—Hickerson Barksdale to Harriet Lowe	Asa B. Douglass
Sept. 27, 1830—Jefferson Baxter to Rebecca Wynn	Robert Gwyn
Jan. 26, 1815—John Harpole to Elisabeth Swingley	George Harpole
Jan. 15, 1831—John W. Jones to Elizabeth Branford	John Yandel
Nov. 23, 1814—William Green to Polly Hooker	William Dunlap
Aug. 18, 1831—Abraham Wright to Martha Smart	Lan Semenes
Nov. 10, 1814—William Handsbrough to Elizabeth Marshall	Robt. Marshall
May 14, 1866—Claiborn Wynne to Eliza Ashworth	Elias Ashworth
March 4, 1810—James Hollard to Elizabeth Walker	George Michie
Jan. 13, '31—William D. Vivrett to Nancy Hickman	Henry Vivrett
July 25, 1815—Joseph Smart to Polly Burnett	Thomas Rhodes
Dec. 18, 1830—McCoy Moore to Ovalina Williams	Wm. Standerfer
Jan. 31, 1831—John Carter to Narcissa Gibson	Thos. Welch
May 1, 1830—Abraham Greer to Mary Ann Bollard	Charles Wilkerson
Aug. 13, 1813—John Berry to Elvira Harris	Sam'l Harris
Jan. 4, 1830—Wm. A. Provine to Nancey F. Bowers	Samuel F. Brown
Oct. 5, 1836—Levi Jones to Elizabeth K. Herald	J. E. Dickinson
June 13, 1815—Henry Smith to Polly Ashford	Graham Jackson
Feb. 4, 1836—Smith Oliver to Sarah Ann Sandors	Robert Hester
Oct. 5, 1836—William Hobbs to Lucretia Wier	Calvin W. Jackson

Names	Surety
Jan. 6, 1831—Fontain Jarrell to Elizabeth Jarrell	George W. Paine
Aug. 22, ——James York to Nancy Blurton	Moses Odam
Jan. 21, 1836—Ed. W. Lester to America Wasson	Chas. W. Cummings
March 15, '36—Richard Barker to Susana Williams	Robert Whitten
Feb. 10, 1860—Thos. B. Lain to Catherine G. Buoy	R. R. Laine

1823

Dec. 10—Chas. McWhirter to Nancy Griffin	Hugh B. McWhirter
Aug. 19—Sylvanus Merritt to Priscilla Bennett	Howard Edwards
Mar. 24—Bryant Tipton to Elizabeth Douglass	Will Spica
Dec. 10—Watkins Johnson to Patsy Edwards	Anderson Loga
Dec. 12—Levi Duke to Sally Bradshaw	Jas. Drake
Dec. 27—Jno. Simpson to Polly Ann Teague	Abner Teague
Aug. 25—Henry Hancock to Priscilla Hancock	Nelson Hancock
Aug. 15—John Coplinger to Martha Bell	Jno. J. Bell
Dec. 4—Robt. Sypert to Priscilla Davis	Thos. Sypert
Dec. 16—Benjamin Hunt to Lucy Mayo	Jno. B. Harris
Aug. 13—Lewis Patterson to Polly Edwards	Samuel C. Gerratt
July 5—Thos. Conyer to Sally Aust	Jno. Conyer
Feb. 15—Wm. Patterson to Happy Edwards	Robt. Baskin
Aug. 27—Wm. Bryant to Cely Higdon	Jas. Allcorn
Dec. 25—Gideon Fox to Unis Bennett	Solomon Warren
July 2—Robt. Williams to Jane Williams	Wm. McIntire
Oct. 6—Henry Fite to Mary Grandstaff	Jno. Grandstaff
Oct. 18—Watkins Owen to Peggy Rias	Robt. Pulley
Aug. 7—Michael Jones to Hannah Dallas	Alpha Phillips
Aug. 17—Henry Brown to Rebecca Mitchell	Taswell Mitchell
Aug. 7—Wm. Colewick to Margaret Steele	Jas. B. Taylor
Aug. 16—Knox Armstrong to Nancy C. Green	Samuel Armstrong
Sept. 12—Joseph Cuthrel to Margaret Spring	Milton W. Grissom
Sept. 12—Wyat Parkman to Patsy Sims	Benjamin Standly
July 21—Jacob Vantrease to Nancy Bass	Jno. Bass
Jan. 22—Wm. Garret to Sarah Welch	Michael McDermon
Dec. 22—Wm. Leeth to Olive Fields	Jno. Barber
Dec. 22—Jefferson Bodin to Peggy Furgason	Thos. L. Bonner
Aug. 2—Leon Bass to Sally Philips	Jno. Bass
July 11—Burwell Reeves to Maria Wilson	Jno. H. Stoneman
June 14—Jno. Craddock to Ruth E. Hicks	Jesse Jennings
Aug. 8—David Echols to Lyster Bradshaw	Jno. Forester
Dec. 4—Jno. Pully to Phebe Franklin	Wm. Owens
Sept. 16—Richard Dortch to Susan Hunt	Thos. Scurlock
Aug. 22—Wm. Ferrill to Elizabeth Wilson	Ewing Wilson
Aug. 7—Henry Ligon to Martha Shephard	Elisha B. Crudup
Sept. 8—Willie Davenport to Lucinda Ward	Jno. Sauls
Feb. 11—Oliver O'Neil to Elizabeth Taylor	David Beard
April 25—Jno. Estes to Scynthia McDaniel	Burwell Reeves

Names	Surety
Jan. 9—John Pemberton to Likey Johnson	Jesse Pemberton
Feb. 3—Benj. Carver to Nancy Lumpkin	Jas. C. Drake
Mar. 30—David King to Lucy Peniel	Ransom Perriman
Jan. 17—Geo. Blaze to Elizabeth Loyd	Lemuel Loyd
May 11—Phillip Johnson to Nancy Carr	John W. Payton
Sept. 2—Henry Hull to Lucy Wright	Jesse Lisle
Sept. 23—Ephraim Sherrill to Polly T. Bell	Samuel Y. Thomas
Oct. 24—Ashley Neil to Elizabeth Water	Joseph B. Lawrence
Feb. 4—John Whitson to Susannah Green	Owen C. Dennis
Feb. 26—Jas. Clemmons to Elizabeth Lee	Wm. Clemmons
Oct. 3—Henry Hobson to Lucy S. Tarver	Jno. H. Dew
Dec. 18—Geo. W. Hughley to Rachel Drennen	Joseph Drennen
Sept. 22—Asa Tatum to Charlotte Harris	Thos. Smith

1822

Names	Surety
Jan. 3—Allen R. Dillard to Emma D. Taylor	Henry Jackson
Mar. 18—Noah A. Suggs to Nancy Tarver	Howell Tarver
Feb. 11—Jas. Wright to Rebecca Kirkpatrick	O. G. Finly
June 5—Reuben Webb to Mary Allen	Gray Webb
Feb. 13—Bennett Webb to Patsey Hull	Jas. Driser
April 30—Wm. Boas to Harriet Simpson	Presly Simpson
Feb. 7—Perrigrim Taylor to Mary Williams	Jno. Afflack
Feb. 14—Enoch Hugle to Polly Walker	Samuel Hugle
Mar. 26—Israel Moore to Susannah Hunt	Jas. Moore
Mar. 20—Jno. Medlin to Fanny Sands	Robt. Anderson
Mar. 2—Isham Baker to Sally Caldwell	Isaac Lawrence
Jan. 19—Howell Tarver to Sally Richmond	Peter Sullivan
May 2—Jas. Mason to Olive Petty	Jas. Moore
Mar. 11—Abraham Sneed to Martha Brown	Jno. McAdow
Feb. 6—Jas. Cason to Jane McKnight	A. H. Wynne
April 30—Franklin Bartlett to Polly Meaks	Geo. L. Smith
Feb. 26—Thos. Burk to Fanny Robertson	Thos. McKnight
May 7—John Harrel to Sally Hutson	Jno. Hutson
Feb. 2—Wm. Howard to Rebecca Edwards	Nathaniel Edwards
Feb. 9—Algernon Piercy to Lucy Lewis	Drewry Dantz
May 6—Alexander Lackey to Elinor Garmany	Wm. Garmany
June 18—Archalack Bass to Rachal Phillips	Leon Bass
May 6—Pleasant Arnold to Synthea Barns	Theo. Arnold
Nov. 27—Archibald Gibson to Fanny Mosely	Hardy H. Leawell
April 2—Brantley Burns to Cela Harrington	B. Modglin
Mar. 16—Ambrose Holland to Rhody Winters	Woodson Layne
Feb. 6—Mathew R. Gibson to Ester Campbell	Geo. A. Campbell
May 21—Jno. Greer to Lidia Sands	Robt. Anderson
Mar. 9—Geo. S. Avery to Judia Chandler	Edings Chandler
April 24—Elijah Adamson to Susanah Hathway	Jesse Pugh
Jan. 30—Wm. Nunor to Nancy Langly	Jno. Cox

Names	Surety
Feb. 22—Jas. Manier to Patsy Irby	Tobias Henderson
Mar. 29—Geo. Phillips to Lucinda Turner	Jere Turner
Aug. 22—Wm. Bryson to Elizabeth Richardson	Samuel C. Odom
Feb. 11—Reuben Jackson to Levina Miller	Dudley Scurlock
April 25—Samuel Conyer to Elizabeth Kenedy	Jno. Conyer
Mar. 24—Abner Wetherly to Mary Edmiston	Samuel Donnell
Feb. 1—Joseph McDement to Anne Duke	Scion Duke
Feb. 21—Allen Dennis to Polly Tipton	Edmond Burk
Feb. 25—Jeremiah Fisher to Sally Drennan	Green B. Lannom
April 3—Samuel S. Mathews to Mary Arnold	Abraham Lasseter
Feb. 22—Eli Thrower to Rebecca Wall	Jno. Hickman
Feb. 19—Jas. Knight to Nancy Merritt	Jno. Merritt
Mar. 9—Theophilus Lambert to Charlotte Reynolds	Jno. Alexander
April 20—Frederick Jolly to Nicey Ames	Cornelius Buck
Dec. 10—Enis Harper to Polly Davis	Jno. Allcorn
Jan. 10—Jno. F. Doak to Elizabeth Hunter	Foster G. Crutcher
Mar. 12—Whitwell Harrington to Syrena Brown	B. Modglin
May 14—Jas. Porterfield to Polly Jennings	Samuel H. Porterfield
Mar. 3—Alford Bettes to Margaret Conyer	Wm. Bettis
Nov. 15—John Ward to Elizabeth Glass	Jno. McCaffry
June 1—Robt. Shepard to Susan Guill	Jno. Shepard
Nov. 19—Fountain Owen to ——— Hancock	Samuel C. Odem

1823

Names	Surety
June 1—Chas. Sullivan to Elizabeth Huddleston	Jacob Sullivan
Nov. 5—Jno. Word to Polly Simpson	Jno. Jennings
—— — Bartley Bowers to Mary Mahafey	Jeremiah Bowers
Dec. 22—Peter Myers to Diana Carter	Thos. Kirkpatrick
Oct. 14—Allen Clemmons to Jincey Young	Wm. Russell
Dec. 8—Wm. Green to Elizabeth Douglass	Robt. Anderson
Oct. 2—Dandridge Moss to Catharine Avans	Jno. Murrey
Oct. 22—Hiram Pursley to Elly Jones	Joel Hunter
Aug. 24—Greenberry Eaton to Jinsey McKinney	Jno. Warnoeh
Sept. 22—Jas. Godfrey to Nancy Whitlock	Jas. Thompson
Oct. 23—Perry Adle to Elizabeth Joiner	Jno. Clampitt
June 24—Leroy Fuston to Patsy Adams	Samuel Little
Oct. 14—Littleberry Wright to Elizabeth Kirkpatrick	——— Walker
June 12—Alexander Hamilton to Jane East	Nicholas Hobson
Dec. 28—Elijah Williams to Polly Clifton	Thos. Guthrie, Thos. Crutcher
Dec. 18—Azor Bone to Hulda Sherrill	Geo. K. Smith
June 30—Benjamin Clifton to Hannah Clifton	L. Sypert
Nov. 12—Jas. Warrick to Lenai Reyton	Hugh Gwyn
Aug. 23—Johnson S. Vaughn to Sally Byter	Wm. Hickman
Nov. 6—Jas. C. Wier to Mary Wier	Jas. Wiers

Names	Surety
Oct. 13—Hope Hancock to Patsey Rogers	Eli Edwards
Oct. 2—Richard Jones to Jane Graves	Bartley Graves
Nov. 29—Ethedred Bass to Nancy Barber	Jno. Bass
June 30—Thos. Pemberton to Polly McHaney	Henry D. Lester
July 7—Jonathan W. Weaver to Elizabeth B. Jones	Thos. Broughton
July 16—Jno. C. Gibson to Sally Ratterce	Geo. A. Campbell
Oct. 23—John Anderson to Jane Roane	A. Roane
June 11—Joseph G. Clendenin to Hannah Kirkpatrick	Wm. McIntone
Dec. 1—Jas. Stephens to Elizabeth Chambers	Jno. Afflack

1825

July 2—Wm. Brison to Sally Debenport	Geo. Brisan
Sept. 14—Edmund York to Ann Carroll	Alsey Garret
Dec. 8—Larkin Keeton to Mary Willerd	Jno. N. Hall

1824

Oct. 24—Charles Bradberry to Nancy Fields	Robertson Wright
July 20—Goodrich Andrews to Aley B. Tarrer	G. B. Andrews
Dec. 21—Thomas H. McCrary to Patsey J. Harlan	James Basford
Jan. 6—Green Chandler to Betsey Lumpkin	William Chandler
Sept. 29—Wm. McDonald to Polly Chandler	Beverly Chumly
Aug. 23—John Rains to Lucinda Cartwright	William Moholland
Mar. 20—Robert Cox to Rebecca Routon	Anderson Cox
Dec. 15—James Hays to Polly Thomas	Thomas Orrin
Sept. 7—William J. Mayo to Sally Eagan	Benjamin Hunt
June 30—Jeremiah Garner to Fanny Tracy	Edward Moore
Nov. 7—Sam'l Doake to Nancy Word	Valentine Kigon
Aug. 10—William Campbell to Polly Warren	Solomon Suggs
Dec. 20—James Spradlin to Margaret Spradlin	Mathew Allen
June 8—Isham Johnson to Susan Smith	Peter Johnson
Dec. 28—James Bond to Sarah Clemmons	Joshua Lester
Feb. 12—William Chester to Sophie M. Hogg	R. M. Burton
Nov. 3—Baker Woodward to Martha Pearcy	George Woodward
Oct. 11—Jefferson Bell to Leathy Johnson	James Johnson
Feb. 18—Elisha Bonds to Elizabeth Truett	Henry Truett
Nov. 7—Ezekiel C. Green to Jane Linch	Amos M. Bond
Mar. 1—Benjamin Sullivan to Polly Sullivan	W. M. Swain
Nov. 15—Hugh Hays to Sally Durk (Dark)	James Hays
Sept. 14—John Rogers to Lucy Goard	Thomas Copeland
Nov. 10—Zacheriah Wortham to Sally Gun	John Puckett
Nov. 1—William Johns to Mary Major	William Major
Sept. 4—John Seatt (Seat) to Abslay Bond	Jordan Johnson
Feb. 24—David Kincade to Sally McWhirter	John Kincade
—— — Jonathan Shore to Jenny Paac	James M. Armstrong

Names	Surety
July 31—Josiah Chandler to Annie Heraldson	Hugh Gwyn (bond unfinished)
Oct. 25—John Hutcherson to Nancy Harvey	Richard Chumly
Mar. 1—James C. Bradshaw to Charlotte Organ	Ewing Wilson
Dec. 22—Robert Chandler to Margaret Calhoon	J. Dew
Dec. 28—Richard Bass to Emily Duke	Isaac Jinkins
Dec. 22—James Arnold to Sarah T. Mitchell	John Gay
Oct. 11—Benjamin Hooken to Martha T. Clemmons	Thomas Partlow
June 28—Joseph Drennon to Lucinda Drennon	James Drennon
Dec. 11—Benjamin B. Coaper to Rebecca Owen	Warren C.Davenport
Dec. 8—Robert D. Reed to Sally Reed	Samuel Donnell
Jan. 23—John W. Avory to Malinda Ann Tarver	Wm. Murray, Jr.
Sept. 13—Washington Thomas to Polly New	Robert Thomas
Nov. 21—Jonathan Baker to Lucy Ann Foster	James Allcorn
Jan. 22—Robert Hallum to Ann T. Dew	Norvall Douglass
Sept. 13—Abel Jones to Sally Baleman	John S. Woollen
Feb. 2—Ansil B. Jolly to Patsey Wright	Philip Smart
Sept. 28—Thomas P. Moore to Tempy Jones	Michael Jones
Mar. 22—Josiah Philips to Polly Bass	Richard Bass
Jan. 31—Samuel Jones to Lucy Winston	John Winston
Aug. 4—John Sims to Elizabeth Coplinger	Robert Corley
Oct. 26—Adam Trout to Sally Dallas	Henry Worye (Rye)
Oct. 23—Hezekiah Davis to Nancy Wilson	Milner Walker
April 30—Orang D. Beardin to Margaret Woodvill	Henry H. Woodvill
Jan. 9—Robert Furgason to Nancy Organ	John Coe
Oct. 11—John Lacky to Jane White	Samuel T. White
Feb. 18—James Neal to Nancy Hearn	George D. Moore
July 15—Anderson Turpin to Corlin Buck	W. Lambeth
Jan. 19—Eden Donnell to Eliza Garmony	Leo Donnell
Oct. 4—James Baker to Levina Donnell	James B. McMurry
Nov. 23—William M. Crook to Rebecca Lassiter	Isaac Sparks
Aug. 13—Charles Wade to Frances Harrison	Henry M. Hancock
Dec. 1—Peter Goard to Dice Smith	Achilles Smith
Nov. 10—Robert Bondurant to Permelia Moseley	E. A. White
Feb. 19—Alexander Kirkpatrick to Lucy Smith	Thomas Bradley
Jan. 7—Newton Cloyd to Elizabeth Williamson	John A. Williamson
Feb. 4—John Cluck to Mary Martin	Thomas Martin
June 30—Hezekiah Brown to Betsey Collings	Anderson Ewing
Dec. 15—Jonathan Turner to Nancy Sneed	John Sneed
Aug. 26—John Cox to Betsey Edwards	Alexander Rutledge
Mar. 2—Wilson Bradshaw to Polly Shickord	Sion Duke
July 28—Henry Vivrett to Polly Hickman	John Hickman
Oct. 16—James Pemberton to Harky Bradly	Thos. P. Moore
Dec. 27—James M. Liveley to Mary Ann Herrito	John M. Greer
Nov. 26—James C. Bond to Mary W. Smith	David K. Donnell

NAMES	SURETY
Oct. 8—Abram Lassiter to Nancy Puckett	John Arnold
Feb. 16—David Baird to Polly Avery	William Wynn
Sept. 20—Alexander Penny to Kitty Harrison	Jesse Wade
Sept. 27—Batt Baird to Elizabeth Askew	Jas. Baird
May 27—Enos Bone to Lucy Hern	James P. Henry
Jan. 14—Samuel Quarls to Parthenia Hines	Zachariah Wortham
July 13—John Bitts to Milly Jolly	William Bitts
Mar. 2—William Reese to Martha Taylor	Thomas Cox
Feb. 23—Gardner Morgan to Polly Chaver	Randolph Morgan
Sept. 7—Nelson Owen to Peggy Duggan	James Duggan
Mar. 2—Thornton Lane to Fanny Haralson	Vincent Harralson
Dec. 8—Young L. Herndon to Sally Kelly	John S. Kennedy
Feb. 8—William Parker to Mary Clouda	William Gray
Oct. 19—John Baird to Elenor Bild	David Baird
June 9—Elijah Vanderpool to Hannah Fuston	John Handly
Feb. 23—George A. Huddleston to Harriet S. Cummings	William Cummings
May 3—William Knight to Lavina Redding	James Knight
Jan. 19—Talbot Jones to Anny Saterfield	John Seat
April 15—Willis Booker to Sally Joplin	Wm. S. Alexander
Dec. 28—Jacob Furgerson to Mary Furgerson	Lemuel Furgerson
Dec. 4—Moses Thompson to Lucinda Donnald	James P. Henry
July 30—Nathaniel Corley to Nancy Turner	Michael Yerger
July 28—Soloman Allman to Elizabeth Puckett	Thos. Allman
Feb. 12—Obediah Freeman to Elizabeth Hancock	Joseph Freeman
Nov. 11—Jonathan Lassiter to Nancy Davis	James Allcorn
July 8—Jones W. Locke to Lucy D. Bonner	(Bat) Bartholomew Figurs
Feb. 14—Jesse Bloodworth to Celia Tucker	Benjamin T. Tucker
Jan. 14—Samuel Quarles to Parthena Hines	John Allcorn
Oct. 9—George Neel to Martha Branch	Joseph B. Lewvner
Dec. 21—Isaac T. Stephenson (Stevenson) to Minerva Norris	Benj. F. Stevenson
Dec. 28—James Cropper to Rhody Holland	Rich'd A. Holland
Feb. 24—William Lawness (sig. Lanius) to Nancy Curd	Jacob Lanius
Oct. 7—Henry Taylor to Mary Betey	Joshua V. Taylor
Sept. 18—Joseph Jinkins to Mary Vantreese	William Vantreese
April 3—James H. Hearn to Rebecca Adkinson	Israel Moore
Aug. 30—James W. Harris to Catsey Smith	Isaac Eagan
Sept. 14—James S. Odom to Mary Francis	Samuel C. Odom
Dec. 20—William Green to Polly Cox	Thomas Cox
May 15—John A. Nettles to Pemmy Cartwright	Jas. Dodds
Aug. 12—Willis Allen to Elizabeth Joyner	Yancy Massey
Sept. 28—Thomas Almond to Margaret (Polly) Ellison	Willis Almond

Names	Surety
Sept. 24—William Eatherly to Elizabeth Bernard	James Williamson
June 16—Robert Milligan to Mary Blanton	James Milligan
June 30—William H. Smith to Lucy W. Pearcy	Drury Dance.
Aug. 5—Thomas Jones to Elizabeth Compton	Joseph L. Green
July 16—Thomas Copeland to Elizabeth Mount	Joshua Copeland
Oct. 5—Cyrus Stuart to Elizabeth Roach	Robert Hallum
Sept. 22—Asa Graves to Sally Jones	Richard Jones
Jan. 12—John Craddock to Lucrecia Arnold	Robert Bumpass
May 31—James Lyon to Priscilla Harris	Jno. White
Sept. 27—Isaac Sparks to Orpha Thompson	John Major
Nov. 29—Thomas Hearn to Elizabeth Nettles	Benjamin Nettles
Nov. 3—Jordan Robertson to Mary Peacock	Sterling Edwards
Sept. 16—Laban O'Neil to Matilda Baker	Jeremiah Brooks
Feb. 4—Frederick Rotramble (sig. Roadtamel) to Celia Maddocks	John B. Harris
Jan. 16—Aaron F. Jones to Nancy T. Buchler	Onessimus Evans
Jan. 5—Ila Douglass to Elizabeth Harris	F. G. Crutcher
Feb. 20—Eli Massy to Mary Davis	Samuel Davis
Nov. 29—Henry Gossett to Polly Dill	John Gossett
June 27—Lesley Hancock to Nancy Smith	Leeander Hancock
July 15—Sam'l Calhoun, Jr., to Martha Figars	T. Bradly
June 27—Robert N. Colso to Frances J. Walters	Jas. Allcorn
Oct. 25—Baily Hutcheson to Betsey Harvy	Rich'd Chumly
—— 9—Reynear H. Mason to Elizabeth Moss	Henry Mason
Jan. 14—Martin Wadkins to Sally Hopkins	Obediah Rich
Oct. 6—Erasmus Jones to Christiana Bond	John Seat
May 5—Levy Stites to Mary Adamson	Jesse Pugh
Aug. 25—Thomas Mason to Nancy Johnson	Sam Brown
April 5—Thomas W. Forbus to Nancy Clifton	Hugh Wiley
April 7—William Mosely to Jemima Turner	Robert N. Coles
Dec. 28—Elijah Clae to Patsey Lane	Patrick Buckley
Sept. 20—Jessey Pue to Rodey Hathaway	John Adamson
May 25—Elisha Cole to Jeney Anderson	James H. Hunt
Feb. 25—Elijah Hodges to Hannah Hubbard	John Ward
June 22—James G. Grubbs to Elizabeth Grubbs	Edmund Sims
June 17—Granville Wammack to Rachael Cropper	Mansfield Massey
Nov. 27—Peter S. Wood to Sarah Seal	William Wood

1825

—— — Jas. Thrift to Elizabeth Sanderson	Edward A. White
Mar. 21—Isaac Brune ——(?) to Midy Helfton	Edward Simpson
Aug. 15—Thos. Lyon to Susannah Livan	Jas. Swan
Aug. 3—Zacariah Keeton to Nancy Redigo	Joseph Fite
Dec. 31—Washington Robertson to Barshaba Williford	Thos. Davis
June 1—Elam Reed to Elizabeth Pentecost	Henry Reed

Names	Surety
Mar. 21—Logan Linch to Elizabeth Wier	Wm. Joiner
Aug. 30—Thos. Patton to Rebecca Patterson	Wm. Thompson
Feb. 1—Jno. Bass to Elizabeth G. Remon	Wm. Beard
Mar. 13—Lovet Caroway to Peggy Schannon	Merritt Caroway
Mar. 23—Flemming Cocke to Martha Williams	Wm. Gray
Nov. 8—Jno. L. Wynne to Minerva Allcorn	Jas. Allcorn
Jan. 11—Thos. Scurlock to Jane Compton	Granvill Mansfield
July 30—John Cunningham to Sally Warren	Moses Cunningham
June 30—Josiah Joiner to Carry Allen	Willis Deer
Jan. 1—Isham Butterworth to Elizabeth Ross	Wm. W. Babb
Jan. 27—Thos. Harrington to Lydia Anglen	Peter Mires
Dec. 10—Absolom Knight to Pernella Dodd	Samuel Ozment
Oct. 14—Armstrong Ozment to Martha Hudson	Absalom Knight
May 5—Drury Shoecraft to Nancy Nickings	Mark Nickings
Sept. 22—James H. Barr to Eliza Miller	Samuel W. Barr
Dec. 23—Jas. New to Mary A. Chanler	Josiah Beasly
Oct. 5—Jas. Devenport to Nancy Mobey	Jas. M. Inman
Aug. 22—Wm. Madox to Sally C. Hancock	Henry M. Hancock
Jan. 4—Hugh George to Polly Gains	Anthony Gains
Aug. 22—Wm. Baird to Lucinda Bennet	Seldon Baird
Nov. 5—Enos McKnight to Sally M. Greer	Winphrey Witherspoon
April 9—Obadiah Gordon to Frances Drake	Sam'l C. McWhirter
Aug. 31—Jas. Cunningham to Elizabeth Patterson	Wm. F. Alexander
Aug. 30—Thos. Willis to Malvina Ruff	Thos. Baget
Sept. 20—Jas. Irby to Sarah Kindred	Thos. Kindred
Oct. 11—Jordan Johnson to Sally Bartlett	Alpha Philips
May 3—Joel B. Holbert to Tursey Sherrill	Zachariah Tolliver
June 16—Wm. H. Blackburn to Sarah Fletcher	Bird Gwill
Sept. 3—Levin Ragsdale to Rebecca Merritt	Asa Ragsdale
Dec. 29—Jno. Brown to Beedy Vivrett	Jas. B. Cole
Jan. 15—Jesse Gibson to Susan T. Hollman	Robt. D. Bell
Mar. 28—Whaley Newby to Elizabeth Cooksey	Jas. Cooksey
Mar. 7—Jas. Campbell to Polly Prichard	Benj. Prichard
April 21—Wm. S. Carruth to Elizabeth Davis	Jesse Jackson
Feb. 2—Epaphredetes Francis to Nancy Cooper	Jas. S. Leeche
June 28—Lemuel Wright to Sarah Drennon	Thos. Drennan
April 11—Horatio Benard to Jane R. Atherly	Evans Mabry
Mar. 23—John G. Brown to Sarah Scott	Moses Brown
Mar. 23—Ezekiel Holloway to Jane Shannon	James Ozment
Oct. 6—John S. Patterson to Harriet Reynolds	William Thompson
Jan. 11—William Joiner to Polly Coe	Harman Lash
Aug. 31—John D. Taylor to Nancy Williams	Henry Young
Sept. 30—Hardy H. Baird to Nancy Baird	Bartholomew Baird
Nov. 19—James T. Sims to Martha Puckett	Leo Donnell
Dec. 2—James Faweal to Sally Faweal	William Cooper

Names	Surety
July 14—John H. Stoneman to Febey Moore	Little B. Moore
Dec. 15—William Williams to Rebecca Jackson	F. G. Crutcher
Dec. 30—Norfleet Nelms to Lydia Deekings	Jesse Cook
Mar. 17—Gabriel Shaw to Locky Organ	Willis Allen
Aug. 31—Alfred M. Hite to Mary Lassiter	William Lassiter
Feb. 1—James Bond to Ruth Florady	William Bond
June 1—Joseph Mingle to Sally Bonds	Thomas Nowlen
Nov. 14—Jonathan Drenan to Lucy G. Liggon	Josiah Ligon
June 15—Joel Fragon to Mary Gilbert	Alexander Rutledge
Oct. 20—Abram Marlow to Rebecca Hanes	John J. Bell
Aug. 4—Moses Odom to Lucy Lawrence	Thomas Barbee
July 29—Mark Leeke to Elizabeth Lewis	William Leeke
April 6—Frederick Aust to Matilda Allen	John Connger
May 13—William Stuart to Mary Tooly	Samuel Massie
Jan. 18—Elisha Bonds to Patsey Bennet	John Meritt
Sept. 25—Benjamin H. Dennis to Rhody Sanders	Johnson Vaughan
July 26—William O. New to Ivy Hamilton	Henry Jackson
Mar. 15—Caleb Taylor to Margaret Glanton	Ransom Howell
Sept. 20—Samuel F. Patterson to Lucy Waters	Nelson G. Alexander
Nov. 28—Charles Bradley to Polly Bradley	William Jackson
Nov. 23—Alfred Clemmons to Elizabeth Young	Allen Clemmons
Aug. 29—Stephen H. Coleman to Nancy P. Harrison	Joshua Harrison
Feb. 21—John Yandell to Elizabeth Jones	James P. Roach
Oct. 18—Zarra Harrelson (Harrison) to Margaret Hepey	John Murray
Sept. 10—Thomas N. Moore to Elizabeth Farver	Joseph T. Bell
Jan. 18—Lewis D. Yarnell to Ann Arnald	J. H. Baird
July 27—Henry Reed to Agness M. Carrath	Robert Reed
April 6—James Viveret to Sally Hill	Henry F. Smith
Nov. 18—Robert Whitten to Elizabeth Cocke	William C. Collins
Sept. 9—Benjamin Nettles to Priscella Mosley	Richard Compton
Nov. 22—Benjamin Bell to Polly Spring	Benjamin Spring
Nov. 23—Lewis Seay to Margaret Ann Rollinan	Thomas Wilson
April 16—John Brown to Sarah Williams	George Benthall
May 18—Samuel R. Wilson to Nancy Goldstone	Anderson Cook
June 16—Samuel Yerger to Hannah E. Johnson	Benjamin S. Litton
Nov. 8—Jno. L. Wynne to Minerva Allcorn	H. L. Donglap
—— — Simon McLendon to Frances Overby	George A. Evans
Mar. 28—Gideon Carter to Martha Dvualt	Abraham Peacock
Dec. 27—Martin Marrs to Mary Marrison	Alexander Marrs
Sept. 21—Isham Joiner to Rachael Eckols	Edmund Jones
—— 13—John Tarpley to Sarah Davis	William New
Jan. 21—John Spurlock to Sinthey Meadoo	John Snead
Oct. 13—William Adkins to Mahala Stublefield	Benjamin Spring

Names	Surety
Dec. 17—David Smith to Mary Cumpton	Jacob Smith, Thomas Barbee
Aug. 1—Thomas Lewis to Elizabeth Hays	James A. Strong
Feb. 23—James Hays to Malindey Night	Wingate Truit
Feb. 15—Granville Mansfield to Frances Scurlock	James Allcorn
May 23—Moses McCrary to Elizabeth Witherly	James Basford
Dec. 26—Levin Woollen to Nancy Peacock	John S. Woollen
Jan. 18—Elisha Bonds to Patsey Bennet	John Merret
May 13—William Stuart to Mary Tooly	Samuel Massie
Feb. 12—Isaac Hollingsworth to Alliminta Justin	William Hollingworth
July 5—William Taylor to Polly Broom	Joel Watkins
April 25—Allen Hill to Sarah Peace	James Allcorn
Mar. 18—Thomas Ames to Sally Ray	Hardy Ames
Aug. 13—James P. Roach to Nelly McNeely	James H. Barr
Oct. 3—John Adamson to Polley Davis	Jesse Pugh
June 23—Greenbury Adams to Sally Periman	Benjamin Periman
Dec. 20—Daniel J. Gutherie to Mary White	Thomas Gutherie
Feb. 5—Alexander Henry to Sarah Carruth	David Walsh
Nov. 12—Allygood Woolard to Elizabeth Hutchison	William L. Sypert
Aug. 22—John Palmer to Margaret Reese	John Cox
Dec. 31—Redding Fields to Polly Ferrington	David Fields
April 12—William Jolly to Martha Golson	Warner Lambeth
Dec. 10—Silas Hedgepath to Rebecca Rice	Leven Woollen
April 13—George D. Cummings to Martha D. Cummings	John Hearn
—— 3—Abner Teogio (Tegue) to Rhody McKnight	Stephen Gallegly
Sept. 6—John Campbell to Melinda Bore (Bone)	Hugh Campbell
July 18—Ezekiel Cloyd to Nancy White	Edward White
Nov. 11—Robert Manning to Nancy Lannum	William Searcy
July 28—James M. Brown to Celia Roach	James H. Barr
Dec. 10—John Haywood to Lucy Wynne	Micajah Haywod
Dec. 6—Jesse Warren to Sally Farmer	Perigren Taylor
Mar. 8—George Benthall to Sally Brown	Littleton Benthal
April 5—Benjamin F. Stepenson (Stevenson) to Elizabeth Willis	Moore T. Moss
Feb. 25—Warren Davenport to Susey Whitlock	James Leech
May 23—Aaron McCrary to Mary Oliver	James Basford
Dec. 22—Julius Blaylock to Irena Bell	Geo. W. Hearn
July 5—Joseph L. Wilson to Margret Barton	Joseph Johnson
Aug. 18—John Mosely to Martha Halbrooks	James O. Lamberth, Samuel Coles
Sept. 26—William Stoboy to Margaret Bay	John Clampett
July 15—William Moore to Elizabeth Brothers	Matthew Hearn
Sept. 7—Thomas Clifton to Mansey Seat	Spencer W. Tally
May 5—Jesse Jackson to Nancy Bouner	James Slate

Names	Surety
Mar. 15—James Martin to Mary Eason	Patrick H. Hegerty
July 21—George Brison to Ester Read	Levey Reade
Oct. 19—Samuel Moseley to Elizabeth Dill	William Allen
Dec. 15—John Traut to Mary Ann Tomlinson	Zealous Johnson
June 6—Stephen Hailey to Ann Gregor	Bemmey B.Beardsley
Nov. 24—Robert N. Nichols to Mary T. Chaney	Jessee M. Wade
April 4—John Prim to Inde Maddox	Frederick Rotramel
Nov. 10—Maben Anderson to Mary McMurray	J. Kirkpatrick
May 7—James Clemmons to ——— ———	Etheldred Clemmons
Jan. 3—Erasmus Tracy to Derusha Taylor	Wiley Garner
June 3—Thomas Martin to Thursey Richardson	Ewing Wilson
Aug. 27—Samuel Baxter to Frances Irby	Jacob Wilhelm
Dec. 3—David Lane to Lucy E. Lane	John Lane
Oct. 28—William Hamilton to Elizabeth Christopher	John McNeely
May 3—Jonathan Patton to Ruth Godfrey	James Thompson
Jan. 3—Hiram Bryant to Mary Wray	Elisha Vaughan
Sept. 24—William Ames to Ann Eagon	Hardy Syfurt
—— 5—Edward Jones to Lucy Lea	Henry H. Harris
Aug. 9—John Allen to Frankey Adams	Zacariah Tommes
Jan. 11—Thomas Alexander to Nancy Jennings	Wm. S. Alexander
Mar. 1—David Briant to Mary Land	Richard Hight
May 9—Simeon Horse to Sally Sneed	Ranson Periman
Aug. 17—Gilpen Hallum to Parthena Graves	Norvall Douglass
July 13—James Manning to Louisa Bobbit	Brittain Odom
Feb. 16—Moses Brown to Tabitha Gardner	Anderson Evans
Mar. 10—Brooking Burnett to Lithe Moss	Regnar H. Mason
Jan. 26—James T. Carruth to Nancy Williams	Thomas Guthrie (?)
July 7—John Hankins to Elizabeth Routen	James Powell
Sept. 27—Berry Grier to Catherine Myres	Aquilla Grier
May 25—James Ozment to Martha Holloway	James R. Allen
1826	1826
Aug. 26—Simpson Bennett to Nancy Jackson	Randal M. Donald
Sept. 14—Joseph Seay to Elizabeth Barker	Robert Burter
May 1—Wm. H. Smith to Jane L. Smith	Joshua W. Smith
Jan. 9—Henry Burnett to Parthena Moss	R. H. Mason
Nov. 20—Wm. B. Gleevs to Harriet Lumpkins	William McNeel
May 5—Timothy Seat to Elizabeth Clifton	Peledge Swindell
Dec. 4—Thomas Barley (Barbee) to Hester Taylor	Joseph Barbee
Feb. 10—Allen Jones to Michie Hutcherson	William L. Sypert
Mar. 13—Caswell S. Sims to Nancy Carter	Thomas Cox
Sept. 5—Wyatt Walker to Jane Petty	John Mason
June 19—Henry Shannon to Margarett Clemmon	William M. Swain
Sept. 30—John Webber to Elizabeth Etherly	F. P. Wood
Aug. 7—David D. McCully to Sarah Drolingden	William Drolingder

Names	Surety
Jan. 12—James Cowan to Nancy Walker	Matthew Horn
Sept. 5—Richard Maddox to Elizabeth Johnson	Larkin Spradlin
July 24—Fountain Robertson to Sarah Cason	Thomas McKnight
Dec. 2—Henry Mathews to Sally Seat	Talbot Jones
Dec. 13—Robert D. Bell to Elizabeth Roane	James Aston
Jan. 30—Richard B. Tate to Rebecah Alexander	James Wilson
Jan. 28—William Vantreece ———	David Grandstaff
Oct. 3—Isaac Whitehead to Sarah Mosley	John Mosley
Sept. 21—Hyram Lea to Elizabeth Lea	Samuel R. Comer
Dec. 4—James S. Bailey to Lucy Puckett	Stanhope Sharp
Sept. 12—John W. Beauchamp to Mary Wilson	James Elizer
Oct. 26—Henry Southern to Bathsheba	Wm. Williams
Aug. 10—Meady White to Sarah Campbell	John C. Gibson
May 23—Thos. Yew Banks to Ann Riddle	Millner Walker
Feb. 3—Samuel Bryson to Mary Millegan	David Milligan
Feb. 15—Turner M. Johnson to Elizabeth Taylor	Willis Dowell
Sept. 18—Edmund Simpson to Rachel Whitton	Stanhope Sharpe
July 11—Alanson F. Doak to Adaline Donnell	L. S. Donnell
Oct. 21—Anderson Walker to Elizabeth Bradley	John H. Swindell
Feb. 8—Harris Campbell to Sarena Hambleton	William O'Neil
Aug. 31—Montgomery Pitner to Jane Wray	William Pitner
Aug. 24—Joseph Bell to Jane Donnell	Jesse M. Wade
Aug. 26—Paschal P. Hudson to Alliphair Hearn	L. S. Donnell
Aug. 26—Edward Freeman to Charlott Everritt	Brinkley Bridges
—— —William McGreggor to Frances H. Graves	Wm. Walker, Jr.
Aug. 8—Cyrus Stuart to Mary S. Gleeves	Robert Campbell
Dec. 22—Jesse Johnson to Rebeccah Stuart	James M. Johnson
Dec. 8—George W. Jones to Christina G. Dance	Elisha Sims
Mar. 18—David Hodges to Mary Rolls	John Rawls
May 17—Drury Mays to Susan M. Williams	John Brown
Jan. 5—Charles Blalock to Palny Tucker	James Mays
June 17—James Daniel to Eliza Smith	Josiah S. McClain
Oct. 26—Edmund Rucker to Lousasa Winchester	Jno. W. Rucker
July 27—James B. Cole to Jacornet Bridges	Aaron Britton
Dec. 14—Henry Walker to Elizabeth Denton	Hubbard Ferrell
June 5—Mark Nickings to Penny Osbrooks	Calvin Nickings
Nov. 21—Thompson Glenn to Julia Scurlock	Jos. L. Wilson
Feb. 16—William England to Seluda Fergerson	James Joby
Aug. 24—Samuel Harlin to Susanna Bradley	Wm. Hodges
Dec. 20—Wm. T. Sherrell to Eleuer M. Thomas	Minetree Jones
Oct. 2—Elisha S. Rhodes to Sally Mosley	J. R. Athworth
Jan. 20—John Taylor to Mariah Edwards	John Gaddy
Feb. 10—John Gunn to Polley Sims	Caswell S. Sims
Jan. 5—Thomas C. Hudson to Cintha-McLeroy	James McLeroy, J. B. Guthrie
Mar. 28—James W. Green to Lucy Ann Bonner	James Allcorn

Names	Surety
Nov. 20—Micajah C. Horn to Sarah Hooper	Byrd Nolen
July 11—John B. Lane to Nancy Arnold	Nathan Williams
Dec. 30—Barna Stewart to Jane Morris	Thomas Gains
Sept. 8—Thomas D. Tarver to Sarah Hallum	John T. Hail
Sept. 15—John P. Johnson to Eliza Mitchell	William Johnson
May 4—John Gay to Mariah A. Clay	Hardy Hunt
Nov. 31—Thomas R. Williams to Mary Henry	Edward G. Jacob
Sept. 5—Wm. M. Dillard to Eliza F. Corley	Robert Corley
July 19—Richard Terrell to Sally Holloway	William Corson
Feb. 7—Thomas Shering to Salley Baxter	Jeremiah Murray
April 1—Nathan Wheeler to Catharine Grandstaff	Thomas Tracy
Aug. 5—William B. Pursley to Hariott Johnson	Robertson Johnson
Nov. 14—Richard Lyon (Lion) tō Ann Swann	Marshall H. Ward
Aug. 19—Henry Morris to Eastor Hearn	Micajah Rogers
Nov. 29—William Alsup to Morning Hill	Solomon Boyd
Feb. 13—William Trusty to Alcy Mitchell	Ishmiel Bradshaw
Sept. 2—William Cason to Mary McKnight	George Smith
June 29—Stephen L. Hearn to Polly G. Hankins	William H. Hearn
Nov. 11—James Cox to Lucy Cox	William Cox
Nov. 20—John N. Taylor to (no name)	Philander Davis
Dec. 20—James Melton to Nancy Palmer	Henry Southern
Dec. 11—Philip Johnson to Elinor Harrison	Robt. Johnson
Nov. 25—Edwin McCorkle to Jane M. Thomas	Wm. Thomas
July 29—Hardin Goodall to Polly Scoby	Thomas B. Ruge
Nov. 1—Asa Ragsdale to Rhoda Ragsdale	Leaven Ragsdale
Dec. 11—Edward Dillard to Martha S. Gold	A. H. Oynall
Oct. 28—Charles Hicks to Clanpa Webb	Willie Dockings
Sept. 20—William McCowen to Mary M. Moseley	James Allcorn
May 13—Isaac Barnett to Nancy Long	James H. Long
April 7—Thomas Short to Elizabeth Pemberton	Jesse Pemberton
Oct. 11—Horatio Bernard to Margarett M. Williamson	Henry T. Smith
Nov. 29—Thomas White to Liney Putman	William Barnett
Sept. 23—Alphy Philips to Elizabeth Edwards	Hez. Cartwright
Dec. 9—Nathan Dillon to Sarah Greer	Williamson Nippen
Sept. 27—Elam Edge to Mary Barbee	Thomas Barbee
Nov. 8—Loven Clifton to Hannah Skean	George Tucker
Feb. 4—Nathaniel Bell to Lusinda Smith	E. Sherill
Aug. 28—Micajah Zachary to Polly Peak	John Peek
Jan. 12—John C. Mondine to Maria Youree	Benjamin Chapman
April 10—John C. Moseley to Sally Jones	Asa Moseley
Oct. 21—Valentine Stull to Susan Rice	Joseph Rutland
Jan. 13—Samuel Smith to Catherine Smith	T. Bradley
Dec. 18—Francis P. Davidson to Sarah Hearn	Thomas Cook
Dec. 7—Reddin Tidwell to Mary Enocks	John Sullivan
May 1—Andrew Thorn to ———	John Lemon

NAMES	SURETY
Aug. 4—James Lanns to Susan Moser	A. C. Carruth
Nov. 11—Henry R. Cox to Purlena Shorter	William Cox
Feb. 1—John K. Parker to Elizabeth Tipton	Fleming Cocke
Sept. 30—Alfred Mathews to Jincy Hollingsworth	Nathan C. Mathews
July 22—David Grindstaff to Margaret Phillips	M. Mathew Hearn
Feb. 14—Solomon Warren to Nancy Howard	Absalom Knight
Sept. 11—John Cloyd to Elizabeth Griffet	John Neuner
April 1—Leeman Hancock to Caty Moxley	Nelson Hancock
Oct. 30—Benjamin Spring to Catherine Spring	Jas. Swann
Mar. 13—John Paisley to Martha Thrower	James Jackson
Sept. 5—Charles Ferris (Fariss) to Susanna Mason	John Mason
1827	1827
April 14—James Booth to Lousiah Graves	Samuel Walker
April 23—Joseph Ingram to Susan Bates	Joseph Blood
Oct. 31—Isaac Ellis to Nancy Jinnings	Jesse B. White
Dec. 12—Stephen Norton to Polly McDaniel	James Walton
Dec. 13—Henry K. Dice to Elizabeth Spring	Daniel Bennett
Dec. 17—William Puckett to Mahala Franklin	B. T. Mottley
Dec. 18—Green Proctor to Margaret Kitrall	Wilbon R. Winter
Aug. 27—David Bass to Harriet Harris	Thomas Cox
Nov. 13—Daniel Freeman to Polly Ann Cunningham	Jefferson Hamilton
Oct. 29—William Thompon to Mirandy Kelly	Daniel Kelley
Mar. 6—Henry F. Smith to Missouri Gleaves	Robert Topp
Oct. 5—Hardy Manning to Lissa Robertson	James Maning
Oct. 23—Joseph Thompson to Elizabeth Dodds	John S. Patterson
Nov. 3—Lindley Baird to Lewarken Medly (Mealley)	Henry Cooley
July 2—David Patterson to Malinda Ethridge	Shadrack C. Smith
Oct. 13—Thomas Branch to Jane Moon	George Neel
Oct. 29—Samuel Capslinger to Rebecca Maricle	John Swan
Mar. 10—Wright M. Weatherly to Ann Bryant	Daniel Williamson
Jan. 29—Jacob Mick to Mary Lott	Henry Robertson
April 27—Josiah Kirkpatrick to Nancy Tilford	John W. Kirkpatrick
Mar. 15—John Reynolds to Abigail Baskins	George Smith
Sept. 25—Hicks Ellis to Lucy Jones	Michael Jones
July 13—Jesse Joynel ———	A. Perkinson
May 18—Arnold Burke to Margarett Smith	Thos. Burk
Jan. 9—George Crutchfield to Amy Hancock	James Allcorn
Nov. 21—Allen Wilson to Elizabeth Davis	James A. Strange
May 31—James M. Irwin to Jane C. Bullard	Leo Donnell
July 3—Martin Rogers to Tempy Warren	Nathan Medyett
May 22—Benjamin Andrews to Polly Parker	James Naylor
June 28—Jesse Bloodworth to Jane Tucker	Wm. Bloodsworth

Names	Surety
April 25—Isaac Dorch to Martha Allen	Adam Harpole
Oct. 9—John W. Tate to Elizabeth Cloyd	Newton Cloyd
Dec. 21—Edward G. Campbell to Seanath Maxwell	Edward G. Jaol
June 20—John Wriston to Lina Edwards	Sam'l Harb
Aug. 25—Benjamin Belt to Sally Reed	Edward G. Campbell
Nov. 27—James P. Scott to Jane C. Carruth	Wm. Scott
Dec. 11—Abraham Massey to Tabitha Hearn	Thomas Davis
Oct. 16—James Walton to Mary Mosier	Stephen Wade
Sept. 3—William Batey to Sarah Grissum	Henry Partin
June 30—Edmund Burton to Amanda Jones	Josiah S. McClain
July 24—Samuel Bond to Elizabeth Milton	Elisha Bond
June 26—Robert Foster to Margaret Rea	David Foster
Sept. 18—John R. Moody to Casander F. Allison	Thos. Allman
June 9—Cornelius W. Bailey (Baley) to Rebecah Patterson	Peter Patterson
Aug. 3—Richard Taylor to Liddy Baird	John Waters
Jan. 4—Wyatt Ramsey to Peggy Rice	William J. Barr
Feb. 1—Briant McDeamon to Elizabeth McDornart	Henry Rutland
June 18—Samuel Sperry to Mourning Wright	John Sperry
—— —Peterson Morris to Catharine Wiley	Thomas Davis
Sept. 3—William Bilbro to Elizabeth Johnson	Jesse B. White
—— —Wm. W. Brooks to Lousana Huddleston	Isaac W. Brooks
July 21—Mekin Ship to Mary Warren	Benton Ship
July 28—Henry Gilliam to Fanny Shaw	Fleming Mitchell
Aug. 8—John Hollingsworth to Nansey Dill	John Gossett
Aug. 22—Daniel McKee to Sarah Thomas	Harry Thomas
Feb. 8—John Perkins to Renanna Sherrill	Alanson Sherrill
Jan. 8—George Smith to Narsissa Davis	Jno. F. Doak
July 31—Achilles Chandler to Cloe Dew	Thomas Cox
Jan. 9—William Barnett to Peggy Gunn	Robert Ramay
Jan. 5—Jacob Keeton to Sally Panter	James A. Strong
Mar. 9—William Johnson to Mary Rice	C. Witner
May 9—George Apperson to Eliza Cole	Edward A. White
Dec. 16—James Hays to Sally Night	James Hays
Dec. 31—Robert P. Martin to Martha A. C. Jones	Aaron F. Jones
Aug. 6—Joel Fusten to Ranney Hollingsworth	Isaac Hollingsworth
Oct. 11—Washington J. Pucket to Frances Bucket	Uriah Jennings
Nov. 24—Mayfield Johnson to Mandane Rutland	Gregory D. Johnson
Sept. 27—Thomas Pettyjohn to Martha M. Davis	P. Anderson
May 14—Davis Crowder to Elizabeth Pugh	Luis Vick
Nov. 17—Chestley Winn (Wynn) to Martha Whitson	James Eagan
Jan. 29—Beverly W. Seay to Mary Bowers	Hezekiah Woodward
—— —Lemuel R. Crutcher to Jane Drenon	Thomas Drennon
April 4—John F. Doak to Colan Q. Harrison	Leo Donald
Mar. 29—John Maxwell to Catherine Williams	W. Maxwell

Names	Surety
April 28—John P. Carter to Mary Lacking	Jesse Medley
Oct. 1—Yancey Massey to Nancy Galaspa	John Dice
Aug. 8—Beverly B. Williams to Patsey Marlow	Meredith Marlow
Mar. 17—Allen Zachary to Margaret Woolard	Thomas Hamilton
Sept. 5—Samuel Creswell to Sarah Mays	James Edding
Jan. 16—Thomas Furgerson to Rebecah Furguson	L. Fergusson
May 21—Joab Heflin to Margarett Moore	James Moor
June 5—Edward Sims to Martha Mayho	John Ferguson
Nov. 10—Hose Ward to Milly Johnson	Edmund W. Lester
Oct. 17—James M. Martin to Mary E. Holland	Albert H. Wynne
Oct. 31—John Mitchell to Elizabeth Crocker	Buller Arnold
Oct. 16—George Tucker to Abagill Hartsfield	Josiah Smith
Nov. 20—Samuel Allison to Malinda Florida	John Bond
Oct. 16—John Summers to Elizabeth Loash	Abner Smith
Sept. 3—Jesse Grimes to Tempey Murry	Cader Bass
Mar. 15—Jesse Bond to Sarah Sypert	Drury Dance
Mar. 5—Conrad Carpenter to Eliza Ann Quarles	J. S. Lester
April 25—Beverly J. Miller to Saluda Stovall	Jac. Hunter
July 10—John R. Rutherford to Mary Hightower	Robert Donaldson
June 18—William Houston to Mary Mann	Brittain Drake
Aug. 14—Preston Hays to Ann Searcy	Hugh Hays
Aug. 9—David C. Richards to Elisabeth C. Parrish	Warren Moore
June 30—Jefferson Hamilton to Rody Cunningham	Josiah Beasley
Aug. 1—Joseph Bryson to Jane Bryson	William Bryson
Sept. 3—Wm. L. Martin to Emily Allcorn	O. B. Hubbons
Aug. 27—John Beard to Margaret Cloyd	David Cloyd
—— —John Nickings to Sally Nickings	Prescoat Nickings
Feb. 24—George Barnfield to Polly Williams	William M. Jutine
April 14—Elisha B. Crudup to Lousiance Alford	Samuel Booth
May 2—Jacob Tilmon to Julia McGrigor	Jno. Shepard
Jan. 27—Richardson Carr to Jemimah Glenn	Wm. Strull
Mar. 28—Claiborn W. Neal to Amy Moore	Isaac Neal
Jan. 18—Harvey Hawkins to Mary Bugg	James L. Hawkins
June 11—George Donnell to Elizabeth E. McMurry	F. G. Crutcher
Oct. 16—Hezekiah Cartwright to Sally Mallan	Wm. Davidson
April 23—Richard Townsend to Sarah A. Phipps	C. W. Cummings
Aug. 26—George R. Pugh to Mary Hopkins	Isaac Pugh
Jan. 10—Walter Carruth to Nancy Keath	Thomas Dean
Aug. 27—William Hunter to Elizabeth Drake	James Allcorn
Dec. 16—John G. Gleeves to Elizabeth Curd	William McNeill
Sept. 4—Alexander J. Compton to Martha Wood	Matthew Compton
Aug. 18—Warrenton Oneal to Isabellar Biles	Wm. S. Swan
Sept. 24—Russel Eskew to Margaret Brown	Thomas Kirkpatrick
May 7—William Ricketts to Sarah Porterfield	James Ricketts
Dec. 4—William Threat to Sophy Mekee	P. W. B. Brien
Aug. 22—George Hunter to Jane Winset	James Winset

Names	Surety
Jan. 31—Joshua Clark to Nancy Bowers	William Hartsfield
Dec. 24—Harry B. Williams to Nancy Copeland	Washington Wilton
April 4—James Merritt to Sally Ferrington	Sherrod Merritt
Dec. 15—Elias Sinclair to Sally McDormet	Thomas Jones
June 16—John A. Neumers to Martha Baird	L. Baird
Mar. 5—Thomas W. Harney to Cynthia Bay	Robt. D. McSpadden
April 27—Thomas Belcher to Deliliz Adamson	Zeddock Mullinall
Sept. 22—George Gaddy to Lucy Bass	Thomas Branch
Sept. 26—James A. Warpole to Nancy P. Tilman	Gregory E. Johnson
Feb. 13—Patrick Youree to Sela Harris	William Chapman
Feb. 5—Elisha Dowell to Elizabeth Barbee	Matthew T. Cart-wright
Sept. 9—Dennis King to Elizabeth Beadle	Edmund W. Lester
May 9—Barna Tipton to Harriet Bridges	John Vivrett
July 20—James Belcher to Rebeckey Talley	David Phillips
Dec. 11—Hartwell Zachary to Anny Willis	William Wray
Dec. 11—William Williams to Nancy Crutchfield (Sig. Williamson)	John A. Williamson
Nov. 26—Robert Law to Ann Telford	Hugh Telford
Dec. 11—Bracston Hill to Polly Tarpley	Jos. McDaniel
Dec. 20—Wm. Maholland to Sally Hopson	Hezekiah Cartwright
Dec. 5—Joseph Rutland to Margaret Thompson	Albert McGrigor
June 15—James W. Booth to Sarah Ealey (Eaby)	Daniel Bass
Mar. 26—Jonathan Hooker to Marget Gwynn	Joshua Hooker
Feb. 27—John D. Morris to Mary Morris	Edward Jones
Mar. 13—James R. Allen to Lusinda Smart	Abraham Wright
May 22—Thomas Tracy to Rutha Hearn	Wiley Garner
Aug. 29—James Eddins to Pothena Brown	Samuel Creswell
Dec. 22—Henry Cooley to Malinda Lunce	Gray Medling
Dec. 1—Thomas Hearn to Sarah Sillaman	John Hearn
Dec. 20—Jeremiah Murry to Rhunry Hesson	William Murry
Nov. 20—Henry Mitchell to Henrietta Jackson	Teopilas T. Gray
Oct. 29—Edward W. Scruggs to Elitha Martin	John H. Drake
Dec. 5—Anderson Wright to Sina Eagan	Wm. Motheral
Mar. 5—Thomas W. Tarpley to Susannah Harvey	George Gaddy
Dec. 20—Lynus Armstrong to Jane Maxwell	Joseph P. Wharten
Nov. 28—Allen H. Bridgers to Sarah Hancock	Joseph Freeman
Dec. 15—Thomas Davis to Jane Donnell	Calvin Donnell
Mar. 16—John L. Allison to Margarett Bond	John Bond
Nov. 19—William Russel to Pirtheny Chandler	William Chandler
Nov. 17—Lot Johnson to Matilda Eason	Isaac Hill
Mar. 3—Jesse Shaw to Polly McKinsey	David Bibs
Mar. 15—William Smith to Liddy Turner	Sam'l Stuart
Aug. 1—Allen Hunt to Rebecah Sanders	Allen Wilkerson
Mar. 7—John Escue to Sarah Lumpkins	Samuel Roberts
Oct. 23—James Warren to Ceila Organ	James Slate
Aug. 29—Merritt Lyon to Nancy Astin	Edward A. White

Names	Surety
Dec. 24—Sterling Edwards to Mahala Puckett	James B. Guthrie
Dec. 28—Thos. B. Applack to Martha W. Warren	Lewis H. Dwyer
Dec. 27—Claibourn Baily to Frances Philips	Robert Wilson
1828	1828
Nov. 22—Washington Williams to Minerva Doak	John Hearn
Jan. 9—Sanders Stephens to Nelly Chambers	Allen Tomlinson
—— —Isaac Hill to Polly Johnson	Phil W. Harrington
April 30—Doak Young to Sarah Reeder	Mathew Hern
Feb. 26—James H. Taylor to Martha Hunter	John Afflack
Nov. 19—Charles W. Cummings to Eliza W. Foster	Ben. T. Mottly
Mar. 22—Robert Corley to Maryan Adams	Samuel Corley
July 1—Alexander Roach to Elizabeth E. Wright	John R. Wright
July 29—John McDaniel to Elizabeth Moore	John Johnson
Sept. 15—Wilee McDonald to Mary Yandle	Matthew Due
—— —William W. Searcy to ———	A. H. Wynne
Sept. 3—Slith Harrison to Harriet Wood	Sam'l Stone
Sept. 26—Gilson Murfrey to Mary Cooksey	Joshua V. Taylor
May 23—Elijah Motsinger to Lucy Harris	Valentine Lion
Mar. 10—Samuel Coles to Calista Walker	John Davis
Sept. 3—Jonathan Whitton to Mary Mount	Chisman ———
July 26—James Smith to Gilley Stewart	Wiley Bodine
Nov. 11—Edmond R. Harrison to Rebecca Hawkins	Alex. Penny
July 9—William Dotson to Elizabeth Heflig	Moses Harrison
Aug. 11—William England to Candis Trovilion	James Trovilion
Aug. 6—Ellison Morris to Tempy Johnson	Joel Graves
Feb. 19—Thomas Fillops to Cassey Jonslan	Benjamin Caley
Dec. 16—Ozburn Eddings to Elizabeth Bone	H. C. Hubbard
—— —Joseph H. Sellers to Polly Gwynn	Sam'l N. McMinn
Jan. 9—Alfred Dukes to Nancy Bradshaw	Joshua Peak
July 26—John T. Lee to Louiza Murry	James U. Lee
Jan. 15—Nathan McCollough to Elizabeth Lanom	Garrett Johnson
Mar. 19—William M. Andrews to Elizabeth Silloman	Geo. D. Moore
Dec. 11—Alexander Michaels to Elira Powell	Willie Powell
Oct. 25—Josiah Philips to Darkus K. Nettles	Benjamin Philips
Sept. 18—John B. Holman to Lavina Randolph	Jesse Gibson
July 4—Allen Blankenship to Eliza J. Spinks	Wm. Mitchell
Jan. 26—Daniel Harpole to Jane D. Allen	George Harpole
July 19—Michael D. Henderson to Elizabeth Wiley	David K. Farr
July 19—Henry Cluck to Mary Robinson	Thos. Burk
Aug. 12—Albert Foster to Lucinda Major	Sam'l Donnell
May 8—William Climer to Jane Lane	Aderson Perry
May 3—Jacob Holdefield to Elizabeth Horn	Richard Horn
Mar. 22—David Fillops to Anney Frances Hart	Peter Fillops
Aug. 2—Clabourne Clark to Sarah Neal	J. Neal (Neel)

Names	Surety
—— —John A. Simmons to Elizabeth Tomlinson	John Trout
Mar. 18—Wm. A. Vowel to Caraline Camell	Albert Foster
Sept. 23—Samuel Patton to Elenor Compton	Charles Compton
July 21—Pervines Fox to Narcissa Bennett	James Baird
Feb. 23—Samuel H. Lasater to Salley Barker	Ambrose Reynolds
Nov. 16—Zedekiah Tate to Zadia Hunt	Tuckmun Perkinson
Nov. 5—John Little to Mattilda Brown	Murphree Camp
Jan. 11—Wm. Wilkerson to Elizabeth Lane	Wm. Climer
Feb. 23—David C. Jackson to Mary Wood	John W. Murray
April 2—John Sanders to Sarah Patterson	John Cummings
June 30—Hyram S. Wroe to Mary D. Hodges	Ozburn Eddings
Jan. 28—Randolph McDaniel to Jane Chambers	John Chambers
Dec. 22—Wm. Lasater to Polly Hill	Abner Hilkeal
Feb. 9—William Smith to Jane Blurton	Malborn Smith
Feb. 7—Anderson Loyd to Lucy Johnson	John Hearn
Mar. 10—Jideon Carter to Lydia Case	Snoden Hickman
Feb. 22—Macom Smith to Elizabeth Young	J. S. Smith
Nov. 29—Peter Patterson to Sarah Patterson	Benton Woods
—— —Abner Upchurch to Nancy Pyland	Wm. Rawls
Aug. 2—Daniel Smith to Amy Neal	C. Clark, Blabamon Clark
Aug. 16—Charles Wright to Margam Hessey	Hollis Wright
Nov. 11—Pleasant Via to Rebecca Tarver	Nelson Tarver
Oct. 18—Littleberry E. Williamson to Rebecca E. Powell	B. Figures
Jan. 13—Ruffin Capel to Lucinda Edins	Allen W. Vick
Feb. 18—Hall J. Winsett to Elizabeth Jarman	Shadrack Jarman
Nov. 14—John Meak to Charlotte J. Morris	Joshua Taylor
Nov. 13—Jesse Pemberton to Saluda Bradley	William Pemberton
Feb. 19—Asa Mosley to Frances M. Snoddy	Media White
Mar. 19—Pleasant G. Belcher to Sally Belcher	James Powell
Oct. 16—Jessee Walden to Martha Turner	Joel Dill
Sept. 15—Thomas V. Wier to Polly Morris	John Pemberton
April 21—Welburn Winter to Mary Dinton	Benjamin Tarver
Dec. 8—William Yindle to Jane Barr	Joseph Barr
July 14—Stokes Zachary to Delila R. Peak	A. Z. Zachary
May 10—James Vaughan to Maria Martin	John P. Martin
Aug. 14—Wm. B. Drake to Ann Robertson	Thomas K. Wynne
Sept. 22—James M. Thompson to Elizabeth Dodd	Joseph Thompson, James Thompson
July 30—Matthew Brown to Elizabeth Walker	John H. B. Coles
Dec. 12—Eclemere Sullivan to Martha M. Stone	W. Thomeson
Feb. 18—John Booker to Lusinda B. Griffin	Green H. Hancock
June 23—Charles Puckett, Jr., to Eliza Lane	George K. Smith
June 6—Hezekiah L. Cartwright to Delila Searcy	John Cox
Aug. 20—Robert Fullerton to Priscilla Clifton	David Berry

Names	Surety
Dec. 13—Sneed Harris to Fany Tilford	Randal McDonald
April 11—James Poe to Elizabeth Lanton	Henry Davis
May 28—Samuel McWhirter to Mary P. Cowen	F. G. Crutcher
Dec. 31—Thomas Estes to Eliza Atkerson	Donnell Freeman
June 8—Wm. S. Scott to Sally Sneed	Thos. Cox
June 26—Daniel Richmond to Mary Bond	T. W. Cummings
Jan. 13—Charles George to Fassti Hughs	George B. Pugh
Jan. 16—Wm. W. Huddleston to Mary B. Tarver	Charles Sullivan
Jan. 3—John Ingram to Eliza Todd	Joshua Clark
Jan. 19—Nelson D. Hancock to Margaret Woodrum	Henry M. Hancock
June 14—Obediah V. Rogers to Sarah Underwood	James Wynne
Aug. 8—Shiely Waters to Nancy Hannon	William Phillips
April 3—Thomas B. Moss to Mourning Davis	William Chapman
Jan. 1—Strother B. Walker to Mariah Akin	John Swan
May 13—William Barker to Martha Winston	William Lasater
Nov. 20—William Carter to Izabella Roan	Wm. M. Chapman
Sept. 23—William Edwards to Patsy Maning	Hames Brown
Aug. 10—Wm. Eddins to Sarah Hooker	Benj. T. Tucker
Mar. 18—Abner Weatherly to Jane Sims	Washington Williams
Oct. 27—Isaac W. Hill to Sarah Baird	William Hill
Jan. 28—Allen Nelson to Sarah Pugh	William Dobson
June 1—John Cates to Ally Johnson	Thos. Chambers
Feb. 8—Michael Bond to Elizabeth King	Thomas King
Dec. 1—Thomas Mitchell to Jane Southworth	John Chambers
Nov. 18—Toliver Turner to Elizabeth Grandstaff	John Grandstaff
Dec. 3—John Wood to Elizabeth Wasson	Wm. Word
April 16—Thomas Baskins to Susan Arnold	Tillman Patterson
Mar. 12—Thomas Brown to Rebecca Boon	Granville Edwards
May 5—Byrd Spurlock to Elizabeth Hancock	George Michie
June 25—Marcus Rieff to Eliza Hulm	Tawrus Rieff
July 2—H. R. Shembridge to Selina Smith	Joseph Smith
Mar. 19—Joseph Moore to Susannah Wood	Robert W. Shelton
April 16—Edwin Duncan to Aley Cooper	John Coe
Oct. 22—William J. Goodwin to Mary McHenry	Jesse Goodwin
July 4—William A. Thompson to Artemisia ———	Jordain Brown
Nov. 26—Coston F. Ballentine to Nancy Taylor	Caleb Taylor
Sept. 24—William Patrick to Pheby Smith	Guinan Las
July 18—Benjamin F. Philips to Mary Devaught	Jno. Perkins
Dec. 22—Wilson Hearn to Elizabeth Winford	John Hearn
June 3—Baxter Bennett to Elizabeth Chandler	Elijah Gholstan
Oct. 15—John H. Reynolds to Jane Barott	Lunsford Bagwell
May 13—Nelson G. Allexander to Mary Patterson	James Carruth
April 17—Edward McMillin to Eliza C. Donnell	John L. Sloan
Jan. 31—John Carr to Mary Biddle	Wm. Gentry
Oct. 2—Alsay Reese to Willey Medling	Richardson Rowland

Names	Surety
Oct. 18—James Haleam to Rebecca Underhill	Edmond Goodenon
Mar. 24—Oliver Oneal to Nancy Clark	David Beard
Feb. 18—Rawlings Henderson to Minerva Kennedy	William H. Henderson
Oct. 27—David B. Smith to Mary Listin	John A. Smith
Nov. 8—John Pemberton to Emaline Mapez	Samuel Bland
June 12—Elijah Jacobs to Jane Bowers	Etheldridge Brantly
Dec. 2—James Coner to Sarah Elliston	John L. Allison
July 29—John B. Arnold to Frances Young	William Young
Dec. 3—Martin Sparks to Rachel J. Marr	Samuel R. Conor
Mar. 7—John A. Dods to Marget M. Thomison	James B. Thompson
Oct. 23—Lewis Patterson to Martha Ward	Tillman Patterson
Oct. 13—Abner Jennings to Cloey F. Lester	Rial C. Jennings

INDEX

A

C

D

E

F

H

I

J

K

L

M

N

O

P

Q

R

S

T

Y